Disciplining Feminism

Disciplining

Feminism

From Social Activism to Academic Discourse

ELLEN MESSER-DAVIDOW

Duke University Press   Durham and London 2002

© 2002 Duke University Press   All rights reserved
Printed in the United States of America on acid-free paper ∞
Designed by Rebecca M. Gimenez   Typeset in Monotype
Dante with Gill Sans display by Keystone Typesetting, Inc.
Library of Congress Cataloging-in-Publication Data
appear on the last printed page of this book.

To Wendy Lynn Jaeger and Michael Charles Jaeger

Contents

Acknowledgments

This book owes its existence to the support of many people. With un-abashed nostalgia, I thank its catalysts: Warren Bennis for introducing me to organizations, David R. Shumway for explaining practice until I finally got it, and David J. Sylvan for encouraging me to do fieldwork.

Generous colleagues read draft chapters and the whole manuscript, sometimes more than once: Andrew Elfenbein, Judith Kegan Gardiner, Evelyn Fox Keller, Annette Kolodny, Bruce Lincoln, Jean O'Barr, Richard Ohmann, Diana Saco, Larry Shillock, David Shumway, and Madelon Sprengnether. The kind comments of sociologists, historians, and political scientists on parts of this book or my related work on social movement organizations assuaged my disciplinary fears: Paul DiMaggio, Stanley N. Katz, Elizabeth Long, Robert Pahre, and Dorothy E. Smith. Audiences who heard excerpts from the book in progress at conferences sponsored by the Modern Language Association, American Studies Association, American Association of Higher Education, and assorted universities supplied encouragement, and reviewers for Duke University Press made helpful suggestions.

Behind-the-scenes wizards made my research possible. Graduate research assistants cheerfully proofed the prose, checked the citations, and somehow kept track of the library books: Larry Shillock, James W. Maertens, Andrea Ghorai, Karen Roggenkamp, Megan Casey, and David Noon. Officials helped me obtain otherwise inaccessible materials: Alexander D. Crary (National Endowment for the Arts), John Hammer (National Humanities Alliance), and Kevin Lane (Office of Sen. Paul Wellstone). Library directors extended the usual and unusual library privileges: Christopher Loring (Director of Reference and Consulting Services, Wilson

Library, University of Minnesota) and Dr. William Miller (Director, Wimberly Library, Florida Atlantic University).

I gratefully acknowledge the University of Minnesota for supporting my research and writing: the Graduate School for a McKnight-Land Grant Professorship (1989–92) and two Grants-in-Aid of Research (1992–93, 1993–94); the Department of English for a fall quarter research leave (1994); and the College of Liberal Arts for a winter quarter research leave (1996) and unpaid winter quarter leaves (1998, 1999).

It is a joy to name the colleagues whose friendship sustained me through the many years it took to shape and reshape this book: Lillian Bridwell-Bowles, Arthur Geffen, Michael Hancher, Joan E. Hartman, Marquita McLean, Richard Leppert, Toni A. H. McNaron, Garth Rockcastle, Gary Thomas, Madelon Sprengnether, Jane Thompkins, and John Watkins. My greatest debt is to four people who gave me their unwavering faith and support: Stanley Fish, Annette Kolodny, my department chair Shirley Nelson Garner, and my editor Ken Wissoker.

With admiration and love, I dedicate this book to my now adult children.

Introduction: Knowing and Doing

Knowing and not doing are equal to not knowing at all. —Fortune cookie,

Vina's Cafe

After thousands of articles and hundreds of books, what can be said that doesn't reiterate the familiar explanations of academic feminism in the United States? The institutional histories have already chronicled its emergence from the activism that swept college campuses; the construction of an infrastructure from programs, publications, and associations; and the continuing struggle for equal opportunity in higher education. The intellectual critiques have already probed the foundational categories that synthesized its discourse, the epistemic modalities that inflected its knowledges, and the identity politics that fissured its community of practitioners. My purpose in reviewing some of these matters is to answer a question about academic feminism as a formation: how did it happen that a bold *cultval* venture launched thirty years ago to transform academic and social institu- $\:\:Q$ tions was itself transformed by them? Since we see things the way we are rather than the way they are, I want to begin with my own story of how I gradually came to understand the conditions of social (trans)formation.

MARRIED AT NINETEEN and mothering two children, I spent the mid-1960s immersed in middle-class suburban domesticity—cooking, cleaning, storytelling, doctoring, and chauffeuring to play groups and nursery school. But one June evening my whirl through this comfortable routine veered into a jolting ride down the road to feminism. That evening, after my husband and I had agreed to divorce, he gripped my arm and said, "If it's the last thing I do, I'll destroy you." And he almost did because for two years I was held hostage by a system of power I couldn't fathom. In order to prove extreme cruelty and gross neglect, one of the few grounds for divorce recognized by the Cincinnati domestic relations court, my attorney insisted that I endure not only my husband's abuse but also the shameful collusion of the authorities who were supposed to protect or serve. Police refused to respond to my calls for help, stores refused to let me use our joint accounts or open my own, and court counselors equivocated on the subject of financial support. Without an employment history or prospects I couldn't rent an apartment and worse, if I did flee with the children, my attorney warned, my husband could countersue for divorce and custody on grounds of desertion. Utterly trapped, I was strung out between the horror of staying at my home and the terror of leaving it.

By winter I was so desperate to do something, anything, that I took to sitting up most of the night in the small room off the garage that had become my bedroom. Searching for a higher authority than the local officials, I paged through the Constitution looking for a section I did not find, the one guaranteeing my rights to personal safety and choice of domicile, and then wrote up my arguments anyway, thinking that the exercise in reasoning repeated night after night would preserve my sanity. Late one night, ill with bronchitis and drenched in terror, I gave up and faced the inevitable: a dark design I couldn't comprehend was destroying me. Stripped of every resource but my own stubbornness, I would go down to the bitter end insisting that they were wrong—the attorneys, the court referees, the credit managers, the police, and my husband were wrong. After a month of fatalism, help came to me unexpectedly during a phone conversation with my best friend, Susanne, who had joined a feminist group in Berkeley. Her explanation of women's oppression and the handful of feminist articles she recommended were floodlights that exposed the divorce machinery for the power system it was.

As the pale March sun began slivering the winter, my recently widowed Aunt Betty and I planned the escape. One Friday morning I fled, bundling the children into my car and our clothes into a borrowed truck. For the rest of the school year, we lived at her house in the same suburban neighborhood. She soothed me through bouts of anguish, cleaned up after my daughter's hamster, and calmly admired the Jewish stars that my five-year-old son had inked on her den sofa. She fed us savory fried chicken and rubbed our backs, managed a restaurant, and confronted my husband when he was obstreperous. Her pluck and competence helped me to realize what I needed to extricate myself from the divorce system—I needed bold tactics. Since my husband had stalled the negotiations on a separation agreement and the court would not rule without it, I would have to force a resolution. Making inquiries, I learned that the domestic court judge owed his position to my husband's attorney, the former chair of the local Republican Party, and worse was rumored to be on the take. I asked a reporter to investigate the rumor, which was confirmed, ironically, when the judge's intermediary approached my father for a payoff (my father refused and eventually a grand jury exposed the judge's activities). Meanwhile, I gathered evidence showing that my husband had appropriated dividend checks made out to me, applied for a loan on my life insurance policy, and forged my signature on tax returns now disputed by the IRS. Then I paid a visit to my attorney. "Tell his attorney," I demanded, "that they have to negotiate a separation agreement." Without a word, he picked up the telephone receiver, slowly dialed a number, and delivered this message: "She's gone berserk. You'd better tell your client to negotiate." The insult ignited my rage, a rage soon to be stoked by the court referee, who confided "Graduate school? Honey, you should be working at a department store," and the welfare lawyer, who shrugged "We can't collect child support; he's out of state." Their words and so many others blazed in front of me like neon signs illuminating the cul-de-sacs of the male power system.

That summer we moved into an apartment with pea-green wallpaper and elegantly carved woodwork on the second floor of a house in Clifton. The south side of this hilly district was occupied by the University of Cincinnati and the north side by a residential quarter of Victorian homes and prewar fourplexes that housed growing families, professionals, and students. Our neighborhood was bisected by a shopping street that was the center of community activity. Kids roved the corner bakery for sticky buns and the five-and-dime for Double-Bubble gum. Grownups posted notices of upcoming events in the window of the Town Meeting Office and gossiped in front of the movie theater. We patronized the health food shop, the India import boutique, and the pharmacy owned by Mr. Pahner, who didn't mind being phoned at home for a late night prescription. Shop owners said, "Saw your daughter and her girlfriends yesterday" or "Your son bought M&Ms after school." Going with the flow, we switched from patio chaises to porch stoops, Pepsi to Kool-Aid, charcoaled steaks to casseroles, and started keeping a penny jar. By the end of summer I was a bell-bottomed, peace-buckled, granny-spectacled chick with two tousled little ones in tow.

That fall I enrolled the kids in an alternative school, started part-time graduate study in the English Department at the University of Cincinnati, and entered the community of graduate students. Winters we had supper in the Ruehlmanns' kitchen; the kids watched TV while Lynne talked about her acting with a local theater group and Bill contrived yet another sortie against the antipornography Citizens for Decent Literature and their vigilante prosecutor Simon Leis. Summers we gathered round the trestle table in the Polks' front yard; the kids played barefooted at mischief while Sally, a Berkeley-style hippie in a gossamer blouse and torn jeans, cooked something with beans, and David, a Berkeley-style radical, ex-pounded on the university's exploitation of teaching assistants. In those days, the English graduate students who were privileged to teach two sections of freshman composition per quarter gratefully subsisted on a $3,500 annual stipend and peanut butter sandwiches the last week of each month. Since childcare facilities were nonexistent, Sally and I traded off babysitting to attend late afternoon graduate seminars. My studying commenced at eight and creaked on past midnight, and my early morn-ing fuzziness dissipated with the surge of adrenaline I always experi-enced on entering McMicken Hall, the building that housed the English department.

Reading literature was a pleasure; learning to do literary studies was a problem. Told that assigned articles were exemplars, I took copious notes, itemizing the facts and tracing the arguments. But I was only skating on surface of the prose; unable to discern the constitutive rules, I couldn't follow them in writing my term papers. A certain something, which I then called "the big picture" and today call "the order of disciplinary dis-course," eluded me. Reckoning that the best defense was a good offense, I tried to evade the rules the professors never explained while trying to figure out what they were. I wrote term papers on unconventional topics and scrambled to gain a vantage point on the big picture by taking courses in linguistics, anthropology, and philosophy. Then one day the director of graduate studies summoned me to his office for the official review of progress and, after squinting at my transcript, gave me this piece of advice: "You'd better decide what discipline you're in." I shaped up quick, finish-ing my course requirements in 1974 and the next year taking my doctoral examinations in four fields—seventeenth-century English literature, Ro-mantic literature, Victorian literature, and critical history and theory.

My apprenticeship, like so many others in the late 1960s and early 1970s, commingled academics and activism. Contrary to the quip, "When the world ends, it will happen ten years later in Cincinnati," this sedate mid-western city had its share of activism pretty much on schedule with the rest of the nation: civil-rights initiatives orchestrated by the black churches and the NAACP chapter, white ministers and rabbis preaching the lessons of Birmingham and Selma to their congregations, citywide black insurgency spiking the long, humid summers, NOW chapters recruiting members, antiwar protests blocking the traffic downtown, and even an underground newspaper that printed New Left analyses next to headshop adverts. But the quip contained a kernel of truth: the city was sedate because the aloof WASP establishment that ruled southern Ohio preferred to smother the activists with proprieties rather than to deploy the brutal tactics that esca-lated the conflicts down south and back east.

In 1969–70, the year I took a seminar on the British Romantic revolu-tions in poetics and politics, antiwar teach-ins filled the Great Hall and demonstrations blanketed the slopes around the administration building. The university administrators responded so indifferently to these events that when we saw the government agents perched on rooftops to photo-graph the crowd we were more relieved than frightened to be considered dangerous radicals. But that May big-time violence erupted in Ohio: after the government announced the Cambodia bombings and the National Guard shot protesting students at Kent State, activists vowed to shut down every university in the state. At Cincinnati, most of the faculty canceled classes, everyone turned out for a mass demonstration, and students oc-cupied the administration building overnight, mindful to stack our pizza boxes in garbage cans before departing the next day. Finally agreeing to entertain the activists' demands, the remote-control president deputized a vice president who, in the time-honored tradition of diplomacy, prefaced the meetings with cordialities and prolonged them with commentaries until he had blunted the activists' forcefulness.

Thankfully, the old decorum melted away when Warren Bennis became president in the fall of 1971. Believing that leaders should stir up a heady brew of change, he held open hours at his office, schmoozed with students lunching at the union, and met with the antiwar, black, and women's groups (I was one of the thirty-some women who crowded into the living room of his home for a confab early that first year). He created laboratories where we could ferment ideas about change: lectures and meetings at the university, Sunday morning synergy brunches and late night suppers at "610" as we dubbed his red brick Victorian home perched on a hillside above Ludlow Avenue. The guests who moved through those burnished scenes were journalists, public leaders, organizational theorists, innovative scholars, and the first famous woman I encountered face-to-face.

The Medical School hall is packed with people occupying every seat, crammed against the walls, and camped in the aisles. Dr. Daniels, the chairman of the Psychiatry Department, squeezes through the doorway and heads for the podium; behind him a short, robust woman wielding a forked tree limb for a cane clumps along in measured steps and takes a seat on the podium. He is several sentences into an effusive introduction when she raises her cane and aims it at the doorway. "You over there, come in. Let the others in." The cane moves rightward, pointing to a bare spot in the sea of bodies and then settles down on the floor with a thump. "Enough introduction," she declares and rises to speak. That evening when I arrive at 610 the dining room lights are dimmed and dozens of candles wink on card tables draped with East Indian printed cloth. We queue at the buffet, loading our plates, and eddy around the tables reading placecards. I sit across from Dr. Margaret Mead, our knees almost touching and my face flushed. As I ransack my memory of anthropology courses in search of an intelligent question, her eyelids droop, her head dips, and her chin hovers only inches above a mound of spaghetti. Gliding by, the president murmurs "tired" and winks as if to reassure me that nothing could be more normal than a famous woman catnapping at the supper table.

My peregrinations through the scenes of change didn't have a destination until 1971 when I drove to Grailville, a retreat managed by radical nuns, to attend a training program for women conducted by the Industrial Areas Foundation (IAF). The founder of the IAF, Saul Alinsky, was the acknowledged dean of a new school of community organizing, a reputation he and his colleagues had earned by helping poor communities organize collective-action projects in Chicago, Rochester, Minneapolis, and other cities. The IAF had come to regard women as an untapped resource for community organizing and, though it harbored no feminist sentiments, had billed the program as "organizing woman power." To prepare for the weekend, we had read Alinsky's *Reveille for Radicals* and *Rules for Radicals,* and then, under the tutelage of trainers Richard Harmon and Grace Lamm, we viewed films of IAF's community-action projects, proposed our own projects, and role played strategic planning and negotiating. Since the logic informing these exercises was already familiar to me from my father's dinnertime stories about Jewish and African-American activism in Cincinnati, learning to do IAF change was easy. The trainers voiced the rules of engagement—enter the arena, act instead of react, convert problems into issues, change institutions not attitudes—that in the heat of rehearsal my pulse put into play. But many of the women objected to Harmon's masculinist style and halted a scheduled session to discuss this problem. The IAF went back to the drawing board and the next year returned to Grailville with a feminist program led by Grace Lamm and Mary Hinz, who taught us how women's groups had mobilized for equal credit policies, employment opportunities, and healthcare benefits. That weekend I met Patricia Durcholz and Janet O'Connor, both University of Cincinnati continuing-education students as thirty-something undergraduate women were called in those days. We discussed the possibility of organizing women on campus and nervously repeated our trainers' advice. "If you get scared," the trainers had said, "you're no good for the project. To be an effective change agent, you have to depersonalize the risk." Was I scared? Sure, but compared to fighting the divorce machine for my life campus activism would be a game. I was ready to play.

That fall a small group of university women huddled in a basement room of McMicken Hall and began to organize the Coalition of Campus Women (CCW). By the end of the academic year we had written bylaws, recruited members, and elected three cochairs for the coming year— professor Elizabeth Bettman, secretary Rose Dalleska, and myself as the graduate student. In 1973–74, the CCW orchestrated a direct-action project: we assembled a list of 125 demands and negotiated them with the administration. Although we knew that activists generally made a few key demands, we considered the long list to be a tactical resource. By forwarding subsets of demands to the administrators in charge of those areas, we would bog them down in a time-consuming process of consultation, and by publicizing the whole list we would shock the university community with the scope of women's inequalities. When the president appointed the provost as his negotiator, we were ready with a strategy. The CCW had designated most of its demands as giveaways to be dropped for the few demands we intended to secure but only after CCW negotiators had tediously haggled over each one. The prolonged haggling would divert administrative energy away from business-as-usual, and the tradeoffs would give us an edge; we could create pressure on the administration by complaining publicly about the numerous demands it rejected. The CCW won most of its short-list items—approval to establish a women's studies program, funding for a library collection of feminist literature, access to law and medical school data on the applicant and admissions pools by gender and race, and an administrative training program for female and minority faculty.

Soon after the women's studies program was launched in 1974, the Women's Studies Advisory Committee (wsac) initiated a series of collaborations between university and community women. Pioneers for Century III, a bicentennial conference held to "bring people together in a new combination,"[1] drew about eight hundred women nationwide. Keynote speakers included United Nations Assistant Secretary Helvi Sipila, U.S. Congresswoman Martha Griffiths, Cincinnati Councilwoman Bobbie Sterne, firebrand attorney Florynce Kennedy, Woman's Bank President Madeline McWhinney, and National Coalition of Labor Vice President Addie Wyatt. Academic women applied feminist scholarship to public issues; social service staff led workshops in consciousness raising, single parenting, and job search techniques; and community activists explained how to design legislative campaigns, manage rape-crisis facilities, mobilize womanpower in volunteer organizations, and build coalitions among Appalachian, African-American, and white women. A few years later, wsac sponsored a conference on the economic consequences of divorce that featured sociologist Lenore Weitzman, local feminist scholars and activists, and women victimized by the divorce process. The conference attracted some five hundred women who angrily confronted the court officials with the injustices they had suffered in the divorce process.

In 1980, Cincinnati feminists again joined forces to found Friends of Women's Studies, a community organization that quickly swelled to some four hundred members and used its dues to establish small grants programs for single mothers returning to the university and for women conducting community-oriented research projects. By 1985, Friends had completed a fundraising drive to endow a visiting professorship in women's studies and had discovered that it could play campus politics with an impunity that faculty and students did not enjoy. When the Friends board was riled by the way the university had handled a student's sexual-harassment complaint, it deputized a subcommittee to get the policy and procedures changed. "The feisty five," as we were dubbed, spoke with the university's trustees and made a presentation at their monthly meeting; since this educational approach had no effect, we lobbied the governor for a feminist appointment to the Board of Trustees and, after three years of determined maneuvering, prevailed.[2]

For every achievement we had plenty of setbacks along the way, but our modus operandi was to convert negatives to positives. We used obstacles as energizers, strategizing with bravado and moving right along. We used defeats to play for future wins; by reminding our opponents that they had wronged university women yet again, we upped the ante and called in our chits. We used "the enemy" as a direct-action tactic, a label affixed to the administration during periods of conflict and revoked during periods of collaboration. Our tensions about race, professional status, and political ideology were tempered by the example of our administrative women. Affirmative action director Marquita McLean, associate dean Myrtis Mosley, and women's studies directors Dana Hiller, Barbara Ramusack, and Laura Strumingher worked with all constituencies and kept their eyes trained on project objectives. The texture of that time is best captured by the 1960s adage "Joy in the struggle"—a joy that continues to bind me over time and distance to those Cincinnati friends.

In 1974, I entered academic activism on the national level. Some months after applying for an appointment to the Modern Language Association (MLA) Commission on the Status of Women (CSW), cochair Elaine Reuben informed me that the CSW had forwarded my name to the MLA Executive Council, which had, however, declined to appoint a graduate student. Hoping that the CSW wouldn't let the matter drop, I conveyed the advice Marquita McLean always gave to Cincinnati feminists: "Regard every setback as an opportunity for more education and activism." The CSW went back to work and secured appointments for two graduate students, Barbara Smith and myself, for the usual three-year terms. At first I waded through the MLA's procedural molasses while the veteran CSW members adroitly played associational politics,[3] but the next year I kicked into strategic gear, organizing the MLA Graduate Student Caucus and suggesting a new project. The CSW had just completed a status study showing that publication was a strong predictor of rank, tenure, and salary. As we pondered the reasons why women were publishing less than men—they were clustered in the lower ranks and less prestigious institutions where teaching loads were heavier—I blurted out, "Why don't we just assume that the publishing industry is sexist and do something about it?" Joan Hartman and I planned a CSW conference in New York that would introduce publishers to the new women's studies scholarship, and afterwards we edited two volumes on the new directions in scholarship and the strategies for getting it into print.[4] That stint on the CSW gave me my first glimpses of how disciplines produced sex-patterned education, employment, and knowledge. How universities operated I was learning through my job at the University of Cincinnati.

After passing my doctoral examinations in 1975, I took what my professors regarded as a detour through a two-year term as administrative assistant to President Bennis. True to form, he designed the position as laboratory work in institutional knowing and doing. For the first two weeks he queried me on the literature he had assigned as my introduction to university management. "What do you think of this article?" he wrote. "Naive structuralism and full of jargon," I replied in a memo. The memo was returned with a comment penned across the top in heavy black ink: "Robert Merton is one of the brightest minds in sociology!!" In ballpoint I scribbled brashly, "Sociology is in trouble," and sent the memo upstairs. That fall Warren put me in charge of presidential communications and gradually added the other duties I would perform for two years—staffing the executive vice presidential search, meeting with governance groups, cosupervising budget studies, and serving on the administration's collective-bargaining strategy committee.

Warren introduced me to the idea of a cleavage between knowing change and doing change because he was constantly pondering the university's convoluted social architecture that dead-ended his change initiatives. For a Harvard lecture, he wrote: "The thinking me sprints out ahead—an article written over the weekend. . . . But the *doing* me limps stubbornly behind. Held back by inertia, by a bureaucracy, by finances, by litigation, by—sometimes it seems—all 38,000 students, 2,600 faculty, 9,000 staff, and all 90,000 of our living alumni and the other 90,000 non-living alumni."[5] He formulated this drag effect as Bennis's First Law of Academic Pseudo-dynamics: "Routine work drives out nonroutine work and smothers to death all creative planning, all fundamental change in the university—or any institution, for that matter."[6] The staff experienced the First Law viscerally. We slogged through the routines, trying to retain our humor by posting a cartoon of two men waist deep in a swamp captioned "When you're up to your ass in alligators, it's hard to remember that your initial objective was clearing the swamp." We lurched through the crises, exhausted by all-night and weekend marathons, and tracked our progress by transferring pages from a looseleaf notebook labeled "active crises" to another notebook labeled "inactive crises." The hours were grueling, but Warren made the learning easy.

In 1977 my terms in the President's Office and on the Women's Commission ended, and as I wrote my dissertation the magic of change seemed to evaporate. By the time I finished, feminist studies had built a nationwide infrastructure and won intellectual legitimacy. While others were celebrating the achievement, I was worrying about a cleavage. The cleavage that had troubled Warren was an institutional problem: the burdensome routine had smothered his creative energies and change initiatives. The cleavage that vexed me was a translation problem: the social change I knew from activism I couldn't reformulate as academic knowledge, and the social change I knew from academic theories I couldn't deploy in activism. The translation problem, I came to realize, was produced by the discontinuous discourses in which I was operating. Through activist discourse I acquired know-how as I did change—like a cat leaping, twisting, and landing on its feet—and through disciplinary discourses I acquired knowledge as I read about change—like a scholar analyzing, criticizing, and arguing. These discourses did not provide two perspectives on "change" as the same thing; rather, their very different sets of practice had constituted "change" as two divergent things. The tactical skills of activism rendered "change" as conflicts to be shaped, whereas the intellectual skills of disciplines had rendered it as schematics to be debated. My simple notion that these discourses had constituted change$_1$ and change$_2$ became more complicated after I moved to the University of Minnesota in 1986.

When I arrived, the dean told me about the History and Society Program (HSP), a social-science research group that met every other week to discuss work in progress by scholars from around the nation and abroad. Through HSP, I came to regard "social change" as an intellectual artifact that the academy had fractured along four sets of fault lines. Disciplines had slivered change into historical developments, economic trends, political realignments, and cultural rifts. Methods had differentiated how change would be investigated and represented: archival research or cliometrics in history, tales or tables in sociology. Theories had inflected the dynamics: change rippled outward from charismatic leaders, gushed forth with working-class insurgency, or burbled up from the gaps between discourses. These divergent ways of modeling change, according to my social-science colleagues, were the surface effects of a deeper divide: the actor / structure dualism in rendering social life. Since my discipline had trained me to focus on individuals (the author, the text), I couldn't see structure until a political scientist used the term in a way that made no sense to me. "What," I blurted out, "do you mean by structure?" He explained it more than once before the concept of organized and organizing social practice loomed on my horizon.

Now I could see HSP as the dramatization of organized and organizing disciplinary practice. While reading history and sociology, the humanities scholars stumbled through thickets of detail and quantification. While reading literary and cultural studies, the social scientists careened down slippery slopes of logic. The tensions that simmered while we read our texts at home boiled over at our meetings where someone was sure to impugn their jargon, methods, or assumptions—but never randomly because we were factionalized by our disciplines and with predictable regularity made fractious comments about them. The social scientists in our group rebuked the humanities authors we read for not gathering empirical data to ground their high-flying theories, and the humanities scholars in our group derided the social-science authors for naively presuming that their data reflected independent realities. When the arguments heated up, someone would cool them down by solemnly noting that academic writing was inaccessible to general readers, a situation we could all deplore together. HSP helped me think about what graduate school had trained me to think with—the disciplinary conventions that ordered our perceptions and practices.

When I returned to the question of what had happened to academic feminism, I realized the methodological obstacles to answering it. Whereas the conventions of literary studies directed me to study academic feminism by reading its texts and joining its theoretical debates, I would have to analyze the forces that formed the field, shaped its objects and objectives, and structured its practices. My HSP colleagues had been saying all along that humanities scholars had to do more than read if they were going to analyze social institutions and practices, but I was held back by fear. How could I investigate objects beyond the pale of my discipline without having been formally trained in the methods for doing so? David Sylvan, a political scientist then at Minnesota, prodded me to do fieldwork—observe organizations, interview actors, collect nonacademic materials—and I delayed this boundary-crossing ramble for as long as possible, first stewing about amateurism until I had a bad case of anxiety and then reading numerous fieldwork textbooks to allay it. When I finally ventured into the field, I had to forget the textbook recipes and flow with the action unfurling uniquely at each event. Shuttling between improvisation in the field and planning at my desk, the shape of the project began to morph and the piles of data to accumulate. By the time I put my fingers to the keyboard, I was paralyzed by the immensity of the task. How was it possible for one scholar to speak about a thirty-year history of academic feminism; about an enterprise institutionalized as thousands of courses, publications, and action projects; and about the feminist specialisms within a single discipline, let alone the feminist knowledge spanning the disciplines? Victimized by my own twist on Bennis's First Law, I was so immersed in scholarly practice that I could no longer get my head above the grass to see the landscape. Routine, Warren would have fondly reminded me, exhausts and eclipses vision.

HOW WAS ACADEMIC FEMINISM formed by the dynamic structures it had set out to transform? This question, like all questions, is posed within assumptions that simultaneously frame what is seen and how it is analyzed. I assume that all social formations are discursively constituted, maintained, and changed and that discourses, especially when institutionalized, consist of a welter of practices fueled by resources and ordered by rules. To understand what happened to academic feminism, I try to synthesize what has been sundered—self-structure and social structure, intellectualization and institutionalization, what is in a discipline and what a discipline is in—and as a result I tell a story that is episodic and contextual. The chapters in part 1 focus on the academy's institutional-disciplinary order that worked on women as they resisted it during the 1950s and 1960s. Those in part 2 concentrate on the formation of feminist studies during the 1970s; starting with the vision of female studies as a hybrid project that would bridge the academy / society divide, they analyze the practices that meshed or fractured feminist studies projects, the venues that formatted feminist studies as an academic discipline, and the forces that proliferated its esoteric knowledges. Returning to the subject of political struggle, the chapters in part 3 examine two arenas of activity in the 1990s—the programs training the third generation of activists and the project to dismantle affirmative action—that will crystallize the future. At a time when feminist and progressive gains are in danger of being swept away, we need to know what deflected our academic initiatives and speculate on how we might redirect them now.

Yet even as I linger at my computer, scanning the incandescent lines burned into the midnight blue screen, I recognize the problem. The social change I did and knew up to the mid-1990s continues to mutate minute by minute, so that by the time these lines are etched onto the pages of a book it will once again have to be done and known as something else.

Part 1. Confronting the Institutional-Disciplinary Order

How an academic system distributes and legitimizes power may well be its most important aspect.—Burton R. Clark, *The Higher Education System* (1983)

In May 1971, *PMLA* and *College English* quietly made history as the first mainstream journals in literary studies to feature the new academic feminism. These debuts were arranged by the Modern Language Association's Commission on the Status of Women, established in 1969 and soon followed by women's committees in many other disciplinary associations. As the scholarly journal of the Modern Language Association, *PMLA* was committed to preserving the disciplinary orthodoxies, but in keeping with its charge to communicate associational business it dutifully printed with the rest of its back matter the CSW's first report on the status of women in modern language departments. *College English,* the organ of the National Council of English Teachers (NCTE), was edited by MLA activist Richard Ohmann and, in keeping with his objective of opening the discipline to radical criticism, devoted the entire May issue to feminist articles.

The *PMLA* report and *College English* articles show us that the first-generation academic feminists were working, like bricoleurs, to solder the discursive bits and pieces they had at hand into a model of the system they had entered and wanted to change. One example will illustrate this point: Florence Howe's "A Report on Women and the Profession," which appeared in *College English.* Drawing on findings of the CSW's study of women's status in the modern languages, she pointed out that women represented more than 65 percent of the beginning graduate students but only 37 percent of the total faculty and, when compared to male faculty, were disproportionately located in the less prestigious colleges, lower ranks, and part-time positions. Then she asked some incisive questions: How does an academic field, "which attracts two-thirds women and one-third men, wind up as a profession with the statistics reversed?" and how do the "men sweep on to the Yales and Harvards, and into the large coeducational universities to dominate . . . the profession?" The statistics and questions made a dynamic structure visible to *College English* readers:

sex patterning within a discipline and across institutions. What caused the sex patterns, Howe speculated, were a "series of interlocking social, political, and economic arrangements" that prevented some women from reaching the gateways to higher education and a set of academic practices that eliminated nearly half of those who had entered the discipline and channeled the rest into its backwaters.[1] It may seem that Howe was combining the bits of traditional discourses—sociology's empirical data with liberalism's egalitarian sentiments—to insist that the modern languages provide women with equal educational and employment opportunities. But the status report she had referenced, like many other status reports and critical articles from the early 1970s, was not merely representing the sex patterns but more importantly was describing how the system had produced them and what women could do to restructure it.

The May 1971 issues of *PMLA* and *College English* appeared at a pivotal moment. Before 1970 academic women could not see the workings of the institutional-disciplinary order they had entered; by 1975 they could consult a burgeoning literature that detailed its sex patterns and described the dynamics producing them. How did they make—that is, discursively produce—the transition from discipline to feminism? That is the subject of the two chapters that follow. Chapter 1 focuses on disciplines: how they socialized disciples as male-gendered practitioners, why they alienated and deauthorized women, and what the women did to reconstitute themselves as feminists. Chapter 2 focuses on institutions: how feminists made systemic sex discrimination visible, what universities did to resist equal opportunity, and why the courts that heard sex-discrimination lawsuits upheld the authority of universities to discriminate. The distribution and legitimation of power, I have to agree with Burton Clark, is the most important and interesting feature of the academic system. My analysis will show that disciplines and institutions could exercise their power to exclude and include, repress and produce, because they could structure their own fields of activity.

1. Disciplining Women

Disciplines are institutionalized formations for organizing schemes of perception, appreciation, and action, and for inculcating them as tools of cognition and communication.—Timothy Lenoir, "The Discipline of Nature and the Nature of Disciplines" (1993)

Result: . . . the subjects . . . "work by themselves" . . . with the exception of the "bad subjects" who on occasion provoke the intervention of one of the detachments of the (repressive) State apparatus. But the vast majority of (good) subjects work all right "all by themselves." . . . They are inserted into practices governed by the rituals of the ISAS.—Louis Althusser, "Ideology and Ideological State Apparatuses (Notes towards an Investigation)" (1970)

Visualize American higher education as a vast industry whose main business is producing, distributing, and consuming knowledge discourses. Its core infrastructure consists of 3,200 universities and colleges and more than 200 disciplines that mesh at specific sites: disciplines are nested in the university as departments and programs, while universities are embedded in a discipline as the departmental members of the disciplinary association. Fueled by resources and authorized by rules, universities and disciplines together govern the duchies they have carved out of higher education's territory. But what exactly do disciplines do for this industry?

First, they produce its knowledge discourses—and let's understand these discourses to consist of not just statements but more fundamentally the knowable objects and knowing subjects. Disciplines constitute "the objects we can study (genes, deviant persons, classic texts) and the relations that obtain among them (mutation, criminality, canonicity)." They "beget the tweedy dons and trendy young turks, plodders and paradigm-smashers, crackpots and classicists" who labor at the industry's knowledge-producing sites—its archives and libraries, clinics and laboratories, classrooms and lecture halls. And, together with academic institutions, they create and maintain the power-prestige hierarchies that order the knowledge enterprise—from instructor to professor, conference presentation to award-winning book, unaccredited program to top-ranked department.[1]

Second, disciplines control the knowledge economy because, as Timothy Lenoir suggests in the first epigraph to this chapter, they are organized and organizing. Each one is organized as an infrastructure of university and college departments, professional associations, and publications; each one organizes by using this infrastructure to assemble, direct, and monitor the processes essential to its functioning. At the macro level a discipline sets the knowledge problems, regulates the market, and distributes the goods, and at the micro level it inculcates and enforces the schemes of perception, cognition, and action that practitioners must use.[2] Consider this mundane example of how a discipline functions simultaneously at both levels to maintain the equilibrium of the knowledge economy: an author submits an article to a nationally prominent journal, which, during the review and revision process, requires her to tone down her truth-claims so they harmonize with the disciplinary orthodoxies.[3]

Finally, disciplines endure through practice, the continuation of practice depends upon reproduction, and reproduction is accomplished by socializing practitioners. When a discipline trains future practitioners, it doesn't just teach them its knowledge contents; it exercises them in its ways of perceiving, thinking, valuing, relating, and acting—thereby, as Althusser notes in the second epigraph, inserting them into its schemes of practice. Once the discipline has credentialed and employed them, it ensures that they continue to observe its "good subject" practices by subjecting them to ongoing evaluations: it rates their teaching performance, appraises their publications, checks their professional service, and tenures or terminates them. Competent practitioners learn (as inept ones do not) to observe the disciplinary norms, and innovative practitioners learn (as merely competent ones do not) which norms they can transgress in order to generate new knowledge. But woe to the practitioner who violates the disciplinary truth—its "ordered procedures for the production, regulation, distribution, circulation, and operation of [true] statements"[4]—because the discipline will regarded her as a bad subject to be subdued or expelled.

In this chapter, I explore how the relay between two disciplinary functions—the socialization of disciples and the ordering of discourse—operated on many of the first-generation feminists who received their training as undergraduate majors or doctoral students during the 1950s and 1960s. The four disciplines I discuss—physics, art history, sociology, and literary studies—are contrast cases in many respects: they investigated natural, social, or artifactual objects, used scientific or humanistic methods, and had unified or diversified cores of knowledge. Yet they all produced painful effects: their female disciples were estranged from everyday experiences, alienated from themselves and others, split into conflicting identities, and deauthorized as disciplinary knowers. These effects were caused by entrenched sexism and something more. I call them discipline effects because the disciplines produced them by doing what disciplines do: organizing their discourses.

Physics: Splitting the Scientist, Eclipsing the Social

For a 1977 volume entitled *Working It Out*, several feminist artists, scholars, and scientists wrote unusually candid and poignant essays about their struggles to live and work as women. None was more harrowing than Evelyn Fox Keller's "The Anomaly of a Woman in Physics," the story of her experiences as a doctoral student at Harvard University during the late 1950s and early 1960s. The story begins at Brandeis University when Keller "fell in love with theoretical physics" during her senior year:

> I fell in love, simultaneously and inextricably, with my professors, with a discipline of pure, precise, definitive thought, and with what I conceived of as its ambitions. I fell in love with the life of the mind. I also fell in love, I might add, with the image of myself striving and succeeding in an area where women had rarely ventured. It was a heady experience. In my adviser's fantasies, I was to rise, unhampered, right to the top. In my private fantasies, I was to be heralded all the way.[5]

What follows this fantasy of her future success—a plausible fantasy since several graduate programs were competing to recruit her—is a horrifying account of her apprenticeship in the Harvard program where she was one of three female doctoral students and the only one who aspired to be a theoretical physicist. Although she easily mastered the skills and generally earned As in her courses, her professors repeatedly undercut her aspirations, telling her that she could never be good enough, that she could not possibly understand what she thought she understood, that her lack of fear was proof of her ignorance, that her ambition was curious, and that no woman had ever succeeded in theoretical physics at Harvard. Thus began two years of "almost unmitigated provocation, insult, and denial" calculated to chasten her for "stubbornly pursuing an obviously male discipline." Shamed and shunned, she struggled to make sense of "the enormous discrepancy between what I expected and what I found."[6]

Intellectually, Keller had expected to be engrossed in pure thought; instead she was exercised in rote computation. Educationally, she had expected an exhilarating adventure; instead she was subjected to a painful trial. Emotionally, she expected to love and be loved; instead she was brutalized. Her professors told her that

> what happened to me at Harvard simply manifested my own confusion, failure, neurosis—in short that *I* had somehow "made" it happen. . . . Now I had to ask *how* I had "made" it happen—what in me required purging? It seemed that my very ambition and seriousness were at fault, and that these qualities—qualities I had always admired in others—had to be given up. Giving up physics, then, seemed to mean giving up parts of me so central to my sense of myself that a meaningful extrication was next to impossible.[7]

On her view, they were demanding not merely that she tone down her seriousness, ambition, and buoyancy but that she give up the self-image she had integrated in college: woman physicist. When Harvard presented those identities as antithetical, Keller was trapped in a struggle to reconcile "my sense of myself as a woman and my identity as a scientist."[8] Her determination to persist in a discipline that was acting to expel her made this contradiction intolerable, and its intolerability incited her further attempts to make sense.

Later I will show that Keller's split subjectivity was a discipline effect that resulted from the way that physics had defined the analyzable objects and analyzing subjects permitted to enter its discursive precincts. To set up that claim, I want to look at the reasons why Keller's initial attempts to make sense of her graduate experience failed. Her undergraduate fantasy used three genres to narrativize the experience she anticipated: (1) the Cartesian myth to figure disciplinary activity as minds engaged in "pure, precise, definitive thought"; (2) the heroic saga to depict her doctoral activity as striving and succeeding in the field; and (3) the romance story to present her emotional activity as falling in love with images of the discipline, the physicist, and her own success. The conventional protagonists of the first two genres are men, but Keller casts herself in these roles; she would be a woman adventuring through a territory women rarely entered. To make sense of the horrid actuality at Harvard, Keller renarrativized using the initiation myth: "I agreed to suspend judgment and to persevere through this stinging 'initiation rite.' In part, then, I believed that I was undergoing some sort of trial that would terminate when I had proven myself, certainly by the time I completed my orals. I need to be stoic only for one year. Unfortunately, that hope turned out to be futile."[9] None of Keller's narratives made sense of the actuality: the Cartesian, heroic, and romance myths were mismatches from the start because she experienced Harvard as profoundly anti-intellectual, educationally obstructionist, and emotionally brutalizing; and the initiation myth became a mismatch when her trial did not terminate. The continuing brutality intensified her rage, which in turn marked her in the eyes of her professors as a student to be ostracized from a discipline that, as she put it, tried "to make itself more powerful by weeding out those sensibilities, emotional and intellectual, that it considers inappropriate."[10]

Reflecting much later on what had been done to her, she finally told a different story: "After two years of virtually continuous denial of my perceptions, my values, and my ambitions—an experience that might then have been described as brainwashing, and ought now be called schizophrenogenic—my demoralization was complete."[11] Through a sociopsychoanalytic lens, she could finally see the socializing process that had split her subjectivity. The professors had constructed her as a bad subject and blamed her for the pain they had caused: they said that she was incompetent and neurotic. Once she introjected the bad-subject characterization, her subjectivity was riven between the self she wanted to be and the self they said she was—between virtuosity and mediocrity, desire and denial, physics and failure. This renarrativization finally showed her what the apprenticeship had done to her. But how did she break through the impasse to become a woman scientist who succeeded in areas where others rarely ventured? Whereas many aspiring women scientists who suffered brutal treatment left the academy, Keller, having determined to remain in it, cleverly exploited the logic of disciplinarity, first by writing her dissertation in the new hybrid science of molecular biology and later by repositioning herself in the new interdisciplinary fields of feminist and science studies. Eventually leaving her science professorship at North-eastern University, she accepted a joint appointment in the departments of rhetoric and women's studies at the University of California, Berkeley, and more recently a professorship in the Program in Science, Technology, and Society at the Massachusetts Institute of Technology, thereby confirming in departmental migration the transition she had made in disciplinary discourses.

Keller's scholarship took as its object of investigation precisely what physics had excluded from its domain. Her first major contribution to feminist science studies, *Reflections on Gender and Science* (1985), examined "the historic conjunction of science and masculinity and the equally his-toric disjunction between science and femininity," and much of her other work analyzed the subjective and social dimensions of scientific practice.[12] My own linking of the Harvard apprenticeship to the later disciplinary and scholarly strategies is justified by Keller's introduction to *Reflections*. "A decade ago," she wrote, " 'the personal is political' was an aphorism. . . . Today, feminist thinkers recognize the conjunction of personal and politi-cal as more than an aphorism: they see it as a method. . . . In short, the logical extension of the personal as political is the scientific as personal."[13] Painfully wedged between two self-constructs, Keller was a resourceful subject who reinvented herself as a critic of what drove her professors to abuse her. But what drove them? The obvious answer is their sexism; the less obvious one is their discipline. The professors, I will argue, were following the disciplinary rules that directed them to extirpate from physics precisely the discourses Keller had used to describe the field and explain her trials.

While Keller was learning physics, Harvard physics professor Gerald Holton was enjoying pedagogical success. His *Introduction to Concepts and Theories in Physical Science*, published in 1952 and in a sixth printing by 1962, was a widely used college textbook that (in both senses of the word) pitched the discipline to apprentice readers. Though written to summarize its "fundamental concepts and theories" and present scientific inquiry "as an integrated and exciting intellectual adventure," the book contains three chapters that uncritically reveal the rules constituting phys-ics' discourse and regulating its knowledge production.[14] As I inspect a few of the rules, I will show how they simultaneously rendered meaningful Keller's fantasy of questing through "a discipline of pure, precise, definitive thought" and rendered meaningless her attempts to make sense of her brutal apprenticeship. Let's begin with Holton's description of physics as

> the ever unfinished quest to discover all facts, the relationships between things, and the laws by which the world runs. . . . we may perhaps agree at the outset that the main business of science is to trace in the chaos and flux of phenomena a consistent structure with order and meaning, that is, to interpret and to transcend direct experience. "The object of all sciences," in Einstein's words, "is to coordinate our experiences and to bring them into a logical system."[15]

To engage his readers, Holton uses the adventure tropes that Keller used, but he immediately differentiates the physics adventure from other adventures. Its objective, to gloss what he says in disciplinary terms, is to transform the messy "nature" of experiential and interpretive discourses into the logical "nature" of scientific discourse.

As Holton goes on to explain the elements of physics—concepts, facts, laws, and theories—it becomes clear that he regards them not as abstractions that represent nature, but as discursive practices that render it. Let's start with concepts. Whereas an interpretive discourse would define the concepts "length" or "speed" linguistically, physics defines them operationally:

> For example, the concept "length of an object" as *used* in science is ultimately defined by the very *operations* involved in making the measurement. The problem "What is the length of a block?" is for all practical purposes identical with the question "What is the difference between those two numbers printed on a specific meter stick which stand directly below two corresponding scratches, entered there to signify local coincidence with the adjacent corners of the block?" This last sentence contained an abbreviated example of what we shall call an *operational definition.*

By performing such operations as measuring and computing, physicists can produce "the 'true meaning'" of the block's length or the comet's speed. Ideally, according to Holton, every concept should be operationally defined because "it is clearly more difficult to misinterpret action than words."[16]

Similarly, whereas an interpretive discourse would define "fact" as accurate information about an actual occurrence, the physicist again resorts to operationalism. A physical fact, Holton emphasizes, is a set of relations apprehended by an observer—but not by just any observer:

> Allow a layman to observe the sky through the new 200-inch telescope, and he will see nothing of interest and understand nothing he sees. But give a trained man only three good looks at a comet through a mediocre instrument, and he will call upon the theories in the field to tell you to a day how soon a comet will return, how fast it is traveling at any moment, what material it is made of, and much else. In short, the pattern we perceive when we note "a fact" is organized and interpreted by a whole system of attitudes and thoughts, memories, beliefs, and learned constructs. It is thought that gives us eyes.[17]

Holton's example indicates (though he might disagree with how I put it) that a fact is constituted by a trained scientist engaged in the combined procedures of bodily perception, instrumentalized detection, and disciplinary discourse. Thus, only by seeing through the discipline's particularly ordered discourse while peering through the telescope's assembly of reflecting and refracting lenses does the observer of a comet apprehend the relations called facts.[18]

To drive home his explanation of concepts and facts, Holton invokes Galileo's distinction between qualities that can be measured and mathematicized and those that cannot. This distinction is the rule that determines which experienced phenomena can be included in physics. In Holton's words, it reduces the

> *eligible* experience to a small fraction of the scientist's total experience, but to precisely that fraction which he could quantify and therefore share fairly unambiguously with his fellows. The ideas of science look so stylized and unreal just because . . . they help us describe those features of experience which the common-sense view of reality cares least about—measurement, mathematical manipulation, numerical prediction, and clear communicability—while failing to describe exactly those most prominent uses of everyday expressions, namely, our feelings, reactions, and other personal developments.[19]

Since the rule excludes phenomena that cannot be quantified and methods that do not quantify, it follows that many statements will be meaningless within the domain of physics—such as Keller's statements about her feelings, her professors' behavior, and even her "vision of theoretical physics as a vehicle for the deepest inquiry into nature—a vision perhaps best personified, in recent times, by Einstein."[20] Just so, Holton declares that "whole statements and even intelligent-sounding, deeply disturbing questions may turn out to be meaningless" and then cites as an example Newton's statement in the *Principia:* "Absolute, true, and mathematical time, of itself, and from its own nature, flows equably and without regard to anything external and by another name is called duration."[21] Since this seemingly profound statement cannot be operationalized, it is meaningless within physics discourse.

Yet physics does not appear to be so purely operationalist when Holton describes how physicists produce knowledge. He divides knowledge production into S[1], which he calls "science in the making," and S[2], which he calls "science as an institution." S[1] has two phases of activity, discovery and operationalization. In discovery, physicists might follow the logical steps of "the well-planned experiment" or they might "let their enthusiasms, their hunches, and their sheer joy of discovery suggest the line of work."[22] Since discovery often involves the very practices—analogizing, guessing, intuiting, feeling—that he previously described as antinomic to operationalizing activity, Holton acknowledges (quoting nuclear physicist H. D. Smyth) the " 'paradox in the method of science. The research man may often think and work like an artist, but he has to talk like a bookkeeper, in terms of facts, figures, and logical sequence of thought.' "[23] How, then, does Holton bridge the disconnects between discovery, operationalization, and the stockpile of physics knowledge? He casts the discovery phase of S[1] as preliminary to the operational phase: "Only when this 'private' stage is over and the individual contribution is formalized in order to be absorbed into 'public' science . . . only then does it begin to be really important that each step, each concept be made clear and meaningful."[24] To follow Holton's metaphorical delineation of S[1] as "science in the making," I would put it this way. The creative activity yields the raw produce— the hunches and guesses. The operationalizing activity turns this produce into the ingredients for scientific cookery—its factual observations, operationalized concepts, and working hypotheses. These ingredients are then transported to S[2] where other physicists put them to the tests that lead to their falsification, verification, or probabilistic confirmation. Thus S[2], or "science as an institution," is the kitchen where the scientific community finally bakes the physics knowledge.[25]

Returning to tropes, Holton binds the fallible physicist to the authoritative institution:

For the scientist's work, like that of any other explorer, must involve the whole man, demanding as it does reflection, observation, experimentation, imagination, and a measure of intuition. Being human, he fails far more often than he succeeds. . . . And yet, the *result* of this uncertain human activity, namely, the growing body of science itself, is undeniably a successful, vigorous enterprise.[26]

Peering through our own discursive telescope, we can see where the shadow of Holton's disciplinary account fell upon Keller's autobiographical account: his scientist-as-explorer language, her use of the exploration myth; his insistence on measurement and mathematics to operationalize concepts, her graduate-school drilling in computation; his rejection of philosophical questions and personal experience as meaningless, her preoccupation with making them meaningful; his rendering of the scientist's confusions and failures, her teachers' renderings of hers. Perhaps most significantly, we can see in his account that the individual scientist always gives way to the institution of science, the authority that determines what qualifies as meaningful experience, how it gets validated, and whether it can be added to the stockpile of physics knowledge. When Keller's professors told her she was failing in the discipline she thought she was mastering, they were following the rules that said philosophical and personal matters were not recognized as "experiences" in physics. Once she challenged their authority by using the discourses that physics had ousted, it was only logical that they would move to oust her. No wonder, then, that her later work was designed to illuminate all of those intelligent and deeply disturbing questions about scientific practice that physics had eclipsed.

Art History: Rehearsing the Viewer, Staging the Artifacts

Lillian S. Robinson and Lise Vogel's 1971 essay, "Modernism and Feminism," presents an excerpt from a letter written by a female graduate student who was being trained in art history while Keller was at Harvard. The letter shows how this discipline organized the visual and interpretive practices of its subjects—both the professional art historian and the occasional museumgoer.

"It is obvious that good art has no sex." So *Art News* tells me. So I have learned to agree. But reading the categorical statement takes me back to my old, "naive" responses. I already had my Master's in art history when my husband and I spent a summer in Europe. One afternoon, at the Alte Pinakothek in Munich, we stopped in front of Boucher's *Reclining Girl*. She is lying on her belly, naked, her elbows supporting the upper part of her rosy body and her legs spread wide apart. My husband looked for a moment and observed with mock pedantry, "Ah yes, a nude of the turn-her-over-and-fuck-her school." But *I* didn't want to turn her over and fuck her. Nor did I want to compete with her candid sexuality. What I felt was her exposure and vulnerability—and I felt that I shared them. We were both supposed to believe that this portrait of a teenaged mistress of Louis XV "is a triumph of simple and memorable design, and shows Boucher's delight in the sheer painting of flesh." As I progressed through graduate school, even such contradictory judgments as this began to come naturally to me too.[27]

This anecdote suggests that Boucher's painting constructs its subject matter and viewer with gendered, sexualized, and classed identities that art history then excludes from its discourse. To show how art history constituted its viewers, I want to begin by contrasting the responses of a properly socialized art historian, the graduate student, and her husband.

An art historian would follow the disciplinary rules that direct him to ignore the eroticized subject matter that positions the portrait in sex-gender discourse and to notice the medium, genre, form, and style that position it in disciplinary discourse. The proper response quoted by the student—that the portrait is "a triumph of simple and memorable design, and shows Boucher's delight in the sheer painting of flesh"—comes from Michael Levey's *A Concise History of Painting from Giotto to Cézanne* (1962), a standard art history textbook that points out how Boucher's design and coloration contribute to the evolution of formal techniques and express his exuberant spirit.[28] By contrast, the graduate student responds empathically to the subject matter and later in her career calls that response "naive," with quotation marks to suggest that this judgment should be attributed elsewhere. Indeed, given the opportunity, her professors would have considered it artless for neglecting the formal and stylistic features and childlike for identifying with the reclining girl's vulnerability. Yet the student's response was complex because it entailed recognizing that she as a woman in a male-dominated, heterosexual economy was susceptible to being in the reclining girl's position and she as a female disciple in a male-dominated disciplinary economy might already be in that position.

Her husband, a linguistics professor, also failed to deliver the proper response. When he commented mockingly, "Ah yes, a nude of the turn-her-over-and-fuck-her school," he did acknowledge the genre conventions that should be noticed, but he also remarked the sexual conventions that should be ignored. Worse, through mock pedantry and coarse language, he ridiculed art history's deportation of sexual features from its scheme of visual and interpretive practice. Robinson and Vogel themselves remarked that art patrons of earlier eras might have enjoyed the blatant sexuality of the nude genre but "today only a naïve or exceptionally candid man admits that facet of his appreciation of a Titian, a Rubens, or a Boucher. . . . We are expected to look at the nude as an exercise in form and design, much as Levey does."[29] Although both the student and her husband transgressed the disciplinary rules, their responses positioned them differently. By performing the prohibited practices, she signaled herself to be a viewer "in the naive" outside of the discipline; by mocking the prescribed and prohibited practices, he signaled himself to be a viewer "in the know" of the discipline.[30] Both transgressed, but the discipline looked down on her, whereas he, by communicating that he knew the conventions and knew what was wrong with them, looked down on the discipline.

During her graduate training, the student apparently performed both sets of interpretive practices, her own and the discipline's, because handling "contradictory judgments . . . began to come naturally." Although disciplinary socialization split her subjectivity, it did not seem to be schizophrenogenic, if by that term we understand the discipline to have produced a subjective dis-integration that impaired the disciple's functioning. Art history's gentler tactics constru(ct)ed her as a naive student who would someday learn the rules; physics' brutal tactics constru(ct)ed Keller as a neurotic one who would never learn the rules. The art history student was able to accommodate both schemes of practices "naturally," gain a critical purchase on the disciplinary rules, and thereby balance her identities as "woman" and "art historian"—at least for a time. After completing her master's degree in art history, she earned a doctorate in literary studies and became (as did Keller) a prominent feminist critic of disciplines. But now I want to return to the issue of how art history disciplined experts and laypersons alike.

Art history's task of ordering its discourse was complicated by the fact that artworks were construed, as physical phenomena were not, by several institutionalized systems: they were the knowledge objects of the academic discipline, the exhibited objects of museums, the transacted objects of art markets, and the aestheticized objects collected by connoisseurs.

Moreover, since art experts regarded artworks as having several modes of existence—material, formal, iconological, geographical-historical, and expressive—they could not distill their object, as physicists distilled theirs, to one set of qualities to be operationalized in one way. An artifact's status as an artwork often depended on material analyses—chemical, X-ray, infrared, and microscopic—that answered questions about its place and time of origin, its authenticity, and its attribution (e.g., as when one artist overpaints part of another's canvas). Once designated as an artwork, its form could not be analyzed and its subject matter interpreted if its surface qualities were ignored. The question, then, is how did the discipline synthesize the object's heterogenous modes of institutionalization and intellectualization.

A brief genealogy of art-historical discourse might begin in the nineteenth century with the rise of the modern museum and the institutionalization of art history in German universities. In the United States, according to Erwin Panofsky, art history "had to fight its way out of an entanglement with practical art instruction, art appreciation, and that amorphous monster 'general education.' "[31] The growth of the discipline was fueled by university departmentalization, and the formation of its discourse was owing to such developments as the founding of photographic archives and reference libraries, the compilation of iconographical indices, and the establishment of the Fogg Museum at Harvard in 1895. The Fogg, explains Donald Preziosi, was not a museum. As "the first institution specifically designed to house the entire disciplinary apparatus of art history," it contained distinctive spaces dedicated to disciplinary purposes: exhibition halls, classrooms, a library of textual materials, and most importantly "an indefinitely expandable archive of uniformly formatted slide and photographic" reproductions of artworks.[32] By juxtaposing these reproductions, art historians could compare artworks along any axis—the material, form, or theme, the oeuvre, school, or geographical location—and thereby fabricate evolutionary narratives. The Fogg supplied the template that departments and museums used to produce art's "history."

But art historians still had to synthesize the artwork's heterogenous features in a coherent interpretive order. This problem was solved by the concept of "style," which was first formulated by Heinrich Wölfflin in his influential *Principles of Art History: The Problem of the Development of Style in Later Art* (1915, English trans. 1932). Wölfflin selected paired paintings, such as Botticelli and de Credi nudes, Hobbema and Ruysdael landscapes, that had nearly identical lines, shapes, and colors and then examined these formal features for differences in such qualities as vitality and languidity, intensity and tranquility. These qualities, he said, indicated "a difference of [artistic] temperament, and that difference penetrates throughout [the paintings], whether we compare the whole or the details. In the drawing of a mere nostril, we have to recognize the essential character of style."[33] Wölfflin formulated "style" by sliding from surface to spirit and un-abashedly prescribed this modus operandi: the art historian, he said, should analyze "style primarily as expression, expression of the temper of an age and a nation as well as expression of the individual temperament."[34] This formula was championed by Panofsky, who heralded the analysis of "materialized form, idea (that is . . . subject matter) and content" as a "recreative synthesis,"[35] and was widely disseminated by Charles R. Jan-sen's *Studying Art History*, the standard art history textbook for several decades.[36]

With style, wrote David Summers, art historians presumably solved the problem of how to synthesize the artwork's modes of existence and ground their own interpretations. They assumed that since the artist, in interpreting and painting what he saw, left traces of his psychology and his culture's spirit on the artwork, they would be able to " 'see through' the surfaces of the work to its meaning."[37] Summers provides a little demon-stration of this method:

> by properly responding to forms, we could see more or less directly into the mind or spirit or world view of artists, places, times, and peoples. . . . The elongated linear forms and nondescriptive colors of Mannerist paintings are to be expected of the paranoid Pontormo or the suicidal Rosso Fiorentino, and such psychological extremities are, in turn, expected of painters working through the sack of Rome, the siege of Florence, and the Reformation.[38]

Once the manipulable archive was joined to the concept of style, art historians could script the coevolution of artifacts and human spirit. And that coevolution was not merely described in textbooks read by disciplin-ary apprentices; it was staged for museumgoers.

When the modern museum emerged in Europe during the early nineteenth century, it introduced galleries to group artifacts, doorways and halls to channel visitors, labels and catalogs to enscript meanings.[39] Through these techniques the museum, Preziosi notes, developed a spa-tial, exhibitionary, and performative format that was the *"correlative* to the discursive space of art history."[40] The traditionally designed multistorey structure was partitioned to organize artifacts geographically and chronologically with finer distinctions by medium or style, artist or school. The visitors did not freely meander and interpret. Entrances, walls, corridors, staircases, railings, and display cases choreographed their routes. Exhibitionary formats (e.g., artifacts arranged in a sequence or a milieu), labels, and catalogs cued them on how to make meaning. Ubiquitous signs and guards tutored them in deportment: no running, touching, loud talking, eating, or photo flashing. The museum didn't present them with a visual narrative; it staged their tour through its narrative and thereby rehearsed them in the disciplinary discourse.[41]

Art-historical discourse, I am arguing, constituted both the expert and layperson. One was trained to produce responses that fell "within the true" of disciplinary analysis, and the other was rehearsed in producing responses that fell "within the know" of museum narratives. In this respect, viewing in art differed from viewing in physics. Holton commented that the layman who looks at the sky through a telescope will "understand nothing he sees," whereas the physicist who peers through the telescope and the disciplinary discourse will see a comet and produce illuminating facts about it. But both the expert and lay viewer can make sense of the artwork because art-historical discourse has already formatted their practices of seeing (through) it.

Sociology: Evacuating the Subject, Scientizing the Social

To explain how a properly socialized disciple could become an undisciplined subject, I turn to an account that feminist sociologist Dorothy E. Smith reprinted in one of her articles. In this account, Catherine Russell, a worker at a Canadian battered women's shelter, reflects on the hostilities that erupted at a conference on battered wives attended by social workers, sociologists, psychologists, and psychiatrists:

> My attitudes on arriving at the conference were fairly consistent with those of the majority. I was there to learn by absorbing theories and facts. . . . Not knowing much, I accepted a position of being low on the hierarchy of people at the symposium; power and worthiness derived from being able to clearly articulate an intellectual perception of a social phenomenon and a theoretical solution to the problem.
>
> My first emotional response at the symposium was to Gene Erring-

ton's speech. She made a strong, angry statement of her reaction to the conference and to the orientation of professionals. I was very uncomfortable and felt antagonistic toward her for making a speech that stirred up the symposium and antagonized a large number of delegates. I didn't want to be identified with the feminists who were giving her a standing ovation—even though I was sitting with that group whose interests coincided with mine. I was accepting the norm that says: "Let's be calm and logical about this. There's no need to get angry. . . ."

The next day I started to realize how I had been affected by the norms of the majority. [I] . . . had been denying others the expression of their feelings and had been valuing people's contributions predominantly on the basis of intellectual consistency, articulation and coolness.

In the first workshop, one woman—in an emotional and somewhat rambling statement—expressed her feeling of being battered by the conference itself. The expression of her feelings was only briefly responded to by the workshop speaker. However, she had spoken for a lot of women at that workshop, in that there was a lot of frustration being experienced . . . at the tone of the conference. Her speaking led other women to speak from their feelings.

And that's when I really started feeling angry. I recognized that my acceptance of the professionals' norms had been a critical factor in my discounting and criticizing Gene the previous day and others during the course of the symposium. . . . Those norms value intellectual perception so highly and emotions so lowly; they are a basic cause of the violence in our culture.[42]

As Russell describes it, the conference was a knowledge economy ordered by a hierarchy and a division. The high-status social scientists—sociologists, psychologists, and psychiatrists—dispensed esoteric knowledge of battering to the low-status social workers, who were supposed to absorb it. The esoteric discourse they used was already sharply demarcated from everyday social discourse and feminist critical discourse by scientific norms that, as Russell put it, "value intellectual perception so highly and emotions so lowly." When the women at the conference tried to introduce the unauthorized discourses, the social scientists maintained their power (as Keller remarked about the physicists) by repudiating the emotional and intellectual sensibilities they considered inappropriate.

At first, when Errington angrily called attention to the conference dynamics and her feminist supporters applauded, Russell did what a good disciple was supposed to do. Although she was sitting with that group and sharing its interests, she used social-science discourse to alienate herself in three ways—from battered women by intellectualizing battering as an object of scientific inquiry, from the feminists by repudiating their emotionality, and from herself by suppressing her knowledge of her own position at the bottom of the professional and gender hierarchies. But she had a different response on the next day when a woman transgressed all three requirements by declaring, in an emotional outburst, that she felt battered by the conference (i.e., she asserted that the social scientists used norms the way batterers used fists). Russell was able to resituate herself with the undisciplined women by performing the practices used in consciousness-raising groups. She heard their comments, witnessed the abuse heaped on them, and empathically shared their anger. Through this process, she came to see that the social-science norms, which the social scientists wielded against female participants who introduced the prohibited discourses, had formed her as a good disciplinary subject.

Russell's transition from disciple to critic was easier than Keller's because her discipline provided intellectual and social resources that physics did not. Russell could use sociological models of social-group norms, hierarchies, and antagonisms to understand the conference hostilities as the effects of intergroup power differentials. But since physics had decreed that the fallible individual should give way to the authoritative institution and had cast conflicts over disciplinary norms as individual pathologies, Keller had to look elsewhere for explanatory models—into discourses that offered her the initiation myth and the schizophrenogenic trope. Tellingly, she concluded her autobiographical account with these words:

> If I was demolished by my graduate school experiences, it was primarily because I failed to define myself as a rebel against norms in which society has heavily invested. In the late fifties, "rebel" was not a meaningful word. Conflicts and obstacles were seen to be internal. . . . An awareness of the political and social realities might have saved me from persisting in a search for affirmation where it could not and would not be given.[43]

In this passage we see Keller's awareness of the social dynamics that physics eclipsed, but her lone-rebel trope reiterates (although inverts the value valence of) its structuring of the social: the individual pitted against the institution. That leads to my final point: the two disciplines also provided different social resources. Sociology had trained a critical mass of women who could band together in conflict situations, and physics had not. To use Althusser's terms, Russell was a bad subject who could work all right with others, but Keller was a bad subject who had to work by herself.

One question remains: why were the social scientists as zealous as the physicists in weeding everyday social discourse out of their domain? The answer resides with the strategies of scientization that the early practitioners used to form the boundaries and core of modern sociology. To dissociate their project from the reform crusades of clergy and improvement societies, the politics of socialists and eugenists, and the community social services, they declared it to be an academic inquiry. But having located their project in the academy they had to distinguish it from traditional social thought, which Jessie Bernard describes as a hodgepodge of moral philosophy, history of civilization, and humanistic speculation, and from the new sciences of economics and politics, which regarded the newcomer as "a mere catch-all for the 'anomalies of fact'" lacking focus and rigor.[44] The decisive move, argue Tom Bottomore and Robert Nisbet in *A History of Sociological Analysis,* occurred when the practitioners decided to make sociology a distinctive "theoretical and empirical science."[45] By using scientific methods, they could differentiate sociology from social thought, and by forming a new object of study—the "conception of 'society'" as "social structure, social systems, and social institutions"[46]—they could differentiate sociology from economics and politics.

The founding fathers installed at the core of sociology what Dorothy Smith describes as convention-structured objectivity practices. The conventions required sociologists to recast multivalent human activities as nominalized constructs, such as "depression" and "family violence," and then to generate data through such methods as interviews, surveys, and opinion polls. The point was to detail the constructs by specifying facts and causes: to identify the "factors" causing "depression" or gauge the "probabilities" that "family violence" would occur under certain conditions.[47] Smith argues that sociology's "facts" and "causes" are not relations that exist among human activities but practices that stabilize the disciplinary discourse. Facticity is the practice "of securing a stable relationship" between a construct (a social activity or event rendered as a sociological construct) and "the statements that can be made about it."[48] Likewise, causality is the practice of webbing the statements that sociologists make about the relations among constructs. To illustrate how the discourse works, Smith quotes a statement about children: "Demographic calculations tell us little of the subcultural processes (social class attitudes), or the more intricate psychosocial processes of the individual family which together provide the motivation to excell and the implementary values which can turn school achievement into career success."[49] Here the author brings nominalized constructs (italicized) into hypothesized causal relations: *subcultural processes* and *family psychosocial processes* provide the *motivation* that produces *school achievement* that amplifies into *career success*. In this statement, constructs are the actors and their causality is the action; gone are the children, parents, teachers, and their lived experiences of feeling, thinking, and acting.

Scientization worked together with gender ideology to reorganize the discipline. With the rise of the research university at the turn of the century, the feminized subfields of home economics and social services were scuttled; other subfields, such as social settlements, sex roles, and marriage and the family, were devalued; and sociologists began appropriating the large-scale surveys conducted by federal and state bureaus. Survey research attracted the grants from government agencies and private foundations that grew sociology, which once again expanded into new territories after World War II when the federal government pumped money into research on such topics as group behavior, organizational dynamics, and social deviance.[50] Paradoxically, the growth of sociology produced the disunity that began to trouble sociologists. They believed that its status as a scientific discipline was endangered by "the coexistence over long periods of a multiplicity of paradigms"[51] and that its status as a public profession was hampered by having no standardized credentialing of professionals, no consistent application of disciplinary knowledge, and little authority with clients.[52] Sociology, it would appear, got caught in a double bind that started when it took on that profitable survey research: as a scientific discipline it needed to maintain a unified core purged of everyday discourse, but as a public profession it needed to put its knowledge to work in everyday arenas.[53]

Reviewing Russell's story through the disciplinary lens, we can see that scientization repeatedly precipitated the conflicts that disrupted the conference. The scientists had expected to observe the usual protocol: they would transfer their esoteric knowledge of battering to the social workers, who would apply it in everyday arenas. When the women objected to this arrangement, the scientists invoked objectivity norms to prevent their insights into power and their emotion-laden language from flowing into the conference's discursive arena. The women then responded by claiming that the scientists were deauthorizing what they—as social workers, as women, and perhaps as past victims—knew about battering. Since scientization already divided the social sciences from everyday discourses, why did the scientists hasten to invoke it? They recognized that the women's statements about people's feelings, thoughts, and actions, if they swarmed into the conference's arena, would recast its sociological discourse as social discourse.

Literary Studies: Obliterating the Critic, Exalting the Text

From the late-nineteenth through the mid-twentieth centuries, while physics, sociology, and art history were consolidating their discourses and as a result enjoying periods of paradigm stability (let's understand *para-digm* in the Kuhnian sense of intellectual framework *and* pattern of practice), literary studies was lurching through long stretches of paradigm proliferation, competition, and shift. Institutionally, it was splintered by language groups housed at first in programs for classical, oriental, and modern languages / literatures and later in specialized university departments—English, French, Spanish, German, East Asian, Arabic, and so on. Discursively, its statements were fissioned into streams emanating from literary history's chronological and contextualizing order, literary theory's nomothetic order, and literary criticism's interpretive and formal orders. And its process of knowledge production, thanks to the methodological eclecticism of literary criticism, looked like the string, woodwind, and percussion instruments of an orchestra trying to braid their dissonant interpretations into a coherent figure. Yet beneath this diversity the discipline's practices were ordered by two basic paradigms during the 1950s and 1960s. One paradigm—let's call it interpretationism—was an open system that allowed sex stereotypes to seep into and steep disciplinary reading and writing. The other paradigm—formalism—was a closed system of textual analysis that excluded other discourses, much as operationalism had banished personal and philosophical discourses from physics and scientization had evacuated everyday social discourse from sociology. The numerous accounts written by first-generation feminists show us how these two patterns of practice produced the painful discipline effects they experienced while traveling along the path from freshman English through graduate training to faculty jobs.

In a 1971 essay, Elaine Showalter examined the undergraduate curriculum from the perspective of the female student, describing course by course the texts she read and the thinking she was taught. The anthologies assigned in freshman English typically devoted 93 percent of their contents to male-authored essays and bore such titles as *The Responsible Man, Conditions of Men, Man in Crisis,* and *Representative Men: Cult Heroes of Our Time.* "By the end of her freshman year," Showalter remarked, the woman student fed on this diet of readings "would be learning, in fact, how to think like a man."[54] Over the next three years, she would encounter the negativity of women—the "martyred mothers, pathetic sisters, and difficult wives" featured in fiction, poetry, and biography, "the myths of female sexuality as seen by Hardy and Lawrence," "the wonders of childbirth as seen by Sterne and Hemingway," and "the long and honorable tradition of literary misogyny." What, Showalter then asked, were the effects of this education on women students?

> The masculine culture . . . is so all-encompassing that few women students can sustain the sense of a positive feminine identity in the face of it. Women are estranged from their own experience and unable to perceive its shape and authenticity, in part because they do not see it mirrored and given resonance by literature. Instead they are expected to identify as readers with a masculine experience and perspective, which is presented as the human one.[55]

For women students, Showalter described this course of undergraduate study as an apprenticeship in "negative capability," a phrase she borrowed from Keats, who used it in the positive sense. A great poet, said Keats, was capable of remaining in a state of uncertainty with no irritable reaching after fact or reason in order to let the beauties of the universe flow into his mind and obliterate all other considerations.[56] Showalter's ironic use of the phrase bared the discipline's standard of competence: to be regarded as capable, the female student would have to endure the obliteration of her female identity that resulted from performing its male-centered, female-negating practices.

Graduate school intensified the apprenticeship in negative capability. Carolyn Heilbrun and Catharine Stimpson reported that they were trained to read

> all works in the light of the conventions of the male critic, who, of course, found only those things that his stringent ideas of maleness had taught him to look for. Not only did we ignore the absences [women's texts and experiences] . . . not only did we defend the sacrifice of

women as only natural, and any defeat of men as life-denying, against the order of nature, to the extent that "to emasculate" became a synonym for "to kill"; but we also assumed that any male writer must be writing from the Freudian convictions of the male critics and professors who taught us.[57]

Male-centered, female-negating conventions also informed Suzanne Juhasz's training in scholarly writing:

> As I wrote my critical papers in graduate school, I tried to learn how to "pass" for male: that is, to write papers that didn't reveal the fact that I was a woman. I wasn't terribly successful. The first draft of my doctoral dissertation was heavily criticized by the male members of the committee (although not by my director, a woman) because of its style. . . . What I had to say about the poetry was fine, but there weren't enough topic sentences and conclusions: what thesis was I trying to prove; why did I write as if I were writing a detective story rather than a piece of scientific research? I wasn't being "logical" enough; I was being too feminine.[58]

To demonstrate her competence, Juhasz would have to replicate the topic sentence / conclusion form of paragraphing and the thesis / proof mode of development. But why did she claim that these seemingly neutral prose conventions were male-gendered? A few years earlier, Mary Ellmann's *Thinking About Women* (1968) showed that prose conventions were sex stereotyped: men's prose, typed as rational, omniscient, and assertive, was taken as meritorious, and women's prose, typed as illogical, formless, and passive, was not. This formula drove the perceptions of ordinary readers and the pronouncements of critics, such as Anthony Burgess's remark that he could gain no pleasure from reading Jane Austen's prose because it "lacks a strong male thrust." What happened was that as the critic read the prose the mere presence or absence of such male-typed conventions as rational argument, omniscient point of view, and assertive style nudged him toward a favorable or unfavorable assessment of the author's competence.[59] Thus in advising Juhasz to use more topic sentences, conclusions, theses, and proofs, her committee members were in effect telling her to use the conventions that signaled writerly competence to readers.

In contrast to interpretationism's leaky perimeters and gender-saturated practices, formalism's impermeable boundaries prevented other discourses from entering its domain; its stringent methods contained the text within a discourse of structure; and its most vigorous strain, New Criticism, sought to monopolize the field of literary criticism. In a recent volume on the birth of feminist literary criticism, French scholar Nancy K. Miller recalled that "formalism reigned supreme" over Columbia University's English Department, and Shakespearean scholar Carol Thomas Nealy confessed that at Smith College she "avoided professors who took a historical or biographical approach (mostly older women, hired as new Ph.D.s in the twenties and thirties . . .) and sought out those who favored the eloquent New Critical analysis of complicated poetic texts (mostly younger men, often recent Yale Ph.D.s)."[60] The New Critics, who were initially clustered at Vanderbilt, Kenyon, Yale, Harvard, and Minnesota, disseminated their method through textbooks, scholarship, and courses that they and their disciples used to train several generations of literary critics—including feminist ones.[61]

Selma R. Burkom, a first-generation feminist who was trained by New Critics in literary studies and logical positivists in philosophy, describes the method. Her professors directed her to "deal only with the empirically verifiable" and rationally analyzable "elements of the text, to be objective, and to control, if not eliminate, most subjective responses." As a result, Burkom, like the female disciples mentioned earlier in this chapter, struggled to "reconcile apparent opposites" within herself—a self that analyzed form and a self that responded with affect. Realizing that her (albeit female-typed) affective and intuitive "self was being denied as fully in philosophy as it had been in English,"[62] she returned to literature in search of characters who

> reconciled within themselves traits stereotypically in opposition. None of the protagonists were definable either by the masculine characteristic cluster—logos, reason, the analytic—or by the feminine cluster—eros, feeling, the synthetic—taken alone. As a graduate student I had experienced my self as split whether I did the "new criticism" or logical empiricism. Now, in literature, I discovered non-divided images of selfhood, which, like the self I had, were constituted not by one thing or another but by both.[63]

Burkom escaped formalism by returning to the interpretationist paradigm, but instead of deploying its male-centered, female-negating conventions she used a comparative and constitutive method. By contrasting images of the integrated self she had found in literature with the split self she had acquired through disciplinary socialization, Burkom could see that she had to conjoin what her disciplines had put asunder: male / female, reason / affect, esoteric knowledge / lived experience. The very act of producing an innovative reading encouraged Burkom and the other women to regard themselves not merely as competent literary critics but as feminist literary critics who could articulate a new professional identity and practice. "I am a feminist and I am a critic," Juhasz crowed, and "the fact that feminism and criticism can come together has brought me several steps closer to my ideal goal of professional life: that it should be integrated with my personal life; that I should be able to function *as a woman* in both spheres."[64] The fact that physics provided no resources for conjoining male / female and reason / affect in science may account for Keller's less triumphal statement: to resolve "the fundamental conflict" between her identities as a woman and a scientist, she wrote, "took a long time, a personal analysis, and the women's movement."[65]

To explain how New Critics ordered their discourse, which in turn produced the split subjectivity experienced by Burkom and others, I draw from two authoritative books: René Wellek and Austin Warren's *Theory of Literature* (1949), widely used as the graduate-level introduction to literary study during the 1950s and 1960s, and W. K. Wimsatt's *The Verbal Icon* (1954), a collection of essays often assigned in graduate seminars. Early in their book, Wellek and Warren used the familiar tactics of division and exclusion to eliminate their competitors in the critical domain. They radically demarcated formal criticism, which they termed the "intrinsic" study of literature, from biographical, psychological, sociological, and historical criticism, which they termed "extrinsic" study. Extrinsic schools of criticism, they said, might explain authorial temperament, cultural themes, or reader responses, but they did not address the literary work's mode of existence.[66] Wimsatt, a Yale colleague of Wellek's, used the same tactics: "Certainly it need not be with a derogatory purpose that one points out personal studies, as distinct from poetic studies, in the realm of literary scholarship. Yet there is a danger of confusing personal and poetic studies. . . . There is a difference between internal and external evidence for the meaning of a poem."[67] Whatever his "purpose," Wimsatt did derogate the so-called personal studies in two influential essays. Critics, he said, committed "the intentional fallacy" when they used biography and history to argue that the poem's meaning was intended by the author or emanated from the zeitgeist, and they committed "the affective fallacy" when they used psychology or aesthetics to argue that the poem's meaning was produced by its readers.[68] In effect, New Critics averted the problem of competing analyses, much as physicists and sociologists did, by excluding the discourses that would produce them.

Having marginalized their competitors for the critical turf, Wellek and Warren then described the elements of their formal discourse. The literary work of art, they claimed, "has a special ontological status. It is neither real (physical, like a statue) nor mental (psychological, like the experience of light or pain) nor ideal (like a triangle). It is a system of norms of ideal concepts which are intersubjective. They must be assumed to exist in collective ideology . . . accessible only through individual mental experiences, based on the sound-structure of its sentences."[69] On their definition, the literary work was concrete because it was realized in written or spoken language, abstract because it had a structure (the plot of a tragedy, the form of a sonnet), and universal because authors and readers participated in the collectively grasped system of formal norms. The task of the New Critic was not to interpret the meaning of the work, despite Wimsatt's reference to the meaning of the poem, but to analyze and evaluate it as a structured language object—"a verbal icon," as Wimsatt put it. "The structure of poems as [both] concrete and universal," he said, "is the principle by which the critic can try to keep the two [analysis and evaluation] together."[70]

New Criticism, like physics and sociology, stringently regulated its practitioners. They were supposed to select a short but complex text (preferably a poem), assume it to be a language object, perform a close reading, and seek a unifying structure.[71] While reading the text, they were supposed to discern relations within it, not references to anything outside of it—the author's life, the social context, the themes recapitulated from elsewhere.[72] The inside / outside distinction was the correlative of Galileo's distinction in physics and, though entirely spurious, did important work for New Criticism. But the grounds on which it disqualified other schools of criticism should have disqualified New Criticism as well because all schools of criticism referred the text to something outside the text: most critics referred it to the conventions of psychology, history, or myth, and New Critics referred it to the conventions of form. The inside / outside distinction also gave the impression that New Criticism, by employing a rigorous method that penetrated to the heart of the object, was scientific— an impression that New Critics buttressed by using agentless phrases or depersonalized pronouns such as Wimsatt's "there is" and "one points out." In New Criticism, as in physics, practitioners were supposed to extirpate their personal feelings, viewpoints, and judgments; but in fact

Wellek, Warren, and Wimsatt left traces of these sentiments in their prose—namely, the judgmental overvoice that designated extrinsic criticism as bad-subject practice and formal analysis as good-subject practice.

Although the New Critic seldom appeared in propria persona, he was typified in Murray Krieger's aptly titled "The Critic as Person and Persona" (1976). In a key passage of the essay, the critic is caught up in a familiar struggle—one we have seen in physics, sociology, and art history—between outsider experiential discourse and insider formal discourse.

> As the critic vainly seeks to capture in his language the object whose language has captured him, he must remain alert to its peculiar and paradoxical nature: it is an object . . . experienced temporally [i.e., because it is read]; but . . . it has formal characteristics that provoke him to claim to find spatial interrelationships within it. . . . But the critic cannot permit his own imposition of spatial structures to deceive him: the object and *its* structures are in movement and so are the structures of his consciousness which interact with it. . . . So there are his ineffable subjective experiences and his reducing or flattening of them to the dimensions of his preconceptions. But can there not also be a normative control that could direct the former and complicate the latter?[73]

The struggle occurs over the imposition of structure at the intersubjective site where the subject meets the object. The critic's already structured consciousness, which gives him access to the poem, wants to redraw the poem in "the contours of his own personality," and the poem's richly detailed features redound on him to complicate his analysis of its structure. Caught between his experiential structures and its formal structures, his preference for crisp design and its presentation of complex detail, the critic must proceed. But how? Krieger cuts through the impasse by distinguishing the critic's preliminary and formal modes of practice, much as Holton specified the physicist's creative and operationalizing modes. To access the poem, the critic apprehends it as "*continuous* with all our other experiences" and constitutes it as "the experienced object." But to convert the "experienced object" into a formally analyzable object he must render it "discontinuous with our other experiences."[74] To move from the experiential mode to the analytical mode, the critic is helped by something that Krieger allusively calls "normative control." Normative control is just another name for New Critical method; it means using formal conventions to discern the poem's structure. Why should the critic submit to that control? Krieger replies, "To the extent that the critic owes his primary fealty to the object that calls him into existence, he must obliterate himself to explain and exalt *it.*"[75]

Krieger's normative control in the discourse of New Criticism points to what I have been saying about the order of discourse in physics, sociology, and art history as well. It is neither the poem that calls the critic into existence nor the critic who calls the poem into existence but New Critical discourse that calls both of them into existence by imposing a scheme of formalizing practices that requires the subject to speak normatively about literary works. Just so, physics called the factual observation and the physicist into existence by imposing a scheme of operationalizing practices, sociology called the construct and the sociologist into existence by imposing a scheme of objectifying practices, and art history called the artifact and art historian into existence by imposing a scheme of narrativizing practices. These schemes of practice—New Criticism's formalism, physics' operationalism, sociology's objectivity, and art history's narrativity—Foucault has named "discipline."

THE DISCIPLINES, I have been arguing, inserted their disciples into normative schemes of practice and thereby produced good subjects who would work all right by themselves. Paradoxically, however, the same preliminary strategies of demarcating and ordering their discourse that enabled the disciplines to produce good subjects also caused them to produce bad ones. All students who enter the university are discursive migrants: they emigrate from their customary social and school discourses into the unfamiliar and difficult discourse of an academic discipline. Once there, they have to learn the intellectual order (the language, content, and skills), the professional order (the character and conduct of practitioners), and the pedagogical order (the learning protocols).[76] Given the complexity and normativity of disciplinary discourse, any student can flounder and experience the effects—the bewilderment of a student who can't grasp the language, the frustration of a student who commits to the intellectual goals but can't achieve competence in the means, and the isolation of a student who masters the intellectual discourse but rejects the professional conduct. One way or another, these feelings destabilize the self, producing doubt that leads to the student's disengagement or determination that fuels his persistence.

But when the disciplinary discourse negates an identity category, the effects are compounded. The stories recounted in this chapter show that the female-negating rules, conventions, and norms operating in all three orders of disciplinary discourse alienated female students from their extra-disciplinary identities and experiences, or split their subjectivities into contradictory modes, or shut down their disciplinary aspirations altogether. Keller's story, because it is the most detailed, provides the best illustration. She easily mastered the skills of physics but rejected its intellectual goal: she "went to graduate school with a vision of theoretical physics as a vehicle for the deepest inquiry into nature. . . . In place of wisdom, I was offered skills."[77] On top of that contradiction, she was committed to the professional order she had envisioned, the life of the mind in a gentle community, but was emotionally battered by the community at Harvard. When her professors told her she was failing in the discipline she thought she was mastering, they were right in two respects. In the discipline's intellectual order, she could not use mathematical skills, the means of operating in physics, to understand deepest nature, a goal that physics had consigned to philosophical discourse. In its professional order, she would not gain admission to the male club of theoretical physics nor could she practice anywhere else in the field if she persisted in using the prohibited discourses. But in the end her professors were wrong because Keller deployed those discourses to understand the nature of physics as social practice.

One question remains: what did female disciples actually do to become feminists who would change the intellectual and professional practices of their disciplines? In a recent article on her graduate student days, Ann Rosalind Jones emphasized that first-generation feminist literary scholars and critics "were evolving a hermeneutic," a "systematic way of interpreting our own statements," a "new signifying practice." Then she linked their practice of learning-to-learn-differently to feminist consciousness-raising (CR):

> It seems clear to me now that the first stages of feminist literary work corresponded to this [CR] process. . . . Early critics read women characters in men's books as we read each other in the consciousness-raising groups: as women placed in oppressive circumstances. The method was not to blame Shakespeare's Cressida or Thackeray's Becky Sharpe but to understand . . . what they were up against. Even more, we read women writers as if they were ourselves: aware of their situation, angry, lucid.[78]

Her description foregrounds the parallels between CR practice and early feminist literary practice: reading analogically to confirm their experiences, reading archaeologically to uncover instances of sexism, reading symptomatically to map patriarchy, and reading constitutively to authorize themselves as feminist knowers and articulate feminist discourse.

By performing analogical readings, feminist literary critics hoped to find in texts what they found in CR groups: stories offering solutions to their "self" problems. Here is Nancy Burr Evans, writing in 1972, about reading Sylvia Plath's *The Bell Jar*, which "set off a succession of shivers as I saw my own experiences mirrored in articulated form. . . . Where else . . . could a woman read so vividly . . . about the perplexing duality of self, the schism between the smiling, enthusiastic public self and the serious, critical private self, for which many of us have felt personally guilty and embarrassed?"[79] Glossing her practice, she said, "I read egocentrically, looking primarily for those ideas and descriptions which most resembled myself or the self I imagined I was to be" (consider how radically analogical reading violated the precepts of physics, sociology, art history, and New Criticism). Moreover, her account of reading *The Bell Jar* was punctuated by the affective comments typically made in CR groups. Said Evans, "I was not alone in my feelings" and "I no longer felt so alienated."[80] Analogical reading, like CR group sharing, gave a woman comparable others, comparability allowed her to legitimate her subjective and social being to herself, self-legitimation gave her a purchase on critical positioning, and critical positioning allowed her to see what disciplinary and everyday socialization had done to her. Through these analogical and critical procedures, Evans arrived at her insight (as had Selma Burkom, quoted earlier): "I was now able to see the ludicrousness . . . of continuing to separate my personal and intellectual self. That the two had to be separated was a fact of which I was constantly reminded by my male professors, but a fact which I nevertheless found difficult to understand let alone support."[81]

From their critical positioning on disciplinary norms and practices, feminist literary critics could perform the archaeological reading. In the dialogue essay written by Heilbrun and Stimpson, one of the authors said that she now read as if she were "a textual archaeologist" trying "to dig up fragments of attitudes about sexuality, sex roles, their genesis, and their justifying ideologies." From the disinterred fragments, she had pieced together two patterns of literary sexism: "The first is the presence of absence. . . . Menstruation, childbirth, or women's rage, for example, are events that are frequently absent from, or deceptively coded in literature. The second pattern is the sexualizing of the principle of activity. . . . Literature has tended to masculinize most activity, particularly worldly activity, even as it has recorded it."[82] By excavating the discipline's textual and social details and reading them as symptoms, feminists could map the contours of its sexist system and figure out where to intervene.

To challenge the academy's knowledge discourse—its procedures for generating subjects, objects, and statements—feminists had to navigate the preliminaries; they had to gain admission to a discipline and win the credentials that authorized them to operate in it. Who was permitted to enter the disciplines and earn credentials, who was then permitted to speak from which positions and about which matters—these were determined by a discriminatory institutional-disciplinary order. In the next chapter, I look at how universities and disciplines (with a little help from federal agencies and courts) coproduced systemic sex discrimination.

2. Constructing Sex Discrimination

The criticisms of the American university that emerged from the feminist movement of the late 1960s and 1970s were directed at both the structure of educational institutions and the conduct and content of scholarly research. University administrations and faculties, and in some fields student bodies as well, were increasingly recognized as places that excluded women, and as a part of their struggle for equal opportunity women demanded an end to overt and covert discriminatory practices.—Ellen Carol Dubois et al. *Feminist Scholarship: Kindling in the Groves of Academe* (1985)

In 1985 when the authors of *Feminist Scholarship* summarized these earlier feminist criticisms of American higher education, many members of the academic community regarded them as substantiated claims, others cav- iled about the details, and a few still considered them to be groundless complaints.[1] However vehemently these colleagues might disagree on the validity of these feminist criticisms, the fact that they could disagree indi- cated that they shared something basic. They understood them to refer to the systemicity of academic sex discrimination—namely, that widespread discriminatory practices had produced sex-patterned inequalities of out- come in academic education and employment. Twenty years earlier, sys- temic sex discrimination did not exist as an object that could be seen and discussed. What made it visible, meaningful, and actionable was the dis- course that academic feminists articulated from the early 1970s onward.

Academic feminists didn't invent the concept of systemic sex discrimination, but they did have to cobble it together from synthetic concepts available in other discourses: "women as an oppressed sex-class" from women's liberation papers, "the white-supremacist system" from the civil rights struggle in the South, "the university as a factory manufacturing knowledge and personnel for the corporate-liberal state" from New Left critique, and the "prohibition of discrimination" from congressional legislation and executive orders.[2] Starting with these borrowed concepts of the class, the system, the academic institution, and the prohibition, feminists had to follow the rules of academic discourse in order to make systemic discrimination visible, meaningful, and actionable in academic arenas. They used survey research and statistical compilations to render sex patterns as the distributions of women and men throughout the academic infrastructure—in disciplines and universities, by educational level and faculty rank. They collected quantitative and qualitative data to show that the patterns were caused by widespread discriminatory practices in student admissions, financial aid, instruction, and advising and in faculty job searches, hiring, promotion, and mentoring. They took action, disseminating these findings, organizing in disciplinary associations and on campuses, meeting with administrators to press for equal opportunity, and taking their demands to faculty senates and committees. When these actions yielded unsatisfactory results, they filed grievances with government agencies and lawsuits in federal courts. At every step along the way, their efforts were resisted by the system they were trying to change. The system was able to resist, I will argue, because it had the power to structure the processes, practices, and resources essential to its functioning.

Systemic discrimination, as I analyze it in this chapter (and again in chapter 7), is a social formation consisting of both activities constructed and meanings construed. From this double view, I will show how the parties to the struggle over discrimination contested it on the fields of construction and construal. The first section, "Sociological Discourse," focuses on construals—the feminist literature that rendered discrimination as sex-patterned outcomes produced by gender-patterned practices and the criticisms that undercut this model. The next section, "Institutional Discourses," focuses on construction—the decision-making architecture of universities that stymied the implementation of affirmative action, and the labyrinthine processes of federal agencies and courts that made remediation difficult. The final section, "Judicial Discourse," brings construal and construction together in the court rulings that diffused or halted institutional discrimination.

Sociological Discourse: Patterning Discrimination

In 1970, when the *American Sociologist* published Alice Rossi's brief report on the status of women in graduate departments of sociology, readers would not have guessed what would follow. Within a few years, academic feminists had generated a new literature that welded research to advocacy: sophisticated studies of disciplines that wove statistical tables and regression analysis into a narrative capped by recommendations, reports on higher education using empirical data and conference discussions as the prelude to policy statements, and articles on the strategies for changing disciplinary and institutional procedures. Most of this literature was issued by the fifty women's committees and caucuses that had formed in thirty-three disciplinary associations between 1968 and 1971 and by the national higher education associations, especially the Office for Women of the American Council of Higher Education, Committee W of the American Association of University Professors, and the American Association of University Women.[3] Although they were given no generic name, the studies, reports, and articles could be labeled as the early feminist sex-discrimination literature.

What the literature made visible was the sex discrimination animating the institutional-disciplinary order that women had entered and wanted to change. It modeled academic discrimination as causes and outcomes bound together in a recursive process. The causes were discriminatory practices that occurred during the institutional processes (admissions, financial aid, hiring, promotion) and routines (mentoring, reference writing, interviewing) that determined which men and women could enter the higher-education system and how they were distributed within it. The outcomes were sex-patterned disciplines and institutions that in turn structured and sanctioned more discriminatory practices. In this section, I look at how the feminist literature modeled sex discrimination across the academy and in the disciplines of physics, sociology, art history, and literary studies.

RENDERING SEX PATTERNS

"The most important single observation about women in the academic world," Patricia Albjerg Graham wrote in 1973, is that their numbers decrease dramatically as the importance of the post increases. Women constitute 41 percent of the undergraduates, 13.5 percent of the doctorate recipients, about 2 percent of the full professors at leading graduate schools of arts and sciences, and no woman holds the position of president of a major coeducational university. When women are found on college faculties, they tend to be concentrated in those fields thought to be particularly suitable for women, i.e., social work, education, home economics, nursing, and library service.[4]

The first pattern that Graham describes is sex stratification: more men rising to the upper levels of education and employment and more women halted at lower levels. The second pattern she describes is sex segregation: men predominating in most disciplines and women ghettoized in a few.

The status studies undertaken during the 1970s used statistical compilations and tables to show that these two patterns typified the distribution of men and women throughout the academic infrastructure. *Across disciplines,* men predominated in the sciences, technologies, and professions and women in the helping fields. *Within disciplines,* men dominated the ranks of full, associate, and assistant professors while women were clustered in temporary and part-time instructorships. *Across academic institutions,* male faculty and students predominated at research universities and prominent liberal arts colleges, women at four-year, women's, and two-year colleges. *Within academic institutions,* men occupied the central administrative positions (e.g., president, provost, and dean) while women were ghettoized in clerical and middle management positions. Finally, *in particular units,* men directed science laboratories or chaired academic departments while women filled support positions. These sex patterns, the status studies argued, correlated with the prestige accorded to disciplines and institutions and with the power vested in jobs.

Since the doctorate was an entrance requirement for most faculty and administrative jobs, the status studies looked for sex patterns in the awarding of this degree. During the first half of the twentieth century, the total number of doctorates awarded rose steadily and the number of women receiving them also increased, but the proportion of female to male recipients did not follow suit. Between 1919–20 and 1943–44, women's share of the total doctorates stagnated between 11.3 and 16.9 percent; after hitting an all-time high of 20.4 percent in 1944–45 (while men were serving in the armed forces), their share plunged to 9 percent in 1953–54 (when men aided by the GI Bill returned to college).[5] The situation slowly improved between 1970 and 1986 because the money the federal government pumped into academic research and student aid in order to edge the United States past the Soviet Union in the Cold War race for techno-

Table 1 Female-Earned Doctorates as a Percentage of Total Doctorates, 1969–70 through 1985–86 (high and low fields within each disciplinary cluster)

	High (%)	Low (%)
Modern Languages		
1969–70	46 (French)	30 (German)
1985–86	74 (French)	52 (German)
Social Sciences		
1969–70	27 (Anthropology)	5 (Economics)
1985–86	52 (Psychology)	20 (Economics)
Natural / Physical Sciences		
1969–70	21 (Bacteriology / Microbiology)	3 (Physics)
1985–86	35 (Bacteriology / Microbiology)	9 (Physics)

Source: Data from Charles J. Anderson et al., comps., *1989–90 Fact Book on Higher Education* (New York: American Council on Education, 1989), 207.

Note: For data showing the same pattern of doctorates for the years 1960 and 1970, see Helen S. Astin, "Career Profiles of Women Doctorates," in Rossi and Calderwood, *Academic Women*, 141.

political supremacy fueled the expansion of higher education. As small colleges swelled into universities offering graduate and professional degrees and universities sprawled into multiversities with branch campuses, the proportion of female-earned doctorates rose slowly from 13.3 percent in 1969–70 to 35 percent in 1985–86.

Yet a closer look at this period of expansion will show that the earning of doctorates was still sex-segregated across the disciplines (table 1). Although the percentage of female-earned doctorates increased within each discipline, women were still more densely clustered in the modern languages than in the sciences and more densely clustered in the lower-prestige empirical sciences than in the higher-prestige quantitative and theoretical ones.

The patterns of stratification and segregation found across disciplines were also documented within disciplines in the reports issued by women's committees of the American Physics Society, American Sociological Association, College Art Association, and Modern Language Association. The first report on physics disclosed a stunning fact: although the *number* of doctorates earned by women had risen from an average of four per year during the 1920s to forty-seven in 1970, the *share* of doctorates earned by women had "dropped from 10% in the 1920's . . . to 2.7% in 1970."[6] The data for 1970–71 showed that something was still working to eliminate women from the field and to segregate the chosen few. That year women comprised 6 percent of all undergraduate students, 2.1 percent of all physicists holding doctorates, and 1.7 percent of all physicists on academic faculties.[7] The few women physicists on academic faculties were segregated by departmental type: at four-year colleges with undergraduate programs, they held 5.8 percent of the full professorships, 4.9 percent of the associate professorships, and 5.2 percent of the assistant professorships, but at the ten universities with the top-ranked doctoral programs women held only .6 percent of the full professorships, 1.1 percent of the associate professorships, and .9 percent of the assistant professorships.[8]

Sociology, with a higher proportion of women, manifested the same patterns. A report on graduate departments noted that in 1968–69 women constituted 33 percent of the graduate students, 15 percent of the faculty members, and 1 percent of the department chairs.[9] More than 50 percent of the full-time male faculty members held full and associate professorships, whereas nearly 75 percent of the full-time female faculty members held untenured assistant professorships and untenurable instructorships (table 2). The patterning of part-time faculty was more stark: 5 percent of the women and 23 percent of the men were full professors, but 70 percent of women and 52 percent of men were instructors or lecturers. As in physics, few women served on sociology faculties at prestigious institutions let alone in the higher ranks of those faculties.[10]

With an even larger concentration of women, the fine arts manifested the same patterning.[11] Although women earned approximately 43 percent of the doctorates awarded from 1966 through 1971, they held only 20.5 percent of all faculty positions and 14.6 percent of the tenured positions from 1970 to 1973.[12] Broken out, the data show women not only thinning out at the higher faculty ranks but lagging far behind men as a percentage of every rank (table 3). Drawing on a previously conducted survey of 164 fine arts departments, the same report documented women's segregation by type of institution. For the years 1970–73, 31 percent of these departments had no men at the rank of full professor but 75 percent had no women at that rank. Although about 22 departments were chaired by women, most were located in small undergraduate colleges and, tellingly, none offered the Ph.D. Similarly, women faculty members were employed by departments granting the A.A., B.A., and B.F.A. degrees, many of which were located in women's colleges and denominational schools, but seldom by university departments granting the M.A., M.F.A., and Ph.D.

Table 2 Distribution of Female and Male Faculty Holding Full-Time
Appointments, 1968–69, through the Ranks in Sociology (as a percentage of sex)

Group	Women (%)	Men (%)
Full professor	10	31
Associate professor	17	22
Assistant professor	41	36
Instructor / lecturer	32	11
Total	100	100

Source: Data from Alice S. Rossi, "Status of Women in Graduate Departments of Sociology,
1968–1969," *American Sociologist* 5.1 (February 1970): 7.

Table 3 Proportion of Female and Male Faculty Holding Full-Time
Appointments, 1970–73, by Rank in the Fine Arts (as a percentage of rank)

Group	Women (%)	Men (%)	Total (%)
Full professor	12.0	88.0	100
Associate professor	17.9	82.1	100
Assistant professor	22.5	77.5	100
Instructor	30.2	69.8	100

Source: Data from Barbara Erlich White and Leon S. White, "Survey on the Status of
Women in College Art Departments," *Art Journal* 32.4 (summer 1973): 420, data from table 1.

degrees.[13] The thinness of women in the tenured ranks and graduate
departments during 1970–73 could not be attributed to a lack of scholarly
productivity because between 1965 and 1971 women "contributed 23.4% of
the articles published in the *Art Bulletin* [the College Art Association jour-
nal] . . . and [wrote] 19% of the books reviewed in the same period.
Significantly these figures are well above the percentages of women in the
fine-arts departments surveyed."[14] "It would appear," wrote Ann Sutherland Harris, "that women in c.a.a. professions face rather more severe
discrimination than do women in m.l.a. fields."[15]

On the contrary, three status studies issued by the MLA Commission
on the Status of Women revealed the tenacity of these patterns in the
modern language fields during the same 1970–73 period.[16] A csw study for
1972–73 showed that women, who then comprised 34 percent of faculty
members in English departments and 35 percent in foreign language departments, were distributed disproportionately in the lower ranks (in-

structor and assistant professor) and at two-year and four-year colleges, while men were distributed disproportionately in the upper ranks (associate and full professor) and at research universities. When regression analysis revealed a correlation among rank, type of institution, and amount of publication, the study's authors hypothesized that a circular dynamic was at work. Since teaching loads determined the time available for scholarship and the prestige accorded to an author's rank and institution often influenced the assessment of the work submitted for publication, women's positioning where teaching loads were heavier and prestige lower contributed to their less impressive publishing records, which in turn made it difficult for them to climb out of that positioning.[17] The subsequent influx of women into the modern languages did not substantially change the sex patterns. By 1986–87, when women earned 56.1 percent of the doctorates in English and 55.2 percent in foreign languages, they were still less likely than their male colleagues to secure tenure-track employment and more likely to take administrative or part-time faculty jobs, conditions that kept them disadvantaged in scholarly publication and career advancement.[18]

EXPLAINING SEX PATTERNS

Feminists argued that the sex patterns were produced by the unequal treatment of men and women that occurred at every step along the career path from graduate student admissions through faculty promotion. At the first step, entrance into graduate programs, the status studies showed that doctoral programs in high-prestige universities and disciplines admitted smaller percentages of women than did those in low-prestige universities and disciplines.[19] Once admitted, female students had substantially higher attrition rates than male students irrespective of their comparable performance levels; that is, regardless of whether their work was rated as excellent, very good, or average to poor, a higher proportion of women than men dropped out.[20] Feminists attributed the disparity in attrition rates to several factors: male students received more financial aid and faculty encouragement than female ones, and male students were less hindered than female ones by the lack of childcare facilities and part-time study.[21] The data on financial aid showed that female students did not receive less aid than male students because they demonstrated less merit; rather, they received less aid when they demonstrated equal or superior merit. For 1966–67 in all disciplines, a greater percentage of undergraduate women consistently achieved higher grade point averages than did undergraduate men; yet, for 1969–70 when some of this cohort had entered graduate school, a smaller percentage of women than men received financial aid.[22] In sum, despite the superior promise of undergraduate women and the comparable or superior performance of graduate women, the flow of symbolic resources (admission to prestigious programs), material resources (financial aid), and social resources (faculty support) was channeled to male students.

In faculty hiring, the next step along the career path, the status studies identified the practices that eliminated or marginalized women. Instead of advertising job openings, departments assembled candidate pools through an "old boys" network without similar outreach to women. Advisers who wrote recommendations for job seekers and faculty who served on search committees allowed inappropriate considerations (e.g., marital status, parenthood, or location of a spouse's job) to enter into their evaluations of women but not men. Universities had antinepotism policies prohibiting the appointment of spouses to the same department and sometimes to the same college; search committees more often invoked the policies against female job candidates than against male ones.[23] In all disciplines (except the few feminized ones), departments hired more men than women, hired men over equally qualified women, staffed part-time and nontenurable positions with a much greater proportion of women, and promoted women at a slower rate than men.[24]

Qualitative data showed that both the formal processes of admissions, financial aid, hiring, and promotion and the individual practices of mentoring and reference writing were driven by sex stereotyping. A report issued by the 1972 Wingspread Conference on the advancement of women in higher education recounted several instances of stereotyping: male professors considered their female graduate students to be incapable of superior performance, assumed that they would give priority to family over careers, and expected them to earn higher grades than men in order to prove their capability and commitment.[25] Other reports quoted comments that professors made to or about women job seekers—such as these made by professors of sociology:

—I can't sponsor you because you are too attractive and my wife would be jealous.
—Will your husband . . . feel threatened?
—Suppose your husband got a job elsewhere?
—Do you intend to have children?
—In spite of the fact that X has six young children to raise, she has always

been a conscientious student and has proven her commitment to the profession.

—She just broke up with her boy friend and so is free to accept a job anywhere in the country.[26]

Such comments were ubiquitous, feminists argued, not simply because academic men were sexist but because so many academic fields were typed as male. When a field is sex-typed, observed sociologist Michelle Patterson, "the sex of the members of the minority becomes occupationally salient"; it cues disciplinarians to limit the number of minority-group members admitted to graduate programs and define those who do enter as deviant—a point most dramatically illustrated by Evelyn Fox Keller's story in chapter 1.[27] On this theory, the stereotype-driven practices in graduate admissions and education reduce the availability of women for faculty positions in a male-dominated field, which in turn reproduces the field's sex-patterned employment and sex-stereotyping practices.

With so many barriers to academic progress, how did some women manage to persevere and succeed? The answer given by feminists was "social density." Alice Rossi argued that the higher the numerical and proportional density of female faculty in a discipline, on a campus, or in a department the more potential they had for mutual support and better retention rates. High social density, she surmised, may "help to explain the early emergence of political action among women in such fields as psychology, sociology, and modern languages"[28] and, as well, the uneven development of the women's studies curriculum (see chapter 4). During the 1960s and 1970s, the disciplines that trained more female practitioners had larger pools of feminists who went on, as faculty members, to produce feminist knowledge and train feminist graduate students. Paradoxically, then, the disciplinary segregation that drove the explosion of feminist scholarship in the humanities[29] also inhibited it in the natural sciences and some social sciences. As neurophysiologist Ruth Bleier observed in 1986, "The feminist discourse on science" is still "hampered in its progress by the fact that there have been so few of us publicly engaged in the project."[30]

The recursiveness of discrimination was most evident where sex-patterned employment was most tenacious—in the physical and natural sciences. Let's start with Sandra Harding's description of employment patterning. As late as the mid-1980s, the two to three hundred scientists who directed academic laboratories were still mostly white men and the nearly two million people who performed scientific and technical work were distributed by sex and race. White men were the ranking research scientists, white women were the technical assistants, the clerks, and occasionally the researchers in less prestigious institutions, and people of color were the maintenance workers.[31] Employment status was the template for distributing resources and thereby shaping careers. Physicist Vera Kistiakowsky remarked in 1980,

> Those scientists who work in leadership positions at the research universities accrue grants and students that result in publications which are in turn rewarded by more grants, students, and prizes in a spiral of success. On the other hand, those who are in secondary positions or at less prestigious institutions (categories in which women have been heavily represented) do not receive this type of support and are unlikely to join the elite. Even women with tenure at major research universities may be outside this circle, whose members are known to each other and who are proposed by one another for leadership or advisory positions, prizes and other forms of recognition.[32]

Kistiakowsky, like other feminists, claimed that because the resource flows were ordered by a gendered prestige economy some academic men accumulated the advantages that fueled successful careers and nearly all academic women accumulated the disadvantages that hindered their careers.

In sum, the feminist literature modeled sex discrimination as practical causes and patterned outcomes bound together in a recursive process. The practices were represented by three types of comparative evidence: qualitative data on the treatment of men and women, statistical data revealing that the inequitable treatment of women pervaded key academic processes (e.g., graduate admissions and faculty hiring), and regression analysis (a metatechnique for analyzing statistical data) that weighed the factors determining men's and women's career advancement (e.g., teaching loads and marital status). The outcomes were presented by statistical tables showing the patterns of segregation and stratification across the academy's infrastructure—by discipline, type of institution, educational level, and faculty rank. Finally, the literature hypothesized that the discriminatory practices produced inequalities in men's and women's academic paths, which aggregatively formed the sex-patterned disciplines and institutions, which in turn selected for the same patterns. In a 1978 book criticizing the discrimination literature, Jonathan R. Cole granted that the early career advantages and disadvantages set in motion a growing inequality among individual scientists, but he argued that this dynamic operated along the lines of merit, not sex. Although he admitted that the sciences had little "pockets of patterned sex-based discrimination" against women, mainly in promotion to the higher ranks, he insisted that "to an extraordinary degree the scientific community distributes its resources and rewards in an equitable fashion."[33] This contradiction—between the feminist claim that sex discrimination was endemic to the academy and Cole's claim that it occurred in little pockets of the academy—can be resolved by looking at how Cole modeled discrimination.

DISAGGREGATING DISCRIMINATION

What troubled Cole was that the status studies had cast discrimination as systemic and recursive. Studies of sex or race discrimination, he wrote, conclude that occupational segregation is both a consequence and a further cause of discrimination; they hold that once the system is in place it continues to segregate workers, not because they possess or lack certain qualifications but because they are perceived to resemble or differ from workers in sex- or race-typed occupations.[34] Cole argued that this conclusion was unfounded because the studies did not observe rigorous standards of measurement and proof—namely, controlling for variables, making strict inferences, and choosing the correct unit of analysis.[35] Let's look more closely at what Cole meant by methodological rigor since his logic will be reprised in the sex-discrimination lawsuits I examine in the section "Judicial Discourse" (below):

Variables. To show that discrimination is the cause of an occupational sex pattern, a study must make the unequal treatment of the two sexes the sole intervening variable. It does that by controlling for (or matching) all other variables—not only the obvious job-related differences (degrees, specialisms, awards) and the social differences (family background, socioeconomic level) but also the effects of past experience on the present occupational situation. If because of differences in their early childhood socialization girls and boys develop different career preferences and aspirations, then their unequal treatment in the occupational situation is not the only intervening variable.

Inferences. A study cannot validly infer from individual cases of discrimination to group discrimination: if, for example, a chemistry department discriminated against three individual female candidates for assistant professor, it does not follow that the department is guilty of discriminating against the class of female job seekers. Nor can a study validly infer from group patterns to individual cases: the fact that chemistry departments nationwide routinely hire men and rarely hire women does not prove that a chemistry department discriminated when it hired a male candidate over a female one. Even if the department was acting on statistics showing that women tend to drop out of chemistry, it is only guilty of what Cole calls "indiscriminate discrimination" against the female candidate it didn't hire.[36]

Units of Analysis. The problem with statistical analysis, said Cole, is that it "can be performed at different levels of aggregation"—for instance, the whole discipline of chemistry or a particular chemistry department and the whole university or one of its departments. The appropriate unit of analysis, he argued, is the smallest unit making "decisions that potentially could be discriminatory."[37]

Under the guide of methodological rigor, Cole reconstrued discrimination. He dehistoricized it by dividing past acts from present ones and cumulative effects from current ones. He disaggregated it by breaking the sex groups into individual cases, the university and the discipline into discrete departments, and the organized processes of admissions, financial aid, and employment into unique decisions. This logic makes systemic discrimination disappear and leaves behind only the single decision contained in the departmental unit. To count as discriminatory, the department's act of inequal treatment cannot be "indiscriminate"; it must be intended for a particular victim.

Cole's own study of women in science shows what happens when this logic is put to work. Using a sample of 565 male and female scientists on academic faculties who were matched for year of doctorate (1957 and 1958), doctorate-granting institution, and specialty, Cole found few differences in their employment status seven years later: men and women were located in departments of equal prestige, men were slightly more likely than women to have won prestigious awards and honors, and men tended to publish more than women. He concluded that there was little discrimination against women apart from promotion to higher ranks,[38] but that conclusion was predetermined by the design of his sample. By using the typical academic career profile, he omitted all those who did not fit it—the many women and the few men who dropped out of graduate training, switched to humanities or professional programs, spent many years earning science doctorates, took nonfaculty jobs in the academy, or sought employment outside the academy. These women, feminists had claimed, were the worst casualties of discrimination. Cole had criticized some discrimination studies for using half-of-the-table logic when they asserted that "only 10 percent of all women applicants received fellowships" without examining the comparable statistics for men.[39] Yet he was guilty of a more egregious half-of-the-table logic by failing to compare the women and men who did not fit the pattern of success selected for his sample.

The divergent conclusions about sex discrimination proffered by Cole and the feminists were caused, I think, by the scope of their studies. Whereas Cole looked for sex discrimination in a small population of successful scientists, feminists looked for it in large populations of students, faculty, and administrators who entered higher education to persevere, stagnate, or drop out. Whereas Cole assumed that university departments were isolatable units that might make discriminatory decisions, feminists assumed that universities and disciplines were coregulators of the decision-making economy that maintained the academy's sex-segregated and sex-stratified territories.

Institutional Discourses: (Re)structuring Decisions

To operate at all, the university must link its academic departments and administrative units in a decision-making structure, but exactly how decision making is structured is hard to pin down if we have to judge from the lived routines. On some days, it resembles a hierarchy with two trajectories: as a board of trustees policy speeds down the line to the administrators charged with publicizing and enforcing it, the departmental budget requests trudge up the line to the administrators who allocate the dollars. On other days, it approximates politics, with faculty members caucusing in cloakrooms and washrooms before thrashing out their decisions on job candidates or curriculum proposals in department meetings. And on bad days the decision process looks like a pool game gone haywire: suggestions, admonitions, and exhortations on how to cope with the latest crisis richochet through wall-to-wall meetings and rapid-fire phone consultations before finally settling into a plan. How decision-making looks depends on the model used to delineate the university as an organization. The corporatist model foregrounds the administration's policies and protocols, the collegial model emphasizes the faculty's disciplinary expertise, and the crisis model stresses the disequilibrium that precipitates decisions.

The architecture of decision making, I will argue in this section, is what made academic discrimination so resistant to change. But first-generation feminists did not start with this insight; having been shut out of academic decision making, they learned its protocols and processes the hard way—through their day-to-day combat with universities, federal agencies, and courts. Although I accord them a large measure of agency by describing their strategic moves and countermoves, I also emphasize that the struggle to halt discrimination and secure equal opportunity was shaped by the already structured fields of activity within which the parties were acting and reacting.

RESISTING AFFIRMATIVE ACTION

The discourse of discrimination can be traced back to postemancipation legislation and constitutional amendments designed to illegalize in the slavelike Black Codes in southern states, but the modern concept of affirmative action as a means of institutionalizing equal opportunity was codified by several federal laws, executive orders, and agency directives issued from 1964 onward. Although the policy architects deplored the long history of oppression suffered by racial minorities and women, their purpose was not to compensate the descendants of victimized peoples but to halt ongoing discrimination and remedy such present effects of past discrimination as underrepresentation, segregation, and stratification in occupational sectors and educational systems. The policies applied to all entities receiving federal funds (government agencies, universities, and businesses), prohibiting them from discriminating on the basis of race, color, religion, national origin, and sex and enjoining them to provide equal opportunities. These mandates were given teeth by assigning oversight and enforcement powers to more than a dozen federal offices and later consolidating these powers in two offices: the Labor Department's Office of Federal Contract Compliance Programs (OFCCP) was authorized to oversee the compliance of government contractors, including universities; and the Equal Employment Opportunity Commission (EEOC) was authorized to investigate complaints of discrimination, issue right-to-sue letters to complainants, and bring lawsuits against discriminatory organizations.[40]

For their part, universities and colleges were required to submit affirmative-action plans and, once these were approved, to disseminate information to all campus units, monitor their compliance, and measure their progress. Campus units were expected to take such positive steps as conducting outreach to racial minorities and women, including qualified members in applicant pools, and ensuring that students and employees received equitable treatment in such matters as financial aid, compensation, working conditions, facility access, and advancement opportunities.

Yet the history of compliance was slow and tortuous. Universities stalled on submitting or implementing affirmative-action plans, mainstream faculty circumvented the procedures, and administrators condoned the intransigence. Worse, many universities made sure that their affirmative-action offices were so underfunded and understaffed that they couldn't handle the work of monitoring and enforcing institutionwide compliance. The resistance on campuses was abetted by federal agencies charged with overseeing compliance. Throughout the 1970s, the EEOC backlogged plans needing approval or revision, ignored many institutions that failed to file plans or establish grievance procedures, and, when presented with evidence of noncompliance, seldom issued "cease and desist" orders or suspended their federal funding.[41]

The various constituencies within universities all discerned the resistance to affirmative action, but they made different sense of it because they differently rendered the institutional decision-making structure. New Leftists, who regarded the administration as a bureaucracy that managed the status quo for the benefit of elites, expected resistance to any democratization. Traditional faculty members, who stood firm on collegial governance, regarded affirmative action as an incursion into their sphere of authority and resistance as the appropriate response. Feminists and racial minorities saw a decision-making structure controlled by white men who resisted affirmative action out of self-interest and ignorance. They were right about control because studies showed that white men predominated in the faculty ranks and all but monopolized the administrative ones. A survey of more than a thousand institutions for the academic year 1975–76 revealed that white men comprised 96 percent of chief executives, 97 percent of executive vice presidents, 92 percent of chief academic officers (e.g., provosts), and more than 90 percent of deans of architecture, agriculture, arts and sciences, business, dentistry, engineering, law, medicine, music, pharmacy, technology, and vocational education. Women and minorities held slightly larger percentages of the administrative jobs in the offices of student affairs, external affairs, and affirmative action, but these peripheral units had little impact on academic, fiscal, and planning activities.[42] Realizing that the decision-making structure had stalled affirmative action, feminists thought that the problem might be solved by appointing more women to administrative positions.

But that initiative was hampered by the entrenched belief that aspiring administrators had to ascend by the proper path: assistant professor → full professor and distinguished scholar → department chair → college dean → provost → president. During the 1970s, few faculty women had achieved the prerequisites of professorial rank, scholarly distinction, and department leadership, and those who did lead the feminized departments of nursing, home economics, and education were easily discounted because these fields had low status at research universities and were absent from liberal arts colleges. To obviate the career path problem, feminists made two moves. On campus, they urged search committees and administrators to recognize that women gained leadership skills in other types of activity, and nationally they launched programs that would position women for academic administration.[43] Higher Education Resource Services (HERS), founded in the early 1970s by Cynthia Secor (a member of the MLA Commission on the Status of Women), offered a four-week residential summer institute that every year since 1976 has trained some seventy to eighty women for administrative careers. The immediate goal was to develop women's skills, and the long-term goal was to create a pool of women qualified for administration and committed to improving the status of other academic women. A year later, in 1977, the American Council on Education established a National Identification Program (ACENIP) under the auspices of its Office for Women in Higher Education. The program built a national network of promising women administrators, recommended them for senior administrative posts, and consulted with institutions on their search processes.[44] But the strategy of moving more women into administrative positions would take decades and even then might not change the decision-making achitecture that stalled the implementation of equal opportunity.

On many campuses, feminists saw the problem. The university had vested the authority to make decisions on academic matters in academic units: the departments, the offices of the deans, provost, and president, and the ubiquitous faculty committees and senates. But then the administration expected the affirmative-action office, which was classified as a nonacademic unit, to take the lead in reorganizing academic decision making and the affirmative-action director, who was classified as a middle manager, to enforce policies resisted by the academic decision makers.[45] When feminists realized that the gritty resistance to affirmative action— coming from faculty members who undermined female colleagues and protégées, department chairs who denigrated equal opportunity procedures, deans who sabotaged "uppity" affirmative-action directors, and central administrators who equivocated—was made possible by the architecture of university decision making, they tried a variety of strategies.

They organized feminist protests, joined forces with other groups seeking to democratize universities, demanded campus commissions on women that could issue reports and recommendations, brought grievances, and filed complaints with the EEOC. Although we tried many of these strategies at the University of Cincinnati, we also recognized that the university would have to insert responsibility and accountability into its formal structure. It would have to write the tasks of ending discrimination and implementing equal opportunity into the job descriptions of every unit head, from department chair to president, and would have to evaluate how well they performed these tasks during term reviews.

INSTITUTIONALIZING CHANGE

That idea was a pipedream until well into the 1980s because the authorities—universities, government agencies, and courts—that had the power to construct and construe the architecture of decision making made even the lawful grievance of discrimination an unwieldy process. When a woman alleged, for instance, that the decision on her tenure was discriminatory, she was required to go through a series of steps at her university, with the EEOC, and in court. Some universities had no grievance committees and directed grievants to the very administrators who had participated in making the negative tenure decision; others had established a grievance committee but had blunted its authority by making it advisory to an administrator and limiting what it could adjudicate. On tenure decisions, the committee was permitted to recommend on questions of procedure (e.g., whether a tenure review had observed the rules of conduct) but not necessarily to entertain questions of merit (e.g., whether evaluations of a candidate's scholarship by outside reviewers and department faculty accurately represented its quality). When a committee did find for the woman and order another tenure review, the administrator could subvert the process of redress by turning the new tenure review over to the original department colleagues, who usually reconfirmed their earlier negative decision.

To take the next step, the grievant had to file a formal complaint with the EEOC, the agency that investigated allegations and issued right-to-sue letters. But the EEOC, which was understaffed and underzealous in enforcing the law, had backlogged complaints needing investigation and requests for right-to-sue letters; the 90,000 unprocessed complaints in 1975 soared to nearly 130,000 in 1977.[46] The structuring of grievance by universities and the EEOC meant that faculty women had to challenge employment discrimination complaint by complaint and, even in victory, with little effect. A woman who won her case might enjoy an individual remedy, but she could not expect her university to revise the policies and practices that produced institutional discrimination, nor could feminists argue that the quantity of complaints, when so many remained unprocessed, supported their claim of systemic discrimination.

When the grievants finally arrived in court, they had to present their cases to judges who were reluctant to adjudicate disputes over academic decision making and seldom found it to be discriminatory.[47] Between 1972 and 1984, according to George R. LaNoue and Barbara A. Lee, the federal courts made "more than three hundred . . . decisions on cases involving college faculty," most brought by women and decided in favor of the defending institutions. Within that pattern, two more patterns were manifested: the courts far more often ruled for the defendant than the plaintiff in class-action lawsuits alleging institutionwide discrimination and in lawsuits alleging discrimination on questions of merit rather than procedure. Of the 160 cases alleging discrimination on questions of the candidates' merits, institutions won 120, plaintiffs won only 34, and the rulings were split in 6 cases. Of the 156 cases alleging discrimination in procedure, institutions won 77, plaintiffs won 58, and rulings were split in 21 cases.[48] Despite the potential of litigation to remedy systemic discrimination, LaNoue and Lee observed in 1987 that "the racial and gender configurations of the American professoriate have changed little in the past decade."[49]

Feminist scholars attributed the difficulty of obtaining remediation to the vast resources that universities could devote to litigation, the sexist attitudes of attorneys and judges, and the complexity of academic discrimination. "In case after case," LaNoue and Lee wrote, the courts admitted "the difficulty of determining, in the academic setting, whether inadequate performance or institutional discrimination have caused plaintiffs to suffer a negative personnel decision. Several commentators have pointed out that the courts seem to have bent civil rights law itself in order to avoid becoming enmeshed in the complexity of these cases."[50] Yet the courts were willing to deal with complexity in other kinds of cases. Mariam K. Chamberlain argued that "the elements of a tenure decision are no more complex than the facts with which a court must grapple in a multi-district antitrust case, or a complex patent or tax case. There is no real reason why the courts should abdicate their statutory mandate in academic employment cases."[51]

There was a reason why so many courts ruled against plaintiffs who brought sex-discrimination lawsuits. The judges who heard them accepted the propositions about university structure put forward by defendants—namely, that the university consisted of autonomous departments; that each department was authorized to make decisions about hiring, tenuring, and promoting its faculty; and that a candidate's performance in disciplinary research and teaching, which weighed heavily in these decisions, was best judged by those who had expertise in these matters. Once the judges accepted this atomistic description of the university, they were unable to see the employment decisions as coproductions of several units. Although they did recognize that a department followed university guidelines when it made decisions on faculty employment, they did not concede the more basic point that the department could make decisions only because centrally mandated policies permitted it to do so. Furthermore, the judges confused the protocol for making an employment decision with the production of that decision; the protocol specified that decision making would originate in a department and then follow a bottom-up trajectory, but the decision itself was not made until all of the participating units had made it. Finally, the judges didn't take the next step. Since university policy and protocol linked several units in employment decision making, the power to discriminate against an individual woman or the class of women was located throughout the institution—in its departments, college- and university-level committees, administrative units, and board of trustees.

Litigation was not an effective strategy for reconfiguring the sex-patterned professoriate for many reasons that feminists have cited—the large numbers of women who suffered university discrimination, the tortuous process of getting to court, the reluctance of courts to intervene in complex academic matters, and the confusion about university structure that informed many of the rulings against plaintiffs. In short, what undercut litigation was the architecture of decision making in all of these institutions—universities, government agencies, and courts. My emphasis on institutionalization in this section is not meant to eclipse the horrors that individual women suffered when they grieved and litigated discrimination. We'll never know the full stories of women who did manage to win in and out of court because many of them were enjoined from discussing their cases. We do know that all of the lawsuits moved slowly and that some, eerily reminiscent of the infamous *Jarndyce v. Jarndyce* in Dickens's *Bleak House*, remained mired in procedure for so long that no favorable ruling could make these victims of protracted agony whole again. Joan

Abramson's grievance against the University of Hawaii, initiated in 1971, was still continuing in 1985. Nancy Shaw's grievance against the University of California at Santa Cruz, initiated in 1982, was concluded in her favor in 1987. Shyamala Rajender's grievance against the University of Minnesota, initiated in 1971, was concluded in her favor in 1980. Regardless of whether the cases were lost or won, the costs to the women pursuing them—in stress, time, financial burden, and lost employment opportunities—were devastating.[52]

Judicial Discourse: Coproducing the Authority to Discriminate

The law provides for two types of complaints, the individual sex-discrimination lawsuit and the class-action lawsuit. The individual lawsuit raises many questions about academic authority—for instance, whether in refusing to tenure an individual a particular department has observed the university guidelines and appropriately exercised its power. The data brought to bear on those questions center on the plaintiff and her institution; they may include explanations of the decision process, documentation of the plaintiff's merits, and comparisons between the plaintiff and other similarly situated individuals. A ruling on that suit affects the parties to it and, when cited as a precedent, may affect the outcome of future lawsuits. By contrast, the class-action lawsuit has more extensive implications. Here a plaintiff (one or more persons) alleges that a university has discriminated not only against her but also against a class of persons that she represents. The data in this type of suit must address questions about the treatment of the plaintiff and the class, about her unit's acts and her institution's patterns of practice. A ruling on that suit immediately affects the large number of persons in the class as well as future lawsuits.

When a class-action lawsuit is filed, the court holds a certification hearing to determine whether the plaintiff may represent a class. At this hearing, according to Federal Rule of Civil Procedure 23(a),

> the plaintiff [must] establish to the satisfaction of the judge that (1) the class is so numerous that joinder of all members is impracticable (the numerosity requirement); (2) there are questions of law or fact common to the class (the commonality requirement); (3) the claims or defenses of the representative party are typical of the claims or defenses of the class (the typicality requirement); and (4) the representative party will fairly and adequately protect the interests of the class. Defendants

in class action claims will routinely attempt to block certification of the class, claiming that it does not meet one or more of the requirements of rule 23(a).[53]

Note that the Rule 23(a) requirements pertain to delineating the class (numerosity, commonality) and the plaintiff's relation to it (typicality of claims, fair representation of interests), not to delineating the university. Yet the certification hearings I examine next will show that how the defending universities delineated their decision-making structure was the critical factor that caused the judges to decertify the class.

PRODUCING THE AUTHORITY TO DISCRIMINATE

In *Michigan State University Faculty Association v. Michigan State University* (1981), university administrators outlined a three-stage tenure process consisting of (1) a "departmental peer review," (2) a conference between the department chairperson and the dean, and (3) a "formal process of recommendation" in which the department's recommendation is reviewed by the dean, the provost, and the president before coming to the board of trustees for its action.[54] Although they described the making of tenure decisions as a process involving individuals from several units (departments, colleges, central administration, and board), the university nevertheless contended that the class of women up for tenure had nothing in common "because the decisions affecting faculty members are made almost exclusively within decentralized, autonomous, academic departments on an individualized basis by different persons pursuant to nonstandardized procedures and widely differing criteria."[55] When Judge Benjamin F. Gibson Jr. wrote his opinion, he reiterated the ambiguity in the university's presentation, on the one hand acknowledging that the criteria for tenure and promotion are "university-wide standards for evaluating faculty" and on the other hand averring that "the implementation of those standards occurs mainly within the individual department."[56] He then concluded that the tenure decision was a departmental act because:

—much of the important decision-making with respect to personnel matters takes place at the department level
—the implementation of . . . [university standards for teaching, research, and service] occurs mainly within the individual department
—the departments act as autonomous units in developing their own governance structure through bylaws, defining their program or mission as a unit, establishing standards and criteria by which performance will be

judged, and establishing procedures for decision-making regarding promotions, tenure, and salary increases.[57]

Note, however, the slippage in his case for departmental autonomy. When
Judge Gibson recast the institutional process as departmental acts, he
could not entirely jettison the participation of the university administration and board in tenure. He said that *much* (not *all*) of the decision making
is performed by departments and that university standards are implemented *mainly* (not *exclusively*) by departments. More importantly, he
ignored the fact that the university, whether through its formal policies
or informal routines, granted the departments the authority to do what
they did.

The university's argument in *Michigan State* was grounded in two presumptions about departmentalized disciplines: first, that the university
had vested the authority to make tenure decisions in the departmental
unit because it could muster the disciplinary expertise required to evaluate
its tenure candidates; and, second, that each tenure candidate was treated
as a unique case because of her particular record of research, teaching, and
service. By convincing Judge Gibson that a uniquely qualified department
made unique tenure decisions, the university effectively undercut the
plaintiff's claim that the decisions on female tenure candidates were comparable or connected. If the decisions were not comparable or connected,
then there could be no institutionwide class of women who had suffered
discrimination through them, nor could there even be a centrally admin-
istered institution to discriminate against them. Indeed, "the point of all
this evidence," Judge Gibson concluded in *Michigan State*, "is that departmental decision-making negates the existence of any common questions
of law or fact to satisfy Rule 23(a)(2) with a University-wide class."[58] The
Michigan State ruling had transposed the commonality and typicality requirements of Rule 23(a). To make a case for classwide discrimination, the
plaintiff would now have to show not only the wholeness of the class
through its commonality and her typicality but also the wholeness of the
university through its centralized decision making. If a judge believes that
the only possible agent of classwide discrimination is a centralized institution consisting of departments that operate in precisely the same way,
then where does he locate the responsibility for discrimination in a university that portrays itself as a decentralized institution? Obviously, he can
hold an individual department responsible for a discriminatory act, but he
will not hold the university responsible for discriminatory acts no matter

how frequent and pervasive they are shown to be. The transposition of commonality and typicality in *Michigan State* had two effects: it placed another burden of proof on the plaintiff and it extended impunity to the defending university.

The influence of *Michigan State* was considerable; not only was it widely cited in certification hearings for new lawsuits, but it was used to reverse certification granted in an older lawsuit. In *Rachelle A. Rosenberg v. University of Cincinnati*, Professor Rosenberg was denied tenure in the Department of English, filed a class-action lawsuit, and won certification at a 1977 hearing. After the *Michigan State* ruling, the university requested another hearing and won class decertification in 1986. Following the *Michigan State* formula, a university administrator testified that "nearly all significant faculty personnel decisions at the University of Cincinnati are made at the level of the faculty member's department including appointment, reappointment, promotion, tenure, determination of initial salary" and that this localization "demonstrate[s] departmental autonomy, decentralized decision-making and peer involvement in personnel decisions."[59] In his preliminary and final rulings, Judge Walter H. Rice repeatedly emphasized that the plaintiff must show that the "institution's structure is sufficiently centralized to allow a common pattern or practice of discrimination to occur."[60] He adduced this requirement from the ruling *for* Michigan State, which was "shown" to have a decentralized structure incapable of classwide discrimination (a point to which I will return later) and also from several rulings *against* corporations, which were shown to have centralized structures capable of classwide discrimination.

Using court rulings against corporations as his guideline, Judge Rice expected the plaintiff to prove that the university had some sort of unifying decision structure: " 'a company-wide policy,' " "a consistent practice within a given department,' " or at least decision making that "originates jointly from the local or departmental unit and the common employer."[61] On his view, the existence of companywide policy, consistent departmental practice, or joint decision making would indicate that departments were operating according to the mandates or within the routines of their institution. The distinction is crucial, he said, because a judge must determine "whether the decision making processes within the university permit a common pattern or practice of discrimination to occur therein."[62] The *Rosenberg* ruling further transposed Rule 23(a). The plaintiff now had to show not only that the university had a unified structure capable of institutionwide discriminatory decisions but also that it had policies codifying or routines regularizing the discriminatory decision making. Finding that the plaintiff did not disclose the existence of a "centralized policy or practice . . . which could create common questions of law or fact sufficient to meet the requirements of Rule 23(a)," Judge Rice decertified the class.[63]

The discursive gymnastics that occurred in these certification hearings are easy to expose. Defendants and judges redefined the university as an aggregation of autonomous departments and its decision-making process as discrete decisions. This redefinition enclosed each tenure candidate and the departmental colleagues who judged her in a single act and separated each tenure decision from others that were made in the same department and across the university, in a given year and over the years. If departments, administrative units, and the board had no shared decision-making process and no history of making decisions, the plaintiff could not identify a cause of classwide discrimination and thus could not support her claim that it had occurred. By contrast, if an institutional process connected these units it would be possible to reason from sex-patterned outcomes to the actions that caused them. Or, as Judge Rice mistakenly reasoned, "where the employment decision originates jointly from the local or departmental unit and the common employer, the commonality / typicality requirement will have been met."[64] That reasoning was wrong because the commonality of a victimized class depends not on where the decision making originates but on which entities participate in it—a crucial point that I will discuss next.

Gutzwiller v. Fenik et al., an individual sex-discrimination suit against the University of Cincinnati, was tried in 1986 and appealed in 1988. The Department of Classics had recommended against tenure for Professor Kathryn Gutzwiller, the arts and sciences dean had recommended for tenure, the provost had recommended against tenure, the president had recommended against tenure, and the board of trustees had denied tenure. Professor Gutzwiller then took her case to the faculty grievance committee, which found a number of irregularities and recommended another tenure review by a specially constituted committee of college faculty. The president, who in his previous job as provost had decided against tenure, agreed to another review but only by the same Classics department faculty who had already voted to deny it. At this point, Professor Gutzwiller declined the review, filed a suit in U.S. District Court, and eventually won on appeal.[65] The Gutzwiller case shows that the decision-making process originates in a department and proceeds through other units that along the way can overturn the decision made at a lower level. The department's decision was reversed by the dean, whose decision was reversed by provost, whose decision was upheld by the president and board, whose decision was to be suspended according to the grievance committee, whose recommendation was modified by the president. This case shows that a decision is not actually produced until it issues from the board of trustees and even then it has the potential to be produced all over again if a university grievance committee so recommends. Applying the insights from *Gutzwiller* to *Michigan State* and *Rosenberg*, I will conclude my analysis of why the judges couldn't see the university's role in producing discrimination.

When the judges compared the corporation and the university, they were confused by differences in their organizational structure and functioning. On one hand, they saw that both the corporation and the university had a hierarchical unit structure. In *Rosenberg*, Judge Rice described the structure by actually naming all the units from top to bottom: the board of trustees, the president, the provost, the deans, the department chairmen, and the department faculties. On the other hand, they saw that corporate decision making followed a top-down trajectory whereas university decision making was represented, in the lawsuits they were adjudicating, as following a bottom-up trajectory. If the department was located at the beginning of the decision-making process and at the bottom of the unit hierarchy, how could its decision continue to be the authoritative one as it ascended the administrative ladder? In *Michigan State*, Judge Gibson rescued departmental authority by minimizing the institutionally mandated standards, ignoring the administrators' involvement in tenure decision making, and declaring the department to be the main actor. In *Rosenberg*, Judge Rice rescued departmental authority in a more sophisticated way by invoking the increased "deference each higher level is required to give to the recommendations of the lower levels of the hierarchy."[66] The departmental recommendation, he noted, ordinarily receives some deference from the dean, more from the provost, and far more from the president and the board. The concept of administrative deference allowed Judge Rice to assert primacy of the department's tenure decision as it proceeded up the line. But, I want to argue, both judges mistook protocol for production. They emphasized the decision's trajectory (the order of units making the decision) and elided the decision's production by all participating units. Whereas Judge Gibson merely eclipsed the administrators' decision making, Judge Rice dampened the effect of their decision making by arguing that they were simply deferring to a lower-level decision. But the *Gutz-willer* case shows that each administrative level has decision-making power that can be exercised by assenting to a lower-level decision or by reversing it. Judge Gibson's own explanation—that the administration is required to defer to lower-level decisions—attests to the fact that deference is just another name for the centrally institutionalized routine of making the decision to assent to other decisions.

This point leads to my last one. The certification hearings recast not only what tenure decisions were and who made them but also how discrimination was manifested and could be proved. Federal agency directives and legal scholarship had delineated two models for construing discrimination and liability. On the individualist model called "disparate treatment," an agent (usually a person or group of persons) discriminates by intentionally performing an act of unequal treatment among similarly situated people of different sexes, races, and so on. As proof, the plaintiff must compare herself to similarly situated men, document the unequal treatment, and show that the agent intended his act to have that effect. On the organizational model called "disparate impact" or "patterns and practices," an organization's procedures for distributing people (i.e., through hiring, promotion, and termination) or distributing benefits (e.g., salaries) result in inequalities among groups by sex, race, and so on. As proof, the plaintiff must document the outcome, identify the procedures, and show that they were not a business necessity.[67] The two models locate the responsibility for discriminatory outcomes in different places. When discrimination is figured as an act that a person intends and performs, the responsibility is located with him, but when it's figured as an occupational pattern that an institution produces the responsibility is located with it. Judges Gibson and Rice used the individualist model to describe the institution. They said that plaintiffs would have to show that the university was a unified agent that expressed its "intention" as centrally mandated policies or centrally routinized practices that in turn caused a classwide discriminatory outcome. In short, they transliterated individual intention as institutional "intention" and then were unable to "find" the university's intention to discriminate. Why?

The judges were unable to find the university's intention to discriminate because they allowed the corporate-university analogy to control their thinking. In cases of corporate discrimination, Mary W. Gray observes, "there would be little doubt that an employer would be responsible and that plant-wide or company-wide statistics could be used to demonstrate a pattern of discrimination whether or not various supervisors acted independently."[68] Because the corporation's executive, supervisory, and employee levels were unified by a top-down chain of command and supervision, judges could hold the top level responsible for the acts that produced lower-level discriminatory outcomes. But Judges Gibson and Rice couldn't see what unified the top administration with the departments, even though they themselves argued that university policy gave departments the authority to make personnel decisions and university custom required administrative deference to their decisions. Obviously, the judges couldn't "find" (both recognize and rule for) tenure discrimination against a class because they couldn't discern a unifying structure of command and supervision that permitted the departments to discriminate. Inadvertently, they were right: the absence of a structure that made all university units responsible and accountable for what they did enabled them to discriminate.

INSTITUTIONALIZING EQUAL TREATMENT

As my last example, I discuss *Shyamala Rajender v. University of Minnesota,* a class-action lawsuit that distributed the responsibility for equal opportunity throughout the university's structure. The events leading to the lawsuit were that the Department of Chemistry had employed Rajender in annually renewable, nontenure-track appointments—a postdoctoral fellowship for three years and a temporary assistant professorship for another three years—before refusing to renew the latter contract for a fourth year. Rajender filed a lawsuit claiming that the department and the university had discriminated against the class of women in their hiring and salary decisions. At the certification hearing, the university repeated the *Michigan State* argument that Rule 23(a) requirements were not satisfied: "because each employment decision concerns unique qualifications of each candidate in the class," the alleged class had no commonality, the plaintiff had no typicality, and thus a ruling for the plaintiff could not remedy the diverse effects that employment decisions had on university women. Judge Miles W. Lord did certify the class because commonality, for him, hinged not on the unity of institutional intention, the similarity of department acts, or the homogeneity of institutionwide outcomes but on whether "a Damoclean threat of sex discrimination hangs over the proposed class."[69] That such a threat was present at the University of Minnesota he concluded from the evidence of disparate impact and treatment. The Department of Chemistry had not hired a woman in a tenure track or tenured position since 1917, and over the years its parent college had hired few women and paid them less than men. The chemistry department chairman, when questioned, acknowledged that the hiring decisions came out of a process that included screening and recommendation by the recruitment committee, concurrence of the department faculty, recommendation by the department chair, and approval by the dean, academic vice president, president, and regents.[70]

Judge Lord broke from the departmental authority / centralized authority dualism by moving outside of the discourse that constituted it. While questioning the university's affirmative-action director, he asked, "The only people that make the hiring decisions and effect compliance or non-compliance with the law are the tenured faculty people in the various departments?" After she replied "yes," he mused: "And apparently that can't ever change until somebody makes . . . a decision that the Regents are responsible for the University and are willing to . . . go right into the hiring process, or send somebody into it . . . to see that they are not biased sexually or racially?" "That's true," she replied. "That," he asserted, "may be what this lawsuit is about . . . whether or not the Regents have an affirmative duty not to so delegate [authority to a department] when the results are as they seem to be in the chemistry department."[71] It might appear that Judge Lord resolved the dualism problem by invoking the corporate model and expecting the regents to exercise their authority by revoking a department's authority to perform discriminatory acts. But the remedy shows otherwise.

After Judge Lord certified the class, the university signed a consent decree that remained in force from 1980 to 1991. The decree set up a special master (an attorney and assistants) to adjudicate claims brought by women and required the university to institute affirmative-action procedures, establish a University Committee on Equal Employment Opportunity for Women, equalize female faculty salaries, and modify the processes of job search, hiring, salary review, contract renewal, tenure, and promotion.[72] The objective was not merely to restructure the decision making but to increase the participation of those who were affected by it. The salary equalization process is a good example. After a university committee documented salary inequities and awarded increases to underpaid female faculty, the university invited each female faculty member to submit further claims based on comparisons of her salary to the salaries of male faculty members with equivalent profiles who were employed in her own department or similar departments.[73] In short, by holding the regents and administrators accountable, reorganizing the institutional processes, and involving the previously excluded class of women in these processes, the resolution of *Rajender* institutionalized the production of equitable decisions as the responsibility of all units and individuals in the university.

RECONSTRUING DISCRIMINATION

To be sure, American universities and colleges are structured as bureaucracies that delegate to a multitude of units the authority to recruit personnel, judge individual worth, and decide what will be done.[74] Without some form of institutionalized accountability—whether it resides with the trustees, the administration, or everyone—these "systems of increased differentiation and specialization," as Warren Bennis observed, "are beautiful mechanisms for the evasion of responsibility and guilt."[75] The evasion of liability was precisely the objective of defending universities when in class certification hearings they followed the logic prescribed by Cole: disaggregate the university into departments, segment the departmental tenure decisions, and reduce the several institutional causes of discrimination to one cause—the department's intentional act of unequal treatment. When the judges agreed with this delineation of university decision making and went on to decertify the class, they not only confirmed the authority of the defending university to continue discriminating, but they also generated the precedents that dispersed the authority to discriminate to other universities. Thus, we should not regard the university delineations of its structure as fact and the judges' decertifications as fact-based rulings that institutionwide discrimination did not occur. Rather, we should view them as moments of discursive production in which construals of discrimination go on, through authorization, to construct more discrimination.

Two decades separate the claims of systemic discrimination made by the early status studies from the restructured decision making at the University of Minnesota when the *Rajender* consent decree expired. All along academic feminists believed that "a greater diffusion of more women in the academic professions" would remedy sex-patterned education, employment, and knowledge.[76] But it didn't. Between 1960 and 1980, higher education experienced an unprecedented era of expansion; the number of academic institutions soared from 2,000 to 3,200, faculty from 235,000 to 685,000, and students from 3.5 million to 12 million.[77] But the price of growth that administrators had anticipated was repeatedly compounded by the soaring costs of fuel, physical-plant maintenance, library materials, healthcare benefits, and high-overhead science laboratories, technology complexes, and medical centers. When soaring costs collided with sluggish revenues, academic institutions were plunged into fiscal crises. The problems may have been less acute for well-endowed colleges than for public universities with high-overhead medical centers, science laboratories, and technology complexes, but all institutions resorted to the same remedies. To increase income, they raised tuition, launched fundraising drives with goals topping $100 million, stepped up their grant applications, and formed corporate research partnerships. To reduce expenses, they deferred facilities maintenance, trimmed extracurricular services, cut library budgets, downsized nonacademic staff, converted full-time faculty lines to part-time instructorships, and even eliminated academic departments. To boost efficiency, they instituted work speedups, larger classes, and time-to-graduation standards. Although the numbers of women flowing into higher education increased steadily throughout the 1970s and 1980s and although they constituted 54 percent of the nationwide enrollment by the mid-1990s, the sex patterns persisted. Today women are still far more clustered than men in the lower-prestige disciplines, the lower-prestige two-year and four-year institutions, the lower faculty ranks, and the part-time faculty positions. Their situation was exacerbated by the fiscal crises and corporate managerialism that reorganized the professoriate into two groups, a professionalized faculty and an expendable workforce. By the mid-1990s, more than 50 percent of recent Ph.D.s were unemployed and 45 percent of employed faculty nationwide held part-time positions, compared to 22 percent in 1970. Those who were disproportionately populating the have-not and have-less groups were women.[78]

In chapters 1 and 2, I delineated the higher-education system that women entered as a coproduction of structure and action. The institutions and disciplines imposed the rules and routines that structured processes and resource flows, and the actors, by performing institutionally and disciplinarily routinized practices, remade their processes and resources. On this view, the actors who performed gendered acts were not creating discrimination; they were remaking what was "already made in the continuity of *praxis*,"[79] and what was already made by the continuity of practice was the architecture of discrimination. Foucault states this point succinctly when he tells us that governors don't have to exercise their power by aiming acts of violence directly at subjects. "To govern," he remarks, "is to structure the possible field of action of others."[80] To discipline and discriminate, I would add, is to do the same.

Part 2. Institutionalizing and Intellectualizing Feminist Studies

A course, a program, a pedagogical method, a way of looking at the world, a new discipline, a movement for change, a critique of male mythology, a feminist cultural revolution . . . the experience of women thinking, talking, working, and being together. —Nancy Hoffman, Cynthia Secor, and Adrian Tinsley, "What Is Women's Studies???" (1972)

*ms.
begin
process*

In the late spring of 1970, an obscure press published a curious item: a khaki-green cover sheet and a stack of unbound pages with three holes punched along the left margin. Photocopied on these pages were the syllabi for seventeen courses taught in 1969–70 and a brief introduction by editor Sheila Tobias, a young professor leaving Cornell to become associate provost at Wesleyan University, situating the courses "in a field that may eventually be called Female Studies."[1] From the editor's tentative tone, the item's shabby format, and the press's word-of-mouth marketing, no one would have expected anything to follow from *Female Studies*. When the loose-leaf *Female Studies II* appeared six months later, in December 1970, it contained the syllabi for sixty-six courses and a note by editor Florence Howe that she knew of thirty-seven others.[2] And when the still loose-leaf *Female Studies III* was published in December 1971, it contained syllabi for fifty-four courses, reports on seventeen women's studies programs, and a notice by editors Howe and Carol Ahlum that they had received syllabi for three hundred courses and knew of three hundred more.

The Tobias volume inaugurated a widely read series of curricular materials that would fuel the development of feminist studies in a resistant academy. Between 1970 and 1975, ten volumes of *Female Studies* were published, five by KNOW Press, a feminist media service founded in 1969 by Jo-Ann Gardner and other members of the Pittsburgh chapter of the National Organization for Women, and five by the Feminist Press, an academic publishing venture founded in 1970 by Howe, Paul Lauter, and others.[3] Most of the volumes were edited by current or former members of the Modern Language Association Commission on the Status of Women, which since its establishment in 1969 had functioned at chairwoman Howe's urging as a "clearing house for information on new curricular developments in feminist studies."[4] Within a few years, the courses and programs were multiplying so rapidly that Howe relocated the clearing-house at the Feminist Press and launched the *Women's Studies Newsletter* to disseminate information on them. The series and the newsletter, together with the outreach of the women's caucuses in the disciplinary associations and the new scholarly feminist journals, drove the exponential growth of the field. By 1973–74, 2,500 courses were offered that year alone, some 4,600 courses had been taught overall, and more than 100 programs had been established.[5]

Today no one would guess that the teachers of these rapidly proliferat-ing courses had virtually no professional authority or resources. Most were adjunct instructors or assistant professors who jeopardized their reputations and their jobs to teach the new courses. " 'A course on *what?* You're kidding," colleagues exclaimed to Barbara A. White when she first taught The Woman-Myth to Northwestern freshmen in the fall of 1970. "And what, by the way, is 'The Woman-Myth?' " The second time around, they were incredulous: " 'What? You're teaching it again? I thought it was just an experiment.' "[6] Mainstream faculty regarded the courses as ill-founded experiments because their topics were not investigated in the disciplines and thus not legitimized by research literatures. Jean O'Barr recounted what happened in 1972 when she asked permission to teach a course on Third World women: "The chairperson looked at me as if I were from another planet and announced that the only way new courses en-tered the curriculum was when a distinguished research literature on the subject existed. I thought about the piles of mimeographed papers on the floor of my study at home. I looked at him and surprised even myself by confidently asserting that there was now an extensive research literature in existence on the subject of Third World women and development."[7]

Bravado such as O'Barr's was commonplace in those days because it was what feminist teachers had to cover for everything they lacked. What they lacked was not merely a research literature to cite as intellectual justification for their course proposals but the fundamentals they needed to propose and teach the courses. They had not settled on a name for their venture—it was variously called female studies, woman studies, women's studies, and feminist studies—nor had they drawn up an exacting descrip-tion to persuade colleagues that it had prospects of becoming a distinctive (let alone distinguished) academic field. They did not have the institutional conveniences to support research and teaching, such as relevant library collections and appropriate course designators, nor did they have a na-tional infrastructure of scholarly conferences, publications, and associations to stabilize the field and spread its activities. But they did have the gumption to envision a bold feminist initiative that would transform the disciplines, bridge the academy / community divide, and fuse scholarly knowledge to social activism.

In subsequent years, thousands of women would institutionalize this initiative, though in a somewhat different form than had been envisioned. To clarify this point, I want to contrast the structures, knowledges, and objectives of female studies with those of feminist studies. In 1970, female studies was barely institutionalized as a hundred courses taught by marginal faculty, a half-dozen emerging programs, and mimeographed "publications." In 1995, feminist studies had a nationwide infrastructure of some 630 women's studies programs, hundreds of curriculum transformation projects, more than eighty campus-based feminist research centers, national associations of feminist scholars, feminist committees and scholarly divisions in every disciplinary association, and thousands of academic-feminist presses, book series, journals, and newsletters. In 1970, its knowledge consisted of little more than skimpy accounts of women's lives and declamations against patriarchy; by 1995, the knowledge base was an extensive body of data, scholarship, and theory in and about the full range of disciplinary and professional fields, social groups, and societies. In 1970, feminists vowed to liberate the classroom; by 1995, such feminist techniques as turn-taking, small-group discussion, and integration of everyday experience were widely used in colleges, high schools, and grade schools. In 1970, we spoke grandiosely of transforming the disciplines; by 1995, we had reconfigured a few and established feminist subfields in the rest. In short, what started as little more than a euphoric vision was realized twenty-five years later as a vast academic-feminist knowledge enterprise.

A large literature has traced the long and arduous route from vision to realization. Institutional histories have recounted the emergence of female studies from the activism sweeping campuses and disciplinary associations in the late 1960s through the founding of such national organizations as the National Women's Studies Association and the National Council for Research on Women a decade later.[8] Review articles have inventoried the rich stocks of feminist knowledge and evaluated their impact on the disciplines. Intellectual critiques have probed the strands of feminist-studies discourse and identified the fundamental flaws—the homogenizing categories, essentializing logic, and totalizing narratives. These studies do important work: they instruct neophytes on the field they have entered, direct scholars and teachers to future projects, and give weary practitioners a pause to celebrate achievements and contemplate problems. But they also follow conventions that I will not observe in the next three chapters. Instead of dividing the work of institutionalization from the work of intellectualization, I will be analyzing the relays between them that formed feminist studies as an academic field. Instead of arguing that feminist studies developed over two decades, I will show that the formation of the field was imploded, its salient features determined by the end of 1972 and its shape fixed by 1976. Instead of assessing the impact of feminist scholarship on the disciplines, I will show that feminist studies became a discipline contained by the academy it had set out to transform. Instead of homing in on the repressive power of its discourse, I will concentrate on its productive power, the rule-bound practices that generated a superabundance of objects and knowledges.

Chapter 3 opens with the vision of female studies as an insurgent project that would fuse academic knowledge to social activism and then analyzes the discursive practices that launched or derailed female-studies projects. Chapter 4 explains why female studies became a cross-discipline formatted by the academy it had set out to transform. Chapter 5 turns to the proliferation of feminist-studies discourse along the crosshatched axes of disciplines, identities, political ideologies, and epistemic assumptions. That diversification, together with other forces impacting the higher-education system, has had many positive effects but also the negative ones of balkanizing academic feminists, dividing us from nonacademic feminists and progressives, and reconstituting social change as an artifact of esoteric discourses. Together these chapters tell a story about the relays between academic institutionalization and intellectualization, the larger forces of socioeconomic change, and the internal rules of discourse that formed the feminist studies we have today.

3. Articulating Projects

The reason we are learning at all is to act on the world. —Marilyn Salzman-Webb, "Feminist Studies: Frill or Necessity?" (1972)

[The activism was] like a jam session, each instrument joining in, playing new music devised and coordinated at the moment. —Tucker Farley, interview (1996)

A failure or break in this constructive process makes action impossible. —Alberto Melucci, "The Process of Collective Identity" (1995)

In November 1971, some ninety women trekked to the University of Pittsburgh for Women and Education: A Feminist Perspective, a three-day conference, and performed a drama that other feminists would enact at conferences and on campuses during the early 1970s. Having assembled to discuss female studies, they agreed on principle that it should be the arm of the movement and debated everything else.[1] What form should it take: a scholarly discipline or an interdisciplinary field, an insurgent academic project or a cluster of women's programs and services based in community centers, a cross-sector network of feminist intellectuals or movement-sponsored schools for political training? Who should make the decisions: movement activists or academic scholars, revolutionaries or reformers, second-wave founders or newcomers? Which of these groups best represented the interests of "the women," that amorphous population invoked as feminism's beneficiaries whenever one faction wanted to disparage the positions taken by others? When the conference papers were published as

Female Studies V (1972), it was clear from a prefatory account that the debates about female studies had shifted the participants' focus to the conference discourse itself—to the matter of who spoke, about what, and from which positions of relative knowledge and authority.

Although all of the conference paper authors understood some of the problems they would confront in institutionalizing female studies, only two—Roberta Salper and Marilyn Salzman-Webb—brought the problematic into view. Early in her paper, Salper alluded to it:

> In a recent article, *The Chronicle of Higher Education* posed the question, "Can Women's Studies be primarily academic or are they sure to become militant and tied to women's liberation?" Setting up this kind of dichotomy between a social movement "out there" and some courses safely nestled within the ivy halls is a very effective way to insure both that the courses do not radically change anyone, and that the Women's Movement does not benefit from the acquisition of skills and other benefits available in the university.[2]

Politically, Salper was right to take the *Chronicle* article to task for presuming that feminists would have to choose between an activist-training project in society and an intellectual program in the academy. But practically feminists did seem to be stuck with an either/or choice because society and the academy were distinctive systems with different sets of rules, institutions, and activities. No matter where they located female studies, they would butt up against limitations to its political effectivity. Community-based projects would be free to catalyze activism but hindered by chronic resource deprivation, whereas university-based programs could access institutional resources but would be restricted to academic activities. The *Chronicle*'s question and the conference debates, though posed from very different positions, turned on the same assumption: feminists could not reconcile the academy's objective of producing and inculcating scholarly knowledge with the movement's objective of making social change.

Salper and Salzman-Webb clarified the problematic that had framed the thinking about institutionalized form. That problematic was the structuring of the social formation—its society/academy divide, its occupational precincts and positional hierarchies, its group antagonisms and individual rivalries. They understood that societal and academic institutions, though managing different arenas of activity, worked together to reproduce this structure. "Rather than building collectivity," Salzman-Webb explained, [universities] divide by competitiveness and grade hierarchies. Rather than creating group solidarity, they create an intellectual elite whose social status . . . is meant to be above those who have never received a higher education. This is not done by accident or through faulty educational theory, but to serve a society that demands a highly technical yet compliant working class. If we are not careful, rather than making any dent in a patriarchal class system, we will instead create careers in academic studies on women and have no relationship with the great majority of women to whom we will become like overseers. So divided, we will all fail to change so pervasive a power dynamic.[3]

Both women recognized that the social formation's structure was the obstacle standing between any vision of female studies and its realization. To evade the divisive strategies and erode the divided sectors, it would have to be a hybrid project.

Salper described an institutionalized form that would bridge the academy / community divide: as planned by a group of San Diego feminists, it was to be a multipurpose Women's Center with several operating units located on the San Diego State College campus (SDSC) and in the San Diego community. But after setting up one of the units, the SDSC Women's Studies Program, the group splintered. Some members took control of the program and others went off to establish a women's center in town, thereby reinscribing the academy / community divide they had hoped to bridge. Twenty-five years later, Salper would tell me about the dynamics that caused the splintering, but at Pittsburgh, just months after leaving a one-year visiting professorship at the SDSC program, she was still hopeful that "to the extent that the university-based programs can create links with other sectors of society, the traditional divisions—student vs. worker, black vs. white, man vs. woman—used to maintain the American Way of Life will be weakened."[4]

For her part, Salzman-Webb was concerned with how to intellectualize female studies when the movement's processes "of collective thought, study and action" were "the antithesis of what universities are all about."

Feminism is a philosophy of knowledge. It is the intellectual understanding of the historical struggle between domination and submission. . . . Such a philosophy cuts across so-called "disciplines" to include psychology (both of the individual and in groups; the colonizer and the colonized); sociology (social forms of power and class development);

economics (uses of power with varied economic bases in history); biology (is there such a thing as biological inferiority?); and of course the study of history, literature and the arts. But this [feminist] study is from a wholly different context: it is the history of what was created both by the dominated and the dominator to sustain or struggle against that domination.[5]

Her statement cleverly meshed the languages of the academy and the movement at a time when, as the *Chronicle*'s question indicated, they were deemed antithetical. By defining female studies as philosophy of knowledge, she recast a political project that universities would ban as a cross-disciplinary inquiry they could respect. By describing its knowledge as analyses of power relations, she recast the disciplinary scholarship that activists would spurn as the tactical knowledge they could deploy in struggle.

Salper and Salzman-Webb presented their audiences with a hybrid female studies that would cut across the disciplines, link universities to communities, and fuse scholarly knowledge to social change. They anticipated its later scope at a time when the actual projects resembled little buoys adrift in the vast archipelago of higher education, and they underscored its political objective—Salper insisting that it train women for the task of "creating real social change" and Salzmann-Webb declaring that "the reason we are learning at all is to act on the world"—at a time when the objective had begun to modulate.[6] That same year other contributors to *Female Studies V* and *Female Studies VI* prophesied that female studies would

—Offer "a new perspective which fully considers the extent of women's oppression" (Devra Lee Davis)
—Instigate paradigm shifts in the disciplines (Ginny Foster)
—Meet the challenge of interdisciplinary work (Gerda Lerner)
—"Break out of the dominant frame of reference in the university, that of specialization and compartmentalization" (Nancy Hoffman et al.)
—Liberate teaching and research (Marcia Landy)
—Breach the divide between theory and practice (Gerda Lerner)
—Precipitate "the destruction of the university as we have known it for the past two hundred years" (Marcia Landy).[7]

The female studies these contributors envisioned still had a hybrid form and an insurgent modality, but its target of change was shifting from society's divided and divisive order to the academy's institutions, disciplines, knowledges, and practices. The academic turn evident in their statements was caused not by individual interests but by the structured forms and structuring forces that would shape female studies as a discipline within a few short years of the Pittsburgh conference.

The question to be addressed in chapters 4, 5, and 6 is this: how was female studies, initially envisioned as a venture that would transform social and academic institutions, itself transformed by them? The answer, abbreviated for now and elaborated in these three chapters, resides in the complex processes of formation. Every new venture, whether a political movement or an academic field, has to go through the processes of incubating, emerging, congealing, and functioning by drawing on existing resources and creating others anew. It incubates because people gather at already existing sites and acquire new ideas and skills; it emerges because they use these bits of discourse to voice grievances, frame issues, envision projects, and devise action plans; and it congeals when, in doing this work, people forge a collective identity. But from the very first moment they enter any arena and begin to act, that arena's already structured venues, resources, and activities work on their venture to format it. New ventures, in short, are formed by the relays between actors' actions and social structures, between intellectualization and institutionalization, between the rules working within the discourse and the forces working on the discourse.

My story begins with the incubation of academic feminism within the matrix of the 1960s movements: the networks of people, the critiques of mainstream education, and the techniques of activism that were transported to academic arenas. Next I focus on radical and feminist activism at two national sites, the American Sociological Association and the Modern Language Association, describing the practices that activists used to secure toeholds in these organizations and use them to leverage new disciplinary policies and knowledges. Last I turn to the grassroots work of launching female studies at conferences and on campuses, examining the practices that feminists used when they derailed their projects or seeded new ones.

Incubating in Movements

According to the standard genealogy, second-wave feminism incubated in two organizational fields—its liberal strain in civil liberties groups, education associations, church councils, labor unions and the remnants of the suffrage movement and its radical strain in the civil rights, New Left, and antiwar movements.[8] While the early conflicts over female studies did turn on this liberal / radical dualism (see "Splintering and Seeding Projects" below), it's more productive to ask where many of the first-generation academic feminists acquired the discursive bits they needed to envision and launch female studies. The answer would have to be that the women who initiated the early feminist projects had learned the skills of political education and organizing at diverse sites. In 1964 alone, they taught in the freedom schools and voter registration classes of the Mississippi Freedom Summer Project and helped to formulate a critique of the multiversity and disrupt its operations in the Berkeley Free Speech Movement. After that they practiced community and campus organizing in Students for a Democratic Society (SDS), revamped continuing education programs for women at Minnesota, Michigan, and other universities, planned conferences for the National Organization for Women, attended antiwar teach-ins, counseled young men on draft resistance, taught courses at left-sponsored free universities, and organized women's workshops in response to the endemic sexism of movement organizations.

If one had to pluck a critical moment from the activism that was sweeping the United States from the mid-1950s to the mid-1970s, it would have to be 1968 and 1969. During those two years, the nation reeled from one cataclysmic event to another, the forces deployed to make change and maintain order collided all over the social field, academic activism came into its own, and second-wave feminism emerged in the academy. In 1968, the civil rights and New Left movements peaked. Through its powerful infrastructure of national and local organizations linked by coordinating councils and communications networks, the civil rights movement had mobilized millions in protest politics. New Left organizations, though not as formally institutionalized and tightly articulated, collaborated in sponsoring antiwar protests in Washington, DC, and other cities that routinely attracted 10,000 to 100,000 participants, and leftist publications had close to 5 million readers. As assassination mowed down beloved leaders, Martin Luther King Jr. in Memphis on April 3 and Robert F. Kennedy in Los Angeles on June 5, the activism that had pounded the nation like a storm intensified, spawning violent tornados that tore through cities and campuses—the insurgency of students at Columbia University in April, the urban uprisings of African Americans over the summer, and the mayhem at the Democratic Party Convention in August when Chicago Mayor

Richard Daley's 12,000 police, 6,000 national guards, and 7,000 army troops battered thousands of protesters along with reporters, campaign staff, and bystanders.

Within this vortex of activism, academic groups had begun to congeal. Early in 1968, the New University Conference (NUC) was founded by radical faculty and graduate students who wanted to catalyze change from within the academy, and in March it held its first annual meeting back-to-back with SDS's national meeting in Chicago. Also in March, the Sociology Liberation Movement was launched by faculty and graduate students at Columbia University and, with SDS and NUC organizers, orchestrated the Columbia protest. These and other groups planned the activism that rocked the meetings of the disciplinary associations in 1968, especially the American Sociological Association in August and the Modern Language Association in December. Meanwhile, on a parallel track that would soon converge with the radical academic groups, women began to build the infrastructure of an independent movement: they proliferated chapters of NOW, organized caucuses in left organizations, formed women's liberation groups in Seattle, San Francisco, Gainesville, Chicago, New York, Boston, and Washington, DC, and held the first small but national feminist conferences at Sandy Springs (Maryland, 1968) and Lake Villa (Illinois, 1969). By 1969–70, the ideas and techniques that percolated at all these sites had bubbled onto a dozen campuses—for instance, Cornell, SUNY Buffalo, Rutgers, Chicago, San Diego State, and Portland State—where instructors offered the first experimental courses on women and entered the disciplinary associations where women's groups sponsored the first feminist sessions.[9]

What the 1960s movements shared was not the same political agenda but a paradigm for making change through structure, action, and education that had been crystallized by the civil rights movement and subsequently developed by the New Left. After emancipation, African Americans began with few resources besides their own determination and labor to found churches, schools, colleges, unions, small businesses, improvement associations, and communications media. This infrastructure was hardened by the establishment of national organizations: the National Association for the Advancement of Colored People (NAACP, 1909) to combat lynching and segregation, the National Urban League (NUL, 1910) to work on economic betterment, the biracial Congress of Racial Equality (CORE, 1942) to organize nonviolent direct action, the Southern Conference Education Fund (SCEF, 1942) and United Negro College Fund (1943) to shore up the financially strapped black schools and colleges, the Southern Christian Leadership Conference (SCLC, 1957) to use the enormous outreach capacity of black churches, and the Student Nonviolent Coordinating Committee (SNCC, 1960) to coordinate the local student groups in the southern sit-in movement. National organizations and community groups were linked by a communications network of black newspapers, magazines, scholarly journals, and organizational newsletters as well as by the contacts made when organizational officials traveled the grassroots and the local people attended training institutes. What African Americans had built was an articulated infrastructure—with vertical linkages connecting national organizations to local communities and horizontal linkages connecting organization to organization and community to community—that was capable of concerted action.

Civil rights activism traveled those vertical and horizontal pathways. When Rosa Parks refused to move to the back of the bus and sparked the Montgomery bus boycott, neither the incident nor the boycott were spontaneous occurrences. Leaders from the local black churches, the NAACP chapter, and the Women's Political Council, some of whom had trained at the Highlander Folk School in Tennessee, had been seeking a precipitant and were poised to rally the black community. Within days of the Parks incident, they had held a mass meeting, distributed flyers announcing a boycott, and formed the Montgomery Improvement Association, which was headed by the young Reverend Martin Luther King Jr., to sustain the year-long boycott through a variety of means that included arranging private transportation, training boycotters, and negotiating with the city. Afterward, southern black ministers who had observed or supported the boycott established SCLC to spread the struggle to other communities.[10] What the movement learned from Montgomery and subsequent projects was that to make social-structural change it would have to deploy five strategies: catalyzing local activism through community education and organizer training, orchestrating direct action (boycotts, sit-ins, marches) to pressure the elites, providing services to the people through parallel organizations (which the New Left called countercultural organizations), working the channels of official politics to change laws and policies, and insinuating movement issues and projects into mainstream arenas.

Besides this tutorial on structure and action, the civil rights struggle in the South showed later activists that education could be an instrument of oppression or liberation. The state-sponsored black schools were so racist that they omitted instruction on civics and African-American history, so underfunded that they barely taught the basics, and so punitive that they expelled students who dared to raise questions about the status quo. By inculcating ignorance and fear, the schools worked hand-in-glove with state-mandated poll taxes and voter registration tests, state-enforced segregation, state-countenanced labor exploitation, and state-condoned vigilante violence to maintain the white-supremacist system. Adding to these insights, the Berkeley Free Speech Movement's (FSM) conflict with the campus administration in 1964–65 showed other activists that universities were the machinery of the corporate-liberal state. They functioned as highly efficient factories that manufactured research for the military-industrial complex and as calcified bureaucracies that used automated registration, large lecture classes, and restrictive in loco parentis rules to interpellate students as the obedient subjects of the state.[11] On the liberation side of the equation, the civil rights movement used several forms of education—organizer training sponsored by the Highlander School as well as by the NAACP and SNCC, academic and practical education at black churches and colleges, and perhaps most importantly political education in the Mississippi freedom schools. The self-empowering pedagogy of the freedom schools enabled the students, black children and adults, to analyze the system of white supremacy, practice democratic processes, and learn the history of the African-American struggle. Other movements added to these forms: conference workshops, campus teach-ins, free universities, and of course feminist consciousness-raising groups.

Most New Leftists admired the civil rights movement but ignored some of the lessons they should have heeded. On the plus side, they drew on the model provided by SNCC: the organizational structure of loosely coordinated local groups, the modalities of participatory decision making in meetings and spontaneous problem solving in the field, the choreography of direct-action events, and the techniques of catalytic education and organizing. On the minus side, they were too alienated from the establishment system—its bureaucratic organizations, centralized decision making, elite politics, and tortuous legal processes—to see that a left organization, even one as large as SDS with its nearly 100,000 members and hundreds of campus chapters in 1968, wasn't a movement. A movement needed formal organizations as well as participant networks, regionally and nationally coordinated initiatives as well as local projects, and strategies for working the levers of official politics as well as for mounting direct action. The Left's antiestablishment choices reverberated at two levels. At the organization level, SDS failed to build a stable national office capable of linking the quickly multiplying chapters and coordinating the massive events it sponsored. It also didn't balance its tactical spontaneity with strategic advance planning, seldom used disruptions of establishment business-as-usual to leverage policy change, couldn't operationalize participatory decision making in mass meetings, and didn't ease the tensions over race, sex, and political ideology that factionalized its membership just as they factionalized SNCC's.[12] At the movement level, the thousands of people mobilized by New Left events were supposed to function as agents of change without the benefit of the hard infrastructure that sustained the civil rights movement: they didn't have networked institutions like the black churches and schools to provide historical continuity and train activists, councils like SCLC and SNCC to coordinate large cross-sector initiatives, and professionalized organizations like the NAACP to revise the laws that ordered the nation's processes.

This paradigm—the structures and strategies, the insights and problems—is what academic activists brought with them when they began to target disciplinary associations and universities. My story about the emergence of female studies at these sites will feature several people whose paths had crossed in the 1960s movements before converging at the sites of academic activism: Dick Flacks, Carol Brown, Jack Roach, Robert Ross, Marlene Dixon, Alice Rossi, Peter Rossi, Heather Booth, Paul Booth, Naomi Weisstein, and Marilyn Salzman-Webb in the social sciences and Louis Kampf, Richard Ohmann, Paul Lauter, Florence Howe, Carol Ohmann, Bruce Franklin, Tucker Farley, Barbara Kessel, and Roberta Salper in the modern languages.[13] For a few years, these and other activists had a nodal point in the academy—a new organization that catalyzed the action in the American Sociological Association (ASA) and the Modern Language Association, the formation of radical caucuses in the disciplines, and the emergence of academic feminism. Early in 1968, as many New Left organizations were disintegrating, a group of radical faculty and students launched the New University Conference (NUC). What motivated them to form an academic organization, said NUC national coordinator Robert Ross, was their dissatisfaction with the anti-intellectualism in many New Left groups or, as regional NUC coordinator Robert Salper remarked more positively, their "desire [to] carry change into the university as graduate students were making the transition to faculty appointments."[14] Ross was well suited to build and coordinate an academic-activist organization with those goals; he was a sociology graduate student at the University of Chicago, a founding member of SDS, and an organizer in Jobs or Income

Now (JOIN), an SDS project that was mobilizing poor biracial communities in northern cities.[15] His academic-activist profile was shared by more than 50 percent of the faculty and student members, who, before joining NUC, had participated in New Left, civil rights, or antiwar activism.[16]

Self-described as "a national organization of radicals who work in and around institutions of higher education," NUC took on the double mission of theorizing "a new, American form of socialism" and replacing "an educational and social system that is an instrument of class, sexual, and racial oppression with one that belongs to the people."[17] Its analysis of the American educational system drew on civil rights and New Left critiques: the primary schools used hierarchical teaching methods to accustom students to obedience and grading to instill the spirit of competition; the secondary schools channeled them into vocational or college preparatory programs; and the universities were partnered with government and industry, receiving material and symbolic capital from them and giving human and intellectual capital back to them. As one NUC member wrote, "Like other so-called private enterprises, elite universities dispose of large quantities of public funds, and often dominate or strongly influence the politics, economy, and demographic nature of the surrounding community." Since the power relay served the State, the antidote was to transform education so that it would furnish the people with the critical knowledges and survival skills they needed. Working from this analysis, NUC pursued the inside-outside strategy of sponsoring radical projects in schools, universities, and disciplinary associations while reaching out to disenfranchised working-class and African-American communities.[18] By 1971, NUC had attracted two thousand members, established sixty campus chapters, and spawned radical caucuses in several disciplinary associations; a year later "it was financially bankrupt and had a surviving membership of some 300 persons.[19] What caused its rapid decline?

Although not remarkably heterogeneous by today's standards, the members had trouble setting a coherent and feasible agenda. Soft-pedaling the situation, Ross said that they had "a conflict about emphasis" because some members identified themselves as teachers in the radical movement and others identified themselves as radical teachers in the university. Literature professor and former NUC member Paul Lauter described the conflict as a coup: the members who wanted to organize the working class wrested control of NUC from those who wanted to transform academic teaching and research.[20] Others thought that NUC, by accommodating both sets of interests, took on more than the members could handle;

the national organization decided to concentrate on formulating a new working-class theory just when the chapters were busy with campus actions and the radical caucuses it had spawned were preoccupied with projects in the disciplines.[21] The common thread in these explanations is identity discourse. When the identities of members oriented them to particular interests, they attempted to stave off conflicts by accommodating diverse projects; but by failing to prioritize the projects they overwhelmed the organization's capacity for effective action and precipitated its disintegration. But the identity discourse also had the positive effect of catalyzing academic feminism.[22] Tucker Farley, then a graduate student in English at Pennsylvania State University, told me she was stewing about the culture of sexism in the SDS and NUC meetings held in Chicago during March 1968. After sitting through the SDS meeting "with Engels and a typewriter, formulating why women should pay attention to women's liberation," she "took that passion and commitment" to NUC's first national meeting a few weeks later. When the feminists attending this meeting discovered that no women were included as speakers, Salzman-Webb recalled, they walked out to form a women's caucus. So effectively did the NUC feminists organize that in 1969 alone they not only dominated the NUC meeting "with issues raised by the Women's Caucus" but also helped to launch the ASA Women's Caucus and the MLA Commission on the Status of Women (see below).[23]

Roberta Salper and Marilyn Salzman-Webb, who will reappear throughout this chapter in my accounts of female studies at national and local sites, were part of this matrix of academic activism. While conducting research in Spain, Salper had participated in student activism and had read an article by Marlene Dixon, a feminist sociologist at the University of Chicago, about women organizing themselves. On her return, she stopped in Chicago for a weekend visit with Dixon, psychologist Naomi Weisstein, and historian Jesse Lemisch that, as she put it, "opened my eyes to the possibility of radicalism and feminism in the United States." After completing her doctorate in romance languages and literatures at Harvard in 1968, she accepted two positions, assistant professor at the University of Pittsburgh and regional coordinator of NUC. Between 1969 and 1971, she served as a member of the newly established MLA Commission on the Status of Women (resigning in 1971 to start a term on the MLA Executive Committee) and held a succession of academic positions: assistant dean of arts and sciences at Pittsburgh in 1969–70, distinguished visiting professor of women's studies at San Diego State College in 1970–71, and associate professor at SUNY, Old Westbury, beginning in fall 1971. Salper's activist and academic experiences informed her vision of social change as an articulatory practice that would have to bridge the divides etched into the academy and society. In a 1970 issue of *NUC Papers,* she wrote, "the most essential, often unperceived need of the people is, in fact, for movements that can organize them around common oppression," and in a 1971 issue of the *NUC Women's Caucus Newsletter* she insisted (just, ironically, as the San Diego feminists splintered over their hybrid Women's Center project) that women's studies "is a political and academic endeavor and the two are inseparable."[24] When I asked Salper why the early feminists categorized one another as activists or academics and as revolutionaries or reformers, she echoed Ross and Lauter's explanation of NUC's troubles. Since most feminists fit into all four categories, she replied, they should have regarded their sisters as having different emphases, but they used the dualisms as an easy way to discredit one group or another.[25]

From 1964 to 1967, while Marilyn Salzman-Webb was a graduate student in educational psychology at the University of Chicago, she joined an activist group formed by people associated with the Educational Psychology and Social Thought programs. The group, which included Heather and Paul Booth, Mickey and Richard Flacks, and Lee Webb, met for study, managed a community education project, and founded an SDS chapter when that organization located its national office in the same Chicago neighborhood.[26] After attending a national SDS conference where female members established a women's caucus and made plans to start women's groups in their home communities, she formed a Chicago women's group with Heather Booth and Paula Goldschmidt that was affiliated with SDS. In 1967, Salzman-Webb moved to Washington, DC, where she wrote for the *Guardian* and *Ramparts,* continued to participate in SDS, served on the planning committees for the feminist conferences at Sandy Springs and Lake Villa, and affiliated with the leftist Institute for Policy Studies (IPS) where she met Charlotte Bunch and Sue Thrasher.[27] The three women, together with others, set up an abortion counseling service (while abortion was still illegal) at a women's center that also sponsored a speakers' bureau and consciousness-raising groups. When I asked Salzman-Webb to talk about the matrix that had fostered her activism, she credited not the male-oriented SDS but the early feminist groups—even though she spoke quite openly about having been savaged by feminists as well as leftist men. For the 1969 Counter-Inaugural, an event organized by the National Mobilization Committee to protest Nixon's inauguration, feminists had chosen two speakers, Shulamith Firestone to represent the pro-woman line and Salzman-Webb to represent the New Left line. As Salzman-Webb began what she described as "a mild speech" about women's reproductive rights and job opportunities, the men standing near the stage screamed "take her into an alley and fuck her." Later that year, when the coordinating committee of the Washington women's center split around the issue of leadership versus collectivity, several members chastized Salzman-Webb for presuming to be a spokesperson and expelled her from the committee.[28] In the fall of 1970, she was appointed to direct the new women's studies program at Goddard College (Vermont). "We are trying to see," she wrote about the program, "what relationship our studies can have in deepening the scope of the movement feeding into action against patriarchy rather than only studying its existence."[29]

My point in providing these vignettes is not to typify left organizations and feminist lives but to set the stage for the discursive work that academic radicals and feminists did. As the discourse of academic change formulated in this matrix radiated outward through member activism on campuses, in disciplinary associations, and at conferences, its modalities of practice— meshing, fracturing, and seeing—were repeated by the women who launched female studies.

Meshing in Disciplinary Associations

History books cannot approximate the activism that was engraved on the memory of those who lived through the midcentury decades of struggle. Participants and bystanders alike were mesmerized by the defiant speeches, the tempestuous clashes, the steady stream of bodies sitting-in, chanting, marching, and surging. They were stunned by those spectacular moments when the forces of government brutalized protesting citizens: Chief "Bull" Connor's police unleashing attack dogs on black adults and children at the Birmingham demonstration in 1963; Alabama Governor George Wallace's state troopers wielding clubs, electric cattle prods, and fire hoses to disperse black marchers at Selma in 1965; Mayor Daley's police and National Guard troops brutalizing thousands at the Democratic Convention; and Ohio Governor James Rhodes's state troopers firing on students, killing four and wounding nine, at Kent State University in 1970. Understandably, then, disruption was the mode of movement activism that loomed large in the minds of the public and lingered in the history books. But I want to argue in what follows that another mode of activism changed disciplinary associations and universities—articulatory practices that linked activists into networks, built alliances among their groups, meshed the divergent discourses of the movement and the academy, and institutionalized the groups that went on to seed radical and feminist projects in the academy.

AT THE ASA

The story of how feminism was institutionalized in the American Sociological Association begins not in 1969 with the birth of the Women's Caucus but during the preceding two years as several groups of activists targeted the association and the discipline. At the 1967 ASA convention in San Francisco, a group of radical graduate students and faculty held an antiwar protest at the Hilton Hotel and attempted to present an antiwar resolution to the membership. When the ASA Council advised the hotel to take whatever legal action was necessary to disband the protest (it took none) and the next day voted the resolution down on the grounds that a scientific society should not take an official stand on policy issues, the group escalated the conflict by holding "a series of hastily assembled *ad hoc* gatherings capped by a mass meeting with one explicit aim: to have the ASA take an official stand against the Vietnam War." According to organizer Jack L. Roach, the group members were ambivalent about their entry into a mainstream institution. On one hand, they realized that the mass meeting had consolidated a network that could sustain the activism; on the other hand, they worried that recourse to associational procedures such as resolutions would convert political activism into professional activity.[30]

In 1968, academic activism picked up momentum. Sociology faculty and students who had attended SDS and NUC meetings that March launched the Sociology Liberation Movement (SLM) at Columbia University. "The idea," said SDS, NUC, and SLM member Dick Flacks, "was to find ways to shake up the discipline and challenge its establishment, starting with the annual [1968] ASA meeting in Boston." SLM activists made plans to sponsor "a series of workshop discussions on the theme 'Knowledge for Whom?',", staff a literature table, picket the hotel, present resolutions, and demonstrate at the keynote speech to be given by Secretary of Health, Education, and Welfare Wilber J. Cohen. When the SLM leaders arrived in Boston, ASA's president threatened them with arrest if they attempted to disrupt the proceedings and, as mollification, permitted them to choose a discussant for the panel responding to Cohen's speech. The keynote event, though not disrupted, looked more like a military enclave than a scholarly convocation; black-armbanded SLM members were spread through the audience and a cordon of police ringed the stage while a thousand people tried to concentrate on the speech. At the Business Meeting, the SLM activists introduced several resolutions that were defeated and one that passed. Horrified by the police brutality that was occurring in Chicago as the ASA was meeting, members voted for the SLM resolution to cancel Chicago as the site of the 1969, 1972, and 1976 conventions. Wisely remarking the groundswell of member opinion, the ASA Council approved the change of venue.[31]

During the spring of 1969, sociology faculty and students intensified their activism and solidified their infrastructure. They demanded that the University of Chicago reinstate radical sociologist Marlene Dixon (the university responded by expelling or suspending many of the students who had protested on her behalf), they formed women's sociology caucuses at Berkeley and Johns Hopkins (see below), and they organized the Eastern and Western Unions of Radical Sociologists. Converging on the ASA at its 1969 convention in San Francisco, an alliance of activists from SLM, Third World Front, and Women's Liberation used the familiar strategies of parallel programs and insurgent politics. At Glide Memorial Church the alliance held a counterconvention of workshops and organizational meetings, and at the Hilton Hotel the SLM sponsored a picket line, a literature table, and truth squads that attended ASA sessions to expose the political entanglements of sociological research.[32] But the activists' resolutions were once again voted down at the Business Meeting, a rebuff they used, according to SLM organizers Jack Roach and Carol Brown, to catalyze the most tumultuous event at the convention. As Ralph H. Turner was about to begin his presidential address to a thousand people, seventy-five SLM members mounted the speaker's platform and conducted a brief memorial service for recently deceased Ho Chi Minh while audience members shook their fists and chanted "throw them out."[33] Afterward the activists began to institutionalize their presence in the ASA; they gained formal recognition of the Caucus of Black Sociologists, merged the SLM and the Union of Radical Sociologists as the Radical Caucus, and founded the Chicano and gay caucuses.

The Women's Caucus, according to Kay Klotzburger, was part of the organization-building phase; it was "announced in June 1969 and made its public debut three months later" at the ASA convention.[34] Early that spring, Alice Rossi had begun working with a women's group at Johns Hopkins where she was a research associate and with the Berkeley Sociology Women's Caucus, founded the previous year.[35] While the two groups prepared materials for the ASA convention—posters and leaflets, papers to be sold at the Women's Caucus table, memoranda to the ASA Council and committees, and resolutions to be presented at the Business Meeting— Rossi conducted a survey "on the status of women as students, faculty, and research personnel in graduate departments of sociology during the academic year 1968–69" that would be used to support the caucus's demands.[36] When the convention opened, however, it was apparent that feminists had organized parallel programs: the Women's Caucus had scheduled its general meeting at the Hilton Hotel, and the Radical Women's Caucus and Berkeley Women's Sociology Caucus were sponsoring sessions at Glide Memorial Church. To bring the hotel and church groups together, Rossi asked the ASA president to reassign a ballroom so that the general meeting could accommodate a larger audience than had been anticipated; he initially refused but relented "when he was confronted with an onerous threat to disrupt the ASA proceedings." The attempt to build bridges almost backfired because the reassignment of the ballroom angered both the ASA members whose event was relocated and the radical feminists, who were counting on a presidential rebuff as the pretext they needed to organize a disruption that, if quelled by the police, would mobilize mass support for their cause.[37]

The ballroom meeting was chaired by Rossi and drew some five hundred people, who, recalled Datha Clapper Brack, "crowded into standing room along the walls, while the overflow milled outside the door trying to find out what was going on inside." As the panel of female faculty and graduate students spoke, Brack was astonished by their mere presence: "In those overwhelmingly male association meetings, I had never before seen a platform occupied entirely by women."[38] Their stories about the sexism they had encountered moved Arlene Kaplan Daniels to tears and insight:

> Suddenly, I recognized the larger pattern in all the slights, snubs, omissions, and patronizing acts that I had shrugged off as my paranoia or my just desserts. . . . As long as I thought I was responsible for events, I could try harder; my fate was within my own control. If I had seen the system as stacked against me, I might have been overcome with rage

and despair and thus immobilized. Without support groups or an ideology of sisterhood, the idea of patterned gender injustice would have been devastating.[39]

The "click"—as the early feminists called these moments of intense insight and affect that overloaded their past experiences with meaning—had a galvanic effect. Both women joined the Women's Caucus, Daniels taking on the jobs of vice president and newsletter editor in 1970 and Brack designing one of the first courses on the sociology of women.

After the panel, the audience discussed the Caucus's ten resolutions "in an atmosphere of mounting tension": the radical women demanded substantive changes, the liberal women eventually assented, and the audience finally approved them. Later Rossi presented the Caucus resolutions and a statement censuring the discipline at the ASA Business Meeting. The Caucus declared that it wanted not pro forma discussions of women's status but structural changes—increased admissions and hiring of women, university childcare and parental leave, new courses on women, inclusion of the topic of sexism in existing courses, and appointment of women to ASA committees and editorial boards. The resolutions, endorsed "in spirit" by the Business Meeting participants and the ASA Council, were published with Rossi's study in ASA's journal, *The American Sociologist,* early in 1970.[40] By then the Women's Caucus was making plans for the 1970 ASA convention in Washington, DC, where it would elect Rossi as its president and would craft several resolutions, among them that ASA establish a committee on women to collect data on women in the profession, approve a section on the Sociology of Sex Roles, and provide free childcare at future meetings.[41]

After the 1970 convention, ASA feminists made the transition from networked activism to institutionalized activism. That December the ASA Council established the Ad Hoc Committee on the Status of Women in Sociology with six members (two of whom were men) and a year later added a graduate student as its seventh member. In 1973 the Ad Hoc Committee, now expanded to nine members (still including two men), published its first report on the status of women in sociology. Modeled on Rossi's earlier report, this one documented the comparative status of female and male graduate students, faculty, and ASA members for the years 1969–72 and the diminishing numbers of women in the field as they moved along the path from undergraduate majors to full professorships.[42] Soon afterward, ASA made the Ad Hoc Committee a standing committee.

Meanwhile, after existing as an informal network for a year and a half, the Women's Caucus was renamed Sociologists for Women in Society (SWS) in February 1971 and restructured as a formal organization with officers and committees to carry out its work. Over the years the two groups worked in tandem, the Committee on Women initiating change from within the ASA and SWS solidifying the grassroots network by organizing the regional caucuses and publishing the *Directory of Members,* the newsletter *SWS Network,* and the journal *Gender and Society,* which was established in 1987. Joining forces, they pressed ASA to transform the Section on Sociology of Sex Roles into the Section on Sociology of Sex and Gender, which by the mid-1990s had grown into the third largest of ASA's scholarly divisions.

Although I will return to ASA activism after discussing the Modern Language Association, I want to make one point now: institutionalization was a necessary but not a sufficient condition for making structural change in the association, the profession, and the discipline. The activism sponsored by ad hoc groups, such as the SLM and the women's caucuses, precipitated the formation of organizations officially sponsored or recognized by the ASA—the Committee on Women, SWS, the Radical Caucus, the Association of Black Sociologists, the Chicano Sociologists, the Sociologists' Gay Caucus, and the new scholarly sections. The formal structures and resources of these groups made it possible for them to carry out sustained projects, but their alliances, said Pamela Roby, who had participated in ASA activism from 1969 onward, made democratization possible. The Committee on Women, SWS, and the Section on Sociology of Sex and Gender collaborated on fostering feminist studies, improving women's status, and (with the other progressive groups) reforming the ASA. During Roby's tenure as SWS president (1978–80), the alliance itself was institutionalized in the form of annual luncheons attended by caucus presidents and section heads.[43]

AT THE *MLA*

Meanwhile, a remarkably similar drama was unfolding at the Modern Language Association where the convergence of antiwar activism and associational reform at the December 1968 convention in New York would bring about the institutionalization of feminism.[44] The idea of taking on the oldest and largest disciplinary association germinated in the fertile ground of two organizations. In March 1968, several dozen MLA members attended NUC's first annual meeting where, according to Tucker Farley, an assortment of people from the social sciences and humanities, SDS, and women's liberation groups talked about academic change strategies. Four of the MLA members attending that meeting—Louis Kampf (who served on NUC's steering committee), Paul Lauter, Richard Ohmann, and Florence Howe—were also board members of Resist, an organization of intellectuals, journalists, and clergy founded in 1967 to support draft resistance and other forms of political organizing. By 1968 Resist had a membership that overlapped other left organizations, a headquarters in New York City, and a small-grants program to seed political projects.[45]

After the NUC meeting, the four Resist members obtained a grant to meet over the summer and share their "thoughts about just what to do" at the MLA convention in December, which initially, according to Kampf and Lauter, "extended little further than 'stirring things up.' "[46] But galvanized by the police brutality in Chicago and the activism at the ASA convention (which Lauter had attended), they began meeting with faculty and graduate students in New York City that fall. From the details of the action they planned, it's clear that they intended to air antiwar issues and recruit supporters by working according to the rules of the convention. Besides scheduling a session that would feature linguist and Resist member Noam Chomsky speaking on the Vietnam War, they demanded that MLA give them a literature table in the exhibition hall, a meeting room for a seminar on teaching literature, and a slot on the respondents' panel at the forum titled "The American Scholar and the Crisis of Our Culture." The night before the convention opened, they held a meeting at Columbia University to brief interested MLA members; some five hundred people showed up to discuss and support the group's events that the MLA had incorporated into its program at the Hilton and Americana hotels.

Usually when an unforeseen event occurs it deflects or hinders the planned action, but this time it sparked a groundswell of support. On the first day of the MLA convention, Howe was hanging posters—picturing Eldridge Cleaver and quoting Blake's proverb "The tygers of wrath are wiser than the horses of instruction"—near the entrance of the Americana. When hotel security guards arrived to remove the posters, a clutch of activists assembled, a scuffle ensued, and the management called the New York City police, who arrested Kampf and a few of his colleagues. The news spread, and the activists hastily caucused outside the ballroom where "The American Scholar and the Crisis of Our Culture" was about to begin. While MLA President Henry Nash Smith welcomed an audience of fifteen hundred people, the activists marched down the aisle and formed a silent vigil line in front of the podium.

Meanwhile the Tactics Committee, which had been set up to orchestrate the planned activism from Ohmann's suite in a small hotel across the street from the Americana, was jolted into high gear and held back-to-back meetings that were open to all interested MLA members. People came and went, bringing with them news of spur-of-the-moment developments and opinions on long-standing issues. When someone proposed nominating Kampf for the MLA second vice presidency as a response to the arrests, the participants held a heated debate on the same issue the ASA activists had addressed—whether a radical group should use its energies to position members inside an establishment institution or to spread movement activism and build counterinstitutions. Farley saw the opening and seized it, arguing that institutionalization was a necessary strategy for women in the discipline; even if they mobilized to voice their concerns and pressure the association, they would still need an MLA-authorized committee to investigate sexism in the profession. After the tactics meeting broke up, Farley and other women prepared a resolution for the MLA Business Meeting that called for the establishment of a committee on women.[47]

On the second day of the convention, the activists used the Chomsky session as an occasion to recruit supporters and escalate the conflict. Inviting the large audience to stay on for a discussion of the arrests, they swelled their numbers, marched to the Americana lobby, and staged a mass sit-in. Hotel management summoned the police, who arrived in riot gear and encircled the protesters while Bruce Franklin led them through a formal discussion of MLA's offer to negotiate. When the parties finally met in a basement room, MLA leaders offered to drop the charges against the arrested members and the activists accepted the gesture, but rumors of the association's intransigence continued to circulate, the New York police remained stationed throughout the convention hotels, and the tension propelled concerned and curious members to the Business Meeting held on the third day. Ordinarily, a few dozen members would show up at the meeting to ratify the Nominating Committee's slate of candidates for associational offices, but this year nearly five hundred members streamed into the ballroom and filled every seat. Most had no knowledge of the resolutions the activists planned to introduce, but they did expect a lively debate on whether the MLA should hold its 1969 convention in Chicago. Having heard that the Executive Council was opposed to relocating it, they were outraged by what they took to be a decision condoning police brutality at the Democratic Convention.

As Joan E. Hartman described that long meeting, the members trudged through a number of procedural questions and votes, some of them concerning the failure of the Committee on Resolutions to forward the activists' resolutions on the Vietnam War and Chicago convention to the Business Meeting. After the last procedural vote, it was clear that a majority would support the activists' resolutions. Ohmann nominated Kampf as second vice president for 1969 (an office succeeding to the 1971 presidency), and the members elected him by a vote of 292 to 187. Then Farley and others called for a committee on women, and the members passed motion as a "sense of the meeting." According to Hartman, the fortuitous conjunction of the police brutality that summer, the arrests at this convention, and the issue of relocating the next convention stirred the members' outrage and produced the large turnout at the Business Meeting, where in turn questions about MLA's blocking of resolutions precipitated a groundswell of support for governance reform.[48]

The groundswell not only motivated the MLA to move the 1969 convention to Denver, but also set in motion the formation of a formal committee and several member caucuses that together would democratize the association. After the 1968 convention, the MLA leadership, realizing that the modest reforms recommended by the existing Study Commission would not satisfy the perturbed membership, established the New Study Commission to recommend a more democratic governance structure. Among the reforms subsequently implemented were the creation of a large Delegate Assembly to share in the governance duties previously carried out by the small Executive Council, the nomination of three candidates for second vice president to replace the single-candidate slate, and the election of delegates and officers by means of mail-in ballots sent to all members.[49] Meanwhile, the activists institutionalized their presence—founding the Radical Caucus and the Women's Caucus for the Modern Languages in 1969, the Gay and Lesbian Caucus a few years later, and new MLA divisions on emerging fields in literary studies from the mid-1970s forward. These groups continued the political, scholarly, and pedagogical initiatives that reconfigured literary studies.

Early in 1969, at the urging of Vice President Kampf, the MLA Executive Council established the Commission on the Status of Women, the first such body in any disciplinary association. The CSW had a mandate to study women's status in modern language departments and in the MLA, where women, although one-third of the nearly thirty thousand members, held few positions on the headquarters' staff, the governance committees, the publication boards, and the executive committees of scholarly divisions. Between 1969 and 1973, the CSW took on several projects: editing volumes of *Female Studies,* organizing sessions on the new feminist scholarship at the MLA conventions, cosponsoring the 1971 Pittsburgh conference, initiating a pamphlet series on professional issues, issuing a report on women's exclusion from MLA's division executive committees and conference sessions, and publishing two nationwide studies of women's status in modern language departments—one documenting the sex-patterned profession and the other addressing admissions, hiring, promotion, compensation, nepotism, parental leave, day care, and affirmative action.[50] By 1973, the CSW was stabilized in its present form, with nine members (including the first two graduate student members) serving three-year terms, and was planning several new projects, including a third status study, advocacy of author-blind review for journal submissions, a conference to educate publishers on women's studies research, and a series of institutes on teaching American women's literature.

The incident that precipitated the founding of the Women's Caucus for the Modern Languages (WCML) occurred during the CSW's scholarly session at the MLA's 1969 convention. Several hundred women listened with rapt attention as Kate Millett read an analysis of patriarchy that would later appear in her *Sexual Politics* and then grew restive as a professor of French delivered a tribute to Yale University for educating women and cited statistics "to prove that, for most of the century, women had earned one-third of Yale's doctorates in several MLA-connected departments." When session chair Florence Howe called for discussion, the "feminist Yale doctorates in the room . . . demanded to know how many of the women the professor bragged about had been hired into Yale's faculty." Angry murmurs were heard, tempers rose, and an uproar seemed imminent. Howe, realizing that "no soothing response was possible, since of course Yale had hired its male doctorates in substantial numbers," avoided an audience riot by spiriting the professor out of the room and then suggesting that the women organize a caucus. Verna Wittrock, an Illinois faculty member, volunteered to lead the planning and huddled with a small group of women at the back of the room. The WCML, "formed with an initial membership of 10," held its first organizational meeting at the MLA's 1970 convention and "quickly grew to more than 500 by 1971."[51]

Soon granted "affiliate organization" status so that it could schedule scholarly sessions and a business meeting at the MLA conventions, the WCML diffused feminist activism and scholarship throughout the grassroots—organizing caucuses in the six MLA regions, managing a fund to aid victims of sex discrimination, publishing the quarterly journal *Concerns,* and establishing the Florence Howe Essay Award, which is still the only one for feminist scholarship among the several awards bestowed by the MLA. Despite tensions between the CSW and WCML that arose from differences in their affiliational status with MLA, access to associational resources, membership size, and politics, the groups collaborated with each other and with the Radical Caucus, the Gay and Lesbian Caucus (GLC), and the MLA Division of Women's Studies in Language and Literature established in 1975. During my years as a CSW member (1974–77) and WCML vice president and president (1991–93), the two groups often coordinated their initiatives, cosponsored or rotated the annual forum allotted by the MLA, and circulated news to their networks. Indeed, it was their networked structure that made that cooperation possible: group memberships overlapped, leaders communicated, and representatives of the WCML, the GLC, and the division usually attended CSW meetings.

Two projects show that networking was the key to effective feminist activism in the association. In 1970, when the MLA Nominating Committee issued a slate of three white male candidates for the 1971 second vice presidency, CSW member Carol Ohmann asked Florence Howe to stand for nomination by member petition. Reluctant to give up her work as CSW chair, Howe agreed only because she thought petitioning was a necessary, if doomed, gesture. But, with help from the CSW, WCML, and Radical Caucus, Ohmann circulated the petitions that put Howe on the ballot; the four-way election split the eleven thousand voting members and gave Howe the second vice presidency by a narrow margin.[52] During 1975 and 1976 the CSW was once again motivated to nominate by petition. First the MLA executive secretary asked the Executive Council to cut the CSW budget and eliminate some of its meeting, and we responded by lobbying Council members to vote against retrenchment. Later that year, when the Nominating Committee proposed all male slates for the second vice presidency and the open seats on the Executive Council, we felt that the MLA was retreating from its obligations not merely to support our work on women's status but to ensure women's participation in associational governance. After Joan Hartman, a CSW member and WCML treasurer, reminded us of the petitioning process, we invited three feminists known for their scholarly and professional achievements to stand for nomination: Jean

Perkins for second vice president and Marilyn Williamson and Micheline Dufault for the Executive Council. Although the petition required only seventy-five signatures, Hartman used the nomination process to lobby for votes, mailing petitions to sympathetic colleagues across the country, who in turn circulated them to colleagues. That fall the members elected Perkins to the vice presidency and Williamson to the Executive Council.[53]

ARTICULATING PRACTICE

From the ASA and MLA stories, I want to extrapolate some points about the emergence of female studies and the modalities of associational activism. First, with 20/20 hindsight it's clear that a nationwide feminist studies could not have been based outside of the academy because the 1960s movements never made feminist education their priority and, more importantly, did not have the infrastructure to sustain it. In the late 1960s, the civil rights movement had split into liberal and black power camps, New Left organizations were disintegrating, and the nascent women's movement consisted of little more than the National Organization for Women and a few dozen women's liberation groups. Through the mid-1970s, the organizational infrastructure of the women's movement was too specialized and beleaguered to support the development of feminist studies. NOW, the largest feminist organization with nearly two hundred chapters and several thousand members, was pursuing a multi-issue agenda and confronting establishment institutions while trying to stave off internal factionalism. Other organizations had specialized interests: The Women's Equity Action League (1968) and Federally Employed Women (1968) were concerned with employment conditions; Human Rights for Women (1968), the Women's Legal Defense Fund (1971), and NOW's Legal and Educational Defense Fund (1971) focused on litigation; and the National Women's Political Caucus (1971) was concerned with electoral politics and public policy. The mass-membership traditional women's organizations, such as the League of Women Voters, Young Women's Christian Association, National Federation of Business and Professional Women, and National Council of Negro Women, were dealing with constituency issues and, although feminism was a growing presence within them, most members were not quite ready to embrace an unabashedly feminist agenda. As for the radical-feminist sector, its groups were too small, too loosely linked, and too evanescent to mount a nationwide project, and the few large groups were stretched thin by their ambitious agendas. The Chicago Women's Liberation Union (1966–77), probably the largest with some two to three hundred active members, was taxed by the demands of maintaining its liberation school, publications program, speakers bureau, underground abortion counseling service, and childcare coalition.[54]

The academy provided a ready-made infrastructure that feminists could, to a certain extent, appropriate for feminist studies; its universities and colleges could house courses, its publications could circulate feminist-studies discourse, and its disciplinary associations could advocate for changes in professional policies and scholarly knowledges. Yet within the academic system I think we need to differentiate the two complementary conditions for building a nationwide feminist studies. The most important one was grassroots labor—the thousands of women (and men) who struggled on their campuses to teach courses, establish programs, and hire faculty while also assembling the infrastructure of feminist journals, presses, conferences, and associations. But to do this campus-by-campus and project-by-project work, feminists needed national apparatuses that furnished the occasions to plan, the mechanisms to coordinate, the venues to circulate, and the authorities to legitimate the projects they launched. That's what the disciplinary associations provided—but only after they themselves were changed. Radical and feminist activists targeted the disciplinary associations not merely to democratize them but to turn them into instruments of wider academic change. To retool the associations, radical and feminist activists had to deploy a variety of articulatory practices. Across many differences, they had to form alliances, win supporters, and mesh the divergent discourses of the movement and the academy.

I don't want to give the impression that the early feminist activists always saw eye-to-eye with radical men. In fact, just as sexism quickly turned Tucker Farley and Marilyn Salzman-Webb into feminists, so it eventually sent Florence Howe and Carol Brown down that road. Howe stressed (as did others who worked with her in those days) that throughout the 1960s she was a civil rights and antiwar activist who had no plans to organize women until circumstances at the MLA drew her to feminism.[55] And Brown recollected that despite "plenty of sexism in the Sociology Liberation Movement" she "was not primarily concerned with women's issues" until the mid-1970s when discrimination on campus and in the ASA transformed her into a self-identified socialist-feminist.[56] Yet the male Left, like the disciplinary associations, provided the women who would launch female studies with an infrastructure—in this case, an already structured field where comrades were networked, activist and academic activities were being meshed, and democratization of associations and universities was underway. Within the overlapped networks of SDS, NUC, ASA, and MLA, feminist projects got off the ground through informal contacts as well as careful planning. During the late 1960s, for example, Florence Howe and Paul Lauter were next-door neighbors of Alice and Peter Rossi in Baltimore. When Howe, who had read Alice's study of women's status in sociology, consulted the Rossis about how to do a similar study of women's status in the modern languages, Peter recommended his student Laura Morlock, who became a coauthor of the CSW's first three status studies.[57] This serendipitous example was really no different in kind from the collaboration of radicals and feminists on big initiatives such as the Glide Church counterconvention at the 1968 ASA meeting, the establishment of the MLA Commission on the Status of Women, and the election of feminists to MLA offices. What made the alliances possible were the linkages they forged by trading for mutual support on their particular issues. At the MLA, Farley told me, the activists said, "If I raise this one, will you talk on it? If you raise that one, I'll talk on it." At the ASA, reported sociologist Pamela Roby, the "caucuses sometimes jointly proposed resolutions and generally supported one another's resolutions."[58] Issue trading, like other articulatory practices, enabled individuals with different priorities to work as a group and groups with different agendas to build coalitions. In subsequent years, the feminist groups in both associations worked in tandem: the small women's committees, officially charged with responsibilities for women's status, incorporated the concerns of the women's caucuses and feminist scholarly divisions into their recommendations, and the large-membership caucuses and divisions pressured the ASA and MLA to implement those recommendations.

In both associations, the convergence of the activists' concerns with the membership's concerns about the flagrant violations of democratic process—Chicago police brutality, research serving the State's interests, and elite associational governance—created a climate favorable to acting on the women's demands at the national conventions. But those superheated moments by themselves would not have supported ongoing feminist change; since ongoing change was resisted by the associations' elite male leadership, feminists needed to win over the mainstream male members as "conscience supporters" who, according to contemporary social-movement theory, lend support to a movement's initiatives without actually joining it. Many of MLA's male members, Hartman stressed, were "natural allies" who had grown accustomed to working with female colleagues in the nonelite modern language departments.[59] Although ASA men had fewer female colleagues in their departments, something like natural alliances was also at work in sociology. The ASA minutes and publications show that when feminists contended that women were disadvantaged by the structuring of the profession male sociologists were predisposed by training to feel an affinity for structural evidence and analysis.

Finally, to make change in the ASA and MLA, the activists had to amalgamate the movement practices of threatening disruptions, holding protests, and making demands with the associational practices of drafting resolutions, speaking at business meetings, and lobbying for issues. Although many MLA members regarded the 1968 radicals as "a 'disciplined' group" prepared to manipulate the convention's procedures and events, they themselves stressed the improvisational nature of their activism. Kampf and Lauter describe the radicals as shuttling between the tactics room and the convention sites, caucusing hastily in hotel hallways, and making forays into sessions.[60] Farley told me that the activism at the 1968 Business Meeting was "like a jam session, each instrument joining in, playing new music devised and coordinated at the moment."[61] Her simile is apt because the association leaders were instructed on governance procedures, but the radicals and feminists learned to play them by ear. Having been shut out of associational governance, Roby observed, feminists "learned through trial and error at the meetings of the ASA, the ISA [International Sociological Association], and several of the regional associations how to submit resolutions. We found that we not only had to write them but turn them into convention offices by certain dates and times. Later we learned to arrange for various members to speak on behalf of each resolution and to assure the passage of resolutions by having enough supporters in the room."[62] Farley similarly commented that the activists had to understand MLA procedures to even be a presence at meetings, let alone to get their resolutions on the table. When a struggle depends in the first place on who can speak, she added, "the most radical thing to do is to teach *Roberts Rules of Order*."[63] Her juxtaposition of radical struggle and *Roberts Rules* points to the fundamental condition for making change that lies behind all of those I have been discussing. The activists had to mesh discontinuous discourses in order to congeal as groups, form group coalitions, and promote movement agendas in academic arenas.

Finally, the episodes of ASA and MLA activism I have described in this chapter illustrate an important point made in chapter 2. To transform academic institutions, activists have to change not merely their decision makers but their decision-making structures. In 1968 this insight eluded a surprising number of ASA and MLA members, both the radicals who believed that the associations had academized them and the traditionalized who believed that the radicals had anarchized the associations. Among the several MLA members who complained about the activism, one even wrote to the House Committee on Un-American Activities and the U.S. Justice Department to allege that radical violence at the 1968 convention had infringed his rights to security and travel.[64] In the 1990s, conservatives reprised this argument, declaring that "tenured radicals" had turned disciplinary associations and universities into "a squalid political battleground."[65] The problem with these haphazard conclusions is that they completely obscure the results. Rather than blunting movement change or destroying associational order, the activism transformed an elitist form of governance that generated inequitable outcomes into a participatory form of governance officially charged with producing equitable outcomes.

Splintering and Seeding Projects

To launch female-studies projects, the early feminists knew that they would have to do several types of articulatory work. They would have to collaborate across differences in political ideology, race and class, movement and academic affiliations, status and skills. They would have to weigh the tradeoffs of locating their projects in left-sponsored free schools, community-based women's centers, or mainstream academic institutions. And if they chose the latter they would somehow have to mesh the radically divergent practices, values, and objectives of the academy and the women's movement. Yet it is clear that their discourses were dividing them—so inevitably did activists and scholars clash over their allegiances to the movement or the university, so predictably did leftists and liberals wrangle about the correct line, and so tediously did the factions invoke "the women" whose interests they claimed to represent. The early feminists were, as it turned out, right to think about differences but wrong to conclude that institutional co-optation, incorrect political analysis, and inadequate representation would derail their projects.

SPLINTERING AT SAN DIEGO, PITTSBURGH, AND SACRAMENTO
In 1969, a feminist rap group at San Diego State College (SDSC) began discussing the idea of a women's studies program and that summer renamed itself the Ad Hoc Committee on Women's Studies. Most of the dozen or so committee members—SDSC instructors, undergraduates, fac-

ulty wives, and community women—had already experienced activism in the Mississippi Freedom Summer Project or the Berkeley Free Speech Movement, local chapters of CORE and SDS, and the recent SDSC demonstrations for ethnic studies.[66] The committee drew up a plan for a hybrid Women's Center: on campus it would have a women's studies program and a women's liberation group; and in the community it would sponsor a research center, a publishing house, an arts center, a childcare facility, and a storefront facility providing information and counseling. The objective in designing a multiprogram and multisite center was to mobilize, coordinate, and serve a broad-based San Diego women's movement that would bridge the divides created by the systems of oppression.

That fall, the Ad Hoc Committee deluged the campus with information on women's studies and, armed with a petition signed by 600 students, approached the SDSC administration for funds to hire program faculty. While faculty volunteers taught five women's studies courses during the spring of 1970, the committee's proposal for a formal ten-course program (accompanied by Alice Rossi's letter of endorsement) made its way through various college committees.[67] By the semester's end, the Faculty Senate had approved the program and the college had allocated funds for a one-year distinguished visiting professorship as well as one and a half instructional positions. Over the summer the committee offered the visiting professorship to Marlene Dixon, an NUC member and radical sociologist at the University of Chicago; Dixon declined but recommended Roberta Salper, who accepted and also recommended Barbara Kessel, another NUC member, for the full-time instructorship.[68] By the time Salper and Kessel arrived at SDSC in the fall of 1970, women's studies was starting to look like a college unit. That year the Ad Hoc Committee was reconstituted as a Board of Women's Studies reporting to the dean of the College of Arts and Letters and authorized to make decisions about the program's budget, hiring, curriculum, events, and publicity; and the next year women's studies would enroll 430 students, offer eight courses, and employ four faculty members.[69]

Meanwhile, the center project was floundering, its route from vision to implementation fraught with discord that splintered the planners. On the dean's advice in the spring of 1970, the Ad Hoc Committee had applied for a $12,000 seed grant from the SDSC Foundation to pay for the salary of a half-time center coordinator and other expenses. After receiving the grant in July, the committee awarded the coordinator job to Carol Rowell Council, an undergraduate student who had been an organizer of the original rap group and the volunteer coordinator of the Ad Hoc Committee. Though well qualified to carry out the duties of fundraising, program planning, and campus-community coordination, Rowell Council found her work stymied by tensions among the various parties to the center project. Administrators expected the Ad Hoc Committee to get behind one or two leaders who would seek foundation funding, foundations wanted not a settled plan but an idea they could shape, and the Ad Hoc Committee insisted on collective decision making while acting in ways that made consensus virtually impossible. The members split into warring camps, one ready to implement the Women's Center as originally designed and the other deeply distrustful of the planners, the design, the SDSC administration, and the foundations. Caught in these breaches, Rowell Council announced herself accountable to none but the yet to be appointed Center board. After a majority on the new Board of Women's Studies voted in fall 1971 to disassociate their program from the Women's Center, she departed to start a Center for Women's Studies and Services at the downtown YWCA that eventually implemented some of the programming detailed in the original plan.[70]

Probing for what had fractured the San Diego feminists, I consulted various sources. In her 1971 Pittsburgh paper, Salper put the blame on a structural dynamic—the power struggle between establishment organizations and the insurgent group that occurs at the moment of institutionalization. She described the San Diego breakup as a concrete instance of "how foundations exert pressure on college administrations to control potentially radical innovation—that is, university programs with the possibility of real linkages with other sectors of society." The SDSC feminists, she suggested, recognized half of the problem: if they located women's studies in universities, they ran the risk of co-optation by a culture of professionalism that would subvert their ends and break their ties to the movement. But they didn't as quickly recognize the other half of the problem: if they located women's studies in movement-sponsored centers or schools, they ran the risk of corruption by a " 'soft culture' . . . that says the best way to be revolutionary is to become a better person by opting out of the system and living a pure life" in the counterculture. "There is no liberated territory in the United States" from which to make the revolution, Salper concluded, because both co-optation by and alienation from mainstream institutions would limit the political impact of women's studies.[71]

After reviewing archived material from the San Diego project, scholar

Catherine Orr blamed the splintering on another dynamic—the crisis of representational legitimacy induced when the San Diego feminists handled their disagreements over institutionalization by discrediting each other. The founding members of the Ad Hoc Committee were typed as authoritarian elitists and the newcomers as vulgar Marxists, the pro-Center members were accused of consorting with the enemy when they discussed plans with activist husbands or male colleagues, and the anti-Center members were suspected of fomenting a gay / straight split when they hung out with lesbian-feminist organizers.[72] Taking hold of the group process, the ad feminam rhetoric intensified the antagonisms, hardened the factions, and escalated the conflict, which in turn spurred the factions to drum up campus and community supporters so they could claim to be representing the interests of "the women." The anti-Center faction, in its bid to prevail over the pro-Center faction, demanded to know how the Center "would meet the needs of San Diego Women" and whether the Center would change "as real women became part of it."[73] When they invoked the "real women," Orr argued, the anti-Center faction excluded several real women from that category—the founders of the rap group, their opponents on the Ad Hoc Committee, and many of the female faculty, students, and staff who didn't agree with their views. Nor did the anti-Center faction, I would add, ponder the feasibility of involving and serving "the women" of San Diego. If they had, they might have recalled that SDS failed to devise an organizational form that could accommodate the direct participation of its mass membership and that smaller organizations, such as NUC, had floundered when they took on too many projects. The committee members never grappled with the problem of how to operationalize decision making by "the women" and services for them because they were too busy re-creating in practice the divisive politics they repudiated in principle.

When I asked Salper and Salzman-Webb in recent interviews about the discord that splintered early feminist groups, they blamed the political climate of that era. Leftists, convinced that government agents had bored into social movements, academic institutions, and foundations to orchestrate domestic counterinsurgency, assiduously watched for signs of betrayal from within and co-optation from without. Salper told me that the members of the San Diego group "were never sure who the enemy was"— others or themselves—and Rowell Council and Joyce Nower, an SDSC faculty member, told Orr that the anti-Center faction regarded any transaction with mainstream institutions or colleagues as compromising the group's solidarity and objectives. Such suspicions, as it turned out, were not the vapors of leftist paranoia. A report issued by the U.S. Senate Select Committee to Study Governmental Operations in 1976 revealed that President Nixon had expanded COINTELPRO, an FBI counterintelligence program initiated to report on communist activity in the 1950s, to surveil, infiltrate, and neutralize an astonishing array of domestic groups from civil rights to black power and liberal reform to radical left. Through the Freedom of Information Act, Salper had recently obtained a four-hundred-page file on her own activities and, although the informers' names were blacked out, had found details that could only have been supplied by movement insiders. Lending credence to this claim, Salzman-Webb told me that former SDS members, by cross-referencing their files, saw "that agents had not merely infiltrated Left groups but were acting as provocateurs" who "accused and silenced group members" and "pushed groups in directions they would not have taken." Looking back at feminism in the early 1970s, Salzman-Webb wondered whether "the women who were fracturing women's groups were provocateurs" intent on magnifying "the tensions in the groups." "That people couldn't get along or had leadership struggles," she added, "isn't the whole story."[74] I think she's right. Something more than the fear of subversion, the issue of representing "the women," and the dilemmas of institutionalization was producing the feminist discord. That something more, I want to show, was the identity discourse that ruptured not only the San Diego project but also the Pittsburgh and Sacramento conferences.

Early in 1971, the MLA Commission on Women and a group of feminists at the University of Pittsburgh began planning "Women and Education: A Feminist Perspective," the first national conference on feminist education (I use the term *education* because its form is precisely what was debated). After consulting with several other women, the organizers settled on a format they hoped would enrich the three-day meeting: it would include paper sessions, workshops on teaching and program building, mealtime discussions, interest-group meetings, films, panels, and a closing plenary. When the papers were published as *Female Studies V* a year later, editor Rae Lee Siporin reported that "the conference as catalyst," as she dubbed it, had set in motion two processes.[75] One was seeding: informed and energized, several participants went home to launch women's studies programs on their own campuses, and two associates of the Feminist Press, Florence Howe and Carol Ahlum, started the *Women's Studies Newsletter*. The other was fracturing: by the second day, most of the participants had factionalized around the issues of their own positionality and process. Undergraduate students felt marginalized by the faculty's loquacity on scholarship and their silence on a film that was screened, graduate students and younger faculty complained that discussions were dominated by prominent scholars, and political activists objected to the academizing of female studies. After voicing their grievances, these groups formed a Revolutionary Feminist Caucus, which demanded that the last morning's schedule be rearranged to accommodate discussions of how feminist education could serve the movement.[76] Most of the Revolutionary feminists favored community-based programs that would teach political and survival skills, but some were willing to consider university-based programs if they were linked to community centers and coadministered by academic, movement, and community women. They were deeply distrustful of the "heavies" in women's studies, the leaders who were concerned with securing the resources needed to build programs and the scholars who insisted on rigorous research. For their part, most of the heavies envisioned an interdisciplinary field that would use critical-historical research, consciousness-raising pedagogy, and other techniques to transform mainstream higher education.

The volleys of statements that ricocheted across the discursive space of the conference were, like those at San Diego, fractious and fracturing. A month later, Elaine Showalter summed up the state of the discourse in her introduction to *Female Studies IV: Teaching About Women* (1971). "The range of definitions of WS [Women's Studies] gives some indication of the controversy surrounding its function in the university and in society," she said, and then added that "Radical feminists see WS as a potential revolutionary force within the university and society" whereas "traditionalists see [it] as a new academic discipline, and are concerned with establishing its legitimacy in terms of research, lectures, papers, exams, and grades."[77] Read literally, her introduction indicated that feminists had polarized around the mission and practices of female studies; read symptomatically, its language pointed to the identity discourse that had splintered the 1960s movement organizations—SNCC, SDS, and NUC—and now the feminist groups in San Diego and Pittsburgh. That discourse presumed that each individual had a fixed identity accommodating only one allegiance and one agenda. When feminists deployed it in their own groups, they typed the speakers, bent the meaning of their statements, and thereby generated the differences that thwarted their work of building the collective agent of activism. The rapid institutionalization of feminist studies only intensified this dynamic. By 1973, a few short years after the idea of a hybrid community-academy form had been broached in San Diego and Pittsburgh, feminist studies consisted of eighty-three women's studies programs and two thousand feminist courses in universities, four-year colleges, and a few community colleges, women's caucuses and committees in the disciplinary associations, a half-dozen feminist scholarly journals, and streams of scholarship welling up from the disciplines.[78] The process of academization was irreversible at that point, but the critics of academic feminist studies fought a fierce rearguard action, as the following examples show.

In April 1973, *Ain't I a Woman?*, a women's liberation newspaper published by an Iowa City collective, printed a scathing article, "Academic Feminists and the Women's Movement" coauthored by Ann Leffler, Dair L. Gillespie, and Elinor Lerner Ratner, three Bay Area feminists who identified themselves as academics and activists. "This is not a sisterly essay," the authors began, because "We believe the women's movement is in danger of co-optation from the right, from small groups of women whose institutional affiliations give them disproportionate power within it. We believe academic women constitute one such group." "The movement," they ended the essay, "should compare its situation with that of academic feminists, and act accordingly. And the phrase is, 'Squash the toadies.'"[79] Between these opening and closing barbs, the authors presented a detailed analysis of the twin dynamics working on feminism: co-optation by universities was shaving groups from without, and factionalism, precipitated by feminists' disparate circumstances, interests, and ideologies, was splintering groups from within. They accused academic feminists of complicity in the shaving and splintering processes; their professional ambitions had turned their loyalties to the academy, and their access to academic resources gave them more power than their movement sisters had to define projects. On the authors' view, these feminists were handing over to the academy what should be the machinery of the movement.

A month later, in May, the identity discourse erupted at "Women's Studies and Feminism: Survival in the 1970's," a West Coast women's studies conference held at Sacramento State College. "A deep cleavage developed," wrote Marilyn Boxer some years later, "when a highly organized group diverted scheduled sessions from their announced purposes. . . . Exhibiting deep distrust of conference planners and movement leaders, the group attacked 'white, middle-class, heterosexual' feminists for attempting to separate women's studies from the radical women's movement" and, faced with "physical as well as verbal confrontation, some of the 700 participants withdrew."[80] The conference speeches, a transcript of its speak-out session, and the postconference articles, all published in the *Report on the West Coast Women's Studies Conference* (1974), reveal that the discursive arena was fractured every which way. As was to be expected, the featured speakers—including Kirsten Amundsen, Rita Mae Brown, Florence Howe, Robin Morgan, and Joan Hoff Wilson—presented different visions of feminist studies; rather than appreciating the diversity of ideas, some of the speakers hurled vituperations at other speakers and some of the participants arrived at the event as organized groups primed for a showdown. The thirty women from the SDSC women's studies program, for instance, notified the planners that they would not pay the four dollars per person registration fee and demanded several changes in the program as well. Once the discord was sparked, the conferees splintered along several fault lines: middle class versus working class, Third World versus white, lesbian versus heterosexual, socialist-feminist versus cultural-feminist, and movement-oriented versus academic-oriented. At a speak-out held on the last day, a few of the women who stepped up to the open mikes thanked the planners for their hard work and many more trashed every aspect of the conference—the events, the fee, the housing and child-care arrangements, the featured speakers and the honoraria they mistakenly assumed had been paid to them, the workshop facilitators, the planners, and the participants. The women they maligned had committed the usual sins of classism, racism, heterosexism, ageism, and intellectual elitism as well as many political heresies inherited from the New Left.[81]

Included in the *Report* were several postconference articles that reflected in a more balanced way on the issues that had been raised. The authors regretted that a conference convened to help women's studies practitioners solve problems had instead multiplied them, but they did not agree on what caused the problems because the identity discourse was still speaking them. "Have we sunk so low in our regard for our sisters," asked Ann Forfreedom, "that we shout accusations. . . ? That we feel good if a woman shakes before speaking? That we use labels . . . to define our enemy, and she is us?" "A few hundred women," wrote Kathleen Barry, turned "a feminist conference into a male left, guilt-tripping, rhetoric bound menagerie." Responding, Loraine Hutchins countered: "She [Barry] says that feminists who struggle with class, race and imperialism are . . . 'the enemy within,' and implies that women left the conference in disgust and disappointment because it had been taken over by women using male left agitating tactics. . . . I felt that many people left in a down state because there was no resolution of conflict, not because one side has seized control."[82]

The feminist groups in San Diego, Pittsburgh, Sacramento, and elsewhere had failed to manage two interactive processes—project formation and collective-identity formation—that are required to launch a venture within any already structured arena. Let's go step by step through the discursive work involved in these processes. To design and implement a feminist-studies project, feminists (like the ASA and MLA activists) would have to blend movement and academic discourses that were already discontinuous in almost every respect—their sites (societal or academic arenas), their actors (oppressors and oppressed or administrators, faculty, and students), their activities (making change or making knowledge), and their modalities (political engagement or scholarly detachment). Not only was it difficult to operationalize the elements of either discourse in the other but both discourses were overstocked with divisive constructs that got in the way of concerted action. Whereas movement discourse was divided by political philosophies, radical / retrograde lines, and loyalists / traitors, academic discourse had its own similarly functioning disciplines, truths / errors, and authorities / underlings. As feminists spoke of these divisions, they let the divisions speak them. By dogmatically proclaiming the one correct version of feminist studies and relentlessly denouncing those who advocated other versions, they were producing not collectivity but the very splintering process they deplored.

As fractious rhetoric began to factionalize a group, the members would refocus from their project to their process. "From the beginning," Salper told me in a recent interview, the San Diego Board of Women's Studies found it "extremely difficult to establish how we were going to interact." At meetings, the board members spent most of their time on issues of positionality and process—their relative status, the weight of their views in exchanges, the procedures for conducting meetings, and their relations with the university and community. When Salper spoke about planning the program's "curriculum, course content, and pedagogy," they "politely discarded" these topics and resumed their debates about positionality and process. The meetings, she observed retrospectively, seemed like "a learning experience": the members were trying to figure out "how to transform movement change into an academic change project and no one knew how to do it." While trying to figure out how to do it, she added, they were guided by feminist ideology, which dictated that they should function as equals, but they weren't equally experienced in activism, equally knowledgeable in academic matters, and equally proficient in decision making. What happened was that they were doing what movement discourse said they should do. When they couldn't figure out how to develop a project, they were supposed to look at their process. But since movement discourse emphasized positional and power differences over instrumental activities, they scrutinized their unequal contributions to the process rather than the details of strategic planning that could realize the project (in chapters 5 and 6, I will address this dynamic in detail). Having made an issue of their differences, they were unable to craft a collective identity or, as Salper put it, they made "connections among clumps of individuals but the larger group never congealed."[83]

To launch any feminist-studies project (whether it is to be located in the academy, the community, or both), individuals have to take collective action, and to take collective action they have to form a collective identity. Collective identity is not a conceptual product, like a job description, that individuals discuss, write up, and perform; it is the practical work of producing linkages among themselves while they negotiate their project's form, objectives, and strategies. "A failure or break in this constructive process" of forming linkages, remarked social-movement theorist Alberto Melucci, "makes the [collective] action impossible."[84] The other side of the constructive process is that the already ordered discourses the group uses and the already structured arenas it enters will shape (or subvert) its collective identity, action, and project. From the first moment that feminists inserted female studies into the academy, the academy was formatting it according to the institutional-disciplinary template that formatted all academic ventures (see chapter 4). In a different arena, feminist education would have taken another form but one nevertheless shaped by the relay between the feminists who were forming and the contexts that were formatting. What happened at San Diego, Pittsburgh, Sacramento, and other sites is that by using the divisive discourses of the movement and academy feminists could not form the collective identity and action they needed to launch the hybrid projects they had envisioned.

I am not claiming that every feminist group either congealed in sisterhood or disintegrated into factions. Rather I am claiming that the fractious rhetoric, the fractured group, and the failed plan were discourse effects. Given the many disarticulations within and between the discourses that feminists used (or that used them), fracturing was an overdetermined result but not an inevitable one. Having examined the articulatory practices of activists at the ASA and MLA, I now want to look at how those practices were deployed at grassroots sites.

SEEDING FROM THE GODDARD EXPERIMENTS

When the students at Goddard College went on strike in the spring of 1970, they demanded a radical studies program that would include a feminist component. College administrators approved a faculty position in women's studies that was held by Marilyn Salzman-Webb for five years. During the fall of 1970, she taught the first women's studies courses and by the following spring had established a program that owed its unusual form of institutionalization to its host. A small experimental college in Vermont, Goddard offered a living-and-learning plan of education that required students to spend four terms in residence and complete other work in their communities; since Goddard's facilities only accommodated four hundred students per term, its fifteen hundred students were always in flux, migrating from their home communities to campus and back home. The students in residence during any one term lived in dormatories organized around particular interests and attended classes in the dormatory lounges. Following Goddard's living-and-learning plan, the women's studies program had an eclectic curriculum that included academic courses on women poets and sex-role differences, skills courses in auto mechanics and carpentry, and CR groups. Typical of the offerings during the 1972 spring term was Feminism Trips Out, which taught the students about women in institutions by sending them on field trips to prisons and mental hospitals as well as by assigning them the usual readings and papers.

Salzman-Webb told me that the Goddard teachers—who included regular faculty members, short-term teachers, and guest speakers—did not know that an extensive, if uneven, literature on women already existed. They started "at the beginning by saying 'We exist and there must be knowledge about women.'" In classes, faculty and students focused on *what* they as women might know. They read Women's Liberation papers to learn about feminist issues, they analyzed literary works from Ibsen to de Beauvoir and Lessing to piece together how women were seen, and they studied history to discover what it included and what could be added to it. In CR groups, they focused on "*how* we as women know—the styles of learning." Overall they wanted to open the disciplines to the subject of women and such new methods as interviewing and collaboration. To exemplify how the Goddard women combined the "what" and "how" of knowing, Salzman-Webb described three projects that crossed various academic / community divides.

Under faculty supervision, the women's studies majors carried out an oral history project—interviewing Vermont women and writing research papers—through which they "[re]discovered the 'witch burnings.'" After leaving Goddard, they grew the project by teaching oral history methods and New England witch burning at other schools. The second project was a course on women's health in which the students assumed the roles of both learner and teacher. When some of the students moved to Boston, they helped form the collective that wrote *Our Bodies, Ourselves* (1973), the guidebook that sparked changes in women's healthcare that are still reverberating through women's communities and healthcare professions today. The last project grew from a faculty CR group that was investigating styles of learning. Three members took this interest with them to other institutions: Mary Field Belenky and Jill Mattuck Tarule eventually collaborated with two more women on the landmark book *Women's Ways of Knowing* (1986), and Virginia Goldner was instrumental in founding the new fields of feminist psychotherapy and family therapy. Perhaps because the Goddard women were transient, arriving at the college from various communities and departing for other communities and universities, Salzman-Webb retrospectively described their activity as cross-fertilization. Their migration across the academic and community divides was the seeding mechanism. The women brought ideas and methods to Goddard where they flourished in the unconventional living-and-learning environment and then carried them to other locations where they sprouted again in new groups.[85]

Salzman-Webb's comment that the Goddard program was trying to feed its studies into action aptly describes the goal of its sister program located at Goddard's Graduate School for Social Change in Cambridge, Massachusetts. Everything about the Cambridge-Goddard School bespoke its status as an alternative institution that hybridized academic learning with the critical analysis taught at free universities and the activist techniques practiced at organizer training institutes (in chapter 6 I will discuss conservative think tanks and training institutes that operate on this model). The M.A. program was designed for students who were "interested in combining research and social action," a goal they obviously could not pursue in conventional graduate programs. The curriculum consisted of year-long social change projects supplemented by weekly seminars, each project undertaken by a collective of faculty and students as their full-time work for that year. All projects were required to have some application to a social-change movement, to produce research findings or provide organizational experience, and to communicate the results to people both within and outside the school. Following that format, the Feminist Studies Program sponsored several projects—in feminist history, cross-cultural studies of women, socialization of children, women and the media, women and the law, the economics of women's oppression, and male sex roles—that were open to degree students and, without charge, to nonstudents who could commit themselves for the year.[86] In her paper for the 1971 Pittsburgh conference, Linda Gordon, a feminist historian at the Cambridge-Goddard School, concluded that it would be difficult to produce women's history without transforming the discipline, the profession, and the university system. "I think," she wrote, "we should consider it as our goal to begin to build up a community of feminist scholars that does not depend so exclusively on the established universities for financial, political, and intellectual support."[87]

HER COMMENT TAKES me back to the problematic that framed the initial thinking about feminist studies. The early feminists knew that different forms of institutionalization were available in mainstream universities, community centers, and counterinstitutions. They recognized that each form came with its own dangers, but they did not quite discern what would form their venture no matter where it was located. In chapters 4 and 5, I will argue that the higher-education system exercised its power not through repression but through production. Fueled by the socioeconomic forces that grew higher education, formatted by the academy's intellectual and educational venues, and fractured by the rules of its own discourse, the project that had set out to feed social change became a discipline that fabricated esoteric knowledge. The *Chronicle* article was inadvertently right to frame the question of feminist studies' form as an either / or eventuality but wrong to suggest that its academicization was an outcome feminists could determine.

I want to end this chapter by juxtaposing two moments in the history of feminist studies. In 1972, KNOW Press issued another curious item: glued into a binder was a stack of pages listing scholarly and movement projects. Today few people know of *Women's Work and Women's Studies 1971,* the first annual feminist bibliography, but its purpose will have a familiar ring. The Barnard College Women's Center compiled it in order "to stimulate interaction between theoretical study and practical approaches" and "to put the results of research into action."[88] After a second volume, the bibliography quietly disappeared in 1973 just as a half-dozen feminist scholarly periodicals were launched, the *Female Studies* series was transferred from the community-based KNOW Press to the academy-oriented Feminist Press, and the hybrid feminist books that combined movement critique with academic criticism waned (see chapter 4). Many years later, when the interaction between academic research and social activism reappeared, it was not a mode of practice in feminist studies but a criticism of feminist studies. Several feminists commented in a 1996 issue of *Signs* that academic-feminist knowledge was irrelevant to women working at feminist policy institutes and issue-advocacy organizations, in labor unions and economic justice groups, and on grassroots projects and national councils. How did we get to the point where bell hooks would observe that feminist scholarship "makes no attempt to engage feminist politics" and Charlotte Bunch would exclaim, "I don't read journals like *Signs* anymore"?[89]

4. Formatting Feminist Studies

By the time I graduated in 1973, activism and scholarly activity were bifurcated. —Jo Freeman, "From Seed to Harvest: Transformations of Feminist Organizations and Scholarship" (1995)

Once a new academic field is envisioned, some modest resources are acquired, and ideas are circulated to others, the hard work of institutionalization has to begin somewhere and fan out everywhere.[1] At this point, as we know from academic history, many worthy ventures are announced with loud fanfare only to founder and fade away because the would-be practitioners lack an organizational infrastructure to sustain and spread their activities. No one hands them an infrastructure; they have to build it by burrowing into academic institutions to appropriate existing platforms, founding their own organizations to sponsor exchange and attract practitioners, and cobbling these bits together in order to develop the field. But from the very first moment the practitioners use the academic system to build the field its already structured organizations and venues act to format their activities.

My task in this chapter is to show that feminist studies was formed by the relays between the practitioners' action and the academic structures during the process of assembling an organizational infrastructure that would sustain and spread the new venture. The formational process traversed three organizational fields: the publishing industry with its commercial, university, and alternative presses; the higher-education system with its universities and colleges; and the disciplines with their national associations and campus departments. By resorting to activism, as we saw in chapter 3, the first-generation academic feminists secured toeholds in disciplinary associations and universities; the venues provided by these institutions and the world of academic publishing were the tools that simultaneously spread feminist studies and shaped it to fit the academy's institutional-disciplinary order.

Turning to Scholarship

Feminist scholars have painted a bleak picture of the structural barriers to diffusing feminist discourse throughout the 1970s. The gatekeepers who determined access to conferences, journals, and presses dismissed feminist work for deviating from political or scholarly orthodoxies and in any case for dwelling on trivial matters that would interest no one but women. By the mid-1980s when feminist studies was an established presence in some disciplines, gatekeeping had not abated in many of the social and natural sciences where "a fairly close network of reviewers" who had "ideas and theories to 'protect' " knew little about feminist research and viewed it "with suspicion, if not outright disdain."[2] The literature on gatekeeping has made at least two important points about the development of academic feminist studies. First, the early feminists used their own venues— conferences, journals, and presses—to pry open the doors of mainstream scholarly venues. And, second, the important work published in these feminist venues gave the lie to the gatekeeping myth that feminist work did not appear in mainstream venues because it lacked the significance and quality to merit publication.

In this section, I approach the matter from another direction. Instead of focusing on how the gatekeepers excluded feminist discourse, I ask how both mainstream and feminist venues shaped it from the late 1960s on. Looking first at publishing during the period when it was reorganized as an industry, I trace the (albeit shifting) interests of publishers and reviewers that split movement critique from academic criticism and molded academic writing according to conventions. Looking next at mainstream and feminist academic venues, I argue that the conferences and journals turned the discourse to scholarship and blunted its transformative potential.

SPLITTING MOVEMENT CRITIQUE AND ACADEMIC CRITICISM:
THE PUBLISHING INDUSTRY

At first glance, academic publishing in 1970 seems very much like academic publishing in 1990 in that its organizational field was divided into commercial, university, and alternative sectors, the latter consisting of small presses and periodicals devoted to the arts, culture, local history, movement politics, and so on. But the resemblance is superficial because during these two decades the quest for profit reorganized everything from the sectors all the way down to the individual books. The once independent commercial publishers were gobbled up by media empires and retooled to market books as commodities; the once stodgy university presses diversified their product lines with textbooks, trade books, mystery novels, and membership services for learned societies; and the once countercultural presses adopted slick direct-mail techniques to build their sales and donor bases. Before the field was transformed into a market economy, the sectors were more cleanly demarcated by the types of work they published, the presses had inflexible interests, and the writings were evaluated for their conformity to the conventions of subject matter, method, presentational style, and authorial status.

When second-wave feminism emerged, the interests and conventions of the publishing world worked against the diffusion of its discourse. By and large, the discourse had minimal impact on left ideas and activities because the male gatekeepers who controlled both the back channels and formal venues of communication were preoccupied with antiwar and anticapitalist issues and didn't want to hear about "the woman question." They ignored feminists in face-to-face conversations, shouted them down in meetings, forgot to invite them to speak at public events, and grudgingly published female-authored articles that applied the accepted modes of left analysis to the important issues. Astonishingly, through 1969, *Liberation, New Left Review, New Left Notes, Leviathan, Radical America,* and *Ramparts* printed far fewer feminist articles than did the homemaker-oriented *McCall's* and *Ladies' Home Journal*; the chic, youth-oriented *Mademoiselle* and *Glamour*; the general-circulation *Time, Newsweek,* and *Life*; and even the scholarly journals of law, psychology, and history. From 1970 on, left periodicals increased their publication of feminist work but only because they were pressured by movement women; some agreed to let the women edit a special issue and others stalled until, as in the case of *Rat,* they were forcibly seized by an angry feminist contingent.[3]

Meanwhile, university presses and scholarly journals (for journals, see below) remained in the grips of managerial and intellectual conservatism. Over the course of a decade, university presses published few more feminist titles than Eleanor Flexner's *Century of Struggle* (Harvard, 1959), Aileen Kraditor's *The Ideas of the Women Suffrage Movement* (Columbia, 1965), Katharine Rogers's *The Troublesome Helpmate: A History of Misogyny in*

Literature (Washington, 1966), editor Eleanor Maccoby's *The Development of Sex Differences* (Stanford, 1966), and Leo Kanowitz's *Women and the Law: The Unfinished Revolution* (New Mexico, 1969). What probably tipped the presses in favor of these books was that they addressed subjects the disciplines recognized (if undervalued) as scholarly ones and their authors had ties to the presses' university sponsors. *The Development of Sex Differences* was a Stanford project: not only was Maccoby a faculty member at the university, but the volume's articles and bibliography came from a working group on sex difference that was meeting at Stanford and funded by the prestigious Social Science Research Council. But very soon two industry trends would compel the university presses to take notice of feminist work: the growth of the feminist publishing sector and the corporatization of the commercial sector.

The feminist sector formed along specialist lines for financial reasons, at first because publishers had scant resources and later because they needed to develop distinctive profiles and products to capture audiences. Newsletters, such as NOW's *Do It Now* and the Women's Equity Action League's *Word Watcher,* reported on organizational activities to a ready-made audience of members and recruits. Movement periodicals, usually published by local collectives whose political slant dictated the contents, proliferated at an astonishing rate but were as likely to fold as to endure because the collectives found themselves buffeted by a shortage of dollars and a surplus of discord. Only *Ms.* magazine, launched in 1972, had the resources to reach a broad audience. The first academic-feminist periodicals, all founded in 1972, immediately carved out niches: historical scholarship was featured in Ann Calderwood's *Feminist Studies,* literary scholarship in Wendy Martin's *Women's Studies,* eighteenth- and nineteenth-century studies in Janet Todd's *Mary Wollstonecraft Newsletter,* bibliographical data in Florence Rush's *Women's Studies Abstracts,* and program resources in the Feminist Press's *Women's Studies Newsletter.* Although it hardly entered an arena crowded with scholarly feminist journals when it debuted in 1975, *Signs* differentiated itself from the others as the most rigorous and prestigious interdisciplinary feminist journal. Among feminist presses, KNOW Press (1969) published an eclectic mixture of materials, but the rest carved out niches: children's literature was claimed by Lollipop Power (1969), women's studies was staked out by the Feminist Press (1970), and creative and self-help genres were divided up along audience lines by the lesbian-feminist Violet Press (1971), Diana Press (1972), and Naiad Press (1973) and the radical-feminist Shameless Hussy Press and Daughters, Inc. (1973).[4]

The second trend began in the 1960s when commercial presses started down the winding road to profitability. Hoping to capture growing markets, the presses sought college textbooks and trade books that could be reprinted in paperback formats. Yet even after Norton hit the jackpot with Betty Friedan's best-selling *The Feminine Mystique* (1963) commercial presses were reluctant to bank on feminist books and careful to select only those that would attract a crossover audience. General readers, they reckoned, could appreciate the irreverent literary criticism in Mary Ellmann's *Thinking About Women* (Harcourt Brace Jovanovich, 1966) and the colloquial social science in Caroline Bird's *Born Female: The High Cost of Keeping Women Down* (McKay, 1968). By the early 1970s, commercial presses had expanded their lines only to find that production costs, especially for paperbacks, had risen more sharply than retail prices at a time when competition in the commercial sector had intensified. As the economics of publishing became more difficult, the independent presses were acquired by "corporations capable of merchandising books worldwide and exploiting book properties simultaneously in several subsidiary markets." Corporate executives, according to then Viking-Penguin editor Martha M. Kinney, retooled the presses as businesses to be managed on profitability principles. Their "expectation that each and every title should not only pay for itself but also return a profit upwards of ten percent" was a drastic change from the traditional expectation that two or three best-selling titles would underwrite a press's less salable but significant books.[5] Profitthink brought commodification to publishing: books were packaged and pitched, their covers designed to attract purchasers and their contents encapsulated for promotions. By the early 1980s, the publishing world had been transformed; a dozen conglomerates owned the once independent commercial presses along with newspapers, magazines, radio and television stations, and entertainment businesses.

If one had to locate a turning point for feminist discourse within the gradual reorganization of publishing, it would have to be 1973; that was the moment when the new academic-feminist journals began churning out feminist scholarship and the commercial presses backed away from feminist trade books that hybridized the elements of movement and academic discourses. The hybrid genre came in two formats: the monograph and the anthology. The monograph, whose lineage could be traced back to Mary Wollstonecraft's *A Vindication of the Rights of Woman* (1792), wove scholarly and movement discourses into a wide-ranging indictment of women's oppression in patriarchal societies. Although none rivaled Friedan's *The Feminine Mystique* as a long-term blockbuster, some came close: press coverage, author appearances, and public controversy boosted Kate Millett's *Sexual Politics* (Doubleday, 1970) and Germaine Greer's *The Female Eunuch* (MacGibbon and Keefe, 1970; McGraw-Hill, 1971) into the ranks of best-sellers. The anthology, formatted something like an almanac, gathered bits and pieces of material—historical feminist documents, contemporary manifestoes, academic and movement papers, personal narratives, and creative writing—to paint a composite picture of women in American society. The best-sellers among more than a dozen anthologies, Robin Morgan's *Sisterhood Is Powerful* (Random House, 1970) and Vivian Gornick and Barbara K. Moran's *Woman in a Sexist Society* (Basic Books, 1971), were stocked by feminist, alternative, and chain bookstores and purchased by movement and academic feminists, high school and college students, and general readers of several descriptions.[6] Since the hybridizing books flared onto the national scene in 1970 and flamed out by the end of 1973, it's tempting to conclude that the publishers rushed them into print when sensationalist media coverage of Women's Lib made them profitable items and dropped them as soon as its controversiality waned. Although the controversiality of feminism certainly influenced both positive and negative publishing decisions, I want to argue that the shift to a market economy accounts for what happened to the hybridizing books and more generally to feminist discourse. Let's start by looking at the receptions accorded to two hybridizing books. Published not quite a year apart, first in hardcover and then in paperback, both had viewpoints that were regarded as blatantly feminist, contents that combined movement critique with academic scholarship, and sales that topped the charts. But they differed in an important respect: one was an anthology and the other a monograph.

Vivian Gornick and Barbara K. Moran's *Woman in Sexist Society: Studies in Power and Powerlessness* was published as a Basic Books hardcover (1971) and a Signet paperback (1972). A big anthology, it contained movement papers, scholarly articles, and creative writing divided into several issue-focused sections. Most of the thirty-five contributors, including several academic women who would soon become leading feminist scholars, were members of Women's Liberation groups who didn't pull their punches in writing trenchant critiques of society and the academy. The editors had purposely aimed for analytical hybridity, scope, and forcefulness in order to demonstrate "that woman's condition" resulted from "a slowly formed, deeply entrenched, extraordinarily pervasive" system of sexism maintained by patriarchal institutions.[7] Reviewers commended not only the individual writings for their eloquence and close reasoning but also the anthology for combining scholarly and creative literature with a commitment to social change. One reviewer said, "This big collection offers great catholicity of perspective, topics, and levels of analysis"; another called it "a lively, challenging anthology of current writing and research by women scholars, authors, and activists"; and even the *Saturday Review*'s Glendy Culligan, who admitted that she considered Women's Libbers a lunatic fringe, praised the anthology's scope and hybridity. *The Nation*'s Margaret Lichtenberg succinctly made the point I want to take up next: she evenhandedly praised both Kate Millett's *Sexual Politics* and Gornick and Moran's *Woman in a Sexist Society* for their powerful voices "raised in the feminist cause" and added that the anthology "is a most appropriate vehicle to present the feminist point of view."[8] But other reviewers would condemn Millett's book for precisely those features that had won praise for the anthology.

When *Sexual Politics* was published as a Doubleday hardcover (1970) and an Avon paperback (1970), it was widely known to have been Millet's dissertation, which she had defended at Columbia University in the spring of that same year. The book looked like a scholarly monograph, with chapters devoted to a hypothesis, a history, and exegeses of several literary authors, topped off by a long list of works cited. But it certainly didn't read like a scholarly monograph. Hybridizing the movement's theory of sex-class domination and Simone de Beauvoir's tour of the disciplines in *The Second Sex,* Millett defined sexual politics as the "arrangements whereby one group of persons is controlled by another" and then proceeded to analyze how a host of arrangements—ideological, biological, social, economic, educational, religious, psychological, and physical—maintained the system of patriarchy.[9] *Sexual Politics* was the butt of unprecedented reviewer hostility.

Reviewers blithely conflated Millett's person with her prose, in one breath smearing her as a member of New York radical-feminist groups and in the next denouncing her writing as belligerent and vanguardist. *The New Republic*'s Jonathan Yardley found the "tone . . . so unflaggingly militant (and irreverent) that only the true-blue feminist will read the book without discomfort," *Newsweek*'s Robert A. Gross styled the author as an "angry successor" to the suffragists, and, not to be outdone, *Time* dubbed Millett "the Mao Tse-tung of Women's Liberation" when it featured her on an August 1970 cover.[10] Moreover, hostile reviewers consistently faulted

Sexual Politics for hybridizing movement and scholarly discourses. *Time* described it as "a polemic suspended awkwardly in academic tradition," and the *Antioch Review* complained that Millett had "clothed her muscular polemic in the ill-fitting costumery of scholarship."[11] Just as vociferously, they objected to its multidisciplinary scope and its slide from social analysis in the early chapters to literary criticism in the later ones on D. H. Lawrence, Henry Miller, Norman Mailer, and Jean Genet. Unable to handle the scope, many reviewers projected their own confusion onto the book. Yardley deemed it "too arbitrarily organized" and "too much of a literary-anthropological-sociological-historical-psychological grabbag to be a clear success in part or in sum," and *Time* opined "it is precisely the broad sweep of that argument that tenders it vulnerable."[12]

No other negative review matched the torrid rhetoric and tortured logic of Norman Mailer's piece for *Harper's*. Undoubtedly stung by the many feminists who had criticized his writings, he characterized Millett as "an honor student in some occult school of thuggee (now open to the ladies via the pressure of Women's Liberation)" who was hunting himself and other authors with a sawed-off shotgun. Invoking scholarly standards, he delineated "the land of Millett" as "a barren and mediocre terrain, its flora reminiscent of a Ph.D. tract, its roads a narrow argument . . . its horizon low," and its landscape littered with the "grit and granite . . . of concept-jargon on every ridge."[13] Although the editors of *Harper's* described Mailer's forty-two-page screed as a "bold analysis of the Women's Liberation Movement,"[14] the logic controlling it was not incisive reason but wounded narcissism. Depicting himself (in the third-person "he"!) as an aspiring Nobel Prize winner taken prisoner in the sex wars, the agonist trumpeted his own sexual and literary conquests, skewered feminist leaders, and confused the ideologies and actualities of sexuality, gender roles, and sex / gender systems.

Since the feminism, scope, and hybridity were no more radical in Millett's book than in the feminist anthology, something else must have heightened the hostility of the reviewers. That something else, I will argue, was the reviewers' growing impotence in the context of the publishing industry's reorganization. By crossing traditionally observed boundaries— between movement critique and scholarly criticism, cultural and academic subject matters, and academic and trade readers—Millett had crafted a powerful case for the pervasiveness of women's oppression in Western cultures. Confounded by the book's scope and hybridity, the reviewers could neither neutralize its arguments nor deter the readers who were rushing to buy it. Within a few months of its publication *Sexual Politics* had sold fifteen thousand copies and gone into a fourth printing, an astounding degree of market penetration for those days.[15] To Doubleday and Avon, the book was a success; to the reviewers, it signaled their failure.

The transformation of publishing into a market economy had put the squeeze on commercial presses whose solution in turn put the squeeze on book reviewers. To differentiate itself from competitors a commercial press had to develop lists that gave it a distinctive profile, but to earn profits it needed books that sold to mixed audiences. The new hybrid feminist genre looked like a solution to this dilemma because its feminism assured a distinctive profile and its scope promised a mixed audience. As for non-hybrid books on the controversial subjects of gender, race, and sexuality, commercial presses drew a wandering line through the sand, publishing the ones that would appeal to a crossover audience of scholarly and general readers and leaving those with specialized subject matter or audiences to alternative publishers.[16] The reviewers were squeezed by these developments and not just intellectually. When commercial presses produced costly hardcover editions, the reviewers stood between a book's publication and its profit by nudging readers toward or away from purchase. But as presses began to produce the cheaper trade paperbacks and promote them directly to readers consumer desire converged with producer profit to erode the ground that reviewers occupied. To edgy reviewers, the impressive sales of *Sexual Politics*, whose scope exceeded their grasp and whose hybridity transgressed scholarly conventions, delivered yet another reminder of their diminishing importance. Finally, if profit motivated commercial presses to pick up the hybridizing genre, then why did they drop it in 1973 just when the market for feminist publications of every kind—polemics, fiction, scholarship, self-help manuals—began to grow exponentially? Once commercial presses had honed the techniques of niche production and direct marketing that brought in profits, the hybridizing genre and its hostile reviewers were rendered obsolete.

The reorganization of publishing as a market economy had a downside and an upside for feminist discourse. On the downside, the competition among commercial publishers to capture market niches worked hand in hand with the lingering conservatism of scholarly publishers to split movement discourse from academic discourse, which in turn was disciplined by feminist and mainstream scholarly venues (see below). On the upside, the quest for profit motivated publishers to grab many feminist books that their sexism might have prompted them to reject, and the subsequent popularity of transgressive work in some disciplines made feminist scholarship a hot property. But the commodification of transgression came a little too late to recuperate the early vision of feminist studies as an academy-based project that would fuel social change because by then what feminist scholars were transgressing was, as the saying goes, purely academic.

FORMATTING FEMINIST WORK:
ACADEMIC CONFERENCES AND PUBLICATIONS

In December 1970, the Modern Language Association Commission on the Status of Women sponsored its first forum at the MLA convention. When the 1970 forum papers were published in a 1971 issue of *College English,* a tilt was apparent. Seven exemplified the new feminist literary scholarship, while only two addressed women's status and two more criticized the traditional curriculum. When the 1971 forum papers were published in a 1972 issue of *College English,* the tilt reappeared. Six scholarly articles filled sixty-five pages, and two articles on the representation of women in freshman textbooks and three on the status of women fitted into thirty-three pages. Subsequently, scholarship captured pride of place in academic journals while curricular and professional matters were banished to the back matter of prestigious journals, the pages of less prestigious journals, and associational reports. When the papers from the CSW's 1972 forum were published in *Women's Studies,* this 1974 issue was entirely given over to scholarly writing—papers and book reviews on the subject of androgyny plus an essay on women's studies research by Wendy Martin and Mary Louise Briscoe.[17] The turn toward scholarship in feminist studies discourse cannot be put down to the co-optation of the CSW because it continued to lead the struggle for disciplinary and professional changes that were strenuously resisted by the MLA, the mainstream journals, and the campus departments. Rather, the turn occurred because the conferences and journals used by feminists were formatting their discourse as scholarship.

By the early 1970s, the MLA's traditionally genteel annual meeting had become an exercise in convention planning and population control. With eight to twelve thousand members attending the convention, the MLA had to design a program that would incorporate their varied scholarly interests yet would fit into the time slots carved out of three days and the meeting rooms provided by two hotels. To do that, it designated the types of events that could be scheduled and then assigned their times (most were seventy-five minutes) and rooms. Because most of the time slots and meeting rooms were allotted the scholarly sessions sponsored by MLA's divisions and by members who had submitted worthy proposals and the remainder to the presidential address, the associational business meetings, and the social occasions sponsored by affiliate organizations, additional events were virtually impossible to schedule. Member groups lacking official recognition were not permitted to schedule events and, with the program filling the hotel facilities, had nowhere to hold impromptu gatherings. Groups recognized by the MLA, such as the Women's Caucus for the Modern Languages and the Radical Caucus, could schedule scholarly sessions but not such nonscholarly ones as a workshop on planning change projects. The program was so rigid and rushed that it even precluded feminist networking—except at the seventy-five minute cash bar that the WCML began sponsoring in the mid-1970s.

The MLA's publications, like its annual conventions, were organized to reflect the hierarchy of interests promoted by the language and literature disciplines—scholarship and criticism at the forefront, pedagogy and curriculum as a distant second, and professional matters in the rear. Accordingly, the centerpiece of MLA's publishing division was *PMLA,* its official and only scholarly journal, followed by the annual bibliographies, editions of literary works, and such items as the style manual, pedagogical and critical anthologies, and eventually the job lists. The journal consisted of six issues—a membership directory, a convention program, and four that published scholarship. The scholarly issues presented up to a dozen articles, bookended by a few pages of front matter and several pages of back matter where the press advertisements took up more space than the governance reports, member letters, and professional announcements. MLA's disregard for feminist scholarship throughout the 1970s was signaled not only by the small number of feminist articles published in *PMLA* (see below) but also by the omission of such taxonomic categories as "women's literature" and "feminist criticism" from the annual bibliographies. Feminist work slipped into print by default: the CSW's studies of women's status appeared in *PMLA* because the MLA was obliged to publish reports of its official committees, and the new feminist scholarship was listed in the bibliographies when it fit the prevailing author and genre categories. The early feminists could not have avoided the formatting of their discourse: lacking their own organizations to circulate feminist work, they had to use the disciplinary conferences and the disciplinary journals that were willing to publish their work. When the CSW tried to arrange publication of the papers from its 1970 and 1971 forums, *PMLA* and other disciplinary journals were unreceptive. The CSW turned to Richard Ohmann, a comrade in MLA activism and the editor of *College English*. Founded in 1939 by the National Council of Teachers of English and historically publishing conventional articles, the journal began under Ohmann's editorship to print innovative, radical, and feminist work. But by the end of 1972 conference papers had other routes to print—the new scholarly feminist journals.

That year MLA member Wendy Martin founded *Women's Studies* as "a forum for the presentation of scholarship and criticism about women in the fields of literature, history, art, sociology, law, political science, economics, anthropology and the sciences."[18] The need for a scholarly feminist journal was probably suggested by Martin's own experiences with "The Feminist Movement," a course she taught at CUNY's Queens College during the spring of 1971. While planning it, she found herself caught between enthusiastic students who wanted an opportunity to rap on women's issues and dubious colleagues who wanted evidence that feminist studies had some academic substance. Deciding that "it was better to be guilty of intellectual overkill than to run the risk of being accused of academic anemia," she opted for an "excessively ambitious" format that included her own lectures, thirty guest lectures, readings from a textbook and books placed on library reserve, and several writing projects. Having scheduled small-group discussions in order to raise the level of feminist awareness, she had to redirect the students away "from sloppy sloganeering to a more thorough understanding of the public and private issues of feminism."[19] When Martin launched *Women's Studies* as a scholarly journal, other academic feminists shared her views on intellectual legitimacy. During the discussion that followed Martin and Briscoe's paper on women's studies research at the 1973 MLA convention, one audience member agonized, "Something needs to be done to convince chairmen and deans that publication in Women's Studies is legitimate for consideration of tenure decisions."[20] That something was the strategy I have been describing: women's committees used the disciplinary conferences to feature feminist papers, which were then parlayed into print at friendly mainstream journals and newly established feminist journals. The objective was to generate research literatures for the new field and publication opportunities for feminists approaching decision points in their careers.

A few years before Martin founded *Women's Studies* to publish feminist scholarship, several feminists in New York City had discussed the idea of a journal that would foster exchange across feminism's academic and community sectors. They put the project in the capable hands of Ann Calderwood, who had a graduate degree in history, a track record in community activism, and experience in alternative publishing. Between 1972 and 1976, she was the "publisher, editor-in-chief, subscription manager, distributor, typesetter, proofreader, and publicist" of *Feminist Studies,* producing the journal from her New York apartment and using her own funds to cover some of the costs. Having conceptualized a journal "produced by, appealing to, and reflecting the values of university scholars and community activists,"[21] Calderwood published a diverse mix of contributors in the early issues—activists, attorneys, journalists, artists, scholars, and graduate students. But that mix, according to Claire Moses, who later edited *Feminist Studies,* resulted as much from the journal's mission as from its need to troll widely for material at a time when relatively little had been produced. "The best sources for getting good material at the time," Moses recalled, "seemed to have been in both history and literature."[22] Perhaps because the csw was channeling feminist literary criticism to *College English* and *Women's Studies,* Calderwood turned to her contacts in history and began publishing work presented at the Berkshire conferences on the history of women.

In 1972, the Berkshire Conference of Women Historians decided to lend support to the nascent field of women's history. The first conference on women's history, organized by Lois Banner and Mary S. Hartman (both assistant professors of history at Douglass College), was held at Douglass in March 1973 and attended by more than six hundred people. When fourteen papers were published as *Clio's Consciousness Raised* (1974), Hartman's introduction identified the research trends in the new field: studying women who did not achieve public prominence but "shared a set of common experiences"; reconstructing social contexts from private papers, domestic manuals, women's magazines, and medical treatises as well as from such conventional sources as public documents; and analyzing ideologies of sex and gender.[23] These trends indicate that feminist historians were translating the movement's issues and especially its slogan that the personal is the political into scholarly subject matters and methods. The next conference, organized by Alberta Arthurs (then dean of admissions at Radcliffe College) and held at Radcliffe in October 1975, drew a surprising crowd of two thousand registrants plus others who dropped in. Afterward the organizing committee summarized the research trends: feminist historians were using the new methods of oral history, psychohistory, and demography to investigate families, women's health, women's roles in professions, churches, and trade unions, and gendered industrialization processes. "The quality of sessions," observed Mary Dunn, "ranged from 'brilliant' to 'dreadful,'" with most offering "good, solid work" and others marred by the "overly-long papers" typical of "academic meetings."[24] Viewed side by side, the comments on the two conferences indicate that even as feminist historians were opening their discipline to new subjects and methods they were becoming disciplined; their research interests were growing more specialized and their evaluative criteria more scholarly.

In her study of feminist journals, Patrice McDermott emphasized that Calderwood's decision to rely on the Berkshire conferences as a source of work

> profoundly altered the identity, content, and politics of *Feminist Studies*. Through this affiliation, the journal was drawn away from the contributors, forms, and arguments of the larger, grass-roots community and deeper into those of the university. *Feminist Studies* became associated with a newly emerging network of scholars who were establishing institutions and negotiating roles within the university rather than the community. It became identified with a particular discipline (women's history) and a particular politics (socialist feminist) and established itself as the foremost publication of feminist social history.

When *Feminist Studies* committed itself to women's history, McDermott observed, it simultaneously committed itself to such disciplinary conventions as "third-person narrative, extensive footnotes, and abstract rational argument instead of the first-person appeals to the authority of emotion and experience found in publications from the feminist community."[25]

In 1975 the prestigious University of Chicago Press began publishing *Signs*.[26] Though announced and received as a bold interdisciplinary venture, the journal hewed to scholarly conventions, as McDermott observed, by seeking articles that provided a "detached, intricately argued, specialized rational analysis" and including "a full page of citation instructions, admonitions, and examples for footnote form in each issue."[27] Besides accepting submissions that already met these exacting standards, *Signs* also shaped submissions to meet them. Jean O'Barr, editor from 1985 to 1990, recalled that when the office received an article on an unusual topic that did not incorporate the scholarly literature, the editors and reviewers gave the author many suggestions—work to read, specialists to contact, analytical refinements to make, and documentation to add. O'Barr told this story to point out that the collaborative review process at

Signs resulted in the publication of an innovative article that would have been eliminated by the yes-or-no review process at a traditional journal. But her story also highlights the paradox of institutionalization: the journal functioned simultaneously to spread innovations and to shape them according to the prevailing scholarly conventions.[28] The trends toward innovation and conventionalism in feminist studies were also hastened by *Signs'* commitment to the review essay, a genre typical of mainstream disciplinary journals. Although *Feminist Studies* usually printed one review essay per year, *Signs* published from two to four per issue. At first the *Signs* essays reviewed new feminist scholarship in the humanities and social sciences, returning to each discipline at regular intervals, and then gradually moved on to feminist work in the natural sciences, professional disciplines, new hybrid fields (e.g., critical science studies), and the topical areas that formed within feminist studies (e.g., mothering). The *Signs* review essays simultaneously drove the proliferation of disciplinary specialisms within feminist studies and of cross-disciplinary syntheses where the specialisms converged.

Although the objectives of feminist conferences and journals were very different from those of mainstream conferences and journals, they had similar effects on the formation of feminist studies. On the one hand, these venues functioned as the instruments of change by publishing the new work that in turn constituted the authority of the practitioners. On the other hand, they functioned as the instruments of discipline by etching scholarly conventions into the published work that in turn was used (as Foucault would have said) for the correct training of future practitioners.

DISCIPLINING FEMINIST SCHOLARSHIP:
MAINSTREAM JOURNALS

First-generation academic feminists will remember 1971 to 1981 as the decade of famines and feasts. Desperately seeking the new scholarship, we foraged the disciplinary journals for tidbits, any raw fact or a pliable theory that could be used in studying women, and we impatiently awaited the feminist journals, each issue a repast of articles trailing footnotes that led us through unfamiliar scholarly forests as if they were crumbs left by Hansel and Gretel. By the late 1970s, we were able to sample the haute cuisine of feminist scholarship. Barbara Smith's "Toward a Black Feminist Criticism" (*Conditions,* 1977) and Deborah McDowell's "New Directions in Black Feminist Criticism" (*Black American Literature Forum,* 1980) paved the way for black feminist studies; Annette Kolodny's "Dancing through the

Minefield" (*Feminist Studies,* 1980) exposed the organizing conventions of literary studies; and Myra Jehlen's "Archimedes and the Paradox of Feminist Criticism" (*Signs,* 1981) navigated the straits between objectivity and subjectivity. The social construction of sexualities was examined by Adrienne Rich's "Compulsory Heterosexuality and Lesbian Existence" (*Signs,* 1980) and Catharine McKinnon's "Feminism, Marxism, Method, and the State" (*Signs,* 1982); of gendered art by Linda Nochlin, Rozsika Parker, Griselda Pollock, and Janet Wolff in feminist and British publications; and of gendered science by Ruth Bleier, Donna Haraway, Evelyn Fox Keller, Sally Gregory Kohlstedt, Marion Lowe, Margaret Rossiter, and others in *Signs.* Since most of us were too engrossed by these articles to consider the matter of where they didn't appear, I want to do so now. Why didn't the Smith and McDowell articles appear in mainstream literary studies journals, or, for that matter, why wasn't "Dancing through the Minefield" published in *Critical Inquiry* or *New Literary History,* two journals that had published other Kolodny articles? What was it about feminist work on the social, cultural, and knowledge formations that made it unpalatable to journals in sociology, art history, and science? To turn the questions around, what sort of feminist work did appear in disciplinary journals?

For sociology, I reviewed the contents of two prominent journals from 1968 through 1982, the ASA's *The American Sociologist* and the University of Chicago Press's *American Journal of Sociology.* From 1968 to 1970, *The American Sociologist (AS)* published one short feminist article.[29] After the ASA recognized the Women's Caucus and established the Committee on Women, its journal dutifully printed material on women's status: the Rossi study in 1970, an account of the Women's Caucus resolutions and two articles on status in 1971, a three-page discussion of opportunities for women and minorities in sociology in 1972, and some references to feminist issues in the minutes of ASA committees.[30] Surprisingly, when *AS* stopped printing accounts of associational business and closed off this route to feminist publication, it gave more space to feminism than it had in previous years. In 1973, it published an article on sexism in introductory texts, a cluster on racial minorities and women in the discipline, and another cluster on sex discrimination.[31] From 1974 through 1976, it continued to print anywhere from one article to one cluster per year on sex differences, status, or discrimination. But not until 1977, after a great deal of groundbreaking feminist sociology had been published by feminist journals and mainstream presses, did *AS* offer readers a sample of this work: Meredith Gould and Rochelle Kern-Daniels's "Toward a Sociological Theory of Gender and Sex."[32] Through 1980, it printed three more articles on women's status but no feminist sociology—a glaring omission considering that its 1979 forum on new directions in research had acknowledged the importance of feminist approaches. By the end of 1982, the only other sample of feminist sociology to appear was Sarah H. Matthews's "Rethinking Sociology through a Feminist Perspective."[33]

The *American Journal of Sociology* (*AJS*) printed no feminist work in 1971, 1974, 1976, and 1981 and typically one or two articles in the other years. Most of these articles took the conventional road to publication by using empirical methods and/or discussing standard (if devalued) disciplinary topics such as marriage, status, and sex roles.[34] Two exceptions interrupt the pattern of disciplinary orthodoxy. In January 1973, *AJS* published a feminist issue edited by Joan Huber and containing essays that interrogated the disciplinary conventions.[35] In March 1977, it featured Rosabeth Moss Kanter's "Some Effects of Proportions on Group Life: Skewed Sex Ratios and Responses to Token Women," an important article that previewed the argument presented in her award-winning *Men and Women of the Corporation* (1977). Kanter turned the discipline's conventional wisdom on its head by showing that gendered patterns of behavior were the effects, not the causes, of men's and women's places in organizational structures. Having published the article, the journal was obliged to print some of the readers' replies it sparked.[36] Its poor record of publishing innovative feminist work seems all the more astonishing after 1972 when it featured the eminent Robert K. Merton's "Insiders and Outsiders: A Chapter in the Sociology of Knowledge," an article that called the question of gatekeeping.[37]

To judge from the articles that appeared in *AS* and *AJS* over this fourteen-year period, the decision makers had drawn a line but not exactly to separate nonfeminist from feminist work. By and large, the journals printed articles that used the standard empirical data and the standard quantitative methods to investigate the standard disciplinary topics and shied away from those that challenged the discipline's conventional wisdom or ways.[38] Since the objectives were to protect sociological doxa and advance research-as-usual, the journals accepted feminist work that appeared to be compensatory. One would expect to find feminist articles that challenged the disciplinary orthodoxies in literary studies because this field had a larger number of journals, a higher proportion of feminist scholars, and a tradition of importing and innovating knowledge. But my review of three prominent journals—*PMLA* and *New Literary History* from 1970 through 1980 and *Critical Inquiry* from 1974 (when it was founded) through 1980—shows that they, too, filtered for type.

PMLA, like its ASA counterpart, was bound to publish associational business and thus printed the CSW's three status studies. Most of its pages were dedicated to scholarship, with each article selected according to disciplinary criteria and each issue assembled to represent national literatures as subdivided by periods, genres, and authors. The contents of the January 1970 issue faithfully reproduced the hierarchies of national literatures and authors; it contained seven articles on major British writers (Spenser, Shakespeare, Milton [two], Pope, and Arnold [two]), two on major American writers (Thoreau and Faulkner), and two on minor examples of other national literatures. Reflecting the discipline's genre preferences, six of these articles were on poetry, three on drama, and two on prose, but poetry entered into even the two articles on Milton and Shakespeare's verse dramas. That year, the only deviation from this formula occurred in the May issue where the gritty fallout from the 1968 activism littered the executive secretary's report, the New Study Commission's correspondence on associational reform, and two articles preaching moderation in the discipline.[39] Only one article in 1970 discussed a woman writer, Gertrude Stein, and that to support its discussion of Alain Robbe-Grillet.[40]

Throughout the 1970s, *PMLA* clung to another orthodoxy, the principle of balanced coverage that prompted it to offset snippets of feminism with samples of tradition. One 1971 issue neatly matched Madelyn Gutwirth's feminist "Madame de Staël, Rousseau, and the Woman Question" with David Sonstroem's traditional "*Wuthering Heights* and the Limits of Vision."[41] Another issue balanced the CSW's first status study with President Maynard Mack's post-1968 exhortation that members should disseminate "the world's great literature" to schools, educated readers, and the media.[42] Several conventional scholarly articles ballasted the 1972 issues against any tremors set off by the CSW's second status study and President Louis Kampf's radical critique of the profession. The 1973 issues printed a stream of conventional articles on women as protagonists—Milton's Eve, Richardson's Pamela, Carroll's Alice, Dickens's Esther, and Woolf's Mrs. Dalloway—and a speck of feminism: a list of women's studies programs in the September directory.[43] The issues for 1974, 1975, 1976, and 1977 would have been bereft of feminism but for *PMLA*'s obligations to print President

Florence Howe's "Literacy and Literature" in May 1974, a member note on women's status in October 1974, the CSW's third status study in January 1976, and the now routine list of women's studies programs. Not until May 1978 did *PMLA* follow up on the 1971 Gutwirth article with another feminist essay—Sandra M. Gilbert's "Patriarchal Poetry and Women Readers."[44] That trend continued in 1979 and 1980, with one feminist article each year and Jean Perkins's presidential address, which called attention to the diversity and inequality of MLA members.[45] In ten years, *PMLA* published four feminist articles that brought the controversial issue of gender to the attention of the profession but by doing precisely what other studies of literature did: they interpreted texts, analyzed genres, discussed authors and readers, and supplied historical contexts without exposing how these constructs and methods organized the discipline.

New Literary History (NLH), launched by Ralph Cohen in 1969 to usher in new thought, deserves credit for that achievement: it circulated European theory in the United States, fostered interdisciplinary work across the human sciences, printed accounts of interesting literature programs, and introduced the format of contributor debates. The authors who appeared in its pages were innovators in the human sciences: hermeneuticist Wilhelm Dilthey, reader-response theorists Wolfgang Iser and Hans Robert Jauss, phenomenologist Georges Poulet, historian Hayden White, anthropologists Claude Lévi-Strauss and Dell Hymes, media guru Marshall McLuhan, composer John Cage, Marxist critic Fredric Jameson, poststructuralists Roland Barthes and Jacques Derrida, and far more literary critics and art historians than can reasonably be listed. Yet from 1970 through 1980 *NLH* published only two feminist essays and one response mentioning feminism. A 1971 issue on modernism and postmodernism included Lillian S. Robinson and Lise Vogel's Marxist-feminist "Modernism and History," and a 1980 issue on narrative included Annette Kolodny's "A Map for Rereading: Or, Gender and the Interpretation of Literary Texts." Although Kolodny's article took on gendered reading conventions, it was more moderate than her sweeping indictment of the discipline in "Dancing through the Minefield," which had been published that same spring in *Feminist Studies*.[46] *NLH,* the premier journal for bringing innovative work to the attention of literary studies practitioners, did not present feminism as a major force in reconfiguring the discipline until well into the 1980s.

When *Critical Inquiry* was founded in 1974 by Sheldon Sacks and others associated with the University of Chicago, it was billed as "A voice for reasoned inquiry into significant creations of the human spirit"[47] and quickly became the other leading journal of theory and criticism in the human sciences. *Critical Inquiry* printed more feminist articles in six years than *PMLA* and *NLH* did in ten, typically including one or two per year with a high of three in 1976 and 1977. These articles did not quite fit the traditional molds: Henry Nash Smith wrote on forgotten best-sellers by women in nineteenth-century America, Carolyn G. Heilbrun on marriage in contemporary fiction, Barbara Currier Bell and Carol Ohmann on Virginia Woolf's criticism, Catharine R. Stimpson on Gertrude Stein's figuration of the body, Susan Fox on Blake's female metaphors, and Sandra M. Gilbert on transvestism in modern literature.[48] *Critical Inquiry* also published three articles on the discipline's androcentrism: Josephine Donovan looking at aesthetics, Lee R. Edwards at models of heroism, and Peter Schwenger at masculine modes of practice.[49] Once again the groundbreaking feminist article was Annette Kolodny's "Some Notes on Defining a 'Feminist Literary Criticism,' " published in 1975 and followed the next year by two replies and Kolodny's response.[50] Although the quantity of feminist work published by *Critical Inquiry* is impressive compared to that of other prominent journals, it nevertheless pales beside the feminist literary scholarship, criticism, and theory that appeared during this period at conferences and in feminist journals, less prestigious mainstream journals, edited collections, and monographs. Moreover, most of its feminist contributors were already nationally recognized scholars who had produced highly regarded books: Heilbrun's *Toward a Theory of Androgyny* (1973), Edwards and Diamond's *The Authority of Experience: Essays in Feminist Criticism* (1977), Gilbert and Gubar's *The Madwoman in the Attic* (1979), and Kolodny's *The Lay of the Land* (1975). Evidently, the visibility factor eased feminist articles into the journal.

The power of journals to filter and shape feminist work is even more evident in the case of the College Art Association's (CAA) *Art Bulletin* (*AB*). Between 1970 and 1980, this journal published only three feminist articles: Carol Duncan's "Happy Mothers and Other New Ideas in French Art" (1973), Norma Broude's "Degas's 'Misogyny' " (1977), and Linda Nochlin's "Lost and *Found*: Once More the Fallen Woman" (1978).[51] The articles braided feminist criticism into the art historical approaches usually featured in the journal. Its traditional articles focused on the individual artwork, artist, genre, or medium in a given period (e.g., panel painting in thirteenth-century Italy) and investigated stock problems: the artwork as a material object (e.g., carbon-dating techniques), an interpretable object referenced to the artist (e.g., his unpublished correspondence) or the visual type (e.g., biblical imagery), and a formal object (e.g., composition). These approaches corresponded to the bibliographical, biographical, representational, and formal modes in literary studies that Lillian S. Robinson had criticized as bourgeois humanism in her 1971 essay "Dwelling in Decencies" (see chapter 1).

In 1980, *AB* began to print clusters of articles on an oeuvre, a school, a multiart grouping (e.g., the arts in seventeenth-century England), or a genre-theme combination (e.g., Romantic landscapes), and in 1983 it included clusters that featured non-Western arts (e.g., Asian and African arts in 1983 and Latin-American arts in 1985) and arts in context (e.g., Baroque painting and its markets in 1984 and architecture and mathematics in 1985). But instead of using the cluster format to link old and new problems (e.g., genres with gender) or to devise new frameworks (e.g., systems of cultural production), the journal only shifted from articles analyzing discrete artworks to those investigating aggregated, neglected, or superficially contextualized artworks. Finally in 1986, *AB* began publishing the new art-historical work, such as interdisciplinary studies of the eighteenth century and poststructural analysis of the female nude genre, and a year later published its first feminist critique. Thalia Gouma-Peterson and Patricia Mathews's "The Feminist Critique of Art History" (1987) combined a review of the (by now not so) new feminist work with a wide-ranging indictment of the discipline's organizing constructs and practices.[52]

WORKING THE MECHANISMS: EVALUATION AND CITATION
Swarming at the heart of the institutional-disciplinary system, as Foucault has observed, are the micromechanisms of evaluation: student examinations, faculty appraisals, program reviews, research proposal ratings, and manuscript readings. The disciplinarians who work these little mechanisms can regulate the scholarly community by punishing transgression and rewarding rectitude and can shape the knowledge core by mandating conventions and moderating claims.[53] Evaluation operates like a feedback loop, as Karin Knorr-Cetina said about the sciences, because

> both the producers and evaluators of knowledge claims are . . . generally members of the same "community." Thus, they are held to *share* a common stock of knowledge and procedures, and presumably common standards of evaluation, professional preferences, and ways of

making a judgment. Furthermore, the validators of a knowledge claim are, at the same time, clients who potentially *need* a scientific result in order to promote their own investigations.

We should not take this comment simplistically to mean that a disciplinary elite monopolizes the production, evaluation, and consumption of knowledge because Knorr-Cetina goes on to explain that knowledge, once published and validated, "become[s] a resource for continuing scientific operations, as well as being a topic of problematisation in further research."[54] Rather we should understand evaluation as recursion: guided by the rules that have already structured a discipline's knowledge, evaluators reproduce the structure of its knowledge.

Publication is probably the most central reproductive mechanism of the disciplinary system. It not only supplies the resources practitioners use to do research and teaching but it also constitutes the expertise they need to join the ranks of those who wield the evaluative mechanisms. In this respect, the feminist journals and presses performed three strategic interventions into the system of evaluation: they delivered knowledges to feminist studies, built the reputations of faculty and students who were evaluated, and gave feminist scholars and scientists the credentials to evaluate. But until well into the 1980s the effects of this strategy were blunted by citation practices. Think of citations as little vehicles that make round-trips: heading outward they transport new knowledge into and around established fields, and heading back they deliver prestige to the knowers. Since disciplinarians rarely (if at all) consulted feminist publications and their bibliographies were slow to index them, feminist scholarship was seldom cited in mainstream venues.

Frequency of mainstream citation was not an important indicator of feminist studies' capital in a large, divergent discipline like literary studies where a great deal of published work was uncited or only cited by a small band of specialists. But in smaller and more convergent disciplines, such as sociology in the 1970s, citation frequency had serious consequences. Since male sociologists outnumbered feminist ones and same-sex correlation strongly influenced citation (i.e., male sociologists cited other male sociologists and rarely cited female ones),[55] the number of people unlikely to cite feminist work far exceeded the number likely to cite it. To complicate matters, the preponderance of feminist sociology was published in feminist venues which mainstream sociologists regarded as nonprestigious if not extradisciplinary.[56] Thus feminist sociologists were trapped in a no-win position: since their work was discredited when published in feminist venues and undercited wherever it was published, they could not achieve the citation frequency required to advance the standing of the field and its practitioners.

The recalcitrance built into the system of evaluation was gradually attenuated by several feminist strategies—namely, increasing the submission of feminist work to mainstream conferences, journals, and presses, adding feminist studies scholars and sympathizers to mainstream evaluative bodies, and modifying mainstream review processes. In the modern languages, for instance, individual members and membership groups (e.g., the csw, wcml, Division of Women's Studies, Gay and Lesbian Caucus, and Radical Caucus) worked together to sponsor a miniconference of sessions within the mla's mainstream convention, and by the 1990s, when feminists served on the executive committees of most scholarly divisions, feminist work authored by both women and men appeared in nearly every convention session. During this same period, they opened disciplinary journals to feminist scholarship by adding feminists to their editorial rosters, instituting author-anonymous review policies, and using feminist studies scholars to review feminist work.[57]

The importance of mainstream and feminist venues cannot be overstated, nor can the paradoxical results be overlooked. They provided the condition of possibility for establishing feminist studies as an academic field. By circulating knowledge, they made it possible for feminists to form an intellectual core, institutionalize women's studies programs and disciplinary subfields, and train future practitioners. By providing opportunities to present work, they constructed the expertise feminists needed to be evaluated and to evaluate. By building up audiences clamoring for more feminist scholarship, they attracted mainstream presses and journals to the field. Once the growing market for feminist scholarship converged with profit-seeking publishers and the national reputations of feminist scholars converged with prestige-hungry departments, feminist studies was transformed from a backwater to a boom town. Yet all along the way something that was happening on campuses worked with the publishing industry to discipline feminist studies.

Establishing Women's Studies

Compared to other new ventures, the institutionalization of women's studies proceeded at an astounding pace. No sooner were the first few female studies courses taught and the first few programs envisioned in

1969 than they multiplied so quickly that all we have are approximate counts over the next few years: 103 courses and 4 programs in December 1970, 600 courses and 17 programs in December 1971, and 4,500 courses and 75 to 110 programs in the 1972–73 academic year. By 1990, women's studies was so widely institutionalized that course estimates fluctuated between 30,000 and 50,000 and programs were reckoned at around 630.[58] But even without definitive numbers it is clear that the growth rate for courses was double or triple that for programs in the first four years and then accelerated when the programs sponsored more courses.

Rather than taking these trends at face value, for after all we know that teaching a course is easier than building a program, I want to interrogate them. What were the campus circumstances favoring course initiatives over program initiatives? What were the course topics, materials, and methods? How did the proliferation of courses affect the formation of the women's studies curriculum? I am pondering these questions, as I did those about publication, for what they tell us about how the institutionalization and intellectualization of the field proceeded together. I will begin with a sketch of women's studies—its courses, programs, and intellectual core—through the mid-1970s and identify the forces that were formatting it. Then I will look at the patterns manifested by a group of robust women's studies programs in the early 1990s.

FORMING WOMEN'S STUDIES PROGRAMS

When Florence Howe and Carol Ahlum published an article on the state of women's studies as of the 1971–72 academic year, they said their purpose was not to advocate for a new field resisted by the academy but to address a "more insistent problem" caused by its rapid emergence: "how to organize, or institutionalize, the courses that are appearing as if by magic on campus after campus across the country; how to understand their appearance, how to gauge their direction."[59] The more than eight hundred courses they had reviewed were stunningly dissimilar—taught by a single instructor, a faculty team, or a cast of campus and community guests lecturers, sweeping across the terrain of women's oppression in the United States or tunneling into a disciplinary topic, and using almost any amalgamation of materials, assignments, and formats. Even the not quite two-dozen programs were so dissimilar that Howe and Ahlum remarked "it would be difficult to find a pair that duplicate each other in aims, organization, relationship to the university, and so on."[60]

We know from reports that the forms of these early programs owed much to the conditions and cultures at their host institutions. The program at Barnard consisted of eleven courses on women in literature, history, and economic and social life that were taught in the "regular Barnard curriculum" and "in keeping with Barnard's academic style." They "appeared," wrote Catharine Stimpson, because the administration "encouraged" faculty members to "share this interest [in women] with students."[61] At SUNY Buffalo, by contrast, a feminist collective had established an insurgent left-feminist unit—a self-governing but university-budgeted College of Women's Studies that offered courses on the systems of oppression, taught academic material along with survival skills, and sponsored projects intended to transform the departmental and professional school curricula.[62] At Cornell, the administration held the Female Studies Program in thrall to the mainstream departmental structure. Although seeded by university grants and coordinated by a half-time director, the program was not permitted to offer for-credit courses or faculty status. Faculty members had to offer courses through "the existing departments," and students taking the only program-sponsored course, a non-credit research seminar, had to find departmental faculty members to give them credit for independent study.[63] The women at Portland State, by contrast, didn't bother to ask for the university's permission when they established the Ad Hoc Women's Institute and Resource Center (WIRC) as an "underground department of women's studies." In 1971, WIRC was teaching eleven courses to four hundred students and planning a curriculum that, as befitting its own genesis, would develop "an intellectual activist consciousness."[64] Indeed, in 1971–72, WIRC offered a three-term introductory course focused on the connections of women's studies to the liberation movement and community, and during the 1972 summer term Amy Kesselman taught Styles of Political Action to a group of students who organized a protest at a community "femininity clinic."[65]

While institutions were shaping the programs, teachers were forming a crosscutting intellectual core. Through the mid-1970s, both program-based and department-based courses assigned two or more of the following texts: Virginia Woolf's *A Room of One's Own*, Simone de Beauvoir's *The Second Sex*, Betty Friedan's *The Feminine Mystique*, Mary Ellmann's *Thinking About Women*, Aileen Kraditor's *Up From the Pedestal*, Eleanor Flexner's *Century of Struggle*, William O'Neill's *Everyone Was Brave*, Leo Kanowitz's *Women and the Law*, Eleanor Maccoby's *The Development of Sex Differences*, Kate Millett's *Sexual Politics*, and the anthologies *Woman in a Sexist Society* and *Sisterhood Is Powerful*. By combining these broad texts with specialized readings, the teachers were forming the field's intellectual core around "women's oppression" as it ramified into disciplinary research topics—for instance, psychology of sex differences, sociology of the family, social histories of women, women's legal and political status, and gendered imagery in the arts. Although specialization inevitably occurs as a field becomes crowded with scholars (see chapter 5 for a discussion of this dynamic), it was hastened in the early years of women's studies by the conjuncture of two financially driven circumstances: the trend in the publishing industry toward the niche marketing of specialized scholarship, and the preference of academic institutions for a curriculum that was assembled from department-based courses.

In 1976, when feminists routinely described women's studies as an interdisciplinary field, the curriculum in most of the 270 programs surveyed for Florence Howe's *Seven Years Later: Women's Studies Programs in 1976* had not taken an interdisciplinary shape. It typically consisted of a tiny core of program-based courses—an introduction, a senior seminar, and a feminist issues course—filled out with several cross-listed department-based courses. Most of the introductions were partitioned along disciplinary lines: two-term courses were divided into social sciences and humanities, and one-term courses were either team taught by a social scientist and a humanities scholar or led by a disciplinary instructor who brought in guest lecturers. The cross-listed courses were also discipline-oriented, and most were based in departments of literature, history, psychology, and sociology with a sprinkling from other departments. The curriculum resembled a multidisciplinary mélange rather than an interdisciplinary hybrid because on most campuses feminists had to use the mainstream departmentalized disciplines to assemble it. But once women's studies programs were securely established, why didn't their curricula morph into an interdisciplinary shape? Howe and Ahlum cited "the essential conservatism of higher education"[66] as an obstacle to interdisciplinarity, and I want to make a finer distinction about what mainstream academics were trying to conserve. In national venues such as conferences and publications, they wanted to protect the intellectual orthodoxies of their disciplines, and on campuses they wanted to preserve the departmentalization that structured university decision making and resource allocation.

The fact that academic institutions were ideologically, materially, and operationally invested in departmentalized disciplines had both upsides and downsides for the formation of the women's studies curriculum. First, it made courses easier to sell than programs: feminists could reassure mainstream faculty and administrators that the addition of a few "qualified" courses to a departmental curriculum posed no threat to its integrity, but they could not similarly quell their anxieties about a program that, by traversing the curricular territory, would breach the departments' authority over their own patches of turf. Second, departmentalization of the university's resources made it easier and cheaper to offer women's studies courses under the aegis of mainstream departments. Feminist teachers could use the resources of their home departments—the topics indicators to list courses, the equipment to duplicate materials, and the staff to schedule classrooms. To offer the same courses in a women's studies unit, feminist faculty had to write up a program proposal, win institutional approval, secure budgeted or borrowed faculty, and obtain funding for support staff or do the work themselves. Administrators naturally recognized that it was far more cost effective and labor efficient to farm the women's studies courses out to mainstream departments than to set them up in a new unit. Consequently, most women's studies curricula were formed as an uneven assortment of department-based courses and a few core courses coordinated by a volunteer committee or part-time director rather than as a coherent hybrid located in a fully funded and freestanding unit. The mélange curriculum persisted through the 1980s because administrators skimped on women's studies budgets, forcing the programs to make do with part-time directors, little staff support, and borrowed faculty members, who had to negotiate women's studies teaching with their home departments and take on women's studies governance as overload work.

Women's studies programs had trouble developing a broad and coherent interdisciplinary curriculum because administrators treated them as institutional units in some respects but not others. While ostensibly allowing the programs to design an undergraduate minor or major, administrators withheld the little mechanisms of faculty lines, faculty teaching assignment, and course approval that mainstream departments wielded to ensure the integrity of their curricula. Without these mechanisms, both underfunded and reasonably funded programs were locked into a course-by-course and department-by-department struggle to patch a curriculum together. For teaching staff, they had to depend on departmental faculty; some departments hired faculty interested in feminist studies, others resisted for as long as possible, and most regarded faculty requests to teach for women's studies as draining labor away from their own curriculum. Since feminist faculty were not uniformly distributed across mainstream departments, women's studies courses erupted un-evenly on most campuses, with the preponderance based in English, his-tory, and sociology; some in the foreign languages, anthropology, psychol-ogy, political science, philosophy, art history, education, and social work; and virtually none in economics, the natural sciences, business, and law. When department-based faculty proposed courses for crosslisting with women's studies, few programs were authorized to conduct a formal review to approve or reject the proposals. Some programs skirted the problem by working with department-based faculty to develop course proposals, but others discovered that course review was a highly contro-versial matter even among their staunch supporters. In 1975, the issue roiled several meetings of the Women's Studies Advisory Council at the University of Cincinnati. Advocates of review argued that WSAC had to be able to screen out courses that were sexist or uninformed by the new feminist scholarship, while critics objected that WSAC lacked the multi-disciplinary expertise to judge the contents and methods of all the courses that might be proposed and in any case was setting itself up for conflicts with "friendly" departments that had already approved these courses.

From my description so far, it should be clear that the institutional conditions and cultures shaping women's studies curricula were backed by several national patterns. One was the disciplinary segregation I described in chapter 2: the training of women (and by extension the feminists) in some disciplines and not others resulted in the uneven departmental hir-ing of feminists that in turn caused the uneven women's studies curricu-lum. Another pattern was stratification: since women disproportionately occupied the lowest and most marginal faculty ranks, they had little lev-erage to teach in women's studies and often suffered for doing so when they came up for contract renewal or tenure review. The third national pattern—that female faculty were disproportionately located at four-year, two-year, and women's colleges rather than in prestigious institutions— did not precisely translate into the curricular possibilities for women's studies on campuses. It was seldom the case that a more robust women's studies curriculum could be built at a women's college with a good track record of hiring feminist faculty than at a university with a mediocre hiring record because many other factors came into play: the size and hetero-geneity of an institution's faculty (as well as its rates of faculty replacement and expansion), the liberalism or conservatism of the institution's sur-rounding community and region, and the strength of organized feminism on the campus and in the community. In 1971, for instance, 127 institutions offered a combined total of 610 women's studies courses. Half of the institutions were doctoral-granting universities, a quarter were four-year coeducational colleges, and roughly a sixth were women's colleges; moreover, half of the institutions were located on the East Coast, a quarter in the Midwest, under a quarter on the West Coast, and only twelve in the South.[67]

The institutional affiliations of the women who contributed hundreds of syllabi and dozens of essays to the *Female Studies* series show that the emergence of women's studies on campuses followed the geography of the New Left, educational reform, and feminist movements.[68] But the names of the *Female Studies* editors and contributors show that an academic network radiating outward from the MLA Commission on the Status of Women boosted its development as a national field. Some were CSW members: Sidonie Cassirer, Mary Anne Ferguson, Joan Hartman, Elaine Hedges, Nancy Jo Hoffman, Florence Howe, Carol Ohmann, Elaine Reuben, Deborah Rosenfelt, Roberta Salper, Cynthia Secor, Elaine Showalter, Catharine Stimpson, and Adrian Tinsley. Others were linked to the CSW as friends of its members and participants in its activities: for instance, Josephine Donovan, Phyllis Franklin, Melanie Kay, Marcia Landy, Wendy Martin, Judith Newton, and Nancy M. Porter in the modern languages; Linda Gordon and Gerda Lerner in history; and Alice Rossi, Pauline Bart, and Arlie Hochschild in sociology. As prominent feminists in their disciplines, they spread women's studies nationally by editing journals and books, organizing conferences, and working through their own disciplinary associations.

What I want to propose from this analysis is a scenario for the institutional and intellectual form(att)ing of feminist studies. The feminists who launched women's studies lacked the academic standing enjoyed by scholars who had established new humanities and science disciplines earlier in the twentieth century. On campuses, their faculty and student status was tenuous, their intellectual credibility was impugned, and their educational agenda was resisted. Yet with boosts from local feminist activism and national feminist activity they managed to parlay little smatterings of courses into small women's studies programs. They started out with cross-disciplinary and cross-sector aspirations, but they met up with disciplinary and institutional limitations. They wanted to hybridize movement and academic discourses, but the national venues they used to circulate their work formatted it according to scholarly conventions. They wanted to link feminist studies to movement activism, but they were located in universities that expected them to perform academic activities. They wanted to build interdisciplinary programs, but they had to assemble the curriculum from courses based in disciplinary departments. By the mid-1970s, feminist studies had formed with internal tensions—between disciplinarity and interdisciplinarity, orthodoxy and heterodoxy, routinization and innovation—that still characterized it in the 1990s.

SURVEYING WOMEN'S STUDIES PROGRAMS

In spring 1992, I wrote to the directors of women's studies programs and departments (henceforth called programs) at thirty-five universities and colleges, asking for information on their founding, faculty, credentialing (e.g., minors, majors, and graduate degrees), curriculum, and other functions (e.g., research projects, lecture series, and conferences) and requesting syllabi for undergraduate and graduate core courses. Besides the twenty-seven programs that sent materials, I already had information on women's studies at three more institutions: the University of Minnesota (my institution), Rutgers University (I was doing fieldwork throughout the state of New Jersey), and Midwestern State (a fictitious name for an institution where I was doing fieldwork).[69] From the survey, I hoped to learn how feminist studies and social change were realized in these programs. What was the form of the curriculum? Had the discourse become cross-disciplinary? Did the programs teach social change as a subject and as a practice? Did they sponsor projects meant to change the academy and society? Diverse as the thirty programs were, my survey revealed some deeply entrenched institutional and intellectual patterns.

First, the form of the 1992 curriculum was still a multidisciplinary mélange. On average, the programs had six program-based courses and fifty cross-listed courses that were oriented toward disciplinary subject matters and methods (the number of crosslisted courses ranged from twelve in small programs to more than eighty in the large ones at Brown and Minnesota). The mélange curriculum, I assumed, held more widely than my sample because I had selected programs with a sizable core faculty or at least several joint faculty lines at a time when most programs still depended heavily on department-based faculty. My impression was bolstered a few years later when a program director attending the National Women's Studies Association's 1997 conference for program directors estimated that 80 percent of the nationwide curriculum consisted of crosslisted, discipline-oriented courses because the programs depended on department-based faculty and the faculty tended to use the "add women and stir" approach.[70] My survey produced some finer distinctions about these crosslisted courses. As I expected, the preponderance came from disciplines that had welcomed or at least tolerated feminist work since 1980: American Studies, anthropology, classics, comparative literature, composition, education, English, French, Italian, German, Spanish and Portuguese, history, sociology, political science, psychology, religion, theater, rhetoric, social work, and speech-communications. But a surprising number were offered in fields less hospitable to feminist work: the courses cross-listed with business management, criminal justice, labor studies, natural resource management, and urban planning were as numerous as those cross-listed with art history, philosophy, and economics. Finally, at institutions with thriving ethnic and area studies programs the interdisciplinary courses cross-listed with African-American, Asian-American, Chicano, Native-American, Judaic, Near-Eastern, and South-Asian studies tugged against the disciplinary tilt of women's studies.

The second curricular pattern I spotted was the disciplinarity of advanced and introductory courses based in the women's studies programs. Some of the advanced courses (e.g., women's biology and feminist philosophy) made it possible for students to study in disciplines that have resisted incorporating feminist work into their curricula, but others (e.g., feminist literary criticism and women's history) repeated the offerings available in mainstream departments. Although the introductory courses invariably criticized disciplinary knowledges, most did not escape the disciplinary form. The Cincinnati program divided both its undergraduate and graduate introductions into separate terms on the social sciences and humanities; the Maryland program offered two separate undergraduate introductions, Women and Society and Women, Art, and Culture, that similarly divided the disciplines; and the doctoral proseminar at CUNY's Graduate Center was team taught by two instructors hailing from these same disciplinary clusters. I know of two courses that problematized disciplinarity itself. Demarcating Disciplinarity, which was taught at Brown's Pembroke Center for Teaching and Research on Women, used *Feminist Scholarship: Kindling in the Groves of Academe* as a launching pad to examine several disciplines. And my quarter of Theory and Method, the two-quarter graduate introduction at Minnesota's Center for Advanced Feminist Studies, focused on the founding of research universities, the emergence of disciplines, and the order of discourse in sample disciplines and feminist studies.

The programs that did offer cross-disciplinary introductions organized them as grids with identity categories crosshatching disciplinary and / or feminist issues. The University of Colorado program described its undergraduate introduction as

> the study of women from an interdisciplinary perspective. The first half of the class examines the notion of a gender-based hierarchy and its effects on women's biological roles, psychological development, and the meaning of sex role socialization. The second half of the course looks at women within the context of the family, the economy, and the political sphere. An overview of social changes is provided through a brief examination of the suffrage campaign and the contemporary women's movement. Throughout the semester, the significance of race and class is brought to bear, particularly with respect to the diversity of women's experience."[71]

As a variation on this form, the University of California at San Diego offered an ambitious undergraduate introduction. The first term surveyed varieties of feminist theories and methods—liberal, socialist-Marxist, radical, lesbian, and others; the second featured such controversial issues as pornography, abortion, occupational discrimination, feminization of poverty, and social movements; and the third term on global feminisms analyzed socioeconomic systems and liberation movements. Although the San Diego trio incorporated a more complex nesting of categories and meshing of methods than the one- or two-term introductions offered elsewhere, it most clearly illustrates the state of the field. Feminist studies, like every other discipline cranked up by exponential growth, had become crowded with specialisms in subject matter, method, and theory that paradoxically drove the proliferation of knowledge and the fragmentation of discourse (see chapter 5).

Not surprisingly, the third curricular pattern revealed by my survey was that the tug between discipline and cross-discipline showed up in the women's studies concentrations. The Maryland program offered an undergraduate concentration in history and three more in disciplinary clusters: art, literature, and music; psychology and sociology with a focus on sex roles; and law, politics, and economics. By contrast, Brown's Pembroke Center had a crosscutting undergraduate concentration: the construction of gender and the category of women as they operated in social, political, economic, and cultural registers. Concentrations at the graduate level seldom broke from the pattern of disciplinary clusters. Students at Cornell could choose their graduate minor from one crosscutting concentration (ideology and culture) and five disciplinary concentrations (history, natural sciences, literature and the arts, psychology and human development, and institutions and societies). Graduate students at Minnesota had two options. They could train for feminist studies in mainstream departments that had strong feminist subfields—the modern languages and literatures, history, American Studies, philosophy, speech-communications, social work, and a few others. Or, once admitted to any department's graduate program, they could also apply for admission to the graduate concentration housed in the Center for Advanced Feminist Studies (CAFS). Presumably the CAFS students were training in two doctoral fields, one in the home discipline and the other in the cross-discipline, but practically CAFS was not as cross-disciplinary as it seemed. Some of its courses were discipline oriented, and others, such as the cross-disciplinary "Theory and Method," usually tilted toward the discipline of the instructor teaching it.[72] What my survey showed to be most immune to disciplinary tilting were the feminist theory courses included in virtually every program's upper division and graduate curricula. Ironically, the level of abstraction in academic feminist theory that made it inaccessible to community feminists seemed to be the common ground where disciplinary feminists met, though not without some invidiousness on the merits of empiricism, social constructivism, and poststructuralism.

Finally, the survey told me what these thirty programs were doing with regard to feminist social change. Nearly all had sponsored curriculum transformation projects at their own institutions, a few were collaborating with women's studies programs at neighboring institutions, and one, the New Jersey Project, had mounted a unique statewide effort to mainstream gender, race, and class into the curricula of all public and private higher-education institutions (see chapter 6). This finding came as no surprise because curriculum transformation had grown into an industry: more than a hundred projects had been mounted nationwide, dozens of articles and books provided advice and resources, and most disciplinary associations had developed materials for revising survey and specialist courses.[73] Change projects geared to helping women students were less common than I had expected. While most programs in my survey offered the usual academic advising and career counseling, only the University of Arizona program operated an ambitious long-term development project, Women in Science and Engineering, that had served more than 3,600 students. Predictably, all of the programs conducted outreach to nonacademic communities through conferences on public policy issues and women's leadership. Only two programs conducted outreach through Friends of Women's Studies organizations that sponsored their own events and supported women's studies through fundraising and lobbying. The five hundred members of Cincinnati's Friends of Women's Studies (founded in 1980) were primarily community women but also alumnae, faculty, and administrators. To build the community membership base, women's studies director Laura Strumingher turned to a network of Cincinnati women who had long worked together in civic organizations and political campaigns and with their help recruited others. But to build the alumnae membership base of Duke's Friends of Women's Studies (founded in 1986), director Jean O'Barr had to begin de novo by identifying university graduates and bringing them back to campus for feminist events.[74]

Every program in my survey taught social change as a subject embedded in such topics courses as women's movements, women and economic development, women in the labor force, the feminization of poverty, and reproductive rights campaigns. Most offered optional internships at local issue advocacy organizations and social service agencies, and a few used the internship as an occasion to teach students about social change: women's studies at the University of Massachusetts in Boston, for example, combined the internship with a seminar on institutions and social change. But social-change practice was rarely taught in campus courses. Women's studies at the University of Michigan offered a trio of action courses that exercised students in group process, decision making, conflict resolution, leadership skills, and change strategies, and a few programs not in my original survey but identified through numerous inquiries included change projects in their undergraduate curriculum. Only one, the Department of Women's Studies at Midwestern State, offered a graduate program in collective action and social change (see chapter 6).

LOOKING BACK

The first-generation academic feminists, as I mentioned in chapter 3, understood the social-change strategies used by the 1960s movements. Once activists had formed a movement, they were supposed to deploy it by catalyzing local activism, orchestrating direct action to pressure elites, insinuating movement projects into mainstream arenas, working the official channels to change laws and policies, and establishing parallel organizations operated by and for the people. While some feminists were inserting feminist studies into the academy, others were setting up parallel organizations—rape-crisis centers, battered women shelters, healthcare services, bookstores, music festivals, policy institutes, and law centers. Although the details of parallel organizations differ from those of feminist studies, the dynamics are similar: they were built during an era of economic and social shifts that formatted them. In the 1970s, progressive movements suffered from chronic revenue shortfalls, steep learning curves, and discontinuities as volunteers came and went—circumstances that made the work of maintaining parallel organizations more difficult. By the end of the decade, parallel service providers that depended on volunteers, such as rape-crisis centers, battered women shelters, and healthcare groups, found their clienteles growing just when labor power was being drained away by employer demands for increased worker productivity, corporate downsizing, and worker needs for supplemental employment. To increase their revenues, they sought government funding, which in turn transformed them into quasi-public agencies that had to bring their activities into compliance with government regulations. When the Reagan and Bush administrations reduced federal support for the service sector, these agencies found themselves mired in the routines of grant writing and donor solicitation they had hoped to avoid in the first place. Other parallel feminist organizations, though not dependent on government funding, were trapped in the same predicament. Nonprofits, such as feminist policy institutes and advocacy groups, had to expend much of their energy on grant writing and donor solicitation to raise operating funds (see chapter 6), and for-profit entities, such as bookstores and music festivals, had to master the fiscal and marketing techniques used by their mainstream competitors. Parallel feminist projects have not evaded the forces shaping their activities any more than feminist studies evaded the academic forces shaping it.

Looking back at the 1971 Pittsburgh conference where Marilyn Salzman-Webb predicted that female studies would produce a "history of what was created both by the dominated and the dominator to sustain or struggle against that domination," I was reminded of Foucault's definition of *genealogy* as "the union of erudite knowledge and local memories which allows us to establish a historical knowledge of struggles and to make use of this knowledge tactically today."[75] In 1996, I asked some first-generation academic feminists to comment on whether feminist studies had lost its genealogical impulse. Tucker Farley, a professor at the City University of New York's Brooklyn College, said that feminist studies was not a purely academic field in every locale and described several projects in New York City that brought feminist studies into community education and labor organizing.[76] Florence Howe, a professor at the City University of New York's Graduate Center and still president of the Feminist Press, didn't know of any program in the United States that was training students to do interdisciplinary and activist feminist studies. When I asked what she meant by those terms, she repeated what a dean had told her in 1973: it meant designing programs that could "fly high enough to spot the enemy installations and solve the problem."[77] When I spoke to Roberta Salper, head of the Division of Humanities and Social Sciences on the Erie campus of Pennsylvania State University, she said that "the venom outside seeps into our skin." Asked for clarification, she replied that her campus and surrounding community were so conservative that she worried about the probity of her administrative decisions, avoided the word *feminism* when she taught courses, and used diplomacy rather than activism to survive.[78]

The comments of these first-generation feminists took me back in time to Foucault, who wrote in 1976:

> is it not perhaps the case that these fragments of genealogies are no sooner . . . put into circulation, than they run the risk of re-codification, re-colonization? In fact, those unitary discourses, which first disqualified and then ignored them when they made their appearance, are, it seems, quite ready . . . to take them back within the fold of their own discourse and to invest them with everything this implies in terms of their effects of knowledge and power.[79]

To socialist feminists Ann Leffler, Dair L. Gillespie, and Elinor Lerner Ratner who wrote in 1973:

> An academic woman *may* submit herself, voluntarily and individually, to the moral sanctions which constitute the movement's control over her. But academic women are formally and collectively responsible solely to the institutions which underwrite them: the universities.[80]

To SDS member Richard Rothstein, who wrote in 1969:

> The regular appearance of new radical books and journals, rather than new projects and organizations, describes our situation. . . . We are a cultural phenomenon, not a political threat.[81]

These comments—notwithstanding their very different foci on the dynamics of discourse, the project of professionalization, or the proliferation of analyses—point to what caused feminist studies to lose its genealogical impulse.

As I look back at feminist studies with institutionalist eyes, I would have to say that the transformations it promised in theory did not pan out in practice, but not for the reasons we anticipated. We understood all too well the power of academic institutions to suppress: they could quash our projects outright or slowly strangle them when evaluation time came. What we did not understand was the power they could exercise by letting us go forward with our projects. Sure enough, the universities with their calcified departments and codified processes, the disciplinary associations with their conference programs and governance protocols, and the publishers with their conventionalized books and journals could format feminist education and knowledge. And sure enough, the routines of maintaining all those courses and programs, scholarly journals and conferences, disciplinary caucuses and feminist associations, exhausted our energies, narrowed our vision, and insulated us. In chapters 3 and 4, I argued that the academy has the power to include and exclude, to stimulate and stifle, because it has the power to structure. As we worked in the academy to institutionalize feminist studies, the academy's institutional-disciplinary order worked on it by structuring our activities and shaping our knowledges. The fate of feminist studies was overdetermined from the start by that relay between institutionalization and intellectualization that disciplines all successful academic-knowledge ventures.

5. Proliferating the Discourse

Conceptually the field of women's studies is much less tidy. In fact, many would claim it is downright messy. Some would say the mess is well deserved, the result of not really being a field. And others would acknowledge the mess and see it as the very sign of intellectual ferment. —Jean O'Barr, *Feminism in Action* (1994)

If feminist studies has surpassed other disciplines during the ripening phase, it has surpassed them in productivity. The seeds that those first feminists planted in the academy when they began to declaim on women's oppression vegetated into the lush, variegated, perplexingly tangled knowledges that now web our field and weave through others. Something about this discourse made it function like a dynamo, generating subfields in mainstream disciplines, multiplying specialisms in its own domain, and forming hybrids along its borders with other fields.

As one indicator of this productivity, we can consider the plethora of objects. Feminist studies reconstru(ct)ed the traditionally fashioned *women* and *men*, denaturalized *sex* and *sexuality*, formulated subjective and social *gender*, modeled *sex-gender systems*, multiplied *identities* and *oppressions*, and problematized all such *categories*. But how were these things I am calling discursive objects formed? They were not formed by plucking words out of the lexicon and assigning them new meanings: "*women* will henceforth signify a variegated population group" or "*multiple oppressions* will denote the intrications of racism, classism, and sexism that produce intensifying effects." Before the definitions came the details: the details swarming within the growing body of scholarship, like the pointillist jots of color applied to a canvas, could be seen at a distance as limning the groupness and variegatedness of women, congealing in the systematicity of sex-gender systems, and filiating one oppression to another. The discourse produced not a succession of objects, with each one giving way to the next, but a coexistence of objects whose longevity has been ensured by ongoing research programs within and across the disciplines. Today literary studies scholars continue to investigate women writers and readers, gendered writing and reading practices, the interactive oppressions that constrain literary and scholarly production, and the unstable categories of literary-studies discourse—just as their feminist colleagues continue to investigate these objects in other fields.

That's why another indicator of productivity is the superabundance of knowledge produced about these objects. We can confirm, if not precisely compute, the quantity of knowledge from the venues where it has appeared over the years—probably ten thousand books, a hundred thousand journal articles and conference papers, and a billion classroom discussions, hallway conversations, and e-mail messages. To guesstimate numbers, you might want to try an exercise I recently tried: an on-line search using the keywords "women," "gender," or "feminism" to call up the book titles or articles. My Lumina search of the library holdings at the University of Minnesota, Twin Cities, and my Luis search of those at the University of Florida suggest that some ten thousand feminist studies books were published between 1980 and 1998—and that is to say nothing of articles, films, videos, audiocassettes, exhibitions, and live performances.[1] The print knowledge alone is so voluminous that practitioners can no longer keep track of the titles, and some of it is so specialized that we can no longer absorb the details. Yet even within the particular literatures each of us reads we encounter the *super* of knowledge's abundance. The traces appear as topical repetitions (everything and anything is gendered), as methodological inflections of a topic (gendering is narrated, quantified, or modeled), and as metadiscourse about the discourse ("gender" as an analytical category is interrogated).

In the previous chapter, I looked at how the institutional machinery feminists used—conferences and publications, departments and programs—disciplined their discourse. This chapter focuses on what drove the discourse to produce the convoy of objects and crush of knowledges, the jostling criticisms and jousting practitioners that, as Jean O'Barr put it, made the field look downright messy. Following her lead, I will examine some of the feminist scholarship, criticism, and theory that constituted three objects: *sex, gender,* and *multiple identities and oppressions.* My purpose is not to review the knowledges as such but to reveal the rules working within and the forces working on the discourses that produced the knowledges.

Subverting Biologized Sex

Today we are so accustomed to analyzing the constructedness of all things that we may not be able to think of biologized sex as it was thought in the human sciences during the 1960s. Sex was the natural force shaping bodies, abilities, and behaviors and thereby structuring society, and this biologized model had oozed into the thinking that determined everyday transactions, public policies, and academic research projects. That was the Western worldview when movement and academic feminists read Shulamith Firestone's *The Dialectic of Sex* (1971).

Firestone was not the first author to look for the causes of women's oppression. Liberals and radicals from the eighteenth century onward had attributed it to political disenfranchisement, legal disabilities, inadequate education, and restricted employment opportunities, and Marxists from Engels onward had described it as an effect of the relations of (re)production in various political economies. Following the first path, Firestone argued that since these arrangements constrained all American women and consigned black and working-class women to a struggle for subsistence, the remedy was to make structural changes—among them, replacing the nuclear family with the communal household, assigning childcare responsibilities to both sexes and social institutions, training women for remunerative employment, and redesigning built environments so they would support individual and community needs.[2] These recommendations would have been familiar to many of her feminist readers because both liberal and radical feminists had been discussing such alternative structures as American countercultural communes and Israeli kibbutzim, equal educational and employment opportunities, free childcare facilities, and affordable community services for women.

Firestone's contribution to feminist critique was not these recommendations, nor was it her use of Marxist analysis to describe women's oppression as rooted in the mode of (re)production because more trenchant left-feminist analyses were published between 1969 and 1975. Her contribution was a strategy for tackling the hypothesis of reproductive determinism: she chipped away the bits of biologized sex and transported them into the

social field. Where biologizers had collapsed the processes of menstruation, pregnancy, and lactation and the activities of infant care, child rearing, and homemaking into a single naturalized category, Firestone transferred the latter activities to the category of social labor. Where they
regarded fertilization and gestation as inalienable reproductive functions,
she speculated about such future possibilities as "test-tube babies." Where
they looked for the cause of women's subordination beneath the social
formation and found sexed bodies, she looked for it in the social formation
and found the sexual division of labor. Marxist theory and feminist critique
gave her the tools to scoop out the topsoil of reproductive determinism
but not to chip into its flinty core—the chromosomal, hormonal, and
developmental processes that feminists in the biological sciences would
soon discuss.

Firestone's strategy spread to the academy where feminist scientists
and scholars began to whittle away at reproductive determinism by arguing that a host of new technologies—birth control, improved pre- and
postnatal care, bottle-feeding, household appliances, and service industries—had freed women from most biological constraints. Here is a typical
statement made by sociologist Joan Huber in 1976:

> Only one biological difference categorically separates women and
> men: No man can bear a child. Yet technology permits humans to tran-
> scend biological characteristics. This common sense observation . . . is
> made only because it is so often forgotten in discussions of women's
> place. That women can bear children is, to date, a fact of nature, but
> that women are assigned the responsibility of rearing children is a man-
> made fact subject to change.[3]

Feminists regarded Huber's common sense observations (though, of
course, she fallaciously attributed childbearing capacity and access to technologies to all women) as a welcome anodyne for the rigidities of nomothetic science. But common sense statements did not qualify for a hearing
in the biological, behavioral, and social sciences because, as Foucault
would have put it, they did not address the sciences' already specified
model of binary and amplifying sex and use their already sanctioned
methods to investigate it.

BINARY SEX

By the time feminist scientists began to address the issue of biological determinism, mainstream biology's model of binary and amplifying sex had

long since permeated the disciplines, grounding not only the sex-difference research in psychology but a whole series of constructs, such culture / nature, public / private spheres, and rationality / sensibility, used to divide the sexes in the social sciences and humanities. Then during the 1970s the stronger claim that genes programmed human behavior gained visibility in the public domain, thanks to splashy media coverage of the new field of sociobiology and its popularizing books such as Lionel Tiger and Robin Fox's *The Imperial Animal* (1971), Edward O. Wilson's *Sociobiology: The New Synthesis* (1974), Richard Dawkins's *The Selfish Gene* (1976), Wilson's *On Human Nature* (1978), and David Barash's *The Whispering Within* (1979).

Mainstream biologists and sociobiologists understood sex differentiation as a process occurring on several biological levels—the genetic, chromosomal, gametic, and physiological—but went on to model it somewhat differently.[4] Mainstream biologists adhered to a moderate binarism and moderate determinism program. They regarded XX and XY as the normal genotypes and their expression in the body's reproductive organs as the normal sex-differentiation process. Normalization, of course, pathologized variations on this model: other chromosomal makeups (XO, XXX, XXY, and XYY) were regarded as aberrations that occurred while the gametic materials mixed to form a new genotype, and "ambiguous" physiological features were considered to be the result of either aberrant genotypes or hormonal conditions that bent the sex-differentiation process in genotypically normal individuals. By contrast, sociobiology had a strong binarism and strong determinism program. Its central doctrine of hereditarianism proclaimed that genes programmed the sexes' and races' social destinies—a concept that Edward O. Wilson illustrated in *On Human Nature* by caroming from the asymmetries of men's and women's physiologies directly to (presumed) differences in their mating behaviors, temperaments, family roles, sports performances, and political activities. Despite a name that seemed to promise an evenhanded synthesis of biology and sociology in studying sex, sociobiology's objectives were not only to biologize the social but to colonize the other disciplines. In *Sociobiology: The New Synthesis,* the field's founding manifesto, Wilson described the social sciences and humanities as "the last branches of biology waiting to be included in the Modern Synthesis [i.e., sociobiology]."[5]

To rethink these two models of sex, several organizations of women in science hosted the Genes and Gender conference in January 1977, and afterward some of the participants carried the rethinking forward by editing the *Genes and Gender* series and feminist anthologies on the biological sciences.[6] They tackled binary sex by subjecting empirical data to critical analysis. For instance, several articles used the clinical literature on intersexing written by John Money, Anke Ehrhardt, and their colleagues. The literature attributed intersexing to problems at two biological levels, the chromosomal and the hormonal. Some individuals had XO, XXY, or XYY chromosomes, which caused the development of "ambiguously sexed" reproductive organs and somatic features during the fetal and pubertal sex-differentiation processes. Others were XY males whose insensitivity to androgen ("testicular feminizing syndrome") or XX females whose prenatal exposure to testosterone-like substances ("adrenogenital syndrome") bent the "normal" sex-differentiation processes. Where Money and his colleagues regarded intersexing as a person problem to be corrected through surgery, hormonal treatment, and counseling, feminists took the opposite approach of regarding it as a knowledge problem created by binary logic and normalizing language.[7]

Feminists used the intersexing literature to criticize the model of binary and amplifying sex. First, this model didn't divide people into male / female categories within any particular biological level. How, for instance, could the XX / XY scheme accommodate people who had XO, XXY, and XYY chromosomes or chromosomal mosaics (i.e., XX pairs in some cells and XY pairs in others) without anomalizing them? Or how could the egg / sperm scheme accommodate people who didn't produce gametes without pathologizing them? Second, the model couldn't define the sex of a person whose features didn't correlate across the levels. What was the sex of an XX person with adrenogenital syndrome who had vestigal ovaries and an enlarged clitoris resembling a penis? Or what was the sex of an XY person with testicular-feminizing syndrome who had breasts and a penis the size of a clitoris?[8] Third, if the model couldn't clearly and consistently demarcate two sexes within and across the biological levels, then how could it undergird the hypothesis that men's and women's biological differences amplified into their behavioral and social differences? Feminists pointed out that the binary model only worked because its language—"abnormal genotypes" and "hermaphroditic ambiguity"—got rid of the empirical anomalies that would challenge its explanatory adequacy. Psychologist Rhoda K. Unger, for instance, commented that "Individuals with Turner's syndrome [XO chromosomal sex] are *not* aberrant females. . . . They are essentially neuter individuals whose external genitalia are similar to those of females. They are defined as female simply because of the inadequacy of our dichotomous classification system for sex."[9] Yet so tenacious was the grip of binary language that Unger herself used the word *neuter* to accommodate cases that did not fit the two-category model.

If the language of sex often snared mainstream researchers and clinicians, it was a resource that sociobiologists exploited for their purposes, as in this passage from Wilson's *On Human Nature:*

> The quintessential female is an individual specialized for making eggs. The large size of the egg enables it to resist drying, to survive adverse periods by consuming stored yolk, to be moved to safety by the parent, and to divide at least a few times after fertilization before needing to ingest nutrients from the outside. The male is defined as the manufacturer of sperm, the little gamete. A sperm is a minimum cellular unit, stripped down to a head packed with DNA and powered by a tail containing just enough stored energy to carry the vehicle to the egg.[10]

Although feminist scientists were appalled by Wilson's linguistic jujitsu, nonscientific readers would not have questioned his metaphors. What he did (and I can't resist using some current metaphors) was to reify the sperm as an Energizer-powered gadget that "keeps on going" to its target and fictionalize the fertilized egg as a sci-fi blob mitotically swelling in its inner-space lair. Wilson might have replied to such criticism that he was only dramatizing the workings of gametes for nonscientific readers, but he was also inculcating the basic concepts of binary sex through the gametic drama and the industrial analogy of individuals specialized for egg or sperm production.

AMPLIFYING SEX

To remodel sex, feminist scientists also had to tackle the ubiquitous amplification hypothesis. In psychology, most research was predicated on the assumption that, as Helen H. Lambert put it, "the genetic and hormonal processes that bring about the sexual differentiation of the reproductive system also operate" to produce differences in male and female perception, cognition, and behavior.[11] Taken further afield, the findings from sex-difference research in biology and psychology informed explanations of human evolution and social organization in anthropology and sociology, practices in education and social services, and advice given to parents in popular childcare manuals. Feminist scientists scrutinized the amplification hypothesis all along the biological-behavioral-social spectrum. Biologists, neurophysiologists, and medical clinicians conducted research on the organismic and environmental factors—from endogenous and exogenous hormones to light cycles and exercise—that contributed to fetal and pubertal sex-differentiation processes. Behavioral scientists identified shortcomings in published studies that alleged a multitude of biologically caused sex differences—from infants' frequency of smiling to children's spatial perception and from high schoolers' mathematical ability to adults' achievement motivation. Social scientists studying non-Western and Western cultures showed that their diverse kinship systems, household and family forms, divisions of labor, social roles, and power relations undermined the hypothesis that biology determined social destiny.[12]

After finding greater social variety, fewer behavioral differences, and many more contributing factors than the traditional literatures asserted, feminist scientists proposed alternatives to the hypothesis that biology determines social destiny. Some suggested using regression analysis to ascertain the relative weights of biological, environmental, and social factors in the sex-differentiation processes. Although this model took the edge off genetic determinism by adding nonbiological factors to the mix, it did not break from the bottom-up logic whereby a set of factors were said to sex individuals. Others suggested using holistic logic to model the production of sex differences as a more complex and prolonged process. Marian Lowe, for instance, argued that the differences in women's and men's long bone growth were produced by a complicated synergy among hereditary factors; increased production of estrogen, which slows bone growth in females; and such social factors as diet, physical activity, stress, and exposure to sunshine, which affect the onset and amount of hormone production.[13] But the impact of feminist critiques was blunted because amplification was not merely a hypothesis to be tested by empirical research but a construct that organized the biological sciences. Sociobiology had been launched precisely to ground behavior and societal organization in biological events, and mainstream biology was invested in amplification because it corresponded to the organization of causal explanations.

MODERN BIOLOGY

Biology's commitment to binary and amplifying sex could probably be traced back to the premodern seventeenth century when the tangled discourses of theology, moral philosophy, and political philosophy conflated what we now distinguish as sex, gender, and sexuality in the doctrine of a divinely determined sexual order. Milton put it succinctly in *Paradise Lost* (1674) when he announced that Adam and Eve were created:

Not equal, as thir sex not equal seem'd;
For contemplation he and valor form'd.
For softness she and sweet attractive Grace.[14]

The doctrine of different faculties, complementary roles, and female subordination was handed down to succeeding generations through school lessons, church sermons, popular genres, and learned literatures and then naturalized by the eighteenth-century natural sciences. The Swedish botanist Linnaeus, for instance, used a sexual system of "female" pistils and "male" stamens to divide the vegetable world into classes, orders, genera, and species. His British popularizers not only borrowed the language of human sex-gender to describe plant functions but adorned their books with etchings of Adam and Eve and Miltonic quotations. The naturalized doctrine lived on in the founding texts of modern biology such as Charles Darwin's *The Descent of Man, and Selection in Relation to Sex* (1871). Man, Darwin echoed Milton, "is considerably taller, heavier, and stronger than woman, with squarer shoulders and more plainly-pronounced muscles"; he is also "more courageous, pugnacious, and energetic than woman, and has a more inventive genius."[15] The Darwinian slide from body to intellect, temperament, and behavior, which arguably was a plausible logic before the modern disciplines partitioned the biological and social territory, metamorphosed into the hereditarian hypothesis of twentieth-century biology.

In the late nineteenth century, biology was institutionalized in research universities and laboratories in Germany and the United States where it began to form specialisms. Driven by departmentalization, research funding, and graduate training, the specialisms developed into what biologist Steven Rose calls "a strange amalgam of different disciplines," each one focused on living organisms at a particular level and producing within-level causal explanations. When asked to explain what causes a frog's muscle to twitch (to use Rose's example), a biochemist would reply that the interdigitation of actin and myosin causes fibrous contractions; a physiologist would describe brain impulses passing down the motor nerve that signal the muscle to contract; and a developmental biologist would proceed from the embryonic specialization of cells to the capacity for muscle twitching.[16] The production of specialized explanations created a knowledge problem: to establish causality, biologists would have to link the within-level explanations up and down the levels.

Two frameworks were available. Holism, which assumed that the properties of a complex system informed the activities of its parts, would produce top-down explanations, and reductionism, which assumed that molecular events informed higher level activities, would produce bottom-up explanations. Rose argues that biology's intellectual commitments over the centuries—to the Cartesian disaggregation of complexities to simples, nineteenth-century mechanical materialism, and late-nineteenth-century hereditarianism—turned it toward reductionism.[17] Other scholars have pointed out that reductionism was not merely an intellectual preference but a possibility realized through innovations—instruments constituting ever smaller objects of investigation and methods of controlling, randomizing, and weighting factors that supported finer cause-and-effect discriminations.[18] So biology's intellectual formation went hand-in-hand with its instrumental and institutional formation, and its intellectual, instrumental, and institutional orders enabled the central dogma of modern molecular biology to emerge. That dogma, formulated by James Watson and Francis Crick in the mid-1950s, holds that DNA is a master molecule whose information flows one way from genes to the realization of the individual's form and function. Today, observed feminist biologist Ruth Hubbard, most biologists, chemists, and physicists "believe that the 'lower' levels, such as atoms and molecules, are more 'basic' and have intrinsically greater explanatory power."[19]

During the twentieth century, these same forces pushed sex-difference research through increasingly lower levels—from fetal sex differentiation to gametes and amphimixis (the union of sperm and egg), to chromosomes and mixis (the mixing of these materials to produce new genotypes), and recently to a sex-determining gene on the Y chromosome.[20] This research, argues Hubbard, does not prove that sex has a determining genetic core because:

> The phenomena we observe at the subatomic, atomic, molecular, cellular, organismic, or societal levels are all taking place simultaneously and constitute a single reality. It is an outcome of Western cultural history and of the history of professionalization that we have developed separate academic disciplines to describe these levels as though they were different phenomena. In fact, the only reason we think in terms of these levels is that we have developed specialties that draw distinctions between them. But the distinctions are not part of nature.[21]

Biology, however, needed reductionism to preserve the coherence of its organisms, the integrity of its causal explanations, and the amalgamation of its disciplines. Given this formation, feminist critiques that challenge bottom-up causality or expose between-level discontinuities appear to shake the reductionist pilasters that support the whole disciplinary edifice. But do these critiques really subvert biologized sex? I am going to argue that they can't—not yet and maybe never.

AN EXAMPLE: BUTLER

Feminist scientists, Ruth Bleier mused in 1986, have "demonstrated, at least to women" that the sciences are social formations whose structures, ideologies, and languages can be analyzed by using the critical-historical methods employed in the humanities.[22] Indeed, such work has been done by feminists from a range of disciplines: neurophysiologist Bleier; biologists Ruth Hubbard, Anne Fausto-Sterling, and Bonnie Spanier; psychologists Rhoda Unger, Suzanne Kessler, and Stephanie Shields; anthropologist Wendy McKenna; philosophers Sandra Harding and Helen Longino; historian Londa Schiebinger; and literary scholar Julia Epstein, to name a few. Although I readily grant that both empirical and critical-historical methods can demystify biologized sex, I don't think they can subvert it. Since *subvert* means overthrowing something at its foundation, we need to be clear about what is at the foundation of biologized sex.

In her celebrated book *Gender Trouble: Feminism and the Subversion of Identity* (1990), philosopher Judith Butler set out "to expose the foundational categories of sex, gender, and desire as effects of a specific formation of power." She argued that all foundationalisms—whether science's use of sex to ground gender or feminism's use of experience to ground the category of women—subscribe to a metaphysics of substance, a Nietzschean phrase referring to the belief that a person is "a substantive thing." Instead of thinking that bodies have a substantive sex (the essentialist version) or that bodied persons signify a substantive sex (the representationalist version), Butler urged her readers to recognize that "the category of 'sex' is itself a *gendered* category, fully politically invested, naturalized but not natural." Once we understand that identities are the "resulting effect of a rule-bound discourse that inserts itself in the pervasive and mundane signifying acts of linguistic life," we can exercise our agency through signifying practices to subvert the constructs they have produced. The subversion of identities, she concluded, can be accomplished by producing "a critical genealogy of the naturalization of sex and of bodies in general" that "establishes as political the very terms through which identity is articulated."[23]

In *Bodies That Matter: On the Discursive Limits of "Sex"* (1993), Butler wanted to clarify "some parts of *Gender Trouble* that have caused confusion" for its readers—including what she meant by performativity, constructedness, materiality, and other terms she had applied to sex, gender, and sexuality. When she used the term *performativity* in the earlier book, she did not mean that "a willful and instrumental subject" could wake up each morning and choose the gender and sex garments she would wear that day. Neither gender nor sex is "an artifice to be taken on or taken off at will and, hence, not an effect of choice." To dispel the liberal-individualist notion of choice and clarify some related issues, she presented an intricate analysis of the power of discourse to materialize sex. Although I cannot do justice to Butler's analysis in a one-sentence summary, I would say that she defines sex as an "ideal construct . . . whose materialization is compelled" by discourses that have the power to produce norms through reiteration and regulation.[24] Butler (like Laclau and Mouffe) emphasizes that discourse consists of rule-bound material(izing) practices stabilized for a time, but she does not, in my opinion, adequately attend to the institutionalization that calcifies discursive practice.

Substantive sex is recalcitrant not merely because high-status sciences promulgate the ideational construct and normative discourses regulate practice. It is recalcitrant because it is entrenched in institutions that study and treat substantive bodies: university departments, laboratories, community hospitals, counseling services, and self-help groups. It is recalcitrant because it is concretized and commodified by industries that sculpt substantive bodies and shape substantive desires: fitness, diet, fashion, cosmetics, plastic surgery, pharmaceuticals, retail, entertainment. . . . Compelling arguments against the presumption of substantive sex may persuade disciplinarians to add a little social analysis to their sex research and may convince clinicians to lighten up on their normalizing treatments, but will the arguments deter the thousands of ordinary people who reproduce this presumption every time they ask for a Viagra prescription, visit a fertility clinic, attend a Weight Watchers meeting, buy a Wonderbra, or climb on a Stairmaster? The work that would have to be done to subvert substantive sex is restructuring the institutionalized and corporatized economies that (re)produce it.

Constru(ct)ing Gender

When feminists adopted the term *gender* in the mid-1970s, Joan W. Scott remarked in a 1986 article on whether it was a useful category of historical analysis, they wanted to reject "the biological determinism implicit in the use of such terms as 'sex' or 'sexual difference'" and to "introduce a relational" mode of analysis into feminist studies at a time when it "focused too narrowly and separately on women."[25] But what began as a solution turned into a problem. Twenty years later, *gender* had accumulated so many definitions, applications, and criticisms that it had become a flashpoint issue debated at conferences and in publications, such as a 1997 issue of *Signs* that featured a long article by Mary Hawkesworth and several responses. Hawkesworth started with a tour of the many ways feminist scholars had operationalized gender—among them, as stereotypes, cognitive schema, and structures of consciousness; as social roles and status, relations among women and men, the social organization of activities, the effects of systems of (re)production; as personality traits, psychic structures, and identity performances; and as media images, cultural ideologies, and the semiotics of the body. Then she asked, "Should this multiplicity of meaning be a source of concern to feminist scholars? Can one concept encompass such a vast terrain? Does deployment of gender as an analytic category enhance our understanding of the various modes of oppression that circumscribe women's lives?"[26] It seems to me that the questions about the numerosity and utility of gender's meanings asked by Hawkesworth and her respondents beg the preliminary question. What was it about their discourses that drove feminist scholars to constitute so many subjective, societal, and symbolic versions of gender? In what follows, I describe some of the transactions within and across disciplines that specified, criticized, revised, and finally undercut gender as a discursive object.

HISTORY AND LITERARY STUDIES

Before cliometrics revealed the slowly fluctuating systems of the *longue durée* and before deconstruction exposed the capricious instabilities of linguistic meaning, history and literary studies delineated the lives and contributions of great men. Although the sister disciplines had different organizing schemes, they deployed similar strategies for disposing of women. Historians took the nation (or some part of it) as their unit of analysis and events, activities, and processes as the phenomena to be explained; literary scholars took the text as their unit of analysis and its form, meaning, and value as the phenomena to be explained. Each discipline had a construct that divided the important phenomena from the unimportant ones—the public sphere in history and the canon in literature. Historians directed their attention to the activities of making laws, governments, wars, and wealth that constituted the public sphere and ignored the everyday activities that occurred in the private sphere. Since most nations had prevented women from assuming public leadership positions, historians could easily discard the few who did influence national developments. The women who acted from quasi-public positions were "passed over as insignificant," and those who held public office "were said to be as ruthless as, or wrote like, or had the brains of men."[27] In literary studies, the task of discarding the thousands of women writers who had been published from the late seventeenth century onward would have been very difficult if scholars had not been able to ignore the many who had faded from disciplinary memory as over time their works went out of print and their names were eliminated from bibliographies. Critics disposed of the rest by deploying the strategies of segregation and denigration used by historians. The first, as Mary Ellmann observed, was to follow the basic "working rule [that] there must always be two literatures like two public toilets, one for Men and one for Women."[28] On this rule, critics used feminine stereotypes to characterize the features of women's texts and then downgraded them for not conforming to the conventions of genre, subject matter, and style exhibited by the canon of male-authored texts. The other strategy was to describe women writers who did measure up to the canonical standards not as exceptionally talented but as exceptionally sexed: they had masculine minds in female bodies. By operationalizing segregation to discard most women and anomalization to explain the few achievers, disciplinarians could preserve the male-gendered public sphere and literary canon.

At first, feminist historians and literary scholars performed the same two tasks of criticizing the sexist statements that littered the disciplinary scholarship and recovering data on women's lives and contributions. Burrowing into the dusty repositories, they found biographies of "women worthies" in the arts, sciences, religion, education, and philanthropy; texts from the *querelle des femmes* on female character; treatises of women's rights; and literary works—the three-decker novels, slim volumes of poetry, and collected letters.[29] The clues in published texts led them to unpublished records—diaries, parish registers, household accounts—that contained the traces of forgotten women. With these materials, they wrote about ordinary as well as notable women and communities as well as individuals. On setting these stories into the narratives of history and literature, they realized that the disciplinary scenarios would have to be reshaped. Instead of an industrial revolution powered by British technology, capital, and colonial trade, history would have to describe an economy congealing more slowly from the activities of women and men who were wage laborers, colonial slaves, and consumers. Instead of a great tradition that leapfrogged from the early eighteenth-century novelists (Defoe, Fielding, Richardson, Smollett, and Sterne) to the early nineteenth-century ones (Austen and Scott), literary history would have to describe the genre innovations made by hundreds of female-authored novels published between these two moments. What happened next was a shift that caused feminist history to diverge from feminist literary criticism.

Feminist historians began to see through the surface of historical narratives to the constructs that disciplinarians had used to select, interpret, and order their data. In a paper prepared for the 1974 Berkshire Conference, Gerda Lerner observed that feminist historians "have applied questions from traditional history to women, and tried to fit women's past into the empty spaces of historical scholarship. . . . Perhaps it would be useful to refer to this work as 'transitional women's history,' seeing it as an inevitable step in the development of new criteria and concepts."[30] While doing research on African-American women and the early twentieth-century pioneers of women's social history, Lerner had encountered constructs—Marxism's class analysis, social history's definition of the family, demography's aggregated populations, and history's periods—that didn't accommodate the new data on women. The exposure of organizing constructs proceeded quickly. In a 1975 review essay, Barbara Sicherman noted that the research on particular communities of women had raised questions about the disciplinary doxa—that women had higher status in preindustrial than industrial nations, that statistical averaging captured the patterns of marriage, childbirth, and widowhood, and that neutral measures were used to gauge societal progress.[31] A year later Joan Kelly declared that the project of restoring women to history indicated that the periods needed different contours and characterizations, that sex was a crosscutting social category, and that theories of socioeconomic change had to accommodate the relationality of the sexes.[32] By 1977, according to Carolyn Lougee, feminist historians were no longer trying "to squeeze women into the orthodox schemes"; they were formulating "their own purposes, criteria, and guidelines," borrowing methods from other disciplines, analyzing the interpenetration of the private and public spheres, and studying women and men relationally.[33]

But feminist literary scholars and critics were still hewing to the disciplinary conventions. Elaine Showalter's review article on work published in 1974 and Annette Kolodny's on work published in 1975 showed that feminists were churning out studies in the traditional scholarly genres: biographies, collected letters, editions, textual interpretations, and studies of literary themes and images. Both reviewers identified methodology as simultaneously a strength and a weakness. Showalter argued that the critical individualism, empiricism, and eclecticism that enabled feminists to recover women writers and reinterpret texts made feminist literary studies look "deceptively easy" to mainstream colleagues who valued "a solid system of critical theory." Kolodny similarly asserted that the "set of interchangeable strategies" used by feminists did not support the development of feminist theory or impress "the larger academic and critical community."[34] The methods they identified as problematical for feminist literary studies I see as paradigmatic for the discipline. Consider, as a piece of evidence, Showalter's "Feminist Criticism in the Wilderness" (1981). Writing at a time when the discipline was preoccupied with high theory, Showalter described feminist criticism as "an empirical orphan in the theoretical storm" because it was still churning out critiques of sexism in literary texts and studies of "the history, styles, themes, genres, and structures of writing by women." In doing this work, feminists used four interpretive schema: biological criticism regarded women's texts as literally or metaphorically bearing the marks of female anatomy, linguistic criticism analyzed the gender differences inscribed in language, psychoanalytic criticism used theories of gendered subjectivity to read texts, and cultural criticism focused on women's traditions. Thus, while feminist historians were working outside and against the disciplinary paradigm by exposing the gendered organization of societal and disciplinary activities, feminist literary critics were still working within the disciplinary paradigm by interpreting the gender traces in literary texts and traditions.[35]

Although the early articles and books can easily be discounted now, they were powerfully illuminating then. Reading them, we experienced the "click," that sudden moment of comprehension laced with anger and elation when for the first time we recognized what the disciplines had done and we saw a way out. We saw ourselves climbing out of our own morass of details, impressions, and hunches to view the summits of gender analysis and theory we would have to scale. In retrospect, I would have to say that feminist historians and literary scholars ascended on the paths already cut by their disciplines. One group, traversing the fields of society, theorized gender as socially organized. The other group, winding through the labyrinths of textuality, theorized it as symbolically inscribed.

PSYCHOLOGY AND ANTHROPOLOGY

During the 1950s and 1960s, psychology was a relentlessly positivist-empiricist science of human behavior that took the subject pool as its unit of analysis, the experiment as its model, measurement as its method, and sex as a variable of one kind or another. When they investigated supposedly neutral topics, psychologists regarded sex as a nuisance variable to be eliminated from research by using male subjects and then generalizing the findings to the human condition.[36] For sex-difference research, they considered it to be an organismic variable because the objective was to demonstrate that the physiology of sex differentiation caused further perceptual, cognitive, temperamental, and behavioral differences.[37] For studies of stereotypes and roles, they treated sex as a social variable that operated from birth onward through various forms of socialization. Through the early 1970s, psychologists used the term *sex* to describe biological traits, social roles, and cognitive schema alike; but *gender* began to appear in behavioral research during the mid-1960s when a few psychologists borrowed the term from grammarians, who used it to denote the inflectional forms of words and the agreement that had to obtain between them (e.g., the feminine singular endings of an adjective-noun pair). Lawrence Kohlberg, for instance, coined the phrase "gender constancy" to denote a child's ability to recognize that a "person's sex is not changed by changing clothes or hair styles, but remains as a constant attribute of the person throughout life" and to perceive that another person's sex is the same as his own. On his model, the child's developmental achievement was to see sex as grammarians saw words—by apprehending the fixed and formal identity beneath the superficial inflections. Though widely hailed as an innovative developmental theorist, Kohlberg did not question the mainstream biological assumption that people had an intrinsic sex; he only wanted to know when and how children grasped this fact of nature.[38]

That was the state of disciplinary affairs when feminists began to review published studies and conduct empirical research.[39] Working in the subfield of sex stereotypes and roles, Inge Broverman and her colleagues (most were clinicians at Worcester and Boston area hospitals) coauthored two groundbreaking articles that were avidly read by academic and movement feminists. The 1970 article showed that psychiatrists, psychologists,

and social workers based patient diagnoses and treatment on stereotypes
—the healthy man as logical, competent, self-confident, and independent
and the healthy woman as emotional, passive, home-oriented, and dependent. The 1972 Broverman et al. article found widespread popular consensus about sex-role standards in the United States: people of both sexes
conformed to sex roles, valued male-typed activities over female-typed
ones, and believed that men were superior to women.[40] By using the
phrase "gender identity" to denote these behaviors and beliefs, the authors
were attempting to redescribe biologized identity as socially learned identity. Although Broverman and her collaborators presented empirically
grounded work, their foray into the social no doubt accounted for the fact
that their articles were published in marginal rather than mainstream
journals—the first one in the *Journal of Consulting Psychology*, the venue for
an applied subfield devalued by the discipline, and the second in a special
feminist issue of the *Journal of Social Issues* (*JSI*), which was the organ of
the Society for the Psychological Study of Social Issues (SPSSI). Formed in
1936 by sociologists and social psychologists who were alarmed by government repression of political dissenters and corporate influence on the
academy, SPSSI focused on analyzing propaganda, lobbying for research on
social problems, and defending colleagues who were being persecuted.
The journal's 1972 feminist issue was titled *New Perspectives on Women* and
featured articles by anthropologists, sociologists, and political scientists as
well as the Broverman study. In keeping with *JSI*'s mission of bringing
"theory and practice into focus on the human problems of the group, the
community, and the nation" and making scientific findings accessible to
general readers,[41] editors Martha Shuch Mednick and Sandra Schwartz
Tangri expressed their hope that academic knowledge could serve progressive social-movement agendas and urged their readers to support all
liberationist struggles against war, capitalism, racism, and sexism.[42] This
approach may have been politically correct in the movements, but it
wasn't practicable in a discipline with a biologized canon that expected its
scientists to hew to the rationalist-empiricist line.

Two years later, Stanford University Press published *The Psychology of
Sex Differences* (1974), an exhaustive and exacting review of more than a
thousand sex-difference studies published during the preceding ten years.
Authors Eleanor Emmons Maccoby and Carol Nagy Jacklin concluded
that many between-sex differences in perception, cognition, temperament, and behavior had been posited but only a few had been proved—
namely that girls demonstrated greater verbal ability, boys performed

better on tests of spatial and mathematical abilities, and males were more aggressive than females. Believing that socialization played a larger role than biology in the formation of children's abilities and behaviors, Maccoby and Jacklin made two social recommendations: societies should choose "the option of minimizing, rather than maximizing, sex differences" and "adults of both sexes [should be] involved in the care of children of both sexes."[43] Their book had the effect of transporting biologized sex differences into the social field where other feminist psychologists were initiating studies of gender stereotyping in the media, popular culture, and professional fields; comparative research on gender roles in diverse cultures and intracultural groups; and longitudinal research on role change during the life course.[44] As feminist psychologists pushed further into the social field, they began to investigate topics studied by feminists in other disciplines—family, work, sexuality, health, discrimination, and violence. These overlaps were the sites where exchange took place and hybridized specialisms formed.

Maccoby and Jacklin's book also discussed several flaws in the design, inference, and reporting of sex-difference research that other feminists would also criticize. An obvious flaw was that most subject pools consisted of white, middle-class, American children, college students, or adults; without comparative data on people from American ethnic or racial minorities, other nations, or lower income levels, the generalizations about biologically based sex differences were unwarranted. Less obvious flaws occurred, for instance, in research that tested children's modalities of perception. From findings that boys perceived more through looking and girls through listening, researchers inferred that sex-differentiated biological causes had produced sex-differentiated spatial and verbal skills. But the research design was faulty: it didn't incorporate data on situational cues that might elicit looking or listening, on the within-sex differences for each modality, and on the children's neurological development, socialization in perception, and preferences for looking or listening. Although the measurements may have been precise, it was unclear which between-sex differences had been measured—biological, social, or situational—and exactly how significant they were relative to within-sex differences.

Feminists were also concerned with the pattern of reporting findings. When research indicated sex differences, the findings were published and publicized, but when research indicated no differences or statistically insignificant ones, the so-called negative result usually went unreported by the researchers and unpublished by journals. Why? Because the negative result was regarded as an instance of the null hypothesis; that is, the result taken to mean that the hypothesized difference did not show in this particular study or with respect to the particular ability being investigated.[45] Since journals seldom published no-difference findings, researchers were spared the appearance of anomalies that would prompt them to question the adequacy of the sex-differences hypothesis. And since psychology did not have a research program on sex similarities, researchers didn't have to interpret no-difference findings as evidence of a sex-similarities hypothesis. Psychology lacked, as Foucault would have said, a discursive context that would make no-difference findings meaningful as challenges to the dominant hypothesis and as facts about men and women.

The obverse of psychology in most respects, anthropology took the social group as its unit of analysis, field research as its method, and the social organization of primate, protohuman, and human groups as the phenomenon it wanted to explain. But in formulating explanations anthropologists tended, as Rayna R. Reiter put it, to "read rather directly from biology to culture"[46] and construct narratives such as the evolutionary one that featured males preserving the species' adaptive traits through competition for reproductive access to females, males honing early human skills and tools through hunting, and males dominating females through the sexual division of productive/reproductive labor. To challenge the "biology-to-culture" paradigm, feminists reviewed the ethnographic literature and conducted their own fieldwork. Primatologists who studied physiologically dimorphic and nondimorphic species documented their plasticity of behavior and diversity of social organization; these findings controverted the twin theses that physiological differences naturally eventuated in male dominance and that data on nonhuman primates could be used to bolster claims about women's subjugation. Anthropologists who did fieldwork in non-Western and Western cultures provided a wealth of comparative data—on the traits ascribed to the sexes, the activities performed by them, the number of sex categories (e.g., male, female, and berdache in some Native-American groups), and the importance of nonsexual categories (e.g., generation or residence)—that undercut biological determinism. Others conducted longitudinal studies on the complex processes—such as environmental events, migration, trading, warfare, and the penetration of Western capitalism—that modified the forms of social organization.[47]

Feminist anthropologists also noted that male anthropologists rarely studied women with the same assiduity as they studied men, obtained data on women from male informants, and set women's roles at "the edges of [their] description" of social organization.[48] But instead of developing a rationalist-empiricist critique of sex-difference research as feminist psychologists had done, they assembled a theory of disciplinary consciousness by drawing on a broad range of social thought: anthropology's distinction between emic and etic perspectives (i.e., the conceptual schemes of the subject population and the researcher), Marx's notion of the proletariat and capitalist standpoints, Dubois's description of the double consciousness of black people in racist society, and Phyllis Kaberry and Jane Goodale's sensitivity to the perspectives of their female subjects.[49] As Rayna Reiter put it,

> All anthropologists wear the blinders of their own civilization in approaching other cultures; our eyes are as conditioned as those of the people we study. Our own academic training reflects, supports, and extends the assumptions of male superiority to which our culture subscribes. The vast majority of anthropologists who survive training, fieldwork, degree-getting, and publishing to give us our information are either men, or women trained by men. We might say that the selection for people who agree on what the important questions are and how they are to be answered is strong, and is strongly male oriented.[50]

Trained to analyze social organization, feminists in anthropology were better equipped than those in literary studies, psychology, and history to constitute gender as a coproduction of social structures and subjective structures.

SEX-GENDER SYSTEMS AND STANDPOINT THEORY

From the mid-1970s to the end of the decade, the several streams of feminist-studies discourse I have sketched—the diminution of biological sex, the formulation of social, subjective, and symbolic gender, and the critiques of disciplinary constructs and methods—were congealing in the twin theories of sex-gender systems and standpoints. Together these theories attempted to integrate what the traditional academic discourses had sundered: subjective, societal, and knowledge formations.

In her groundbreaking article "The Traffic in Women: Notes on the 'Political Economy' of Sex" (1975), Gayle Rubin, who was then a doctoral student in anthropology at the University of Michigan, set herself the daunting task of rethinking the "genesis of women's oppression and social subordination" and the changes that would have to be made "in order to achieve a society without gender hierarchy." Engaging the work of Freud, Deutsch, Horney, Lacan, Marx, Engels, Althusser, Balibar, Mauss, Lévi-Strauss, Derrida, and Wittig, Rubin described her method as an exegetical reading that would move "from the explicit content" of the texts to their "presuppositions and implications."[51] But she did not stop at exposing the problematics of psychoanalysis, Marxism, and structuralism; rather, she went on to invert traditional formulations of sex. Where traditionalists claimed that biological sex expressed itself as differences in personality and behavior, she counterclaimed that socially organized gender suppressed the similarities in personality and behavior. Where they defined the incest taboo as an explicit prohibition of certain heterosexual unions, she redefined it as an implicit prohibition of homosexual unions. Where they credited the sexual division of labor with ensuring the mutual dependency of the sexes, she criticized it for dividing them into mutually exclusive categories.

Integrating these bits, Rubin articulated the proposition that sexed, gendered, and sexual identities were the effects of people's insertion into an economy of reproduction with its relations of kinship and household, exchange and ownership that she called the sex-gender system. Rubin cautioned her readers that "sex-gender system," like "political economy," was a generic phrase that designated a domain, not a type, to be analyzed. Just as political economies came in feudal, socialist, or capitalist forms, so sex-gender systems were organized in a variety of ways. When feminists used the term *patriarchy* to refer to all nonegalitarian systems, they were making a mistake that would be analogous to using *capitalism* to refer to all political economies that devalued, exploited, or oppressed workers; as a result of using the generic term to denote specific systems, they concluded that women's oppression was a trans-historical and -cultural phenomenon. From her analysis, Rubin extrapolated two lessons for contemporary feminists: they "should not aim for the elimination of men, but for the elimination of the social system which creates sexism and gender" and they should realize that the social system can only "be reorganized through political action."[52]

By the late 1970s, feminists had theorized sex-gender systems and standpoints. The sex-gender system consisted of the multivalent arrangements—material, social, and symbolic—that produced sex, gender, and sexuality. Described by Sandra Harding in 1983 as an "*organic* social variable" like race and class, the sex-gender system was organic because it organized "social life throughout most recorded history and in every culture today" and variable because it was "expressed in differing intensities and forms in different cultures and classes." In contemporary Western societies, it took the form of "a system of male-dominance made possible by men's control of women's productive and reproductive labor, where 'reproduction' is broadly construed to include sexuality, family life, and kinship formations, as well as the birthing which biologically reproduces the species."[53] Standpoint theory was indebted to Marxist thought when it premiered and then picked up ethnomethodological, multicultural, and poststructural inflections in the work of Dorothy E. Smith, Nancy Hartsock, Sandra Harding, Patricia Hill Collins, and others.[54] It was developed to refute the disciplinary epistemology, which, as Harding summarized it, claimed that "only the impersonal, disinterested, socially anonymous representatives of human reason" who used rigorous and value-neutral methods were "capable of producing [true] knowledge."[55] Standpoint theorists started with the gendered, classed, and raced social formation and went on to argue that individuals were differentially positioned in its web of relations, which in turn shaped their different consciousness of reality and their (mis)representations of it.

Standpoint theory was perhaps best exemplified in the work of black women sociologists. In her many discussions of black women's consciousness, Patricia Hill Collins pointed out that the countless black women who worked in privileged white households and establishments were positioned as outsiders-within mainstream American society; their insider knowledge demystified the ideology that whites succeeded through superior talents, and their outsider status gave them a critical perspective on the racism that maintained white advantage. Moreover, since most black women were located at the intersection of racism, sexism, and classism, they understood these systems as interlocking oppressions that produced intensified effects. Bearing this consciousness, Collins argued, black women sociologists would be wary of sociological doctrine and insider status.[56] Collins's remarks aptly describe the sociological standpoint deployed ten years earlier in Joyce A. Ladner's *Tomorrow's Tomorrow* (1971), a groundbreaking study of adolescent black girls growing up in the infamous Pruitt-Ingoe housing project in St. Louis. Rejecting the discipline's pathologizing model of black self-hatred and deviance model of black family life, Ladner wanted to show that the Pruitt-Ingoe girls and women were strong people coping with not only the harsh circumstances of racism, poverty, and sexism but also a double-bind—namely, that society expected them to conform to white, middle-class norms while denying them the resources they needed to do so. Lest her sociological readers get caught up in the affecting interview material and miss her inversion of the disciplinary perspective, Ladner made it perfectly clear: "It is only when the analysis of the oppressive forces which produce various forms of anti-social behavior has been conducted that we can reverse the conceptualization of pathology. *The society, instead of its members, becomes pathological.*" And lest her white, middle-class, feminist readers confuse their problems with those of black women, she set them straight: black women never had "the protective shelters which society has imposed on white women" nor the luxury of struggling "over equalization of power in interpersonal relations" with men.[57]

The title of Harding's essay posed a question that I want to answer: "Why Has the Sex/Gender System Become Visible Only Now?" Sex-gender systems and standpoints emerged when feminists consolidated the work they had been doing in their discrete disciplines. On the ontological plane, feminists chipped little bits of human behavior away from biologized sex and transported them to the social field where they began constru(ct)ing gender within the precincts of their disciplines. Historical gender consisted of people performing socially organized activities whereas anthropological gender foregrounded the forms of social organization that specified people's positions and activities. Psychological gender emphasized the identity schema that people learned and enacted whereas literary gender focused on the linguistically constituted differences inscribed in people's texts and conversations. Meanwhile, on the epistemological plane, feminists had shifted from claiming that disciplinary knowledges misrepresented the real natures of women and men to asserting that disciplinary methods and constructs generated what passed for truth about people and societies. When these ontological and epistemological bits came together as a social constructivist paradigm, feminists could theorize subject, societal, and knowledge formations.

AN EXAMPLE: CHODOROW

Having conceptualized this expansive cross-disciplinary model of subject, societal, and knowledge formation, feminists were constrained by their disciplines when they attempted to investigate it. Consider the reception accorded to Nancy Chodorow's *The Reproduction of Mothering: Psychoanalysis and the Sociology of Gender* (1978). In this book and some preliminary articles, Chodorow had used the discourses of psychoanalysis and social psychology to theorize the reproduction of gender identity in families where mothers did the intersubjective and caretaking work of parenting. Her work was based on what the twin theories had posited: the coproduction of social and self structures. It showed that the asymmetrical family was a matrix where psychosocial practices produced gendered subjects whose practices as adults renewed society's gendered processes. Chodorow's work was more widely dispersed across the disciplines than that of any other single feminist scholar up to that time and probably for a long while afterward. The book was read by feminists from a range of disciplines, the theory was widely hailed and debated, and the analysis was applied in such areas as moral development, education, political philosophy, psychoanalysis, literary studies, history, and philosophy of science.[58]

Nevertheless, the responses to Chodorow's work highlight the difficulties that discipline-trained feminists have had in appraising, let alone doing, cross-disciplinary analysis. In a 1981 *Signs* forum on *The Reproduction of Mothering,* two contributors faulted her theory on different methodological grounds. Sociologist Judith Lorber confessed that she had read the book as "primarily an exegesis of psychoanalytic theory and, therefore, in my eyes, a lesser contribution to the sociology of gender" than Chodorow's earlier articles. Lorber found "the evidence [from patient and therapist accounts] too narrow to support her conclusions" and complained about the lack of "social structural and behavioral analyses." Alice Rossi, who identified herself as "a developmental biosocial scientist, with strong research inclinations to behavior science," was unprepared for "so extended an exegesis of psychoanalytic theory" and spent "a good deal of time" translating "some of Chodorow's terms and concepts." Because Chodorow had rejected "theories in biology and developmental psychology" and relied on clinical cases, Rossi declared, "the book cannot be viewed as the expression of substantiated, tested theory."[59] The disciplinary predilections evident in Lorber's wanting more social-structural analysis and Rossi's wanting more biobehavioral evidence continued to inform the critiques of Chodorow's work. In 1988, philosopher Elizabeth V. Spelman challenged the theory with a closely reasoned, text-based rebuttal of its logic that was typical of her discipline, and in 1989 microstructural sociologists Ralph Larossa, Maureen Mulligan Larossa, and Barbara J. Risman challenged it with empirical research on fathers' parenting practices.[60] For her part, Chodorow understandably mistook her critics' disciplinary leanings for an antipathy to psychoanalytic theory because when she answered them in *Feminism and Psychoanalytic Theory* (1989) she restated its value and her commitment to it.[61] All of Chodorow's critics seemed to be doing the same thing: they were judging the adequacy of the data and inferences that grounded her theory. But they were also doing different things: when they addressed a cross-disciplinary model of identity formation, they were performing distinctively disciplinary practices.

During this same period, Chodorow's theory of gender identity formation was also criticized for its identity logic. In her celebrated article "Compulsory Heterosexuality and Lesbian Existence" (1980), Adrienne Rich argued that Chodorow, by failing to examine the institutionalized strategies—sexual, affective, economic, educational, political, and legal—that compelled heterosexual identity and family form, was stuck trying to reform hetero-mothering instead of trying to subvert the hetero-regime itself. Ten years later when *Signs* (1990) published another forum on mothering, the issue editors granted that Chodorow had intended to unmask "the myth of the ideal mother [as] a central tool of patriarchy" but warned their readers to be chary of theories positing "the universality of the experience of motherhood across culture, color, class, and history."[62] To illustrate the diverse providers and practices of what Chodorow had called mothering, they included articles on government homes in mid–twentieth-century Belgian Africa, childcare services in the United States today, and households in Tudor England.

From my discussion in this section, it should be clear that when feminist scholars and scientists investigated sex-gender systems they were doing precisely what standpoint theory predicted they would do. Positioned by disciplinary, identity, and political discourses, they were generating new knowledges and critiques of these knowledges according to their positions within these crosshatched discourses. The knowledges and critiques brought home a sobering realization about sex-gender systems: understanding these complex and expansive economies would be difficult and in the end inadequate, because to map any social formation feminists would need an analysis that captured its diversified identities and oppressions.

Multiplying Identities and Oppressions

Everyone from senior scholars to undergraduate students knows that the most contentious issue in feminist studies has been the practitioners' identity politics. Everyone has encountered criticisms of feminists bearing privileged identities—white, heterosexual, and upper or middle class—for ignoring, marginalizing, or actively oppressing people of other races, ethnicities, nationalities, sexualities, and classes. The grievance modality of identity discourse, as I shall call it, has been extraordinarily productive within feminism as well as U.S. culture and society; it spawned, as Susan Stanford Friedman explained in a recent article, ritualized scripts of accusation, denial, and confession that pit "us" against "them."[63] Although the framing of grievances is an important step in the construction of collective identity and action, this grievance discourse has been counterproductive for progressives and feminists because its ritualization has a numbing effect (as ritualization always does) that causes us to reiterate claims that fuel identity-group hostilities that in turn sabotage the work of building the alliances needed to make academic and societal change.

The story of identity politics within and around academic feminism is, I think, more complicated than ritualized claims acknowledge. Academic identity discourses unspooled themselves in four modalities: scholarship on the lives and times of identity groups, critical-historical analyses of oppressions, theories synthesizing subject and social formation, and grievances about academic delimitation. By delimitation, I mean determinations of who does and doesn't speak, write, and act on which issues, in which venues, and through which conventions. Using African-American women as my example, I want to look at academic delimitation—the sites where it occurred and the agents who effected it—and then segue into the modeling of multiple identities and oppressions.

ACADEMIC INSTITUTIONS

In previous chapters, we saw that the power to delimit populations and discourses was dispersed throughout the academic apparatus. It was wielded by committees that made decisions on admissions, student aid, and research grants; by faculty who determined employment, education, and knowledges; by editors and reviewers who vetted submissions for publication; by organizers who chose conference formats and presentations; and even by the mass media that conferred newsworthiness on scholarly issues. To judge from the outcomes, the higher-education system continued to delimit racial minorities while it grew exponentially from 1960 to 1980, lurched through a series of fiscal crises from the mid-1970s to the mid-1980s, and modulated into a corporatized form during the prosperous 1990s.

Two trends that started in the mid-1970s should have converged with the expansion of higher education to open its gates to racial minorities: academic institutions implemented antidiscrimination policies and affirmative-action plans, and the gap in high-school graduation rates between some racial minorities (especially African Americans) and whites narrowed.[64] But expansion, affirmative action, and improved graduation rates had minimal impact on the racial composition of the student body and the professoriate. From 1980 to the mid-1990s, the percentage of white high school graduates enrolling in college rose and that of African-American and Hispanic-American high school graduates declined. In 1995, the numbers of minority-group students enrolling in college began to increase but their proportions in the nationwide enrollment remained low: for the 1997 enrollment, .8 percent were Native Americans, 8 percent were Hispanic Americans, and 10.6 percent were African Americans. During this same period, the total number of doctorates awarded increased, but both the number and the proportional share earned by racial minorities remained small. For 1996 doctorates, less than .5 percent went to Native Americans, 2.5 percent to Hispanic Americans, and 4.6 percent to African Americans.[65] For African Americans (and perhaps other groups), the gross percentages are somewhat misleading for two reasons. First, they were not evenly distributed across the disciplines: in 1996, African Americans received 10 percent of the doctorates in education but only 2 percent of the doctorates in many of the natural sciences, social sciences, and humanities. English and American literature, a field that awarded nearly 60 percent of its doctorates to (predominantly white) women from 1993 on, granted a minuscule share to African Americans. Of 819 doctorates awarded in 1993, 759 went to whites and 18 to African Americans (2.2 percent). Of 943 doctorates awarded in 1994, 780 went to whites and 26 to African Americans (3.3 percent). Of 1,080 doctorates awarded in 1995, 883 went to whites and 18 to African Americans (1.6 percent).[66] Second, African-American recipients of these literature doctorates had earned their undergraduate degrees at twenty-one institutions, of which eighteen were historically black colleges. Without the historically black colleges, which were educating about 100,000 students annually, African-American enrollments at the undergraduate and graduate levels would have been even smaller.

Two decades after academic institutions had set out to remedy discrimination, the racial profile of the faculty had barely changed: in 1970 whites held 91 percent of the faculty positions nationwide, and in 1991 they held 88 percent.[67] I don't want to discount the discrimination that continued to operate in employment decision making at some academic institutions, but I do want to argue that those institutions making genuine efforts to recruit and retain African-American faculty were hindered by the process of recursive racism. Operating from birth onward, many forms of discrimination—whether intentional or inadvertent—determined how communities distributed material and social resources, how elementary and secondary schools provided education, how colleges selected applicants, whether campus climates fostered or retarded student development, and how graduate programs selected and trained future practitioners. These forms of discrimination had shrunk the pool of African Americans as they moved through the pipelines leading to terminal graduate degrees and thereby produced too few potential faculty members to staff the predominantly white institutions competing to recruit them. As the demand produced by the institutions' commitment to diversity outran the supply limited by systemic racism, tokenism was revived. The old type of professionalized racism, which heightened the visibility and stereotypicality of African Americans, modulated into a more virulent strain as universities and colleges raised their productivity standards for faculty members. African-American faculty members were expected not merely to shoulder the usual duties but to mentor students of color, represent the "minority-group perspective" on committees, and, in the case of African-American women, work for women's interests. But these tasks took time away from their research and teaching, the activities that carried the most weight in promotion and salary decisions. This situation was doubly discriminatory: the higher service expectations for African-American faculty members were de facto performance standards not imposed on others, and the heavier service loads sabotaged their career advancement.[68] Although the details varied by institution and discipline, the accurate claim about delimitation would be this: the many forms of discrimination that filtered African Americans out of the pipelines leading to and through higher education sustained the predominantly white faculties that affirmative action had promised to open to African Americans. Now three decades after academic institutions implemented affirmative action, the process of recursive racism, far more than the intentions and actions of individuals, continues to produce the racial patterning of student and faculty populations—a dynamic that recent court rulings on discrimination lawsuits refuse to acknowledge, as we will see in chapter 7.

PRESSES AND JOURNALS

In the academic system, publication determines the linked fates of aspiring professors and emerging discourses. Between 1970 and the early 1980s, while commercial and university presses increased their publication of academic-feminist books, they published little more than a dozen academic books by and about African-American women. Most were literary anthologies and reprints; a few were source materials and social analyses.[69] One could attribute the paucity of books not to disinterest on the part of mainstream presses but to the fact that scholars in emerging fields debut their research in article form before writing full-length studies. Yet the articles by and about African-American women were published not in the leading disciplinary journals but in African-American studies collections, hybrid feminist anthologies, and a few academic journals, such as *College English, Journal of Marriage and the Family,* and *Social Problems,* that had opened their pages to feminist work. Mainstream presses and journals claimed that they published little work by and about African-American women because little work was being done, but the evidence doesn't support that claim.

In her aptly titled "Black Women in and out of Print" (1982), Erlene Stetson reviewed the status of publications by and about African-American women in literary studies as well as the related fields of history and social science. Her findings were grim. Most published books—from slave narratives and antislavery treatises to fiction, poetry, biography, and scholarship—had gone out of print, suggesting that the publishing industry was ignoring the texts needed for research and teaching. Most published bibliographies were outdated compilations of material on "the negro in America," and only five, all published between 1972 and 1980, focused on African-American women, suggesting that the publishing industry was slow to supply the most essential tool for directing scholars and students through the field. As for primary materials on African-American women, the documents preserved in libraries and archives were seldom cataloged, the records of women's clubs reposed in the organizational files, and the personal papers stored in attics and closets had yet to be located. "Generations of neglect," Stetson wrote, "have left to us the essential tasks of discovering, documenting, publishing, and interpreting the works of black women."[70] This literature was out of print because it was blocked by the white male establishment that controlled preservation and publication. Reckoning that the only routes to print were the alternative venues, Stetson urged them to open their pages to work by and about women of color.

Stetson was right because most of the work we now regard as formative of black feminist studies appeared in alternative venues between 1975 and 1983. Special issues on African-American women were published by *The Black Scholar* (1975, 1978, 1979), the lesbian-feminist *Conditions* (1979) and

Heresies (1979), and the movement-oriented *Off Our Backs* (1979), and books by and about African-American women were published by the Kennikat, South End, Long Haul, Crossing, Persephone, and Feminist presses.[71] During this same period, African-American women were establishing their own venues: *Sojourner: A Third World Women's Newsletter* (1977); *Truth: The Newsletter of the Association of Black Women Historians* (1979); Kitchen Table / Women of Color Press (1983), whose inaugural volume was Barbara Smith's *Home Girls: A Black Feminist Anthology* (1983); and *SAGE: A Scholarly Journal on Black Women* (1984). Finally in the early 1980s, university and commercial presses began to publish a small but steadily increasing number of books by and about African-American women.[72] The pattern that emerges from this abbreviated review suggests that African-American women, by using the sidebar strategy of publishing their work in alternative venues and creating an audience for it, slowly pried open some of the doors to mainstream publishing. Whereas political ideology made alternative venues the most receptive to their work and profit-think made commercial presses more receptive than subsidized university presses (until the economics of university press publishing changed in the mid-1980s), the conservatism of the leading disciplinary journals made them the last holdouts.

The pattern in mainstream publishing has its counterpart when we look at specific feminist venues. On one hand, the hybrid anthologies published by commercial presses between 1970 and 1974 featured diverse authors writing on identity-linked issues. Robin Morgan's *Sisterhood Is Powerful* (1970) and Leslie Tanner's *Voices from Women's Liberation* (1970), for instance, contained writings by and about black, Chicana, lesbian, white, teenage, and older women; women working in factories, offices, media outlets, the armed forces, hospitals, and schools; and women using childcare and welfare services. And feminist presses, as we have seen, published out-of-print and new texts by and about working-class women, lesbians, and women of color. On the other hand, the leading feminist scholarly journals were slower to print work on African-American women than work on other identity groups. From 1972 to 1980, *Feminist Studies* featured numerous articles on family, work, unions, industrialization, and feminist movements, and by 1983 it had published articles on psychoanalytic theory, French feminism, conservative antifeminism, and lesbian criticism. Yet the journal had printed only a half-dozen articles by and about African-American women.[73] Similarly, *Signs* published work in many new areas: two special issues on women and development in India, Africa, Malaysia,

Latin America, and the Middle East (1977, 1981), a cluster on French feminism (1981), pioneering articles on lesbianism (1980, 1982), and "The Lesbian Issue" (1982). But this journal printed only four articles by and/or about African-American women, all of which appeared between 1975 and 1979.[74] About half of the by-and-about articles in both journals were bold reformulations of academic orthodoxies, and the other half, though presenting new knowledges, took conventional approaches. The turning point occurred in the mid-1980s. Only after mainstream venues and feminist journals had churned out white feminist scholarship for fifteen years did they make a serious commitment to disseminate African-American women's scholarship and criticism.

FEMINIST STUDIES' INTELLECTUAL CORE

Finally, I want to consider the claim that feminist-studies discourse formed along the axis of sex-gender difference and consequently did not accommodate the differences of race, ethnicity, nationality, class, and sexuality. First, the claim doesn't accurately represent the early difference discourse I have described: feminist historians and anthropologists studying a range of national, ethnic, racial, and economic groups; feminist psychologists criticizing research that used homogeneous subject populations; and feminist scientists contesting genetic determinism's racist and sexist agenda (feminist literary critics, I admit, were slower to diversify their work). Second, the claim oversimplifies feminism's history of modeling the interactive systems of racism, capitalism, and sexism in the United States.

Let's start with what women did to constitute what they could not see or say as individuals whose experiences were personalized, whose problems were pathologized, and whose subjection passed for common sense. They had to articulate *groupness* by linking individualized experience to individualized experience, and they had to limn *oppression* by connecting those experiences to social arrangements. Once they could see, as Ethel Klein said, that their previously personalized problems had "a social cause and probably a political solution," they could begin building a mass movement for social change.[75] The articulatory work of constru(ct)ing *women's oppression* began at the premobilization sites where women gathered— networks radiating outward from the President's Commission on the Status of Women and the Labor Department's Office of Women in the early 1960s; meetings of civil rights, New Left, and antiwar organizations in the mid-1960s; and the National Organization for Women Chapters, feminist liberation groups, and consciousness-raising groups that mushroomed across the country at the end of the decade. The bits of discourse—facts, statistics, insights—crafted at these sites congealed into political issues.

Rereading some of the early publications—the President's Commission on the Status of Women's *American Women,* NOW's newsletters, the radical-feminists' position papers, and the mass market feminist anthologies—I was struck by the plethora of issues they politicized for future feminist generations. A representative list would have to include orgasm, birth control, abortion, heterosexuality, lesbianism, marriage, divorce, housework, parenting, aging, education, occupations, volunteer activities, healthcare, childcare, welfare, consumerism, militarism, rape, assault, the media, the arts, the academic disciplines, and legal, political, and economic status. As these issues emerged, feminists took them into public arenas; they were the slogans shouted at protests, the demands negotiated with mainstream authorities, the claims pursued through litigation, and the bills introduced in legislatures. Through these activities, feminists pressed for changes in policy and practice such as legalization of abortion, protocols for treating rape victims and prosecuting offenders, and admission of women to trade schools, unions, and male-typed jobs. From this brief description, I want to extract two points. First, the discursive process of forming *women's oppression* was tessellation from bits. Experience by experience, insight by insight, issue by issue, demand by demand, negotiation by negotiation, feminists assembled the variegated *system of women's oppression in the contemporary United States.* Second, the group and the oppression were the nodes that every social-movement discourse needs to conjoin its statements in political analysis and its subjects in collective action. To say that the movement constituted a unitary and transhistorical category is to make the reductionist mistake of distilling praxis to signification.

Not to ignore signification, however, I will look at how the first-generation feminists did conceptualize the systematicity of racism and sexism. Although the media coverage of the civil rights struggle was seldom analytical, television and photography at least made it possible for white bystanders to grasp the scope of racism by capturing the steady stream of black bodies sitting, marching, and chanting, only to be halted by the battalions of uniformed white bodies beating, arresting, and shooting. Whites who joined the civil rights struggle in the South saw firsthand the systematicity of racism and the carefully orchestrated change initiatives. Other whites learned about racism in university classrooms when they read Ralph Ellison's *Invisible Man* (1952), James Baldwin's *Go Tell It on* the Mountain (1953), Gunnar Myrdal's An American Dilemma (1944), and Eleanor Flexner's Century of Struggle (1959), a richly detailed account of the links between the emancipation and women's rights movements. Myrdal's publicly controversial but academically respected book contained an appendix analogizing "the woman problem" to "the Negro problem" that was used as a model in the early writings on women. Sociologist Helen Hacker's "Women as a Minority Group" (1951) presented an elaborate table of resemblances in the castelike status of African Americans and women in the United States. Former SNCC organizers Casey Hayden and Mary King's "Sex and Caste" (1965), a short position paper circulated to SDS women and published in Liberation, analogized the sexual caste system to the racial caste system and listed similarities in the treatment of the two groups—the biologizing of differences, menial employment, legal inequality, and disrespect. Caroline Bird's widely read Born Female (1968) paralleled the race and sex maps of the United States, noting similarities in the status, stereotyping, and legal disabilities of the two groups.[76] The parallels were inapt but that was inevitable because analogizing, which uses a known category to conceptualize an unknown category, could not capture the interactivity of racism and sexism before the system of sexism had been limned.

Yet from the start feminists—white and black, academic and activist— were trying to formulate what we now call multiple identities and interactive oppressions. Gerda Lerner's "New Approaches to the Study of Women" (1969) sounded a warning about analogy: "Women's position has variously been likened to that of the slaves, oppressed ethnic or racial minorities, or economically deprived groups. But these comparisons quickly prove inadequate" because women (unlike slaves) were never denied freedom and personhood and women (unlike an oppressed racial or economic group) did not uniformly share a low social or economic status. Since women's circumstances differ by nationality, race, class, status, and other factors, Lerner cautioned, sex is "too vast and diffuse [a category] to serve as a valid point of departure" for scholarship.[77] That year Gayle Rubin's "Woman as Nigger" (1969), published in a University of Michigan student newspaper and reprinted in a trade anthology, took on "The basic premise of women's liberation . . . that women are an exploited class, like black people." Both populations, she said, suffer from "dynamic system[s] of social, political, economic, and psychological pressures" that oppress them as groups: black people "are oppressed as workers, but their blackness makes them more vulnerable than white workers. They are a class within a class. Women form a class within every class."[78] Instead of merely analogizing, Rubin made it possible to see the nesting of classism, racism, and sexism or, to put it the other way around, to see that poor black women were situated at the conjuncture of three oppressions. Yet she was also attuned to the fact that most women were not conscious of gender oppression and reiterated for them a truism of 1960s movements: first organize around your own oppression and then build alliances with other movements in order "to alter the power relationships that oppress Vietnamese, blacks, poor people, and ourselves."[79]

In 1970, several feminist anthologies presented articles written by African-American academics and activists who had been working on the more complex agenda of integrating race, class, and gender analytics. Frances M. Beale, a SNCC board member and program specialist with the National Council of Negro Women, argued that the circumstances of black women differed from those of black men and white women; race and sex situated them for "double jeopardy" in the socioeconomic system and for breach positioning among the movements for racial, gender, and economic justice. White feminist groups that were not antiracist and anticapitalist as well as antisexist, Beale declared, had "nothing in common with the black woman's struggle." Attorney Pauli Murray, a longtime civil rights activist and a NOW founder, similarly explained that since most black women were "triply handicapped" by institutionalized racism, classism, and sexism they had to cope with "multiple disadvantages" in education, employment, healthcare, and other services while assuming family responsibilities. Mary Ann Weathers positioned black women in tension with both black men and white women and discussed the differences among black women who were poor and middle class, younger and older, with and without children.[80] What distinguished all of these articles, from Lerner through Weathers, was that they moved from analogy to analysis, from a static system of castes to a dynamic system of oppressions, from one-category mobilization to coalitional struggle.

By the late 1970s, socialist feminists had braided the strands of class and gender into a dual-systems theory in order, as Zillah Eisenstein said in her work on capitalist patriarchy, "to emphasize the mutually reinforcing dialectical relationship between capitalist class structure and hierarchical sexual structuring."[81] But others pointed out its inadequacies. Women's lives, wrote Iris Young, are "not conditioned by two distinct systems of social relations which have distinct structures, movements, and histories." Nor, added Emily Hicks, could class and gender relations be understood without attending to the differences in race, sexuality, and ethnicity within the two categories.[82] Black feminist scholars published empirically based analyses of the interconnectivity of systemic oppressions. Jacquelyn Dowd Hall's 1983 article on the lynching of black people and the rape of black women showed that both emanated from the tangled themes of racial and gender mythology—white male chivalry, white female purity, black male sexual aggression, and black female promiscuity—that white men used to incite violence against black people and secure the complicity of white women in it. On her analysis, lynching and rape were the cogwheels that meshed the grinding machinery of the white supremacist and patriarchal systems in the post-Reconstruction south.[83] Deborah K. King's 1988 article argued that both the dual-systems model (racism plus sexism) and the triple-systems model (racism plus sexism plus classism) incorrectly cast the effects of oppression as additive. Using data on the socioeconomic status, educational attainment, and income levels of four groups (white men, black men, white women, and black women), she showed that the three systems of oppression had multiplicative and intensifying effects on the lives of black women.[84]

Over the years, feminists from a large array of marginalized or oppressed racial, ethnic, national, class, religious, sexual, and age groups demanded a discourse that more completely modeled identities, more complexly analyzed systemic oppressions, and more critically reflected on the state of academic-feminist knowledge. They were not alone. Many of those maligned white, middle-class, heterosexual feminists were seeking the same.

AN EXAMPLE: KOLODNY

The demand that feminist studies complexify its identity discourse motivated the production of illuminating work and sometimes motivated the censure of illuminating work. As an example, I want to consider some responses to Annette Kolodny's "Dancing Through the Minefield: Some Observations on the Theory, Practice, and Politics of a Feminist Literary Criticism," an essay that won the Florence Howe Award for feminist literary criticism in 1979 and appeared as the lead article in a 1980 issue of *Feminist Studies*. After summarizing the first decade of feminist literary scholarship and criticism, Kolodny asked why that work was ignored by mainstream scholars and answered by exposing the discipline's organizing constructs and practices. First she asserted that literary history was "a fiction" based on another fiction—the canon of great works that served as the model for charting the "continuities and discontinuities . . . between works, genres, and authors." Next she argued that scholars were trained to read canonical texts and continued to use the canonical strategies to read other texts. Rather than engaging texts in all their specificity and variety, the strategies predisposed them to value the texts that resembled canonical ones and devalue those that did not. Finally, since determinations of merit were contingent not on the presumably intrinsic aesthetic qualities of texts but the strategies used to read them, she urged feminists to "reexamine . . . the inherent biases and assumptions informing the critical methods which (in part) shape our aesthetic responses."[85] To break out of the disciplinary paradigm, feminist critics would have to initiate "a playful pluralism": "Only by employing a plurality of methods will we protect ourselves from the temptation of so oversimplifying any text [that we become unresponsive to its multivalence]. . . . whatever our predilection let us not generate from it a straightjacket that limits the scope of possible analysis."[86] The pluralism that Kolodny recommended was a methodological repertoire that would allow feminist critics to zigzag around the paradigmatic mines buried in the disciplinary field they wanted to rehabilitate.

It was no small irony that, when *Feminist Studies* published a forum on Kolodny's essay in 1982, the three respondents deployed paradigmatic feminist strategies to interpret the essay. Applying political typology, Judith Kegan Gardiner aligned most of Kolodny's ideas with liberal feminism and only a few with radical and socialist feminisms. Using identity critique, Elly Bulkin argued that Kolodny's analytic categories excluded the work of lesbian, black, Chicana, Third World, working-class, and poor women and went on to excoriate feminist scholars who selected such work as Kolodny's for publication and awards. Borrowing from Marxist analysis, Rena Grasso Patterson asserted that Kolodny's focus on textual meaning and value "derives from, and shares, the structuralist abstraction" of literature from its material, social, and historical conditions—a claim that blatantly misrepresented Kolodny's exposé of the discipline's historically specific and materially instantiated practices, which had produced its abstracted texts. Ironically, the respondents were doing precisely what Kolodny had criticized disciplinarians for doing: their reading strategies produced what they saw "in" the essay and eclipsed the radical disciplinary critique they should also have seen.[87]

Finally, the respondents all misread Kolodny's methodological pluralism as bourgeois doctrine. For Patterson, the word *pluralism* signaled Kolodny's "basic affinity not with feminism as I have defined it, but with liberal academic thought." Feminist thought, said Patterson, had built a "coherent theoretical foundation" by analyzing "the systematization of male supremacy in all its dimensions—including its interdependence with racism, classism, and heterosexism," whereas liberal academic thought promulgated the "greatest bourgeois theme of all, the myth of pluralism, with its consequent rejection of ideological commitment as 'too simple' to embrace the (necessary complex) truth."[88] Politically and intellectually speaking, Patterson was right to champion feminist criticism that analyzed cultural production within the interconnected systems of oppression, but wrong to use twisted logic to discredit Kolodny's work. On her reasoning, methodological pluralism was equivalent to liberal-academic pluralism, liberal-academic pluralism rejected ideological commitment as too simple, and therefore Kolodny in recommending methodological pluralism lacked a commitment to feminism. The best that can be said about their repudiation of methodological pluralism is that the respondents temporarily forgot recent history—namely that renegade literary critics (including feminist ones) had used methodological pluralism to break formalism's stranglehold on the discipline and that the social movements, whose ideological commitments the respondents praised, had used methodological pluralism—the deployment of diverse analytical and activist strategies—in their political struggles.

If I had to identify what Kolodny didn't do, it is what other feminist literary critics weren't doing at the time: social-structural analysis of cultural systems like the analyses of socioeconomic systems in the social sciences. If I had to identify what she did do that they weren't doing, it is what we now call the "strong program" of constructivism. Kolodny was asking literary critics to shift their attention from texts as objects to the institutionally organized practices that had constru(ct)ed them as disciplinary objects. She advocated methodological pluralism not to turn literary studies into a bourgeois, laissez-faire enterprise but to turn it into a critical-historical project that could expose and change the order of disciplinary discourse.

Producing the Predicament

Sometime around 1990 when feminist studies had become "downright messy" (as Jean O'Barr said), its practitioners took another look at the field. They saw, as editors Mariane Hirsh and Evelyn Fox Keller put it in *Conflicts in Feminism,* that after "a decade of intense mutual criticism and internal divisiveness . . . the feminist illusion of 'sisterhood' and the 'dream of a common language' gave way to the realities of fractured discourses."[89] They saw the factions hunkered down in the discursive trenches: minimizers and maximizers, essentialists and social constructivists, materialists and poststructuralists, second-wave generation and third-wave generation.[90] They saw problems in feminist studies, but of course they did not precisely agree on what those problems were. Here are a few recent takes on that subject.

For political scientist and former *Signs* editor Jean O'Barr, the problem was that the scholarly productivity, which had constituted the object of inquiry, eventually dissolved it:

> The more work that appeared on women in the disciplines, the more the basic category Women disappeared. . . . Women's studies scholarship became incredibly richer because scholars recognized and investigated the pervasive differences among women, while wondering what unified the field.

The solution, said O'Barr, was "to increase our research into . . . the heterogeneity of women's experiences while keeping our focus on the shared nature of those experiences" and "to work out the complex symbolic relationships between the representations of women in texts of every kind and the realities of women's daily lives."[91]

For feminist and Chicano studies scholar Chéla Sandoval, the problem was the homogeneity of the category "women": the predominantly white women's movement had been organized on the single axis of male dominance / female subjugation, and white feminist scholars had followed suit by focusing on " 'their oppression as women' while continuing 'to ignore difference.' "

> The publication of *This Bridge Called My Back* in 1981 made the presence of U.S. third world feminism impossible to ignore, but soon the writings and theoretical challenges of U.S. third world feminists were marginalized into the category of mere "description." . . . If, during the 1980s, U.S. third world feminism had become a theoretical problem . . . to be solved for hegemonic feminism, then perhaps a theory of difference—but imported from Europe—could subsume if not solve it.[92]

Sandoval's solution was that hegemonic feminists should acquire what U.S. Third World feminists already had: a consciousness of difference that would enable them to understand the varied forms of oppression and make tactical use of that knowledge.

For philosophers Kathryn Pyne Addelson and Elizabeth Potter, the problem was the academicization of women and "women." The early feminist intellectuals

> helped write position statements that analyzed the historical moment in which a revolutionary group found itself and that set forth strategies to bring about social change. When the authors . . . wrote of "all women," they were making rallying calls for political unity. . . . They were not making statements about "objective knowledge of true propositions about all women." They addressed a constituency to be organized, not a category to be described.

Today feminist scholars and scientists, though rejecting epistemological individualism, are professional individualists who spin arguments about the a priori abstractions of sexism, racism, and classism and produce esoteric knowledges that most people cannot understand. The remedy, said Addelson and Potter, was to permeate "the boundaries between classrooms and communities, research and lived experience, academic and everyday knowers" so that feminist-studies knowledge could be deployed in political struggle.[93]

Finally, for Indiana University Press Assistant Director Joan Catapano and Rutgers University Press Director Marlie P. Wasserman, the problem was that feminist scholarship, once revolutionary, had become repetitious. Many of the manuscripts they reviewed

> rework a select group of much-read theorists in often heavy-handed, unimaginative ways. . . . Even authors who have written groundbreaking books in the past seem to repeat themselves. The last few publishing seasons have produced neither major theoretical breakthroughs nor major syntheses. . . . It seems ironic that women's studies courses, programs, and enrollments continue to grow as intellectual discussions run out of steam.

The directors noted such reiterative trends as "more emphasis on gender and less on women's or feminist concerns," "a shift away from engaged feminist discussion to [superstar] performance," and slavish attempts to "recreate [the field] in the image of the traditional disciplines." Although reaffirming their commitment to publishing feminist books (which comprised 20 to 25 percent of their press lists), Catapano and Wasserman were not optimistic. "Perhaps," they speculated, feminist studies "has succumbed to the inevitable. All revolutionary movements either dissipate or are institutionalized."[94]

These feminists were pointing in the right directions when they identified the problems in feminist studies as modulating objects and objectives, abstract and reiterative knowledges, theorizations of the epistemic domain, and intellectualization of the social struggle. In this final subsection, I want to get at what drove feminist studies to generate problems.

THE MATERIALITY OF ACADEMIC KNOWLEDGE PRODUCTION

Feminist studies was institutionalized midway through an era of expansion that, among its many effects, accelerated the processes of disciplinary specialization, interdiscursivity, and hybridization. As the disciplines trained and hired more scholars who then produced more scholarship, their intellectual cores became crowded, and the crowding in turn motivated the scholars to specialize by subject matter, method, or theory, a trend that was boosted during the late 1970s when academic institutions hoisted their publishing requirements for faculty and profit-driven presses carved out intellectual niches. Density in the intellectual core, as the work of Mattei Dogan and Robert Pahre shows, has negative and positive effects on knowledge production. As knowledges accumulate and topics are exhausted, scholars who remain in the core engage in raging debates over minutiae that would be ignored in underpopulated fields, but those who want to produce innovative knowledge turn to interdiscursive activities. They can import from other discourses to rejuvenate the cores of their specialisms and, if successful, will form the divergent subfields that over time will fracture their discipline. Or they can turn their attention to interstitial problems—unclaimed, multiply claimed, and complex intellectual problems—that exist because disciplines have carved up the knowledge territory with overlaps and fissures. Collaboration-minded scholars will form discursive trading zones and, with institutionalized homes and resources, may be able to fuse their specialist knowledge fragments into a new hybrid field. Thus, during the decades when specialization was fragmenting the disciplines, interdiscursivity was working to recombine the knowledge fragments into such hybrid fields as urban, area, ethnic, and feminist studies, which then generated their own specialisms.[95]

The trends to specialization and commodification in higher education supported the institutionalization of feminist studies and shaped its discourse. Universities seeking tuition revenues upped their funding of women's studies courses because they attracted high enrollments, departments recruiting faculty to teach their multiplying specialisms and student majors eventually hired feminist faculty, and presses competing to wring profits from niche markets published specialized feminist books. The trajectory of disciplinary growth (specialization → fragmentation → hybridization) and the trajectory of commodification (product proliferation in a competitive field → product differentiation to draw consumers away from other choices → product obsolescence to motivate new purchases) worked together to intensify the production of differences within feminist-studies discourse.[96]

For simplicity's sake, visualize feminist studies in the mid-1980s as a field with four axes of specialization: political ideologies, social identities, disciplines, and epistemic assumptions (which I discuss below). First, each axis generates its own specialisms; for instance, an identities scholar could specialize in one or more races, sexes, ethnicities, nationalities, or sexualities. Second, each axis mutates new specialisms wherever it crosses the others. Consider research on the topic of transsexualism: the product could be a history of its formation in medical discourse or a sociology of a transsexual movement (discipline-based specializations), a study of transsexual practices and meanings in a Native-American community or in an African-American community (identity-based specializations), a justification or a critique of the laws (politics-based specializations), an analysis of personality or performativity (episteme-based specializations). Third, the positioning of scholars on these axes generates criticisms and contests— the discipline-based and identity-linked objections to Chodorow's theory of mothering and the identity-linked and politically based readings of Kolodny's article on literary studies. Last, positioning on the axes generates the knowledge repetitions noted by Catapano and Wasserman; anything and everything can be analyzed for gendering (Revlon advertisements, work in a physics laboratory, international human rights discourse), subjected to transgressive readings (*Pamela,* the Mall of America, the Islamic veil), or examined through a theoretical lens (the many applications of a theory).

What happened in feminist studies is this. Specialization and commodification drove the proliferation of particularized knowledges, which invited specialist criticisms, which sparked the metadiscourse about how to produce more adequate knowledges, which, once they were produced, went spinning through the same routines.

During the early 1960s, literary studies in the United States dropped its trade barriers and began importing European theories that gradually leached into other disciplines. By the early 1970s when feminists were just beginning to envision female studies, mainstream scholars had already organized numerous conferences, seminars, journal issues, and collections to disseminate poststructuralist discourse. Although we can find references to Lacan, Derrida, and Foucault in the work of a few U.S. feminists before 1975, it's probably safe to say that poststructuralism was ushered into the field by feminists trained in French language and literature and / or associated with the theorists at Yale, Johns Hopkins, Cornell, Irvine, and Berkeley. They circulated it through translations and essays published in *Diacritics, Signs, Feminist Studies,* and *Yale French Studies,* translations collected in Elaine Marks and Isabelle de Courtivron's *New French Feminisms* (1980), and such book-length engagements as Jane Gallop's *The Daughter's Seduction* (1982).[97]

Poststructuralism threatened or promised a radical departure from critical thinking-as-usual because instead of targeting specific disciplinary knowledges it took aim at the conceptual scaffolding of the modern knowledge enterprise. Claiming that all categories were unstable linguistic articulations, poststructuralists used such methods as deconstructive reading, discourse analysis, and psychoanalytic interpretation to dissolve the continuities that glued Western knowledge together: the originary event with its chain of effects; the unified identity with its interests and intentions; the chains of influence; the history of traditions; and the narrative of progress. American feminists were divided: some regarded deconstructive methods as convergent with feminism's critical-historical analyses, but others, such as Linda Alcoff, contended that they would make for "a wholly negative feminism, deconstructing everything and refusing to construct anything."[98] When the dust settled, feminists who had been preoccupied with the old couplets of men / women, sex / gender, identities / oppressions, and mainstream disciplines / feminist studies now had a new metacouplet to ponder: the modern / postmodern epistemes.

Debating the new couplet, most feminists insistently returned to the problem of agency. Alcoff criticized modernist approaches for ontologizing *women* as biologically sexed or socially gendered individuals dwelling in the realm of the real and poststructuralist ones for nominalizing *women* as an indeterminable category situated in the domain of language. Both, she argued, posited an overdetermination (biological, social, or linguistic) that seemed to deny the possibility of feminist agency for social change. Christine de Stefano objected that poststructuralist approaches were deconstructing the category of human agency "at the moment in Western history when previously silenced populations have begun to speak for themselves and on behalf of their subjectivities." And Susan Bordo contended that both the modernist "view from nowhere" and the postmodernist "dream of everywhere" evidenced a utopic desire to escape from a material world where people situated in physical and social bodies produced knowledges.[99]

Strung out between the modernist and postmodernist epistemes, realist and nominalist assumptions, constructivist and deconstructive methods, stability and permutability, feminist-studies discourse had entered a zone of liminality it had to escape. One escape strategy recalled the Marxism / feminism accommodation; if feminists modified some of the poststructuralist methods, they could use them to dismantle modernist constructs without disabling their own analytics and activism.[100] Another resembled the New University Conference's accommodation: feminists could regard modernists and postmodernists as having different emphases. Modernists, said Nancy Fraser and Linda Nicholson, "offer robust conceptions of social criticism, but they tend at times to lapse into foundationalism and essentialism," whereas "postmodernists offer sophisticated and persuasive criticisms of foundationalism and essentialism, but their conceptions of social criticism tend to be anemic." The third strategy was to synthesize the social and symbolic, the local and general, the materialized and theorized, so that postmodern feminist work, wrote Fraser and Nicholson, "would look more like a tapestry composed of threads of many different hues than one woven in a single color."[101]

Stepping back from the issues that were debated, I want to summarize what happened to the discourse. To clarify poststructuralism's difficult concepts and methods, feminists produced exegeses that in turn sparked debates about using its concepts and methods: would they dissolve feminist studies' objects and deter its objectives or would they give it a more potent arsenal for achieving its intellectual and political objectives? Debates polarized the modern episteme with its material order and the postmodern episteme with its symbolic one, and polarization prompted feminists to seek a synthesis. Indeed, we now have a synthesis in feminist studies, cultural studies, and social studies of science: studies showing that thousands of tiny adjustments, innovations, and disappearances simultaneously produce the material order of bodies, instruments, and built spaces *and* the symbolic order of categories, logics, and frames.

THE RULES OF DISCOURSE

Although I have been arguing that our field's tangled profusion of knowledges should not be regarded as luxurient blooms cultivated in a significatory hothouse, I now want to bring signification back into the picture by looking at feminist studies as a rule-governed system that produces, modifies, and circulates enunciations (by enunciations I mean not just linguistic and nonlinguistic acts but who performs them, from which positions, and in which ways). The early feminist groups professed the ideals of inclusivity and equality and tried to operationalize them by using such techniques as respectful listening and turn taking in discussions, collective decision making, and rotation of organizational duties.[102] Nevertheless, many of these groups—from the large formal NOW to the small women's liberation cells—played out scenarios of factionalization that were repeated, as we saw in chapter 3, by the groups trying to envision or launch feminist-studies projects.[103] The groups ran into trouble because the operationalization of inclusivity and equality was complicated by the difference rule, which bid feminists to assert their particular identities, ideologies, and affiliations and demand parity in their individual involvement and resources—as we saw in the conflicts among white women and women of color, revolutionaries and reformers, and movement and academic feminists at conferences and on campuses.

For feminist studies, the difficulty of reconciling the ideals of inclusivity and equality with its difference rule was compounded by the fact that it had to operationalize the ideals within academic institutions that were governed by a very different set of rules. The inclusivity rule specified that feminist studies should be open to faculty and students of marginalized classes, races, and ethnicities, but academic institutions, operating on the exclusivity rule, admitted so few women faculty and students from the marginalized groups that they were bound to be a minority presence in the field. The inclusivity rule also specified that women's studies programs should involve community feminists in their governance and instructional activities, but academic institutions, operating on the inequality rule, refused community feminists an active role on the grounds that they lacked academic credentials and expertise. To counteract these situations, feminist-studies faculty worked for the implementation of affirmative action and brought community feminists into the programs as guest lecturers, advisory board members, and internship providers. Nevertheless, the academy's exclusivity and inequality, which feminist studies could not remedy, set its difference rule in motion. This rule bid the practitioners, and especially those marginalized by the academy and society, to scrutinize their own identity-linked disparities and take action.

But then, following the academy's rule that issues should be intellectualized (i.e., researched and analyzed according to disciplinary conventions) and presented in publications, symposia, and classrooms, the marginalized women made inclusivity / exclusivity and equality / inequality the subject of their scholarship and teaching. To a certain extent, they could use feminist and mainstream academic venues to circulate their criticisms of exclusion and inequality, but they lacked the academic and extra-academic resources to change the procedures of the higher-education system that produced exclusion and inequality.[104] As a contrast case, consider how conservatives entered feminism's arenas. From the mid-1970s to the mid-1980s, the small band of critics who demonized feminism were mostly conservative men speaking to other conservatives through conservative organizations and publications; as such, they were speaking outside of feminism and often outside of the mainstream. By the early 1990s, the critical themes hadn't changed much, but the critics' modality had. The new critics were conservative women from the community and academy who called themselves equal-rights feminists and claimed to represent other women, who, like themselves, were determined to recapture feminism from the IDPOL crowd (identity politics and ideological policing), which had hijacked it.[105] Backed by conservative organizations and communicating through the mainstream media, they were able to position themselves within feminism's activist and academic arenas.

The civil rights and New Left movements had laid the groundwork for feminism's self-reflexivity rule by preaching "organize around your own oppression," practicing self-criticism, and unpacking the objectivity claims of official information. Feminism went deeper into self-reflexivity by specifying that women would be both the subjects and the objects of its discourse: they were at once the knowers and known of movement analysis, the agents and beneficiaries of movement activism. Transplanted to the nascent field of feminist studies, self-reflexivity was operationalized as a relay between its not yet legitimated subject and its not yet limned object. As a result, the early practitioners tended to skate between the two: they knew the object of inquiry because they were (like) the object and had experienced the object's experiences, which had constituted their viewpoints, which in turn gave them a better purchase than others on knowledge of that object. Once academic feminists had formulated gender as the coproduction of subject, societal, and knowledge formations, they had to locate themselves within this relay. As Jane Flax put it more simply, "I will be moving back and forth between thinking about gender relations and thinking about how I am thinking—or could think—about them."[106] Flax could no longer just think about gendered relations as an object; now she had to think about herself as a subject produced by gendered social relations and thus disposed to think about them in certain ways.

Finally, I want to consider how feminist studies' rules functioned with its four axes of specialization to proliferate knowledge discourse. As feminist studies came to include more diverse practitioners (the inclusivity rule said it should) who worked on the premise that "you know according to who and how you are constituted" (the self-reflexivity rule said they should), they generated streams of knowledge particularized according to their identity, disciplinary, and / or political positions (the difference rule said they should). To synthesize these distinctive and sometimes discordant knowledges, feminists formulated sex-gender systems / standpoints and multiple identities / interactive oppressions. But then all this work collided with poststructuralist critique, jamming feminist-studies discourse between epistemic levels. When feminists theorized sex-gender systems / standpoints and multiple oppressions / identities, they were thinking about subject, societal, and knowledge formations. When they produced exegeses of poststructuralism, they were thinking about poststructuralist thinking about modernist thinking. When they debated these approaches, they solidified an epistemic plane where they could think comparatively about modern, postmodern, and feminist modes of thinking about subject, societal, and knowledge formations. But once they began thinking within the poststructuralist paradigm, they were snared by its hyper-reflexivity. Poststructuralist discourse was premised on a significatory universe where subjects could only traipse back and forth between the reflexively redounding signifiers and signifieds. On that premise, feminists were thinking in an echo chamber: they were THINKING ABOUT THE (thinking about the [*thinking about the* {*thinking about the*}. . . .]). This development completed the discursive transformation of "social change." Whereas female studies had cast it as a practical objective to be achieved by collective analysis and action and feminist studies had recast it as a subject matter to be investigated, poststructuralism internalized social change to the workings of signification.

TO RECAP THE DYNAMICS I examined in this chapter, feminist studies, like other flourishing disciplines fueled by the expanding higher-education system and the corporatized publishing industry, was able to proliferate objects, knowledges, and specialisms within its domain and to breed hybrids along its borders with other fields. But its axes of specialization and rules of discourse volatilized these processes. Having limned a knowledge object, feminists then worked on specifying it according to their positioning on the disciplinary, identity, and political axes. The specifications of an object invited criticisms by differently positioned feminists, the criticisms motivated theorizations of the object, and the theorizations pushed the debates to a more abstract level, which in turn sent us spinning through another (re)formation process and spiraling into the metadiscursive stratosphere. Ensconced in our institutions, we demanded inclusivity from systems of selectivity, we sought equality from orders of ranking, and we fought for parity in economies of scarcity. And when we felt the effects of institutional exclusions, inequalities, and disparities, we did what the self-reflexivity rule said we should do: we debated our positionalities and practices within feminist studies without acknowledging that they, too, were the effects of trying to operationalize our discourse within the academy's rule-governed routines.

Although I have characterized feminist studies as a disunified field with a volatile intellectual core and a discordant scholarly community, others would argue that it has had far too much unity, stability, and consensus. But that is exactly my point: feminist studies is an institutionalized formation that produces an abundance of differences and hence problems. Warren Bennis once said, "A problem is something you have, but a predicament is something that has you." We have problems in feminist studies because feminist studies is the predicament that has us.

Part 3. Crystallizing the Future

There is no way back to 1968. —Bill Readings, *The University in Ruins* (1996)

"It's the beginning of the end," I said to Joan Hartman the night after Ronald Reagan was elected to the presidency. Thinking only of his power to appoint Supreme Court justices who would erode liberalized abortion law, I didn't anticipate what came to pass.

Phyllis Schlafly's Eagle Forum led the campaign that halted state ratification of the Equal Rights Amendment and the heads of federal agencies pulled back from enforcing antidiscrimination law. Jerry Falwell's Moral Majority issued waves of direct mail exhorting Christians to quell homosexuality, teen sexuality, single-mother sexuality, extramarital sexuality, sex education in schools, and sexual themes in Hollywood films, TV sit-coms, rock videos, and fashion industry ads while the president cozied up to the Christian Right at prayer breakfasts. Prodemca supported genocidal regimes in Central America, and pro-lifers bombed abortion clinics in the United States. The Christian textbook movement demanded equal time for creation science, and public officials advocated voucher plans that would redirect public school funding into religious and private schools. The Chairmen of the National Endowment for the Humanities (NEH), William Bennett and Lynne Cheney, demonized new trends in the humanities, Congress slashed the NEH budget, and conservatives on NEH review committees manipulated the awards process. Conservative legal centers took retrograde lawsuits to federal courts where conservative judges obligingly eroded female reproductive choice, affirmative action, and church-state separation.

In 1987, I began doing research on the new conservative movement—its emergence in the 1960s, the formation of its organizational infrastructure in the 1970s, and its political initiatives in the 1980s.[1] That research showed me, to borrow Bill Readings's phrasing, that there was no way back to the 1960s when activists in the New Left, antiwar, and women's movements had intended to transform the structures of consciousness and society, no way back to the 1970s when feminists had launched an insurgent field that would link academic knowledge to social activism, and no way back to the 1980s when progressive scholars had argued that the new critical studies would subvert power at the sites of its production. There was no way back because over the years the modalities of social change had shifted from activist networks to organizational infrastructures, from group techniques to nationwide technologies, from specialized intrasector projects to strategic cross-sector campaigns, and from consciousness raising to reality making. We missed the shift because over the years we got stuck in our own discourse of social maintenance and change, rather like callers to an automated telephone system who cycle through prerecorded messages and never converse with the real operators.

Even as organizations are us and we are them—they by fabricating our desires and organizing our practices, we by performing the routines that constitute their structures and processes—they are also something more. They are the nodes a movement must construct to connect its activities, the repositories of resources it must access, the instruments for leveraging change it must use, and the entities it must re-form. Consider, for a moment, the lessons we can learn from the organizational biographies of social movements: the work of the Montgomery Improvement Society in sustaining a yearlong bus boycott and the NAACP in crafting desegregation lawsuits; the catalytic organizing of SNCC in the deep south and SDS on college campuses; the feminist consciousness-raising groups that mushroomed across the nation; the radical and feminist caucuses that carved niches into the academic infrastructure to appropriate the resources of disciplinary associations and universities; the academic enterprise that feminists finally institutionalized; and the tightly meshed, highly technologized organizations that the conservative movement has used to seize control of political parties, legislatures, church councils, and school boards. Articulated organizations are now the agencies of social maintenance and change.

My task in these final chapters is to sail along with the ongoing flows of social change and speculate about how they might congeal into a future. As I compare conservative and feminist change agency today, I will rotate my analytical lens to bring into focus how organizations function as the middle term in coproducing actors and structures. In chapter 6, I set the stage by describing a nationwide conservative network and a statewide feminist network. Then I focus on four hybrid programs—embedded in these networks and perched between the academy and society—that are training the third generation of movement activists and national leaders. Chapter 7 returns to a struggle that hasn't gone away—the struggle over discrimination discussed in previous chapters. Only this time conservatives have seized the initiative from liberals and progressives by mounting a wide-ranging campaign to dismantle affirmative action and restructure the nation's economy of opportunity.

Social change is not merely the work performed in the present; it is the process of crystallizing a future. As a feminist scholar and activist, I am appalled by conservatism's vision of society, alarmed by its successes, and worried that the profound changes now sweeping through our nation will sweep democracy away. By analyzing some recent episodes of change, I hope to show that academic feminism's liberationist projects, unless reoriented to that reality, may be capsized by the larger political forces contending for the future.

6. Remaking Change Agency

From 1991 through 1994, I was an itinerant scholar who drove the midwestern byways and Garden State freeways, rode the rails of the Chicago El and the DC Metro, bussed to the Virginia suburbs, and walked the paths meandering through campuses. My destinations were feminist and conservative organizations, my purpose to study how they were making change.

Virtually all of the conservative organizations—national think tanks, training schools, and interest groups—were hybrids in form and function. They had arrogated intellectual legitimacy by issuing research studies, cultural capital by providing student scholarships and programs, and the veneer of stewardship by using the rhetoric of public benefaction. But they were managed on business principles and coordinated like a cartel intent on driving competitors out of the public policy agora. They pitched plans to donors, spun issues in the media, mobilized supporters, delivered proposals to public officials, and clinched the sales by mustering squads of paid lobbyists backed by citizen letter-writing campaigns. Although some organizations had multi-issue agendas and others had carved out niches, such as family policy or business deregulation, they were able to mount cross-sector operations because they drew their associates from overlapping conservative networks in government, business, the professions, education, and the media.

Most of the feminist organizations, by contrast, were firmly planted within a societal sector. Inside the academy, feminist programs, research centers, and publications were preoccupied with esoteric knowledges and loosely connected, if at all, by the National Women's Studies Association and the National Council for Research on Women. Outside the academy, small policy institutes conducted research on women's issues, political action organizations provided campaign training and financial support for women candidates, and advocacy was divided among the multi-issue National Organization for Women and several organizations that specialized in identity and issue clusters—for instance, the Women and Poverty Project, the National Abortion Rights Action League, the National Institute for Women of Color, and the Older Women's League. Finally, poised between the academic and policy arenas, the American Association of University Women, Committee W of the American Association of University Professors, and the Office for Women of the American Council on Education addressed education policy issues and sponsored gender equity projects.

Although they had racked up many achievements, the feminist organizations impressed me as lacking the long-range vision, robust purposefulness, and coherent agenda I saw at conservative organizations. One contributing factor was that conservatives, but not feminists, had mastered the techniques of capitalization—direct-mail solicitation, endowment fundraising, and foundation support. Consider just foundation support. Between 1992 and 1994 alone, twelve conservative foundations poured nearly $80 million into eighteen conservative think tanks and interest-advocacy organizations and $88.9 million into conservative academic programs—for research, curriculum development, professorships, fellowships, lecture series, and book projects.[1] in 1995, the top five conservative institutes received $77 million from foundations while the top eight progressive institutes (none were feminist) received only $16.6 million.[2] To take a closer look, the revenues of the Heritage Foundation, the leading conservative think tank, shot up from $19.3 million in 1991 to $29.7 million in 1995; those 1995 revenues, approximately 25 percent of which were supplied by conservative foundations, supported a staff of more than 150 people, a large array of research and advocacy programs, a high-tech communications system, and a national network of conservative organizations.[3] Smaller conservative think tanks were by no means impoverished; between 1992 and 1994, conservative foundations bestowed approximately $7 million on the American Enterprise Institute, $5 million on the Free Congress Foundation, $4 million on the Cato Institute, and more than $3 million each on the Hudson Institute and the Hoover Institution.[4]

Throughout the 1990s, mainstream and progressive foundations remained wary of the strategic grantmaking practiced by their conservative counterparts, and feminist policy institutes (as well as nonfeminist progressive ones) continued to struggle.[5] At its founding, the Center for Women Policy Studies (1972), said Director Leslie R. Wolfe, had aspired to be a feminist Brookings Institute but couldn't capture the funds needed to expand; in 1992, the center's seven staff members were maintaining a dozen programs in policy studies and leadership development.[6] The Institute for Women's Policy Research (1987) aimed to be the feminist movement's premier think tank, but its 1992 revenues of $500,000—60 percent from foundations, 20 percent from government, 10 percent from memberships, and 10 percent from income-producing activities—didn't support this ambition. Yet Director Heidi Hartman and seven staffers somehow managed to keep the research, publications, and conferences afloat.[7] The Women's Research and Education Institute (WREI, 1977), which was established to provide research for women in Congress, did enjoy ten years of congressional funding at $1 million annually. When this largesse was reduced to occasional project support, said Executive Director Betty Parsons Dooley, WREI diversified its revenue sources and in 1992 received $700,000 primarily from foundations, corporations, and fundraising events. Still, its six staff members were scrambling to keep up with congressional requests while managing ongoing policy research, a congressional fellowships program for young women, and national conferences.[8]

A second factor that made feminist groups seem less purposeful than conservative ones was the structuring of the organizational field. Conservatives had established umbrella councils to coordinate both within-sector and cross-sector change initiatives. For instance, the Philanthropy Roundtable's member foundations and donors divided up the task of funding the array of organizations, the State Policy Network's thirty-seven state-level think tanks shared materials and plans, and the American Legislative Exchange Council's state and federal legislators met annually to discuss policy strategies. Their coordination was facilitated by regularly scheduled convocations and the high-tech communications system mentioned earlier—cable TV, radio, e-mail, and Web sites. By contrast, feminist umbrella organizations—such as the National Women's Studies Association, Women in Foundations, Women in Communications, and Business and Professional Women USA—functioned as within-sector professional associations rather than cross-sector political councils. Feminist organizations did join two kinds of political coalitions: the short-term local or state campaign on such issues as childcare, welfare, housing, or pollution; and national progressive councils, such as the Leadership Conference on Civil

Rights and the Rainbow / PUSH Coalition, whose members included unions, professional associations, civil liberties groups, churches, and identity-linked organizations.[9] Cross-sector coalition building among women's groups seemed to be a recent undertaking: Women's Ways USA (1995) was established to federate 660 national women's organizations, and Women's Roundtable (1996) was founded by feminist scholars, writers, and activists to counter the media success of the antifeminist Independent Women's Forum and Women's Freedom Network.[10]

The third factor was identity discourse. While conservative leaders were crafting a new discourse to solidify the movement's economic, social, cultural, and religious factions, feminist leaders were fumbling opportunities to speak across their divided sectors. In 1992, the Heritage Foundation's annual Resource Bank Meeting (see below) showcased a new rhetoric that meshed the interests of conservative factions in a battle plan for the 1990s. That same year the Ford Foundation invited thirty-five feminists to discuss overlaps between academic feminist studies and nonacademic policy institutes. Commenting on the Ford meeting, WREI executive director Betty Parsons Dooley said, "There wasn't a declarative sentence available during the whole day; the discussion was framed in impenetrable ways."[11]

What I found, in short, was that conservative entrepreneurs had built an organizational infrastructure that was better financed, technologized, and instrumentalized than that of the feminist movement. The networks and training programs I examine in this chapter were chosen to illustrate the conditions for making social and academic change in the 1990s. I intend to show how these conditions—everything from dollars to discourse—operate at three levels: the field of action, the individual organization, and the actors.

Networking the Field

We must rebuild the institutional base needed to make the conservative agenda a reality, not only in Washington but throughout the nation. — *The Heritage Foundation 1991 Annual Report*

We had to play the role of change agent—one who creates an environment and set of activities which facilitate the work of others who have an interest in planning and implementing change.—Edward D. Goldberg, "New Jersey's Model for Stimulating Change" (1986)

These quotations allude to very different ways of using organizations to make social-structural change. The first refers to an organizational infrastructure that sets the agenda and engineers the changes to be imposed upon ordinary people, the second to organizations that spark the formation of a grassroots network and provide resources that stoke the changes it wants to make. In this section, we will see how the Heritage Foundation orchestrated coalition building among the conservative movement's warring factions so that they could act in concert to implement a national policy agenda. Then we will look at a feminist project, facilitated by the New Jersey Department of Higher Education, that in turn helped faculty who wanted to transform the curricula of universities and colleges.

THE RESOURCE BANK

When I first heard about the Heritage Foundation's Resource Bank, I assumed that it was a computerized data bank of policy experts who could deliver public lectures and speak to the media because Heritage president Edwin Feulner described it as "in touch with 1,600 scholars and 400 organizations worldwide."[12] But that phrase, "in touch," did not capture what the Resource Bank was doing through its Internet facilities and regularly scheduled events. The central event was the annual meeting, a convocation of conservative leaders in the academy, media, government, foundations, and movement organizations; though far smaller than Christian Coalition meetings that regularly drew thousands, the Fifteenth Annual Resource Bank meeting held in April 1992 was instrumental in reconsolidating a factionalized movement.

It was no coincidence that the Heritage Foundation convened this meeting on the two days preceding the Philadelphia Society's annual meeting and in the same Chicago hotel. Founded in the mid-1960s as a forum for discussion among paleoconservatives, neoconservatives, and libertarians, the Philadelphia Society had become the scene of rancorous debates between social and economic conservatives during the late 1980s.[13] When asked about the strife in a 1991 interview, Feulner had admonished the warring factions: "Conservatism is going to have to involve coalitions between people who don't always agree with each other if it is going to be a broader-based movement and become a governing majority for the future. You don't build a majority by writing off a large chunk of individuals who ought to be part of your movement. Successful politics consists of addition and multiplication, not subtraction and division."[14] The details of the 1992 Resource Bank Meeting were designed to reunite a movement wracked by discord and win over the voters who would hand conservatives rule of the nation. The title, Ideas Have Consequences: A Conservative Battleplan for the 1990s, gestured to paleoconservative Richard Weaver's classic book, *Ideas Have Consequences,* and signaled Feulner's call-to-action strategy for rebuilding the Reagan era coalition. The program quoted his interview statement on coalition building, and the invited conferees represented virtually every conservative organization in the United States as well as many organizations abroad.[15] The keynote speakers made the objectives clear, Feulner by reflecting on the themes announced in the interview and Wisconsin Governor Tommy Thompson by presenting his state's "workfare" and school voucher programs as examples of how ideas translated into policy have economic and social consequences.

Speakers at the five panels debuted a new rhetoric that would function like a multipurpose tool with one gadget used to rivet conservative factions, another to clasp unaligned citizens, and a third to split liberal coalitions. At the session Building New Grassroots Coalitions: Family Policy and Economic Growth, the moderator set the tone by asking, "Can economic conservatives learn anything from family-value conservatives, and vice-versa?" and "Is there a symbiotic relationship between activism and academic research?" Following this lead, the panelists dispensed examples and advice. One reported that his Pennsylvania think tank had spent $10 million setting up a statewide Internet network to foster communication between economic and social conservatives who then formed an alliance that managed to get school choice legislation passed. A second urged the audience to "repackage the economic agenda into pro-family terms" that would be attractive to voters. Instead of denouncing regulations for interfering with free-market dynamics, conservatives should say that pollution controls, by increasing the price of cars, force mothers to take jobs in order to help their families afford them.[16] Similarly, at the panel Conservatives and Congress: Can We Prevail? a speaker advised the audience not to "say 'the federal debt is $40 trillion' but rather 'your family's share this year is $40,000.'"[17]

At both panels, the speakers and the audience members regarded rhetoric as a tool that could wedge into liberally aligned constituencies. By learning "to speak to Democrats and use their language,"[18] conservatives could win over moderate Democrat voters, and by describing themselves as generating citizen "choices" and thereby "empowering the people" they could make conservativism more palatable to left-leaning and populist constituencies. But a speaker who didn't want to alienate the traditional values groups noted that the language of "responsibility" rather than "choice" was more appropriate for welfare policy because the system was too permissive and the clients too promiscuous. When an audience member pointed out that the movement was having trouble recruiting women, one panelist criticized think tank publications for using language that appealed to men, and another, well-schooled in encomium, said that women were going to be "the hands and feet of the movement" in his state. When an audience member asked how conservatives could reach out to blacks, one panelist said that his state organization hired black staffers in the hope that they would talk up conservative issues in their communities.[19]

To dispel any lingering impression that conservative discourse was all talk and no action, I want to review how the movement was translating the idea of "choice" into practice. Applied to tactics, choice dictated that conservatives shift from defensively criticizing liberal policies to proposing their own. Applied to recruitment, choice rhetoric would persuade ordinary people that conservative policies would give them more options for education, employment, healthcare, religion, and other social goods. Applied to structural change, choice suggested an economic strategy that would complement the movement's electoral politics. To restructure the social formation, conservatives would create a marketplace of competitive service providers and even governments. "We have to create a market of local governments, we have to expand them by scores," exhorted a speaker at the panel Reinventing Federalism, so that individuals "can choose their government by living in one or moving away into another."[20] I wasn't sure how a marketplace of governments could be created until the panelists urged the audience to introduce state-level reforms along the lines of California's anti-affirmative action initiatives and Wisconsin's workfare-welfare program. Then I realized that by implementing these "reforms" conservative governments could drive the have-nots into liberal counties and states that continued to fund social services. If the objective of shifting the overhead costs from conservative governments to liberal ones was to build the prosperity of the former while bankrupting the latter, the result would surely be a nation divided into ghettos and gated communities.[21]

At the closing panel of the 1992 Resource Bank Meeting, Free Congress Foundation (FCF) Senior Vice President Michael Schwartz reflected on conservatism's progress. The small meetings of Washington conservatives that Paul Weyrich had initiated twenty years earlier when he founded the Heritage Foundation and the Free Congress Foundation had grown into an organizational infrastructure that sustained and spread the nationwide conservative movement.[22] When I spoke privately with Schwartz, he confirmed my impression that professionally managed, high-tech conservative organizations had saturated the recruitment and training territory. The FCF reached out to the grassroots by holding workshops in the states and beaming its more cost-effective National Empowerment Television (NET) into 11 million homes and offices. The NET programs were formatted to mobilize viewers: on the November 1992 broadcast of *Family Forum Live,* for instance, speakers from three organizations recruited viewers to their projects—establishing church shelters for pregnant women, lobbying against the proposed Freedom of Choice Act, and organizing school choice campaigns to break the public school funding monopoly—while FCF's camera repeatedly flashed their addresses and 800 numbers on TV screens.[23] The Heritage Foundation took a more traditional approach to leadership training. Its 1992–93 lecture series entitled Defining Conservatism, said Feulner in a press release, would "outline concrete strategies needed to recapture American culture from the death grip of the liberal establishment" and would "define the principles that should guide and unify a vigorous conservative movement." Widely publicized and attended by overflow crowds, the lectures outlined conservative initiatives in the areas of foreign relations, taxes, healthcare, families, school vouchers, religion, philanthropy, drugs, crime, political correctness on campuses, and feminism (masterminding the latter was neoconservative Midge Decter).[24]

Yet Heritage and FCF's capacity to train activists paled beside that of such mass membership organizations as Pat Robertson's Christian Coalition, Beverly LeHaye's Concerned Women of America, and several organizations dedicated to preparing the third generation. The Leadership Institute (LI) operated four schools to train young conservatives for the movement (in such skills as leadership, grassroots organizing, and direct-mail fundraising) and five to train them for professions (Foreign Service, Capitol Hill staffing, legislative management, broadcast journalism, and student publications).[25] The LI graduated 3,950 students from 1987 through 1991, with record highs of 1,002 graduates in 1991 and thirty-three training programs in 1992.[26] The National Journalism Center (NJC), whose mission was to "help talented young people break into the media" and correct its liberal bias, sponsored a twelve-week program held four times a year and training 60 to 80 students annually.[27] The students took courses on conservative journalism and "common-sense economics" while interning at media outlets. In 1990, NJC estimated that "500 of our alumni are working in media and media-related posts" at major news services, networks, and newspapers and at virtually every conservative media venue.[28] The Intercollegiate Studies Institute (ISI), founded to promote traditional education and free enterprise, reached more than 100,000 college students annually through its summer institutes, conferences, lectures, and publications. Besides supporting a network of conservative student newspapers on campuses,[29] ISI poured $200,000 a year into fellowships for graduate students who promised to pursue academic careers.[30] The Young America's Foundation (YAF) sponsored a wide array of projects—regional leadership conferences, summer institutes, lectures, student scholarships and internships, C-Span coverage, Internet service, and publications. Its star-studded student conference featured authors Tom Clancy and Dinesh D'Souza; talk show ideologues Rush Limbaugh, Oliver North, and G. Gordon Liddy; Congressmen Newt Gingrich and Dick Armey; Senators Jesse Helms and Phil Gramm; and Supreme Court Justice Clarence Thomas.[31]

Reflecting on my travels through conservatism, I was struck by several conditions for making social and academic change. First, the agencies of change are not the astute leaders and hardworking followers but the tightly networked national and state organizations. Conservative organizations frame issues, mobilize workers and voters, win elections, and staff government institutions; then the elected officials and the staff work together on revising public policies and redirecting public resources.[32] In short, the movement uses this organizational infrastructure to weld social activism to formal political and governmental processes, thereby creating a hybrid agency that amplifies change across the sectors of society. Second, the conservative rhetoric of citizen choices and group coalitions sounds democratic, but let's look at what it was doing from the Reagan presidency through the Gingrich Congress. The citizen choice rhetoric cloaked the movement's stealth bombers as they dropped their payloads on public schools, affirmative action laws, poverty programs, universal healthcare proposals, consumer protection regulations, and immigration policies. A citizen's choice depends in the first place on whether she has the wherewithal to exercise it. Without the money, driving skills, license, and product knowledge, she can't exercise the choice of buying a car, and without the car her choices in everything else—employment, housing, healthcare, childcare, education, and leisure activities—are narrowed. The dismantling of programs that help have-not citizens will not produce empowerment; rather, they will produce a "new economic exclusionism" that codifies in the policies of the land the deepening divide between haves and have-nots.[33]

Finally, conservatives were using the coalition discourse to wedge into such traditionally left-of-center populations as African Americans, Hispanic Americans, women, and Jews in the hope of assimilating the more prosperous or tradition-minded members into their movement. Typically, the outreach programs at the organizations I studied did not invite minorities to collaborate as equal partners; they exported conservative ideas to minority communities and groomed token individuals as conservative leaders. Since the one-way scheme of traffic was predicated on what these folks could do for conservatism, I wasn't surprised that the organizations had few racial minority members. But I was surprised to find so many white women serving as vice presidents and program directors in organizations that promulgated traditional ideals of family and domesticity. At first I thought that the ideological division of woman into warrior and wife would come back to vex the movement, but then I realized that the female leaders were role-modeling an identity updated for our times. That identity, the "new conservative woman," integrates the educational and professional opportunities that middle-class women have come to expect with the family values and free-market economics that conservatism espouses.

The conservative discourse of choices and coalitions was identity politics by another name; it was geared to re-forming identities and realigning populations in order to assemble the critical mass of voters and leaders that would secure conservative rule of the nation. One might argue that every movement has to use identity discourse to catalyze collective action. That's true. But it takes a widely institutionalized, highly technologized, and tightly coordinated movement to reconfigure the social formation.

THE NEW JERSEY PROJECT

Since the feminist movement had no equivalent of the Heritage Foundation's Resource Bank, I began looking for other types of feminist networks and discovered one when I visited Rutgers University in 1991 to observe Celebration of Our Work. Sponsored by Douglass College's Institute for Research on Women (IRW), this annual day-long conference was attended by New Jersey women in education, business, government, and other sectors. Speaking with the conferees, I learned that IRW was administering the New Jersey Project, a statewide program aiming to integrate the scholarship on gender, race, and class into college and university curricula.

Although the project was officially launched in 1986, the idea had been germinating for some time at the New Jersey Department of Higher Education (DHE). When the state accumulated a budget surplus in the early 1980s, Governor Thomas Keane allocated curriculum development funds to the DHE. After consulting with New Jersey faculty and out-of-state scholars, the DHE selected four areas for development: technological literacy, gender integration, multicultural studies, and global-international education. Meanwhile, a few campuses were already sponsoring modest gender and multicultural projects. At William Paterson College, faculty members in women's studies and black studies had initiated a Race and Gender Project in 1981 to design and teach a new course titled Racism and Sexism in the United States. Building on the course, coordinator and philosophy professor Paula Rothenberg wrote a proposal in 1984 for a college-wide curriculum project.[34] At Drew University, Wendy Kolmar, who was hired "as a consultant to get women's studies off the ground" and then appointed program director, had secured four consecutive grants to help faculty members integrate scholarship on women into their courses.[35]

After the DHE decided to support a statewide project on gender integration, Assistant Chancellor Edward D. Goldberg invited IRW director Catharine Stimpson and her associates to submit a proposal.[36] Taking the proposal process as an opportunity to create a network, the IRW held a meeting that was attended by several New Jersey faculty women, sought advice from curriculum transformation projects in other states, and contacted individuals who had participated in the American Council of Education's National Identity Program, the Mid-Atlantic division of the National Women's Studies Association, and the Celebration of Our Work conferences.[37] Funded by the DHE for three years, the New Jersey Project was led by IRW director Carol Smith (Stimpson's successor), with Ferris Olin serving as associate director and Rider College professor Judith S. Johnston as liaison to the DHE and other campuses. By the end of the first year, it had held four faculty workshops focused on specific disciplines, a two-week summer institute for faculty teams from several campuses, and meetings to help the teams rework their institute applications as grant proposals for DHE funding of campus integration projects.[38] During the second and third years, the project continued to sponsor these events while its staff worked on recruiting faculty from more campuses, publicizing the project at state and national meetings, and publishing a newsletter.[39] Overall, between 1986 and 1989, hundreds of New Jersey faculty members attended project events, thirty-two of the state's fifty-six institutions sent teams to the summer institutes, and forty curriculum projects at nineteen institutions won DHE grants.[40]

When Assistant Chancellor Goldberg asked Paula Rothenberg to direct the second phase at William Paterson College, the DHE budget did not permit the same level of financial commitment. To cope with reduced funding, Rothenberg shortened the summer institutes to four days but broadened the project's scope by including materials on race, class, and sexuality, increasing the number of men who participated in the summer institute (25 percent of the 1991 and 1992 participants were men), and launching a women-of-color network that began organizing its own events. To harden its infrastructure, Rothenberg organized New Jersey colleges and universities into three regional networks, each one sponsoring events to stimulate integration projects at member campuses, and tied the campuses together with an events hotline, a video archive, the *New Jersey Project Newsletter,* and *Transformations,* a journal founded in 1990.[41] In April 1993, the New Jersey Project hosted The Inclusive Curriculum: Setting Our Own Agenda, a national conference that attracted some eight hundred participants and showcased feminist scholars speaking on curriculum integration.[42] No sooner did the project celebrate its transition to a third phase at the conference than it collided with a new financial reality. When Governor Christine Whitman and the legislature trimmed the state budget, they eliminated the Department of Higher Education and, through an oversight, omitted the New Jersey Project from the higher-education appropriations bill for the next year. Thrust into fundraising, Rothenberg and her supporters secured a $100,000 discretionary grant from the Office of the Governor and $55,000 in state appropriations for two years, the time they needed to generate income from grants, a corporate campaign, a partnership program with colleges and universities, and publications.[43]

The New Jersey Project's discourse of diversity and inclusivity informed its design of the 1992 summer institute, which was held retreat style at Rutgers' Continuing Education Center from May 30 to June 2. The institute's purpose was to acquaint college teachers with the new scholarship on gender, race, ethnicity, class, and sexuality and help them plan integration projects for their home institutions.[44] Both the speakers and the participants, forty-three faculty members who came as teams from fourteen New Jersey institutions, were diversified by discipline, sex, race, class, and sexuality.[45] The program began with general sessions on rethinking society and scholarship, broke into workshops on particular disciplines, and concluded with general sessions on pedagogy and strategies for institutionalizing their projects. Besides these sessions, the participants attended evening keynote speeches and cultural events, joined in spontaneous mealtime conversations, and used spare moments to browse the resource display and peruse the hefty readings packet.[46] Yet for all of their enthusiasm about the institute's riches, they sometimes found its discourse hard to do. Participant reactions to three of the sessions and the comments they wrote on their evaluations suggest that identity discourse complicated the task of learning how to make curricular change.

Speaking in two sessions held on the second day of the institute, psychology professor James Anderson deftly touched all the bases for changing disciplinary knowledges—intellectual, personal, and social. At the morning session, he introduced himself as "feminist, Afrocentric, pro-Hispanic, [and] pro-Asian" in order, he said pointedly, to role-model the concepts of multiple identities and reciprocal support. Then he offered a protocol for intellectual change—historicize disciplinary knowledges, think critically about them, and build new models for the study of race, gender, and class—and demonstrated how it could work on racist social science.[47] In the companion session held that afternoon, Anderson moved on to the personal and social dimensions of disciplinary change. When you approach your colleagues, he advised the audience, "asking them to ask new questions about the discipline is the least threatening thing you can do; you're dead in the water if you start with a blistering criticism." His own procedure was "to generate a bunch of questions that people can't answer by using the traditional assumptions and models of their discipline" but to make sure the questions were posed in disciplinary terms so that colleagues had "a base line" for answering.[48] Anderson's approach was to initiate the change process well within people's comfort zones and then gradually move them along.

The speaker at dinner that evening was philosophy professor Marilyn Frye, who discussed "whiteliness," an attitude that took white privilege for granted and ignored the perspectives of people of color. Many of the participants experienced her talk as verging beyond their comfort zones: some walked out of the discussion period, others sat in glum silence, a few voiced objections, and afterward several held a heated discussion in the lounge while Frye played pool in a nearby room. At the time I attributed their responses to the problems of discipline in both senses of that word. I assumed that Frye's lengthy chains of reasoning, which were characteristic of the philosophical style of argument, may have been difficult for non-philosophers to follow in oral presentation and that her unvarnished self-criticism may have suggested to participants who were willing to eliminate the whiteliness that had seeped into their college courses that they would have to abase themselves in the process.[49]

Later that summer Rothenberg sent me two sets of participant evaluations, a reflection page written the day after Frye's talk and a longer evaluation completed at the end of the institute.[50] Reading the reflections, I realized that I was wrong because only two participants said they were taxed by Frye's philosophical style.[51] The others had followed her presentation and described it as "provocative," but the reactions it provoked varied. For three, her talk precipitated insights they welcomed, as this example shows:

> Marilyn's vision that we need to come together as women with all the differences fully functioning is exactly where and how I see myself wanting and needing to make a contribution.[52]

For others, the talk provoked defensiveness. One questioned her feelings:

> I found myself getting defensive and I began to ponder why. Is it because I'm white and I identify with what she said? Is it because I love the men in my life? I'm not sure. . . . I know she shook me up and I needed that. I need to do a lot more thinking about all the things she said. (respondent's ellipses)

A second deflected her feelings:

> I found strong objections from myself and many others to the premise that some of us are not entitled to be considered feminist in our thinking due to our birth culture, race, & gender.

Yet another resorted to self-silencing:

> My reaction to the provocative talk by Marilyn Frye. . . . (respondent's ellipsis)

For this participant, something was too threatening to be inscribed on a sheet that would be read by the institute organizers.

More information was provided by the final evaluation forms where the participants rated the institute presentations on a scale from 1 as low to 5 as high. For Frye's talk, ten participants gave it high marks (5 or 4), six gave it low ones low (1 or 2), and seven chose the median number 3, which could indicate a rating of so-so quality or could mean something else. Since nearly all of the participants who submitted reflections and wrote comments in the space provided on final evaluations had described Frye's presentation as provocative, I interpreted the group of seven as refusing to select a rating that would reveal their own positioning. But what was it that they refused to position themselves on? They unabashedly positioned themselves on other matters, lavishly praising the institute as stimulating and well-organized, the presentations as informative, the workshops and materials as helpful, and the networking with colleagues as exhilarating. A few, however, indicated that the institute's discourse of diversity was most difficult to do when it seemed to target their personalized "selves." For example: "I came here to find out about myself—in a way that others perceive me—as a male white teacher. . . . Coming away from this conference, I can't be the same as going into it—but I'm not sure how. . . . Nothing is easy!" It would be wrong to conclude that the participants at this institute were tripped up by self-reflection and critical analysis that those at the Resource Bank Meeting did not practice. Conservatives did ponder the differences that had produced discord within their movement and the differences within other groups that their movement could exploit. What distinguished the two events was whether the participants were asked to focus their self-reflection and critical analysis on their own identities in order to change those identities.

When the process of critical self-reflection occurs in the presence of others, the discomfort that some people feel can become an obstacle to self-change. Anderson's use of nonthreatening procedures to help people change their disciplinary assumptions and practices reminded me of the advice I had heard twenty years earlier at the Industrial Areas Foundation (IAF) training programs for women: you have to depersonalize the risk because, the IAF trainers told us, once you fear for your "self" you won't be effective in the change process. Since making change is by definition a risk-taking activity, a would-be change agent has to step outside her comfort zone in order to learn the change-making techniques but also has to stay firmly planted within it in order to use those techniques in a change project. Ideally, a training process would enlarge, even while reinforcing, the zone of comfort wherein the "self" dwells. Or as one institute participant wrote on her evaluation form,

> I think being uncomfortable is necessary; however, the reactions from my colleagues have shown me that, not that they're not ready for such provocation, but that they *are* and 4 days of intense throwing at them of ideas and suggestions is making them not thoughtful and reflective, but defensive and sensitive (to themselves not to others). So I think that what is necessary is a much *longer* process—one that goes on for several weeks. (respondent's emphasis)

How long the training process takes depends upon the person's capacity to accommodate the identity changes asked of her; some who attended the New Jersey Project Summer Institute needed "a much *longer* process." By contrast, the participants at the Resource Bank Meeting did not need a much longer process because the speakers did not attempt to edge them outside their comfort zones. The speakers affirmed the identities the participants already had, gave them skills they needed to work for a coalitional agenda, and sent them into the world radiating purposefulness.

Since identity-linked purpose has to be realized in material practice, I want to mention the fortuitous confluence of structural circumstances—educational, demographic, geographic, financial—that supported the formation of a feminist network in New Jersey and the success of the New Jersey Project. First, a critical mass of academic feminists had assembled at Douglass College in the early 1970s and somewhat later at other public and private institutions throughout the state. By the time the DHE decided to fund a statewide gender integration project, these institutions had flourishing academic-feminist communities and experienced feminist leaders. When we spoke, Chancellor Goldberg made a point of acknowledging feminist leaders: Catharine Stimpson, who, as the founder of *Signs* and director of the IRW, was regarded as the foremost expert in gender scholarship; Dean Mary Hartman, who provided strong institutional support; Carol Smith and Ferris Olin, who bestowed "intellectual lustre" on the project; and Paula Rothenberg, who "came on board with new goals, new energy, and political sense."[53]

Second, New Jersey's geography, demography, and social architecture were conducive to a statewide project. Since fifty-six institutions of higher education were crowded into a small state that could be driven border-to-border in four hours, the project leaders could count on attracting faculty to events wherever they were located. They could also count on the state's heterogeneous student population to welcome gender, race, and class scholarship. Statistics generated by DHE showed that, in 1985, 55 percent of all New Jersey college students were women, 56 percent of Hispanic students were women, and 63 percent of African-American students were women. Even with an accessible and interested population, information about the project might have traveled more slowly were it not for the linkages among faculty at diverse institutions that women's groups and the DHE had created for previous projects. These infrastructural features made the job of building a statewide project much easier than it would have been in larger and less cohesive states.[54]

Third, the success of the project was made possible by the DHE's philosophy. In the mid-1980s, Chancellor Goldberg told me, the DHE "had decided to move away from regulation as a primary coordinating mechanism and toward a catalytic role; it felt that planning, suggesting, seeding, and furnishing inventive funding would engender more change than regulation would." As his comment suggests, the DHE catalyzed grassroots change by forming advisory groups to involve faculty in the planning process, funding resource centers for curriculum development, and establishing a competitive grants program to support campus-based projects.[55] Besides seeding grassroots change, the chancellor and assistant chancellor personally spoke at an initial conference to brief campus administrators on the project, praised the project in annual DHE reports to state government, and helped project leaders work with the legislature's Budget Committee.[56] Finally, the New Jersey Project was more fortunate than most academic-feminist programs that experienced slow starvation as their host universities and colleges coped with revenue shortfalls from the 1980s onward. Between 1986 and 1990, the DHE committed a total of $1,456,000 to the New Jersey Project—$360,000 for the first phase, $200,000 for the second phase, and $896,000 to support forty campus-based projects at participating institutions across the state—and later the state gave it bridge funding until it could begin generating income.[57] People who do their networking through Rolodexes, chance encounters, and brief collaborations may be able to sponsor modest change projects, but to make structural change they need an organizational infrastructure linked by communications technologies, stoked with dollars, and sponsoring ongoing activities.

As superb examples of this infrastructure, the Heritage Resource Bank and the New Jersey Project have many features in common: they are coordinated by central offices; institutionalized through an array of training programs, events, and technologies; and oriented toward long-term goals. Yet I also want to foreground some differences. The first is scope and objective: while the Resource Bank was acting across the sectors of Civil Society and the State to build a conservative governing majority, the New Jersey Project was acting within the higher-education sector to integrate curricula. I make this point not to criticize the New Jersey Project but to suggest that the transformation of material practices and processes has to occur in two directions—revising the rules and raising the consciousnesses. The second difference bears on efficacy: conservative organizations, as private enterprises funded by foundations, donors, and income-producing activities, are free to pursue political objectives, but academy-based feminist projects, despite the inflated claims of political efficacy attributed to them, are constrained by their hosts' intellectual and educational missions. The third difference—that mainstream foundations have shied away from the strategic grantmaking practiced by conservative ones—should remind us that the nation will get what its funders pay for. What the nation is likely to get for its future leaders and citizens I explore in the next section.

Training the Third Generation

To educate leaders for the Republic—Fund for American Studies and Georgetown University (1993)

Encouraging, inspiring, and facilitating the interest of young women in politics and public leadership—Center for the American Woman and Politics, Rutgers University (1994)

Training activists and leaders who wish to promote social change in a variety of settings—Graduate Program in Women's Studies, Midwestern State University (1991)

Social-change initiatives, I have been arguing, are conditioned by a movement's structural features—its tightly or loosely linked organizations, cross-sector or only intrasector operations, and coherent or contested agendas. Now I want to shift my focus from the organizational field to some of the individual programs designed to produce what conservatives call "the third generation" and feminists call "the third wave." The programs described in this section are neither random selections nor matched pairs; they are the best examples I could find of hybrids operating across the academic / political divide and training college students for public leadership and movement activism. The programs differ in many respects— their selection of students, staff, and speakers, their content and pedagogy, their duration and follow-up—which I will describe. But since I want to probe how they go about constituting change agents, I will be addressing these questions. How do the programs delineate the nation's economic, political, and social systems? What skills and opportunities do they offer the students? What self-awareness and other-awareness do they encourage the students to develop? And how does identity discourse, whether submerged or surfaced, drive their activities?

AT GEORGETOWN UNIVERSITY

As New Left criticisms of American racism, capitalism, and imperialism were sweeping college campuses during the mid-1960s, a group of conservatives met to plan an organization that would inculcate the young with an appreciation of the American system as they saw it. The Charles Edison Fund was founded in 1967 by James Buckley and Walter H. Judd with the help of Buckley campaign chairman David Jones and Georgetown economics professor Lev Dobriansky. After receiving IRS 501(c)(3) status as a tax-exempt educational organization, the Edison Fund commenced operations in 1970 with the Institute for Comparative Economic and Political Systems (ICPES), a six-week summer program for college students held at Georgetown University. In succeeding years, the Edison Fund changed its name to the Fund for American Studies (FAS) and established three more summer programs: the Institute on Political Journalism (IPJ) in 1985, the Bryce Harlow Institute on Business and Government Affairs in 1990 (both at Georgetown), and the Institute on Political Economy in 1993 at Charles University in Czechoslovakia. The next year FAS inaugurated an ambitious program that would give its three thousand alumni, most of whom were working in government, business, and the media, additional training in public leadership.[58]

By 1993, the institutes were a booming enterprise in every sense of the word: they had campus recruiters, nationwide corporate partners and private donors, internship providers in the Washington metropolitan area, and a steady supply of students. That summer 127 students enrolled in ICPES, 68 in IPJ, and 42 in the Harlow program. Since a student's outlay to attend an institute—$3,000 for Georgetown tuition and housing, plus travel and per diem expenses—didn't cover the actual per student cost to the institutes, FAS underwrote the deficit by providing per student subsidies of $1,800 for ICPES, $3,600 for IPJ, and $4,200 for the Harlow Institute. In addition, FAS awarded full scholarships to about one-third of the ICPES students and more than half of the IPJ students, while each of the corporations hosting the Harlow internships sponsored one student.[59] If these numbers are correct, a quick calculation shows that FAS spent nearly $650,000 on subsidies and $250,000 on scholarships for a total outlay of close to a million dollars in 1993 alone.

The partnership sponsoring the institutes was something of a puzzle to me. Clearly FAS gained an intellectual legitimacy and educational capability it would not have had on its own, but why would Georgetown University hitch itself to FAS? To find out whether something more than summer school revenues cemented the union, I asked the people who managed the institutes to describe the partnership: Georgetown Dean of Summer and Continuing Education Michael J. Collins and FAS staff directors Marina C. Sheridan (ICPES) and Lawrence F. Guillemette Jr. (IPJ). Collins said the partners' "goals conjoin": both were founded "to educate leaders for the Republic" and believed their education should include practical as well as intellectual preparation for "responsible leadership and transformation." I learned of their ideological synchronicity when, in separate interviews, Collins told me that FAS wanted to show young people the superiority of the American system through comparative political and economic education[60] and Sheridan and Guillemette said that the institutes compared our system of government "to other systems in the hope that the students will see ours as best."[61] Although Collins emphasized that FAS respected the university's autonomy in academic matters—the summer school selected the professors who in turn designed the courses—I wondered whether the institutes might be practicing conservative politics voluntarily, so to speak.

When I asked Dean Collins whether the institutes promoted conservatism, he hedged, on the one hand averring that FAS never imposed an ideological litmus test on the professors, speakers, and students and on the other hand acknowledging that several professors taught from a conservative perspective and most guest speakers "tilted toward the conservative viewpoint."[62] My fieldwork disclosed more than a tilt toward conservatism on both sides of the partnership. The institute boards (like FAS's own boards of trustees, advisers, and alumni) were heavily weighted with conservatives, and the institute internship providers selected by FAS ranged from far right to centrist (none were feminist or progressive).[63] Two of the four Georgetown professors teaching ICPES and IPJ courses presented only conservative economics, a third advocated conservative ethics, and the fourth used a variety of theories to analyze the democratization processes of Western nations.[64] Finally, the students attending the 1993 institutes were diversified by region, type of academic institution, and gender (more than 50 percent of IPJ and 40 percent of ICPES students were women) but not by race or political beliefs. One ICPES student told me that "the liberal students kind of cluster together and feel somewhat besieged"; that sentiment was repeated by the half-dozen left-of-center students and the few students of color who spoke with me during class breaks or informal suppers.[65]

For six weeks, from June 10 to July 23, the students lived in dorms on the hillsides of the gracious, tree-shaded Georgetown campus. In the mornings they interned at congressional offices, public agencies, media organizations, and interest-advocacy groups; during the afternoons they attended classes (two courses per institute) and informal discussions facilitated by FAS staff; and some evenings they trooped to lectures featuring public leaders. For two weeks, one in June and one in July, I lived in another Georgetown dormitory and observed the activities of ICPES and IPJ. What I found at the institutes was not the blatant ideologizing I had observed at the Free Congress Foundation and the Leadership Institute but a subtler blending of ingredients.

Formulaic Learning. Students attending the Institute for Political Journalism took two courses, Economics in Public Policy and Ethics and the Media, each meeting three times a week as well as in occasional joint sessions. The economics course used two texts, Edwin Mansfield and Nariman Behravesh's *Economics USA* (Norton, 1992) and Thomas Swartz and Frank Bonello's *Taking Sides* (Guilford, 1993), supplemented by information in lectures and handouts. The professor, a veteran teacher for IPJ, covered six topics geared to illuminating the dynamics of the free-market system: supply and demand, national income determination, the role of government, the monetary system and financial markets, international economic issues, and major public policy issues. The stated purpose of the course was to teach students about economic policy issues and connect economic policy to the issues addressed in the Ethics and Media course, but the actual purpose was to inculcate a type of conservative economics that I would describe as abstract positivism.[66]

Presenting the American economy as an abstract model shorn of human behavior, real-life consequences, and historical contingency, the professor concentrated on exercising the students in formulas that captured the hypothetical market system's operations; for instance, they practiced using a supply-demand equation to ascertain the market's shifts away from and return to equilibrium. When the students raised messy normative issues, the professor brought them back to abstract positivism with humorous reminders. To the student who asked, "When a recession causes people's income to go down, does demand go down?" he replied, "Leave recession out of it; stay with the micro. We're supposed to compartmentalize the parts."[67] When he asked the students to explain what would happen if the government increased the minimum wage, one student replied that demand would increase because people would have more dollars to spend, a second surmised that unemployment would increase because employers would try to offset higher wages by firing workers, and a third thought that on balance supply and demand would stay the same. "Too cosmic," the professor joked. "You're feeding in too much; you must be thinking of becoming political scientists."[68] These classroom moments, as well as many others I could have recounted, showed that the students were expected to decontextualize economic activities, recast them as an abstract puzzle, reduce the puzzle to simples, and formulaically determine how the simples would operate in a "perfect" market. The formulaic logic evacuated people from economic activity and with them any consideration of real-life constraints and consequences flowing from economic policies.

The IPJ ethics course took a more nuanced approach to policy issues or so it seemed at the outset when the professor defined *ethics* as giving moral meaning to action through the practice of reflecting on whether what we do is congruent with what we believe to be good. Having promised that the students would wrestle with the question of what was good, the professor then presented four ethical frameworks that delimited their answers. The first framework defined four components that commonly enter in people's ethical decision making: facts, biases and loyalties, beliefs and values, and principles and norms. The professor emphasized that biases and loyalties, which resulted from "perspective[s] based on our education, our class, our race, our gender," caused us to "load the facts" and thus distort our perception of the situations calling for ethical decisions. We should eliminate identity-driven biases and loyalties from ethical decision making, he said, and let ourselves be guided instead by the beliefs and values derived from moral principles and societal norms. In class discussions, the students dutifully applied this framework without noticing that it was the normative counterpart of abstract economics. Ethical principles and norms, like economic formulas, would operate on the unvarnished facts to extract the right answers.[69]

It came as no surprise when the professor next presented three principle-based frameworks that would generate the right answers. With Kantian ethics, the decision maker would use universal principles "accepted by all people in all times" to analyze a situation. This approach is valuable, he said, because it "gets away from individual preferences and subjectivism"—or, in other words, from those identity-driven biases. The students had few criticisms of this model. With utilitarian ethics, the decision maker would calculate the comparative weight of the good and harmful consequences expected to ensue from decisions. The students were more critical here, pointing out that a determination of good would have to precede a calculation of consequences, that predicting the consequences might be impossible, and that an evil system such as slavery could be rationalized as benefiting more people than it harmed.

The professor called the last framework "distributive justice," but instead of presenting it in social-structural terms so that the students could analyze the distribution of social goods he defined it in individualist terms as fairness to the parties to a particular situation. Accordingly, the students defined media fairness as covering all sides of a story or, as one said (whether ironically or sincerely, I could not tell), "representing the opinions of the victim and the perpetrator" of a crime. The professor did complicate the issue of fairness by asking whether it meant guaranteeing everyone the same outcome or guaranteeing everyone merit-based outcomes. Is it fair, he asked, to give "everyone in this class an A?" or to give "each man his due—and each woman?" This exchange followed:

STUDENT: You base the grade on performance.
STUDENT: You get what you deserve.
STUDENT: What about making the grade proportional to the person's capacity to contribute?
PROFESSOR: Do students have the right to an A or the right to try earning an A? Does a right to healthcare mean that all people pay the same costs or that people pay proportionately as they can afford?[70]

Although his questions were thought provoking, they did not provoke further thoughts on whether fundamental distributive injustices undermined the notion of merit-based outcomes. The class did not consider how citizens' material and social circumstances from birth forward had already positioned them for advantage or disadvantage before they tried to speak to the media, earn grades, and pay for healthcare, nor how the media, education systems, and government institutions participated in the economy of distributive injustice.

Midway through the course, the professor set the stage for a theory of the State that would synthesize the four ethics frameworks. He declared that the identity-driven biases distorting ethical decision making were also disintegrating the nation:

> We have a breakdown of consensus. . . . The glue is gone and we're falling apart. . . . And also the disciplines we use to understand ourselves—sociology, political science, economics—are fractured. Too many approaches and no single perspective. When we try to think coherently . . . we have enormous difficulty because we no longer have common assumptions.[71]

"How," asked a student, "do you get back to coherence without infringing upon individual rights?" The professor answered, "When we stress rights, we pit people against each other—children's rights, animal rights. We need a new framework for thinking about rights with regard to community membership and responsibility rather than [with regard to] individualism." That framework was civic republicanism, the professor's theory of the State.

As preparation, the professor had assigned William M. Sullivan's *Reconstructing Public Philosophy* (1982), a book that counterpoints liberalism and civic republicanism, and then following Sullivan's lead he gradually set up the dualism. First he made common-sense remarks such as "We have mutual responsibilities and obligations, as well as individual ones" and "The issue isn't my rights versus yours, but our rights. The 'us' should have a more permanent place in our thinking." Then to civic republicanism he linked founding doctrine, classical humanist values, social coherence, and national rebirth, and to liberalism he linked identity-driven interests, moral relativism, social disintegration, and national decline. Once he had clarified the principles of civic republicanism—the normativity of universal human nature, conservative values, competitive enterprise, and philanthropy for the unfortunates—I could see that the State would be governed by a rationalist oligarchy that garbed its formulaic policy decisions in cozy communitarian rhetoric. Most of the students embraced the theory, but a few tried to imagine a State that would accommodate differences. "Are you thinking," one asked, "about a homogeneous country, a melting pot? Or are we a mosaic of differences?" Another suggested that society was a salad bowl in which the ingredients, though blended, retain their distinctive identities, and a third asked, "What about the idea of civic liberalism?" For his part, the professor reiterated that civic republicanism glued the pieces together.[72]

My concern that the students, once exercised in economics formulas and ethics frameworks, would not analyze real-life circumstances was heightened at a joint session facilitated by the two professors. To prepare, the students had read an article by Milton Friedman arguing that the market should be allowed to do its work and a case study of Ford Pintos whose defective gas tanks were prone to rupturing. The discussion was initiated with this question: "What is Ford's responsibility, knowing that the gas tanks were faulty but at a time when no laws required the industry to recall and repair defective automobiles?" To the student who said that the company should repair the Pintos, a professor replied that Ford had estimated a cost of $500 to repair each of the millions of vehicles already sold. To the student who said that responsible behavior would increase Ford's long-term profits, a professor exclaimed "caveat emptor" and explained that the buyer should assume responsibility for finding out about product defects. This exchange followed:

> STUDENT: How are we supposed to find out about fatal flaws in cars?
> PROFESSOR: The flaws are known—now what?
> STUDENT: Everyone knows Volvos are better than Pintos, so we should buy Volvos.
> STUDENT: What happens if you can't afford a Volvo?
> STUDENT: Ford could give buyers the option of an exploding gas tank at one price and a nonexploding gas tank at $500 more.[73]

No one discussed how the consumers' wherewithal to research flaws, purchase a car, and seek redress was already determined by distributive inequalities. Using economics formulas and ethics frameworks, the class redescribed a complex problem as a corporate gain-loss equation, recast corporate responsibility as caveat emptor, and then reluctantly emptied buyer choice of the wherewithal necessary to implement that choice—namely, discretionary income and informed decision making. By concentrating on two abstract categories, the corporation and the consumer, the class skirted the consequences for real-life Pinto victims—property loss, bodily damage, and sometimes death.

Reflecting on the IPJ courses, I concluded that the professors had not so much ignored distributive inequalities as redefined them in conservative terms. The economics professor described the distribution of "merit goods" (e.g., welfare, food stamps, and Medicare) as disrupting the competition that would perfect the market, and the ethics professor similarly described the identity-driven conflicts as disrupting the consensus that would perfect civil society. What they failed to clarify, even in their own terms, was the link between their models: the nation's imperfect economic, political, and social systems had constituted the identity groups now pitched in conflict over distributive justice.

The Disappearance of Diversity. Two sessions facilitated by IPJ director Larry Guillemette revealed how the institute's identity discourse worked. Since the purpose of these sessions was to teach the students how to forge an agreement to disagree when discussing political and policy issues, Guillemette asked them to observe these rules: (1) support your own position, (2) understand your opponents' positions, (3) disagree respectfully with your fellow students, and (4) harbor no ill feelings for those whose opinions differ from your own.

At the first session, Guillemette invited them to share their impressions of politics and life in Washington, DC. Their comments are so telling that I quote them at length. On the federal government:

> "The bureaucracy is unbelievable; I hate government."
> "Congress is spending $18 million to rebuild the subway loop around Capitol Hill so that it goes marginally faster."
> "I thought senators were concerned about their constituencies, but everything is well orchestrated. They're not saying 'Lets go in and do something for Montana today.'"
> "One thing rubs me the wrong way—Congress members' focus on celebrity, media coverage, positions, and status."

On power-brokering in the capital:

> "The Republicans and Democrats are strong on tradition—the tradition of beating up new ideas and newcomers."
> "My [internship] boss says DC works because you either succeed or fail; if you fail, you're replaced."

"I came to my internship in a senator's office as an idealist and was disillusioned on the first day. All of the staff have a 'place'; you're never allowed to forget you're an intern."

"I arrived as a cynic about [power brokers'] egos, but I'm amazed by the level of incompetence in DC."

On everyday life in the capital:

"I come to DC every summer and see the homeless on the streets. How can you insulate yourself? But people do—they live in affluent neighborhoods, get on the Metro, and look straight ahead. I'm amazed by the apathy."

"I used to be prejudiced against the homeless, but I recently talked to a homeless man to find out what his life is like."

"We need healthcare reform. I was in the hospital for eight days to have my appendix out and the bill was $10,000. What do homeless people do?"

"The homeless die in the streets."

"I was surprised by the racial segregation in a city that's 80 percent black. California has more races represented in more professions. Here people yell racial insults at each other on M Street on Saturday night."

These remarks show that the students' critical awareness was based in the identity-linked perspectives and values that the professors had banished from their courses. By contrasting life in their home communities with that in Washington, they could see violent incongruities and virulent hypocrisies: they were disgusted by the behavior of politicians, disturbed by the plight of the homeless, concerned about the entrenched racism, and astonished by the apathy of the privileged. Some of the students took the next step of reflecting on how their perspectives and values had changed. One arrived an idealist and was immediately disillusioned, another had his cynicism deepened, a third was disabused of a prejudice. Only one student "came as an idealist and will leave with my idealism intact." Her internship provider, a woman who had launched a now-booming business from her home, reinforced the student's belief that a person could succeed through hard work.[74]

The students' critical faculties retreated during the second session when Guillemette invited them to debate two policy issues resembling those discussed in their classes. "Should U.S. taxpayers be required to bail out people who had houses in flood-prone zones?" he asked, referring to Federal Emergency Management Agency (FEMA) assistance to the Iowa flood victims. The students replied,

> "Individuals who built houses in risky places shouldn't be assisted but should have their own insurance."
> "If a city council makes the wrong decision [about building locations], government should help people."
> "The flood is a disaster, but FEMA is stupidly set up to reward stupid behavior."
> "The most fertile farmland is . . . adjacent to the Mississippi River, so the location of farms is *not* a quixotic choice."

Having learned that choices entail costs in the economics course and that rights entail responsibilities in the ethics course, the students meshed these concepts into a new formula—those who have the right to choose also have the responsibility to pay—that prompted them to identify the guilty parties. The first student fingered the individuals who chose where to build their homes, the second coimplicated the city council for its zoning ordinances, and the third excoriated the feds for setting up a relief agency to reward irresponsible citizen behavior. Trying to get away from the guilt formula, the fourth student exonerated those who did not have free choice (farmers) but implicitly left the blame with those who did (home and business owners). Finally, several students followed Guillemette's hint that FEMA was misusing money still owned by the taxpayers. One student made the utilitarian argument that FEMA had an ethical responsibility to weigh the lesser cost to taxpayers of helping flood victims against the greater cost of not helping them: "more homeless, more people on welfare, more people sucking the system in some way." This scathing comment went unremarked because the class never discussed flood victims' ruined lives or views on federal assistance.

The second issue the students debated was President Clinton's shifting position on gays and lesbians in the military. The president, Guillemette explained, had initially favored a policy permitting gays and lesbians to serve openly, but after encountering opposition he had decided to support the "don't ask, don't tell" policy and put the administration to work on lowering the gay and lesbian community's expectations. By failing to impart information on various policy options and implying that no heterosexuals preferred the open inclusion policy, Guillemette left the students to flounder in their own heterosexual identity dilemmas. Some were strung out between making anxious comments on homosexuality and declaring that gays and lesbians should have equal employment opportunities. Others were torn between their concurrence with the "don't ask, don't tell" policy and their desire to avoid being labeled homophobic for it. Veering away from these dilemmas, the students situated responsibility elsewhere, as this exchange shows.

> "The military has always discriminated."
> "If the military doesn't want gays, it should be able to reject them as well as whomever else it doesn't want—whether the reasons are too short or tall, flat feet, or gay."
> "Are you saying that being homosexual equals being deficient?"
> "No, I'm saying that our military, which is the best in the world, has a right to choose and reject whoever it wants."

Since Guillemette did not introduce the idea that military recruitment could be based on objective job descriptions and retention on actual job performance, the students set about determining who was authorized to make policy and should take the heat. One blamed the president as commander in chief, and another pointed out that since presidential decisions are subject to congressional approval the blame should be shared.

As I saw it, the students used the rights-responsibilities formula learned in their ethics class to project their homophobia onto the military and then denied the military's homophobia by converting it into the military's right, as subject to presidential and congressional policy, to make recruitment and retention decisions. Only two students considered how gays and lesbians might feel about the "don't ask, don't tell" policy. One, who had interviewed a discharged lesbian, observed that "people shouldn't have to hide things." Another, perhaps alluding to Guillemette's omissions, said she "appreciated it when people spoke about the issue based on information and experience, part of which was talking to gay people about how they feel."[75] But in the main the application of economics formulas and ethical frameworks had evacuated from the discussion the people who were affected by public policies and with them the responsibility of the students as future leaders to understand the circumstances and views of citizens affected by those policies.

Identity Affirmations. The FAS staff directors arranged for me to interview four students and their internship providers. Meeting the students at nearby Georgetown restaurants, I asked open-ended questions—"Tell me about your internship," "What did you learn at the Institute?" and "Will you go home the same person or a different one?"—and then followed their leads. Meeting the internship providers at their offices, I asked about their organizations, the duties of their interns, and their views of the FAS-Georgetown institutes.[76] The interview data revealed that identity discourse at the institutes worked in similar ways to that discourse at the Heritage Foundation's Resource Bank Meeting.

David was an IPJ intern at the Media Research Center (MRC), a right-wing media watchdog and lobbying organization founded in 1987 by L. Brent Bozell and Brent H. Baker. The MRC's mission, according to Sandra L. Crawford (director of the entertainment division), was to document liberal bias in the media, create market pressure on them, and thereby bring conservative themes and activities into news and entertainment. David's job was to view TV shows and write articles about their liberal bias. When I asked how he recognized liberal bias, he said that MRC had given him a list of fifty types—for instance, more numerous mentions of Clinton than Bush, more pro than con mentions of Clinton, portrayals of Mormons as rabid polygamists, and dramas featuring children who don't respect their parents. David regarded MRC's philosophy as congruent with his own "moderate conservatism" and described the internship as "ideal" because MRC gave him the same assignments as full-time staff and offered him a paid internship for the rest of the summer. Crawford said that the internships provided mutual benefits: the young people had "a test drive," and MRC had a "good farm team." Indeed, MRC had added several former interns to its full-time staff.[77]

Kevin was an ICPES intern at the NFIB Foundation, the research and education arm of the National Federation of Independent Business (NFIB), a lobbying organization that supported "the preservation of the American free-enterprise economic system based on private ownership, fair competition and the opportunity to become an entrepreneur."[78] The foundation's "front burner" issues, said Kimberly K. Brandow (coordinator of the Small Business Research Institute), were government regulations and employer rights. When Kevin told me that his research on these two issues was geared to showing that "we have a Democratic administration whose philosophy may in part be unconstitutional," I asked for clarification. He explained that the government, by imposing costly regulations that diminished business and stockholder profits, was violating the "takings clause [of the Constitution], which says that government cannot deny someone the right to their property." Kevin described NFIB's "nonpartisan philosophy" as congruent with his own and praised ICPES for acknowledging his motivation and competence. "When your teacher assumes you are competent," he said, "the teacher will receive competence," adding that he felt "loyalty [to FAS] because of this positive experience." Brandow told me that NFIB had invited the FAS interns to stay through the summer in paid positions and later might hire them to do contract work.[79]

Betsy was an ICPES intern at the Legal Services Corporation (LSC), a congressionally funded nonprofit corporation that monitors and awards grants to local agencies providing civil legal services to the poor. She worked in the Monitoring Division preparing memoranda on local agency problems and proudly told me that LSC had given her an office, a computer, and access to case files. Kenneth F. Boehm (assistant to the president and counsel to the board of directors) said LSC was so impressed with previous FAS interns that it was now hosting five who were assigned to do legal and financial analysis. Betsy praised LSC for teaching her "about the world, herself, and the future" and ICPES for providing "not just an exciting but a fulfilling experience." The students "came from all over with different expectations and priorities": some were "gifted and know so much," some "cut out every night to party," and others, like herself, worked. She concluded the interview by exclaiming, "If you were in a group with everybody like yourself, what would you learn from that?"[80]

Diane was an IPJ intern at Pasha Publications, a company providing newsletters and digests to operators in the energy, environmental, aerospace, and defense industries. From her assignments in the first two areas, Diane praised Pasha for being concerned "not just with mine regulations but with mine operators' lives" and criticized the Environmental Protection Agency (EPA) for spending its funds on lawsuits to "find out which companies were responsible twenty years ago instead of cleaning up the waste [at 1,200 hazardous sites] and helping people [who were victims]." A maverick at IPJ, she liked the ethics course more than the economics course because she learned better from "real-life issues and stories than from mechanics," adding "I don't like dealing with numbers because they act in their own ways." What she appreciated most was the opportunity to interact with students who had a "really amazing diversity of opinion and background." The students sometimes "got into huge arguments in class and outside" because "we only have our own experiences, and if you remember that you won't expect people to agree with you." Yet she "ended up not liking some people because of their viewpoints," avoided raising issues that would "cause tension between me and other people," and didn't "hang around with people I disagree with politically." The result, she observed, was that "nobody changed anyone's mind."[81]

Although identity discourse was officially submerged, it nevertheless determined who the institutes had chosen to train as future leaders and how they were training them. The institutes had diversified their student bodies by region, academic institution, and sex but not by race, sexuality, and political ideology. In teaching policy analysis, the institutes did not invite homeless people, victims of faulty products, or gays and lesbians to speak on the policies affecting them, nor did they provide materials and methods for getting at the life circumstances of excluded populations. While exercising the students in economics formulas and ethical frameworks, the staff steered them away from messy normative matters. When left to their own logics, the students did notice poverty, racism, and so forth, but their observations went nowhere: Guillemette didn't build on them, the economics professor ruled them out of bounds, and the ethics professor declared them to be divisive. The laissez-faire rule of "agreeing to disagree respectfully" operated to protect the status quo in classes and peer groups: on those occasions when the students expressed conflicting viewpoints, they withdrew from further engagement, hung out in clusters, and, as Diane noted, rarely changed anybody's mind.

Yet the students regarded their summer at Georgetown as an enriching experience and rightly so because the institutes cultivated their identities. The professors assumed that they were motivated, competent, and knowledgeable, the internship providers gave them full-fledged duties and entré into later employment, and the FAS staff treated them as future leaders in the important world of policy formation. The pedagogical reinforcement and professionalizing trajectory were an identity discourse. By affirming who the students were and speeding them toward whom they hoped to be, the institutes won their gratitude and commitment to the conservative cause—a cause the institutes served by spotting the talent and funneling it into conservative organizations. But in tendering the promissory note of national leadership the institutes had omitted the quid pro quo sentence— the one saying that leaders have a responsibility to understand the problems of diverse citizens and to collaborate with them on the solutions.

AT RUTGERS UNIVERSITY

Soon after becoming the president of Wells College in 1976, former Texas legislator Frances Farenthold began working with others who were troubled by the underrepresentation of women in political office and the neglect of women's needs in policy formation. The group sought Carnegie Foundation funding "to create a network of women's colleges" that would take on the task of "building the next generation of [women] leaders" and in 1978 launched the Public Leadership Education Network (PLEN) with five small women's colleges as its members.[82] By 1992, PLEN had sixteen colleges and a headquarters staff that coordinated the annual programs held in Washington, DC—a public leadership career conference, a two-week seminar on women and public policy, and a student semester that combined classes, internships, and site briefings—and lent support to the member colleges whose activities included hosting conferences, founding institutes, and designing new courses.[83]

Ruth Mandel, a PLEN cofounder and director of the Center for the American Woman and Politics (CAWP) at Rutgers University, had secured a Kellogg Foundation grant to fund NEW Leadership, a summer institute that would train young women in public and political leadership. Each year, from 1991 through 1994, CAWP invited twelve colleges and universities (six were PLEN members) to send two incoming juniors, along with a faculty or staff adviser, to the institute.[84] The center's commitment to diversity by race, region, and type of institution was reflected in the institute's content, staff, and guest speakers as well as the students. For the 1991 and 1992 student cohorts—18 percent were Hispanic, 11 percent were African American, 11 percent were Asian American, and 4 percent were "other"—and the proportions for women of color increased for the 1993 and 1994 student cohorts. More students described themselves as liberal than conservative, but most said they were independents rather than political party supporters.[85]

The 1994 institute, held from June 6 through June 16, was a perfectly choreographed whirlwind of activities designed, according to NEW Leadership coordinator Tobi Walker, to provide the students with knowledge of women in politics, contact with experienced women leaders, leadership skills, and a project opportunity.[86] Living in fourplex apartment dormitories on the bucolic New Brunswick campus were twenty-four students, twelve advisers from their home campuses, and three faculty in residence (FIRS)—a former congresswoman, a Texas legislator, and a consultant to the California Senate. Also in attendance were NEW Leadership staff members, CAWP Director Ruth Mandel, PLEN Director Marianne Alexander, and PLEN Program Director Sharon Stoneback. The busy days on campus, filled with sessions held at the sprawling nineteenth-century manse that housed CAWP, were interspersed with field trips to Trenton, New York City, and Washington, DC, where the students had briefings on government and conversations with leaders.

Experiential Learning. The FAS-Georgetown institutes had divided dormitory living from classroom learning and had used a formal school pedagogy on most occasions—the lecture-discussion format for evening events and the question-answer protocol in classrooms. By contrast, NEW Leadership used a living-and-learning pedagogy that blended the intellectual, practical, and personal.[87] Whatever the occasion—a panel of speakers or a stroll back to the dorm, a skills workshop or a bus trip to the state capital—the students had conversations with the resident staff and accomplished public leaders who invariably shared personal anecdotes and answered questions about their lives.

The learning components of NEW Leadership were not only more integrated but also more varied than those at the FAS-Georgetown institutes. On campus, the students attended informational sessions on the history of women in American politics, women's impact in politics, models of leadership, women's global leadership, and young women in politics. They practiced public speaking and other skills in workshops, discussed their interests in focus groups, and analyzed group process in other sessions. They participated in conversations with Bella Abzug (former New York congresswoman), Liz Abzug (director for Federal Affairs and Programs, New York State Urban Development Corporation), and Geraldine Ferraro (former New York congresswoman and chair of the U.S. Delegation to the United Nations Human Rights Commission). Their conversations with the CAWP staff members, FIRS, and campus advisers took place at early morning dorm breakfasts, on the front porch of the manse between sessions, across banquet tables, and during late evening walks.

The same pedagogy was used on the field trips. In Trenton, the students convened in the Senate chamber for legislative role-playing directed by FIR Debra Danburg, a Texas legislator, and a legislative overview lecture by Eagleton Institute professor Alan Rosenthal. They had conversations with Jane Kenney, chief of policy and planning for the governor; Judy Shaw, chief of staff for the governor; Melanie Griffin, director of the New Jersey Commission on Sex Discrimination; and Linda Bowker, director of the New Jersey Division on Women. In Washington, after touring the halls of Congress, they had conversations with Supreme Court Justice Ruth Bader Ginsburg, Secretary of Energy Hazel O'Leary, and Congresswomen Patsy Mink (D-Hawaii), Marge Roukema (R-N.J.), and Jolene Unsoeld (D-

Wash.). Later they broke into small groups and conversed with legislative assistants and staff at public policy organizations.

Since the program was too brief to include internships, its application component consisted of campus-team projects. At the institute, each team designed a public leadership education project for its home institution or community, wrote a proposal, and drew up a budget. After approving the projects, NEW Leadership seeded each team with a $1,000 grant and monitored its work throughout the year. Returning to the next summer institute, the teams presented their projects to the new crop of students and spoke with the staff about what they had learned.[88]

Diversity Discourse. The institute taught the practices of political leadership in a diverse and often divided democracy. The staff provided a broad definition of politics that added to electoral and governmental activities the many forms of citizen engagement with public issues. That definition in turn meant that they could teach a range of leadership skills, those needed to navigate formal processes, mobilize citizens, plan events, raise funds, and advocate for issues. The student field trip to Trenton was an object lesson in how the diversity practices of government officials and citizens could come together in policy decisions. That morning Professor Rosenthal described the New Jersey legislature as a microcosm of the nation's pluralistic society where the diverse needs of communities, the competing demands for resources, and the sheer number of bills threatened to swamp a decision-making process that legislators held together through negotiation. Later that day the governor's chief of staff, Judy Shaw, gave the students a succinct example of negotiation, describing the state budget as not simply a policy document listing items to be funded but an agreement with citizens reached through a long process of round-table discussions, call-ins, write-ins, and consultations. The goal of the process, she said, was to incorporate diverse citizen interests without pitting the races, genders, and regions against one another.[89]

The information imparted at NEW Leadership was always enlivened with real-life stories illustrating the strategies for cementing individual and coalitional alliances. Debra Danburg, for instance, told the students that to form a working relationship with the "bubbas," the good old boys who represented rural districts in the Texas legislature, she had to "reach out, way out, beyond her comfort level and go and live with them for a while. That's the only way I'll get to understand them." She also boned up on the concerns of their constituents so that when they came to the legislature they didn't dismiss her as a "city person." The bubbas, she added, may be her enemies on some issues, but they are the best leaders their districts have to offer and her own "colleagues and friends, too." Other NEW Leadership staff members spoke about strategic alliances among women in public offices. Sue Carroll, a senior research associate at CAWP, pointed out that women who did not identify themselves as feminists were nearly as likely as feminists to give priority to issues that concerned women and children, to analyze seemingly neutral policies for their differential impact on women and men, and to mentor younger women.[90] Or, as Ruth Mandel put it, diverse women could "find common cause around *some* items on the agenda but not *all* of them."[91]

Several NEW Leadership speakers described coalition building among interest groups. Political consultant Sandy Aguilar recounted how the pro-life and pro-choice women in her home state of West Virginia had found common cause in advocating for a childcare bill but once the bill was passed had returned to their own causes. The reason why more coalitions form around a short single-issue campaign than endure through a prolonged multi-issue struggle became evident when political activist Nancy Amidei presented another example. This one was a food and nutrition policy coalition of mothers, teachers, college students, senior citizens, nutritionists, medical specialists, farmers, supermarket chains, and the health food sector. The more diverse the coalition, she remarked, the greater its potential for political clout but also for discord and disintegration. A coalition, Amidei cautioned the students, "only works if member groups pledge not to work *against* each other's issues for a particular campaign; groups are not required to work *for* but they can't work *against*." "That," as Aguilar said about the short-term pro-life and pro-choice alliance for a childcare bill, "is what coalition building means."[92]

To exercise the students in diversity practice, NEW Leadership staff asked them to observe rules of discussion similar to those at the FAS-Georgetown institutes: the students would hear a range of views from speakers, should question those views in a respectful manner, and should argue ideas without attacking persons. But they also implemented turn taking so that more vocal students would not dominate group discussions, encouraged students with minority views or unaddressed issues to voice them, and invited students reluctant to speak in public to talk privately with staff members.[93] Where the FAS-Georgetown protocol culminated in disengagements that submerged differences, the NEW Leadership protocol supported ongoing engagements that surfaced differences. But even with this support the students found diversity practice hard to do and for reasons that reminded me of the identity complications at the New Jersey Project's summer institute.

Identity Complications. On the first day of the institute, former New York Congresswoman Bella Abzug and her daughter Liz Abzug, the director for federal affairs and programs at the New York State Urban Development Corporation, were the featured speakers at a session entitled Women, Politics, and Leadership: An Intergenerational Conversation. Both speakers acknowledged feminism for giving women new opportunities in personal and public life, and during the discussion period that followed a student confessed that "many students were apprehensive about identifying as a feminist." Liz replied that some "people think *feminist* means *lesbian*; it's all right to use another word," and Bella added, "The word may be a problem, but feminism is a vision of the world—a world with equal justice, a clean environment, elimination of poverty and war." After a second student pointed out that the feminists on her campus let people "define their own issues—race, class, sexuality," a third asked, "What role can conservative women play in the movement?" "Good question," Bella replied, "but that depends on what you mean by 'conservative.' If you mean including a pro-life position, I don't agree, but if you mean including conservative economics, I can understand. We have a pro-choice agenda and recognize Republican women who have tried to move their party toward that position." The student then objected to Bella's earlier comment that Margaret Thatcher was practicing male politics rather than working to change the power structures and declared that she herself respected Thatcher's sex and politics.[94]

The exchange might seem to have been about who can enter feminism's precincts—with Bella Abzug insisting on a pro-choice litmus test and two students arguing that women should decide for themselves whether they were feminists. But the exchange went to the heart of NEW Leadership's identity complications. Its official discourse had specified "women's leadership" as a capacious category that included women of diverse ideologies, party affiliations, and leadership practices and had left "feminist leadership" as an unspecified category. Knowing the negative connotations that feminism had acquired, the apprehensive students wanted more specification before they were willing to identify themselves with it. This discourse created further complications for the student who admired Thatcher. She wanted to envision a role for conservative women in the women's movement, but Bella's specification of it as embracing the pro-choice agenda and eschewing male-typed power politics positioned the student in a breach. What she wanted, I would argue, was something like the "new conservative woman" identity crafted by the Heritage network discourse—a woman who is accorded the equal educational and employment opportunities advocated by feminists and thereby positioned to work on the conservative agenda for traditional values and free-market economics.

As the institute progressed, the students routinely asked the guest speakers, "Are you a feminist?" They posed the question, I thought, less to ascertain the speakers' identities than to decide whether they would identify themselves as a woman leader or a feminist leader. The speakers affirmed both options. A panel of young women holding public offices in New Jersey replied that they did not call themselves feminists but unstintingly worked "to bring women along" and gratefully acknowledged the important changes won by the feminist movement.[95] Supreme Court Justice Ruth Bader Ginsburg defined feminism as a movement for all women's equality so that the talents of that half of humankind could be utilized. Both women and men could be counted as feminists and share in life's work; women should not be protected from courtrooms and men from parenting.[96] Congresswoman Marge Roukema (R-N.J.) told the students that she considered herself a feminist and raised feminist issues while campaigning in a conservative rural part of her district. The majority of Republican women serving in the House, she added, supported women's equal opportunities and reproductive choice.[97] Collectively, these speakers enlarged feminism's domain by accommodating women and men, Democrats and Republicans, outspoken advocates and tacitly grateful beneficiaries.

Naturally, I wondered why NEW Leadership associates seldom spoke of feminism when they had the option of describing it in inclusive terms. PLEN Program Director Sharon Stoneback said that the PLEN staff didn't use the term because it "turns off" both funders and "a lot of women ... at [the] member colleges." PLEN Director Marianne Alexander explained that PLEN and CAWP were neutral organizations that did not promote feminism or any other ideology to students. Ruth Mandel added that CAWP didn't identify itself with ideological agendas because it was trying to do the difficult work of linking women across parties, jobs, generations, races, and classes. Since "feminism" was, as Mandel put it, "a charged, or potentially controversial, label,"[98] I concluded that they expected references to feminism to diminish PLEN's and CAWP's effectiveness in public and political arenas. But feminism was only one cause of the identity anxiety that gripped the students.

Midway through the institute, NEW Leadership Coordinator Tobi Walker facilitated a rap session and invited the students to ask questions, which she then wrote on a poster.

What is feminism?
What does it mean to be inclusive?
What are tolerance and acceptance?
What does it mean to be racist?
What do you do when you're in a group and feel alienated and isolated?
How do you handle fear and conflict?
How do you challenge your own comfort zone?

Walker initiated the discussion by observing that "When we talk about the future of the nation and the world, we have to talk with people who are different from ourselves and who may have challenging and scary ideas. We have to maintain our own identities while growing, changing, and making space at the table for people who look different and have different ideas." After some generalizations, the students focused on themselves.

Much of the discussion revolved around the interactions between African-American and white students outside of the institute's formal sessions. "I notice segregation going on," one African-American student said, "because whites don't join African-American groups when they walk or ride in the van." Other African-American students offered these explanations:

"There are so few black people that we're just happy to see each other."
"We should admit we have cliques, but the African-American students feel we're making an effort and the white students aren't."
"Sometimes [when we talk] it's a black woman thing, but sometimes [when we talk] it's a *woman* thing."

A white student who felt unwelcome to join the African-American groups commented that "segregation goes both ways," and a second confessed that she didn't approach African-American students because she was afraid to initiate conversation. But other white students reported having good conversations with African-American, Asian-American, and white students, and one said that her only problem was "getting around to all the wonderful women here." Underscoring the point, an African-American student chimed in, "Don't be afraid to talk to people."

Clearly many of the students feared something—a something at the heart of Walker's comment that "we have to maintain our own identities." The something they feared, I would argue, was less the challenging ideas broached by others than their own fumbling attempts to respond. The issue became clearer when Walker asked them "Do you want your comfort zone pushed?" Most students replied that they did, but one didn't want it pushed at all, a second didn't want it pushed in private conversations, and a third was willing to push it herself but didn't want others to do so. Although not explicitly defined, *comfort zone* seemed to designate a region of interaction that permitted the student to remain securely anchored in her identity as it was then constituted. The boundary of the comfort zone varied by student and situation. But for most students pushing beyond the comfort zone was easier to do when they were in institute sessions than in peer groups and easier when they pushed than when they were pushed—in short, easier when they felt more in control.

What allowed the students to feel in control? At institute sessions the discussion protocol made interactions fairly predictable, and in peer groups student skills made interactions manageable. But some students knew they didn't have those skills because during the rap session one admitted that she feared offending someone, a second pointed out that not everyone had the tools to confront an offense, and a third asked how she could deal with tense interactions. They were saying that a person finds it easier to push beyond her comfort zone when interactions are structured or structurable to minimize the risks to the "self." What feels like self-risk or self-security varies because, as one of the campus advisers put it, "people don't *have* a comfort zone; it's contingent on the situation."[99] This theory that a diversity situation needs to be structured or structurable to minimize identity risks can be applied to the other institutes I have described. At the New Jersey Project Institute, some of the participants needed more time to assimilate the skills for structuring a diversity situation before they were willing to push beyond their comfort zones and take interactive risks. At the FAS-Georgetown institutes the situation was already structured to leave the students in their comfort zones; the materials and speakers minimized their exposure to diversity, and the laissez-faire protocol disengaged them from risky confrontations.

When I visited Midwestern State during spring quarter 1991, it typified those baccalaureate state colleges that had expanded into multipurpose universities during the 1980s. The new 300 acre campus, accommodating 13,000 undergraduate students (mostly state residents) and 3,000 graduate and professional students, sprawled across a plateau overlooking a town of 45,000 people. The town, though not yet boasting citified prosperity, was buoyed by a stable mix of agriculture, industry, business, and new corporate divisions attracted to the area by its low overhead costs and middle American work ethic.

After its founding in 1973, the Midwestern Department of Women's Studies had followed the usual pattern of development—winning approval for a minor in 1975, adding B.A. and B.S. programs in 1980, launching a graduate concentration through the Division of Continuing Studies, and parlaying the concentration into an M.S. program in 1986.[100] Yet this department was unique among women's studies programs, for it unabashedly taught activism. A brochure told prospective majors that "One objective of the Women's Studies program is to foster praxis, the process of putting theory into practice. Student activism is encouraged as an integral part of the learning process." Another brochure described the M.S. program as "oriented toward training activists and leaders who wish to promote social change in a variety of settings."[101] Indeed the department's curriculum, though stocked with the usual elective courses, had a required core of action-oriented courses; the four taken by majors assigned change analysis and small-group projects, and the four taken by M.S. students expected them to stage individual and collective social-change projects.

Institutionalized Problems. The department's scope of activity—it taught some three dozen courses, supervised student internships and change projects, and hosted numerous events—struck me as miraculous when I learned of its chronic problems. Never staffed by more than four full-time faculty whose stay averaged two to five years, it had only three core faculty members in 1990–91. Hillary, a British sociologist who had participated in the democratic socialist movement, held a tenure-track appointment and served as chair. Louise, a longtime Native-American community activist, had deferred her doctoral examinations in sociology to take an annually renewable appointment. Diane, a Chicano-white activist for racial, economic, and environmental issues, also held a temporary appointment while she completed a political science dissertation.[102] When I asked about the high rate of faculty turnover, the core and affiliate faculty members gave me the same explanation. To cope with the university's growing student body during an era of chronic underfunding, administrators had limited faculty hiring to lower salaried positions with heavier teaching loads, which in turn prevented the temporary hires from completing their doctorates and the tenure-track hires from meeting their research requirements. When administrators downsized to cover further budget shortfalls, they were bound by the faculty union's seniority rule to terminate recent hires and thus had little flexibility in considering the staffing needs of such burgeoning departments as women's studies.[103] The revolving door set in motion by these institutional policies was speeded by the department's own dilemmas.

The women's studies faculty believed, Diane said, that "we have to institutionalize the 'doing' of change—put it in courses and give credit for learning to 'do'"; yet they also understood that "institutionalization changes us and our program."[104] Speaking with me about how institutionalization had changed the department, the faculty and students insistently returned to the M.S. program as if it were a little motor generating painful jolts of electricity that radiated outward. When the department offered a graduate concentration under the aegis of the Division of Continuing Studies, it attracted local women who wanted to use their training in community activism. But once the concentration was revamped as an M.S. program located in the Graduate School, the department gained academic credibility and attracted a more diverse body of students who were seeking intellectual preparation for scholarly or professional careers (typically, the 1991 cohort had two in-state students and twelve hailing from distant states and other nations).[105] The new scholarly tilt heightened the existing tensions between town and gown feminists, professional and working-class identities, and core and affiliated faculty.

Mina, a women's studies graduate hired as the associate director of university fundraising, told me that community women regarded university women as classist, a perception (she carefully explained) that was owing to distributive inequalities: university women had access to resources not available in the community and, more fundamentally, enjoyed the benefits accruing from higher education. Perhaps because her academic education and employment had propelled her into a life that no one in her working-class family had experienced, she said in a voice tinged with sadness, "We go into and change organizations, but then 'we' become more like 'them.'" Diane, a women's studies faculty member, observed that "the university is like a priesthood with its own ways of talking and learning and its own work attitudes. There's more realism about factory work and relations with coworkers; in academe you get all this 'love one's job' stuff." Reflecting on her academic career after leaving her Chicano working-class community, she said "I was separated from life as I know it" and "find it painful to return to family and friends."[106]

Since the community women expected women's studies to reach across the university / community divide, the faculty hoped that "adding activist or service requirements to every course would increase our community visibility."[107] But adding more of anything to the curriculum only heightened the existing tensions between the core and affiliated faculty. John, a professor of sociology, pointed out that women's studies offered numerous general education courses because "they were the 'material base' that brought in funding for the graduate program 'superstructure.'" Since the core faculty was preoccupied with keeping the graduate program and undergraduate major afloat, the affiliated faculty was ghettoized in the general education and crosslisted disciplinary courses.[108] Candace, a professor of political science, put it bluntly: "The graduate program is obliterating the undergraduate program. This is partly a function of numbers. There are three core faculty: two teach nine quarter-courses a year, and the director teaches six quarter courses—for a total of a twenty-four-quarter capability in women's studies."[109] In this economy of scarcity, the familiar relay between institutionalization and intellectualization functioned less to turn an activist department into a scholarly one than to throw spanners into all of its machinery.

Activist Learning. Despite its many constraints, the department was teaching undergraduate and graduate students the practices of social change in the courses I observed during spring quarter 1991. To analyze its pedagogy, I turn to what happened in Collective Analysis and Action (CAA), a core course in the M.S. program designed to teach the entering cohort of fourteen students "how we work change."[110] Meeting twice a week from late March through early June, the students read *Women and the Politics of Empowerment,* the *AAUW Community Action Tool Catalog,* and other materials; they discussed theories and practices of social change, wrote weekly thought papers, and presented personal change projects.[111] But CAA's centerpiece was a collective-action project that exercised the students in all the gritty details of making change.

Instructor Louise acquainted them with the ground rules for collective action. When people mobilize to act on problems that are at once experienced personally and amplified systematically, she said, they will trigger conflicts over beliefs and needs. Allies must agree among themselves on the principles that will guide their collaboration, and when they act they must show respect for their opponents by giving them a chance to participate in the solution. Following this advice, the students decided to use a feminist perspective, a group responsibility and consensus model, and nonviolent action; then they assembled a list of possible projects that included protesting budget cuts to the Women's Center and library, lobbying for the appointment of a student representative to the state board of regents, and holding a "Take Back the Night" rally. After conducting a feasibility assessment of each project, they settled on protesting the budget cuts. By the fourth week of class, they had drawn up a flow chart of their actions and administrative reactions, had role-played how to work with allies, and had chosen Students Concerned about the Budget (SCAB) as the name of the campus coalition they would form.

From the fifth week on, the students mushed through the avalanche of details, some of which I repeat here to illustrate the complexity of planning a change project:

— They drafted and circulated a petition to be signed by students, faculty, staff, and community members and decided to deliver copies to the governor, local legislators, university administrators, and newspapers.
— To generate interest in the budget issue, they produced materials— fact sheets, a "gripe-vine" for browsers to inscribe, and petitions to be signed—for an information table they staffed at the student union.
— After choosing May 8 as the date of a mass demonstration, they reserved campus facilities and equipment, invited speakers, made posters and leaflets, drafted a sample letter for the letter-writing campaign to be sparked by the demonstration, and set volunteer schedules for the big day.
— To attract the large crowd and media coverage that were needed to put pressure on the administration, the students placed leaflets on cars, mailed more than four hundred letters, stuffed fliers into the student newspaper, distributed press releases, and alerted the radio and TV news programs.
— To finance the project, they secured dollar and in-kind contributions from a variety of sources—themselves, student associations, the university, and community organizations.

On May 6, with the demonstration less than forty-eight hours away, the CAA class buzzed with details: remind the invited speakers and administrators, deliver the fliers, attach SCAB logos to the organizers' armbands, bring extension cords, show up at the predemonstration meeting. . . .

The demonstration came off pretty much as planned, attracting good media coverage and a big turnout that impressed the financial vice president, who said "It's good to see the campus alive" and subsequently retrenched an administrative office instead of the Women's Center and library. When asked to evaluate their project at the May 13 class, the students were "flying on a 'high' ": they had won the budget battle, had shown "grace under pressure," and had achieved "a cohesiveness on that day that was lacking before." Only with Louise's repeated prodding did they voice some misgivings: they hadn't done enough to let everyone know what was going on and hadn't brought as many student groups into the sponsoring coalition as they had hoped. But with two and a half weeks of class left, they had to hustle through the remaining chores: sending thank-you notes to speakers, allies, media, and administrators; delivering the petition to the university president, legislators, and the governor; and arranging for media coverage in the state capital.[112] Their rush to the finish line reminded me of an evaluation imparted four weeks earlier when I interviewed Oona, director of the Women's Center. She remarked that change requires sustained action and the CAA project, though well conceptualized, was a one-shot effort that would end with spring quarter. The M.S. program, she added, should teach the analysis of social change and leave the practice to internships at community-based organizations. She was right that change takes time, but I couldn't help thinking that the program was crimped less by the quarter system than the inadequate funding that complicated everything else.[113]

Identity Complications. If feminism was a malcontent ostracized by the FAS-Georgetown institutes and a shadow flitting into NEW Leadership, it was business-as-usual in Midwestern's Department of Women's Studies, though not without a few grumblings. A departmental review for the 1984–90 period noted that undergraduate students had a "degree of feminism" problem with the courses: some nonmajors rated them as too feminist, some majors rated them as not feminist enough, and among the majors some wanted more intellectual analysis and others more activism.[114] The graduate students had a problem not with feminism but with differences in their own experiences, resources, and aspirations. Sue, a middle-aged white woman who described herself as "a hard-core activist" in local union organizing, said that others benefited from the program but she had found it a tepid experience compared to "the real McCoy." Having enjoyed the "emotional bonding" and astute strategizing of union organizing, she was put off by the students' power struggles and simple collective-action projects. "Activism," she remarked, "encourages you to think more [than academic study does]."[115] Anne, a white Canadian feminist, credited the program's skill training and action projects with getting her a postgraduate job as the administrative coordinator of a Canadian committee on the status of women. Though intending to pursue a doctorate later, she criticized the students with doctoral ambitions who did not take activism as seriously as they took scholarship.[116] Leslie, a young white graduate of a Missouri university, had enrolled in the M.S. program for "personal satisfaction, not professional credentialing." The courses had crystallized her vague "feminist feelings" by showing her "the systematic way that all oppressions work" and by "demystifying activism." After earning a Ph.D., she intended to use what she had learned at Midwestern in college teaching and community volunteerism.[117] Rosa, a Latina who had grown up in New York City, chose the program "because it was cheap," but as a single mother rearing two children she nevertheless felt the crunch on her budget and her time. Since she intended to earn a humanities doctorate and teach at the college level, she was disappointed by the program's emphasis on social science and activism, which she didn't foresee using except "on faculty discrimination issues."[118]

Making inquiries about the student power struggles, I received different explanations. Louise acknowledged that some of the CAA students had formed cliques, resisted course projects, and engaged in "butt biting" outside the class, but she regarded their behavior as part of the process of learning to do change. Sue felt that the students were hyper-critical of differences in skill and effort compared to union organizers, who understood that the newcomers who walked the picket line were putting out just as much effort as the old-timers who planned the boycott. Department chair Hillary thought the students were acting out "the various conflicts among women" of different races, classes, generations, and sexualities that were submerged "in the early days of the movement [when] it was easier to come together and fight 'the oppressor.'" Rosa, emphasizing class differences, said the instigators of the CAA tensions "had access to resources that others didn't—knowledge, experience, equipment"—and maneuvered covertly so that they could continue appearing "nice" in class.[119] Indeed, the six CAA students I interviewed all noted that the conflicts were played out in extramural maneuvering rather than surfaced in classroom discussions. On May 15, the tensions finally surfaced when a CAA student sent a letter to her classmates. Ostensibly writing to say that a family obligation prevented her from attending class, the student tallied her own contributions to the collective-action project and complained that some of her classmates had repeatedly interrupted her work day with requests for advice or materials to be duplicated on her office's equipment. The students, she said, had failed to demand that slackers do their share of the work, failed to respond to the working-class women who objected to the SCAB acronym, and failed to discuss how well the class was living up to its ideal of leaderless collectivism. The letter writer concluded that they had fallen into the trap of believing that their primary "goal was to accomplish something outside the class" when it "should have been to learn from our project, not just how to change the world, but also how to change ourselves."[120]

My conclusion was that the student behaviors—the public nicety and private "butt biting," the concerns about who accessed the resources and who carried the workload, the complaints about activist and scholarly training—were effects that emanated from the department's structural double bind. The variables of life circumstances, skills, and postdegree aspirations that diversified the graduate students caused them to have not merely different expectations for the department but a quantity of expectations that a department of limited means could not possibly satisfy. When the students' egalitarian principles collided with their unmet individual expectations, they aimed their dissatisfaction at each other, the matters at hand, and even the departmental ethos of collective identity and action. Their behavior may seem to have little in common with the other groups described in this book, but I would argue that it all comes down to the same dynamic: whenever diverse people come together to set a group agenda, the tensions that arise from their different identities, interests, skills, and needs always tug against collective goals. The many groups described in this book differed not in whether they experienced this dynamic but in how they responded to it. The ASA and MLA groups responded by deploying articulatory practices that meshed activist and academic discourses, the feminists at San Diego and Pittsburgh by amplifying their differences and forming factions, the Heritage Resource Bank by using a discourse that reintegrated the interests and objectives of conservative factions, the FAS-Georgetown institutes by minimizing student diversity and short-circuiting conflicts, and the New Jersey Project and NEW Leadership by teaching diversity skills to their students.

THE PROGRAMS I HAVE DESCRIBED were not just training the third generation in leadership skills; they were inculcating visions of America as it is and should be. The government of a diverse and divided society, they were saying, should be entrusted to a conservative oligarchy, democratic negotiations, or collective processes. As the third generation moves into public leadership positions, what kind of America is likely to await it?

7. Playing by the New Rules

The successes of history belong to those who are capable of seizing these rules, to replace those who had used them, to disguise themselves so as to pervert them, invert their meaning, and redirect them against those who had initially imposed them.—Michel Foucault, "Nietzsche, Genealogy, History" (1977)

At this moment in the history of a diverse and divided people, the social movements locked in a struggle to determine the nation's future are not evenly matched. Progressives, having spent the last two decades proliferating identities and interests, are still tying to make change from the margins: working in policy institutes and issue-advocacy organizations to influence government policy processes, working in communities to sponsor alternative programs, working in academic sanctuaries to train students who will carry the new critical discourses into the world of real politics. But conservatives, having seized control of several presidential administrations and congressional terms, more than half of the state legislatures and governorships, countless local governments, and most of the federal judicial system, have been setting the national agenda. Using the meshed machineries of their movement and the State, they are inverting the meaning of egalitarian principles, perverting the purpose of democratic laws, and bringing the nation closer to that hegemonic moment when patterned injustice can no longer be seen and said.

The shape of the nation in the twenty-first century will depend upon the rules—the laws that define rights and wrongs and the policies that determine how socioeconomic goods are distributed. In this last chapter, I return to the subject of affirmative action because what in reality is only a limited attempt to provide equal opportunity has been transformed into another one of those political flashpoints that blind leaders and citizens to the fundamental problem that we still do not have distributive justice. After analyzing some of the conservative strategies for dismantling affirmative action, I want to ponder the rights and wrongs and then suggest what progressives might do.

PRODUCING POLICY INITIATIVES

Antidiscrimination law, as I mentioned in chapter 2, had a tortuous history of institutionalization in higher education: many universities balked at submitting affirmative-action plans, individual complainants stumbled through complex grievance processes, enforcement agencies backlogged complaints needing investigation, lawsuits dragged on at terrible cost to plaintiffs, and courts ruled more often for defendants than for the plaintiffs alleging discrimination. By the early 1980s, most academic institutions had implemented equal opportunity policies and recognized diversity as a desideratum of campus life. Over the next two decades, the gains made by white women were uneven; female students continued to be underrepresented in the science and technology fields, and female faculty were still scarce in the higher ranks and prestigious institutions. Far worse, racial minorities had been making slight gains in undergraduate, graduate, and professional education that seemed in danger of reversal in the late 1990s as their applications to graduate and professional schools declined in many states. What got in the way of equal opportunity, besides the usual welter of economic and social circumstances, were the actions of conservative public officials from 1980 forward.

When President Reagan took office in 1981, the Heritage Foundation and American Enterprise Institute were ready: they handed him an agenda for a conservative revolution that included the repeal of affirmative action through governmental and judicial activism and provided him with names from the talent banks they had assembled for federal appointments. Federal agencies, they said, had been pandering to special interests by enforcing antidiscrimination laws and funding programs for female, minority, and learning-challenged students. The solution was to restructure the education system. Relieve the Department of Education of its cabinet-level status and most of its functions, cut federal budgets and transmit block grants to the states to use as they saw fit, institute a voucher system that would siphon money away from public schools to private and religious ones, shift college student aid from scholarships to loans, eliminate federal civil rights enforcement, and dismantle affirmative action.[1] Movement leaders and government officials began waging a public relations war against affirmative action. The Department of Education's Secretary William Bennett and Assistant Secretary Chester Finn declared that it had lowered educational standards, and the Department of Justice's Attorney General William French Smith and Assistant Attorney General William Bradford Reynolds denounced it for imposing "quotas" on white men and giving "preferences" to minorities and women.[2] In an unprecedented coup in 1984, President Reagan sacked four of the six members serving on the purportedly independent U.S. Commission on Civil Rights and appointed new members who were hostile to affirmative action. His administration also worked the agencies and courts—slashing the Office of Contract Compliance Programs and Equal Employment Opportunity Commission budgets and retrenching their compliance activities, appointing conservative judges, and directing the Justice Department to oppose affirmative action.[3] This activism prepared the ground for the next development.

In 1987 two men affiliated with New York neoconservative groups founded the National Association of Scholars (NAS) to mobilize dissent and make change inside the academy. In 1989 two staffers from the right-wing Washington Legal Foundation established the Center for Individual Rights (CIR) to specialize in litigation against institutional policies on affirmative action, sexual harassment, and religion. And in 1990 another small group launched the Madison Center for Educational Affairs (MCEA) to build a network of conservative student newspapers that would ignite controversies over programs addressing racial, gender, and sexual inequalities on college campuses. The NAS, CIR, and MCEA worked with the rest of the movement's machinery to produce anti-affirmative action initiatives: academic groups trolled for complaints, legal centers crafted complaints as lawsuits, and advocacy organizations joined conservative legislators and regents in orchestrating the policy rollbacks. Here's a sample of the initiatives directed at higher education:

1994. In *Podberesky,* crafted by the Washington Legal Foundation, a federal district court ruled that the University of Maryland's scholarship program for minority students was illegal, the Fourth Circuit U.S. Court of Appeals upheld that ruling, and the Supreme Court let the decision stand.[4]

1995. California Governor Pete Wilson called for an end to affirmative action, and the University of California Board of Regents banned the use of race-sensitive criteria in student admissions, financial aid, and other processes.

1995–97. The NAS and other conservative groups launched the California Civil Rights Initiative to abolish affirmative action in public universities and agencies. Appearing on the November 1996 ballot, Proposition 209 was approved by 54 percent of the voters and then taken to court. In April 1997, it was ruled constitutional by the Ninth Circuit U.S. Court of Appeals, and in November 1997 the Supreme Court let that decision stand. Emboldened by this success, conservatives led by black California businessman Ward Connerly formed the American Civil Rights Institute (ACRI) to launch voter referenda in other states.[5]

1996. The Arizona Board of Regents ordered all public universities to provide an inventory of their affirmative action programs and began scrutinizing programs that helped racial minorities and women; then the board president called for an end to race-sensitive criteria, declaring "Nothing's off the table until the regents say it's off the table."

1996. In *Hopwood,* crafted by the CIR, the Fifth Circuit U.S. Court of Appeals ruled that the University of Texas Law School admissions process discriminated against four white applicants when it used race as a factor and conducted a double-track process. The ruling applied to institutions in Texas, Louisiana, and Mississippi, and the Supreme Court's decision to let it stand has import for all institutions using race-sensitive criteria.[6]

1996. Twelve-year-old Jane Doe, represented by the CIR, sued Texas A&M University for not admitting her to a science camp designed as an outreach program for Hispanic students and sued the National Science Foundation (NSF) for funding the camp. Settling out of court, the university and NSF paid her $20,000.[7]

1996. Jack W. Daly, represented by the CIR, sued the University of North Carolina for targeting awards to minorities and for reserving eight of its thirty-two trustee seats for women and minorities. He claimed that he was the victim of race and sex discrimination because he was ineligible to compete for four of the eight trustee seats vacated that spring.[8]

1996. John K. Hartman, a Central Michigan University professor represented by the CIR, sued the Bowling Green University Journalism Department for hiring a black female applicant rather than himself and sued the Journalism Council, the accrediting agency that required the department to develop a plan for improving its recruitment of female and minority scholars. After the state civil rights commission found that he had not proved university discrimination, a federal district court ruled in his favor and awarded him $122,000 in damages.[9]

1996. When the Dole-Canady bill was tabled, House Speaker Newt Gingrich and Senate Majority Leader Trent Lott commented that for the duration of the election year Republicans would forego sweeping repeal of affirmative action and instead chip away with legislation that would prohibit federal grants and programs benefiting minorities. Why? They were worried about losing women voters.[10]

1997. The CIR crafted three *Hopwood* look-alikes. *Katuria E. Smith v. University of Washington Law School* (March) was brought by a white plaintiff claiming that the Law School had denied her admission on racially discriminatory grounds. *Jennifer Gratz and Patrick Hamacher v. Bollinger et al.* (October), a class-action suit filed on behalf of white plaintiffs, claimed that the University of Michigan's College of Literature, Science, and the Arts had denied them admission on racially discriminatory grounds. *Barbara Grutter v. Bollinger et al.* (December), another class-action suit, made the same claim against Michigan's Law School. Working behind the scenes, conservative state legislators had sought out applicants willing to sue and forwarded their names to the CIR.[11]

1998. The ACRI organized Initiative 200 to ban affirmative action in Washington state, and the voters passed this referendum in November 1998.

1999. The ACRI launched the Florida Civil Rights Initiative and Republican Governor Jeb Bush, in an effort to preempt it, proposed the somewhat less draconian One Florida Initiative. After the state university board approved the plan, progressive groups—including the NAACP, the Rainbow / PUSH Coalition, and NOW, began to organize protests.

These examples, as well as many others I could have cited, reveal the conservative plan for dismantling affirmative action in higher education. Target the most vulnerable populations—African, Hispanic, and Native Americans. Intervene in university admissions and financial aid to further constrict the flow of these populations into higher education, itself the gateway to employment opportunity, upward economic mobility, and citizen participation. Splinter the protected category of women by finding white ones who are willing to sue on grounds of racial discrimination. Craft lawsuits to pit individual against group so as to redefine affirmative action as "preferences" for racial minority groups that cause "reverse discrimination" against white individuals. Launch state-by-state policy initiatives to abolish programs geared to helping disadvantaged groups on the specious logic that they are not "blind" to gender, race, and ethnicity.

MAKING THE NEW RULES

In our democratic system, rules organize most of what transpires in social life; they regulate institutional processes, individual practices, and resource flows. It comes as no surprise, then, that movements seeking to make structural change would target their initiatives to the rules, but some types of rules are more effective than others in amplifying change throughout the system. Obviously, congressional legislation is the most expedient route because in one stroke it mandates nationwide change. State legislation, though geographically limited, can catalyze structural change elsewhere because a victory in one state gives legitimacy to the movement's framing of an issue, raises public consciousness, and inspires activists to lobby for similar legislation in other states. By comparison, litigation seems to be a tedious way to make structural change; an issue must be raised case by case, each case takes time to craft and litigate, and, if taken to a higher court, it may have to be appealed on a point that is tangential to the main issue.

Nevertheless, the judicial system has a built-in logic that amplifies change—the logic of class-action lawsuits, precedents, principles, and ascending levels. We have already seen in chapter 2 that a ruling for the plaintiff in a class-action lawsuit on university discrimination spreads change because it applies to a large group of people and mandates new institutional procedures. The precedent, as we also saw, is a ruling on a previous lawsuit that is invoked in a current one to buttress the plaintiff or defendant's argument and guide the judge's deliberations. Since the precedent comes with definitions and decisions, it functions in later lawsuits to disperse discrimination or equal opportunity as both meanings construed and activities (re)constructed. The most potent tool of change, however, is a lawsuit deliberately crafted to (re)formulate a principle that structures some part of the social formation—as do statements of principle that specify the rights and protections granted to citizens, the activities permitted to organizations, and the operational scope of the legislative, executive, and judicial branches of state and federal governments. The current anti-affirmative action lawsuits, I will argue, are principle-targeting initiatives crafted to redefine discrimination and dismantle the affirmative-action programs devised to give historically excluded racial groups access to higher education. Finally, as a lawsuit ascends from federal district court up to the Supreme Court, favorable rulings on it can shift the whole discourse. What the circuit court says applies to all the states falling within its jurisdiction and invites look-alike lawsuits in other districts; what the Supreme Court says is the law of the land. In the ways I have outlined, the judicial system's built-in logic propels the changes wrought by a single successful lawsuit through the byways of the nation's institutional processes and citizen practices.

Embedded at the core of judicial discourse is that unresolved paradox, as I explained in chapter 2, between discrimination against the individual and discrimination against the group. In discrimination lawsuits brought against universities, judges have clung to the individualist model; they not only have handed down a higher proportion of pro-plaintiff rulings in individual lawsuits than in class action lawsuits but have used individualist logic to decertify the class in class-action lawsuits. Exploiting this judicial preference for the individualist model, conservatives have crafted anti-affirmative action lawsuits to claim that affirmative-action procedures ostensibly devised to eliminate discrimination against racial minority groups actually discriminate against individual whites. Adjudicating these lawsuits, judges have failed to harmonize the group and the individual claims to equal opportunity, treatment, and protection and, as conservative attorneys intend, have made group discrimination disappear. To show how this strategy works, I will examine two landmark cases.[12] The Supreme Court ruling on *Regents of University of California v. Bakke* (1978) presented both ways to think about discrimination—historical and systemic discrimination against racial minority groups and reverse discrimination against individual whites. The federal court that ruled on *Hopwood v. Texas* (1997) went down the individualist path and found that a remedy for racial minority group discrimination had caused reverse discrimination against the white plaintiffs. The ruling was, to paraphrase Yogi Berra, déjà vu all over again in the history of judicial racism but this time with a twist: where the egregious ruling in *Plessy v. Ferguson* (1896) deployed racist discourse to maintain the system of racial discrimination, the ruling in *Hopwood* used antiracist rhetoric and perverted logic to do the same job.

In *Bakke,* the Supreme Court ruled that the University of California had discriminated against Allan Bakke, a white applicant to the Medical School on the Davis campus. The school had one hundred slots for the entering class, eighty-four designated for general admissions applicants and sixteen designated for minority, economically disadvantaged, and educationally disadvantaged applicants. For the two tracks, it conducted separate admissions processes using somewhat different standards. Lawyers for the plaintiff characterized the numerical arrangement as imposing a quota on Bakke and the other general applicants, who could compete for no more than eighty-four slots, but not on minority and disadvantaged applicants, who could compete for all one hundred slots. Lawyers for the university described the sixteen set-aside slots as an admissions goal, not a quota, and argued that the admissions program was designed to remedy historical discrimination against the minority and disadvantaged groups. Although the Supreme Court ruled five to four that the admissions program was illegal, the justices were so fractured on the matters of the case that every one dissented in part.

The key splits concerned the entity—the individual or the group—to which rights were guaranteed and the conditions under which a university might use race as a factor in admissions decision making. Bakke claimed that the admissions program had violated two of his rights. It violated his right to nondiscrimination as codified by Title VI of the Civil Rights Act of 1964, which states that "no person," on the basis of race, color, or national origin, can be excluded from or subjected to discrimination by programs receiving federal financial assistance. And it violated his right to equal protection as provided by section 1 of the Fourteenth Amendment to the Constitution, which says that no state can "deny to any person within its jurisdiction the equal protection of the law." The singular terms *no person* and *any person* would seem to legitimate using the individualist definition of *discrimination,* but that is not warranted by the texts of these two documents. Title VII of the Civil Rights Act of 1964 defines the term *person* as including one or more individuals, and section 1 of the Fourteenth Amendment uses plural terms before using the singular term: "All *persons* born or naturalized in the United States . . . are *citizens* of the United States and of the State wherein they reside. No State shall make or enforce any law which shall abridge the privileges or immunities of *citizens*" (my emphasis). Moreover, the historical context shows that the framers of these two documents were thinking of racial group injustice. Congressional discussion of the bill, which the justices included in the *Bakke* opinion, indicated that it was intended to put an end to the exclusionary and discriminatory treatment of African Americans as a racial group. And the Fourteenth Amendment (1868) was surrounded by legislation that specifically addressed the circumstances of African Americans: the Thirteenth Amendment (1865) abolishing slavery, the Civil Rights Act of 1866 outlawing Black Codes in the South (racist laws and practices immuring African Americans in slavelike conditions), and the Fifteenth Amendment (1870) prohibiting the denial of citizen voting rights on grounds of race, color, or previous servitude. Despite the textual and historical evidence for thinking of discrimination in both the plural and the singular, the *Bakke* justices fractured around the same questions that vexed the courts in previous twentieth-century desegregation and discrimination litigation. Were rights and protections attached to the individual and / or the group? Did the law permit attention to race in order to remedy invidious racial group discrimination or did it mandate color-blindness?

Four justices, thinking in the plural and of the historical context, upheld the Medical School's admissions program as a remedy for the long history of national and educational discrimination suffered by the minority and disadvantaged groups in question. Four more justices, thinking in the singular, argued that the program violated Bakke's nondiscrimination rights. By attaching those rights only to the individual, they could see Bakke, but not the minority and disadvantaged groups, as victimized. Although Justice Powell concluded that the program violated Bakke's nondiscrimination and equal protection rights, he attempted to resolve the individual / group dilemma. He argued that the achievement of a diverse student body was a compelling educational and national interest because it brought to campus a multiplicity of experiences, viewpoints, and ideas that would safeguard academic freedom, enrich student training, and equip graduates to serve humanity. Diversity, he wrote, was a goal that justified the use of race as one of several factors (but not as the sole determining factor) in admissions decision making.[13] But the trend that began in *Bakke* of disaggregating groups to individuals and attaching rights to individuals was escalated through a series of lawsuits challenging set-aside contracts awarded to minority contractors, layoffs of white employees who had seniority over minority employees, job promotions of women and minorities, and university scholarships targeted to minority students.

The Center for Individual Rights then crafted *Hopwood* to assert the primacy of the individual and redefine the key terms in the discourse of discrimination. In 1997 the Supreme Court let stand a 1996 decision by the Fifth Circuit U.S. Court of Appeals, which had ruled in favor of four white plaintiffs, three men and a woman, who claimed that the University of Texas had discriminated against them as applicants to the Law School. To evaluate the potential of applicants, the Law School considered the grade point average (GPA), the Law School Aptitude Test score (LSAT), other indicators of undergraduate education (e.g., strength of training, difficulty of the major, and grade inflation), state residency or nonresidency, background, and life experiences. Using these criteria, it sorted the applications into three categories—presumptive admit, presumptive deny, and a middle group that was most intensely reviewed by the admissions committee. The Texas admissions program did not have set-aside slots, as did the UC-Davis program, but it did separate African-American and Mexican-American applicants from white and other racial-minority applicants by requiring different GPA and LSAT levels and using a minority subcommittee to rank and recommend applicants from the first two groups. The white plaintiffs, whose scores placed them in the middle group of applicants, argued that they would have been admitted if the Law School had maintained only one applicant pool, one GPA-LSAT level, and one committee to review applicants. Since race was the intervening variable, they claimed that the admissions program violated their nondiscrimination and equal protection rights under the Fourteenth Amendment.

In court, the university counsel argued that the Law School used race as a factor in admissions decision making to further two compelling national interests. First, the admissions program was an affirmative remedy for the long history of racial discrimination in the state's education systems and for the present effects of racism at the university—such effects as its bad reputation in minority communities, the atmosphere of racial hostility on campus, and the underrepresentation of African Americans and Mexican Americans in the student body. Second, the admissions program helped the Law School obtain the benefits that flow from having a diverse student body—namely, the mixture of experiences, viewpoints, and ideas that, according to Justice Powell in *Bakke,* would enrich the education of students and equip them to serve humanity after graduation. But following the new rules, the CIR pitted group against individual, arguing that the admissions program had conferred and withheld benefits based on the applicants' racial group membership and thereby had violated the rights of the individual plaintiffs. Where the university counsel cast the admissions program as a remedy for systemic discrimination against African Americans and Mexican Americans, the CIR cast it as a systematic process of discrimination against individual whites. Where the university counsel cast the outcome of the admissions process as an educational desideratum, the CIR cast it as a constitutional transgression. The problem with the Fifth Circuit Court ruling was not that the judges found the admissions program illegal but that the written opinion backing that finding inverted civil rights discourse and made group discrimination disappear.

Proceeding on the assumption that diversity meant a student body that offered a multiplicity of distinctive life experiences and viewpoints, the judges immediately undercut Justice Powell's claim that race could be used as one of many admissions factors geared to diversifying the student body. As the first step, they argued that the use of race only achieves "a student body that looks different" and as such is no more rational than using physical size or blood type to identify applicants who have different experiences and viewpoints.[14] By distilling the meaning of *race* to physiological traits, such as skin color and facial features, they stripped race of the nation's racialist organization of people's socioeconomic circumstances that in turn had produced their racially differentiated experiences and viewpoints. As the second step, the judges quoted from an article written by conservative judge Richard A. Posner, who stated that "the use of a racial characteristic to establish a presumption that the individual also possesses other, and socially relevant, characteristics . . . underlies most prejudice and bigotry in modern America.' "[15] Posner sounds like he is invoking the civil rights movement's well-known rejoinder to the racist stereotype of African Americans as lacking the intelligence, motivation, and maturity for certain types of education and employment, but he made this comment in an article that depicted affirmative action as the practice of preferring racial minorities over whites. Thus the Posner comment together with the judges' quotation of it should be seen as advancing three conservative objectives. The comment's antiracist rhetoric cloaks the conservative attack on affirmative action in high-toned moral garb. The comment's blithe conflation of biobehavioral racist stereotyping with the analysis and remediation of socially organized racism supports the conservative argument that our thinking should be race blind. Finally, the comment's inscription in a court ruling that outlaws the use of race as a factor in college admissions invites other lawsuits that construe any programmatic attention to race as racism and to sex as sexism—for instance, ethnic student clubs, multicultural research projects, women's counseling centers, and women's studies programs.

Having outlawed the use of race as an admissions factor, the judges then enumerated the factors that a university "may reasonably consider" in evaluating applicants and diversifying the student body: musical, athletic, or intellectual abilities; extracurricular activities; home region; kinship to alumni; and socioeconomic background. To quote them, "A university may properly favor one applicant over another because of his ability to play the cello, make a downfield tackle, or understand chaos theory."[16] Their logic was flawed for several reasons that I want to discuss in turn. First, some of the admissions factors the judges sanctioned are irrelevant to the applicant's suitability for legal education. By trying out an applicant scenario, we can see the problem: "Because I have a parent who graduated from this law school, I'm well qualified for legal education." Obviously, alumni kinship doesn't speak to the applicant's abilities, accomplishments, and potential, nor would it diversify the student body. At a law school that historically enrolled white, upper middle-class students, the use of alumni kinship as an admissions factor would work to continue this student body profile.

Second, some of the factors sanctioned by the judges are uncertain indicators of applicants' abilities and diversity. Let's try this applicant scenario: "Because I (1) play cello in the college ensemble, (2) quarterback on a winning team, or (3) understand chaos theory, I am well qualified for legal education and will bring a distinctive viewpoint to the university." One might be tempted to infer that each of these applicants has demonstrated such abilities as concentration and perseverance that would suit him for legal study. But the inference is unwarranted not only because some applicants who participated in the activities may not have honed those abilities but also because some applicants were situated in childhood communities, high schools, and colleges that didn't provide music ensembles, football teams, or instruction in chaos theory. When the judges factored these activities into the admissions process, they put the cart before the horse: the question of whether applicants had honed their abilities by participating in these activities is secondary to the question of whether applicants had *access* to these activities. If an admissions committee did not consider whether applicants had access to the activities, it would be predisposed to favor the haves over the have-nots. But the judges made an even more fundamental mistake when they implied that musical, athletic, and theoretical activities diversify a student body. Such activities do furnish individuals with particular experiences, skills, and perhaps viewpoints. But these differences are the surface effects of the deeper socioeconomic dynamics that produce social-group differentiation. Or, to put it the other way around, the inequitable distribution of socioeconomic resources (family income, housing, healthcare, education, recreation, and much more) is what differentiates the lived experiences of classes, races, and sexes, which in turn shapes the viewpoints of individuals from birth forward.[17]

Finally, to consider the validity of home region as an admissions factor, let's try this scenario: "Because I've lived up to now in (1) Beverly Hills, (2) an Appalachian village, or (3) China, I am well suited for legal education and will bring a distinctive viewpoint to the university." Home regions do not indicate an applicant's abilities, but they may indicate that she has distinctive life experiences and viewpoints. It's easy to see that the student from China would bring distinctive ideas to her classes on international law and U.S. law because, unlike most homegrown students, she knows the Chinese system and has critical distance from the American one. Distinctive experience might be claimed for the Beverly Hills student who applies to a law school with a student body hailing predominantly from Appalachia or China. My point is that what makes a student's regional experience and viewpoint distinctive are their differences from the prevailing ones. I have left the Appalachian student for last because no matter that we think we're considering her region we're also considering her socioeconomic circumstances. Are we confused? No, because in the United States socioeconomic circumstances correlate with regions, though not so categorically as they do with races.

Although the judges decreed that using race as an admissions factor was invidious, discriminatory, and illegal, they didn't seem to notice that using marital and parental circumstances as factors is also invidious, discriminatory, and illegal. They said that the Law School admissions committee could legitimately consider Cheryl Hopwood's life as the thirty-two-year-old wife of an Armed Forces member and the mother of a severely handicapped child to be a plus or a minus. If a plus, the admissions committee would see her as having experiences that would enrich the student body; if a minus, it would see her as having burdens that would constrain her academic performance.[18] The fallacies here are more complicated. First, marital and parental circumstances such as Hopwood's do not necessarily produce distinctive experiences and viewpoints; another applicant in the same circumstances, if blessed with family wealth, household employees, and a private school for the child, might have experiences and viewpoints similar to those of other relatively privileged applicants. Second, the judges' slapdash formulation, if put into practice, would discriminate no matter which way the admissions committee went. Imagine the negative scenario as the committee evaluates Hopwood's potential: "Her parental burden will limit her time and energy for study, and her husband's transfer to another military base will prevent her from completing the program." If it rejects her on these grounds—as indeed many committees did reject women, but not men, during the 1960s and 1970s—it discriminates against her. Now imagine the positive scenario as the committee ranks the middle-group applicants: "We should give (1) ten extra points to Cheryl because she's caring for a handicapped child, (2) five extra points to Jim because he's caring for two healthy children, and (3) no extra points to Sam because he has no children. Of course, if Sam can show that he's helping to raise his sister's handicapped child. . . ." Even if the committee assigns a plus value to parental circumstances, it discriminates against applicants who are not parenting. Still, I think that marital and parental circumstances do have a place in the deliberations. Since circumstances such as Hopwood's might explain why an applicant attended a small local college rather than an elite out-of-state university or why she took six years rather than four to earn an undergraduate degree, a sensitive admissions committee would refrain from making snap judgments about applicants based on the prestige of the undergraduate institution or time to graduation.

Once the Fifth Circuit judges had stripped race of its meaning and pumped up the other factors, they got down to the main business of eliminating the two goals that the university cited to justify its use of race as a factor in admissions: achieving student body diversity and remedying racial discrimination. On the first one, the judges declared that the achievement of student body diversity "is not a compelling interest under the Fourteenth Amendment."[19] Indeed student body diversity is not mentioned anywhere in the Constitution as a compelling national interest, but it is one of the *means* by which we can achieve compelling national interests such as citizen equality and productivity. It's hard to imagine how these interests can be achieved without giving historically excluded social groups access to higher education and without teaching students to understand and respect social differences. But to bolster their dismissal of student body diversity the judges first asserted the primacy of the individual by quoting from *Shelley v. Kraemer* (1948): "the rights created by . . . the Fourteenth Amendment are, by its terms, guaranteed to the individual. The rights established are personal rights." Then they discredited Justice Powell's opinion that diversity was a compelling educational interest by repeatedly calling it a "single-Justice opinion."[20]

Stepping back, we can see that the judges played fast and loose with the individual/group dilemma: Powell's opinion, weighed against the two four-justice opinions, is deemed invalid because it is individual, whereas each *Hopwood* plaintiff's claim to the nondiscrimination right, weighed against the African-American and Hispanic-American group claims to the same right, is deemed valid because it is individual. The judges went on to say that since Justice Powell's opinion didn't garner majority support it was not a binding precedent, meaning that they were not obliged to follow it in reaching their conclusions. By this rhetorical sleight-of-hand, they substituted the number of votes supporting an opinion for the merits of the opinion. If an opinion assumes the status of a binding precedent from the number of votes it garnered and not necessarily from its accuracy, fairness, and wisdom in analyzing a complex welter of facts and circumstances, then precedential guidance is determined by the rules of a cynical game wherein judges can pluck from history either the plural or singular terms, the wrong or right reasoning, and the vicious or virtuous interpretations that suit their purposes.[21]

At last the judges considered the second goal: the university had argued that the admissions program was a justifiable remedy for "Texas's well-documented history of discrimination in education," which had several damaging effects on current minority applicants and students. To eliminate this justification, the judges invoked two principles established in previous lawsuits: an institution was supposed to devise "narrow remedies" for discrimination, and a judge was supposed to apply "strict scrutiny" to any remedy that distinguished among people on the basis of such suspect categories as race and ethnicity.[22] A proper remedy, the judges declared, would focus on discrimination by a particular unit, such as a primary school or a law school; thus the Texas Law School could not justify its admissions program on the basis of discrimination elsewhere in the state's systems of primary, secondary, and higher education.[23] As for the matter of its own discrimination, the Law School would need to document the history, prove that the present effects were of sufficient magnitude to justify a remedial program, and narrowly tailor the remedy to only those effects.[24]

These conclusions, when compared to other parts of the *Hopwood* opinion, point up three flaws in the strict scrutiny test. First, the judges carefully scrutinized race as a factor in admissions decision making but did not as carefully scrutinize the factors they would permit to give some applicants an edge—athletic, musical, and theoretical activities; alumni kinship; and marital status and parental circumstances. Second, they applied half-the-table logic in scrutinizing the matter of discrimination against one applicant group (four whites) but not in scrutinizing the matter of discrimination against other applicant groups (African and Mexican Americans). Last, they scrutinized the moment of selecting people from the applicant pool but not the process that produced the applicant pool. Why didn't they have to consider whether Texas's race-patterned education—which determined the inequalities built into school funding, instructional quality, extracurricular activities, and student testing—had already prevented many African-American and Mexican-American students from applying to the Law School and had disadvantaged many who did apply? Since the legal system functions case by case, the judges could regard these moments of discrimination as extraneous to the matter at hand and wait for African-American and Mexican-American students to bring their own lawsuits to court.

The *Hopwood* opinion is an exercise in casuistry. Its scrupulous adherence to legal conventions—principles cited, authorities invoked, definitions provided—masks the specious logic that constructs a framework for evading the responsibility of courts, legislatures, and institutions to act against patterned discrimination. By segmenting discrimination into discrete sites and times, this logic erases historical patterns, present effects, and victimized groups. By recasting remedial attention to racism against groups as reverse discrimination against individuals, this logic justifies the dismantling of programs that enhance the life circumstances of disadvantaged populations. By substituting the number of votes garnered by a prior legal opinion for the merits of the opinion, this logic allows judges to pick the justifications that serve the conservative movement's policy agenda. And that is the crux of conservative judicial activism: bending jurisprudence to fit political objectives.

Let us recall Foucault's cautionary observation about truth. He tells us that claims regarded as true do not in themselves communicate objective truths; rather, they are regarded as communicating truths when they appear "within the true" as constituted by the rules of a discourse. Conservative judges have partnered themselves with other conservative leaders to play a cynical political game. The job of the judges is to produce a new discourse of truth about discrimination that will falsify virtually all claims about patterned discrimination. Then conservative politicians can get on with their job of revoking affirmative-action remedies for the systemic inequalities that ostensibly don't exist and conservative intellectuals can get on with their job of inculcating blindness to the social categories that organize the inequitable distribution of economic, social, and political goods. Once we are blind, conservatism's so-called meritocracy will be able to function like its free-market economy—with impunity.

Once we are blind, the disparities among citizens will appear to be generated "naturally."

WHAT'S RIGHT AND WHAT'S LEFT—TO DO?

Our society's goods—rights, responsibilities, and respect; housing, education, and employment; wages, wealth, and consumption—are still unjustly apportioned by class, race, ethnicity, and sex and, moreover, apportioned from the moment of birth forward.[25] Affirmative action is not a sweeping remedy for these distributive injustices but merely a narrow intervention into educational, employment, and contracting processes. It does not mandate equal opportunities outside these processes—for instance, the facilities available to people residing in prosperous suburbs versus inner-city ghettoes, the healthcare offered to the comfortably employed but not the underemployed and unemployed, the criminal justice meted out differentially to whites and people of color, and the industrial pollution left to corrode some neighborhoods and cleaned out of others. Nor does it alleviate the conditions that prevent people from reaching the gateways to higher education, comfortable employment, and business contracts: the toddlers who don't get innoculations or even breakfast, the kids growing up in urban war zones or rural poverty, the inner-city teens lacking transportation to summer jobs, the workfare moms cut off for staying home with sick kids, and the would-be minority business owners who can't get capitalized. If we as a nation were serious about providing citizens with basic life needs, constitutionally guaranteed rights, and equal opportunities, then we would have to act affirmatively from the moment of birth forward. Right now 25 percent of the nation's children, disproportionately children from minority races and ethnicities, live in poverty.[26] Will they survive that early life? What competitive credentials will they bring many years later to the college and job market gateways? Besides these casualties of poverty, poverty that seeds other deprivations throughout the life course, how many children in more comfortable circumstances—but weighed down by racism, sexism, or homophobia—will falter while trying to navigate through the gateways that open onto a better life?

What's wrong with the conservative movement is its pernicious morality and self-defeating myopia. The movement has created flashpoint issues to blind citizens to its destruction of programs that attempt to provide a head start in early life and some modest help along the way—"welfare queens" to trim family assistance programs, "school choice" to siphon government funds from public education, "tax-and-spend government" to take care of the rest, and "meritocracy" to hide the machinery of distributive injustice. In America, conservatives say, people who congregate at "starting lines" and compete on "level playing fields" can succeed through talent and hard work. We don't need affirmative action, say the hardliners, because what look like race- and sex-patterned discriminatory outcomes are really only the socioeconomic disparities that naturally result from competition when the meritocracy is functioning properly. Perhaps, say the moderates, we should give the deserving economically deprived kids a little developmental boost. As Richard D. Kahlenberg puts it, "If we are trying to provide genuine equal opportunity . . . class-based affirmative action would apply with most force at 'meritocratic crisis points' relatively *early* in life." But what Kahlenberg intends looks more like a belated talent search than an early developmental boost: "for people in their late teens who are applying to college or for an entry-level job, being economically disadvantaged is not at all their 'fault' and yet may hide their true potential."[27] Boosting a select group of economically disadvantaged teens (selected, according to Kahlenberg's formula, for their intrinsic potential and innocence) does too little, too late, for too few.

The movement may win its battle to dismantle affirmative action, but the victory will be pyrrhic and pointless. What, the movement needs to ask itself, does it portend for the nation's future that one-quarter of the adult population will have been damaged by all manner of deprivation, degradation, and discrimination and yet expected to function as productive citizens? What will happen if these citizens are ruled by privileged leaders who are blind to the causes of their misery? What kind of diversity will society have—the kind that wracks the nation or the kind that renews it? Conservative leaders invoke the adage that ideas have consequences when they are translated into public policies, voter realignments, and political rule. Another adage, which these leaders have overlooked, is the one they will discover sooner or later: consequences expose pretenses and, when pernicious, provoke insurrections.

What's wrong with too many of the nation's public officials is that their political behavior is determined by pollsters and spinmeisters who shape the issue itinerary, by interests that deliver the campaign funds with the policy packages, and by party whips who demand loyalty to partisan agendas. These officials have lost sight of the bottom line, which is that each of us—of whatever race, ethnicity, religion, sex, or sexuality—is a human being who enjoys and suffers one life of uncertain duration that is situated in the collective living that the people of this nation do together. What that means, as I see it, is that public policies have to foster both individual lives and collective living. To formulate policy options, public officials will have to acquaint themselves with people's circumstances, needs, and demands. To analyze the potential effects of policy options, they will have to think outside of the individual / group box; individual successes do not invalidate the "groupness" of a disadvantaged population, nor do the privileges accorded to a group mean that individual members are never disadvantaged. To solve economic and social problems, they will have to reconceptualize their own jobs: rather than declaiming and mandating, they should be orchestrating the democratic processes that promote distributive justice and comity among the nation's diverse peoples.

Finally, I want to talk about what went wrong for progressives in the academy. It was not simply that the conservative movement had amassed the financial, human, and organizational resources to attack our projects: feminist, African-American, cultural, gay / lesbian, and other studies. We also made ourselves vulnerable by internalizing to academic discourses what we set out to analyze and change in society. Despite our professed concern with societal problems, our scholarly practices have recast them as discursive artifacts. The "problems" we now address get fabricated at the sites where esoteric theories collide, abstract categories rupture, and arcane knowledges avalanche. Our discursive insularity may have been set in motion by the relay between institutionalization and intellectualization that disciplines all insurgent projects. But we became too driven by the imperative to criticize, too engrossed in particularizing identities and issues, and too busy sustaining our organizations on scant resources to keep the gradually shifting conditions of social change in view. And, sure enough, the gritty routine of doing all that work exhausted our energies, eclipsed our vision, and insulated us.

I do not want to be misunderstood as exhorting people to rush from their college classrooms, campaign offices, policy institutes, and battered women shelters into the streets. Social-structural change will not be made through 1960s-style protests, nor will it be made by organizations so specialized that they no longer constitute even a loosely networked movement. The solution today is not to abandon the national and local organizations we built but to retool them for greater political effectivity. For those who want to attempt that task, what's left to do is what feminists and progressives have not yet done successfully—use the wherewithal we already have to build the cross-sector infrastructure we need. Here are some suggestions to consider:

—Develop a hard network—with data bases, Internet communication, and regular events—that reaches across the sectors of the academy and society to connect those who are concerned with public issues.
—Form a council of academic and activist organizations to coordinate progressive projects across the breaches that now divide identity- and issue-based groups.
—Identify public issues that can be the occasion for local, regional, or national coalition building.
—Learn how to deploy cross-sector problem-solving teams in research on public issues, how to design academic research for use in public arenas, and how to translate research findings into forms accessible to policy-makers, the media, and other nonacademic publics.
—Provide training for academics and activists in media, lobbying, legislative, and fundraising skills.

Much more could be said about how to counter the politics of denigration and destruction—but not here. Such discussions are best held in private meetings, meetings attended by representatives of diverse constituencies who believe that, however different people are, they still do their collective living together, who know that coalition building is the work of producing mutual commitment, and who remember that the key to mutual commitment is flexibility. To make common cause, member groups will have to work together across sectors, in shifting combinations, and on some but not all issues, variously leading or supporting the other members.

In spring 1986, just before I left Cincinnati for a wholly consuming academic life at the University of Minnesota, a national pro-life organization sent its emissaries to stir up the town. One evening they held a public rally, and before dawn of the next morning unknown persons had bombed the Planned Parenthood Clinic, making it one more casualty of the organized forces that had bombed nearly thirty clinics, picketed many more venues, and harassed staffers at their own homes. Concerned Cincinnatians quickly formed a coalition and held a counterrally to expose the pattern of violence. One of the speakers was the Rev. Maurice McCracken, a feisty octogenarian and civil rights activist whose words on that occasion I want to repeat now. "In times such as these," he told the crowd, "there are no innocent bystanders. If you're a bystander, you're not innocent." Progressive scholars have paid a steep price for our achievements. While concentrating on our struggles to launch new knowledge projects in the academy, we became bystanders to the political struggles for everything else in the social field. Now that we have institutionalized these projects, isn't it time to call the question: knowledge for what? The answer is, as it always has been, up to each of you. But I hope this book convinces at least some of you to put progressive organizations and knowledges to work in the struggle over the nation's future.

Notes

Introduction: Knowing and Doing

1   From the conference program, "Pioneers for Century III: A National Bicentennial Conference," Cincinnati, Ohio, 22–25 April 1976, 1.

2   For the story of this project, see my "Changing the System: The Board of Trustees Caper," *Women's Studies Quarterly* 18.3–4 (fall-winter 1990): 136–46.

3   The 1974–75 members were Gloria DeSole, Joan Hartman, Leonore Hoffman, Jean Perkins, Deborah Rosenfelt, Cynthia Secor, Barbara Smith, Adrian Tinsley, and myself. Occasionally dropping in on our meetings was Florence Howe, the first CSW chair, founding mother of women's studies, and president of the Feminist Press.

4   See Joan E. Hartman and Ellen Messer-Davidow, Introduction to *Women in Print I: Opportunities for Women's Studies Research in Language and Literature*, ed. Joan E. Hartman and Ellen Messer-Davidow (New York: Modern Language Association, 1982), 1–9; and *Women in Print II: Opportunities for Women's Studies Publication in Language and Literature*, ed. Joan E. Hartman and Ellen Messer-Davidow (New York: Modern Language Association, 1982).

5   This quotation comes from my typescript copy of "Collage: One Life in the Day of a University President," a lecture that Warren Bennis gave at the Harvard University Graduate School of Education in fall 1976. It has not been published.

6   See the autobiographical essay in Warren Bennis, *An Invented Life: Reflections on Leadership and Change* (Reading, MA: Addison-Wesley, 1993), 1–40 (quotation, 29).

Part 1: Confronting the Institutional-Disciplinary Order

1   Florence Howe, "A Report on Women and the Profession," *College English* 32.8 (May 1971): 847–54 (first and second quotations, 850, third quotation, 852). The CSW report from which she draws is Florence Howe, Laura Morlock, and Richard Berk, "The Status of Women in Modern Language Departments: A Report of the Modern Language Association Commission on the Status of Women in the Profession," *PMLA* 86.3 (May 1971): 459–68. At the time when Howe quoted some of its findings—for instance, that although 55 percent of graduate students were women only about 10 percent of their teachers were women and that "the percentage of women among the

teaching faculty declines as the course level rises" (848)—the circumstances of women faculty as a group were so unknown that the data would have shocked readers.

Chapter 1: Disciplining Women

1   Ellen Messer-Davidow, David R. Shumway, and David J. Sylvan, Preface to *Knowledges: Historical and Critical Studies in Disciplinarity*, ed. Ellen Messer-Davidow, David R. Shumway, and David J. Sylvan (Charlottesville: University Press of Virginia, 1993), vii (both quotations). Systems of higher education are described in Burton R. Clark, *The Higher Education System: Academic Organization in Cross-national Perspective* (Berkeley: University of California Press, 1983). For the forms and functions of disciplines, see the essays in Messer-Davidow et al., *Knowledges;* David R. Shumway and Ellen Messer-Davidow, "Disciplinarity: An Introduction," *Poetics Today* 12.2 (1991): 201–25; and Tony Becher, *Academic Tribes and Territories: Intellectual Enquiry and the Culture of Disciplines* (Milton Keynes, U.K.: Society for Research into Higher Education / Open University Press, 1989).

2   Timothy Lenoir, "The Discipline of Nature and the Nature of Disciplines," in Messer-Davidow et al., *Knowledges,* 72.

3   For case studies of how journals wield scientific and scholarly discourse to modify authorial claims, see Greg Myers, "The Social Construction of Two Biologists' Articles," in Messer-Davidow et al., *Knowledges,* 327–67; Ed Cohen, "Are We (Not) What We Are Becoming? Gay 'Identity,' 'Gay Studies,' and the Disciplining of Knowledge," in Messer-Davidow et al., *Knowledges,* 397–421; and Patricia J. Williams, "The Death of the Profane," in *Debating Affirmative Action: Race, Gender, Ethnicity, and the Politics of Inclusion,* ed. Nicolaus Mills (New York: Dell, 1994), 117–25. Williams tells the story of what happened to an article on racism that included, as an example, a personal incident: a Benetton store open to white shoppers barred her from entering. Instead of the routine editorial process of making minor corrections to a typescript, the journal subjected hers to three rounds of editing. In the first, it converted her phrasing to the agentless-passive, omitting her person and feelings from the Benetton incident; in the second round, it excised the store's name on the rationale that it wouldn't print unverified defamations; and finally it deleted all references to the author's race, saying that the purpose of law-review articles was to discuss legal principles not personal details. These editorial tactics made the Benetton incident incapable of exemplifying institutionalized racism and on principle would disqualify any qualitative data—that is, descriptions of people's experiences—from supporting the larger argument that the law permitted and perpetuated institutionalized racism.

4   Michel Foucault, "Truth and Power," in *Power / Knowledge: Selected Interviews and Other Writings, 1972–1977,* ed. Colin Gordon, trans. Colin Gordon, Leo Marshall, John Mepham, and Kate Soper (New York: Pantheon, 1980), 133. Also see Foucault's comments on truth in "Two Lectures," in ibid., 93.

5   Evelyn Fox Keller, "The Anomaly of a Woman in Physics," in *Working It Out: 23 Women Writers, Artists, Scientists, and Scholars Talk About Their Lives and Work,* ed. Sara Ruddick and Pamela Daniels (New York: Pantheon, 1977), 78–79.

6   Keller, "Anomaly," 87 (first quotation), 81 (second and third quotations).

7   Ibid., 88–89.

8   Ibid., 89.

9   Ibid., 86.

10 Ibid., 84–85.

11 Ibid., 88.

12 Evelyn Fox Keller, *Reflections on Gender and Science* (New Haven: Yale University Press, 1985), 4 (quotation).

13 Ibid., 9.

14 Gerald Holton, *Introduction to Concepts and Theories in Physical Science* (Reading, MA: Addison-Wesley, 1952), xiii.

15 Ibid., 216.

16 Ibid., 222 (long quotation and two short quotations).

17 Ibid., 247.

18 I am not claiming that Holton's explanation of "fact" as relations observed by the physicist is the definitive one today. Studies of physics by philosophers of science, sociologists of science, and anthropologists have complicated the status of physical facts by debating the extent to which they are constru(ct)ed by instruments, practices, and theories. See, for instance, *Observation, Experiment, and Hypothesis in Modern Physical Science,* ed. Peter Achinstein and Owen Hannaway (Cambridge: MIT Press, 1985); Andrew Pickering, *Constructing Quarks: A Sociological History of Particle Physics* (Chicago: University of Chicago Press, 1984); and Sharon Traweek, *Beamtimes and Lifetimes: The World of High Energy Physicists* (Cambridge: Harvard University Press, 1988).

19 Holton, *Introduction,* 226–27.

20 Keller, "Anomaly," 83.

21 Holton, *Introduction,* 224–25.

22 Ibid., 235.

23 Ibid., 236.

24 Ibid.

25 See ibid., 248–50.

26 Ibid., 218. It is no accident that the opening chapters of introductory physics textbooks provide a narrative of the discipline's intellectual progress with pictures of individuals, from the ancients to the founding fathers of modern physics, dotting the margins. See, for instance, F. K. Richtmyer, E. H. Kennard, and John N. Cooper, *Introduction to Modern Physics,* 6th ed. (New York: McGraw-Hill, 1969); and J. J. G. McCue, *The World of Atoms: An Introduction to Physical Science* (New York: Ronald Press, 1956).

27 Lillian S. Robinson and Lise Vogel, "Modernism and History," in Lillian S. Robinson, *Sex, Class, and Culture* (Bloomington: Indiana University Press, 1978), 24–25 (originally published in *New Literary History* 3.1 [autumn 1971]: 177–97). I am grateful to Lillian Robinson for providing information about the graduate student and her husband (whose names she asked me to withhold). It helped me analyze their responses to the

painting and to contextualize the student's anecdote in her subsequent career (personal communication, August 1994).

28   See Michael Levey, *A Concise History of Painting from Giotto to Cézanne* (New York: Praeger, 1962), 216–17 (for comments on Boucher).

29   Robinson and Vogel, "Modernism," 31.

30   I am, of course, echoing Foucault (he borrowed the idea from Georges Canguilhem) who explained that before a statement can even be appraised as true or false it must be posed "within the true" as constituted by the discourse; that is, it must address the objects and use the concepts already recognized by the discourse. See Michel Foucault, "The Discourse on Language," in Foucault, *The Archaeology of Knowledge and the Discourse on Language,* trans. A. M. Sheridan Smith (New York: Pantheon, 1972), 223–24.

31   Erwin Panofsky, *Meaning in the Visual Arts* (Garden City, NY: Anchor, 1955), 324. Symptomatically, *Art Bulletin,* founded in 1913 and soon recognized as the leading journal in the field, initially published articles on art instruction and appreciation as well as art-historical scholarship and only began featuring scholarship in the 1920s.

32   Donald Preziosi, "The Question of Art History," *Critical Inquiry* 18.2 (winter 1992): 365 (first quotation), 369 (second quotation).

33   Heinrich Wölfflin, *Principles of Art History: The Problem of the Development of Style in Later Art,* trans. of 7th German ed. (New York: Dover, 1932), 2.

34   Wölfflin wrote, "We shall realise that a certain conception of form is necessarily bound up with a certain tonality and shall gradually come to understand the whole complex of personal characteristics of style as the expression of a certain temperament" (ibid., 6 [quotation here], 10 [quotation in the text]).

35   Panofsky, *Meaning,* 16; see also 14–17.

36   See Charles R. Jansen, *Studying Art History* (Englewood Cliffs, NJ: Prentice-Hall, 1986), 6, 11–12.

37   David Summers, " 'Form,' Nineteenth-Century Metaphysics, and the Problem of Art Historical Description," *Critical Inquiry* 15.2 (winter 1989): 379. For other explanations of how artworks are not merely seen but seen through, see Tony Bennett, *The Birth of the Museum: History, Theory, and Politics* (London: Routledge, 1995), 35; and Donald Preziosi, "Seeing through Art History," in Messer-Davidow et al., *Knowledges,* 215–31.

38   David Summers, "Form and Gender," in *Visual Culture: Images and Interpretations,* ed. Norman Bryson, Michael Ann Holly, and Keith Moxey (Hanover, NH: Wesleyan University Press, 1994), 384–85. Summers is not a true believer; he commented that these "physiognomic inferences from presumably expressive forms . . . began to appear circular, to explain too much too quickly; or to explain nothing at all" (385).

39   For a discussion of the disciplinary techniques used by these early museums, see Eilean Hooper-Greenhill, *Museums and the Shaping of Modern Knowledge* (London: Routledge, 1992), 167–90.

40   Preziosi, "Seeing," 225.

41   Although he puts it a bit differently, see Bennett, *Birth,* 96.

42   Dorothy E. Smith, *The Everyday World as Problematic: A Feminist Sociology* (Boston:

Northeastern University Press, 1987), 71–72, quoted from Catherine Russell, letter in *Kinesis* 5 (February 1977).

43 Keller, "Anomaly," 90–91.

44 Jessie Bernard, "Re-viewing the Impact of Women's Studies on Sociology," in *The Impact of Feminist Research in the Academy,* ed. Christie Farnham (Bloomington: Indiana University Press, 1987), 197.

45 Tom Bottomore and Robert Nisbet, Introduction to *A History of Sociological Analysis,* ed. Tom Bottomore and Robert Nisbet (New York: Basic Books, 1978), viii; also see viii–x.

46 Ibid., viii.

47 See Dorothy E. Smith, "Sociological Theory: Methods of Writing Patriarchy," in *Feminism and Sociological Theory,* ed. Ruth A. Wallace (Newbury Park, CA: Sage, 1989), 35, 44–49; and *The Conceptual Practices of Power: A Feminist Sociology of Knowledge* (Boston: Northeastern University Press, 1990), 32–33. Since we're used to thinking about objectivity as defined in the scientific and philosophical traditions, Smith's understanding of it may be difficult to grasp. When scientists use the term to support their truth claims, they mean that by eliminating their personal biases, feelings, and interests from research they can produce knowledge that accurately represents reality. By contrast, philosophers such as Allan Megill describe the term *objectivity* as operating in a linguistic binary with *subjectivity:* the one seeks to exclude or contain the other (see Allan Megill, "Introduction: Four Senses of Objectivity," *Annals of Scholarship* 8.3–4 [summer–fall 1991]: 301–20). Smith combines sociological and discourse theory to describe objectivity as the convention-organized practices of constructing and construing the elements of sociological discourse—namely, the objects and relations investigated.

To illustrate Smith's point about how sociological discourse recasts the social, I offer this observation made by Robert Merton in 1972. Sociological conventions, he writes, require us "to ignore such intense human experiences as pain, suffering, humiliation, and so on. In this context, analytically useful concepts such as social stratification, social exchange, reward system, dysfunction, symbolic interaction, etc., are altogether bland in the fairly precise sense of being unperturbing, suave, and soothing in effect. To say this is not to imply that the conceptual repertoire of sociology . . . must be purged of such impersonal concepts and filled with sentiment-laden substitutes. But it should be noted that analytically useful as these impersonal concepts are for certain problems, they also serve to exclude from the attention of the social scientist the intense feelings of pain and suffering that are the experience of some people caught up in the social patterns under examination." According to Merton, sociologists have ignored pain and suffering not because they are inhumane but because they use concepts formed precisely by excluding the affective and other elements of everyday discourse (quoted in Bernard, "Re-viewing," 209).

48 Smith, *Conceptual Practices,* 70 (first quotation), 71 (second quotation).

49 Smith, "Sociological Theory," 49; she is quoting from *Family, Class and Education: A Reader,* ed. Maurice Craft (London: Longman, 1970), 7.

50 See Bernard, "Re-viewing," 197; Martin Bulmer, "The Growth of Applied Sociology after 1945: The Prewar Establishment of the Postwar Infrastructure," in *Sociology and Its Publics: The Forms and Fates of Disciplinary Organization,* ed. Terence C. Halliday and Morris Janowitz (Chicago: University of Chicago Press, 1992), 318–35; William Buxton and Stephen P. Turner, "From Education to Expertise: Sociology as a 'Profession,'" in Halliday and Janowitz, *Sociology,* 373–404; and Lewis A. Coser, "American Trends," in Bottomore and Nisbet, *History,* 311–17.

51 Bottomore and Nisbet, Introduction to Bottomore and Nisbet, ix.

52 See Terence C. Halliday, "Introduction: Sociology's Fragile Professionalism," in Halliday and Janowitz, *Sociology,* 12–15.

53 For this concern with sociology as a profession, see ibid., 5–9. I don't want to oversimplify sociology as a disciplinary formation. It has been riven not only by its disciplinary and professional objectives but by its empirical and interpretive paradigms, its quantitative and qualitative methods, and, as Bottomore and Nisbet point out, its many schools: Marxist, positivist, functionalist, interactionist, phenomenological, structuralist, and so on. Thus I would have to argue, as Craig Calhoun does, that sociology has two historical trajectories: the project of scientization that tried to make it a bounded discipline with a uniform intellectual core and the forces of growth, specialization, and importation that made it a variegated discipline. After examining sociology's trade with other fields—the social sciences, history, law, education, and women's studies—Calhoun concludes that the discipline has imported knowledge from fields such as economics that advance its scientization and has blockaded knowledge from less scientific fields. Tellingly, feminist research has been "slow to penetrate the mainstream journals of sociology," and even the research published in important feminist journals such as *Signs* is seldom cited by sociologists. On Calhoun's view, the attempt to trade up the scientific scale has promoted a degree of schematization, simplification, and specialization that impoverishes sociological work. See Craig Calhoun, "Sociology, Other Disciplines, and the Project of a General Understanding of Social Life," in Halliday and Janowitz, *Sociology,* 137–95.

54 Elaine Showalter, "Women and the Literary Curriculum," *College English* 32.8 (May 1971): 855. Showalter's claim, in 1971, that freshman English anthologies excluded women writers was not an exaggeration. That year, Jean S. Mullen conducted two surveys: the preliminary survey of 21 freshman English anthologies found that the overall proportion of female to male authors was 7 to 93 percent, and the full survey of 122 anthologies found that they contained 472 female-authored and 5,795 male-authored texts, for a proportion of 7.53 percent to 92.47 percent. Of these anthologies, the few edited by women and the one edited by students contained the highest percentages of women writers. See Jean S. Mullen, "Freshman Textbooks," *College English* 34.1 (October 1972): 79–84.

55 Showalter, "Women," 856 (four short quotations above and this long one).

56 I am closely paraphrasing from John Keats's letter to his brothers, George and Thomas Keats, written on 21 December 1817.

57 Carolyn Heilbrun and Catharine Stimpson, "Theories of Feminist Criticism: A Di-

alogue," in *Feminist Literary Criticism: Explorations in Theory,* ed. Josephine Donovan (Lexington: University Press of Kentucky, 1975), 64–65.

58   Suzanne Juhasz, "Feminist Criticism: My Theory and Practice," in Catherine L. Blecki, Barbara C. Gelpi, Suzanne Juhasz, and Selma R. Burkom, *Feminist Literary Criticism: A Symposium* (San Jose: Diotima, 1974), 10.

59   Mary Ellmann, *Thinking About Women* (New York: Harcourt Brace Jovanovich, 1968), 23 (quotation), 150 (for Ellmann's explanation of how male-typed prose conventions elicit a favorable critical judgment).

60   Nancy K. Miller, "Decades," in *Changing Subjects: The Making of Feminist Literary Criticism,* ed. Gayle Greene and Coppélia Kahn (London and New York: Routledge, 1993), 35; Carol Thomas Neely, "Loss and Recovery: Homes Away From Home," in ibid., 183.

61   For discussions of New Criticism's history and practices, see René Wellek, "American Literary Scholarship," in René Wellek, *Concepts of Criticism,* ed. Stephen G. Nichols Jr. (New Haven: Yale University Press, 1963), 296–315; Vincent Leitch, *American Literary Criticism from the 30s to the 80s* (New York: Columbia University Press, 1988), 24–59; William E. Cain, *The Crisis in Criticism: Theory, Literature, and Reform in English Studies* (Baltimore: Johns Hopkins University Press, 1984), 85–121; and David R. Shumway, *Creating American Civilization: A Genealogy of American Literature as an Academic Discipline* (Minneapolis: University of Minnesota Press, 1994), 208–18, 221–36.

62   Selma R. Burkom, "Feminist Criticism: Humanism," in Blecki et al., *Feminist Literary Criticism,* 17 (all quotations above).

63   Ibid., 18.

64   Juhasz, "Feminist Criticism," 16.

65   Keller, "Anomaly," 89.

66   See René Wellek and Austin Warren, *Theory of Literature,* 3d ed. (New York: Harcourt, Brace & World, 1956), 73.

67   W. K. Wimsatt Jr., *The Verbal Icon: Studies in the Meaning of Poetry* (Lexington: University of Kentucky Press, [1954] 1967), 10.

68   See W. K. Wimsatt, "The Intentional Fallacy" and "The Affective Fallacy," in ibid., 3–18, 21–39.

69   Wellek and Warren, *Theory,* 156.

70   Wimsatt, *Verbal Icon,* x (first quotation), 82 (second quotation).

71   I have abbreviated Vincent Leitch's description of practice in his *American Literary Criticism,* 30–35.

72   See W. K. Wimsatt, "What to Say about a Poem," in *Hateful Contraries: Studies in Literature and Criticism* (Lexington: University of Kentucky Press, 1966), 215–44.

73   Murray Krieger, *Theory of Criticism: A Tradition and Its System* (Baltimore: Johns Hopkins University Press, 1976), 39.

74   Ibid., 41.

75   Ibid., 44.

76   Here and below I draw heavily from Basil Bernstein's *Class, Codes and Control,* vol. 3, *Towards a Theory of Educational Transmission* (London: Routledge & Kegan Paul, 1975),

31–38 (on the three orders of disciplinary discourse), 40–46 (on the effects when students falter).

77 Keller, "Anomaly," 83.

78 Ann Rosalind Jones, "Imaginary Gardens with Real Frogs in Them: Feminist Euphoria and the Franco-American Divide, 1976–88," in Greene and Kahn, *Changing Subjects,* 66 (first quotation), 68–69 (other quotations).

79 Nancy Burr Evans, "The Value and Peril for Women of Reading Women Writers," in *Images of Women in Fiction: Feminist Perspectives,* ed. Susan Koppelman Cornillon, rev. ed. (Bowling Green: Bowling Green University Popular Press, 1973), 309–10.

80 Ibid., 311 (first quotation), 310 (second quotation), 311 (third and fourth quotations).

81 Ibid., 312.

82 Heilbrun and Stimpson, "Theories of Feminist Criticism: A Dialogue," in Donovan, *Feminist Literary Criticism,* 62 (all quotes).

Chapter 2: Constructing Sex Discrimination

1 Ellen Carol Dubois, Gail Paradise Kelly, Elizabeth Lapovsky Kennedy, Carolyn W. Korsmeyer, and Lillian S. Robinson, *Feminist Scholarship: Kindling in the Groves of Academe* (Urbana: University of Illinois Press, 1985), 2.

2 For readers who are interested in the civil rights and New Left movements, I suggest the following as places to start.

For the civil rights movement, see Doug McAdam, *Political Process and the Development of Black Insurgency, 1930–1970* (Chicago: University of Chicago Press, 1982); Aldon D. Morris, *The Origins of the Civil Rights Movement: Black Communities Organizing for Change* (New York: Free Press, 1984); James Laue, *Direct Action and Desegregation, 1960–62* (Brooklyn: Carlson, 1989); Clayborne Carson, *In Struggle: SNCC and the Black Awakening of the 1960s,* new ed. (Cambridge: Harvard University Press, 1995); and Doug McAdam, *Freedom Summer* (New York: Oxford University Press, 1988).

For the New Left, see Todd Gitlin, *The Sixties: Years of Hope, Days of Rage* (New York: Bantam, 1987); James Miller, *Democracy Is in the Streets: From Port Huron to the Siege of Chicago* (New York: Simon and Schuster, 1987); Wini Breines, *Community and Organization in the New Left, 1962–1968;* new ed. (New Brunswick, NJ: Rutgers University Press, 1989); and Max Heirich, *The Spiral of Conflict: Berkeley 1964* (New York: Columbia University Press, 1971).

For source material, the analyses of systematicity and critiques of education can be pieced together from the writings of movement members. See Paul Jacobs and Saul Landau, *The New Radicals: A Report with Documents* (New York: Vintage, 1966); *The New Left: A Collection of Essays,* ed. Priscilla Long (Boston: Porter Sargent, 1969); *The New Left: A Documentary History,* ed. Massimo Teodori (Indianapolis: Bobbs-Merrill, 1969); *The American Left: Radical Political Thought in the Twentieth Century,* ed. Loren Baritz (New York: Basic Books, 1971); *The Student Voice 1960–1965: Periodical of the Student Nonviolent Coordinating Committee,* ed. Clayborne Carson (Westport, CT: Meckler, 1990); and *"Takin' It to the Streets": A Sixties Reader,* ed. Alexander Bloom and Wini Breines (New York: Oxford University Press, 1995).

Elsewhere in this book, I will be citing materials on early feminism and antidiscrimination laws.

3   For general accounts of women's committees, commissions, and caucuses, see Ruth M. Oltman, "Women in the Professional Caucuses," *American Behavioral Sciences* 15.2 (November–December 1971): 281–302; Kay Klotzberger, "Political Action by Academic Women," in *Academic Women on the Move,* ed. Alice S. Rossi and Ann Calderwood (New York: Russell Sage Foundation, 1973), 359–91; Anne M. Briscoe, "Phenomenon of the Seventies: The Women's Caucuses," *Signs* 4.1 (autumn 1978): 152–58; and "Women's Groups in the Professional Associations," in *Women in Academe: Progress and Prospects,* ed. Mariam K. Chamberlain (New York: Russell Sage Foundation, 1988), 275–89.

On the Committee on Women in Physics, see "Women in Physics," The Report of the Committee on the Status of Women in Physics, *Bulletin of the American Physical Society,* 2d ser., 17.6 (June 1972): 740–53; GBL, "Discrimination against Women in Physics," *Physics Today* 25.7 (July 1972): 61–62; and Committee on the Status of Women in Physics, "Twenty Years Later CSWP Is Still Going Strong," *American Physical Society News* 1.6 (June 1992): 11–15.

On the College Art Association Women's Caucus, see Mary Stofflet, "Women's Caucus for Art at the C.A.A.," *Feminist Art Journal* 5.2 (summer 1976): 38–40.

On the Modern Language Association Commission on the Status of Women in the Profession and the Women's Caucus for the Modern Languages, see E. Diggs, "Rebels in the MLA," *Social Policy* 1.2 (July–August 1970): 57–59; Virginia Barber, "The Women's Revolt in the MLA," in *Women on Campus: The Unfinished Liberation,* ed. Editors of *Change* (New Rochelle, NY: Change, 1975), 85–94; Introduction to *Women in Print I: Opportunities for Women's Studies Research in Language and Literature,* ed. Joan E. Hartman and Ellen Messer-Davidow (New York: Modern Language Association, 1982); and Florence Howe, "What Was It Like Then?" in *Courage and Tools,* ed. Joanne Glasgow and Angela Ingram (New York: Modern Language Association, 1990).

As these citations indicate, we have scattered vignettes of the women's committees, commissions, and caucuses; what we need are substantial histories of their formation, projects, and change strategies as well as their collaborative work across disciplines.

4   Patricia Albjerg Graham, "Status Transitions of Women Students, Faculty, and Administrators," in Rossi and Calderwood, *Academic Women,* 163.

5   Pamela Roby, "Institutional Barriers to Women Students in Higher Education," in Rossi and Calderwood, *Academic Women,* 40. As readers peruse the findings that follow, it is important to keep in mind that the status studies, especially those emanating from different disciplines, did not format their data in the same way. In discussing the distribution by faculty rank in a particular discipline, one might compare the percentages of women and men at each rank, while another might compare the distribution of each sex among the four faculty ranks, but both formats show women clustered in the lower two ranks and men clustered in the higher.

6   "Women in Physics," 747.

7   Ibid., 742, 746, 750. Also see Betsy Ancker-Johnson, "Women's Lib and Physics," *Physics Teacher* 10.9 (December 1972): 499–507. Although physicists holding doctorates worked in government, national laboratories, industry, and the academy, I focus on the academy because it employed 58 percent of women physicists.

8   "Women in Physics," 752.

9   Alice S. Rossi, "Status of Women in Graduate Departments of Sociology, 1968–1969," *The American Sociologist* 5.1 (February 1970): 2, 5, 11.

10 Ibid., 7–8.

11 See Ann Sutherland Harris, "The Second Sex in Academe," *ART in America*, May–June 1972, 18–19 (it provides data on women and men in four full-time ranks for the years 1963 through 1971); Ann Sutherland Harris, "Women in College Art Departments and Museums," *Art Journal* 32.4 (summer 1973): 417–19 (it presents data collected by *Art Journal* for the years 1960 through 1965 and by the College Art Association Women's Caucus from a survey of 164 departments for the year 1970–71); and Barbara Erlich White and Leon S. White, "Survey on the Status of Women in College Art Departments," *Art Journal* 32.4 (summer 1973): 420–22 (it provides data on 164 departments, most for the years 1970 through 1973).

12 Harris, "Women," 417 (first percentage); White and White, "Survey," 422 (second and third percentages).

13 White and White, "Survey," 421–22.

14 Harris, "Second Sex," 19.

15 Harris, "Women," 418.

16 See Florence Howe, Laura Morlock, and Richard Berk, "The Status of Women in Modern Language Departments: A Report of the Modern Language Association Commission on the Status of Women in the Profession," *PMLA* 86.3 (May 1971): 459–68; Laura Morlock et al., "Affirmative Action for Women in 1971: A Report of the Modern Language Association Commission on the Status of Women in the Profession," *PMLA* 87.3 (May 1972): 530–40; and Joan E. Hartman, Laura Morlock, Jean A. Perkins, and Adrian Tinsley, "Study III. Women in Modern Language Departments, 1972–73: A Report by the Commission on the Status of Women in the Profession," *PMLA* 91.1 (January 1976): 124–36.

17 Hartman et al., "Study III," 124–36. In those days, for readers who may not know, journals had not yet instituted author-blind reviews of submissions. The manuscripts were sent to readers with the author's name, rank, department, and institution on the cover page.

18 Bettina J. Huber, Denise M. Pinney, David E. Lawrence, and Denise Bourassa Knight, "MLA Surveys of Ph.D. Placement: Most Recent Findings and Decade-Long Trends," *ADFL Bulletin* 20.3 (April 1989): 20–30. Huber and her colleagues note that sex-patterned employment was more clear-cut in the foreign languages than in English. The 1979–80 pattern—that men in the foreign languages "were more likely to have tenure-track appointments, while women were more likely to have part-time appointments" (21)—was somewhat less pronounced in 1986–87.

19   See Alice S. Rossi, "Summary and Prospects," in Rossi and Calderwood, *Academic Women*, 509; Rossi, "Status," 3; and Joyce M. Mitchell and Rachel R. Starr, "A Regional Approach for Analyzing the Recruitment of Academic Women," *American Behavioral Scientist* 15 (November–December 1971): 190–202.

20   See Rossi, "Status," 5 (the data on attrition rates used by Rossi pertained to sociology departments at the Universities of Chicago and Wisconsin); and Michelle Patterson and Lucy Sells, "Women Dropouts from Higher Education," in Rossi and Calderwood, *Academic Women*, 84–89.

21   For a summary of the attrition problem and its causes, see Mina Rees, "The Graduate Education of Women," in *Women in Higher Education*, ed. W. Todd Furniss and Patricia Albjerg Graham (Washington, DC: American Council on Education, 1974), 178–87.

22   Roby, "Institutional Barriers," 41–42, 47–50. The pattern in sociology was typical of those in other disciplines. For 1971–72, 37.5 percent of female graduate students and 62.5 percent of male ones received financial aid (Ad Hoc Committee on the Status of Women in the Profession, *The Status of Women in Sociology, 1968–1972* [Washington, DC: American Sociological Association, 1973], 22).

23   See Laura Morlock, "Discipline Variation in the Status of Academic Women," in Rossi and Calderwood, *Academic Women*, 264–66; and Heather Sigworth, "Issues in Nepotism Rules," in Furniss and Graham, *Women*, 117. Morlock mentions a 1972 study of the modern languages showing that departments without antinepotism policies employed far higher percentages of women at all professorial ranks than did those with written or unwritten policies. Sigworth mentions studies showing that these policies were widespread: one 1970 survey reported that 74 percent of the 42 land grant universities responding to the questionnaire had written antinepotism policies, and another 1970 survey showed that 35 percent of all universities and colleges had specific antinepotism rules.

24   See Morlock, "Discipline Variation," 273–74, 276–77; Lora H. Robinson, "Institutional Variation in the Status of Academic Women," in Rossi and Calderwood, *Academic Women*, 210–12; and Sheila Tobias and Margaret L. Rumbarger, "Rearrangements in Faculty Schedules: Full-Status Part-Time Faculty," in Furniss and Graham, *Women*, 128–37.

25   Esther M. Westervelt, *Women's Higher Education: Some Unanswered Questions* (Racine, WI: Johnson Foundation, 1972), 7–8 (report of the Wingspread Conference). The Wingspread Conference, probably the first national feminist conference on women in higher education, was attended by representatives of universities, education associations, government agencies, foundations, and women's organizations.

      Personal anecdotes from this period also show that women were discouraged from pursuing advanced degrees. See *Working It Out: 23 Women Writers, Artists, Scientists, and Scholars Talk About Their Lives and Work*, ed. Sara Ruddick and Pamela Daniels (New York: Pantheon, 1977); and *The Road Retaken: Women Reenter the Academy*, ed. Irene Thompson and Audrey Roberts (New York: Modern Language Association, 1985). For discussions of attitudes toward women, see Roby, "Institutional Barriers," 52; Pepper Schwartz and Janet Lever, "Women in the Male World of Higher Education," in Rossi and Calderwood, *Academic Women*, 57–77; and Graham, "Status Transitions," in Rossi and Calderwood, *Academic Women*, 164–67.

26 *Status of Women in Sociology*, 24, 25, 27. For a fuller sampling of such comments, see Schwartz and Lever, "Women," 57–77; Harris, "Second Sex," 284–85; "Women in Physics," 748; and Nancy Jo Hoffman, "Sexism in Letters of Recommendation," *MLA Newsletter*, September 1972, 5–6.

27 Michelle Patterson, "Sex and Specialization in Academe and the Professions," in Rossi and Calderwood, *Academic Women*, 313–14 (two quotations above). As a contrast to her own theory that stereotype-driven practices cumulatively (re)produce sex-segregated fields, Patterson mentions the two theories of sex segregation prevalent at that time. The pressure theory held that most of the women who are interested in a male-dominated field "are guided by significant others . . . into specialties that are considered appropriate for women," while the few who do enter it are discouraged by male professors and drop out. By contrast, the preference theory held "that women are genuinely attracted by, pulled by their own interests toward the specialties in which they are found." Patterson argued that both theories ignored the prior facts: in a society that maintained a rigid sex-role system, women had few alternatives to seek and, once they were socialized into choosing appropriately female roles, had little motivation to seek them (330 [first quotation], 329 [second quotation]).

28 Rossi, "Summary," 518.

29 Compare the programs of the Modern Language Association conventions in 1970 and 1989. Of the 171 scholarly sessions in 1970, 9 (5 percent) concerned women's literature, feminist criticism, gender, and women's status and another 7 (4 percent) included at least one feminist paper (*PMLA* 85.6 [November 1970]). Of the 680 scholarly sessions in 1989, 143 (21 percent) concerned women's literature, feminist criticism, gender, and women's status and another 81 (12 percent) included at least one feminist paper (*PMLA* 104.6 [November 1989]).

30 Ruth Bleier, "Lab Coat: Robe of Innocence or Klansman's Sheet?" in *Feminist Studies / Critical Studies*, ed. Teresa de Lauretis (Bloomington: Indiana University Press, 1986), 56.

31 For descriptions of the organization of scientific labor in the 1980s, see Sandra Harding, *The Science Question in Feminism* (Ithaca, NY: Cornell University Press, 1986), 68–78; and Sharon Traweek, *Beamtimes and Lifetimes: The World of High Energy Physicists* (Cambridge: Harvard University Press, 1988), 24–36, 115–17.

32 Vera Kistiakowsky, "Women in Physics: Unnecessary, Injurious, and Out of Place?" *Physics Today* 33.2 (February 1980): 39. For a detailed account of how the hierarchical work site patterns authority and activity, see Terry Shinn, "Scientific Disciplines and Organizational Specificity: The Social and Cognitive Configuration of Laboratory Activities," in *Scientific Establishments and Hierarchies*, ed. Norbert Elias, Herminio Martins, and Richard Whitley (Dordrecht: Reidel, 1982), 239–54. In scientific laboratories, according to Shinn, the research director selects the scientific program, the investigations to be carried out, and the specific research strategies. He disperses the material resources and assigns the tasks. The senior and junior scientists link the director's

program to the daily work of realizing it, and the laboratory assistants and technicians carry out the routine work of experiment or observation, equipment maintenance, and provision of materials. The pattern of decision making is hierarchical, and the flow of communications reinforces it. Vertical communications, usually in the form of written memoranda initiated and received by the director, predominate, while horizontal ones, in the form of oral exchanges among individuals of the same stratum, are seen as less important. In short, the research director shapes both the careers of scientists and the production of knowledge by controlling the organization of resources and practices.

33 Jonathan R. Cole, *Fair Science: Women in the Scientific Community* (New York: Free Press, 1979), 7–8 (on accumulation of advantage and disadvantage), 300 (quotations).

34 Ibid., 26.

35 Ibid., 21.

36 Ibid., 33 (first quotation), 34 (second quotation).

37 Ibid., 36.

38 See ibid., 51–91.

39 Ibid., 36.

40 This body of law includes: (1) President John F. Kennedy's Executive Order 10925 (1961) prohibiting discrimination by government contractors on the basis of race, creed, color, and national origin; (2) the Equal Pay Act of 1964, prohibiting pay discrimination; (3) the Civil Rights Act of 1964, especially Title VI, Title VII, and other sections, prohibiting discrimination by virtually all public and private employers on the basis of race, color, religion, national origin, and sex (this act was amended in 1972 to include many activities at public and private academic institutions); (4) President Lyndon Johnson's Executive Order 11246 (1965), prohibiting discrimination by federal contractors (including educational institutions) on the basis of race, color, religion and national origin; and (5) President Johnson's Executive Order 11375 (1968), amending the previous one by adding sex to the list and further prohibiting discrimination by the federal government itself. Many discrimination lawsuits also invoke section 1 of the Fourteenth Amendment to the Constitution (1868), which prohibits the states from abridging the privileges and immunities of citizens of the United States and from denying equal protection under the law to persons within their jurisdictions.

Initially, the oversight responsibilities were divided among several federal agencies. The Equal Employment Opportunity Commission (EEOC), established in 1964, handled the Title VII compliance of private and state employers, the Civil Service Commission handled the Title VII compliance of federal employers, and the Office of Civil Rights in the Department of Health, Education, and Welfare, together with smaller federal offices, shared other compliance responsibilities. When the EEOC balked at dealing with several types of sex discrimination brought to its attention by the federal and state commissions on women (established in the early 1960s), the ensuing hostilities sparked the formation of the National Organization for Women in 1966.

For accounts of the resistance to affirmative action in the early years, see Jo Freeman, "Women on the Move: The Roots of Revolt," in Rossi and Calderwood, *Aca-*

demic Women, 5–9; Jo Freeman, *The Politics of Women's Liberation* (New York: McKay, 1975), 52–56, 75–80; Judith Hole and Ellen Levine, *Rebirth of Feminism* (New York: Quadrangle, 1971), 28–48; Bernice Sandler, "A Little Help from Our Government: WEAL and Contract Compliance," in Rossi and Calderwood, *Academic Women,* 439–62; Bernice Sandler, "The Hand That Rocked the Cradle Has Learned to Rock the Boat," *New Directions in Institutional Research* 3 (1974): 1–21; *Making Affirmative Action Work in Higher Education* (San Francisco: Jossey-Bass, 1975) (a report of the Carnegie Council on Policy Studies in Higher Education); and Joan Abramson, *Old Boys, New Women: The Politics of Sex Discrimination* (New York: Praeger, 1979).

41 See Jennie Farley, "Women versus Academe: Who's Winning?" *Journal of Social Issues* 41.4 (1985): 112; and Athena Theodore, *The Campus Troublemakers: Academic Women in Protest* (Houston: Cap and Gown, 1986), 83–90.

42 See Carol Van Alstyne, R. Frank Mensel, Julie S. Withers, and F. Stephen Malott, *Women and Minorities in Administration of Higher Education Institutions: Employment Patterns and Salary Comparisons* (Washington, DC: College and University Personnel Association, 1977), 2, 27. The study grouped the schools as white coeducational institutions, white women's colleges, white men's colleges, and minority institutions. At white coeducational institutions, the distribution for 448 affirmative action directors for 1975–76 was 32 percent white women, 17 percent minority women, 33 percent minority men, and 18 percent white men. White women's colleges and white men's colleges had no affirmative action administrators, and minority institutions had only 3.

    Also see Carol Frances and R. Frank Mensel, *Women and Minorities in Administration of Higher Education Institutions: Employment Patterns and Salary Comparisons 1978–79 and An Analysis of Progress Toward Affirmative Action Goals 1975–76 to 1978–79* (Washington, DC: College and University Personnel Association, 1981). This study showed that the profile of women and minorities in higher-education administration had scarcely changed by the 1978–79 academic year. White men held 74.5 percent of the top positions and continued their predominance, upward of 85 percent, in such academic positions as dean, provost, academic vice president, and president.

43 For general discussions of the problem, see Jacquelyn A. Mattfeld, "Many Are Called, But Few Are Chosen," in Furniss and Graham, *Women,* 121–27; and Barbara Krohn, "The Puzzling Case of the Missing Ms.," *Nation's Schools and Colleges* 1.3 (November 1974): 32–38.

    For strategies for increasing the number of women administrators, see J. Barry McGannon, "Tooling Up in the Talent Pool: A Proposal for Regional Administrative Internship Programs for Women," paper presented at the American Council on Education Meeting, October 1972, ERIC document ED–071–188 EA–004–783, 6 October 1972; Patricia Stringer, "Grooming Women for Leadership," *Change* 9.2 (February 1977): 21–24, 26; "Women in Educational Administration," in Chamberlain, *Women in Academe,* 317–31; and Donna Shavlik and Judy Toucher, "Toward a New Era of Leadership: The National Identification Program," in *Women in Higher Education Administra-*

tion, ed. Adrian Tinsley, Cynthia Secor, and Sheila Kaplan (San Francisco: Jossey-Bass, 1984), 47–58.

For case studies of campus advocacy, see Dee L. R. Graham, Patricia O'Reilly, and Edna I. Rawlings, "Costs and Benefits of Advocacy for Faculty Women: A Case Study," *Journal of Social Issues* 41.4 (1985): 85–98 (on the University of Cincinnati); and Gloria DeSole and Meredith Butler, "Building an Effective Model for Institutional Change: Women's Committees as Catalyst," *Initiatives* 53.2 (summer 1990): 1–10 (on State University of New York, Albany).

44 See Cynthia Secor, "Preparing the Individual for Institutional Leadership: The Summer Institute," in Tinsley, Secor, and Kaplan, *Women in Higher Education Administration,* 27; Donna Shavlik and Judy Toucher, "Toward a New Era of Leadership," in Tinsley, Secor, and Kaplan, *Women in Higher Education Administration,* 47–58; and Mariam K. Chamberlain, "Women in Educational Administration," in Chamberlain, *Women in Academe,* 317–31. Before ACENIP was officially launched, Emily Taylor, director of ACE's Office of Women in Higher Education, barnstormed the country. At the University of Cincinnati, she spoke to some thirty women (including myself), selected by the affirmative action director, about identifying potential women administrators on our campus and setting up a regional identification network.

45 The importance of faculty and administrative leadership in the success of affirmative action is stressed in Judith P. Newcombe and Clinton F. Conrad, "A Theory of Mandated Academic Change," *Journal of Higher Education* 52.6 (November–December 1981): 555–77; Patricia B. Hyer, "Affirmative Action for Women Faculty: Case Studies of Three Successful Institutions," *Journal of Higher Education* 56.3 (May–June 1985): 282–99; and Charlotte Hanna, "The Organizational Context for Affirmative Action for Women Faculty," *Journal of Higher Education* 59.4 (July–August 1988): 390–411.

46 For data on unprocessed complaints and other problems, see the Carnegie Council on Policy Studies in Higher Education, *Making Affirmative Action Work in Higher Education,* 162 and elsewhere; and Abramson, *Old Boys,* 58–59. For specific examples of bungled complaints, see Theodore, *Campus Troublemakers,* 105–17.

47 See Mary W. Gray, "The Halls of Ivy and the Halls of Justice: Resisting Sex Discrimination against Faculty Women," *Academe* 71.5 (September–October 1985): 33–41; and Farley, "Women versus Academe," 114.

48 George R. LaNoue and Barbara A. Lee, *Academics in Court: The Consequences of Faculty Discrimination Litigation* (Ann Arbor: University of Michigan Press, 1987), 30.

49 Ibid., 20.

50 Ibid., 20–21. Also see Mary W. Gray, "Legal Perspectives on Sex Equity in Faculty Employment," *Journal of Social Issues* 41.4 (1985): 121–22; and Theodore *Campus Troublemakers,* 125–26. Theodore observes that judges were in awe of the university, reluctant to interfere in its affairs, and loath to substitute their opinions for the faculty's professional judgments.

51 Chamberlain, *Women in Academe,* 182.

52 See Abramson, *Old Boys,* for individual horror stories; Graham et al., "Costs," 85–98; and Gray, "Halls," 33–41. Gray reports that "the costs, exclusive of attorney's fees, of pursuing litigation can amount to several hundred thousand dollars for the plaintiffs in a single class action" (40).

53 LaNoue and Lee, *Academics in Court,* 122–23.

54 *Michigan State University Faculty Association v. Michigan State University,* 32 Federal Rules Service 2d, 1294.

55 Ibid., 1293.

56 *Michigan State University Faculty Association v. Michigan State University,* no. G76–640 CA5, 93 Federal Rules Decisions, 57.

57 *Michigan State University Faculty Association v. Michigan State University* 32 Federal Rules Service 2d, 1294.

58 Ibid., 1297.

59 Thomas Wagner, Affidavit, *Rachelle A. Rosenberg v. University of Cincinnati,* Civil Action No. C–1–77–39 (Rice, J.), 3, 4.

60 Judge Walter H. Rice, "Decision and Entry Setting Limited Evidentiary Hearing on Defendants' Motion to Decertify Class (Doc. no. 71)," *Rachelle A. Rosenberg v. University of Cincinnati,* Case no. C–1–77–039, 29 September 1986, 8, 16; *Rachelle A. Rosenberg v. University of Cincinnati,* 654 Federal Supplement, 775, 778, 780; *Rachelle A. Rosenberg v. University of Cincinnati,* 118 Federal Rules Decisions, 591–96.

61 *Rachelle A. Rosenberg v. University of Cincinnati,* 654 Federal Register, 777, 778.

62 *Rachelle A. Rosenberg v. University of Cincinnati,* 654 Federal Supplement, 778.

63 *Rachelle A. Rosenberg v. University of Cincinnati,* 118 Federal Rules Decisions, 596.

64 *Rachelle A. Rosenberg v. University of Cincinnati,* 654 Federal Supplement, 778.

65 See *Kathryn J. Gutzwiller v. Bernard C. Fenik et al.,* United States Court of Appeals for the Sixth Circuit Full Text Publication, nos. 86–3852, 86–3854, 86–3916.

66 *Rachelle A. Rosenberg v. University of Cincinnati,* 118 Federal Rules Decisions, 592–94. On deference, see Hanna, "Organizational Context," 390–411.

67 See Gray, "Halls," 37; and Gray, "Legal Perspectives," 125–26, 129. Gray notes that many judges do consider documented patterns to be proof of discrimination.

68 Gray, "Halls," 39.

69 Judge Miles W. Lord, "Memorandum Accompanying Order of February 13, 1978," Civil 4–73–435, United States District Court, District of Minnesota, Fourth Division, 7 (also see 8).

70 Attorneys for the Plaintiff, "Memorandum in Support of Motion for Order Determining that Action Is Maintainable as a Class Action," *Rajender v. University of Minnesota,* United States District Court, District of Minnesota, Fourth Division, Civil 4–73–435, 8–9, 11, and exhibit A, 2–3.

71 LaNoue and Lee, *Academics in Court,* 205–6.

72 See "Consent Decree from *Rajender v. The University of Minnesota,*" *Journal of College and University Law* 8.2 (1981–82): 219–53.

73 The comparisons revealed that salary inequities were linked to sex in three ways: the sex of similarly ranked faculty members within a given department, the predomi-

nance of one sex or the other within a department, and the sex segregation across departments. In other words, a female associate professor in American Studies had a lower salary than her male counterpart in political science, even though they both worked on American politics and had comparable records of achievement in research, teaching, and service.

74   See Burton R. Clark, *The Higher Education System: Academic Organization in Cross-National Perspective* (Berkeley: University of California Press, 1983), 118.

75   Warren Bennis, "The Pornography of Everyday Life," *New York Times,* 28 November 1976, 4E, 15.

76   Joyce M. Mitchell and Rachel R. Starr, "A Regional Approach for Analyzing the Recruitment of Academic Women," *American Behavioral Scientist* 15.2 (November–December 1971): 183.

77   Clark Kerr, *The Great Transformation in Higher Education, 1960–1980* (Albany: State University of New York Press, 1991), xiv–xv.

78   While the numbers and proportions of female graduate students and faculty rose from the early 1970s to the early 1990s, the gender gaps in faculty salary, tenure, and employment in part-time faculty positions, at two-year colleges versus universities, and in administrative positions increased during that period. See Betty M. Vetter and Eleanor L. Babco, *Professional Women and Minorities: A Manpower Resource Service* (Washington, DC: Scientific Manpower Committee, 1975).

In physics, a study comparing the periods 1960–69 and 1970–79 shows that the slight rise in female-earned Ph.D.s was owing not to the admission of more women into graduate programs but to the perseverance of women beyond the M.A. level. During the same decade, the percentage of women faculty in physics declined in almost all ranks at all types of institutions. See Vera Kistiakowsky, "Women in Physics and Astronomy," *Annals of the New York Academy of Sciences* 323 (April 20, 1979): 41, 44; and Kistiakowsky, "Women in Physics," 35.

In the modern languages, the percentages of women employed as full-time faculty increased slowly in the ranks of full, associate, and assistant professors throughout the 1980s, but the disturbing news in 1980 was that: (1) the percentages of women at the ranks of instructor and lecturer had increased far more dramatically than those at the higher ranks; (2) the increases occurred disproportionately at two-year institutions; and (3) the increase in female faculty approximated the increase in female-earned doctorates only in the lower ranks and at the institutions already heavily female. See Huber et al., "MLA Surveys," 20–30.

For the effects of fiscal crisis and corporate managerialism, see Randy Martin, "Introduction: Education as National Pedagogy," in *Chalk Lines: The Politics of Work in the Managed University,* ed. Randy Martin (Durham, NC: Duke University Press, 1998), 1–29; Gary Rhoades and Sheila Slaughter, "Academic Capitalism, Managed Professionals, and Supply-Side Higher Education," in Martin, *Chalk Lines,* 33–68; Vincent Tirelli, "Adjuncts and More Adjuncts: Labor Segmentation and the Transformation of Higher Education," in Martin, *Chalk Lines,* 181–201; and Ernst Benjamin, "A Faculty Response to the Fiscal Crisis: From Defense to Offense," in *Higher Education Under*

Fire: Politics, Economics, and the Crisis of the Humanities, ed. Michael Bérubé and Cary Nelson (New York: Routledge, 1995), 52–72.

In other words, the greater diffusion of women in the academy appears to have maintained, not remedied, sex patterning within and across the disciplines and institutions. For this conclusion, see "Twenty Years Later CSWP Is Still Going Strong," American Physical Society News 1.6 (June 1992): 12–13.

79 Anthony Giddens, The Constitution of Society: Outline of the Theory of Structuration (Berkeley: University of California Press, 1984), 171 (first quotation); Anthony Giddens, Social Theory and Modern Sociology (Cambridge, U.K.: Polity, 1987), 220 (second quotation).

80 Michel Foucault, "The Subject and Power," in Michel Foucault: Beyond Structuralism and Hermeneutics, ed. Hubert L. Dreyfus and Paul Rabinow, 2d ed. (Chicago: University of Chicago Press, 1983), 221.

Part 2: Institutionalizing and Intellectualizing Feminist Studies

1 Sheila Tobias, Introduction to Female Studies I, ed. Sheila Tobias (Pittsburgh: KNOW Press, 1970), n.p.[i].

2 Female Studies II, ed. Florence Howe (Pittsburgh: KNOW Press, 1970).

3 Dr. Jo-Ann Gardner and eighteen other members of NOW's Pittsburgh chapter launched KNOW Press under the motto "Freedom of the press belongs to those who own the press." The press was a hybrid media enterprise that functioned as a national clearinghouse for feminist news, a publisher of pamphlets, bibliographies, and a newsletter, and a distributor of short, duplicated papers written by movement and academic feminists. Roberta Salper described Gardner as an "entrepreneurial" activist—an apt characterization of a woman who, in 1969 alone, helped to found KNOW, worked on other NOW projects with Wilma Scott Heide (chairwoman of the NOW board of dirctors), launched the Association for Women in Psychology at the American Psychological Association's annual meeting, and met with producer Joan Cooney about the sex-role stereotyping on Sesame Street, a popular children's television program. This information is from Jo Freeman, The Politics of Women's Liberation (New York: McKay, 1975), 157–58; Polly Joan and Andrea Chesman, Guide to Women's Publishing (Paradise, CA: Dustbooks, 1978), 144–47; Judith Hole and Ellen Levine, Rebirth of Feminism (New York: Quadrangle, 1971), 346, 250–51, 102; and Roberta Salper, telephone interview with author, 18 October 1996.

4 Acknowledgments to Female Studies III, ed. Florence Howe and Carol Ahlum (Pittsburgh: KNOW Press, 1971), i.

5 Florence Howe, "Women and the Power to Change," in Women and the Power to Change, ed. Florence Howe (New York: McGraw-Hill, 1975), 154.

6 Barbara A. White, "Up from the Podium: Feminist Revolution in the Classroom," in Female Studies IV: Teaching about Women, ed. Elaine Showalter and Carol Ohmann (Pittsburgh: KNOW Press, 1971), 28.

7 Jean O'Barr, Feminism in Action (Chapel Hill: University of North Carolina Press, 1994), 95.

8 See, for instance, Florence Howe and Carol Ahlum, "Women's Studies and Social

Change," in *Academic Women on the Move,* ed. Alice S. Rossi and Ann Calderwood (New York: Russell Sage Foundation, 1973), 396–99; Sheila Tobias, "Women's Studies: Its Origin, Organization, and Prospects," in *The Higher Education of Women: Essays in Honor of Rosemary Parks,* ed. Helen S. Astin and Werner Z. Hirsch (New York: Praeger, 1978), 80–82; Florence Howe and Paul Lauter, *The Impact of Women's Studies on the Campus and the Disciplines* (Washington, DC: National Institute of Education, 1980), 21–23, 39–42, 47–55; and Marilyn J. Boxer, "For and About Women: The Theory and Practice of Women's Studies in the United States," *Signs* 7.3 (spring 1982): esp. 661–74.

Chapter 3: Articulating Projects

1   In the early years, this project was variously called female studies, women's studies, and feminist studies. In chapters 3, 4, and 5, I use the terms *female studies* to denote the project during the emerging and envisioning stages, *women's studies* to refer to women's studies programs and courses, and *feminist studies* to indicate the larger enterprise of feminist research and teaching as institutionalized in mainstream disciplinary departments and women's studies programs, in feminist research institutes, in disciplinary and feminist associations, and in the publishing sector.

2   Roberta Salper, "Women's Studies," in *Female Studies V,* ed. Rae Lee Siporin (Pittsburgh: KNOW Press, 1972), 100.

3   Marilyn Salzman-Webb, "Feminist Studies: Frill or Necessity?" in *Female Studies V,* 64–65.

4   Salper, "Women's Studies," 100.

5   Salzman-Webb, "Feminist Studies," 64 (short quotations), 66–67 (long quotation).

6   Salper, "Women's Studies," 105; Salzman-Webb, "Feminist Studies," 66 (see also 64).

7   Devra Lee Davis, "The Woman in the Moon: Prolegomenon for Women's Studies," in *Female Studies V,* 20; Ginny Foster, "Women as Liberators," in *Female Studies VI,* ed. Nancy Hoffman, Cynthia Secor, and Adrian Tinsley (Old Westbury, NY: Feminist Press, 1972), 20–21; Gerda Lerner, "On the Teaching and Organization of Feminist Studies," in *Female Studies V,* 34, 36; Marcia Landy, "Women, Education, and Social Power," in *Female Studies V,* 63, 62.

8   For an explanation of what are called incubation or premobilization structures (e.g., the occasions, organizations, and networks where people can acquire skills and congeal around a new set of interests, see Hank Johnston, Enrique Laraña, and Joseph R. Gusfield, "Identities, Grievances, and New Social Movements," in *New Social Movements: From Ideology to Identity,* ed. Enrique Laraña, Hank Johnston, and Joseph R. Gusfield (Philadelphia: Temple University Press, 1994), 24–25.

   For studies of second-wave feminism that take this approach, see Carol Mueller, "Conflict Networks and the Origins of Women's Liberation," in Laraña et al., *New Social Movements,* 234–63; Leila Rupp and Verta Taylor, *Survival in the Doldrums: The American Women's Rights Movement, 1945 to the 1960s* (New York: Oxford University Press, 1987); and Susan M. Hartmann, *The Other Feminists: Activists in the Liberal Establishment* (New Haven, CT: Yale University Press, 1998). Studies of the civil rights movement that pioneered this approach include Doug McAdam, *Political Process and the Development of Black Insurgency, 1930–1970* (Chicago: University of Chicago Press, 1982); and Aldon Morris, *The Origins of the Civil Rights Movement: Black Communities Organizing for Change* (New York: Free Press, 1984).

I have some reservations about Mueller's use of the phrase "cultural laboratories," which is borrowed from Alberto Melucci, *Nomads of the Present: Social Movements and Individual Needs in Contemporary Society* (Philadelphia: Temple University Press, 1989), to describe the organizations in which second-wave feminism incubated. In the context of sociology and political science, which have been dominated by social-structural analysis (e.g., Marxist, resource-mobilization, and structural strain theories), the new social-movement literature provides a welcome emphasis on the cultural work of constru(ct)ing collective identities, issues, opportunities, and public awareness. But I think we need to distinguish the kinds of skills that women who would become second-wave feminists learned in cultural organizations (e.g., civic clubs, church councils, arts societies, and professional associations) from those learned in organizations that engaged in politics, broadly defined to include a variety of official, direct-action, and catalytic strategies (e.g., political parties, advocacy organizations, legal defense funds, unions, and of course social movement organizations). At the same time, I want to point out that skills and activities formerly associated with particular sectors—business, education, culture, media, and politics—have been meshed by the conservative movement. In chapter 6, I will describe how it deploys the techniques of fundraising, cable television programming, lobbying, activist training, and much more to make change.

9 For publications that trace the affiliations of first-generation movement feminists to civil rights, New Left, and feminist organizations, see Sara Evans, *Personal Politics: The Roots of Women's Liberation in the Civil Rights Movement and the New Left* (New York: Vintage, 1980); Alice Echols, *Daring to Be Bad: Radical Feminism in America, 1967–1975* (Minneapolis: University of Minnesota Press, 1989); *The Feminist Memoir Project: Voices from Women's Liberation,* ed. Rachel Blau DuPlessis and Ann Snitow (New York: Three Rivers Press, 1998); and Ruth Rosen, *The World Split Open: How the Modern Women's Movement Changed America* (New York: Putnam, 2000), which contains the most detailed information on first-generation affiliations. But to reconstruct the overlapping networks in which first-generation *academic feminists* linked up, one would have to compare the rosters of academic organizations, conferences, and publications to data on participants in the civil rights, liberal, New Left, and educational reform movements.

10 For accounts of the organized networking, planning, and coordination at Montgomery and elsewhere, see Juan Williams, *Eyes on the Prize: America's Civil Rights Years, 1954–1965* (New York: Penguin, 1987), 59–89; Lewis M. Killian, "Organization, Rationality, and Spontaneity in the Civil Rights Movement," in *Collective Behavior and Social Movements,* ed. Russell L. Curtis Jr. and Benigno E. Aguirre (Boston: Allyn and Bacon, 1993), 209–25; and Aldon Morris, "Black Southern Sit-In Movement: An Analysis of Internal Organization," in Curtis and Aguirre, *Collective Behavior,* 361–80.

11 For documents written by participants in the civil rights and New Left movements,

see Paul Jacobs and Saul Landau, *The New Radicals: A Report with Documents* (New York: Vintage, 1966); *The New Left: A Documentary History,* ed. Massimo Teodori (Indianapolis: Bobbs-Merrill, 1969); *The New Left: A Collection of Essays,* ed. Priscilla Long (Boston: Porter Sargent, 1969); *The Student Voice, 1960–1965: Periodical of the Student Nonviolent Coordinating Committee,* ed. Clayborne Carson (Westport, CT: Meckler, 1990); and *"Takin' It to the Streets": A Sixties Reader,* ed. Alexander Bloom and Wini Breines (New York: Oxford University Press, 1995).

For useful histories that also discuss the movements' social and educational critiques and change projects, see Doug McAdam, *Freedom Summer* (New York: Oxford University Press, 1988); Max Heirich, *The Spiral of Conflict: Berkeley 1964* (New York: Columbia University Press, 1971); and James Miller, *Democracy Is in the Streets: From Port Huron to the Siege of Chicago* (New York: Simon and Schuster, 1987), which reprints SDS's "Port Huron Statement."

12   These points are made in Wini Breines, *Community and Organization in the New Left, 1962–1968,* new ed. (New Brunswick, NJ: Rutgers University Press, 1989). But the problems can also be seen in Miller's *Democracy* and Todd Gitlin's *The Sixties: Years of Hope, Days of Rage* (New York: Bantam, 1987).

13   Others belonging to NUC were Frank Battaglia, Ellen Cantarow, Kate Ellis, John McDermott, Ruth Mischeloff, Elaine Reuben, Lillian Robinson, and Martha Vicinus from the modern languages, sociologists Pauline Bart and Jo Freeman, and radical feminist Shulamith Firestone.

My sources emphasized that MLA activists had multiple and overlapping memberships in NUC, SDS, Resist, and other antiwar groups, women's liberation groups, and MLA committees and caucuses. Howe, Salper, Ohmann, and Reuben served on the MLA Commission on the Status of Women; Kampf and Howe were elected MLA second vice president, a position that automatically turned over to first vice president and president; and Salper was elected to the MLA Executive Council. But almost all of NUC's modern language members took active roles in the discipline: they were leaders of the Radical Caucus, the Women's Caucus, and the Gay and Lesbian Caucus; members of the executive committees for the new scholarly divisions; and editors of *Radical Teacher, College English, Female Studies,* and the *Women's Review of Books,* to name a few.

Over the years, sociologists have produced a large literature describing their activism in the NUC and other left organizations, at the American Sociological Association, and on their home campuses. By blending facts and analyses with personal reflections, their writings vividly convey both the structure and texture of social change at that time. To my surprise, I found that the literature written by activists in the modern languages was so skimpy that I had to speak with some of them to obtain basic information about their participation in NUC and MLA activism. My information comes from telephone interviews with Paul Lauter, 11 August 1996; Florence Howe, 14 August 1996; Joan E. Hartman, 29 August 1996 and e-mail answers to my e-mail queries, August 1996; Tucker Farley, 25 September 1996 and notes written on a copy of the telephone interview transcript, February 1997; Roberta Salper, 18 October 1996 and 17 January 1997; and Marilyn Salzman-Webb, 18 October 1996 and 7 December 1996. Pamella Tucker Farley, as she was known in the 1960s, later chose to go by the name of Tucker Farley, a preference I observe in this book.

14 Fred L. Pincus and Howard J. Erlich, "The New University Conference: A Study of Former Members," *Critical Sociology* 15.2 (summer 1988): 145 (Ross); Salper, telephone interview with author, 18 October 1996.

15 Robert J. S. Ross, "At the Center and the Edge: Notes on a Life in and out of Sociology and the New Left," *Critical Sociology* 15.2 (summer 1988): 79–84; Robert J. S. Ross, "Primary Groups in Social Movements: A Memoir and Interpretation," in *Toward a History of the New Left: Essays from within the Movement,* ed. R. David Myers (Brooklyn: Carlson, 1989), 158. For SDS's Economic Research and Action Projects (ERAP) and Jobs or Income Now (JOIN), see Breines, *Community.*

16 Pincus and Erlich, "New University Conference," 146.

17 *NUC Papers* 3 (fall 1970): front matter.

18 See "The Open Up the Schools Program: OUTS Political Perspective II," *NUC Papers* 3 (fall 1970): 7 (quotation); "The Open Up the Schools Program: OUTS Political Perspective I," *NUC Papers* 3 (fall 1970): 1; and the fourteen papers printed in "The Open Up the Schools Program," ed. Beth Lehman, *NUC Papers* 3 (1971). To avoid confusion, I want to point out that these articles appeared in two different publications bearing the same title. The first two articles appeared in the fall 1970 issue of a newsletter titled *NUC Papers;* the third one appeared in a 1971 booklet of fifty-five pages also titled *NUC Papers* and edited by Beth Lehman.

19 Pincus and Erlich, "New University Conference," 145.

20 Ross, "At the Center," 86; Paul Lauter, telephone interview with author, 11 August 1996.

21 Dick Flacks, "The Sociology Liberation Movement: Some Lessons and Legacies," in *Radical Sociologists and the Movement: Experiences, Lessons, and Legacies,* ed. Martin Oppenheimer, Martin J. Murray, and Rhonda F. Levine (Philadelphia: Temple University Press, 1991), 24; Pincus and Erlich, "New University Conference," 146.

22 By disintegration, I mean the factionalization within and collapse of particular organizations; their members went on to seed new organizations and movements, taking with them critiques and strategies. This point is elaborated in Carl Boggs, "Rethinking the Sixties Legacy: From New Left to New Social Movements," in *Social Movements: Critiques, Concepts, Case-Studies,* ed. Stanford M. Lyman (New York: New York University Press, 1995), 331–55.

23 Tucker Farley, telephone interview with author, 25 September 1996; Marilyn Salzman-Webb, telephone interview with author, 7 December 1996; Martin Oppenheimer, Martin J. Murray, and Rhonda F. Levine, "Introduction: The Movement and the Academy," in Oppenheimer et al., *Radical Sociologists,* 10 (quotation on the Women's Caucus).

24 Roberta Salper and Barbara Kessel, "Case Study: Women's Studies," *NUC Papers* 3 (fall 1970): 40; Roberta Salper, "Women's Studies: Theory and Practice," *NUC Women's*

Caucus Newsletter, 7 April 1971, quoted in "Introduction: Teaching About Women, 1971," in *Female Studies IV,* 1.

25 Information in this paragraph, unless otherwise cited, is from Salper, telephone interview with author, 18 October 1996; and Salper, follow-up telephone conversation, 17 January 1997. For accounts of Chicago feminism, its origins in SDS and NUC, and the women who launched it, see Roberta Salper, "The Development of the American Women's Liberation Movement, 1967–1971," in *Female Liberation: History and Current Politics,* ed. Roberta Salper (New York: Knopf, 1972), 169–70, 174–75; Judith Hole and Ellen Levine, *Rebirth of Feminism* (New York: Quadrangle, 1971), 112–15; and Sara Evans, *Personal Politics,* 193–211.

26 Through the Student Woodlawn Area Project, Salzman-Webb launched a school based on the Mississippi Freedom Summer schools to teach children and train their mothers to teach there. The project, she said, was a good fit with SDS's JOIN projects in Chicago and other cities. With pilot money from the U.S. Office of Educational Opportunity, the school she launched became a model for the Head Start programs and the small-school concept now used in public school systems.

27 For accounts of the conferences, see Echols, *Daring to Be Bad,* 104–14. My information comes from Salzman-Webb, telephone interview with author, 7 December 1996; and Salzman-Webb, notes to the author on a draft chapter, February 1997.

28 For two accounts of the Counter-Inaugural, see Gitlin, *The Sixties,* 362–64; and Echols, *Daring to Be Bad,* 114–20. Salzman-Webb said that Gitlin's account was inaccurate, particularly his claim that after the Counter-Inaugural she received a threatening phone call from Kathie Wilkerson, an SDS member later turned Weatherman. Salzman-Webb told me that Wilkerson, a good friend, told her the phone call had been made by a government infiltrator mimicking her (Salzman-Webb, telephone interview with author, 7 December 1996). Echols (*Daring to be Bad,* 205) mentions Salzman-Webb's expulsion from the coordinating committee, but Salzman-Webb told me she couldn't remember whether the committee did or did not expel her. She did recall that several committee members were horrified by the attack and, with herself, went off to start *Off Our Backs,* a feminist periodical.

29 Marilyn Salzman-Webb, "Feminist Studies Program, Goddard College," in *Female Studies III,* ed. Florence Howe and Carol Ahlum (Pittsburgh: KNOW Press, 1971), 157.

30 Jack L. Roach, "The Radical Sociology Movement: A Short History and Commentary," *The American Sociologist* 5.3 (August 1970): 226 (quotation 226).

31 Information from Flacks, "Sociology Liberation Movement," 18–19 (quotation 18); Roach, "Radical Sociology Movement," 227–28; "Minutes of the First 1968 ASA Business Meeting, Wednesday, August 28, 1968," *The American Sociologist* 3.4 (November 1968): 321–23; "Minutes of the Second 1968 ASA Business Meeting, Thursday, August 29, 1968," *The American Sociologist,* 3.4 (November 1968): 324–25; and "Minutes of the Second 1969 Council Meeting, Friday, August 30, 1968," *The American Sociologist* 3.4 (November 1968): 325.

32 Information from Roach, "Radical Sociology Movement," 229–31; Oppenheimer et al., "Introduction," 7–10; Carol A. Brown, "The Early Years of the Sociology Libera-

tion Movement," in Oppenheimer et al., *Radical Sociologists*, 43–53; Flacks, "Sociology Liberation Movement," 17–27; and Ross, "At the Center," 203.

33 Brown, "Early Years," 47; Roach, "Radical Sociology Movement," 224 (quotation).

34 Kay Klotzburger, "Political Action by Academic Women," in *Academic Women on the Move*, ed. Alice Rossi and Ann Calderwood (New York: Russell Sage Foundation, 1973), 380.

35 Since Dr. Rossi declined to be interviewed for this book, I have taken my information from published sources, including Alice Rossi, "Women—Terms of Liberation," *Dissent* 17 (November–December 1970): 531–41. On Berkeley feminism and activism, see Arlie Russell Hochschild, "Inside the Clockwork of Male Careers," in *Gender and the Academic Experience: Berkeley Women Sociologists*, ed. Kathryn P. Meadow Orlans and Ruth A. Wallace (Lincoln: University of Nebraska Press, 1994), 135–38 (an account of the first meeting of the Women's Caucus); Ruth Dixon-Mueller, "Accidental Tourist," in Orlans and Wallace, *Gender*, 207–8; Lillian B. Rubin, "An Unanticipated Life," in Orlans and Wallace, *Gender*, 239, 241; and Jane E. Prather, "Acquiring an Academic Room of One's Own," in *Individual Voices, Collective Visions: Fifty Years of Women in Sociology*, ed. Ann Goetting and Sarah Fenstermaker (Philadelphia: Temple University Press, 1995), 76–79.

36 See Alice Rossi, "Status of Women in Graduate Departments of Sociology, 1968–1969," *The American Sociologist* 5.1 (September 1970): 1–12 (quotation 1); and Klotzburger, "Political Action," 380–84.

37 Klotzburger, "Political Action," 381 (quotation); Rossi, "Status," 12 (quotation); Pamela Roby, "Women and the ASA: Degendering Organizational Structures and Processes, 1964–1974," *The American Sociologist* 25.1 (spring 1992): 23–25.

38 Datha Clapper Brack, "Writing Papers and Stirring Soup: Career and Family in the Baby Boom Years," in Goetting and Fenstermaker, *Individual Voices*, 29. Rossi lists the panelists as Ann Leffler and Lucy Sells (graduate students), Barbara Laslett and Arlie Hochschild (faculty on first appointments), and Marlene Dixon and herself (faculty in later stages of their careers) (see Rossi, "Status," 12). Jane E. Prather, then a sociology graduate student at Berkeley, mentions serving on a panel of graduate students at a 1969 Women's Caucus event and angrily speaking about the problems of women in the discipline (see Prather, "Acquiring an Academic Room," 79).

39 Arlene Kaplan Daniels, "When We Were All Boys Together: Graduate School in the Fifties and Beyond," in Orlans and Wallace, *Gender*, 36–37.

40 Information from Klotzburger, "Political Action," 381 (quotation and account of ballroom discussion); "Women's Caucus Statement and Resolutions to the General Business Meeting of the American Sociological Association, September 3, 1969," rpt. in Oppenheimer et al., *Radical Sociologists*, 256; "Minutes of the First Business Meeting . . . Wednesday, September 3, 1969," *The American Sociologist* 5.1 (February 1970): 62–65; and "Minutes of the 1970 Council Meeting, Wednesday, September 3, 1969," *The American Sociologist* 5.1 (February 1970): 59–60.

41 The fourth resolution, asking ASA to declare its support for the Equal Rights Amendment, was defeated. Information from Klotzburger, "Political Action," 382; "Minutes

of the First Business Meeting, Tuesday, September 1, 1970," *The American Sociologist* 6.1 (February 1971): 65–66 (Committee on Women); and "Minutes of the Second Business Meeting, Wednesday, September 2, 1970," *The American Sociologist* 6.1 (February 1971): 70–71 (Sociology of Sex Roles Division, child care, Equal Rights Amendment).

42   *The Status of Women in Sociology 1968–1972: Report to the American Sociological Association of the Ad Hoc Committee on the Status of Women in the Profession* (Washington, DC: American Sociological Association, 1973). Also see Roby, "Women and the ASA," 39.

43   Roby, "Women and the ASA," 27–28, 32–33, 37–39.

44   Published sources on the 1968 MLA activism described here and below include: Louis Kampf and Paul Lauter, Introduction to *The Politics of Literature: Dissenting Essays on the Teaching of English*, ed. Louis Kampf and Paul Lauter (New York: Pantheon, 1970), 34–40; Richard Ohmann, *English in America: A Radical View of the Profession* (New York: Oxford University Press, 1976), 27–50; Vincent B. Leitch, *American Literary Criticism from the 30s to the 80s* (New York: Columbia University Press, 1988), 371–73; "Statement by Henry Nash Smith, 1969 MLA President," *PMLA* 84.2 (March 1969): 344; "Statement by John Hurt Fisher, MLA Executive Secretary," *PMLA* 84.2 (March 1969): 345–46; and "Statement by Louis Kampf, 1969 MLA Second Vice President," *PMLA* 84.2 (March 1969): 347–48.

My interview sources supplied many of the factual and atmospheric details: Paul Lauter, telephone interview with author, 11 August 1996; Florence Howe, telephone interview with author, 14 August 1996; Joan E. Hartman, telephone interview with author, 29 August 1996; Joan E. Hartman, answers to e-mail queries, August 1996; Tucker Farley, telephone interview with author, 25 September 1996; Tucker Farley, notes to the author on transcript of telephone interview, February 1997; and Roberta Salper, telephone interview with author, 18 October 1996.

45   Information on MLA members attending the NUC meeting from Tucker Farley, telephone interview with author, 25 September 1996; information on Resist and planning the MLA action (here and below) from Paul Lauter, telephone interview with author, 11 August 1996.

46   Kampf and Lauter, "Introduction," 34 (quotations).

47   Paul Lauter, telephone interview with author, 11 August 1996; Tucker Farley, telephone interview with author, 25 September 1996.

48   Joan E. Hartman, telephone interview with author, 29 August 1996; Tucker Farley, telephone interview with author, 25 September 1996. For the resolutions and procedural votes, see "Actions of the 1968 Business Meeting, 29 December 1968," *PMLA* 84.5 (September 1969): 1231–33.

49   "Report of the Executive Secretary," *PMLA* 85.3 (May 1970): 535–36; "Summary of Correspondence to the New Study Commission," *PMLA* 85.3 (May 1970): 550, 552, 554, 556; "Informal Comments on Proposed Constitutional Amendments, December 1970," *PMLA* 85.6 (November 1970): 1247–50.

50   For the CSW's origins and other details, see Virginia Barber, "The Women's Revolt in the MLA," in *Women on Campus: The Unfinished Liberation* (New Rochelle, NY: Change, 1975), 85–94; Florence Howe, "What Was It Like Then?" in *Courage and Tools:*

The Florence Howe Award for Feminist Scholarship, 1974–1989, ed. Joanne Glasgow and Angela Ingram (New York: Modern Language Association, 1990), ix–xii; Klotzburger, "Political Action," 359–91; and Ellen DuBois et al., Feminist Scholarship, 3.

51 Howe, "What Was It Like Then?" x (first, second, and third quotations); and Barber, "Women's Revolt," 86 (fourth and fifth quotations). Additional descriptions of the CSW event are from Florence Howe, telephone interview with author, 14 August 1996; Roberta Salper, telephone interview with author, 18 October 1996; and Joan E. Hartman, answers to e-mail queries, August 1996.

The birth of the WCML was no accident. Howe told me that she thought the CSW could not be effective without a caucus to pressure it and the MLA. Salper, who served on the CSW from 1969 to 1971, added that Howe had discussed the idea of organizing a women's caucus with Lauter and Kampf, CSW members, and Verna Wittrock and planned the CSW's December event to precipitate its formation. This tactic, Salper remarked, was used "all the time in civil rights and antiwar organizing." What exactly was the tactic? The best example comes from the Berkeley Free Speech Movement. Campus activists repeatedly invited the administration's insults, crack-downs, and rebuffs, which they then used to recruit supporters and escalate the conflict (see Heirich, The Spiral of Conflict. This tactic was also deployed, as we have seen, by activists at the 1968 conventions of the ASA and MLA.

52 The one discrepancy among my sources concerns who orchestrated the petition to nominate Howe for the second vice presidency; Lauter credits the Radical Caucus, Howe credits Carol Ohmann and the WCML, and Barber credits the CSW and WCML.

53 Information from author's recollections and Joan E. Hartman, telephone interview with author, 29 August 1996.

54 See Margaret Strobel, "Consciousness and Action: Historical Agency in the Chicago Women's Liberation Union," in Provoking Agents: Gender and Agency in Theory and Practice, ed. Judith Kegan Gardiner (Urbana: University of Illinois Press, 1995), 52–68.

55 Florence Howe, telephone interview with author, 14 August 1996; Roberta Salper, telephone interview with author, 18 October 1996.

56 Brown, "Early Years," 49–51 (quotations 49).

57 Florence Howe, telephone interview with author, 14 August 1996.

58 Tucker Farley, telephone interview with author, 25 September 1996; Roby, "Women and the ASA," 37.

59 Joan E. Hartman, telephone interview with author, 29 August 1996.

60 Kampf and Lauter, "Introduction," 37–38 (quotation above, 38).

61 Tucker Farley, telephone interview with author, 25 September 1996.

62 Roby, "Women and the ASA," 37.

63 Tucker Farley, telephone interview with author, 25 September 1996. In notes to the author (February 1997), Farley observed, "we learned the trade union lesson for democratic participation in the meeting" and wrote at length about feminist activism in the New York area during the 1970s: the first women's studies course she taught, the Women's Labor Project, and drives for childcare and healthcare. Farley's, Salper's, and Salzman-Webb's responses to a draft of this chapter persuaded me that we will not

have a richly textured and complexly woven tapestry of those early days until the participants write their own narratives.

64 For a sampling of letters to Louis Kampf and the MLA, see Ohmann, *English in America,* 35–37, 39, 47 (this letter).

65 See, for instance, Stephen H. Balch and Herbert I. London, "The Tenured Left," *Commentary* 82.4 (October 1986): 41–51; John P. Roche, "The New Left Vigilantes," *National Review,* 8 December 1989, 34–35; and "The Academic Left Strikes Back," *New Criterion* 10.3 (November 1991): 1–2 (quotation 1).

66 Published sources for information on the San Diego project include: Roberta Salper and Barbara Kessel, "Case Study," 40–41; Nancy Hollander, "Women's Studies Program, San Diego State College," in *Female Studies III,* 174–75; Roberta Salper, "Women's Studies," in *Female Studies V;* and Roberta Salper, "Women's Studies," *Ramparts* 10.6 (December 1971): 56–60 (this article is a version of the *Female Studies V* essay). For other details, I am indebted to Catherine Orr's dissertation, "Representing Women / Disciplining Feminism: Activism, Professionalism, and Women's Studies," University of Minnesota, June 1998 (chapter 2 is a case study of the San Diego program); and Roberta Salper, telephone interview with author, 18 October 1996.

67 Salper, "Women's Studies," 101; Orr, "Representing Women," 55–58.

68 Information on the proposal, Rossi letter, and recruitment from Orr, "Representing Women," 57–59; information on recruitment also from Roberta Salper, telephone interview with author, 18 October 1996.

69 Program statistics for 1971–72 are from Helen S. Astin and Allison Parelman, "Women's Studies in American Colleges and Universities," *International Social Science Journal* 25.3 (1973): 398.

70 Salper, "Women's Studies," 101–3.

71 Ibid., 102 (first quotation), 104 (second and third quotations).

72 Examples of these accusations appear in Orr, "Representing Women," 62–63, 67–68.

73 Ibid., 86. In "Case Study" their article on women's studies at San Diego, Roberta Salper and Barbara Kessel wrote: "Who are 'the people' and how can their needs be defined? For a Women's Studies Program within a university, the 'people' are obviously those women enrolled in the classes of a program openly designed to redress some of the injustices society has fostered [*sic*] on them" (40). Although the referent of "the women" could vary, the exclusions from it seldom did because feminist discourse reiterated the elite / bourgeois / proletariat division standard in Left theory. "The women" who were agents and beneficiaries in this discourse (like "the people" in NUC discourse) seldom included women working in university administration, business management, or social services, serving as volunteers in civic and political organizations, or engaged full time in homemaking—virtually all of whom were exploited or oppressed in those days.

74 Rowell Council and Nower's opinion is summarized in Orr, "Representing Women," 70. Other information and quotations are from Roberta Salper, telephone interview with author, 18 October 1996; and Marilyn Salzman-Webb, telephone interview with

author, 7 December 1996. For COINTELPRO's targets and strategies, see Bloom and Breines's brief description in *Takin' It to the Streets*, 363–72.

75 Information on the conference from Rae Lee Siporin, "Women and Education: The Conference as Catalyst," in *Female Studies V*, iii–xiv (quotation iii).

76 Ibid., x.

77 Elaine Showalter, "Introduction: Teaching About Women, 1971," in *Female Studies IV*, i (first quotation), vii (other quotations).

78 Program and course data from Deborah Silverton Rosenfelt, "Introduction," in *Female Studies VII: Going Strong, New Courses / New Programs*, ed. Deborah Silverton Rosenfelt (Old Westbury, NY: Feminist Press, 1973), iii, ix.

79 Ann Leffler, Dair L. Gillespie, and Elinor Lerner Ratner, "Academic Feminists and the Women's Movement," *Ain't I A Woman* 4.1 (April 1973): 1 (opening quotation), 21 (closing quotation).

80 Marilyn J. Boxer, "For and About Women: The Theory and Practice of Women's Studies in the United States," *Signs* 7.3 (spring 1982): 668–69.

81 See *Report on the West Coast Women's Studies Conference*, comp. Editorial Staff of the Women's Studies Board (Sacramento: Sacramento State University Women's Studies Board, 1974), esp. 49–77 (the speak-out) and 78–143 (statements and articles written afterward). I am grateful to Amy Kesselman for lending me her copy of the *Report*.

Curious about the timing of the *Ain't I A Woman* article and the Sacramento conference, I asked Deborah Rosenfelt (who attended and wrote about the conference) if she knew whether Gillespie, Leffler, and Ratner were there. She was "fairly certain" but not "100% positive" that Gillespie was at Sacramento as part of the Socialist Workers Party contingent (Rosenfelt, answer to e-mail query, 19 May 1999). Since the *Report* makes it clear that some two hundred women, not a handful, roiled the conference and since this same scenario occurred at many other events, I have to conclude that the discourse was widely diffused.

82 Ann Forfreedom, "Whither Women's Studies?" *Report on the West Coast Women's Studies Conference*, 113; Kathleen Barry, "The Fear of Feminism or What Makes Women's Liberation Laugh," in ibid., 115; Loraine Hutchins, "Letter to the Editor about Feminist Priorities," in ibid., 135.

83 Roberta Salper, telephone interview with author, 18 October 1996. Salper told me that at San Diego State she wanted to concentrate on teaching her classes, writing a book, and developing the academic program. But Orr ("Representing Women"), drawing on documents from that time, portrays Salper as actively siding with the anti-Center students in their opposition to Rowell Council and other original Ad Hoc Committee members.

84 On collective-identity formation, see Alberto Melucci, "The Process of Collective Identity," in *Social Movements and Culture*, ed. Hank Johnston and Bert Klandermans (Minneapolis: University of Minnesota Press, 1995), 41–63 (quotation 44).

85 Information in these paragraphs from Marilyn Salzman-Webb, telephone interview with author, 7 December 1996; and Marilyn Salzman-Webb, "Feminist Studies Program, Goddard College," in *Female Studies III*, 157–58.

86 Linda Gordon, "Radical Feminist Studies Program, Cambridge-Goddard Graduate School for Social Change, Cambridge, Massachusetts," in *Female Studies III*, 147–48 (quotation 147).

87 Linda Gordon, "Towards a Feminist History," in *Female Studies V*, 52.

88 *Women's Work and Women's Studies 1972*, ed. Dicki Lou Ellis, Kathleen Graves, Kirsten Grimstad, Dorothy Marks, Fannette Pollack, Jan Thompson, and Mary Elizabeth Wexford (Pittsburgh: KNOW Press, 1973), [iv]. Also see *Women's Work and Women's Studies, 1971*, ed. Kirsten Drake, Dorothy Marks, and Mary Wexford (Pittsburgh: KNOW Press, 1972).

89 See bell hooks, with Tanya McKinnon, "Sisterhood: Beyond Public and Private," *Signs* 21.4 (summer 1996): 814–29 (quotation 817); and Heidi Hartman, Ellen Bravo, Charlotte Bunch, Nancy Hartsock, Roberta Spalter-Roth, Linda Williams, and Maria Blanco, "Bringing Together Feminist Theory and Practice: A Collective Interview," *Signs* 21.4 (summer 1996): 917–51 (quotation 923).

Chapter 4: Formatting Feminist Studies

1 In this chapter and the next one, I draw on two literatures, one dubbed "the new institutionalism" and the other "the new knowledge studies," that provide important insights into the forms of new academic ventures and the processes of institutionalizing them.

The first literature shows, among other things, that institutionalization occurs at three distinctive but interpenetrating levels: the activities within an organization, the transactions among organizations, and the structuring of the organizational field. For an example of this analysis, see Paul J. DiMaggio, "Constructing an Organizational Field as a Professional Project: U.S. Art Museums, 1920–1940," in *The New Institutionalism in Organizational Analysis*, ed. Walter W. Powell and Paul J. DiMaggio (Chicago: University of Chicago Press, 1991), 267–92. In the case of feminist studies, we would ask different questions about the levels: how did a university's structure shape the project that was institutionalized on that campus, how were the resources of disciplinary associations used to leverage the institutionalization of feminist studies in universities, and how was the formation of feminist studies as a nationwide field conditioned by trends affecting the higher-education system and the publishing industry?

The second literature deals more specifically with the formation of disciplinary and interdisciplinary ventures. The work on new disciplines shows us that the founders, especially when they have reputations in already established disciplines, can attract the homes and resources they need by devising an intellectual agenda that appeals to institutions, but from that very first moment of agenda setting the institutions have acted and will continue to act on the new discipline's knowledge-producing objectives and practices. For an example of this analysis with case studies, see Timothy Lenoir, "The Discipline of Nature and the Nature of Disciplines," in *Knowledges: Historical and Critical Studies in Disciplinarity*, ed. Ellen Messer-Davidow, David R. Shumway, and David J. Sylvan (Charlottesville: University Press of Virginia, 1993), 70–103.

Finally, for the diverse institutional forms and institutionalizing strategies of inter-disciplinary ventures, see Julie Thompson Klein, *Interdisciplinarity: History, Theory, and Practice* (Detroit: Wayne State University Press, 1990); "Across the Boundaries," *Social Epistemology* 4.3 (July–September 1990), 267–80; and *Crossing Boundaries: Knowledge, Disciplinarities, and Interdisciplinarities* (Charlottesville: University Press of Virginia, 1996).

2   Judith A. Cook and Mary Margaret Fonow, "Am I My Sister's Gatekeeper? Cautionary Tales from the Academic Hierarchy," in *A Feminist Ethic for Social Science Research,* ed. Nebraska Sociological Feminist Collective (Lewiston, NY: Mellen, 1988), 209 (quotation). Also see Suzanna Rose, "Women Biologists and the 'Old Boy' Network," *Women's Studies International Forum* 12.3 (1989): 349–54.

3   For instance, feminists edited a special issue of *Radical America* (4.2 [February 1970]) containing essays by Marlene Dixon, Gail Paradise Kelly, Mari Jo Buhle, and others; and "Women Unite," a special issue of *Leviathan* (2.2 [May 1970]). For an account of the 1970 feminist takeover of *Rat*, a prominent New Left underground newspaper, see Robin Morgan, *Going Too Far: The Personal Chronicle of a Feminist* (New York: Vintage, 1978), 115–30. For the types of venues that published feminist articles through 1970, I consulted Lucinda Cisler, *Women: A Bibliography* (New York: Lucinda Cisler, 1970); and Lucinda Cisler, "A Selected Bibliography on Women," in Judith Hole and Ellen Levine, *Rebirth of Feminism* (New York: Quadrangle, 1971), 451–71.

4   The first decade of feminist presses and periodicals is described in Carol Erlich, "The Woman Book Industry," in *Changing Women in a Changing Society,* ed. Joan Huber (Chicago: University of Chicago Press, 1973), 268–82; Jean Collins, "The Feminist Press," in *Women on Campus: The Unfinished Liberation* (New Rochelle, NY: Change, 1975), 102–9; and *Women in Print II: Opportunities for Women's Studies Publication in Language and Literature,* ed. Joan E. Hartman and Ellen Messer-Davidow (New York: Modern Language Association, 1982), which contains essays about feminist presses and journals as well as mainstream and alternative venues receptive to feminist work.

5   Martha M. Kinney, "Boards and Paper: Feminist Writing and Trade Publishing," in *Women in Print II,* 45.

6   Besides *Sisterhood Is Powerful: An Anthology of Writing from the Women's Liberation Movement,* ed. Robin Morgan (New York: Random House, 1970); and *Woman in a Sexist Society: Studies in Power and Powerlessness,* ed. Vivian Gornick and Barbara K. Moran (New York: Basic Books, 1971), see *The Black Woman: An Anthology,* ed. Toni Cade (New York: Mentor, 1970); *Voices of the New Feminism,* ed. Mary Lou Thompson (Boston: Beacon, 1970); *Voices from Women's Liberation,* ed. Leslie B. Tanner (New York: Mentor, 1970); *Women's Liberation: Blueprint for the Future,* ed. Sookie Stambler (New York: Ace, 1970); *Female Liberation: History and Current Politics,* ed. Roberta Salper (New York: Knopf, 1971); *From Feminism to Liberation,* ed. Edith Hoshino Altbach (Cambridge, MA, and London: Schenkman, 1971); *Liberation Now! Writings from the Women's Liberation Movement,* ed. Deborah Babcox and Madeline Belkin (New York: Dell, 1971); *Up Against the Wall, Mother: On Women's Liberation,* ed. Elsie Adams

and Mary Louise Briscoe (Beverly Hills, CA: Glencoe, 1971); *Radical Feminism,* ed. Anne Koedt, Ellen Levine, and Anita Rapone (New York: Quadrangle, 1973); and *Amazon Expedition: A Lesbian Anthology,* ed. Phyllis Birkby et al. (Washington, NJ: Times Change Press, 1973).

7   Vivian Gornick and Barbara K. Moran, Introduction to Gornick and Moran, *Woman,* xix (both quotations). Among the landmark essays appearing in this anthology were Elaine Showalter's "Women Writers and the Double Critical Standard," Linda Nochlin's "Why Are There No Great Women Artists?" and Naomi Weisstein's "Psychology Constructs the Female." Other contributors who were or soon became leading feminist scholars include Pauline Bart and Jessie Bernard in sociology, Phyllis Chesler and Nancy Chodorow in psychoanalytic theory, Ruby Leavitt in anthropology, and Wendy Martin and Catharine Stimpson in literary studies.

8   Two unattributed reviewer quotations in Gornick and Moran, *Woman,* unnumbered pages preceding title page; Glendy Culligan, "Born Free But Not Liberated," *Saturday Review,* 5 June 1971, 25–28; Margaret Lichtenberg, "Power and Powerlessness," *The Nation,* 8 November 1971, 475.

9   Kate Millett, *Sexual Politics* (Garden City, NY: Doubleday, 1970), 23.

10 Jonathan Yardley, "Women's Lib Gets Rough," *The New Republic,* 1 August 1970, 30; Robert A. Gross, "How Men Use Women," *Newsweek,* 27 July 1970, 72; "Who's Come a Long Way, Baby?" *Time,* 31 August 1970, 16 and cover illustration.

11 "Who's Come a Long Way, Baby?" 16; "Review of *Sexual Politics,*" *Antioch Review* 30.2 (September 1970): 263. For other negative comments on the discursive mix, see Gross, "How Men Use Women," 74; Yardley, "Women's Lib," 26, 30–32; and R. Z. S., "Up Against the Men's Room Wall," *Time,* 3 August 1970, 70–71. For positive comments, see Barbara Hardy, "De Beauvoir, Lessing—now Kate Millett," *New York Times Book Review,* 6 September 1970, 8, 10, 12; and for ambiguous ones, see Nancy R. McWilliams, "An intelligent women's guide to feminism," *Commonweal,* 1 October 1970, 25–26.

12 Yardley, "Women's Lib," 30 (first quotation), 32 (second quotation); "Who's Come a Long Way, Baby?" 20.

13 Norman Mailer, "The Prisoner of Sex," *Harper's,* March 1971, 60 ("honor student" quotation), 62 (other quotations).

14 "About This Issue," *Harper's,* March 1971, 4.

15 "Who's Come a Long Way, Baby?" 16.

16 For instance, commercial presses published Joyce Ladner's *Tomorrow's Tomorrow* (Doubleday, 1971), Gerda Lerner's *Black Women in White America* (Pantheon, 1972), and Jill Johnston's *Lesbian Nation* (Simon and Schuster, 1973). But *Notes from the First Year* (1968), *Notes from the Second Year* (1970), and *Notes from the Third Year* (1971) were self-published by a New York Women's Liberation group; Jeannette Foster's out-of-print *Sex Variant Women in Literature* (Daughters of Bilitis, 1967) was republished by Diana Press (1975); and Del Martin and Phyllis Lyon's *Lesbian/Woman* was published by Glide Press (1972) before it was picked up by Bantam (1973).

17 See *Women's Studies* 2.2 (1974).

18 The statement of purpose appeared in the front matter of each issue of *Women's Studies.*

19 Wendy Martin, "Teaching Women's Studies—Some Problems and Discoveries," in *Female Studies IV: Teaching About Women,* ed. Elaine Showalter and Carol Ohmann (Pittsburgh: KNOW Press, 1971), 9–10 (all quotations).

20 Wendy Martin and Mary Louise Briscoe, "Women's Studies: Problems in Research," *Women's Studies* 2.2 (1974): 259. A summary of the MLA audience discussion is appended to the article.

21 My information, as well as some of my analytical points, come from Patrice McDermott's wonderful study of feminist journals, *Politics and Scholarship: Feminist Academic Journals and the Production of Knowledge* (Urbana: University of Illinois Press, 1994), 65 (first quotation), 64 (second quotation).

22 Quoted in ibid., 68.

23 Mary S. Hartman, Introduction to *Clio's Consciousness Raised: New Perspectives on the History of Women,* ed. Mary S. Hartman and Lois Banner (New York: Harper Torchbooks, 1974), vii–xii.

24 Information on both conferences from Mary Dunn, "Second Berkshire Conference on the History of Women," *Women's Studies Newsletter* 3.2 (spring 1975): 7–8 (quotations 7); and Barbara Sicherman, "Review Essay: American History," *Signs* 1.2 (winter 1975): 462.

25 McDermott, *Politics,* 71 (long quotation), 69 (short quotation).

26 After five years under founding editor Catharine Stimpson at Barnard College and Rutgers University, *Signs* was edited by Barbara Gelpi at Stanford University (1980–85), Jean O'Barr at Duke University (1985–90), Ruth-Ellen Joeres and Barbara Laslett at the University of Minnesota (1990–95), and Carolyn Allen and Judith A. Howard at the University of Washington (1995–2000). For accounts of the journal, see Catharine R. Stimpson, "The Making of *Signs,*" *Radical Teacher* 6 (December 1977): 23–25; and Jean O'Barr, "What Is It Like to Edit *Signs?*" in Jean O'Barr, *Feminism in Action* (Chapel Hill: University of North Carolina Press, 1994), 200–218.

27 McDermott, *Politics,* 100 (first quotation), 99 (second quotation).

28 O'Barr, *Feminism,* 203–5. Most mainstream disciplinary journals eventually modified their yes-or-no decision making by giving manuscript reviewers the option of recommending that the author revise and resubmit.

29 Ann E. Davis, "Women as a Minority Group in Higher Academics," *The American Sociologist* 4.2 (May 1969): 95–99.

30 Cherry Carter Kinney, "Reflections on the 1969 Resolutions of the Women's Caucus," *The American Sociologist* 6.1 (February 1971): 19–22; Michelle Patterson, "Alice in Wonderland: A Study of Women Faculty in Graduate Departments of Sociology," *The American Sociologist* 6.3 (August 1971): 225–34; Michael A. La Sorte, "Sex Differences in Salary among Academic Sociology Teachers," *The American Sociologist* 6.4 (November 1971): 304–7; Maurice Jackson, "Minorities and Women in Sociology: Are Opportunities Changing?" *The American Sociologist* 6.4 (November 1974): 3–5.

31 Joseph W. Schneider and Sally I. Hacker, "Sex Role Imagery and the Use of the Generic 'Man' in Introductory Texts: A Case in the Sociology of Sociology," *The American Sociologist* 8.1 (February 1973): 12–18. For clusters, see *The American Sociologist* 8.3 (August 1973); and 8.4 (November 1973).

32 Meredith Gould and Rochelle Kern-Daniels, "Toward a Sociological Theory of Gender and Sex," *The American Sociologist* 12.4 (November 1977): 183–89.

33 Sarah H. Matthews, "Rethinking Sociology through a Feminist Perspective," *The American Sociologist* 17.1 (February 1982): 29–39.

34 On marriage, see Susan Orden and Norman Bradburn, "Working Wives and Marriage Happiness," *American Journal of Sociology* 74.1 (July 1968): 392–407; Alan Bayer, "Marriage Plans and Educational Aspirations," *American Journal of Sociology* 75.2 (September 1969); 239–44; Kathleen V. Ritter and Lowell L. Hargens, "Occupational Positions and Class Identifications of Married Working Women," *American Journal of Sociology* 80.4 (January 1975): 934–48; and Linda Waite, "Working Wives and the Family Life Cycle," *American Journal of Sociology* 86.2 (September 1980): 272–94. On status, see Cynthia Fuchs Epstein, "Encountering the Male Establishment: Sex-Status Limits on Women's Careers in the Professions," *American Journal of Sociology* 75.6 (May 1970): 965–82. On sex roles, see Marianne Abeles Ferber and Joan A. Huber, "Sex of Student and Instructor: A Study of Student Bias," *American Journal of Sociology* 80.4 (January 1975): 949–63; Adeline Levine and Janice Crumrine, "Women and the Fear of Success," *American Journal of Sociology* 80.4 (January 1975): 964–74; and Karen Oppenheimer Mason, "U.S. Women's Sex-Role Ideology, 1970," *American Journal of Sociology* 80.5 (March 1975): 1212–19.

35 The issue was republished in book form as *Women in a Changing Society,* ed. Joan Huber (Chicago: University of Chicago Press, 1973).

36 Rosabeth Moss Kanter, "Some Effects of Proportions on Group Life: Skewed Sex Ratios and Responses to Token Women," *American Journal of Sociology* 82.5 (March 1977): 965–90. The responses were Eve Spangler, Marsha A. Gordon, and Ronald M. Pipkin, "Token Women: An Empirical Test of Kanter's Hypothesis," *American Journal of Sociology* 84.1 (July 1978): 160–70; and several brief comments in the same journal (84.6 [May 1979]: 1438–41).

37 Robert K. Merton, "Insiders and Outsiders: A Chapter in the Sociology of Knowledge," *American Journal of Sociology* 78.1 (July 1972): 9–47.

38 A survey of three journals (the *American Journal of Sociology,* the *American Sociological Review,* and *Social Problems*) traced the increasing publication of empirically based articles using statistical presentations over the course of more than half a century and argued that funders of sociological research drove the trend to scientization; by the time of the last period surveyed, 1955 through 1964, more than 80 percent of the articles published used statistical presentations (James L. McCartney, "On Being Scientific: Changing Styles of Presentation of Sociological Research," *The American Sociologist* 5.1 [February 1970]: 30–35). A survey of recent publishing history found that less than 12 percent of the articles published in major sociology journals from 1974 through 1983 were theoretical, qualitative, or otherwise nonempirical (Linda Grant,

Kathryn B. Ward, and Xue Lan Rong, "Is There an Association between Gender and Method in Sociological Research?" *American Sociological Review* 52.6 [December 1987]: 856–62).

Research on women sociologists who studied gender showed that they used qualitative methods more often than quantitative ones but that more of the published work by women sociologists used quantitative methods (Linda Grant and Kathryn B. Ward, "Gender and Publishing in Sociology," *Gender and Society* 5.2 [June 1991]: 207–23). On the basis of such data, feminist sociologists reached two conclusions: that mainstream sociology journals tend to publish empirically based and quantitative work and to reject qualitative work, and that women sociologists seek to publish their quantitative work in mainstream journals and their qualitative work in feminist ones (Marlene Mackie, "Female Sociologists' Productivity, Collegial Relations, and Research Style Examined through Journal Publications," *Sociology and Social Research* 69.2 [January 1985]: 189–209).

39   See Frederick Crews, "Do Literary Studies Have an Ideology?" *PMLA* 85.3 (May 1970): 423–28; Rima Drell Reck, "The Politics of Literature," *PMLA* 85.3 (May 1970): 429–32; the executive secretary's report, *PMLA* 85.3 (May 1970): 535–39; and the New Study Commission correspondence, *PMLA* 85.3 (May 1970): 550–55.

40   Strother B. Perry, "Gertrude Stein at Marienbad," *PMLA* 85.5 (October 1970): 1096–1105.

41   Madelyn Gutwirth, "Madame de Staël, Rousseau, and the Woman Question," *PMLA* 86.1 (January 1971): 100–109; David Sonstroem, "*Wuthering Heights* and the Limits of Vision," *PMLA* 86.1 (January 1971): 51–62.

42   Maynard Mack, "To See It Feelingly," *PMLA* 86.3 (May 1971): 363–74 (Mack quotation from the abstract preceding the article, 359).

43   Stella P. Revard, "Eve and the Doctrine of Responsibility in *Paradise Lost*," *PMLA* 88.1 (January 1973): 69–78; Stuart Wilson, "Richardson's *Pamela*," *PMLA* 88.1 (January 1973): 79–91; James R. Kincaid, "Alice's Invasion of Wonderland," *PMLA* 88.1 (January 1973): 91–99; Alex Zwerdling, "Esther Summerson Rehabilitated," *PMLA* 88.3 (May 1973): 429–39; and Jean M. Wyatt, "*Mrs. Dalloway:* Literary Allusion as Structural Metaphor," *PMLA* 88.3 (May 1973): 440–51.

44   Sandra M. Gilbert, "Patriarchal Poetry and Women Readers," *PMLA* 93.3 (May 1978): 368–82.

45   Mary Carruthers, "The Wife of Bath and the Painting of Lions," *PMLA* 94.2 (March 1979): 209–22 (discusses the legal status of women); Mary Poovey, "My Hideous Progeny: Mary Shelley and the Feminization of Romanticism," *PMLA* 95.3 (May 1980): 332–47 (discusses the author's model of the female artist).

46   Lillian S. Robinson and Lise Vogel, "Modernism and History," *New Literary History* 3.1 (autumn 1971): 177–200; Annette Kolodny, "A Map for Rereading; Or, Gender and the Interpretation of Literary Texts," *New Literary History* 11.3 (spring 1980): 451–68. The response to other articles that touches briefly on feminism is Verena Andermatt-Conley, "A Doll's Story," *New Literary History* 9.1 (autumn 1977): 181–88.

47   Statement of purpose in the table of contents, *Critical Inquiry* 1.1 (September 1974).

48 Henry Nash Smith, "The Scribbling Women and the Cosmic Success Story," *Critical Inquiry* 1.1 (September 1974): 47–70; Carolyn Heilbrun, "Marriage and Contemporary Fiction," *Critical Inquiry* 5.2 (winter 1978): 309–23; Barbara Currier Bell and Carol Ohmann, "Virginia Woolf's Criticism: A Polemical Preface," *Critical Inquiry* 1.2 (December 1974): 361–72; Catharine R. Stimpson, "The Mind, the Body, and Gertrude Stein," *Critical Inquiry* 3.3 (spring 1977): 489–506; Susan Fox, "The Female as Metaphor in William Blake's Poetry," *Critical Inquiry* 3.3 (spring 1977): 507–20; Sandra M. Gilbert, "Costumes of the Mind: Transvestism as Metaphor in Modern Literature," *Critical Inquiry* 7.2 (winter 1980): 391–418.

49 Josephine Donovan, "Feminism and Aesthetics," *Critical Inquiry* 3.3 (spring 1977): 605–10; Lee R. Edwards, "The Labors of Psyche: Toward a Theory of Female Heroism," *Critical Inquiry* 6.1 (autumn 1979): 33–50; Peter Schwenger, "The Masculine Mode," *Critical Inquiry* 5.4 (summer 1979): 621–34.

50 Annette Kolodny, "Some Notes on Defining a 'Feminist Literary Criticism,'" *Critical Inquiry* 2.1 (autumn 1975): 75–92. Also see William W. Morgan, "Feminism and Literary Study: A Reply to Annette Kolodny"; Beverly Voloshin, "A Historical Note on Women's Fiction: A Reply to Annette Kolodny"; and Annette Kolodny, "The Feminist as Literary Critic," all in *Critical Inquiry* 2.4 (summer 1976): 807–16, 817–20, and 821–32, respectively.

51 Carol Duncan, "Happy Mothers and Other New Ideas in French Art," *Art Bulletin* 55.4 (December 1973): 570–83; Norma Braude, "Degas's Misogyny," *Art Bulletin* 59.1 (March 1977): 95–107; and Linda Nochlin, "Lost and *Found*: Once More the Fallen Woman," *Art Bulletin* 60.1 (March 1978): 139–53.

52 Thalia Gouma Peterson and Patricia Mathews, "The Feminist Critique of Art History, *Art Bulletin* 69.3 (September 1987): 326–57.

53 For detailed case studies of how the journal evaluation process works, see Greg Myers, "The Social Construction of Two Biologists' Articles," in *Knowledges: Historical and Critical Studies in Disciplinarity*, ed. Ellen Messer-Davidow, David R. Shumway, and David J. Sylvan (Charlottesville: University Press of Virginia, 1993), 327–67; and Ed Cohen, "Are We (Not) What We Are Becoming? Gay 'Identity,' 'Gay Studies,' and the Disciplining of Knowledge," in Messer-Davidow et al., *Knowledges*, 397–421. Although the authors describe journals in two very different disciplines—biology and literary studies—the processes of article review, revision, and eventual acceptance similarly result in the toning down of the author's claims so that they do not call into question the discipline's current assumptions.

54 Karin D. Knorr-Cetina, *The Manufacture of Knowledge: An Essay on the Constructivist and Contextual Nature of Science* (Oxford: Pergamon, 1981), 7 (long and short quotations).

55 Ethel D. Klein and Lillian Robbins, "Social-Psychological Issues in Sex Discrimination," *Journal of Social Issues* 41.4 (1985): 139.

56 See Ruth A. Wallace, Introduction to *Feminism and Sociological Theory*, ed. Ruth A. Wallace (Newbury Park, CA: Sage, 1989), 9.

57 For the importance of author-anonymous review, see Domna C. Stanton, "What's in a Name? The Case for Author-Anonymous Reviewing," in *Women in Print II*, 65–77;

and "What's in a Name"? Re-visiting Author Anonymous Reviewing," *PMLA* 112.2 (March 1997): 191–97. Stanton took the lead for the MLA Commission on the Status of Women in 1976 when it advocated an author-anonymous review policy to *PMLA;* as editor of that journal in 1997, she was defending the policy against critics who wanted to suspend it.

58   An exact count of courses and programs for any given year has never been available. *Female Studies I* (1970) printed seventeen syllabi, *Female Studies II* (1970) printed sixty-six syllabi and noted the existence of thirty-seven more courses, and *Female Studies III* (1971) noted the existence of six hundred courses and contained brief reports on seventeen programs—at Barnard College, State University of New York at Buffalo, Cambridge-Goddard Graduate School, Chicago Liberation School, Cornell University, Douglass College at Rutgers University, the Five Colleges in Amherst (Amherst, Hampshire, Mt. Holyoke, University of Massachusetts, and Smith), Goddard College, Laney College, University of Pittsburgh, Portland State University, City University of New York at Richmond, Sacramento State College, San Diego State College, San Francisco State College, Towson State College, and University of Washington (editors Florence Howe and Carol Ahlum noted that programs were being organized on another dozen campuses).

For additional information, I have drawn on the pamphlet "The Guide to Current Female Studies III," produced by the Feminist Press, summer 1973; Florence Howe, "The First Ten Years Are the Easiest," in *Index to the First Ten Years, 1972–1982,* comp. Jo Baird, Shirley Frank, and Beth Stafford (Old Westbury, NY: Feminist Press, 1983) (the index covers the *Women's Studies Newsletter, Women's Studies Quarterly,* and *Women's Studies International*); and the *NWSA Directory of Women's Studies Programs, Women's Centers, and Women's Research Centers* (College Park, MD: National Women's Studies Association, 1990), which lists 627 programs.

The literature on women's studies is now vast. For a historical sense of its development, see Florence Howe and Carol Ahlum, "Women's Studies and Social Change," in *Academic Women on the Move,* ed. Alice S. Rossi and Ann Calderwood (New York: Russell Sage Foundation, 1973), 393–424; Barbara Sicherman, "The Invisible Woman: The Case for Women's Studies," in *Women in Higher Education,* ed. W. Todd Furniss and Patricia Albjerg Graham (Washington, DC: American Council on Education, 1974), 155–77; Catharine R. Stimpson, "The New Feminism and Women's Studies," in *Women on Campus: The Unfinished Revolution* (New Rochelle, NY: Change, 1975), 69–84; Florence Howe, *Seven Years Later: Women's Studies Programs in 1976* (Washington, DC: National Advisory Council on Women's Educational Programs, 1977); Marilyn J. Boxer, "For and About Women: The Theory and Practice of Women's Studies in the United States," *Signs* 7.3 (spring 1982): 661–95; Paula R. Holleran, "The Feminist Curriculum: Issues for Survival in Academe," *Journal of Thought* 20.3 (fall 1985): 25–36; Maxine Baca Zinn, Lynn Weber Cannon, Elizabeth Higginbotham, and Bonnie Thornton Dill, "The Cost of Exclusionary Practice in Women's Studies," *Signs* 11.2 (winter 1986): 290–303; Catharine Stimpson and Nina Kressner Cobb, *Women's Studies in the United States* (New York: Ford Foundation, 1986); Johnella E. Butler et al., *Liberal Learning and* the *Women's Studies Major* (College Park, MD: National Women's Studies Association, 1991); *The Courage to Question: Women's Studies and Student Learning,* ed. Caryn Mc-Tighe Musil (Washington, DC: Association of American Colleges / National Women's Studies Association, 1992), 1–15; and Marilyn J. Boxer, *When Women Ask the Questions: Creating Women's Studies in America* (Baltimore: Johns Hopkins University Press, 1998).

59 Howe and Ahlum, "Women's Studies," 393.

60 Ibid., 394.

61 Catharine R. Stimpson, "Women's Studies, Barnard College," in *Female Studies III,* 140.

62 "College of Women's Studies, State University of N.Y. at Buffalo," in *Female Studies III,* 142–46.

63 Steering Committee, "Female Studies Program, Cornell University," in *Female Studies III,* 152.

64 Nancy Hoffman, "Ad Hoc Women's Institute and Resource Center, Portland State University," in *Female Studies III,* 164 (first quotation), 165 (second quotation).

65 Information from Nancy M. Porter, "A Nuts and Bolts View of Women's Studies," in *Female Studies VI: Closer to the Ground, Women's Classes, Criticism, Programs—1972,* ed. Nancy Hoffman, Cynthia Secor, and Adrian Tinsley (Old Westbury, NY: Feminist Press, 1972), 170–71; Samantha Willow, "Rounding Our Corners," in *Female Studies VI,* 209–11.

66 Howe and Ahlum, "Women's Studies," 413.

67 Ibid., 402–3.

68 Howe and Ahlum make this point in ibid., 414.

69 From a list of some six hundred women's studies programs, I made a shorter list of several hundred that seemed to be stabilized as large or medium-sized programs and read descriptions of them in their university or college bulletins. From that reading, I assembled a list of thirty-five programs plus the programs at the University of Minnesota where I teach and at a university where I was doing fieldwork. The women's studies programs responding to my initial query letter or my follow-up letter were at the University of Arizona, Brown University, University of California (Berkeley, Los Angeles, and San Diego), University of Cincinnati, City University of New York (Graduate Center), University of Colorado, University of Connecticut, Cornell University, Denison University, Duke University, University of Illinois (Urbana-Champaign), Indiana University, University of Iowa, University of Maryland, University of Massachusetts (Amherst and Boston), University of Michigan, University of New Mexico, Ohio State University, Ohio University, Stanford University, State University of New York (Albany and Binghamton), University of Virginia, and University of Wisconsin. The programs that did not respond were at the University of Alabama, Amherst College, University of California (Davis and Irvine), University of Kentucky, Rutgers University, Smith College, and State University of New York (Buffalo). While doing fieldwork in New Jersey, I obtained information on the Rutgers program.

70 I neglected to get the name of the program director who made this comment at The Next Twenty-Five Years: A Participatory Conference on Women's Studies Program

Administration, sponsored by the Arizona State University Women's Studies Program, Tempe, 13–15 February 1997.

71 The University of Colorado women's studies program sent me a typed sheet (dated spring 1992) containing this description and the syllabus for the introductory course. The syllabus moves through a series of topics: biology, reproduction, psychology, sex-role socialization, family forms, family violence, the economy, and feminist movements.

72 In fall 1998, after two years of planning, CAFS was reorganized as a research center, and the Department of Women's Studies, which had expanded its core faculty, took over graduate education, incorporating the concentration and launching a doctoral program. The curriculum is still a crosshatched grid of identities, disciplines, feminist issues, and theories and methods.

73 To sample the large literature on curriculum transformation projects, see *Toward a Balanced Curriculum: A Sourcebook for Initiating Gender Integration Projects,* ed. Bonnie Spanier, Alexander Bloom, and Darlene Boroviak (Cambridge, MA: Schenkman, 1984); Betty Schmitz, *Integrating Women's Studies into the Curriculum: A Guide and Bibliography* (Old Westbury, NY: Feminist Press, 1985); *Changing Our Minds: Feminist Transformations of Knowledge,* ed. Susan Hardy Aiken, Karen Anderson, Myra Dinnerstein, Judy Nolte Lensink, and Patricia MacCorquodale (Albany: State University of New York Press, 1988); "Curricular and Institutional Change," a double issue on curriculum transformation, *Women's Studies Quarterly* 18.1–2 (spring–summer 1990); *Transforming the Curriculum: Ethnic Studies and Women's Studies,* ed. Johnnella E. Butler and John C. Walter (Albany: State University of New York Press, 1991); and *Mainstreaming Minority Women's Studies Programs* (New York: National Council for Research on Women, 1991). In *Mainstreaming,* Mariam Chamberlain estimated that some eighty mainstreaming projects had been conducted by 1985 and argued that race and ethnicity needed to be integrated into both traditional and women's studies curricula. Among the associations developing feminist curricular materials are the American Historical Association, Organization of American Historians, American Political Science Association, American Psychological Association, American Sociological Association, Association of American Geographers, and Speech Communication Association.

74 On Cincinnati's Friends of Women's Studies, see Theresa D. Balayon, "A History of the Women's Studies Program," *Forum: A Women's Studies Quarterly* 11.2 (winter 1985): 3–4; Laura S. Strumingher, "The Birth and Growth of 'Friends of Women's Studies' at the University of Cincinnati," *Frontiers* 8.3 (1986): 83–86; and Ellen Messer-Davidow, "Changing the System: The Board of Trustees Caper," *Women's Studies Quarterly* 18.3–4 (fall–winter 1990): 41–55. On Duke's Friends of Women's Studies, see O'Barr, *Feminism,* 219–38.

75 Michel Foucault, "Two Lectures," in Foucault, *Power / Knowledge: Selected Interviews and Other Writings 1972–1977,* ed. Colin Gordon, trans. Colin Gordon, Leo Marshall, John Mepham, and Kate Soper (New York: Pantheon, 1980), 83.

76   Tucker Farley, telephone interview with author, 25 September 1996; Tucker Farley's notes, written after reading an early draft of this chapter in February 1997.

77   Florence Howe, telephone interview with author, 14 August 1996.

78   Roberta Salper, telephone interview with author, 18 October 1996.

79   Foucault, "Two Lectures," 86.

80   Ann Leffler, Dair L. Gillespie, and Elinor Lerner Ratner, "Academic Feminists and the Women's Movement," *Ain't I A Woman* 4.1 (April 1973): 9.

81   Richard Rothstein, "Evolution of the ERAP Organizers," in *The New Left: A Collection of Essays*, ed. Priscilla Long (Boston: Porter Sargent, 1969), 272.

Chapter 5: Proliferating the Discourse

1   In early 1999, I did a Lumina search of the library holdings at the University of Minnesota, Twin Cities, for book titles under four keywords: it yielded 839 titles under *women's studies*, 4,091 under *feminism*, 3,382 under *gender*, and 41,838 under *women*. These gross numbers were misleading because Lumina did not let me limit the search to titles published between 1970 and 1998, eliminate duplication of titles across the categories, or scan for nonfeminist and antifeminist titles. Given these problems, I tried some breakouts by year of publication:

Year	Feminism	Gender	Women
1980	67	19	803
1985	134	71	1,095
1990	188	156	1,285
1995	249	328	1,823
1998	235	468	1,589

Then I did a Luis search of the library holdings at the University of Florida broken out for the same years of publication.

Year	Feminism	Gender	Women
1980	49	10	729
1985	110	68	900
1990	148	145	1,092
1995	218	348	1,605
1998	174	278	1,241

Scanning the titles, I found that the following circumstances at both Minnesota and Florida would reduce the estimated numbers of feminist-studies publications: (1) in 1980, a substantial number of the titles listed under "women" were nonfeminist books from traditional fields or government sources, but in the later years most were feminist books; (2) in 1980, almost half the titles listed under *gender* were nonfeminist books from traditional fields, but in the later years almost all were feminist or gay-lesbian studies books; and (3) the titles listed under *feminism* were feminist books, except for a few antifeminist books in later years. Concentrating on the Minnesota holdings, I averaged the titles published during these five years, divided by three to reduce for duplication and nonfeminist listings, and then multiplied by the eighteen years (1980–98). With this method, I estimated that roughly 10,200 feminist books were published between 1980 and 1998. The estimate is conservative because I did not consider feminist books (published in the United States and abroad) that were not acquired by Minnesota.

2   See Shulamith Firestone, *The Dialectic of Sex: The Case for Feminist Revolution* (New York: Bantam, 1971), 8–31, 72–94, 113–17, 205–42.

3   Joan Huber, "Toward a Sociotechnological Theory of the Women's Movement," *Social Problems* 23.4 (April 1976): 372.

4   The baseline dynamics are that the egg and the sperm (gametes) each bear twenty-three chromosomes, which on uniting form the twenty-three chromosomal pairs found in human cells. To make up the chromosomal pair that determines sex, the egg donates an X chromosome and the sperm donates either an X or a Y chromosome; the resulting XX is regarded as the female genotype and the XY as the male genotype. Some of the genes carried on these chromosomes activate and direct the sex-differentiation process; a gene on the Y chromosome, for instance, releases a substance that triggers the formation of the Wolffian system that under "normal" conditions develops into the male reproductive system. Sex differentiation continues up to birth and afterward and is accelerated by hormonal processes that occur during puberty.

5   Edward O. Wilson, *Sociobiology: The New Synthesis* (Cambridge: Harvard University Press, 1975), 4.

6   The Genes and Gender Conference was cosponsored by the Association for Women in Science, the Committee for Women in the American Museum of Natural History, the Ad Hoc Committee for Women in Science in the New York Academy of Sciences, and the Division for the Psychology of Women of the American Psychological Association. See *Genes and Gender I,* ed. Betty Rosoff and Ethel Tobach (New York: Gordian, 1978), 7–8; and *Genes and Gender II,* ed. Ruth Hubbard and Marian Lowe (New York: Gordian, 1979), 7–8.

7   See John Money and Anke Ehrhardt, *Man and Woman, Boy and Girl* (Baltimore: Johns Hopkins University Press, 1972). For feminist responses to the literature and treatment of intersexing, see Freda Salzman, "Aggression and Gender: A Critique of the Nature-Nurture Question for Humans," in *Genes and Gender II,* 71–89; Marian Lowe and Ruth Hubbard, "Sociobiology and Biosociology: Can Science Prove the Biological Basis of Sex Differences in Behavior?" in *Genes and Gender II,* 111; Janice G. Raymond, "Transsexualism: An Issue of Sex-Role Stereotyping," in *Genes and Gender II,* 131–41; Suzanne J. Kessler and Wendy McKenna, *Gender: An Ethnomethodological Approach* (New York: Wiley, 1978), 42–80; Rhoda K. Unger, *Female and Male: Psychological Perspectives* (New York: Harper & Row, 1978), 105–45; Suzanne J. Kessler, "The Medical Construction of Gender: Case Management of Intersexed Infants," *Signs* 16.1 (autumn 1990): 3–26; Anne Fausto-Sterling, "The Five Sexes," *The Sciences* (March–April 1993): 20–24; and Suzanne J. Kessler, *Lessons from the Intersexed* (New Brunswick, NJ: Rutgers University Press, 1998).

8 See Kessler and McKenna, *Gender,* 51–55. When Olympics officials suspect that ostensibly female entrants are men who have taken hormones to feminize their appearance, they subject them to genetic testing. Unaware of genetic mosaics, they have disqualified female entrants on the basis of obtaining an XY result from a small tissue swipe. See Alison Carlson, "Chromosome Count," *Ms.,* October 1988, 40, 42–44.

9 Unger, *Female,* 112, 105–45.

10 Edward O. Wilson, *On Human Nature* (Cambridge: Harvard University Press, 1978), 123–24.

11 Helen H. Lambert, "Biology and Equality: A Perspective on Sex Differences," *Signs* 4.1 (autumn 1978): 99.

12 For critiques of sex-difference research from the biological sciences, see ibid., 97–117; Marian Lowe, "Sociobiology and Sex Differences," *Signs* 4.1 (autumn 1978): 118–25; *Women Look at Biology Looking at Women,* ed. Ruth Hubbard, Mary Sue Henifin, and Barbara Fried (Cambridge, MA: Schenkman, 1979); *Genes and Gender IV,* ed. Myra Fooden, Susan Gordon, and Betty Hughley (New York: Gordian, 1983); *Woman's Nature: Rationalizations of Inequality,* ed. Marian Lowe and Ruth Hubbard (New York: Pergamon, 1983); Ruth Bleier, *Science and Gender: A Critique of Biology and Its Theories on Women* (New York: Pergamon, 1984); Ruth Bleier, "Sex Differences Research: Science or Belief?" in *Feminist Approaches to Science,* ed. Ruth Bleier (New York: Pergamon, 1986), 147–64; Anne Fausto-Sterling, *Myths of Gender: Biological Theories about Women and Men* (New York: Basic Books, 1985); Lynda Birke, *Women, Feminism and Biology* (New York: Methuen, 1986); Ruth Hubbard, *The Politics of Women's Biology* (New Brunswick, NJ: Rutgers University Press, 1990); and Sue V. Rosser, *Biology and Feminism: A Dynamic Interaction* (New York: Twayne, 1992). Philosopher Helen E. Longino also deals with this subject in *Science as Social Knowledge* (Princeton: Princeton University Press, 1990), 103–32. Later I will cite critiques of sex-difference research by feminists in psychology and anthropology.

13 See Marian Lowe's model in her "The Dialectic of Biology and Culture," in Lowe and Hubbard, *Woman's Nature,* 39–62; and Hubbard's account of the multifactor and interactive models in Hubbard, *Politics,* 105–17.

14 John Milton, *Paradise Lost* (1674), in *Complete Poems and Major Prose,* ed. Merritt Y. Hughes (New York: Odyssey, 1957), 4:296–98.

15 Charles Darwin, *The Descent of Man, and Selection in Relation to Sex,* 2 vols. (London: Murray, 1871), 2:316. For discussions of the discourse of sex and sexuality during these periods, see Ruth Hubbard, "Have Only Men Evolved?" in Hubbard et al., *Women,* 7–35 (still the most readable and rollicking short tour of the history of the "biology is social destiny" doctrine); Londa Schiebinger, *The Mind Has No Sex: Women in the Origins of Modern Science* (Cambridge: Harvard University Press, 1989); and *Science and Sensibility: Gender and Scientific Inquiry, 1780–1945,* ed. Marina Benjamin (Oxford: Blackwell, 1991), especially Londa Schiebinger's "The Private Life of Plants: Sexual Politics in Carl Linnaeus and Erasmus Darwin," 121–43.

16 Steven Rose, "The Roots and Social Functions of Biological Reductionism," in *Reductionism in Academic Disciplines,* ed. Arthur Peacocke (Guildford, Surrey, U.K.:

Society for Research into Higher Education NFER-NELSON, 1985), 26–28 (quotation 26).

17   Ibid., 29–37.

18   Birke, *Women*, 57–58.

19   Hubbard, *Politics*, 107–8.

20   For a critique of the discovery of a sex-determining gene, see Anne Fausto-Sterling, "Life in the XY Corral," *Women's Studies International Forum* 12.3 (1989): 319–31.

21   Hubbard, *Politics*, 116.

22   Ruth Bleier, "Lab Coat: Robe of Innocence of Klansman's Sheet?" in *Feminist Studies / Critical Studies*, ed. Teresa de Lauretis (Bloomington: Indiana University Press, 1986), 62.

23   Judith Butler, *Gender Trouble: Feminism and the Subversion of Identity* (New York: Routledge, 1990), xi (first quotation), 20 (second quotation), 112 (third quotation), 145 (fourth quotation), 147 (fifth quotation), 148 (sixth quotation); also see 6–8. For an argument against the dismantling of substantive sex, see Evelyn Fox Keller, "Holding the Center of Feminist Theory," *Women's Studies International Quarterly* 12.3 (1989): 315–16.

24   Judith Butler, *Bodies That Matter: On the Discursive Limits of "Sex"* (New York: Routledge, 1993), xii (first quotation), x (second quotation), 1 (third and fourth quotations). Also see her scheme for reformulating the materiality of bodies on pages 2–3.

25   Joan W. Scott, "Gender: A Useful Category of Historical Analysis," *American Historical Review* 91.5 (December 1986): 1054.

26   Mary Hawkesworth, "Confounding Gender," *Signs* 22.3 (spring 1997): 649–85 (quotation 651, tour of gender 650–51). Also see the replies by Wendy McKenna and Suzanne Kessler, Steven G. Smith, Joan Wallach Scott, R. W. Connell, and Mary Hawkesworth in the same issue, 687–713.

27   For discussions of the public and private spheres, see Gerda Lerner, "New Approaches to the Study of Women in American History," in Gerda Lerner, *The Majority Finds Its Past: Placing Women in History* (New York: Oxford University Press, 1979), 3–14 (first quotation 3) (rpt. from *The Journal of Social History* 3.1 [fall 1969]: 53–62); and Joan Kelly, "The Social Relations of the Sexes: Methodological Implications of Women's History," in Joan Kelly, *Women, History, and Theory: The Essays of Joan Kelly* (Chicago: University of Chicago Press, 1984), 1–18 (second quotation 2) (rpt. from *Signs* 1.4 [summer 1976]: 809–23). For similar reflections on political science, see Nannerl O. Keohane, "Speaking from Silence: Women and the Science of Politics," in *A Feminist Perspective in the Academy: The Difference It Makes*, ed. Elizabeth Langland and Walter Gove (Chicago: University of Chicago Press, 1983), 87.

28   Mary Ellmann, *Thinking About Women* (New York: Harcourt Brace Jovanovich, 1968), 32–33.

29   See Natalie Zemon Davis, " 'Women's History' in Transition: The European Case," *Feminist Studies* 3.3–4 (spring–summer 1976): 83–103; and Joan Kelly, "Early Feminist Theory and the *Querelle des Femmes*, 1400–1789," in Kelly, *Women*, 65–109 (rpt. from *Signs* 8.1 [autumn 1982]: 4–28).

These two essays don't quite capture the range and significance of the genres feminist scholars found. In eighteenth-century England, for example, biographies, conduct books, and short essays were the preferred genres for edifying young women; the real-life actions in biography dramatized the lessons in duty, morality, piety. And patriotism they were expected to learn, while the colloquial style of the conduct book (usually written as if they were letters or conversations) and short informal essay was believed to be suited to their weak intellects. The many feminist treatises published during the radical 1790s—among them Catharine Macaulay's *Letters on Education* (1790), Mary Wollstonecraft's *A Vindication of the Rights of Woman* (1792), Mary Hays's *An Appeal to the Men of Great Britain in behalf of the Women* (1798), Priscilla Wakefield's *Reflections on the Present Condition of the Female Sex* (1798), and Mary Ann Radcliffe's *The Female Advocate: or, An Attempt to Recover the Rights of Women from Male Usurpation* (1799)—were a road map feminist scholars used to develop analyses of women's legal, political, economic, educational, and social status in Britain and the United States. Most of the 1790s feminist writers were not the liberals they were later said to be. They wrote about the sexual ideology that shaped women's lives, the pernicious class system in England, women's low status in other cultures, and in some cases the abolition of the slave trade—all considered dangerously radical positions then.

30 Gerda Lerner, "Placing Women in History: Definitions and Challenges," in Lerner, *Majority*, 149–50 (this paper was delivered at the 1974 Berkshire Conference).

31 Barbara Sicherman, "Review Essay: American History," *Signs* 1.2 (winter 1975): 461–85 (esp. 463). The inadequacies of traditional history and the possibilities for feminist history were suggested to Gerda Lerner, Joan Kelly, and others by early social histories, such as Georgiana Hill's *Women in English Life from Medieval to Modern Times* (1896), Alice Clark's *Working Life of Women in the Seventeenth Century* (1919), Ivy Pinchbeck's *Women Workers and the Industrial Revolution* (1930), and Mary Beard's *Woman as a Force in History* (1946).

32 Kelly, "Social Relations," 1–18. Tamara K. Hareven uses the reformulation of period, category, and theory in "Modernization and Family History: Perspectives on Social Change," *Signs* 2.1 (autumn 1976): 190–206.

33 Carolyn C. Lougee, "Review Essay: Modern European History," *Signs* 2.3 (spring 1977): 628–50 (quotation 629). Carroll Smith-Rosenberg's "The New Woman and the New History," *Feminist Studies* 3.1–2 (fall 1975): 185–98, addresses many of the issues raised by the feminists I have cited: for instance, the study of male-female and female-female relations; the reevaluation of canons, periods, and theories; the focus on the so-called private sphere activities; and methods borrowed from anthropology, sociology, and psychology.

For a theoretically pitched discussion of how discourses constru(ct)ed the social order, see Joan Kelly, "The Doubled Vision of Feminist Theory: A Postscript to the 'Women and Power' Conference," in Kelly, *Women*, 51–64 (rpt. from *Feminist Studies* 5.1 [spring 1979]: 216–27). History, she said, had foregrounded the public sphere and backgrounded the private one, Marxist analysis had foregrounded class and backgrounded racial and gender groups, and radical feminism had emphasized psychic, sexual, and ideological structures while socialist feminism had emphasized social structures. In the aggregate, feminist work showed that social relations traversed the presumably divided spheres (public / domestic, productive / reproductive, psychic / social) and that the systems of gender, race, and class operated simultaneously to produce social order.

The formation of feminist history I have been describing can be seen at a glance in *Liberating Women's History: Theoretical and Critical Essays,* ed. Berenice A. Carroll (Urbana: University of Illinois Press, 1976), which contains critiques of traditional history, examples of the new feminist history, and reflections on feminist history as a field.

34 Elaine Showalter, "Review Essay: Literary Criticism," *Signs* 1.2 (winter 1975): 436 (both quotations); Annette Kolodny, "Review Essay: Literary Criticism," *Signs* 2.2 (winter 1976): 420 (first quotation), 421 (second quotation).

35 Elaine Showalter, "Feminist Criticism in the Wilderness," *Critical Inquiry* 8.2 (winter 1981): 180 (first quotation), 184 (second quotation); but see the whole essay (179–205).

To dispel any confusion about Showalter's claim and mine, I want to make two points. First, Showalter accurately described the two types of feminist criticism: "feminist critique," as exemplified by Judith Fetterley, *The Resisting Reader: A Feminist Approach to American Fiction* (Bloomington: Indiana University Press, 1977); and "gynocritics" (or woman-centered scholarship), as exemplified by Patricia M. Spacks, *The Female Imagination* (New York: Knopf, 1975); Ellen Moers, *Literary Women: The Great Writers* (New York: Doubleday, 1976); Elaine Showalter, *A Literature of Their Own: British Women Novelists from Brontë to Lessing* (Princeton, NJ: Princeton University Press, 1977); and Sandra Gilbert and Susan Gubar, *Shakespeare's Sisters: Feminist Essays on Women Poets* (Bloomington: Indiana University Press, 1979). Gilbert and Gubar's *The Madwoman in the Attic: The Woman Writer and the Nineteenth-Century Literary Imagination* (New Haven, CT: Yale University Press, 1979) combined the two approaches. In all of these books the authors did what most literary critics did: they discussed individual texts and authors; texts grouped by oeuvre, school, and period; and texts gendered by genre, theme, and style. Books that didn't fit the disciplinary paradigm discussed the material and social conditions of literary production: for instance, Tillie Olsen, *Silences* (New York: Delacorte, 1978); Lillian S. Robinson, *Sex, Class, and Culture* (Bloomington: Indiana University Press, 1978); and Adrienne Rich, *On Lies, Secrets, and Silences* (New York: Norton, 1979).

Second, Showalter and Kolodny were concerned with the effects of feminist literary critics' individualism, empiricism, and eclecticism on feminist criticism. While I agree that individualism made it difficult for critics to refocus from authors and texts to the systems of literary production, circulation, and consumption, I do not believe that empiricism and eclecticism were necessarily obstacles; what hindered the development of social-structural analysis and theorizing in feminist literary studies was too little (not too much) empiricism and eclecticism. Most feminist literary critics didn't follow the analyses and theories of social, economic, political, and legal systems in other disciplines.

36 In studies asking psychologists why they didn't include women in their subject pools, the respondents cited these reasons: the researcher knew that sex differences existed but was not interested in investigating them; the researcher knew that sex differences existed and wanted to reduce the variables that entered into his study; the researcher was investigating a hypothesis that applied only to the male sex; the researcher assumed that males were more representative of the human race than were females; the pool of subjects available for research was male; and the pool of subjects would be too large to study if females were included. See Mary Brown Parlee, "Review Essay: Psychology," *Signs* 1.1 (autumn 1975): 125–27.

37 The sex- and race-difference research in psychology came in two strains. Strong determinists controlled for social factors so as to show the weight of biological factors in producing sex or race differences. Virulent determinists—such as Berkeley psychologist Arthur Jensen, Harvard psychologist Richard Herrnstein, and Stanford physicist William Shockley—held that genes programmed the races and argued that racial minorities in the United States exhibited a lower intelligence, fewer talents, and a greater propensity for crime. The findings from both strains of research were published in a range of venues from scientific journals to the *Harvard Educational Review*, from the *Atlantic Monthly* to the news media. Snapped up by public leaders who did not make fine discriminations about scientific evidence or social consequences, the difference studies informed labor legislation, healthcare policy, and educational practice. For a chilling account of how racist research on intelligence, the diseases of sickle cell anemia and hypertension, and XYY and XXY chromosomal combinations entered into public policy, healthcare, and education, see Inez Smith Reid, "Viewpoint: Science, Politics, and Race," *Signs* 1.2 (winter 1975): 397–422.

38 The term *gender* was used by several contributors to *The Development of Sex Differences*, ed. Eleanor E. Maccoby (Stanford, CA: Stanford University Press, 1966), a book that grew out of a working group on sex differences meeting at Stanford between 1962 and 1964. Some of the essays repeated and others repudiated the doxa of mainstream biology, Freudian theory, developmental psychology, and anthropology. As an example of repetition, see Roy G. D'Andrade, "Sex Differences and Cultural Institutions," in Maccoby, *Development*, 174–204. As an example of repudiation, see Lawrence Kohlberg, "A Cognitive-Developmental Analysis of Children's Sex-Role Concepts and Attitudes," in Maccoby, *Development*, 82–173.

Kohlberg's explanation of gender constancy is usefully summarized in Eleanor E. Maccoby and Carol Nagy Jacklin, *The Psychology of Sex Differences* (Stanford, CA: Stanford University Press, 1974), 290 (quotation above), 302, 364. His formulation of gender constancy was based on Piaget's explanation of the stage in cognitive development at which a child can recognize attribute constancy (e.g., the child realizes that the quantity of water that fills a small glass to the brim is not diminished when the water is poured into a large glass and fills it only halfway). What Piaget's attribute constancy shared with biology's sex and grammar's gender was the concept of an intrinsic and fixed formal identity. So, in formulating "gender constancy," Kohlberg performed the very cognitive maneuver he and Piaget had described; he recognized what the seemingly different discourses of early cognitive development, biological sex, and grammar shared—namely, the core concept of an intrinsic and fixed formal identity. But he also performed a heavy-handed normalizing maneuver by describing gender constancy as a developmental achievement because, on that definition, everyone who today believes that sex and sexuality are not intrinsic and fixed formal identities would have to be seen as developmentally retarded.

39   For a brief history of the psychology of women subfield, see Florence L. Denmark and Linda C. Fernandez, "Historical Development of the Psychology of Women," in *Psychology of Women: A Handbook of Issues and Theories*, ed. Florence L. Denmark and Michele A. Paludi (Westport, CT: Greenwood, 1993), 3–22. The early feminist psychologists worked in several arenas: clinical practice (e.g., psychotherapy, counseling, social services, and testing); disciplinary subfields (including sex stereotypes, roles, and differences); and such hybrid ventures as the feminist project of rethinking psychoanalytic theory, which, from its earliest years, traversed several disciplines. Since the scope of feminist psychology exceeds what I can address in this brief section, I look at the work on sex stereotypes, roles, and differences.

To sample the literature on the psychology of women, see Judith Bardwick, *The Psychology of Women* (New York: Harper & Row, 1970); Julia Sherman, *On the Psychology of Women* (Springfield, IL: Thomas, 1971); *Female Psychology: The Emerging Self*, ed. Sue Cox (Chicago: Science Research Associates, 1976); Jean Baker Miller, *Toward a New Psychology of Women* (Boston: Beacon, 1976); Virginia O'Leary, *Toward Understanding Women* (Monterey, CA: Brooks / Cole, 1977); Julia Sherman and Florence L. Denmark, *The Psychology of Women: Future Directions of Research* (New York: Psychological Dimensions, 1978); *Psychology of Women*, ed. Juanita Williams (New York: Norton, 1979); Stephanie A. Shields, "The Variability Hypothesis: The History of a Biological Model of Sex Differences in Intelligence," *Signs* 7.4 (summer 1982): 769–97; *Women, Gender, and Social Psychology*, ed. Virginia E. O'Leary, Rhoda K. Unger, and B. S. Wallston (Hillsdale, NJ: Erlbaum, 1985); and *Lesbian Psychologies: Explorations and Challenges*, ed. Boston Lesbian Psychologies Collective (Urbana: University of Illinois Press, 1987).

To sample early discussions of psychoanalytic theory, see Simone de Beauvoir, *The Second Sex*, trans. H. M. Parshley (New York: Knopf, 1953); Betty Friedan, *The Feminine Mystique* (New York: Norton, 1963); Kate Millett, *Sexual Politics* (New York: Doubleday, 1970); Shulamith Firestone, *The Dialectic of Sex: The Case for Feminist Revolution* (New York: Bantam, 1971); Phyllis Chesler, *Women and Madness* (New York: Doubleday, 1972); *Psychoanalysis and Women*, ed. Jean Baker Miller (New York: Brunner / Mazell, 1973); and Juliet Mitchell, *Psychoanalysis and Feminism* (New York: Pantheon, 1974), the most important analysis of that time.

40   Inge K. Broverman et al., "Sex-Role Stereotypes and Clinical Judgments of Mental Health," *Journal of Consulting Psychology* 34 (1970): 232–42; Inge K. Broverman et al., "Sex-Role Stereotypes: A Current Appraisal," *Journal of Social Issues* 28.2 (1972): 59–79.

41   Alfred McClung Lee's "Steps Taken Toward Liberating Sociologists," in *Radical Sociologists and the Movement: Experiences, Lessons, and Legacies*, ed. Martin Oppenheimer,

Martin J. Murray, and Rhonda F. Levine (Philadelphia: Temple University Press, 1991), 31–33 (on spssi); and "Statement of Purpose," *Journal of Social Issues* 28.2 (1972): front matter, n.p. (on *JSI*'s mission).

42 Martha Shuch Mednick and Sandra Schwartz Tangri, "New Social Psychological Perspectives on Women," *Journal of Social Issues* 28.2 (1972): 13–14.

43 Maccoby and Jacklin, *Psychology*, 374 (first quotation), 373 (second quotation).

44 For specific examples, see Sandra L. Bem, "The Measurement of Psychological Androgyny," *Journal of Consulting and Clinical Psychology* 88 (1974): 155–62; L. Z. McArthur and B. G. Resko, "The Portrayal of Men and Women in American Television Commercials," *Journal of Social Psychology* 97 (1975): 209–20; Janice Gump, "A Comparative Analysis of Black and White Women's Sex-Role Attitudes," *Journal of Consulting and Clinical Psychology* 43 (1975): 858–63; Diane K. Lewis, "The Black Family: Socialization and Sex Roles," *Phylon* 36.3 (1975): 221–27; and M. R. Malson, "Black Women's Sex Roles: The Social Context for a New Ideology," *Journal of Social Issues* 39.3 (1983): 101–13.

The shift in terminology from *sex* to *gender* was noted by Reesa M. Vaughter in "Review Essay: Psychology," *Signs* 2.1 (autumn 1976): 123. She used *sex roles* to denote only the irreducible reproductive features and functions (e.g., ovulation, menstruation, gestation, lactation, spermatogenesis, and ejaculation), *sex-role identity* to denote one's experience of the self as physiologically sexed, and *gender* to indicate that identities and roles arise from a social system organized around the assigning of sex.

45 See Maccoby and Jacklin, *Psychology*, 3–6, 8–10, 17–19; and Rhoda K. Unger, *Female and Male: Psychological Perspectives* (New York: Harper & Row, 1979), 4. Many years ago, when Unger was writing articles about methodological problems in psychology, we had a conversation about the null hypothesis from which I also draw here. For subsequent reviews of method, see Carol N. Jacklin, "Methodological Issues in the Study of Sex-Related Differences," in *Methodological Issues in Sex Roles and Social Change,* ed. J. Wirtenberg and B. L. Jackson (New York: Praeger, 1983), 173–96; Kay Deux, "From Individual Differences to Social Categories: Analysis of a Decade's Research on Gender," *American Psychologist* 39 (1984): 105–16; and Vita Carulli Rabinowitz and Jeri A. Sechzer, "Feminist Perspectives on Research Methods," in Denmark and Paludi, *Psychology,* 23–66.

46 Rayna R. Reiter, Introduction to *Toward an Anthropology of Women,* ed. Rayna R. Reiter (New York: Monthly Review Press, 1975), 12.

47 To sample the work, see *Woman, Culture, and Society,* ed. Michelle Zimbalist Rosaldo and Louise Lamphere (Stanford, CA: Stanford University Press, 1974); Reiter, *Toward an Anthropology; Perceiving Women,* ed. Shirley Ardener (London: Dent, 1975); Jane B. Lancaster, *Primate Behavior and the Emergence of Human Culture* (New York: Holt, Rinehart & Winston, 1975); Nancy Tanner and Adrienne L. Zihlman, "Women in Evolution, Part I: Innovation and Selection in Human Origins," *Signs* 1.3 (spring 1976): 585–608; Adrienne L. Zihlman, "Women in Evolution, Part II: Susbsistence and Social Organization among Early Hominids," *Signs* 4.1 (autumn 1978): 4–20; and Donna Haraway, "Animal Sociology and a Natural Economy of the Body Politic, Part II: The

Past Is the Contested Zone—Human Nature and Theories of Production and Reproduction in Primate Behavior Studies," *Signs* 4.1 (autumn 1978): 37–60. For an overview of the many factors contributing to the social organization of the sexes, see Peggy R. Sanday, "Female Status in the Public Domain," in Rosaldo and Lamphere, *Woman,* 189–206.

The review essays published in *Signs*—Carol B. Stack et al., "Review Essay: Anthropology," *Signs* 1.1 (autumn 1975): 147–59; and Louise Lamphere, "Review Essay: Anthropology," *Signs* 2.3 (spring 1977): 612–27—show that the early feminist work took one or more of three paths: (1) criticizing the traditional work in primatology, archaeology, and anthropology; (2) providing empirically based accounts of human evolution, non-Western cultures, and communities in Western societies; and / or (3) refuting biologistic theories of male domination / female subordination and presenting new theories. For a later essay that brings out the cross-cultural and intracultural texture of feminist anthropology, see Micaela di Leonardo, "Contingencies of Value in Feminist Anthropology," in *(En)Gendering Knowledge: Feminists in Academe,* ed. Joan E. Hartman and Ellen Messer-Davidow (Knoxville: University of Tennessee Press, 1991), 140–58.

48   See Reiter, "Introduction," 11–19 (quotation 12); and Michele Zimbalist Rosaldo and Louise Lamphere, Preface and Introduction to Rosaldo and Lamphere *Woman,* v–vi, 1–15. The anthropological literature discusses the problems of access in doing fieldwork. If a male researcher is not permitted to observe a certain transaction among women and the women are reluctant to report to him, then he is placed in the position of either using male informants or minimizing his account. In earlier years the problem of inadequate access and description was an effect of the predominantly male discipline; today it is obviated by putting more women anthropologists in the field and by using a male-female team of anthropologists.

49   See, for instance, Ruby Rohrlich-Leavitt, Barbara Sykes, and Elizabeth Weatherford, "Aboriginal Woman: Male and Female Anthropological Perspectives," in Reiter, *Toward an Anthropology,* 110–26.

50   Reiter, "Introduction," 13–14.

51   Gayle Rubin, "The Traffic in Women: Notes on the 'Political Economy' of Sex," in Reiter, *Toward an Anthropology,* 157 (first and second quotations), 159 (third and fourth quotations). I don't want to give the impression that Rubin was the only feminist reading this wide range of works in the mid-1970s. See Mitchell, *Psychoanalysis and Feminism*; and Catharine MacKinnon, "Feminism, Marxism, Method, and the State: An Agenda for Theory," *Signs* 7.3 (1982): 514–44 (MacKinnon notes that she wrote an early version in 1973 and circulated it for criticism).

52   Rubin, "Traffic," 165–68.

53   Sandra Harding, "Why Has the Sex / Gender System Become Visible Only Now?" in *Discovering Reality: Feminist Perspectives on Epistemology, Metaphysics, Methodology, and Philosophy of Science,* ed. Sandra Harding and Merrill B. Hintikka (Dordrecht: Reidel, 1983), 312 (first three quotations), 311 (fourth quotation).

54 To sample the literature, see Dorothy E. Smith, "Women's Perspective as a Radical Critique of Sociology," *Sociological Inquiry* 44 (1974): 7–14; Dorothy E. Smith, "A Sociology for Women," in *The Prism of Sex: Essays in the Sociology of Knowledge,* ed. Julia A. Sherman and Evelyn Torton Beck (Madison: University of Wisconsin Press, 1979), 135–87; Nancy Hartsock, "The Feminist Standpoint: Developing the Ground for a Specifically Feminist Historical Materialism," in Harding and Hintikka, *Discovering Reality,* 283–310; Nancy Hartsock, *Money, Sex, and Power* (New York: Longman, 1983); Dorothy E. Smith, *The Everyday World as Problematic: A Feminist Sociology* (Boston: Northeastern University Press, 1987), esp. 78–88, 105–17; Patricia Hill Collins, *Black Feminist Thought: Knowledge, Consciousness, and the Politics of Empowerment* (New York: HarperCollins, 1991), esp. 21–39, 201–19; Sandra Harding, *Whose Science? Whose Knowledge? Thinking from Women's Lives* (Ithaca, NY: Cornell University Press, 1991), esp. 169–87, 268–95; Sandra Harding, "Rethinking Standpoint Epistemology: 'What Is Strong Objectivity?' " in *Feminist Epistemologies,* ed. Linda Alcoff and Elizabeth Potter (New York: Routledge, 1993), 49–82; and Bat-Ami Bar On, "Marginality and Epistemic Privilege," in Alcoff and Potter, *Feminist Epistemologies,* 83–100.

55 Sandra Harding, "Who Knows? Identities and Feminist Epistemology," in Hartman and Messer-Davidow, *(En)Gendering Knowledge,* 101.

56 Patricia Hill Collins, "Learning from the Outsider Within: The Sociological Significance of Black Feminist Thought," in Hartman and Messer-Davidow, *(En)Gendering Knowledge,* 55, 47.

57 Joyce A. Ladner, *Tomorrow's Tomorrow: The Black Woman,* 25th anniversary ed. (Lincoln: University of Nebraska Press, 1995), 101 (first quotation), 283 (second and third quotations). To understand how Ladner designed her research, see the two introductions and the conclusion.

58 For applications, see Nancy Chodorow, *The Reproduction of Mothering: Psychoanalysis and the Sociology of Gender* (Berkeley: University of California Press, 1978). Carol Gilligan, *In a Different Voice: Psychological Theory and Women's Development* (Cambridge: Harvard University Press, 1982); Mary Field Belenky, Blythe McVicker Clinchy, Nancy Rule Goldberger, and Jill Mattuck Tarule, *Women's Ways of Knowing: The Development of Self, Voice, and Mind* (New York: Basic Books, 1986); Jane Flax, "Political Philosophy and the Patriarchal Unconscious: A Psychoanalytic Perspective on Epistemology and Metaphysics," in Harding and Hintikka, *Discovering Reality,* 245–81; Judith Kegan Gardiner, "On Female Identity and Writing by Women," *Critical Inquiry* 8.2 (winter 1981): 347–61; Coppélia Kahn, "The Hand That Rocks the Cradle: Recent Gender Theories and Their Implications," in *The (M)other Tongue: Essays in Feminist Psychoanalytic Interpretation,* ed. Shirley Nelson Garner, Claire Kahane, and Madelon Sprengnether (Ithaca, NY: Cornell University Press, 1985), 72–88; Gayle Greene, "Women and Men in Doris Lessing's *Golden Notebook:* Divided Selves," in Garner et al., *(M)other Tongue,* 280–305; Evelyn Fox Keller, *Reflections on Gender and Science* (New Haven, CT: Yale University Press, 1985); and Susan R. Bordo, *The Flight to Objectivity: Essays on Cartesianism and Culture* (Albany: State University of New York Press, 1987).

59   See Judith Lorber, Rose Laub Coser, Alice S. Rossi, and Nancy Chodorow, "On *The Reproduction of Mothering*: A Methodological Debate," *Signs* 6.3 (spring 1981): 482–514 (Lorber quotations 482–83; Rossi quotations 493–94).

60   Elizabeth V. Spelman, *Inessential Woman: Problems of Exclusion in Feminist Thought* (Boston: Beacon, 1988), 80–113. See also Ralph Larossa and Maureen Mulligan Larossa's "Baby Case: Fathers vs. Mothers," Barbara J. Risman's "Can Men 'Mother'? Life as a Single Father," both in *Gender in Intimate Relationships: A Microstructural Approach*, ed. Barbara J. Risman and Pepper Schwartz (Belmont, CA: Wadsworth, 1989), 138–54, 155–64, respectively.

61   Nancy J. Chodorow, *Feminism and Psychoanalytic Theory* (New Haven, CT: Yale University Press, 1989), esp. "Introduction: Feminism and Psychoanalytic Theory."

62   Adrienne Rich, "Compulsory Heterosexuality and Lesbian Existence," *Signs* 5.4 (summer 1980): 631–60; and Deborah Pope, Naomi Quinn, and Mary Wyer, "Editorial," *Signs* 15.3 (spring 1990): 446 (both quotations).

63   Susan Stanford Friedman, "Beyond White and Other: Relationality and Narratives of Race in Feminist Discourse," *Signs* 21.1 (autumn 1995): 1–49; for examples of the scripts, see 9–11.

64   See David Karen, "The Politics of Class, Race, and Gender: Access to Higher Education in the United States, 1960–1986," *American Journal of Higher Education* 99.2 (February 1991): 208–37.

65   Scott Carlson, "Minority Students Posted Slight Increase in College Enrollment in 1997, Report Says," *Chronicle of Higher Education*, 17 December 1999, A53; Denise K. Magner, "Number of Minority Ph.D.'s Reached an All-Time High in 1996," *Chronicle of Higher Education*, 21 November 1997, A10–11. I have also consulted the *Statistical Abstract of the United States*, 119th ed. (Washington, DC: U.S. Bureau of the Census, 1999). Although statistics are useful tools for gauging patterns, I want to mention some problems. First, the Census Bureau includes American Indians, Eskimos, and Aleuts in the category "Native American," but many other sources do not specify the groups included in that category. Second, sources using the category "Hispanic American" do not capture differences among the groups it includes—for instance, differences in enrollment, field, and degree for Cuban Americans and Chicanos. Third, many sources do not indicate which categories were designated by individuals of mixed races and ethnicities. Finally, comparative proportionality is difficult to ascertain. To determine whether a racial minority group is equitably represented in higher education, most people compare its percentage of the nationwide college enrollment to its percentage of the total U.S. population. But the apt comparison would be the racial minority group's percentage of the total enrollment to its percentage of the college-age cohort within the total U.S. population (probably individuals who are seventeen to thirty years old). Even so, each college-age cohort would need to be nuanced by factors that we know have a differential impact on the races and sexes. Incarceration, poverty, illness, and death, for instance, disproportionately reduce the male cohorts of African and Native Americans.

66 Data from Delores H. Thurgood and Julie E. Clarke, *Doctorate Recipients from United States Universities: Summary Report 1993* (Washington, DC: National Academy of Sciences, 1995), 23, 24, 49, 52; Robert O. Simmons and Delores H. Thurgood, *Doctorate Recipients from United States Universities: Summary Report 1994* (Washington, DC: National Academy of Sciences, 1995), 49, 52; and Peter H. Henderson, Julie E. Clarke, and Mary A. Reynolds, *Doctorate Recipients from United States Universities: Summary Report 1995* (Washington, DC: National Academy of Sciences, 1996), 105, 108.

67 Alison Schneider, "Affirmative Action's Impact on Academe Has Been Minimal, a New Book Argues," *Chronicle of Higher Education*, 24 March 2000, A20.

68 See Nellie McKay's comments in "Naming the Problem That Led to the Question 'Who Shall Teach African American Literature?'; or, Are We Ready to Disband the Wheatley Court?" *PMLA* 113.3 (May 1998): 363–64.

69 For this period, the list of mainstream press publications intended for academic readers or crossover audiences would include the following. Anthologies: Toni Cade's *The Black Woman: An Anthology* (New York: Mentor, 1970); Mary Helen Washington's *Black-Eyed Susans: Classic Stories by and about Black Women* (New York: Doubleday, 1975); Roseann P. Bell et al.'s *Sturdy Black Bridges: Visions of Black Women in Literature* (New York: Doubleday, 1979); and Washington's *Midnight Birds: Stories of Contemporary Black Women Writers* (New York: Doubleday, 1980). Reprints: *The Poems of Phillis Wheatley* (Chapel Hill: University of North Carolina Press, 1966) and, thanks to the interest in Zora Neale Hurston sparked by Robert Hemenway's 1977 biography, Hurston's *Mules and Men* (Bloomington: Indiana University Press, 1978), *Their Eyes Were Watching God* (Urbana: University of Illinois Press, 1978), and the Hurston reader, *I Love Myself When I Am Laughing* (Old Westbury, NY: Feminist Press, 1979). Source material: Gerda Lerner's *Black Women in White America* (New York: Vintage, 1972). Social analysis: Joyce Ladner's *Tomorrow's Tomorrow* (New York: Doubleday, 1971); Michelle Wallace's *Black Macho and the Myth of the SuperWoman* (New York: Dial, 1978); and Phyllis Wallace's collection *Black Women in the Labor Force* (Cambridge: MIT Press, 1980).

70 Erlene Stetson, "Black Women in and out of Print," in *Women in Print I: Opportunities for Women's Studies Research in Language and Literature*, ed. Joan E. Hartman and Ellen Messer-Davidow (New York: Modern Language Association, 1982), 87–107 (quotation 94).

71 Besides bibliographies, biographies, and literary reprints (fiction, poetry, drama, and nonfiction), these presses published, for instance, Sharon Harley and Rosalyn Terborg-Penn's *The Afro-American Woman: Struggles and Images* (Port Washington, NY: Kennikat Press, 1978); Dorothy Sterling's *Black Foremothers* (Old Westbury: Feminist Press, 1979); Cherríe Moraga and Gloria Anzaldua's *This Bridge Called My Back: Writings by Radical Women of Color* (Watertown, MA: Persephone Press, 1981); bell hooks's *Ain't I a Woman: Black Women and Feminism* (Boston: South End, 1981); hooks's *Feminist Theory: From Margin to Center* (Boston: South End, 1984); Gloria Hull, Patricia Bell-Scott, and Barbara Smith's *All the Women Are White, All the Blacks Are Men, But Some of Us Are Brave: Black Women's Studies* (Old Westbury: Feminist Press, 1982); Audre

Lorde's *Sister Outsider: Essays and Speeches* (Trumansburg, NY: Crossing, 1983); and Elly Bulkin, Minnie Bruce Pratt, and Barbara Smith's *Yours in Struggle* (Brooklyn: Long Haul, 1984).

72 Notably, Barbara Christian's *Black Women Novelists: The Development of a Tradition, 1892–1976* (Westport, CT: Greenwood, 1980); Angela Davis's *Women, Race, and Class* (New York: Random House, 1981); Erlene Stetson's anthology *Black Sister: Poetry by Black American Women, 1746–1980* (Bloomington: Indiana University Press, 1981); Trudier Harris's *From Mammies to Militants: Domestics in Black American Literature* (Philadelphia: Temple University Press, 1982); and Paula Giddings's *When and Where I Enter: The Impact of Black Women on Race and Sex in America* (New York: William Morrow, 1984).

73 See Margaret A. Simons, "Racism and Feminism: A Schism in the Sisterhood," *Feminist Studies* 5.2 (summer 1979): 385–401; Gloria T. Hull, "Researching Alice Dunbar-Nelson: A Personal and Literary Perspective," *Feminist Studies* 6.2 (summer 1980): 314–20; Bernice Johnson Reagon, "My Black Mothers and Sisters or on Beginning a Cultural Autobiography," *Feminist Studies* 8.1 (spring 1982): 81–96; Jacqueline Jones, " 'My Mother Was Much of a Woman': Black Women, Work, and the Family under Slavery," *Feminist Studies* 8.2 (summer 1982): 235–70; Suzanne Lebsock, "Free Black Women and the Question of Matriarchy: Petersburg, Virginia," *Feminist Studies* 8.2 (summer 1982): 271–90; and Paul Lauter, "Race and Gender in the Shaping of the American Literary Canon: A Case Study from the Twenties," *Feminist Studies* 9.3 (fall 1983): 435–64. During this decade, *Feminist Studies* also published some poetry by women of color and articles on issues of race and gender in the civil rights movement. See, for instance, Mary Aickin Rothchild's "White Women Volunteers in the Freedom Summers: Their Life and Work in a Movement for Social Change"; and Wini Breines's "A Review Essay: Sara Evans's *Personal Politics*," both in *Feminist Studies* 5.3 (fall 1979): 466–94, 495–506, respectively.

74 Inez Reid Smith, "Viewpoint: Science, Politics, and Race," *Signs* 1.2 (winter 1975): 397–422; Walter R. Allen, "Family Roles, Occupational Statuses, and Achievement Orientations among Black Women in the United States," *Signs* 4.4 (summer 1979): 470–86; Diane K. Lewis, "A Response to Inequality: Black Women, Racism, and Sexism," *Signs* 3.2 (winter 1977): 339–61; Bonnie Thornton Dill, "The Dialectics of Black Womanhood," *Signs* 4.3 (spring 1979): 543–55. Although it was not focused exclusively on African-American women, I include the Smith article because in many ways it was the most radical analysis of institutionalized racism published by *Signs* during this decade.

75 Ethel Klein, "The Diffusion of Consciousness in the United States and Western Europe," in *The Women's Movements of the United States and Western Europe*, ed. Mary Fainsod Katzenstein and Carol McClurg Mueller (Philadelphia: Temple University Press, 1987), 24.

76 See Gunnar Myrdal, *An American Dilemma: The Negro Problem and Modern Democracy* (New York: Harper & Row, 1944); Helen Hacker, "Women as a Minority Group," *Social Forces* 30 (October 1951): 60–69; Casey Hayden and Mary King, "Sex and Caste," *Liberation* 10.2 (April 1966), 35–36; and Caroline Bird, *Born Female: The High Cost of Keeping Women Down* (New York: David McKay, 1968), chap. 6.

77 Lerner, "New Approaches to the Study of Women," in Lerner, *Majority,* 8 (first quotation), 10 (second quotation) (rpt. from the *Journal for Social History* 3.1 [fall 1969]: 53–62).

78 Gayle Rubin, "Woman as Nigger," in *Masculine / Feminine: Readings in Sexual Mythology and the Liberation of Women,* ed. Betty Roszak and Theodore Roszak (New York: Harper, 1969), 231; originally published in *The Argus* (1969), a University of Michigan newspaper, Rubin took her title from Jerry Farber's *The Student as Nigger* (1969), which circulated widely in the New Left, educational reform, and women's movements. Rubin's essay drew on a variety of sources, including sociologists Myrdal, Hacker, and Julius Lester, psychologists Daryl and Sandra Bem, philosophers Sartre and de Beauvoir, literary texts, movement writings, and a People Against Racism training session she had attended.

79 Rubin, "Woman as Nigger," 240.

80 Frances M. Beale, "Double Jeopardy: To Be Black and Female," in *Sisterhood Is Powerful: An Anthology of Writings from the Women's Liberation Movement,* ed. Robin Morgan (New York: Random House, 1970), 350; Pauli Murray, "The Liberation of Black Women," in *Voices of the New Feminism,* ed. Mary Lou Thompson (Boston: Beacon, 1970), 100 (first quotation), 101 (second quotation); and Mary Ann Weathers, "An Argument for Black Women's Liberation As a Revolutionary Force," in *Voices from Women's Liberation,* ed. Leslie B. Tanner (New York: Mentor, 1970), 303–7. White feminist Marlene Dixon made similar points about interlocking oppressions and struggles in "Why Women's Liberation?" *Ramparts* 8.6 (December 1969): 58–63.

81 Zillah Eisenstein, "Developing a Theory of Capitalist Patriarchy and Socialist Feminism," in *Capitalist Patriarchy and the Case for Socialist Feminism,* ed. Zillah R. Eisenstein (New York: Monthly Review Press, 1979), 5.

82 Iris Young, "Beyond the Unhappy Marriage: A Critique of the Dual Systems Theory," in *Women and Revolution: A Discussion of the Unhappy Marriage of Marxism and Feminism,* ed. Lydia Sargent (Boston: South End, 1981), 44; Emily Hicks, "Cultural Marxism: Nonsynchrony and Feminist Practice," in Sargent, *Women and Revolution,* 219–37.

83 Jacqueline Dowd Hall, " 'The Mind That Burns in Each Body': Women, Rape, and Racial Violence," in *Powers of Desire: The Politics of Sexuality,* ed. Ann Snitow, Christine Stansell, and Sharon Thompson (New York: Monthly Review Press, 1983), 328–49.

84 Deborah K. King, "Multiple Jeopardy, Multiple Consciousness: The Context of a Black Feminist Ideology," *Signs* 14.1 (autumn 1988): 42–72.

85 Annette Kolodny, "Dancing Through the Minefield: Some Observations on the Theory, Practice, and Politics of a Feminist Literary Criticism," *Feminist Studies* 6.1 (spring 1980): 8–9 (all quotations).

86 Ibid., 16 (first quotation), 19 (second quotation).

87 Rena Grasso Patterson, in Judith Kegan Gardiner, Elly Bulkin, Rena Grasso Patterson, and Annette Kolodny, "An Interchange on Feminist Criticism: On 'Dancing Through the Minefield,' " *Feminist Studies* 8.3 (fall 1982): 659. For the entire interchange, see pages 629–75. Interestingly, all of the authors were veterans of feminist struggle who understood how the social and intellectual orders worked to create conflicts. Gar-

diner, an activist in the Chicago Women's Liberation Union during the 1970s, was a professor of English and women's studies at the University of Illinois in Chicago and had published on identity issues. Bulkin, a longtime Jewish lesbian-feminist activist in New York, a founding editor of *Conditions,* and an editor of two lesbian anthologies, also worked on identity issues, including the Arab-Israeli conflict. Patterson, an activist living in New York City, had been coordinator of the radical Women's Studies College at the State University of New York in Buffalo. Kolodny, at that point the author of a book and several articles, had won an out-of-court settlement of her sex-discrimination and anti-Semitism lawsuit against the University of New Hampshire, had established a legal defense fund to help other academic women, and after several years of unofficial blacklisting would settle into a faculty position at Rennselaer Polytechnic Institute.

88   Patterson, "Interchange," 659 (all quotations). In the second quotation, Patterson is quoting from Lillian Robinson, "Dwelling in Decencies: Radical Criticism and the Feminist Perspective," *College English* 32 (May 1971).

89   Marianne Hirsch and Eveyln Fox Keller, "Introduction: January 4, 1990," in *Conflicts in Feminism,* ed. Marianne Hirsch and Evelyn Fox Keller (New York: Routledge, 1990), 1.

90   See, for instance, Hirsch and Keller, *Conflicts,* esp. Ann Snitow, "A Gender Diary," 9–43; Elspeth Probyn, *Sexing the Self: Gendered Positions in Cultural Studies* (New York: Routledge, 1993); *Feminism Beside Itself,* ed. Diane Elam and Robyn Wiegman (New York: Routledge, 1995), esp. Cyraina Johnson-Roullier, "The Singularity of Multiplicity: Feminism and the Pitfalls of Valorization," 179–96; *Generations: Academic Feminists in Dialogue,* ed. Devony Looser and E. Ann Kaplan (Minneapolis: University of Minnesota Press, 1997); and *Third Wave Agenda: Being Feminist, Doing Feminism,* ed. Leslie Heywood and Jenifer Drake (Minneapolis: University of Minnesota Press, 1997).

91   Jean O'Barr, *Feminism in Action* (Chapel Hill: University of North Carolina Press, 1994), 280.

92   Chéla Sandoval, "Feminist Forms of Agency and Oppositional Consciousness: U.S. Third World Feminist Criticism," in *Provoking Agents: Gender and Agency in Theory and Practice,* ed. Judith Kegan Gardiner (Urbana: University of Illinois Press, 1995), 210–11.

93   Kathryn Pyne Addelson and Elizabeth Potter, "Making Knowledge," in Hartman and Messer-Davidow, *(En)Gendering Knowledge,* 273 (first and second quotations), 275 (third quotation).

94   Joan Catapano and Marlie P. Wasserman, "Is Publishing Perishing?" *Women's Review of Books* 15.5 (February 1998): 22 (all quotations).

95   In this paragraph, I draw on Mattei Dogan and Robert Pahre, *Creative Marginality: Innovation at the Intersections of Social Sciences* (Boulder: Westview, 1990), 29–36, 53–62; and Julie Thompson Klein, *Crossing Boundaries: Knowledge, Disciplinarities, and Interdisciplinarities* (Charlottesville: University Press of Virginia, 1996), esp. 22–27, 42–52.

96   For a fuller discussion of comodification and fragmentation, see Norman Fairclough, *Discourse and Social Change* (Cambridge, U.K.: Polity, 1992), 218–23.

97   For the influx of poststructuralism into American literary studies, see Vincent B. Leitch, *American Literary Criticism from the 30s to the 80s* (New York: Columbia Univer-

sity Press, 1988), esp. 238–308; and *The Structuralist Controversy: The Languages of Criticism and the Sciences of Man,* ed. Richard Macksey and Eugenio Donato, 2d ed. (Baltimore: Johns Hopkins University Press, 1972), esp. xv–xix.

English translations published during the 1970s include Foucault's *The Order of Things* (1970), *The Archaeology of Knowledge* (1972), *The Birth of the Clinic* (1975), *Discipline and Punish* (1977), *Language, Counter-Memory, Practice* (1977), and *The History of Sexuality,* vol. 1 (1978); Derrida's *Speech and Phenomenon* (1973), *Of Grammatology* (1976), and *Writing and Difference* (1978); Jean-François Lyotard's *The Postmodern Condition* (1977); Gilles Deleuze and Felix Guattari's *Anti-Oedipus* (1977); and Lacan's *Ecrits* (1977) and *The Four Fundamental Concepts of Psychoanalysis* (1978).

For accounts of French feminism in France and the United States, see Claire Duchen, *Feminism in France from May '68 to Mitterrand* (London: Routledge & Kegan Paul, 1986); *The Future of Difference,* ed. Hester Eisenstein and Alice Jardine (Boston: Hall, 1980); and Jane Gallop, *Around 1981: Academic Feminist Literary Theory* (New York: Routledge, 1992).

98 Linda Alcoff, "Cultural Feminism versus Post-Structuralism," *Signs* 13.3 (spring 1988): 418.

99 Christine De Stefano, "Dilemmas of Difference: Feminism, Modernity, and Postmodernism," in *Feminism/Postmodernism,* ed. Linda J. Nicholson (New York: Routledge, 1990), 75; Susan R. Bordo, "Feminism, Postmodernism, and Gender-Scepticism," in Nicholson, *Feminism/Postmodernism,* 145. For a recent collection of criticisms, see *Radically Speaking: Feminism Reclaimed,* ed. Diane Bell and Renate Klein (North Melbourne, Australia: Spinifex, 1996).

100 See Leslie Wahl Rabine, "A Feminist Politics of Non-Identity," *Feminist Studies* 14.1 (spring 1988): 11–31; Joan W. Scott, "Deconstructing Equality-Versus-Difference: Or, the Uses of Post-structuralist Theory for Feminism," *Feminist Studies* 14.1 (spring 1988): 33–50; and Mary Poovey, "Feminism and Deconstruction," *Feminist Studies* 14.1 (spring 1988): 51–65.

101 Nancy Fraser and Linda J. Nicholson, "Social Criticism without Philosophy," in Nicholson, *Feminism/Postmodernism,* 20 (first quotation), 35 (second quotation).

102 I am using the term *enunciations* rather than *statements* to avoid a problem in the translation of Michael Foucault's *The Archaeology of Knowledge and the Discourse on Language,* trans. A. M. Sheridan Smith (New York: Pantheon, 1972). When the translator uses *statements* to render Foucault's *enoncés,* he doesn't capture the referents of the latter term in the *Archaeology* as well as Foucault's *The Birth of the Clinic* and *Discipline and Punish.* In these texts, enunciations are not just verbal or written statements but also instruments, gestures, and actions brought together in meaningfully structured relations. For instance, in handwriting exercise, rifle maneuvers, and ausculation, the actor performs a complex articulation of the body part and the instrument, the gesture and the posture, the self and the other(s).

I borrow the concept of operationalization from Robert Pahre's "Mathematical Discourse and Crossdisciplinary Communities: The Case of Political Economy," *Social Epistemology* 10.1 (January–March 1996): 55–73. Pahre demonstrates that a scholar who borrows from another discourse can take a concept with its operationalization in the donor discourse or without its operationalization in the donor discourse—as occurs when literary scholars apply sociological analysis to literary production versus merely reading literary texts through a sociological lens.

103   The explanations of why feminist groups failed to be inclusive or egalitarian focus on different causes. Jo Freeman foregrounds organizational structure in "The Tyranny of Structurelessness," *Berkeley Journal of Sociology* 17 (1972–73): 151–64, and in *The Politics of Women's Liberation* (New York: McKay, 1975), 71–102, 103–46. Barbara Ryan stresses ideological conflict in "Ideological Purity and Feminism: The U.S. Women's Movement from 1966 to 1975," *Gender and Society* 3.2 (June 1989): 239–57, and in *Feminism and the Women's Movement: Dynamics of Change in Social Movement Ideology and Activism* (New York: Routledge, 1992), 53–64. The contributors to *The Feminist Memoir Project: Voices from Women's Liberation,* ed. Rachel Blau DuPlessis and Ann Snitow (New York: Three Rivers, 1998), variously describe movement inclusivity or exclusivity and group solidarity or conflict.

104   Later inclusivity, equality, and difference were the themes of the "equality versus difference" debates, which focused on the proper analytic to be used in feminist research and the positions to be taken on public policy. With regard to public policy, the sameness / difference and equality / inequality rules produced such positions as: female employees should have access to pregnancy and childbirth leaves not available to male employees, female employees should have the same amount of medical leave as male employees even if they have to work under physical circumstances not borne by male employees, employees of both sexes should have the same leave allotment but to be used for purposes they designate, and employees should have leave allotments adjustable to their life circumstances. With respect to feminist objectives, the rules produced such dualistic positions as: feminist research should retain its focus on women or should crosshatch this category with racial, ethnic, national, sexual, and class differences and feminist research should advocate for equal treatment or for situationally sensitive treatment.

Four articles on the equality versus difference problem, now conveniently reprinted together in *Feminist Social Thought: A Reader,* ed. Diana Tietjens Meyers (New York: Routledge, 1997), are particularly edifying: Wendy W. Williams, "The Equality Crisis: Some Reflections on Culture, Courts, and Feminism," 696–713; Christine A. Littleton, "Reconstructing Sexual Equality," 715–34; Joan W. Scott, "Deconstructing Equality-Versus-Difference: Or, the Uses of Poststructuralist Theory for Feminism," 759–70; and Chantal Mouffe, "Feminism, Citizenship, and Radical Democratic Politics," 532–44. Mouffe and Littleton do the best job of untangling the problem by moving outside of its constitutive rules. Both start with the assumption that everyone is different from everyone else. Where Mouffe theorizes a radical democracy that recognizes plural differences and seeks plural social goods, Littleton examines concrete policy measures that would make differences costless to their bearers.

105   For early conservative criticisms, see Midge Decter's *The New Chastity and Other Arguments Against Women's Liberation* (New York: Coward, McCann and Geohegan,

1972), George Gilder's *Sexual Suicide* (New York: Quadrangle, 1973), and Nicholas Davidson's *The Failure of Feminism* (New York: Prometheus, 1988) as well as a steady stream of articles published by *The American Spectator, The New Republic, National Review,* and *Commentary.* For later ones, see Katherine Kersten, "What Do Women Want? A Conservative Feminist Manifesto," *Policy Review* 56 (spring 1991): 4–15; Christina Hoff Sommers, *Who Stole Feminism? How Women Have Betrayed Women* (New York: Simon and Schuster, 1994); and Daphne Patai and Noretta Koertge, *Professing Feminism: Cautionary Tales from the Strange World of Women's Studies* (New York: Basic Books, 1994).

106 Jane Flax, "Postmodernism and Gender Relations in Feminist Theory," *Signs* 12.4 (summer 1987): 623.

Part 3: Crystallizing the Future

1 See my "Manufacturing the Attack on Liberalized Higher Education," *Social Text* 36 (fall 1993): 40–80; "Who (Ac)Counts and How," *MMLA Journal* 27.1 (spring 1994): 26–41; and "Dollars for Scholars: The Real Politics of Humanities Scholarship and Programs," in *The Politics of Research,* ed. E. Ann Kaplan and George Levine (New Brunswick, NJ: Rutgers University Press, 1997), 193–233.

Chapter 6: Remaking Change Agency

1 Sally Covington, *Moving a Public Policy Agenda: The Strategic Philanthropy of Conservative Foundations* (Washington, DC: National Committee for Responsive Philanthropy, July 1997), 13–15 (think tank grants), 7–8 (academic grants). Also see *Buying a Movement: Right-Wing Foundations and American Politics* (Washington, DC: People for the American Way, 1996). Covington's breakdown of where the $88.9 million in academic grants went is so stunning that it bears repeating here: $23 million to conservative academic programs and curricula; $16.8 million to student training, primarily in law, economics, political science, and public policy; $7.8 million to academic-change organizations such as the National Association of Scholars; $7.6 million to university chairs and professorships; $5.7 million to research centers; $6.1 million to domestic policy research; $4.6 million to foreign policy research; $3.1 million to teach judges how to apply economic principles in legal decision making; and $2.1 million to book projects.

2 Covington, *Moving,* 38.

3 *The Heritage Foundation 1991 Annual Report* (Washington, DC: Heritage Foundation, n.d.), 28 (1991 revenues); Covington, *Moving,* 13 (1995 revenues); Charles L. Heatherly (vice president for academic relations, Heritage Foundation), interview with author, Heritage Foundation, Washington, DC, 6 April 1992 (percentages and staffing).

4 Covington, *Moving,* 14.

5 On the reluctance of mainstream foundations to practice strategic grantmaking, see Sally Covington and Larry Parachini, *Foundations in the Newt Era* (Washington, DC: National Committee for Responsive Philanthropy, 1995). I do want to acknowledge that strategic funding is a complicated issue. The Rockefeller Foundation, for instance, has been funding about two dozen academic centers that sponsor social-

justice research, but whether the research is strategic depends upon its applicability to policy formation and other types of social-change practice.

6 Leslie R. Wolfe (president, Center for Women Policy Studies), interview with author, Center for Women Policy Studies, Washington, DC, 10 June 1992; and "Center for Women Policy Studies," brochure, Washington, DC, Center for Women Policy Studies, n.d.

7 Heidi Hartman (director, Institute for Women's Policy Research), interview with author, Institute for Women's Policy Research, Washington, DC, 23 November 1992; "List of Publications, Spring 1992," Institute for Women's Policy Research, May 1992, mimeo, 6 pp.; Heidi Hartman and Roberta Spalter-Roth, "Why an Institute for Women's Policy Research?" Institute for Women's Policy Research, October 1991, mimeo, 4 pp.; conference program, Exploring the Quincentennial: The Policy Challenges of Gender, Diversity, and International Exchange, Third Women's Policy Research Conference, cosponsored by the Institute for Women's Policy Research and the American University Department of Sociology, American University, Washington, DC, 15–16 May 1992.

8 Betty Parsons Dooley (executive director, Women's Research and Education Institute), interview with author, Women's Research and Education Institute, Washington, DC, 23 November 1992; untitled brochure, Washington, DC, WREI, n.d.; "WREI Awards Ten Congressional Fellowships," press release, Women's Research and Education Institute, October 1992; "WREI Congressional Fellowships, 1992–1993," program information, Washington, DC, WREI, n.d.

9 For studies of feminist social change in the political, policy, grassroots, and community service sectors, see Kay Lehman Schlozman, "Representing Women in Washington: Sisterhood and Pressure Politics," in *Women, Politics, and Change*, ed. Louise A. Tilly and Patricia Gurin (New York: Russell Sage Foundation, 1990), 339–82; *Feminist Organizations: Harvest of the New Women's Movement*, ed. Myra Marx Ferree and Patricia Yancey Martin (Philadelphia: Temple University Press, 1995); *Women Transforming Politics*, ed. Cathy J. Cohen, Kathleen B. Jones, and Joan C. Tronto (New York: New York University Press, 1997); and *Community Activism and Feminist Politics: Organizing Across Race, Class, and Gender*, ed. Nancy A. Naples (New York: Routledge, 1998).

10 Information from "Women's Groups Organizing Another National Federation," *Responsive Philanthropy* (fall 1994): 1–2 (on Women's Ways USA); and Joan E. Berlin, cover letter and "The Women's Roundtable," statement of purpose, April 1996.

11 Betty Parsons Dooley, interview with author, 23 November 1992. The Ford meeting was held on 12 November 1992.

12 Adam Meyerson's interview of Edwin J. Feulner, Jr., "Building the New Establishment," *Policy Review* 58 (fall 1991): 9.

13 See Paul Gottfried, *The Conservative Movement*, rev. ed. (New York: Twayne, 1993), 91–92.

14 Feulner, "Building," 13.

15 The information in this section, unless otherwise cited, comes from my notes while

attending Ideas Have Consequences: A Conservative Battleplan for the 1990s, the Fifteenth Annual Resource Bank Meeting, Heritage Foundation, Chicago, IL, 23–24 April 1992; and the conference program and expected attendance list (Heritage Foundation, n.d.), both of which were included in the registration packet.

16   Author's notes, Building New Grassroots Coalitions: Family Policy and Economic Growth, Fifteenth Annual Resource Bank Meeting. The moderator was John Cooper (president, James Madison Institute for Public Policy Studies); the panelists were Robert Rector (policy analyst, Heritage Foundation), Gary Palmer (executive director, Alabama Family Alliance), and Don Eberly (president, Commonwealth Foundation [a Pennsylvania think tank]).

17   Author's notes, Conservatives and Congress: How We Can Prevail? Fifteenth Annual Resource Bank Meeting. The moderator was Kate Walsh O'Beirne (vice president of government relations, Heritage Foundation), and the panelists were Doug Badger (assistant staff director, Senate Republican Policy Committee) and Becca Tice (legislative director, Office of Congressman Charles Stenholm [D-Tex.]).

18   Author's notes, Conservatives and Congress: How We Can Prevail? Fifteenth Annual Resource Bank Meeting.

19   Author's notes, Building New Grassroots Coalitions: Family Policy and Economic Growth, Fifteenth Annual Resource Bank Meeting.

20   Author's notes, Reinventing Federalism, Fifteenth Annual Resource Bank Meeting. The moderator was Charles Heatherly (vice president for academic relations, Heritage Foundation), and the panelists were William Bennett (Cultural Policy Studies Distinguished Fellow, Heritage Foundation), Donald Devine (president, Citizens for America), and Tex Lezar (president, Texas Public Policy Foundation).

21   For diametrically opposed assessments of Wisconsin's w-2 (workfare-welfare) program, see Governor Tommy Thompson's interview with Adam Meyerson, "Land of Milk and Money," *Policy Review* 56 (spring 1991): 31–35; and "In Our Own Words: Mothers' Perspectives on Welfare Reform," a report prepared for the Stewart Mott Foundation by the Women and Poverty Public Education Initiative, 1997. (As of May 2001, copies can be obtained from Anne Statham, outreach coordinator, Women's Studies Consortium Outreach Program, University of Wisconsin, Parkside, 900 Woods Road, Box 2000, Kenosha, WI 53141–2000). "In Our Own Words" reports on a large-scale study conducted by women's studies faculty at the University of Wisconsin; it uses quantitative as well as qualitative data from four in-depth interviews with each of two hundred women to analyze the effects of w-2 on women's and children's lives. Contrary to the conservative myth, these welfare mothers were committed to leading economically and socially productive lives and "rank[ed] education as their number one concern." But w-2 locked them into "low-level jobs with little hope of advancing to a position that offers benefits and a family-supporting wage" (quotations from letter to the author, Katherine A. Rhoades [professor of Women's Studies, University of Wisconsin, Eau Claire], 17 February 1998). Indeed, the majority of state workfare-welfare programs allow recipients only short-term job training or two years of postsecondary education in vocational programs—and that on top of the onerous

requirement of year-round employment (see Peter Schmidt, "States Discourage Welfare Recipients From Pursuing a Higher Education," *Chronicle of Higher Education*, 23 January 1998, A34).

22 Author's notes, Tomorrow's Town Hall: Technology as Empowerment, Fifteenth Annual Resource Bank Meeting.

23 Information from Michael Schwartz (senior vice president, Coalition for America Broadcasting Network), interviews with author, Free Congress Foundation, Washington, DC, 10 June 1992 (quotations from this date) and 24 November 1992; *Family Forum Live,* author's observation, Free Congress Foundation, Washington, DC, 17 November 1992; and *Annual Report, 1995* (Washington, DC: Free Congress Research and Education Foundation, n.d.). The November 1992 broadcast of *Family Forum Live* featured Gary Thomas (Christian Action Council), Darla St. Martin and Doug Johnson (National Right to Life), and Chip Mellor (Institute for Justice).

24 "Heritage Foundation to Host Lecture Series on 'Defining Conservatism,'" press release, Heritage Foundation, Washington, DC, 15 October 1992, 2 pp. (Feulner quotation). Other information from "Defining Conservatism," double-sided flier, Heritage Foundation, Washington, DC [1992], 1 p.; "Shaping America's Values Debate," single-sided flier, Heritage Foundation, Washington, DC, [1992], 1 p.; and author's notes, "Ideas and Strategies to Unite the Conservative Majority," lecture by Paul Weyrich (president, Free Congress Foundation), Heritage Foundation, Washington, DC, 24 November 1992. Series speakers included Heritage Fellows William Bennett and Edwin Meese, Heritage vice presidents Kate Walsh O'Beirne and Stuart Butler, perennial favorites Jeane Kirkpatrick and Dinesh D'Souza, and the heads of other organizations: Free Congress Foundation (FCF) President Weyrich, Intercollegiate Studies Institute (ISI) President Cribb, National Association of Scholars (NAS) President Steve Balch, Madison Center for Educational Affairs (MCEA) Executive Vice President Charles Horner, Center for the Study of Popular Culture President David Horowitz, and Bradley Foundation President Michael Joyce.

25 Information from William Forrest (vice president for programs, Leadership Institute), interview with author, Leadership Institute, Springfield, VA, 9 June 1992; assorted program announcements from William Forrest; and *The Leadership Institute Prospectus* (Springfield, VA: Leadership Institute, n.d.).

26 Congressman Dick Armey, direct mail letter, Leadership Institute, 8 June 1991, 5; *Building Leadership: The Newsletter of the Leadership Institute* 6.1 (1992): 1, 5.

27 Chris Warden (editor, National Journalism Center), interview with author, National Journalism Center, Washington, DC, 3 April 1992; Mal Klein (associate editor, National Journalism Center), interview with author, National Journalism Center, Washington, DC, 3 April 1992.

28 *E&RI 1990 Annual Report* (Washington, DC: Education and Research Institute, n.d.), 1, 6–9; montage of newsclips displayed at the National Journalism Center, n.d.

29 My research on ISI was so extensive that I cannot cite all the materials I gathered. They include seventeen issues of *The Intercollegiate Review* (1989–97), twenty-one issues of *Campus* (1991–97), dozens of fliers and direct mail letters, a speakers directory, a guide

to campus activism, and observation of The Upper Midwest Leadership Conference, Minneapolis, MN, 10 October 1992. The ISI acquired the Collegiate Network (some eighty student newspapers) from the Madison Center on Educational Affairs.

30 In return for tuition and $3,000, ISI's Weaver fellows "must do graduate work for the purpose of teaching at the college level." In return for a $10,000 grant, Salvatori fellows "must do graduate work in a field related to the American Founding" and prepare "for a lifelong teaching career in the liberal arts or social sciences at the college level." Information from "The Richard M. Weaver Fellowship Awards Program of the Intercollegiate Studies Institute for Graduate Studies during the 1993–94 Academic Year," double-sided flier with information and application form, Bryn Mawr, PA, Intercollegiate Studies Association, n.d., 1 p.; and "ISI Salvatori Fellowship Program," double-sided flier with information and application form, Bryn Mawr, PA, Intercollegiate Studies Association, n.d., 1 p. (but for the 1993–94 academic year). Although its organizational fliers say that ISI spends a minimum of $125,000 per year on these fellowships, Christopher Long, an ISI associate, mentioned $200,000 per year at ISI's Upper Midwest Leadership Conference (cosponsored by the Fund for American Studies and Young America's Foundation), Minneapolis, MN, 10 October 1992.

31 For the period 1992 through 1996, I examined thirteen issues of *Campus Leader: A Newsletter for Student Leaders from Young America's Foundation* and ten issues of *Libertas: The Voice of Freedom on Campus.*

32 For a study of how this process worked in the case of the National Endowment for the Humanities, see my "Dollars for Scholars: The Real Politics of Humanities Scholarship and Programs," in *The Politics of Research,* ed. E. Ann Kaplan and George Levine (New Brunswick, NJ: Rutgers University Press, 1997), 193–233.

33 For the concepts of conservatism's stealth rhetoric and exclusionary politics, I am indebted to Amy Ansell, "The Color of America's Culture Wars," a typescript paper she shared with me.

34 Paula Rothenberg (director, New Jersey Project), interview with author, William Paterson College, Wayne, NJ, 30 March 1992.

35 Wendy Kolmar (director of women's studies, Drew University), interview with author, Madison, NJ, 29 May 1992.

36 Edward D. Goldberg (chancellor, Department of Higher Education), interview with author, Department of Higher Education, Trenton, NJ, 2 June 1992. At the DHE, the New Jersey Project was under the jurisdiction of Assistant Chancellor Goldberg, who became chancellor in 1991.

37 Judith L. Johnston, "The Challenges of the First Year," in *The New Jersey Project: Integrating the Scholarship on Gender, 1986–1989,* ed. Carol H. Smith and Ferris Olin (New Brunswick, NJ: Institute for Research on Women, 1990), 11–16.

38 My information comes from "The New Jersey Project: Integrating the Scholarship on Gender," *Network* (fall 1986): 1; Carol Smith, "Creating a State-Wide Network," in Smith and Olin, *New Jersey Project,* 1–7; Judith S. Johnston (professor of English, Rider College) and Ferris Olin (executive officer, Institute for Research on Women, Rutgers

University), joint interview with author, New Brunswick, NJ, 21 May 1991; and Paula Rothenberg and Wendy Kolmar, interviews with author, cited above.

39 Connie Murray, "The Second Year of the Project: Consolidating the Gains of the First Year," in Smith and Olin, *New Jersey Project,* 17–19; and Corann Okorodudu, "The Third Year: Increasing National Visibility," in Smith and Olin, *New Jersey Project,* 20–25.

40 Numbers from Paula Rothenberg, "The New Jersey Project Enters Its Second Phase," *Women's Studies Quarterly* 18.1–2 (spring–summer 1990): 119.

41 Information on the second phase from Paula Rothenberg, interview with author, 30 March 1992; and Rothenberg's notes written on my interview transcript, 4 August 1992. I consulted a number of publications and documents: Rothenberg, "The New Jersey Project": 119–22; Paula Rothenberg, "The New Jersey Project 1989–90 Year End Report" (n.d.); Paula Rothenberg, "The New Jersey Project: Integrating the Scholarship on Gender, Final Report, July 1991, 1990–91 Academic Year"; Paula Rothenberg, "The New Jersey Project: Integrating the Scholarship on Gender, Preliminary Report, February 1, 1992, 1991–92 Academic Year"; issues of *The New Jersey Project Newsletter;* issues of *Transformations,* the New Jersey Project journal; and assorted conference programs, event announcements, and summer institute applications and programs sent to me by Professor Rothenberg.

42 Conference Program The Inclusive Curriculum: Setting Our Own Agenda, the New Jersey Project, cosponsored with the New Jersey Multicultural Studies Project and the New Jersey College and University Coalition of Women's Education, Parsippany, NJ, 16–18 April 1993; author's notes from the conference.

43 Information from *The New Jersey Project Newsletter,* spring 1995, fall 1995, and fall 1996. The New Jersey Project expanded the journal *Transformations* and began charging subscribers, who had previously received free copies. Its first book, *Creating an Inclusive College Curriculum: A Teaching Sourcebook from the New Jersey Project* (ed. Charles Flint, Ellen Friedman, Wendy Kolmar, and Paula Rothenberg [New York: Teachers College Press, 1995]), sold out within a year and was reprinted in 1996.

44 Announcement of the 1992 Summer Institute circulated to invite applications, Wayne, NJ, New Jersey Project, n.d., double-sided, typed page.

45 Participants' institutions were private colleges (Centenary, Felician), community and county colleges (Camden County, Morris County, Essex County, Hudson County, Passaic County, Sussex County), four-year state colleges (Montclair, Ramopo, Trenton, William Paterson), and research universities (Princeton, Rutgers). Their disciplines included African-American studies, anthropology, art, art history, biology, business, education, English, English as a second language, health sciences, history, legal studies, mathematics, media production, psychology, sociology, and Spanish. Information from a typed list of participants, New Jersey Project 1992 Summer Institute; a typed list of participants by discipline, New Jersey Project 1992 Summer Institute; and a typed list of guest speakers, New Jersey Project 1992 Summer Institute.

46 Unless otherwise cited, my information comes from my notes on the New Jersey Project Summer Institute, Rutgers University, 30 May–2 June 1992; the typed pro-

gram, New Jersey Project 1992 Summer Institute; and the readings packet, New Jersey Project 1992 Summer Institute.

47   Author's notes, Rethinking the Disciplines, New Jersey Project Summer Institute, Rutgers University, 31 May 1992.

48   Author's notes, Discipline Workshops, New Jersey Project Summer Institute, Rutgers University, 31 May 1992.

49   Author's notes during and after Marilyn Frye's talk, New Jersey Project Summer Institute, 30 May 1992.

50   Of the forty-three participants, thirty-four submitted the reflection sheets written the morning after Frye's talk and twenty-seven submitted the five-page evaluations written at the end of the institute.

51   One wrote, "I find her provocative / thoughtful, but feel excluded by her philosophy." The other wrote, "Her work . . . would better have been presented during the day, when I was more awake. I feel I need to read the essays, because I am sure I missed a good part of what she said."

52   A second wrote, "Marilyn Frye opened my mind to a totally new way of thinking, and at my age, this is some accomplishment!" The third wrote, "She went beyond the typical rhetoric of [illegible word] gender theory to introduce ideas that were problematic. . . . This is far more useful than the 'preaching to the converted.' "

53   Edward D. Goldberg (chancellor, Department of Higher Education), interview with author, 2 June 1992; Goldberg's comments written on my interview transcript, 5 August 1992.

54   Population statistics taken from Johnston, "Challenge," 13. Edward D. Goldberg reported in a 1985 speech that the state had nineteen community colleges, one multi-campus state university (Rutgers), nine other state universities, one technological university, sixteen private colleges, eight theological colleges, one medical and dental university, and one proprietary institution licensed to offer degrees (Edward D. Goldberg, "New Jersey's Model for Stimulating Change," in *The State University of New York: The New Liberal Arts, Curriculum in Transition* [Albany: State University of New York Press, 1986], 47–60). Other information in this paragraph is from Irma Lester (professor, Writing Department, Brookdale Community College, Lincroft, NJ), interview with author, Rutgers University, 21 May 1991; Mary S. Hartman, "The Ivory Tower and the Real World: Scholarship and Activism in the Garden State," keynote address, Ninth Annual Celebration of Our Work, Rutgers University, New Brunswick, NJ, 21 May 1991; and Judith L. Johnston, "Telling Our Stories: The Academy and Change," *Women's Studies Quarterly* 18.3–4 (fall–winter 1990): 119–27.

55   Goldberg, "New Jersey's Model," 51–52.

56   Chancellor Goldberg sent me two speeches. In "Remarks on the Occasion of His Swearing In as the Third Chancellor of the New Jersey Higher Education System" (Trenton, NJ, 1 March 1991), he praised the state's gender and multicultural projects. In an untitled speech (delivered at Changing the Subject(s): A Celebration of Six Years of Curriculum Change in New Jersey, New Jersey Project Statewide Conference,

Brookdale Community College, 1 November 1991), he admonished critics who labeled the inclusive curriculum with "the disparaging term, 'political correctness,'" reminding them and his audience that good faculty members are constantly revising their courses to enrich the content and methods.

57 Edward D. Goldberg, "The Development of Higher Education's Involvement in the New Jersey Project," in Smith and Olin, *New Jersey Project,* 8–9.

58 Roger R. Ream (executive vice president, Fund for American Studies), interview with author, Fund for American Studies, Washington, DC, 17 November 1992; Michael J. Collins (dean, School for Summer and Continuing Education, Georgetown University), interview with author, Georgetown University, Washington, DC, 17 November 1992; Fund for American Studies promotional video shown to author on 17 November 1992.

59 Marina C. Sheridan (FAS staff director, ICPES) and Lawrence F. Guillemette Jr. (FAS staff director, IPJ), joint interview with author, Washington, DC, 13 July 1993; Roger R. Ream, interview with author, 11 November 1992.

60 Michael J. Collins, interviews with author, Georgetown University, Washington, DC, 17 November 1992 and 18 June 1993. Also see Michael J. Collins, letter dated 15 September 1992, in *1992 Program Report* (Washington, DC: Fund for American Studies, 1992), [v].

61 Marina C. Sheridan and Lawrence F. Guillemette Jr., joint interview with author, 13 July 1993.

62 Michael J. Collins, interviews with author, 17 November 1992 and 18 June 1993. The School of Summer and Continuing Education arranged for the institute courses, and FAS arranged for student internships, site briefings, and evening lecture events—hence Dean Collins's distinctions about how and where conservatism was manifested.

63 Serving on these boards were associates of the American Enterprise Institute, Citizens for a Sound Economy, Fund for a Conservative Majority, Heritage Foundation, Institute for Justice, Intercollegiate Studies Institute, Lincoln Institute, National Journalism Center, *The New Republic,* and Young America's Foundation. There were no associates from such liberal organizations as the Brookings Institute, American Civil Liberties Union, and People for the American Way (information from *1992 Program Report* [Washington, DC: Fund for American Studies, 1992]).

64 One professor told me that the textbook he had written based on his institute courses was "so right-wing that no one would publish it" and he was "thinking about [sending it to] the Intercollegiate Studies Institute" (author's notes from an after-class discussion with the instructor of Comparative Economic Systems, Institute for Comparative Political and Economic Systems, Georgetown University, 15 June 1993).

65 Author's notes, supper with ICPES professor and four ICPES students, Georgetown, 17 June 1993. An IPJ internship provider who styled herself the "token liberal" on the FAS Alumni Board told me that when her interns complained about IPJ's conservatism she would tell them, "you'd better get used to it because you need to understand the people in power" (Ellen Smith [editor, Pasha Publications], interview with author, Arlington, VA, 15 July 1993). Two liberal female students told me that they were

annoyed with the institute for including no women as instructors and only one, Jeane Kirkpatrick, as a guest speaker. On another occasion, two progressive students, one male and one female, rolled their eyes while saying that they were resigned to the institutes' conservatism.

66 Information from author's conversations with the professors, week of 14 June 1993, Georgetown University, Washington, DC; and syllabus for "Economics in Public Policy," 1993 Institute on Political Journalism, Fund for American Studies and George-town University, one-page, double-sided handout (purpose of course). Noninstitute students in Georgetown's summer school could enroll in the IPJ courses and earn six undergraduate credits (*Georgetown University Summer School 1993* [Washington, DC: Georgetown University, n.d.], 68). In contrast to the purpose described on the course syllabus, FAS's IPJ director Larry Guillemette told me that the goal of the two IPJ courses was to inculcate "ethical leadership and economics literacy" because "the media are an unregulated profession lacking ethical standards" and an understanding of "how the free-market economy works" (Marina C. Sheridan and Lawrence F. Guillemette Jr., joint interview with author, 13 July 1993).

67 Author's notes, "Economics in Public Policy," Georgetown University, 14 June 1993.

68 "Economics in Public Policy," 16 June 1993.

69 Author's notes, "Ethics and the Media," Georgetown University, 14 June 1993.

70 "Ethics and the Media," 14 June and 16 June 1993.

71 "Ethics and the Media," 12 July 1993.

72 All information from "Ethics and the Media," 12, 14, and 16 July 1993.

73 Author's notes, joint session of "Economics in Public Policy" and "Ethics and the Media," Georgetown University, 16 June 1993.

74 Author's notes, discussion session facilitated by Lawrence F. Guillemette Jr., George-town University, 14 July 1993.

75 Author's notes, discussion session facilitated by Lawrence F. Guillemette, George-town University, 16 July 1993.

76 To ensure the anonymity of the students, I have given them pseudonyms and have changed other identifying details. For the internship providers, I use the names of the organizations and their officials.

77 David, interview with author, Georgetown Inn, 15 July 1993; Sandra L. Crawford (director of the Entertainment Division, Media Research Center), interview with author, Media Research Center, Alexandria, VA, 15 July 1993. Brent Bozell, MRC co-founder, is the brother-in-law of James Buckley, a founder of the Fund for American Studies.

78 "Philosophy and Mission Statement," in *NFIB Foundation* (Washington, DC: NFIB Foundation, n.d.), 2–3 (quotation 2). David R. Jones, president of the NFIB Founda-tion, is also president (and a founder) of the Fund for American Studies. David Cullen, NFIB vice president for public affairs, serves on the Institute for Political Journalism Board of Visitors. John Molloy, NFIB vice president for government affairs, serves on the Harlow Institute Board of Visitors. Information from *1992 Program Report* (Wash-ington, DC: Fund for American Studies, 1992), 46, 50, 51.

79 Kevin, interview with author, Dean and DeLucca, Georgetown, 17 July 1993; Kimberly R. Brandow (coordinator, NFIB Small Business Research Institute), interview with author, National Federation of Independent Business, Washington, DC, 14 July 1993. Kevin's explanation of the takings clause was a truncated version of the conservative one. Traditionally, the takings clause of the Fifth Amendment to the Constitution, which states "nor shall private property be taken for public use, without just compensation," has been understood as requiring a county government, for instance, to pay homeowners a fair market price when appropriating their properties to build a highway. The conservative interpretation starts with two assumptions: that government-imposed regulations interfere with free-market enterprise, which functions through the mechanisms of competition and profit, and demand and supply; and that enterprises have an almost absolute right to possess and dispose of their property. On these assumptions, conservatives argue that when government imposes reporting regulations on a business it takes some of the profits rightfully owned by stockholders or when it imposes environmental requirements on a factory it curbs the owners' right to use their facilities as they see fit.

80 Betsy, interview with author, Paolo's, Georgetown, 13 July 1993; Kenneth F. Boehm (assistant to the president and counsel to the board, Legal Services Corporation), interview with author, Legal Services Corporation, Washington, DC, 14 July 1993. The president of the United States appoints and the Senate confirms LSC board members, who in turn select the LSC president and staff, then consisting of some 130 specialists in relevant areas of legal services and finance.

81 Diane, interview with author, Dean and Delucca, Georgetown, 17 July 1993; Ellen Smith (editor, Pasha Publications), interview with author, Rosslyn, VA, 15 July 1993. Smith serves on the FAS Alumni Board.

82 Katherine E. Kleeman, "Learning to Lead: Public Leadership Education Programs for Women," pamphlet, Washington, DC, PLEN, 1984, 6. The founding colleges were Wells (Aurora, NY), Carlow (Pittsburgh), Goucher (Baltimore), Spelman (Atlanta), and Stephens (Columbia, MO).

83 Information from Marianne Alexander (director, PLEN), interview with author, PLEN, Washington, DC, 12 June 1992; Kleeman, "Learning to Lead," 2–3, 16–32; "PLEN Public Policy Programs, 1991–92," flier, Washington, DC, PLEN, n.d.; "PLEN Public Policy Programs, 1992–93," flier, Washington, DC, PLEN, n.d.; and "PLEN: A Washington Seminar 1992 Application," flier, Washington, DC, PLEN, n.d.

84 Debra L. Dodson, with the assistance of Tobi Walker, "New Leadership: A Preliminary Evaluation Report," Center for the American Woman and Politics, Eagleton Institute, Rutgers University, n.d. (ca. 1994), 7, 4, typescript.

85 Ibid., 7.

86 Author's notes, remarks by Tobi Walker (coordinator, NEW Leadership) at the opening dinner, Rutgers University, 6 June 1994.

87 Sharon Stoneback described this pedagogy as "experiential learning" (Sharon Stoneback [program director, PLEN], interview with author, Rutgers University, 10 June 1994).

88 Dodson, "New Leadership," 5–6. All other information from author's notes, NEW Leadership, Rutgers University, 6–16 June 1994.

89 Author's notes, Legislative Overview (Alan Rosenthal, professor, Eagleton Institute), Trenton, NJ, 8 June 1994; author's notes, Conversation with Judy Shaw (chief of staff, Office of Governor Christine Todd Whitman), Trenton, NJ, 8 June 1994.

90 Author's notes, The Impact of Women in Politics (Sue Carroll, CAWP Senior Research Associate), Rutgers University, 7 June 1994.

91 Author's notes, Women, Politics, and Leadership: An Intergenerational Conversation, Rutgers University, 7 June 1994 (my emphasis).

92 Author's notes, Sandy Aguiler, Political Skills: Essential Tools for Public Leadership, Rutgers University, 12 June 1994; author's notes, Nancy Amidei (teacher / writer / advocate), Advocacy and the Political Process: An Exercise, Rutgers University, 15 June 1994 (my emphasis). The panelists in Political Skills were Sandy Aguilar (political consultant), Debra Danburg (state representative, Texas), Liz Hager (state representative, New Hampshire), Holly Mitchell (consultant, California Senate Committee on Health and Human Services), and Claudine Schneider (chair, RENEW America, and former congresswoman, Rhode Island).

93 Author's notes, Logistics meeting conducted by Tobi Walker (coordinator, NEW Leadership), and Debra Liebowitz (program associate, NEW Leadership), Rutgers University, 7 June 1994; author's notes from the rap session facilitated by Tobi Walker, Rutgers University, 12 June 1994.

94 Author's notes, Bella Abzug and Liz Abzug, Women, Politics, and Leadership: An Intergenerational Conversation, Rutgers University, 7 June 1994.

95 Author's notes, Young Women and Politics, Rutgers University, 11 June 1994. The panelists were Sarah Clarke (city councilmember, Highland Park, NJ), Deb De Santis (deputy commissioner, New Jersey Department of Community Affairs), Promita Gupta (legislative director, U.S. Student Association), and Nelida Valentin (executive director, New Jersey Human Services Advisory Council).

96 Author's notes, Ruth Bader Ginsburg (Associate Justice U.S. Supreme Court), The Supreme Court, Washington, DC, 13 June 1994.

97 Author's notes, Visits with Congresswomen, Washington, DC, 13 June 1994. The speakers were Congresswomen Patsy Mink (D-Hawaii), Marge Roukema (R-NJ), and Joelene Unsoeld (D-Wash.).

98 Sharon Stoneback (program director, PLEN), interview with author, 10 June 1994; Marianne Alexander (director, PLEN), interview with author, Rutgers University, 7 June 1994; Ruth Mandel (director, Center for the American Woman and Politics), interview with author, Rutgers University, 12 June 1994.

99 All information from author's notes on the rap session facilitated by Tobi Walker, Rutgers University, 12 June 1994.

100 To preserve the anonymity of the department, I have assigned pseudonyms to the university, faculty, staff, and students and have removed identifying markers from the materials cited. Unless specifically cited, the information in this paragraph is taken from: "Women's Studies," brochure, Department of Women's Studies, Midwestern

State University, 1990; "Graduate Study in Women's Studies," brochure, Department of Women's Studies, Midwestern State University, 1989; "1984–1990 Program Evaluation: Women's Studies" (1990), institutional document supplied by the Department of Women's Studies, spring 1991; and a short article written by the program's first coordinator that was published in a small leftist journal (citation is withheld because it would reveal the identity of the department). Additional information from Diane (instructor in women's studies), interview with author, Midwestern State University, 29 April 1991; and Candace (professor of political science and affiliate professor of women's studies), interview with author, Midwestern State University, 29 April 1991.

101 "Women's Studies" (first quotation); "Graduate Study in Women's Studies" (second quotation).

102 Hillary (assistant professor and chair of women's studies), interview with author, Midwestern State University, 15 April 1991; Louise (instructor in women's studies), interview with author, Midwestern State University, 15 April 1991; Diane (instructor in women's studies), interview with author, Midwestern State University, 29 April 1991; Sheryl (professor of English and affiliate professor of women's studies), interview with author, Midwestern State University, 6 May 1991.

103 Diane, interview with author, Midwestern State University, 6 May 1991; Sheryl, interview with author, 6 May 1991; John (assistant professor of sociology and affiliate professor of women's studies), interview with author, Midwestern State University, 30 April 1991.

104 Diane, interview with author, 29 April 1991 (first quotation) and 6 May 1991 (second quotation).

105 Hillary, interview with author, 15 April 1991.

106 Mina (associate director of fundraising), interview with author, Midwestern State University, 15 April 1991; Diane, interview with author, 6 May 1991.

107 "1984–1990 Program Evaluation," 38–39. I have omitted the reviewer's name and institution to preserve the anonymity of the department.

108 John, interview with author, 30 April 1991.

109 Candace, interview with author, 29 April 1991.

110 Louise, Midwestern State University, interview with author, 15 April 1991.

111 Women and the Politics of Empowerment, ed. Ann Bookman and Sandra Morgan (Philadelphia: Temple University Press, 1988); AAUW Community Action Tool Catalog: Techniques and Strategies for Successful Action Programs (Washington, DC: American Association of University Women, 1981).

112 Information from Louise's syllabus for "Collective Analysis and Action," spring quarter 1991; Louise's "The Theoretical Basis for Change" (one-page typed class handout); "Student Notes from CAA," 1 April 1991 (one-page typed summary); "Student Notes from CAA," 3 April 1991 (one-page typed summary); author's notes from CAA, 15 April 1991; "Student Notes from CAA" (two-page typed summary), 24 April 1991; author's notes from CAA, 29 April 1991; "Student Notes from CAA" (three-page typed summary), 1 May 1991; author's notes from CAA, 6 May 1991; author's notes from CAA,

13 May 1991; author's notes from CAA, 15 May 1991; and Louise's memorandum to CAA class, 15 May 1991.

113   Oona (director of the Women's Center), interview with author, Midwestern State University, 15 April 1991.

114   "1984–1990 Program Evaluation," 28.

115   Sue, interview with author, Midwestern State University, 29 May 1991.

116   Anne, interview with author, Midwestern State University, 29 May 1991.

117   Leslie, interview with author, Midwestern State University, 29 May 1991.

118   Rosa, interview with author, Midwestern State University, 29 May 1991.

119   Louise, interview with author, 15 April 1991; Sue, interview with author, 29 May 1991; Hillary, interview with author, 15 April 1991; Rosa, interview with author, 29 May 1991.

120   Signed letter to the class (two pages, single-spaced and typed), undated but distributed on 15 May 1991. I have omitted the writer's name.

Chapter 7: Playing by the New Rules

1   See *Mandate for Leadership: Policy Management in a Conservative Administration,* ed. Charles L. Heatherly (Washington, DC: Heritage Foundation, 1981); *Mandate for Leadership II: Continuing the Conservative Revolution* (Washington, DC: Heritage Foundation, 1984); and *A New Agenda for Education,* ed. Eileen M. Gardiner (Washington, DC: Heritage Foundation, 1985).

2   For conservative critiques of affirmative action, see Walter E. Williams, "Race, Scholarship, and Affirmative Action," *National Review,* 5 May 1989, 36–38; Thomas Sowell, " 'Affirmative Action': A Worldwide Disaster," *Commentary* 88.6 (December 1989): 21–41; Abigail M. Thernstrom, "On the Scarcity of Black Professors," *Commentary* 90.1 (July 1990): 22–26; Frederick R. Lynch, "Surviving Affirmative Action (More or Less), *Commentary* 90.2 (August 1990): 44–47; James Workman, "Gender Norming," *New Republic,* 1 July 1991, 16, 18; and Chester E. Finn Jr., "Quotas and the Bush Administration," *Commentary* 92.5 (November 1992): 17–23. Books, also numerous now, include: Barry Gross, *Discrimination in Reverse: Is Turnabout Fair Play?* (New York: New York University Press, 1978); Terry Eastland and William Bennett, *Counting by Race: Equality from the Founding Fathers to Bakke and Weber* (New York: Basic Books, 1979); Abigail M. Thernstrom, *Whose Votes Count? Affirmative Action and Minority Voting Rights* (Cambridge: Harvard University Press, 1987); Frederick R. Lynch, *Invisible Victims: White Males and the Crisis of Affirmative Action* (Westport, CT: Greenwood, 1989); Thomas Sowell, *Preferential Policies* (New York: Morrow, 1990); Dinesh D'Souza, *Illiberal Education: The Politics of Race and Sex on Campus* (New York: Vintage, 1991); Dinesh D'Souza, *The End of Racism* (New York: Free Press, 1995); and Terry Eastland, *Ending Affirmative Action: The Case for Colorblind Justice* (New York: Basic Books, 1996).

3   Information on the Reagan record is drawn from *Affirmative Action to Open the Doors of Job Opportunity* (Washington, DC: Citizens' Commission on Civil Rights, 1984), 89–120.

4   Among the several hearings, see *Podberesky v. Kirwan,* 956 Federal Reporter, 2d Series (Fourth Circuit), 52–57, decided 31 January 1992; and 38 Federal Reporter, 3d Series (Fourth Circuit), 147–62, decided 27 October 1994.

5   Peter Schmidt and Douglas Lederman, "Legal Barriers Removed to California's Ban on Racial Preferences," *Chronicle of Higher Education,* 5 September 1997, A47; "Affirmative-action ban stands," *Minneapolis Star Tribune,* 4 November 1997, A1, A13; "Proposition 209 Timeline" (three typescript pages), included in the section on "State and Local Affirmative Action Initiatives: A 1997 Update," looseleaf notebook prepared by the Leadership Conference on Civil Rights, November 1997. For an account of the several anti-affirmative action initiatives in California, see Kathleen Morris, "Through the Looking Glass: Recent Developments in Affirmative Action," *Berkeley Women's Law Journal* 11 (1996): 182–93.

6   See *Cheryl Hopwood v. State of Texas,* 78 Federal Reporter, 3d Series (Fifth Circuit), 932–68, decided 18 March 1996. Also see *Chronicle of Higher Education,* 29 March 1996, A26–38, B2–3 (text of ruling, articles, and opinion pieces); Douglas Lederman, "Texas Asks High Court to Uphold Legality of Affirmative Action," *Chronicle of Higher Education,* 10 May 1996, A25, A38; and "High Court Refuses to Hear Appeal of Ruling That Barred Considering Race in Admissions," *Chronicle of Higher Education,* 12 July 1996, A25, A29.

7   Douglas Lederman, "Growing Attacks on Affirmative Action," *Chronicle of Higher Education,* 26 April 1996, A30.

8   Ibid., A30.

9   Denise K. Magner, "Job Applicant Sues Bowling Green U. and Accreditor," *Chronicle of Higher Education,* 12 July 1996, A16; "White Professor Wins $122,000 in Bias Case," *Chronicle of Higher Education,* 27 March 1998, A14.

10 "Bill to end affirmative action on hold, GOP leaders say," *Minneapolis Star Tribune,* 15 July 1996, A4.

11 Information from Douglas Lederman, "New Lawsuits May Help Determine What's Legal in Affirmative Action," *Chronicle of Higher Education,* 21 March 1997, A34–35; Douglas Lederman, "Suit Challenges Affirmative Action in Admissions at U. of Michigan," *Chronicle of Higher Education,* 24 October 1997, A27–28; "Civil-Rights Groups Barred from Mich. Suit," *Chronicle of Higher Education,* 17 July 1998, A40; and "Active Case Summaries," Center for Individual Rights web site, September 1998: ⟨http: // www.wdn.com / cir / cs-sum.htm⟩.

12 The literature on the legislation and lawsuits concerning discrimination and affirmative action is vast. For two useful summaries of concepts and cases, see Carl E. Brody Jr., "A Historical Review of Affirmative Action and the Interpretation of Its Legislative Intent by the Supreme Court," *Akron Law Review* 29.2 (winter 1996): 291–334; and Peter Frankel, "Title VII and the Supreme Court: The Evolution of Affirmative Action," *Glendale Law Review* 8.1–2 (winter–summer 1988): 102–31.

13 *Regents of the University of California v. Bakke,* 96 Supreme Court Reporter (1978): 2733–2815, decided 28 June 1978.

14 *Cheryl J. Hopwood v. State of Texas,* 78 Federal Reporter, 3d Series (decided 22 April 1996): 945 (both quotations).

15 Ibid., 946. The judges were quoting from Richard A. Posner, "The DeFunis Case and the Constitutionality of Preferential Treatment of Racial Minorities," 1974 Supreme Court Review, 12.

16 Ibid. (both quotations).

17 Since the shaping of experience and viewpoint is a complicated matter, I want to clarify three points. I am not arguing that the shape of any group's experience is unchanging in time or homogeneous in all places (the history of African Americans, for instance, attests to the fact that it is neither). Nor am I arguing that individuals are determined by the circumstances of their birth and youth because every individual is a migrant who travels through several experiential arenas. And I am also not arguing that each individual occupies a single location in the social formation because, as so much research reminds us, we are multiply situated in positions of privilege and privation with respect to class, race, ethnicity, sex, and so on. What I am arguing is that the inequitable distribution of socioeconomic resources should be seen as a structure that structures the experience of differentially situated individuals by supplying or withholding what they need, enabling and constraining their actions, and setting the horizon of their aspirations and opportunities.

18 *Hopwood v. Texas,* 946–47.

19 Ibid., 944.

20 Ibid., 941 (first quotation), 944 (second quotation).

21 Since a law professor who attended one of my talks on anti-affirmative action litigation asked me to explain more fully what I meant by "the precedent function," I take this opportunity to do so. In thinking about "the precedent," I took my lead from Foucault, who regarded "the author" as a construct that permitted practitioners to perform certain organizing functions in literary-studies discourse: grouping texts under the name of the author, interpreting texts through the lens of author biography and psychology, and organizing literary history by means of such continuities as author-to-author influence and author aggregation into schools.

    In judicial discourse, the precedent functions (1) heuristically by guiding an attorney's crafting of a new case, the in-court analysis of claims and counterclaims, and the judge's opinion; (2) articulatively by linking the discursive bits (the facts, analyses, and arguments) of one case to those of others; (3) historically by suturing cases into lines of exemplars that can be demarcated from inapposite lines; and of course (4) productively by sparking more litigation and procuring similar rulings.

    Since in most lawsuits the parties can and do cite divergent precedents to support their competing claims, judges have to determine the force of the precedents. It is here that the concept of "binding precedent" enters. If the obligation to consider the precedential case (its "bindingness") depends upon how many Supreme Court justices concurred in the majority and minority opinions, it doesn't matter what the numbers are (e.g., 8 to 1, 7 to 2, 6 to 3, or 5 to 4) because what happens is that the signifier (the number of votes) stands for a signified (the reasoning) that may or may not be meritorious. I would make a similar argument against those who gauge the bindingness of a ruling according to the level at which it was rendered. While it is true that a Supreme Court ruling binds as "the law of the land" whereas district and appellate court rulings do not, that de jure obligation is an artifact of the hierarchical organization of our judicial system that still does not speak to the issue of merits of reasoning.

Of course, what people recognize as meritorious reasoning in a case may not be so meritorious because that recognition itself is often achieved by looking to legal, political, and social principles that were previously established to protect unjust majoritarian interests and values. For an account of how majoritarianism has conditioned the Supreme Court's reception to claims made by racial minorities, see Girardeau A. Spann, "Pure Politics," in *Critical Race Theory: The Cutting Edge,* ed. Richard Delgado (Philadelphia: Temple University Press, 1995), 21–34.

Plessy v. Ferguson exemplifies the claims I am making. Brought by Homer Plessy, a man of Caucasian and African descent who was prosecuted for sitting in a whites-only train compartment, *Plessy* was decided by the Supreme Court in 1896. The ruling not only affirmed the legality of a Louisiana statute mandating segregated railroad coaches but established the "separate but equal" principle whose seemingly democratic language justified the system of racial segregation and masked the inferior provisions made for African Americans. For more than half a century, in case after case brought to challenge racial segregation in housing, transportation, education, and other areas, defendants and judges cited the *Plessy* principle as the precedent for maintaining racial segregation. Even in *Brown v. Board of Education,* when the Supreme Court finally overturned *Plessy* in 1954, a lower court had ruled that the segregation policy of the Topeka, Kansas, schools was legal because it complied with the *Plessy* ruling. See the discussion of the ruling's majoritarian sentiments and continuing influence in A. Leon Higginbotham Jr., *Shades of Freedom: Racial Politics and the Presumptions of the American Legal Process* (Oxford: Oxford University Press, 1996), 108–18.

22   From the early 1940s through the mid-1970s, the Supreme Court formulated and began applying three levels of review to discrimination lawsuits: rational basis, heightened (or intermediate) scrutiny, and strict scrutiny. In rational-basis review, a court considers whether a procedure or policy that makes distinctions among people is (1) reasonable, nondiscriminatory, and thus constitutional or (2) arbitrary, discriminatory, and thus unconstitutional. In the heightened-scrutiny review, which was developed to deal with claims of sex discrimination, a court considers the same matters and expects a defendant to show that a distinction based on sex has an important and valid objective. The bona fide occupational qualification (BFOQ) would fall into this category. A university might be able to argue convincingly that "female sex" is a BFOQ for the job of resident counselor in the women's dorm, but it could not argue that "female sex" is a BFOQ for the job of adviser in the undergraduate college office. In the strict scrutiny review, which is applied to cases alleging the violation of basic civil

rights or the invidious use of the "suspect" categories of race, ethnicity, and religion, a court addresses the same matters and requires the defendant to show that the procedure or policy in question serves a compelling national interest. Thus Justice Powell argued in *Bakke* that the use of race as one of several factors in medical school admissions was justified by the long history of racism and its present effects on higher education and the nation. But even if the defending university can meet the strict-scrutiny test it also has to demonstrate that narrower and less suspect remedies will not do the job of serving the compelling national interest.

23 *Hopwood v. Texas,* 948–51.

24 Ibid., 951–54.

25 As a few examples of how race and gender organize three interactive systems of social goods—housing, employment, and education—see Thomas D. Boston, *Race, Class, and Conservatism* (Boston: Unwin Hyman, 1988); Rosemary T. Cunningham, "Market Segmentation: The Role of Race in Housing Markets" and Louise Laurence and Robert L. Moore, "Gender and Race and the Decision to Go to College," both in *Introducing Race and Gender into Economics,* ed. Robin L. Bartlett (London and New York: Routledge, 1997), 42–51 and 52–66; "Forum—In Pursuit of a Dream Deferred: Linking Housing and Education," *Minnesota Law Review* 80.4 (April 1996): 743–910.

26 Barbara A. Bergmann, *In Defense of Affirmative Action* (New York: Basic Books, 1996), 11.

27 Richard D. Kahlenberg, *The Remedy: Class, Race, and Affirmative Action* (New York: Basic Books, 1996), 123.

Works Cited

Published Works and Unpublished Documents

AAUW Community Action Tool Catalog: Techniques and Strategies for Successful Action Programs. Washington, DC: American Association of University Women, 1981.

"About This Issue." *Harper's,* March 1971, 4.

Abramson, Joan. *Old Boys, New Women: The Politics of Sex Discrimination.* New York: Praeger, 1979.

"The Academic Left Strikes Back." *New Criterion* 10.3 (1991): 1–2.

Achinstein, Peter, and Owen Hannaway, eds. *Observation, Experiment, and Hypothesis in Modern Physical Science.* Cambridge: MIT Press, 1985.

Adams, Elsie, and Mary Louise Briscoe, eds. *Up Against the Wall, Mother: On Women's Liberation.* Beverly Hills, CA: Glencoe, 1971.

Addelson, Kathryn Pyne, and Elizabeth Potter. "Making Knowledge." In Hartman and Messer-Davidow, *(En)Gendering Knowledge,* 1991. 259–77.

"Affirmative-action ban stands." *Minneapolis Star Tribune,* 4 November 1997, A1, A13.

Aiken, Susan Hardy, Karen Anderson, Myra Dinnerstein, Judy Nolte Lensink, and Patricia MacCorquodale, eds. *Changing Our Minds: Feminist Transformations of Knowledge.* Albany: State University of New York Press, 1988.

Alcoff, Linda. "Cultural Feminism versus Post-Structuralism." *Signs* 13 (1988): 405–36.

——, and Elizabeth Potter, eds. *Feminist Epistemologies.* New York: Routledge, 1993.

Allen, Walter R. "Family Roles, Occupational Statuses, and Achievement Orientations among Black Women in the United States." *Signs* 4 (1979): 470–86.

Altbach, Edith Hoshino, ed. *From Feminism to Liberation.* Cambridge, MA, and London: Schenkman, 1971.

American Sociological Association, Ad Hoc Committee on the Status of Women in the Profession. *The Status of Women in Sociology 1968–1972.* Washington, DC: American Sociological Association, 1973. Booklet. 60 pp.

——. "Minutes of the First 1968 ASA Business Meeting, Wednesday, August 28, 1968." *The American Sociologist* 3 (1968): 321–23.

——. "Minutes of the Second 1968 ASA Business Meeting, Thursday, August 29, 1968." *The American Sociologist* 3 (1968): 324–25.

———. "Minutes of the Second 1969 Council Meeting, Friday, August 30, 1968." *The American Sociologist* 3 (1968): 325–26.

———. "Minutes of the First Business Meeting, Wednesday, September 3, 1969." *The American Sociologist* 5 (1970): 62–68.

———. "Minutes of the 1970 Council Meeting, Friday, September 5, 1969." *The American Sociologist* 5 (1970): 60–62.

———. "Minutes of the First Business Meeting, Tuesday, September 1, 1970." *The American Sociolgist* 6 (1971): 65–67.

———. "Minutes of the Second Business Meeting, Wednesday, September 2, 1970." *The American Sociologist* 6 (1971): 68–71.

———. "Women's Caucus Statement and Resolutions to the General Business Meeting of the American Sociological Association, September 3, 1969." In Oppenheimer et al., *Radical Sociologists*, 225–58.

The American Sociologist 8.3 (August 1973).

———. 8.4 (November 1973).

Ancker-Johnson, Betsy. "Women's Lib and Physics." *Physics Teacher* 10 (1972): 499–507.

Andermatt-Conley, Verena. "A Doll's Story." *New Literary History* 9 (1977): 181–88.

Andersen, Charles J., Deborah J. Carter, and Andrew G. Malizio, with Boichi San, comp. *1989–90 Fact Book on Higher Education*. New York: American Council on Education, 1989.

Ansell, Amy. "The Color of America's Culture Wars." Typescript supplied by Amy Ansell.

Ardener, Shirley, ed. *Perceiving Women*. London: J. M. Dent; and New York: John Wiley, 1975.

Astin, Helen S. "Career Profiles of Women Doctorates." In Rossi and Calderwood, *Academic Women*, 139–61.

———, and Allison Parelman. "Women's Studies in American Colleges and Universities." *International Social Science Journal* 25 (1973): 389–400.

Babcox, Deborah, and Madeline Belkin, eds. *Liberation Now! Writings from the Women's Liberation Movement*. New York: Dell, 1971.

Balayon, Theresa D. "A History of the Women's Studies Program." *Forum: A Women's Studies Quarterly* 11.2 (1985): 3–4.

Balch, Stephen H., and Herbert I. London. "The Tenured Left." *Commentary* 82.4 (1986): 41–51.

Barber, Virginia. "The Women's Revolt in the MLA." In *Women on Campus*, 85–94.

Bardwick, Judith. *The Psychology of Women*. New York: Harper & Row, 1970.

Baritz, Loren, ed. *The American Left: Radical Political Thought in the Twentieth Century*. New York: Basic Books, 1971.

Bar On, Bat-Ami. "Marginality and Epistemic Privilege." In Alcoff and Potter, *Feminist Epistemologies*, 83–100.

Barry, Kathleen. "The Fear of Feminism or What Makes Women's Liberation Laugh." In Sacramento State University Women's Studies Board, *Report*, 115–16.

Bartlett, Robin L., ed. *Introducing Race and Gender into Economics*. London and New York: Routledge, 1997.

Bayer, Alan. "Marriage Plans and Educational Aspirations." *American Journal of Sociology* 75 (1969): 239–44.

Beale, Frances M. "Double Jeopardy: To Be Black and Female." In Morgan, *Sisterhood*, 340–53.

Beauvoir, Simone de. *The Second Sex.* Trans. H. M. Parshley. New York: Knopf, 1953.

Becher, Tony. *Academic Tribes and Territories: Intellectual Enquiry and the Culture of Disciplines.* Milton Keynes, UK: Society for Research into Higher Education, and Open University Press, 1989.

Belenky, Mary Field, Blythe McVicker Clinchy, Nancy Rule Goldberger, and Jill Mattuck Tarule. *Women's Ways of Knowing: The Development of Self, Voice, and Mind.* New York: Basic Books, 1986.

Bell, Barbara Currier, and Carol Ohmann. "Virginia Woolf's Criticism: A Polemical Preface." *Critical Inquiry* 1 (1974): 361–72.

Bell, Diane, and Renate Klein, eds. *Radically Speaking: Feminism Reclaimed.* North Melbourne, Australia: Spinifex, 1996.

Bell, Roseann P., Bettye J. Parker, and Beverly Guy-Sheftell, eds. *Sturdy Black Bridges: Visions of Black Women in Literature.* New York: Doubleday, 1979.

Bem, Sandra L. "The Measurement of Psychological Androgyny." *Journal of Consulting and Clinical Psychology* 88 (1974): 155–66.

Benjamin, Ernst. "A Faculty Response to the Fiscal Crisis: From Defense to Offense." In Bérubé and Nelson, *Higher Education,* 52–72.

Bennett, Tony. *The Birth of the Modern Museum: History, Politics, Theory.* London and New York: Routledge, 1995.

Bennis, Warren. "Collage: One Life in the Day of a University President." 1976. Typescript. 32 pp.

———. *An Invented Life: Reflections on Leadership and Change.* Reading, MA: Addison-Wesley, 1993.

———. "The Pornography of Everyday Life." *New York Times,* 28 November 1976, 4E, 15.

Bergmann, Barbara A. *In Defense of Affirmative Action.* New York: Basic Books, 1996.

Berlin, Joan E. "The Women's Roundtable." Direct mail cover letter and statement of purpose, April 1996.

Bernard, Jessie. "Re-viewing the Impact of Women's Studies on Sociology." In Farnham, *Impact,* 193–216.

Bernstein, Basil. *Class, Codes and Control.* Vol. 3: *Towards a Theory of Educational Transmission.* London: Routledge & Kegan Paul, 1973.

Bérubé, Michael, and Cary Nelson, eds. *Higher Education under Fire: Politics, Economics, and the Crisis of the Humanities.* New York: Routledge, 1995.

"Bill to end affirmative action on hold, GOP leaders say." *Minneapolis Star Tribune,* 15 July 1996, A4.

Bird, Caroline. *Born Female: The High Cost of Keeping Women Down.* New York: David McKay, 1968.

Birke, Lynda. *Women, Feminism and Biology.* New York: Methuen, 1986.

Birkby, Phyllis, Bertha Harris, Jill Johnston, Esther Newton, and Jane O'Wyatt, eds. *Amazon Expedition: A Lesbian Anthology.* Washington, NJ: Times Change, 1973.

Blecki, Catherine L., Barbara C. Gelpi, Suzanne Juhasz, and Selma R. Burkom, eds. *Feminist Literary Criticism: A Symposium.* San Jose: Diotima, 1974.

Bleier, Ruth. "Lab Coat: Robe of Innocence or Klansman's Sheet?" In Lauretis, *Feminist Studies,* 55–66.

——. "Sex Differences Research: Science of Belief?" In Bleier, *Feminist Approaches,* 147–64.

——. *Science and Gender: A Critique of Biology and Its Theories on Women.* New York: Pergamon, 1984.

——. ed. *Feminist Approaches to Science.* New York: Pergamon, 1986.

Bloom, Alexander, and Wini Breines, eds. *"Takin' It to the Streets": A Sixties Reader.* New York: Oxford University Press, 1995.

Boggs, Carl. "Rethinking the Sixties Legacy: From New Left to New Social Movements." In *Social Movements: Critiques, Concepts, Case-Studies.* Ed. Stanford M. Lyman. New York: New York University Press, 1995. 331–55.

Bookman, Ann, and Sandra Morgan, eds. *Women and the Politics of Empowerment.* Philadelphia: Temple University Press, 1988.

Bordo, Susan R. "Feminism, Postmodernism, and Gender-Scepticism." In Nicholson, *Feminism / Postmodernism,* 133–56.

——. *The Flight to Objectivity: Essays on Cartesianism and Culture.* Albany: State University of New York Press, 1987.

Boston Lesbian Psychologies Collective, ed. *Lesbian Psychologies: Explorations and Challenges.* Urbana: University of Illinois Press, 1987.

Boston, Thomas D. *Race, Class and Conservatism.* Boston: Unwin Hyman, 1988.

Bottomore, Tom and Robert Nisbet, eds. *A History of Sociological Analysis.* New York: Basic Books, 1978.

——. Introduction to Bottomore and Nisbet, *History,* vii–xiv.

Boxer, Marilyn J. "For and About Women: The Theory and Practice of Women's Studies in the United States." *Signs* 7 (1982): 661–95.

——. *When Women Ask the Questions: Creating Women's Studies in America.* Baltimore: Johns Hopkins University Press, 1998.

Brack, Datha Clapper. "Writing Papers and Stirring Soup: Career and Family in the Baby Boom Years." In Goetting and Fenstermaker, *Individual Voices,* 23–36.

Braude, Norma. "Degas's Misogyny." *Art Bulletin* 59 (1977): 95–107.

Breines, Wini. *Community and Organization in the New Left, 1962–1968.* New ed. New Brunswick: Rutgers University Press, 1989.

——. "A Review Essay: Sara Evans's *Personal Politics.*" *Feminist Studies* 5 (1979): 495–506.

Briscoe, Anne M. "Phenomenon of the Seventies: The Women's Caucuses." *Signs* 4 (1978): 152–58.

Brody, Carl E., Jr. "A Historical Review of Affirmative Action and the Interpretation of Its Legislative Intent by the Supreme Court." *Akron Law Review* 29 (winter 1996): 291–334.

Broverman, Inge K., Susan Raymond-Vogel, Donald Broverman, Frank E. Clarkson, and

Paul S. Rosenkrantz. "Sex-Role Stereotypes: A Current Appraisal." *Journal of Consulting and Clinical Psychology* 34 (1970): 59–78.

Broverman, Donald M., Frank E. Clarkson, Paul S. Rosenkrantz, and Susan Vogel. "Sex-Role Stereotypes and Clinical Judgments of Mental Health." *Journal of Consulting and Clinical Psychology* 34 (1970): 1–7.

Brown, Carol A. "The Early Years of the Sociology Liberation Movement." In Oppenheimer et al., *Radical Sociologists*, 43–53.

Bulkin, Elly, Minnie Bruce Pratt, and Barbara Smith. *Yours in Struggle.* Brooklyn: Long Haul, 1984.

Bulmer, Martin. "The Growth of Applied Sociology after 1945: The Prewar Establishment of the Postwar Infrastructure." In Halliday and Janowitz, *Sociology*, 318–35.

Burkom, Selma R. "Feminist Criticism: Humanism." In Blecki et al., *Feminist Literary Criticism*, 17–19.

Butler, Johnella E., and John Walter, eds. *Transforming the Curriculum: Ethnic Studies and Women's Studies.* Albany: State University of New York Press, 1991.

Butler, Johnella E., et al. *Liberal Learning and the Women's Studies Major.* College Park, MD: National Women's Studies Association, 1991.

Butler, Judith. *Bodies That Matter: On the Discursive Limits of "Sex."* New York: Routledge, 1993.

———. *Gender Trouble: Feminism and the Subversion of Identity.* New York: Routledge, 1990.

Buxton, William, and Stephen P. Turner. "From Education to Expertise: Sociology as a 'Profession.'" In Halliday and Janowitz, *Sociology*, 373–407.

Cade, Toni, ed. *The Black Woman: An Anthology.* New York: Mentor, 1970.

Cain, William E. *The Crisis in Criticism: Theory, Literature, and Reform in English Studies.* Baltimore, MD: Johns Hopkins University Press, 1984.

Calhoun, Craig. "Sociology, Other Disciplines, and the Project of a General Understanding of Social Life." In Halliday and Janowitz, *Sociology*, 137–95.

Carlson, Alison. "Chromosome Count." *Ms.*, October 1988, 40, 42–44.

Carlson, Scott. "Minority Students Posted Slight Increase in College Enrollment in 1997, Report Says." *Chronicle of Higher Education*, 17 December 1999, A53.

Carnegie Council on Policy Studies in Higher Education. *Making Affirmative Action Work in Higher Education.* San Francisco: Jossey-Bass, 1975.

Carroll, Berenice, ed. *Liberating Women's History: Theoretical and Critical Essays.* Urbana: University of Illinois Press, 1976.

Carruthers, Mary. "The Wife of Bath and the Painting of Lions." *PMLA* 94 (1979): 209–22.

Carson, Clayborne. *In Struggle: SNCC and the Black Awakening of the 1960s.* New ed. Cambridge: Harvard University Press, 1995.

———, ed. *The Student Voice 1960–1965: Periodical of the Student Nonviolent Coordinating Committee.* Westport, CT: Meckler, 1990.

Catapano, Joan, and Marlie P. Wasserman. "Is Publishing Perishing?" *Women's Review of Books*, February 1998, 22.

Center for Individual Rights. "Active Case Summaries." Center for Individual Rights Web Site, September 1998: ⟨http://www.wdn.com/cir/cs-sum.htm⟩.

Center for Women Policy Studies. "Center for Women Policy Studies." Brochure, Washington, DC, n.d.

Chamberlain, Mariam K., ed. *Women in Academe: Progress and Prospects.* New York: Russell Sage Foundation, 1988.

Chesler, Phyllis. *Women and Madness.* New York: Doubleday, 1972.

Chodorow, Nancy. *Feminism and Psychoanalytic Theory.* New Haven, CT: Yale University Press, 1989.

———. *The Reproduction of Mothering: Psychoanalysis and the Sociology of Gender.* Berkeley: University of California Press, 1978.

Christian, Barbara. *Black Women Novelists: The Development of a Tradition, 1892–1976.* Westport, CT: Greenwood, 1980.

Cisler, Lucinda, comp. "A Selected Bibliography on Women." In Hole and Levine, *Rebirth,* 451–71.

Citizens' Commission on Civil Rights. *Affirmative Action to Open the Doors of Job Opportunities.* Washington, DC: Citizens' Commission on Civil Rights, 1984.

"Civil-Rights Groups Barred from Mich. Suit." *Chronicle of Higher Education,* 17 July 1998, A40.

Clark, Burton R. *The Higher Education System: Academic Organization in Cross-National Perspective.* Berkeley: University of California Press, 1983.

Cohen, Cathy J., Kathleen B. Jones, and Joan C. Tronto, eds. *Women Transforming Politics.* New York: New York University Press, 1997.

Cohen, Ed. "Are We (Not) What We Are Becoming? Gay 'Identity,' 'Gay Studies,' and the Disciplining of Knowledge." In Messer-Davidow et al., *Knowledges,* 397–421.

Cole, Jonathan R. *Fair Science: Women in the Scientific Community.* New York: Free Press, 1979.

"College of Women's Studies, State University of N.Y. at Buffalo." In *Female Studies III,* 142–46.

Collins, Jean. "The Feminist Press." In *Women on Campus,* 102–9.

Collins, Patricia Hill. *Black Feminist Thought: Knowledge, Consciousness, and the Politics of Empowerment.* New York: HarperCollins, 1991.

———. "Learning from the Outsider Within: The Sociological Significance of Black Feminist Thought." In Hartman and Messer-Davidow, *(En)Gendering Knowledge,* 40–65.

Committee on the Status of Women in Physics. "Twenty Years Later, CSWP Is Still Going Strong." *American Physical Society News* 1.6 (1992): 740–53.

———. "Women in Physics." *Bulletin of the American Physical Society,* series 2, 17 (1972): 740–53.

Cook, Judith A., and Mary Margaret Fonow. "Am I My Sister's Gatekeeper? Cautionary Tales from the Academic Hierarchy." In *A Feminist Ethic for Social Science Research.* Ed. Nebraska Sociological Feminist Collective. Lewiston, NY: Edwin Mellen, 1988. 201–35.

Cornillon, Susan Koppelman, ed. *Images of Women in Fiction: Feminist Perspectives.* Rev. ed. Bowling Green: Bowling Green University Popular Press, 1973.

Coser, Lewis A. "American Trends." In Bottomore and Nisbet, *History,* 311–17.

Covington, Sally. *Moving a Public Policy Agenda: The Strategic Philanthropy of Conservative Foundations*. Washington, DC: National Committee for Responsive Philanthropy, 1997.

——, and Larry Parachini. *Foundations in the Newt Era*. Washington, DC: National Committee for Responsive Philanthropy, 1995.

Cox, Sue, ed. *Female Psychology: The Emerging Self*. Chicago: Science Research Associates, 1976.

Crews, Frederick. "Do Literary Studies Have an Ideology?" *PMLA* 85 (1970): 423–28.

Critical Inquiry 1.1 (1974).

Culligan, Glendy. "Born Free But Not Liberated." *Saturday Review*, 5 June 1971, 25–28.

Cunningham, Rosemary T. "Market Segmentation: The Role of Race in Housing Markets." In Bartlett, *Introducing Race*, 42–51.

"Curricular and Institutional Change." Special double issue of *Women's Studies Quarterly* 18.1–2 (1990).

Curtis, Russell L., Jr., and Benigno E. Aguirre, eds. *Collective Behavior and Social Movements*. Boston: Allyn and Bacon, 1993.

D'Andrade, Roy G. "Sex Differences and Cultural Institutions." In Maccoby, *Development*, 174–204.

Daniels, Arlene Kaplan. "When We Were All Boys Together: Graduate School in the Fifties and Beyond." In Orlans and Wallace, *Gender*, 27–43.

Darwin, Charles. *The Descent of Man, and Selection in Relation to Sex*. 2 vols. London: Murray, 1871.

Davidson, Nicholas. *The Failure of Feminism*. New York: Prometheus, 1988.

Davis, Angela. *Women, Race, and Class*. New York: Random House, 1981.

Davis, Ann E. "Women as a Minority Group in Higher Academics." *The American Sociologist* 4 (1969): 95–99.

Davis, Devra Lee. "The Woman in the Moon: Prolegomenon for Women's Studies." In *Female Studies V*, 17–28.

Davis, Natalie Zemon. " 'Women's History' in Transition: The European Case." *Feminist Studies* 3.3–4 (1976): 83–103.

Decter, Midge. *The New Chastity and Other Arguments Against Women's Liberation*. New York: Coward, McCann and Geohegan, 1972.

Denmark, Florence L., and Linda C. Fernandez. "Historical Development of the Psychology of Women." In Denmark and Paludi, *Psychology*, 3–22.

Denmark, Florence L., and Michele A. Paludi, eds. *Psychology of Women: A Handbook of Issues and Theories*. Westport, CT: Greenwood, 1993.

DeSole, Gloria, and Meredith Butler. "Building an Effective Model for Institutional Change: Women's Committees as Catalyst." *Initiatives* 53.2 (1990): 1–10.

Deux, Kay. "From Individual Differences to Social Categories: Analysis of a Decade's Research on Gender." *American Psychologist* 39 (1984): 105–16.

Diggs, E. "Rebels in the MLA." *Social Policy* 1.2 (1970): 57–59.

Dill, Bonnie Thornton. "The Dialectics of Black Womanhood." *Signs* 4 (1979): 543–55.

DiMaggio, Paul J. "Constructing an Organizational Field as a Professional Project: U.S. Art

Museums, 1920–1940." In *The New Institutionalism in Organizational Analysis.* Ed. Walter W. Powell and Paul J. DiMaggio. Chicago: University of Chicago Press, 1991. 267–92.

Dixon, Marlene. "Why Women's Liberation?" *Ramparts* 8.6 (December 1969): 57–63.

Dixon-Mueller, Ruth. "Accidental Tourist." In Orlans and Wallace, *Gender,* 201–18.

Dogan, Mattei, and Robert Pahre. *Creative Marginality: Innovation at the Intersections of Social Sciences.* Boulder, CO: Westview, 1990.

Donovan, Josephine. "Feminism and Aesthetics." *Critical Inquiry* 3 (1977): 605–10.

D'Souza, Dinesh. *The End of Racism.* New York: Free Press, 1995.

——. *Illiberal Education: The Politics of Race and Sex on Campus.* New York: Vintage, 1991.

Dubois, Ellen Carol, Gail Paradise Kelly, Elizabeth Lapovsky Kennedy, Carolyn W. Korsmeyer, and Lillian S. Robinson. *Feminist Scholarship: Kindling in the Groves of Academe.* Urbana: University of Illinois Press, 1985.

Duchen, Claire. *Feminism in France from May '68 to Mitterrand.* London: Routledge & Kegan Paul, 1986.

Duncan, Carol. "Happy Mothers and Other New Ideas in French Art." *Art Bulletin* 55 (1973): 570–83.

Dunn, Mary. "Second Berkshire Conference on the History of Women." *Women's Studies Newsletter* 3.2 (1975): 7–8.

DuPlessis, Rachel Blau, and Ann Snitow, eds. *The Feminist Memoir Project: Voices from Women's Liberation.* New York: Three Rivers, 1998.

Eastland, Terry. *Ending Affirmative Action: The Case for Colorblind Justice.* New York: Basic Books, 1996.

——, and William Bennett. *Counting by Race: Equality from the Founding Fathers to Bakke and Weber.* New York: Basic Books, 1979.

Echols, Alice. *Daring to Be Bad: Radical Feminism in America, 1967–1975.* Minneapolis: University of Minnesota Press, 1989.

Edwards, Lee. "The Labors of Psyche: Toward a Theory of Female Heroism." *Critical Inquiry* 6 (1979): 33–50.

Eisenstein, Hester, and Alice Jardine, eds. *The Future of Difference.* Boston: Hall, 1980.

Eisenstein, Zillah R. "Developing a Theory of Capitalist Patriarchy and Socialist Feminism." In *Capitalist Patriarchy and the Case for Socialist Feminism.* Ed. Zillah R. Eisenstein. New York: Monthly Review Press, 1979. 5–40.

Ellmann, Mary. *Thinking About Women.* New York: Harcourt Brace Jovanovich, 1968.

Epstein, Cynthia Fuchs. "Encountering the Male Establishment: Sex-Status Limits on Women's Careers in the Professions." *American Journal of Sociology* 75 (1970): 965–82.

Erlich, Carol. "The Woman Book Industry." In Huber, *Changing Women,* 268–82.

Evans, Nancy Burr. "The Value and Peril for Women of Reading Women Writers." In Cornillon, *Images,* 308–14.

Evans, Sara. *Personal Politics: The Roots of Women's Liberation in the Civil Rights Movement and the New Left.* New York: Vintage, 1980.

Fairclough, Norman. *Discourse and Social Change.* Cambridge, UK: Polity, 1992.

Farley, Jennie. "Women versus Academe: Who's Winning?" *Journal of Social Issues* 41.4 (1985): 111–19.

Farnham, Christie, ed. *The Impact of Feminist Research in the Academy.* Bloomington: Indiana University Press, 1987.

Fausto-Sterling, Anne. "The Five Sexes." *The Sciences* (March–April 1993): 20–24.

——. "Life in the XY Corral." *Women's Studies International Forum* 12 (1989): 319–31.

——. *Myths of Gender: Biological Theories about Women and Men.* New York: Basic Books, 1985.

Female Studies I. Ed. Sheila Tobias. Pittsburgh: KNOW Press, 1970.

Female Studies II. Ed. Florence Howe. Pittsburgh: KNOW Press, 1970.

Female Studies III. Ed. Florence Howe and Carol Ahlum. Pittsburgh: KNOW Press, 1971.

Female Studies IV: Teaching About Women. Ed. Elaine Showalter and Carol Ohmann. Pittsburgh: KNOW Press, 1971.

Female Studies V. Ed. Rae Lee Siporin. Pittsburgh: KNOW Press, 1972.

Female Studies VI: Closer to the Ground, Women's Classes, Criticism, Programs—1972. Ed. Nancy Hoffman, Cynthia Secor, and Adrian Tinsley. Old Westbury, NY: Feminist Press, 1972.

Female Studies VII: Going Strong, New Courses / New Programs. Ed. Deborah Silverton Rosenfelt. Old Westbury, NY: Feminist Press, 1973.

Ferber, Marianne Abeles, and Joan A. Huber. "Sex of Student and Instructor: A Study of Student Bias." *American Journal of Sociology* 80 (1975): 949–63.

Ferree, Myra Marx, and Patricia Yancey Martin, eds. *Feminist Organizations: Harvest of the New Women's Movement.* Philadelphia: Temple University Press, 1995.

Feulner, Edwin J., Jr. "Building the New Establishment: An interview with Adam Meyerson. *Policy Review* 58 (1991): 6–16.

Finn, Chester E., Jr. "Quotas and the Bush Administration." *Commentary* 92.5 (November 1992): 17–23.

Firestone, Shulamith. *The Dialectic of Sex: The Case for Feminist Revolution.* New York: Bantam, 1971.

Flacks, Dick [Richard]. "The Sociology Liberation Movement: Some Lessons and Legacies." In Oppenheimer et al., *Radical Sociologists,* 17–27.

Flax, Jane. "Political Philosophy and the Patriarchal Unconscious: A Psychoanalytic Perspective on Epistemology and Metaphysics." In Harding and Hintikka, *Discovering Reality,* 245–81.

——. "Postmodernism and Gender Relations in Feminist Theory." *Signs* 12 (1987): 621–43.

Flint, Charles, Ellen Friedman, Wendy Kolmar, and Paula Rothenberg, eds. *Creating an Inclusive College Curriculum: A Teaching Sourcebook from the New Jersey Project.* New York: Teachers College, 1995.

Forfreedom, Ann. "Whither Women's Studies." In Sacramento State University Women's Studies Board, *Report,* 112–13.

"Forum: In Pursuit of a Dream Deferred—Linking Housing and Education." *Minnesota Law Review* 80 (1996): 743–910.

Foster, Ginny. "Women as Liberators." In *Female Studies VI*, 6–35.

Foster, Jeannette. *Sex Variant Women in Literature*. San Francisco: Daughters of Bilitis, 1967. Rpt. Baltimore, MD: Diana, 1975.

Foucault, Michel. "Afterword: The Subject and Power." Appended to Hubert L. Dreyfus and Paul Rabinow, *Michel Foucault: Beyond Structuralism and Hermeneutics*. 2d ed. Chicago: University of Chicago Press, 1983. 208–26.

——. *The Archaeology of Knowledge and the Discourse on Language*. Trans. A. M. Sheridan Smith. New York: Pantheon, 1972.

——. "The Discourse on Language." In Foucault, *Archaeology*, 1972, 215–37.

——. "Truth and Power." In *Power/Knowledge: Selected Interviews and Other Writings, 1972–1977*. Ed. Colin Gordon. Trans. Colin Gordon, Leo Marshall, John Mepham, and Kate Soper. New York: Pantheon, 1980. 109–33.

——. "Two Lectures." In *Power/Knowledge: Selected Interviews and Other Writings 1972–1977*. Ed. Colin Gordon. Trans. Colin Gordon, Leo Marshall, John Mepham, and Kate Soper. New York: Pantheon, 1980. 78–108.

Fox, Susan. "The Female as Metaphor in William Blake's Poetry." *Critical Inquiry* 3 (1977): 507–20.

Frances, Carol, and R. Frank Mensel. *Women and Minorities in Administration of Higher Education Institutions: Employment Patterns and Salary Comparisons 1978–79 and An Analysis of Progress Toward Affirmative Action Goals 1975–76 to 1978–79*. Washington, DC: College and University Personnel Association, 1981.

Frankel, Peter. "Title VII and the Supreme Court: The Evolution of Affirmative Action." *Glendale Law Review* 8.1–2 (1988): 102–31.

Fraser, Nancy, and Linda J. Nicholson. "Social Criticism without Philosophy." In Nicholson, *Feminism/Postmodernism*, 19–38.

Free Congress Foundation. *Annual Report, 1995*. Washington, DC, n.d.

Freeman, Jo. *The Politics of Women's Liberation*. New York: McKay, 1975.

——. "The Tyranny of Structurelessness." *Berkeley Journal of Sociology* 17 (1972–73): 151–64.

——. "Women on the Move: The Roots of Revolt." In Rossi and Calderwood, *Academic Women*, 1–32.

Friedan, Betty. *The Feminine Mystique*. New York: Norton, 1963.

Friedman, Susan Stanford. "Beyond White and Other: Relationality and Narratives of Race in Feminist Discourse." *Signs* 21 (1995): 1–49.

Fund for American Studies. *1992 Program Report*. Washington, DC: Fund for American Studies, 1992.

——. Collins, Michael J. Letter dated 15 September 1992. In Fund for American Studies, *1992 Program Report*, v.

——. Promotional video shown to author at Fund for American Studies, Washington, DC, 17 November 1992.

Fund for American Studies and Georgetown University Institutes. Course syllabus for Economics in Public Policy. 1993 Institute on Political Journalism, Fund for American Studies/Georgetown University, Handout. 1 p.

Furniss, W. Todd, and Patricia Albjerg Graham, eds. *Women in Higher Education.* Washington, DC: American Council on Education, 1974.

Gallop, Jane. *Around 1981: Academic Feminist Literary Theory.* New York: Routledge, 1992.

Gardiner, Judith Kegan. "On Female Identity and Writing by Women." *Critical Inquiry* 8 (1981): 347–61.

——, ed. *Provoking Agents: Gender and Agency in Theory and Practice.* Urbana: University of Illinois Press, 1995.

——, Elly Bulkin, Rena Grasso Patterson, and Annette Kolodny. "An Interchange on Feminist Criticism: On 'Dancing Through the Minefield.' " *Feminist Studies* 8 (1982): 629–75.

Garner, Shirley Nelson, Claire Kahane, and Madelon Sprengnether, eds. *The (M)other Tongue: Essays in Feminist Psychoanalytic Interpretation.* Ithaca, NY: Cornell University Press, 1985.

GBL. "Discrimination against women in physics." *Physics Today* 25.7 (1972): 61–62.

Genes and Gender I. Ed. Betty Rosoff and Ethel Toback. New York: Gordian, 1978.

Genes and Gender II: Pitfalls of Research on Sex and Gender. Ed. Ruth Hubbard and Marian Lowe. New York: Gordian, 1979.

Genes and Gender IV: The Second X and Women's Health. Ed. Myra Fooden, Susan Gordon, and Betty Hughley. New York: Gordian, 1983.

Georgetown University Summer School 1993. Bulletin, Georgetown University, n.d.

Giddens, Anthony. *The Constitution of Society: Outline of the Theory of Structuration.* Berkeley: University of California Press, 1984.

——. *Social Theory and Modern Sociology.* Cambridge, UK: Polity, 1987.

Giddings, Paula. *When and Where I Enter: The Impact of Black Women on Race and Sex in America.* New York: Morrow, 1984.

Gilbert, Sandra M. "Costumes of the Mind: Transvestism as Metaphor in Modern Literature." *Critical Inquiry* 7 (1980): 391–418.

——. "Patriarchal Poetry and Women Readers." *PMLA* 93 (1978): 368–82.

Gilder, George. *Sexual Suicide.* New York: Quadrangle, 1973.

Gilligan, Carol. *In a Different Voice: Psychological Theory and Women's Development.* Cambridge: Harvard University Press, 1982.

Gitlin, Todd. *The Sixties: Years of Hope, Days of Rage.* New York: Bantam, 1987.

Goetting, Ann, and Sara Fenstermaker, eds. *Individual Voices, Collective Visions: Fifty Years of Women in Sociology.* Philadelphia: Temple University Press, 1995.

Goldberg, Edward D. "The Development of Higher Education's Involvement in the New Jersey Project." In Smith and Olin, *New Jersey Project,* 8–10.

——. "New Jersey's Model for Stimulating Change." In *The State University of New York: The New Liberal Arts—Curriculum in Transition.* Albany: State University of New York Press, 1986. 47–60.

——. "Remarks on the Occasion of His Swearing In as the Third Chancellor of the New Jersey Higher Education System." Trenton, NJ, 1 March 1991. Typescript supplied by Edward D. Goldberg.

——. Untitled speech given at the conference Changing the Subject(s): A Celebration of

Six Years of Curriculum Change in New Jersey. New Jersey Project Statewide Conference, Brookdale Community College, 1 November 1991. Typescript supplied by Edward D. Goldberg.

Gordon, Linda. "Radical Feminist Studies Program, Cambridge-Goddard Graduate School for Social Change, Cambridge, Massachusetts." In *Female Studies III*, 147–48.

Gornick, Vivian, and Barbara K. Moran. Introduction to Gornick and Moran, *Woman*, xiii–xxxii.

——, eds. *Woman in a Sexist Society: Studies in Power and Powerlessness.* New York: Basic Books, 1971.

Gottfried, Paul. *The Conservative Movement.* Rev. ed. New York: Twayne, 1993.

Gould, Meredith, and Rochelle Kern-Daniels. "Toward a Sociological Theory of Gender and Sex." *The American Sociologist* 12 (1977): 182–89.

Graham, Dee L. R., Patricia O'Reilly, and Edna I. Rawlings. "Costs and Benefits of Advocacy for Faculty Women: A Case Study." *Journal of Social Issues* 41.4 (1985): 85–98.

Graham, Patricia Albjerg. "Status Transitions of Women Students, Faculty, and Administrators." In Rossi and Calderwood, *Academic Women*, 163–72.

Grant, Linda, and Kathryn B. Ward. "Gender and Publishing in Sociology." *Gender and Society* 5 (1991): 207–23.

Grant, Linda, Kathryn B. Ward, and Xue Lan Rong. "Is There an Association between Gender and Method in Sociological Research?" *American Sociological Review* 52 (1987): 856–62.

Gray, Mary W. "The Halls of Ivy and the Halls of Justice: Resisting Sex Discrimination Against Faculty Women." *Academe* 71.5 (1985): 33–41.

——. "Legal Perspectives on Sex Equity in Faculty Employment." *Journal of Social Issues* 41.4 (1985): 121–34.

Greene, Gayle. "Women and Men in Doris Lessing's *Golden Notebook:* Divided Selves." In Garner et al., *(M)other Tongue*, 280–305.

——, and Coppélia Kahn, eds. *Changing Subjects: The Making of Feminist Literary Criticism.* London and New York: Routledge, 1993.

Gross, Barry. *Discrimination in Reverse: Is Turnabout Fair Play?* New York: New York University Press, 1978.

Gross, Robert A. "How Men Use Women." *Newsweek*, 25 July 1970, 72–74.

"The Guide to Current Female Studies III." Old Westbury, NY: Feminist Press, 1973. Pamphlet.

Gump, Janice. "A Comparative Analysis of Black and White Women's Sex-Role Attitudes." *Journal of Consulting and Clinical Psychology* 43 (1975): 858–63.

Gutwirth, Madelyn. "Madame de Staël, Rousseau, and the Woman Question." *PMLA* 86 (1971): 100–109.

Hacker, Helen. "Women as a Minority Group." *Social Forces* 30 (October 1951): 60–69.

Hall, Jacqueline Dowd. " 'The Mind That Burns in Each Body': Women, Rape, and Racial Violence." In *Powers of Desire: The Politics of Sexuality.* Ed. Ann Snitow, Christine Stansell, and Sharon Thompson. New York: Monthly Review Press, 1983. 328–49.

Halliday, Terence C. "Introduction: Sociology's Fragile Professionalism." In Halliday and Janowitz, *Sociology*, 3–42.

———, and Morris Janowitz, eds. *Sociology and Its Publics: The Forms and Fates of Disciplinary Organization*. Chicago: University of Chicago Press, 1992.

Hanna, Charlotte. "The Organizational Context for Affirmative Action for Women Faculty." *Journal of Higher Education* 59 (1988): 390–411.

Haraway, Donna. "Animal Sociology and a Natural Economy of the Body Politic, Part II: The Past Is the Contested Zone—Human Nature and Theories of Production and Reproduction in Primate Behavior Studies." *Signs* 4 (1978): 37–60.

Harding, Sandra. *The Science Question in Feminism*. Ithaca, NY: Cornell University Press, 1986.

———. "Rethinking Standpoint Epistemology: 'What Is Strong Objectivity?' " In Alcoff and Potter, *Feminist Epistemologies*, 49–82.

———. "Who Knows? Identities and Feminist Epistemology." In Hartman and Messer-Davidow, *(En)Gendering Knowledge*, 100–115.

———. *Whose Science? Whose Knowledge? Thinking from Women's Lives*. Ithaca, NY: Cornell University Press, 1991.

———. "Why Has the Sex / Gender System Become Visible Only Now?" In Harding and Hintikka, *Discovering Reality*, 311–24.

———, and Merrill B. Hintikka, eds. *Discovering Reality: Feminist Perspectives on Epistemology, Metaphysics, Methodology, and Philosophy of Science*. Dordrecht, Holland: D. Reidel, 1983.

Hardy, Barbara. "De Beauvoir, Lessing—Now Kate Millett." *New York Times Book Review*, 6 September 1970, 8, 10, 12.

Hareven, Tamara K. "Modernization and Family History: Perspectives on Social Change." *Signs* 2 (1976): 190–206.

Harley, Sharon, and Rosalyn Terborg-Penn, eds. *The Afro-American Woman: Struggles and Images*. Port Washington, NY: Kennikat, 1978.

Harris, Ann Sutherland. "The Second Sex in Academe." *ART in America* (May–June 1972): 418–19.

———. "The Second Sex in Academe." *AAUP Bulletin* 56 (1970): 283–95.

———. "Women in College Art Departments and Museums." *Art Journal* 32 (1973): 417–19.

Harris, Trudier. *From Mammies to Militants: Domestics in Black American Literature*. Philadelphia: Temple University Press, 1982.

Hartman, Heidi, Ellen Bravo, Charlotte Bunch, Nancy Hartsock, Roberta Spalter-Roth, Linda Williams, and Maria Blanco. "Bringing Together Feminist Theory and Practice: A Collective Interview." *Signs* 21 (1996): 917–51.

Hartman, Joan E., and Ellen Messer-Davidow. Introduction to Hartman and Messer-Davidow, *Women in Print* I, 1–9.

———, eds. *Women in Print I: Opportunities for Women's Studies Research in Language and Literature*. New York: Modern Language Association, 1982.

———. *Women in Print II: Opportunities for Women's Studies Publication in Language and Literature*. New York: Modern Language Association, 1982.

——. *(En)Gendering Knowledge: Feminists in Academe.* Knoxville: University of Tennessee Press, 1991.

Hartman, Mary S. "The Ivory Tower and the Real World: Scholarship and Activism in the Garden State." Keynote address at the conference Ninth Annual Celebration of Our Work. Rutgers University, New Brunswick, NJ, 21 May 1991. Typescript supplied by Mary S. Hartman.

——. Preface to *Clio's Consciousness Raised: New Perspectives on the History of Women.* New York: Harper Torchbooks, 1974, vii–xii.

Hartmann, Susan M. *The Other Feminists: Activists in the Liberal Establishment.* New Haven, CT: Yale University Press, 1998.

Hartsock, Nancy. "The Feminist Standpoint: Developing the Ground for a Specifically Feminist Historical Materialism." In Harding and Hintikka, *Discovering Reality,* 283–310.

——. *Money, Sex, and Power.* New York: Longman, 1983.

Hawkesworth, Mary. "Confounding Gender." *Signs* 22 (1997): 649–85. Also see replies by Wendy McKenna and Suzanne Kessler, Steven G. Smith, Joan Wallach Scott, R. W. Connell, and Mary Hawkesworth in the same issue, 687–713.

Hayden, Casey, and Mary King. "Sex and Caste." *Liberation* 10.2 (1966): 35–36.

Heilbrun, Carolyn. "Marriage and Contemporary Fiction." *Critical Inquiry* 5 (1978): 309–23.

——, and Catharine Stimpson. "Theories of Feminist Criticism: A Dialogue." In *Feminist Literary Criticism: Explorations in Theory.* Ed. Josephine Donovan. Lexington: University Press of Kentucky, 1975. 61–73.

Heirich, Max. *The Spiral of Conflict: Berkeley, 1964.* New York: Columbia University Press, 1971.

Henderson, Peter H., Julie E. Clarke, and Mary A. Reynolds. *Doctorate Recipients from United States Universities: Summary Report 1995.* Washington, DC: National Academy of Sciences, 1996.

Heritage Foundation. *A New Agenda for Education.* Ed. Eileen M. Gardiner. Washington, DC: Heritage Foundation, 1985.

——. "Defining Conservatism." Flier, Washington, DC, [1992]. 1 p.

——. *The Heritage Foundation 1991 Annual Report.* Washington, DC: Heritage Foundation, n.d.

——. "Heritage Foundation to Host Lecture Series on 'Defining Conservatism.' " Press release, Washington, DC, 15 October 1992. 2 pp.

——. "Ideas Have Consequences: A Conservative Battleplan for the 1990s." Expected attendance list included in registration packet for the Fifteenth Annual Resource Bank Meeting, Chicago, 23–24 April 1992.

——. "Ideas Have Consequences: A Conservative Battleplan for the 1990s." Program for the Fifteenth Annual Resource Bank Meeting, Chicago, 23–24 April 1992.

——. *Mandate for Leadership: Policy Management in a Conservative Administration.* Ed. Charles L. Heatherly. Washington, DC: Heritage Foundation, 1981.

——. *Mandate for Leadership II: Continuing the Conservative Revolution.* Washington DC: Heritage Foundation, 1984.

——. "Shaping America's Values Debate." Flier, Washington, DC, [1992], 1 p.

Heywood, Leslie, and Jennifer Drake, eds. *Third Wave Agenda: Being Feminist, Doing Feminism.* Minneapolis: University of Minnesota Press, 1997.

Hicks, Emily. "Cultural Marxism: Nonsynchrony and Feminist Practice." In Sargent, *Women,* 219–37.

Higginbotham, A. Leon, Jr. *Shades of Freedom: Racial Politics and the Presumptions of the American Legal Process.* Oxford: Oxford University Press, 1996.

"High Court Refuses to Hear Appeal of Ruling That Barred Considering Race in Admissions." *Chronicle of Higher Education,* 12 July 1996, A25, A29.

Hirsch, Marianne, and Evelyn Fox Keller. "Introduction: January 4, 1990." In Hirsch and Keller, *Conflicts,* 1–5.

——, eds. *Conflicts in Feminism.* New York: Routledge, 1990.

Hochschild, Arlie Russell. "Inside the Clockwork of Male Careers." In Orlans and Wallace, *Gender,* 125–39.

Hoffman, Nancy Jo. "Ad Hoc Women's Institute and Resource Center, Portland State University." In *Female Studies III,* 164–67.

——. "Sexism in Letters of Recommendation." *MLA Newsletter,* September 1972, 5–6.

Hole, Judith, and Ellen Levine. *Rebirth of Feminism.* New York: Quadrangle, 1971.

Hollander, Nancy. "Women's Studies Program, San Diego State College." In *Female Studies III,* 174–75.

Holleran, Paula R. "The Feminist Curriculum: Issues for Survival in Academe." *Journal of Thought* 20.3 (1985): 25–36.

Holton, Gerald. *Introduction to Concepts and Theories in Physical Science.* Reading, MA: Addison-Wesley, 1952.

hooks, bell. *Ain't I a Woman: Black Women and Feminism.* Boston: South End, 1981.

——. *Feminist Theory: From Margin to Center.* Boston: South End, 1984.

——. "Sisterhood: Beyond Public and Private." *Signs* 21 (1996): 814–29. Interview with Tanya McKinnon.

Hooper-Greenhill, Eilean. *Museums and the Shaping of Modern Knowledge.* London and New York: Routledge, 1992.

Howe, Florence. "The First Ten Years Are the Easiest." In *Index to the First Ten Years.* Comp. Jo Baird, Shirley Frank, and Beth Stafford. Old Westbury, NY: Feminist Press, 1983.

——. "A Report on Women and the Profession." *College English* 32 (1971): 847–54.

——. *Seven Years Later: Women's Studies Programs in 1976.* Washington, DC: National Advisory Council on Women's Educational Programs, 1977.

——. "What Was It Like Then?" In *Courage and Tools: The Florence Howe Award for Feminist Scholarship, 1974–1989.* Ed. Joanne Glasgow and Angela Ingram. New York: MLA, 1990. ix–xii.

——. "Women and the Power to Change." In *Women and the Power to Change.* Ed. Florence Howe. New York: McGraw-Hill, 1975. 127–71.

——, and Carol Ahlum. "Women's Studies and Social Change." In Rossi and Calderwood, *Academic Women,* 393–424.

Howe, Florence, and Paul Lauter. *The Impact of Women's Studies on the Campus and the Dis-*

ciplines. Washington, DC: National Institute of Education, 1980. Report to U.S. Department of Health, Education, and Welfare.

——, Laura Morlock, and Richard Berk. "The Status of Women in Modern Language Departments: A Report of the Modern Language Association Commission on the Status of Women in the Profession." *PMLA* 86.3 (May 1971): 459–68.

Hubbard, Ruth. "Have Only Men Evolved?" In Hubbard et al., *Women*, 7–35.

——. *The Politics of Women's Biology.* New Brunswick, NJ: Rutgers University Press, 1990.

——, Mary Sue Henifin, and Barbara Fried, eds. *Women Look at Biology Looking at Women.* Cambridge, MA: Schenkman, 1979.

Huber, Bettina J., Denise M. Pinney, David E. Lawrence, and Denise Bourassa Knight. "MLA Surveys of Ph.D. Placement: Most Recent Findings and Decade-Long Trends." *ADFL Bulletin* 20.3 (1989): 20–30.

Huber, Joan. "Toward a Sociotechnological Theory of the Women's Movement." *Social Problems* 23 (1976): 371–88.

——, ed. *Changing Women in a Changing Society.* Chicago: University of Chicago Press, 1973.

Hull, Gloria T. "Researching Alice Dunbar-Nelson: A Personal and Literary Perspective." *Feminist Studies* 6 (1980): 314–20.

——, Patricia Bell-Scott, and Barbara Smith, eds. *All the Women Are White, All the Blacks Are Men, But Some of Us Are Brave: Black Women's Studies.* Old Westbury, NY: Feminist Press, 1982.

Hurston, Zora Neale. *I Love Myself When I Am Laughing . . . : A Zora Neale Hurston Reader.* Ed. Alice Walker. Old Westbury, NY: Feminist Press, 1979.

——. *Mules and Men.* Bloomington: Indiana University Press, 1978.

——. *Their Eyes Were Watching God.* Urbana: University of Illinois Press, 1978.

Hutchins, Loraine. "Letter to the Editor about Feminist Priorities." In Sacramento State University Women's Studies Board, *Report*, 135.

Hyer, Patricia B. "Affirmative Action for Women Faculty: Case Studies of Three Successful Institutions." *Journal of Higher Education* 56 (1985): 282–99.

Institute for Women's Policy Research. "Exploring the Quincentennial: The Policy Challenges of Gender, Diversity, and International Exchange." Conference program for Third Women's Policy Research Conference, Washington, DC, 15–16 May 1992.

——. Hartman, Heidi, and Roberta Spalter-Roth. "Why an Institute for Women's Policy Research?" Statement. Washington, DC, October 1991. 4 pp.

——. "List of Publications, Spring 1992." List, Washington, DC, May 1992. 6 pp.

Intercollegiate Studies Institute. *Campus*, 21 issues, 1991–97.

——. *Intercollegiate Review*, 17 issues, 1989–97.

——. "ISI Salvatori Fellowship Program." Flier, Bryn Mawr, PA, n.d. 1 p.

——. "The Richard M. Weaver Fellowship Awards Program of the Intercollege Studies Institute for Graduate Students during the 1993–94 Academic Year." Flier, Bryn Mawr, PA, n.d. 1 p.

Jacklin, Carol N. "Methodological Issues in the Study of Sex-Related Differences." In *Sex Role Research: Measuring Social Change.* Ed. Barbara L. Richardson and Jeana Wirtenberg. New York: Praeger, 1983. 93–100.

Jackson, Maurice. "Minorities and Women in Sociology: Are Opportunities Changing?" *The American Sociologist* 6 (1971): 3–5.

Jacobs, Paul, and Saul Landau. *The New Radicals: A Report with Documents.* New York: Vintage, 1966.

Jansen, Charles R. *Studying Art History.* Englewood Cliffs, NJ: Prentice-Hall, 1986.

Johnson-Roullier, Cyraina. "The Singularity of Multiplicity: Feminism and the Pitfalls of Valorization." In *Feminism Beside Itself.* Ed. Diane Elam and Robyn Wiegman. New York: Routledge, 1995. 179–96.

Johnston, Hank, Enrique Laraña, and Joseph R. Gusfield. "Identities, Grievances, and New Social Movements." In Laraña et al., *New Social Movements,* 3–35.

Johnston, Jill. *Lesbian Nation.* New York: Simon and Schuster, 1973.

Johnston, Judith L. "The Challenges of the First Year." In Smith and Olin, *New Jersey Project,* 11–16.

———. "Telling Our Stories: The Academy and Change." *Women's Studies Quarterly* 18. 3–4 (1990): 118–27.

Jones, Ann Rosalind. "Imaginary Gardens with Real Frogs in Them: Feminist Euphoria and the Franco-American Divide, 1976–88." In Greene and Kahn, *Changing Subjects,* 64–82.

Jones, Jacqueline. " 'My Mother Was Much of a Woman': Black Women, Work, and the Family under Slavery." *Feminist Studies* 8 (1982): 235–70.

Journal of Social Issues 28.2 (1972).

Juhasz, Suzanne. "Feminist Criticism: My Theory and Practice." In Blecki et al., *Feminist Literary Criticism,* 10–16.

Kahlenberg, Richard D. *The Remedy: Class, Race, and Affirmative Action.* New York: Basic Books, 1996.

Kahn, Coppélia. "The Hand That Rocks the Cradle: Recent Gender Theories and Their Implications." In Garner et al., *(M)other Tongue,* 72–88.

Kampf, Louis, and Paul Lauter, eds. *The Politics of Literature: Dissenting Essays on the Teaching of English.* New York: Pantheon, 1970.

Kanter, Rosabeth Moss. "Some Effects of Proportions on Group Life: Skewed Sex Ratios and Responses to Token Women." *American Journal of Sociology* 82 (1977): 965–90.

Karen, David. "The Politics of Class, Race, and Gender: Access to Higher Education in the United States, 1960–1986." *American Journal of Higher Education* 99 (1991): 208–37.

Keller, Evelyn Fox. "The Anomaly of a Woman in Physics." In *Working It Out: 23 Women Writers, Artists, Scientists, and Scholars Talk About Their Lives and Works.* Ed. Sara Ruddick and Pamela Daniels. New York: Pantheon, 1977. 77–91.

———. "Holding the Center of Feminist Theory." *Women's Studies International Forum* 12 (1989): 313–18.

———. *Reflections on Gender and Science.* New Haven, CT: Yale University Press, 1985.

Kelly, Joan. "The Doubled Vision of Feminist Theory: A Postscript to the 'Women and Power' Conference." In Kelly, *Women,* 51–64. Rpt. from *Feminist Studies* 5 (1979): 216–27.

——. "Early Feminist Theory and the *Querelle des Femmes*, 1400–1789." In Kelly, *Women*, 65–109. Rpt. from *Signs* 8 (1982): 4–28.

——. "The Social Relations of the Sexes: Methodological Implications of Women's History." In Kelly, *Women*, 1–18. Rpt. from *Signs* 1 (1976): 1–18.

——. *Women, History, and Theory: The Essays of Joan Kelly.* Chicago: University of Chicago Press, 1984.

Keohane, Nannerl O. "Speaking from Silence: Women and the Science of Politics." In *A Feminist Perspective in the Academy: The Difference It Makes.* Ed. Elizabeth Langland and Walter Gove. Chicago: University of Chicago Press, 1983. 86–100.

Kerr, Clark. *The Great Transformation in Higher Education, 1960–1980.* Albany: State University of New York Press, 1991.

Kersten, Katherine. "What Do Women Want? A Conservative Feminist Manifesto." *Policy Review* 56 (1991): 4–15.

Kessler, Suzanne J. *Lessons from the Intersexed.* New Brunswick, NJ: Rutgers University Press, 1998.

——. "The Medical Construction of Gender: Case Management of Intersexed Infants." *Signs* 16 (1990): 3–26.

——, and Wendy McKenna. *Gender: An Ethnomethodological Approach.* New York: John Wiley, 1978.

Killian, Lewis M. "Organization, Rationality, and Spontaneity in the Civil Rights Movement." In Curtis and Aguirre, *Collective Behavior* 209–25.

Kincaid, James R. "Alice's Invasion of Wonderland." *PMLA* 88 (1973): 91–99.

King, Deborah K. "Multiple Jeopardy, Multiple Consciousness: The Context of a Black Feminist Ideology." *Signs* 14 (1988): 42–72.

Kinney, Cherry Carter. "Reflections on the 1969 Resolution of the Women's Caucus." *The American Sociologist* 6 (1971): 19–22.

Kinney, Martha M. "Boards and Paper: Feminist Writing and Trade Publishing." In Hartman and Messer-Davidow, *Women in Print* II, 41–55.

Kistiakowsky, Vera. "Women in Physics: Unnecessary, Injurious, and Out of Place?" *Physics Today*, February 1980, 32–40.

——. "Women in Physics and Astronomy." *Annals of the New York Academy of Sciences* 323 (20 April 1979): 35–47.

Kleeman, Katherine E. *Learning to Lead: Public Leadership Education Programs for Women.* Pamphlet, Washington, DC: PLEN, 1984.

Klein, Ethel. "The Diffusion of Consciousness in the United States and Western Europe." In *The Women's Movements of the United States and Western Europe.* Ed. Mary Fainsod Katzenstein and Carol McClurg Mueller. Philadelphia: Temple University Press, 1987. 23–43.

——, and Lillian Robbins. "Social-Psychological Issues in Sex Discrimination," *Journal of Social Issues* 41.4 (1985): 135–54.

Klein, Julie Thompson. "Across the Boundaries." *Social Epistemology* 4 (1990): 267–80.

——. *Crossing Boundaries: Knowledge, Disciplinarities, and Interdisciplinarities.* Charlottesville: University Press of Virginia, 1996.

——. *Interdisciplinarity: History, Theory, and Practice.* Detroit: Wayne State University Press, 1990.

Klotzberger, Kay. "Political Action by Academic Women." In Rossi and Calderwood, *Academic Women,* 359–91.

Knorr-Cetina, Karen D. *The Manufacture of Knowledge: An Essay on the Constructivist and Contextual Nature of Science.* Oxford: Pergamon, 1981.

Koedt, Anne, Ellen Levine, and Anita Rapone, eds. *Radical Feminism.* New York: Quadrangle, 1973.

Kohlberg, Lawrence. "A Cognitive-Developmental Analysis of Children's Sex-Role Concepts and Attitudes." In Maccoby, *Development,* 82–173.

Kolodny, Annette. "Dancing Through the Minefield: Some Observations on the Theory, Practice, and Politics of a Feminist Literary Criticism." *Feminist Studies* 6 (1980): 1–25.

——. "The Feminist as Literary Critic." *Critical Inquiry* 2 (1976): 821–32.

——. "A Map for Rereading: Or, Gender and the Interpretation of Literary Texts." *New Literary History* 11 (1980): 451–68.

——. "Review Essay: Literary Criticism." *Signs* 2 (1976): 404–21.

——. "Some Notes on Defining a 'Feminist Literary Criticism.'" *Critical Inquiry* 2 (1975): 75–92.

Krieger, Murray. *Theory of Criticism: A Tradition and Its System.* Baltimore: Johns Hopkins University Press, 1976.

Krohn, Barbara. "The Puzzling Case of the Missing Ms." *Nation's Schools and Colleges* 1.3 (1974): 32–38.

Ladner, Joyce A. *Tomorrow's Tomorrow: The Black Woman.* 25th anniversary ed. Lincoln: University of Nebraska Press, 1995. Original publication, New York: Doubleday, 1971.

Lambert, Helen H. "Biology and Equality: A Perspective on Sex Differences." *Signs* 4 (1978): 97–117.

Lamphere, Louise. "Review Essay: Anthropology." *Signs* 2 (1977): 612–27.

Lancaster, Jane B. *Primate Behavior and the Emergence of Human Culture.* New York: Holt, Rinehart & Winston, 1975.

Landy, Marcia. "Women, Education, and Social Power." In *Female Studies V,* 53–63.

LaNoue, George R., and Barbara A. Lee. *Academics in Court: The Consequences of Faculty Discrimination Litigation.* Ann Arbor: University of Michigan Press, 1987.

Laraña, Enrique, Hank Johnston, and Joseph R. Gusfield, eds. *New Social Movements: From Ideology to Identity.* Philadelphia: Temple University Press, 1994.

Larossa, Ralph, and Maureen Mulligan Larossa. "Baby Case: Fathers vs. Mothers." In Risman and Schwartz, *Gender,* 138–54.

La Sorte, Michelle A. "Sex Differences in Salary among Academic Sociology Teachers." *The American Sociologist* 6 (1971): 304–7.

Laue, James. *Direct Action and Desegregation, 1960–62.* Brooklyn: Carlson, 1989.

Lauretis, Teresa de, ed. *Feminist Studies / Critical Studies.* Bloomington: Indiana University Press, 1986.

Lauter, Paul. "Race and Gender in the Shaping of the American Literary Canon: A Case Study from the Twenties." *Feminist Studies* 9 (1983): 435–64.

Leadership Conference on Civil Rights. "Proposition 209 Timeline." In a looseleaf note-book on anti-affirmative action initiatives prepared by the Leadership Conference on Civil Rights, November 1997.

Leadership Institute, U.S. congressman Dick Armey. Direct-mail letter circulated by the Leadership Institute, 8 June 1991.

———. *Building Leadership: The Newsletter of the Leadership Institute* 6.1 (1992).

———. *The Leadership Institute Prospectus.* Springfield, VA: Leadership Institute, n.d.

Lebsock, Suzanne. "Free Black Women and the Question of Matriarchy: Petersburg, Virginia." *Feminist Studies* 8 (1982): 271–90.

Lederman, Douglas. "Growing Attacks on Affirmative Action." *Chronicle of Higher Education,* 26 April 1996, A30.

———. "New Lawsuits May Help Determine What's Legal in Affirmative Action." *Chronicle of Higher Education,* 21 March 1997, A34–35.

———. "Suit Challenges Affirmative Action in Admissions at U. of Michigan." *Chronicle of Higher Education,* 24 October 1997, A27–28.

———. "Texas Asks High Court to Uphold Legality of Affirmative Action." *Chronicle of Higher Education,* 10 May 1996, A25, A38.

Lee, Alfred McClung. "Steps Taken Toward Liberating Sociologists." In Oppenheimer et al., *Radical Sociologists,* 28–42.

Leffler, Ann, Dair L. Gillespie, and Elinor Lerner Ratner. "Academic Feminists and the Women's Movement." *Ain't I A Woman* 4 (1973): 1–21.

Lehman, Beth, ed. *The Open Up the Schools Program.* NUC Papers, no. 3. N.p.: N.p., 1971. Booklet. 55 pp.

Leitch, Vincent. *American Literary Criticism from the 30s to the 80s.* New York: Columbia University Press, 1988.

Lenoir, Timothy. "The Discipline of Nature and the Nature of Disciplines." In Messer-Davidow et al., *Knowledges,* 70–103.

Leonardo, Micaela di. "Contingencies of Value in Feminist Anthropology." In Hartman and Messer-Davidow, *(En)Gendering Knowledge,* 140–58.

Lerner, Gerda. *Black Women in White America.* New York: Pantheon, 1972.

———. *The Majority Finds Its Past: Placing Women in History.* New York: Oxford University Press, 1979.

———. "New Approaches to the Study of Women in American History." In Lerner, *Majority,* 3–14. Rpt. from *Journal of Social History* 3 (1969): 53–62.

———. "Placing Women in History: Definitions and Challenges." In Lerner, *Majority,* 145–59.

———. "On the Teaching and Organization of Feminist Studies." In *Female Studies V,* 34–37.

Levey, Michael. *A Concise History of Painting from Giotto to Cèzanne.* New York: Praeger, 1962.

Levine, Adeline, and Janice Crumrine. "Women and the Fear of Success." *American Journal of Sociology* 80 (1975): 964–74.

Lewis, Diane K. "A Response to Inequality: Black Women, Racism, and Sexism." *Signs* 3 (1977): 339–61.

——. "The Black Family: Socialization and Sex Roles." *Phylon* 36 (1975): 221–27.

Lichtenberg, Margaret. "Power and Powerlessness." *The Nation,* 8 November 1971, 473–75.

Littleton, Christine A. "Reconstructing Sexual Equality." In Meyers, *Feminist Social Thought,* 696–713.

Long, Priscilla, ed. *The New Left: A Collection of Essays.* Boston: Porter Sargent, 1969.

Longino, Helen E. *Science as Social Knowledge.* Princeton, NJ: Princeton University Press, 1990.

Looser, Devony, and E. Ann Kaplan, eds. *Generations: Academic Feminists in Dialogue.* Minneapolis: University of Minnesota Press, 1997.

Lorber, Judith, Rose Laub Coser, Alice S. Rossi, and Nancy Chodorow. "On *The Reproduction of Mothering:* A Methodological Debate." *Signs* 6 (1981): 482–514.

Lorde, Audre. *Sister Outsider: Essays and Speeches.* Trumansburg, NY: Crossing, 1983.

Lougee, Carolyn C. "Review Essay: Modern European History." *Signs* 2 (1977): 185–98.

Lowe, Marian. "The Dialectic of Biology and Culture." In Lowe and Hubbard, *Woman's Nature,* 39–62.

——. "Sociobiology and Sex Differences." *Signs* 4 (1978): 118–25.

——, and Ruth Hubbard. "Sociobiology and Biosociology: Can Science Prove the Biological Basis of Sex Differences in Behavior?" In *Genes and Gender II,* 91–111.

——, eds. *Woman's Nature: Rationalizations of Inequality.* New York: Pergamon, 1983.

Lynch, Frederick R. *Invisible Victims: White Males and the Crisis of Affirmative Action.* Westport, CT: Greenwood, 1989.

——. "Surviving Affirmative Action (More or Less)." *Commentary* 90.2 (August 1990): 44–47.

Maccoby, Eleanor E., ed. *The Development of Sex Differences.* Stanford, CA: Stanford University Press, 1966.

Maccoby, Eleanor E., and Carol Nagy Jacklin. *The Psychology of Sex Differences.* Stanford, CA: Stanford University Press, 1974.

Mack, Maynard. "To See It Feelingly." *PMLA* 86 (1971): 363–74.

Mackie, Marlene. "Female Sociologists' Productivity, Collegial Relations, and Research Style Examined through Journal Publications." *Sociology and Social Research* 69 (1985): 189–209.

Magner, Denise K. "Job Applicant Sues Bowling Green U. and Accreditor." *Chronicle of Higher Education,* 12 July 1996, A16.

——. "Number of Minority Ph.D.'s Reached an All-Time High in 1996." *Chronicle of Higher Education,* 21 November 1997, A10–11.

Mailer, Norman. "The Prisoner of Sex." *Harper's,* March 1971, 41–46, 48, 50, 52–60, 62–66, 68–72, 77–92.

Mainstreaming Minority Women's Studies Programs. New York: National Council for Research on Women, 1991. Booklet. 30 pp.

Malson, M. R. "Black Women's Sex Roles: The Social Context for a New Ideology." *Journal of Social Issues* 39.3 (1983): 101–13.

Martin, Del, and Phyllis Lyon. *Lesbian / Woman.* San Francisco: Glide, 1972. Rpt. New York: Bantam, 1973.

Martin, Randy. "Introduction: Education as National Pedagogy." In Martin, *Chalk Lines*, 1–29.

——, ed. *Chalk Lines: The Politics of Work in the Managed University*. Durham, NC: Duke University Press, 1998.

Martin, Wendy. "Teaching Women's Studies—Some Problems and Discoveries." *Female Studies IV*, 9–13.

——, and Mary Louise Briscoe. "Women's Studies: Problems in Research." *Women's Studies* 2 (1974): 249–59.

Mason, Karen Oppenheimer. "U.S. Women's Sex-Role Ideology, 1970." *American Journal of Sociology* 80 (1975): 1212–19.

Mattfeld, Jacqueline A. "Many Are Called, But Few Are Chosen." In Furniss and Graham, *Women*, 121–27.

Matthews, Sarah H. "Rethinking Sociology through a Feminist Perspective." *The American Sociologist* 17 (1982): 29–39.

MacKinnon, Catharine. "Feminism, Marxism, Method, and the State: An Agenda for Theory." *Signs* 7 (1982): 514–44.

Macksey, Richard, and Eugenio Donato, eds. *The Structuralist Controversy: The Languages of Criticism and the Sciences of Man*. 2d ed. Baltimore: Johns Hopkins University Press, 1972.

McAdam, Doug. *Freedom Summer*. New York: Oxford University Press, 1988.

——. *Political Process and the Development of Black Insurgency, 1930–1970*. Chicago: University of Chicago Press, 1982.

McArthur, L. Z., and B. G. Resko. "The Portrayal of Men and Women in American Television Commercials." *Journal of Social Psychology* 97 (1975): 209–20.

McCartney, James L. "On Being Scientific: Changing Styles of Presentation of Sociological Research." *The American Sociologist* 5 (1970): 30–35.

McCue, J. J. G. *The World of Atoms: An Introduction to Physical Science*. New York: Ronald, 1956.

McDermott, Patrice. *Politics and Scholarship: Feminist Academic Journals and the Production of Knowledge*. Urbana: University of Illinois Press, 1994.

McGannon, J. Barry. "Tooling Up in the Talent Pool: A Proposal for Regional Administrative Internship Programs for Women." Paper presented at the American Council on Education Meeting, 6 October 1972. ERIC Document ED–071–188, EA–004–783.

McKay, Nellie. "Naming the Problem That Led to the Question 'Who Shall Teach African American Literature?' or, Are We Ready to Disband the Wheatley Court?" *PMLA* 113 (1998): 359–69.

McWilliams, Nancy R. "An intelligent women's guide to feminism." *Commonweal*, 1 October 1970, 25–26.

Mednick, Martha Shuch, and Sandra Schwartz Tangri. "New Social Psychological Perspectives on Women." *Journal of Social Issues* 28.2 (1972): 1–16.

Megill, Allan. "Introduction: Four Senses of Objectivity." *Annals of Scholarship* 8 (1991): 301–20.

Melucci, Alberto. *Nomads of the Present: Social Movements and Individual Needs in Contemporary Society.* Philadelphia: Temple University Press, 1989.

——. "The Process of Collective Identity." In *Social Movements and Culture.* Ed. Hank Johnston and Bert Klandermans. Minneapolis: University of Minnesota Press, 1995. 41–63.

Merton, Robert K. "Insiders and Outsiders: A Chapter in the Sociology of Knowledge." *American Journal of Sociology* 78 (1972): 9–47.

Messer-Davidow, Ellen. "Changing the System: The Board of Trustees Caper." *Women's Studies Quarterly* 18.3–4 (1976): 41–55.

——. "Dollars for Scholars: The Real Politics of Humanities Scholarship and Programs." In *The Politics of Research.* Ed. E. Ann Kaplan and George Levine. New Brunswick, NJ: Rutgers University Press, 1997, 193–233.

——. "Manufacturing the Attack on Liberalized Higher Education." *Social Text* 36 (1993): 40–80.

——. "Who (Ac)Counts and How." *MMLA Journal* 27 (1994): 26–41.

——, David R. Shumway, and David J. Sylvan, eds. *Knowledges: Historical and Critical Studies in Disciplinarity.* Charlottesville: University Press of Virginia, 1993.

——. Preface to Messer-Davidow et al., *Knowledges,* vii–viii.

Meyers, Diana Tietjens, ed. *Feminist Social Thought: A Reader.* New York: Routledge, 1997.

Miller, James. *Democracy Is in the Streets: From Port Huron to the Siege of Chicago.* New York: Simon and Schuster, 1987.

Miller, Jean Baker. *Toward a New Psychology of Women.* Boston: Beacon, 1976.

——, ed. *Psychoanalysis and Women.* New York: Brunner, 1973.

Miller, Nancy K. "Decades." In Greene and Kahn, *Changing Subjects,* 31–47.

Milton, John. *Paradise Lost: Complete Poems and Major Prose.* Ed. Merritt Y. Hughes. New York: Odyssey, [1674] 1957.

Midwestern State University. Course syllabus for "Collective Analysis and Action," spring quarter, 1991.

——. "Graduate Study in Women's Studies." Department of Women's Studies, 1989. Brochure.

——. "Louise" (instructor). Typed memorandum to "Collective Analysis and Action" students, 15 May 1991. 1 p.

——. "1984–1990 Program Evaluation: Women's Studies," spring 1991. Institutional document supplied by the chair of Women's Studies.

——. Student to CAA classmates. Typed letter distributed in class on 15 May 1991. 2 pp.

——. "Student Notes from CAA." Typed summary, 1 April 1991. 1 p.

——. "Student Notes from CAA." Typed summary, 3 April 1991. 1 p.

——. "Student Notes from CAA." Typed summary, 1 May 1991. 3 pp.

——. "The Theoretical Basis for Change." Typed handout for "Collective Analysis and Action" course, n.d. 1 p.

——. "Women's Studies." Department of Women's Studies, 1990. Brochure.

Mitchell, Joyce M., and Rachel R. Starr. "A Regional Approach for Analyzing the Recruitment of Academic Women." *American Behavioral Scientist* 15 (1971): 190–202.

Mitchell, Juliet. *Psychoanalysis and Feminism.* New York: Pantheon, 1974.

Modern Language Association. "Actions of the 1968 Business Meeting, 29 December 1968." *PMLA* 84 (1969): 1231–33.

——. Convention Program. *PMLA* 85 (1970).

——. Convention Program. *PMLA* 104 (1989).

——. Hartman, Joan E., Laura Morlock, Jean A. Perkins, and Adrian Tinsley. "Study III: Women in Modern Language Departments, 1972–73: A Report by the Commission on the Status of Women in the Profession." *PMLA* 91 (1976): 124–36.

——. Howe, Florence, Laura Morlock, and Richard Berk. "The Status of Women in Modern Language Departments: A Report of the Modern Language Association Commission on the Status of Women in the Profession." *PMLA* 86 (1971): 459–68.

——. "Informal Comments on Proposed Constitutional Amendments, December 1970." *PMLA* 85 (1970): 1247–50.

——. Morlock, Laura, et al. "Affirmative Action for Women in 1971: A Report of the Modern Language Association Commission on the Status of Women in the Profession." *PMLA* 87 (1972): 530–40.

——. "Report of the Executive Secretary." *PMLA* 85 (1970): 535–39.

——. "Statement by Henry Nash Smith, 1969 MLA President." *PMLA* 84 (1969): 344.

——. "Statement by John Hurt Fisher, MLA Executive Secretary." *PMLA* 84 (1969): 345–46.

——. "Statement by Louis Kampf, 1969 MLA Second Vice President." *PMLA* 84 (1969): 347–48.

——. "Summary of Correspondence to the New Study Commission." *PMLA* 85 (1970): 550–56.

Money, John, and Anke Ehrhardt. *Man and Woman, Boy and Girl.* Baltimore, MD: Johns Hopkins University Press, 1972.

Moore, Robert L. "Gender and Race and the Decision to Go to College." In Bartlett, *Introducing Race,* 52–66.

Moraga, Cherríe, and Gloria Anzaldua, eds. *This Bridge Called My Back: Writings by Radical Women of Color.* Watertown, MA: Persephone, 1981.

Morgan, Robin, *Going Too Far: The Personal Chronicle of a Feminist.* New York: Vintage, 1978.

——, ed. *Sisterhood Is Powerful: An Anthology of Writing from the Women's Liberation Movement.* New York: Random House, 1970.

Morgan, William W. "Feminism and Literary Study: A Reply to Annette Kolodny." *Critical Inquiry* 2 (1976): 807–16.

Morlock, Laura. "Discipline Variation in the Status of Academic Women." In Rossi and Calderwood, *Academic Women,* 255–312.

Morris, Aldon. "Black Southern Sit-In Movement: An Analysis of Internal Organization." In Curtis and Aguirre, *Collective Behavior,* 361–80.

——. *The Origins of the Civil Rights Movement: Black Communities Organizing for Change.* New York: Free Press, 1984.

Morris, Kathleen. "Through the Looking Glass: Recent Developments in Affirmative Action." *Berkeley Women's Law Journal* 11 (1996): 182–93.

Mueller, Carol. "Conflict Networks and the Origins of Women's Liberation." In Laraña et al., *New Social Movements*, 234–63.

Mullen, Jean S. "Freshman Textbooks." *College English* 34 (1972): 79–84.

Murray, Connie. "The Second Year of the Project: Consolidating the Gains of the First Year." In Smith and Olin, *New Jersey Project*, 17–19.

Murray, Pauli. "The Liberation of Black Women." In Thompson, *Voices*, 87–102.

Musil, Caryn McTighe, ed. *The Courage to Question: Women's Studies and Student Learning.* Washington, DC: Association of American Colleges, 1992.

Mouffe, Chantal. "Feminism, Citizenship, and Radical Democratic Politics." In Meyers, *Feminist Social Thought*, 532–44.

Myers, Greg. "The Social Construction of Two Biologists' Articles." In Messer-Davidow et al., *Knowledges*, 327–67.

Myrdal, Gunnar. *An American Dilemma: The Negro Problem and Modern Democracy.* New York: Harper & Row, 1944.

Naples, Nancy A., ed. *Community Activism and Feminist Politics: Organizing Across Race, Class, and Gender.* New York: Routledge, 1998.

National Journalism Center. *E&RI 1990 Annual Report.* Washington, DC: Education and Research Institute, n.d.

———. Montage of newsclips (n.d.) on display at the National Journalism Center, April 1992.

Neely, Carol Thomas. "Loss and Recovery: Homes Away From Home." In Greene and Kahn, *Changing Subjects*, 180–94.

Newcombe, Judith P., and Clinton F. Conrad. "A Theory of Mandated Academic Change." *Journal of Higher Education* 52 (1981): 555–77.

New Jersey Project. Announcement of the 1992 Summer Institute, n.d. 1 p.

———. Guest Speakers. 1992 Summer Institute. Typed list included in registration packet, n.d.

———. "The New Jersey Project: Integrating the Scholarship on Gender." *Network* (Fall 1986): 1.

———. *The New Jersey Project Newsletter,* spring 1995, fall 1995, and fall 1996.

———. Participants. 1992 Summer Institute. Typed list included in registration packet, n.d.

———. Participants by Discipline. 1992 Summer Institute. Typed list included in registration packet, n.d.

———. Program for the conference The Inclusive Curriculum: Setting Our Own Agenda, Parsippany, NJ, 16–18 April 1993.

———. Program for the 1992 Summer Institute, included in registration packet, n.d.

———. Readings packet for 1992 Summer Institute, distributed at registration, n.d.

———. Rothenberg, Paula. "The New Jersey Project: Integrating the Scholarship on Gender, Final Report—July 1991, 1990–91 Academic Year." Typescript supplied by Paula Rothenberg. 16 pp.

———. Rothenberg, Paula. "The New Jersey Project 1989–90 Year End Report," n.d. Type-script supplied by Paula Rothenberg. 13 pp.

NEW Leadership. Dodson, Debra L., with the assistance of Tobi Walker. "New Leadership: A Preliminary Evaluation Report." Center for the American Woman and Politics, Rutgers University, ca. 1994. Typescript supplied by Tobi Walker. 31 pp.

NFIB Foundation. *The NFIB Foundation*. Washington, DC: National Federation of Independent Business, n.d. Booklet.

Nicholson, Linda J., ed. *Feminism / Postmodernism*. New York: Routledge, 1990.

Nochlin, Linda. "Lost and Found: Once More the Fallen Woman." *Art Bulletin* 60 (1978): 139–53.

——. "Why Are There No Great Women Artists?" In Gornick and Moran, *Woman*, 480–510.

Notes from the First Year: Women's Liberation. New York: N.p., 1968.

Notes from the Second Year: Women's Liberation. New York: Radical Feminists, 1970.

Notes from the Third Year: Women's Liberation. New York: N.p., 1971.

O'Barr, Jean. *Feminism in Action*. Chapel Hill: University of North Carolina Press, 1994.

Ohmann, Richard. *English in America: A Radical View of the Profession*. New York: Oxford University Press, 1976.

Okorodudu, Corann. "The Third Year: Increasing National Visibility." In Smith and Olin, *New Jersey Project*, 20–25.

O'Leary, Virginia. *Toward Understanding Women*. Monterey, CA: Brooks / Cole, 1977.

——, Rhoda K. Unger, and B. S. Wallston, eds. *Women, Gender, and Social Psychology*. Hillsdale, NJ: Erlbaum, 1985.

Oltman, Ruth M. "Women in the Professional Caucuses." *American Behavioral Sciences* 15 (1971): 281–302.

"The Open Up the Schools Program: OUTS Political Perspective I." *NUC Papers* 3 (fall 1970): 1–4.

"The Open Up the Schools Program: OUTS Political Perspective II." *NUC Papers* 3 (fall 1970): 5–10.

Oppenheimer, Martin, Martin J. Murray, and Rhonda F. Levine. "Introduction: The Movement and the Academy." In Oppenheimer et al., *Radical Sociologists*, 3–14.

——, eds. *Radical Sociologists and the Movement: Experiences, Lessons, and Legacies*. Philadelphia: Temple University Press, 1991.

Orden, Susan, and Norman Bradburn. "Working Wives and Marriage Happiness." *American Journal of Sociology* 74 (1968): 392–407.

Orlans, Kathryn P. Meadow, and Ruth A. Wallace, eds. *Gender and the Academic Experience: Berkeley Women Sociologists*. Lincoln: University of Nebraska Press, 1995.

Orr, Catherine. "Representing Women / Disciplining Feminism: Activism, Professionalism, and Women's Studies." Ph.D. diss. University of Minnesota, June 1998.

Pahre, Robert. "Mathematical Discourse and Crossdisciplinary Communities: The Case of Political Economy." *Social Epistemology* 10 (1996): 55–73.

Panofsky, Erwin. *Meaning in the Visual Arts*. Garden City, NY: Anchor, 1955.

Parlee, Mary Brown. "Review Essay: Psychology." *Signs* 1 (1975): 119–38.

Patai, Daphne, and Noretta Koertge. *Professing Feminism: Cautionary Tales from the Strange World of Women's Studies*. New York: Basic Books, 1994.

Patterson, Michelle. "Alice in Wonderland: A Study of Women Faculty in Graduate Departments of Sociology." *The American Sociologist* 6 (1971): 225–34.

———. "Sex Specialization in Academe and the Professions." In Rossi and Calderwood, *Academic Women*, 313–31.

———, and Lucy Sells. "Women Dropouts from Higher Education." In Rossi and Calderwood, *Academic Women*, 79–91.

People for the American Way. *Buying a Movement: Right-Wing Foundations and American Politics*. Washington, DC: People for the American Way, 1996.

Perry, Strother B. "Gertrude Stein at Marienbad." *PMLA* 85 (1970): 1096–1105.

Peterson, Thalia Gouma, and Patricia Mathews. "The Feminist Critique of Art History." *Art Bulletin* 69 (1987): 226–57.

Pickering, Andrew. *Constructing Quarks: A Sociological History of Particle Physics*. Chicago: University of Chicago Press, 1984.

Pincus, Fred L., and Howard J. Erlich. "The New University Conference: A Study of Former Members." *Critical Sociology* 15 (1988): 145–47.

Poovey, Mary. "Feminism and Deconstruction." *Feminist Studies* 14 (1988): 51–65.

———. "My Hideous Progeny: Mary Shelley and the Feminization of Romanticism." *PMLA* 95 (1980): 332–47.

Pope, Deborah, Naomi Quinn, and Mary Wyer. "Editorial." *Signs* 15 (1990): 441–46.

Porter, Nancy M. "A Nuts and Bolts View of Women's Studies." In *Female Studies VI*, 167–77.

Prather, Jane E. "Acquiring an Academic Room of One's Own." In Goetting and Fenstermaker, *Individual Voices*, 69–86.

Preziosi, Donald. "The Question of Art History." *Critical Inquiry* 18 (1992): 363–80.

———. "Seeing through Art History." In Messer-Davidow et al., *Knowledges*, 215–31.

Probyn, Elspeth. *Sexing the Self: Gendered Positions in Cultural Studies*. New York: Routledge, 1993.

Public Leadership Education Network. "PLEN Public Policy Programs, 1991–92." Washington, DC: PLEN, n.d. Flier.

———. "PLEN Public Policy Programs 1992–93." Washington, DC: PLEN, n.d. Flier.

———. "PLEN: A Washington Seminar 1992 Application." Washington, DC: PLEN, n.d. Flier.

Rabine, Leslie Wahl. "A Feminist Politics of Non-Identity." *Feminist Studies* 14 (1988): 11–31.

Rabinowitz, Vita Carulli, and Jeri A. Sechzer. "Feminist Perspectives on Research Methods." In Denmark and Paludi, *Psychology*, 23–66.

Radical America 4.2 (1970).

Raymond, Janice G. "Transsexualism: An Issue of Sex-Role Stereotyping." In *Genes and Gender II*, 131–41.

Reagon, Bernice Johnson. "My Black Mothers and Sisters or on Beginning a Cultural Autobiography." *Feminist Studies* 8 (1982): 81–96.

Reck, Rima Drell. "The Politics of Literature." *PMLA* 85 (1970): 429–32.

Rees, Mina. "The Graduate Education of Women." In Furniss and Graham, *Women*, 178–87.

Reid, Inez Smith. "Viewpoint: Science, Politics, and Race." *Signs* 1 (1975): 397–422.

Reiter, Rayna R. Introduction to Reiter, *Toward an Anthropology*, 11–19.

——, ed. *Toward an Anthropology of Women*. New York: Monthly Review Press, 1975.

Revard, Stella P. "Eve and the Doctrine of Responsibility in *Paradise Lost.*" *PMLA* 88 (1973): 69–78.

"Review of *Sexual Politics.*" *Antioch Review* 30 (1970): 263.

Rhoades, Gary, and Sheila Slaughter. "Academic Capitalism, Managed Professionals, and Supply-Side Higher Education." In Martin, *Chalk Lines*, 33–68.

Rich, Adrienne. "Compulsory Heterosexuality and Lesbian Existence." *Signs* 5 (1980): 631–60.

Richtmyer, F. K., E. H. Kennard, and John N. Cooper. *Introduction to Modern Physics*. 6th ed. New York: McGraw-Hill, 1969.

Risman, Barbara J. "Can Men 'Mother'? Life as a Single Father." In Risman and Schwartz, *Gender*, 155–64.

——, and Pepper Schwartz, eds. *Gender in Intimate Relationships: A Microstructural Approach*. Belmont, CA: Wadsworth, 1989.

Ritter, Kathleen V., and Lowell L. Hargens. "Occupational Positions and Class Identifications of Married Working Women." *American Journal of Sociology* 80 (1975): 934–48.

Roach, Jack L. "The Radical Sociology Movement: A Short History and Commentary." *The American Sociologist* 5 (1970): 224–33.

Robinson, Lillian S. "Dwelling in Decencies: Radical Criticism and the Feminist Perspective." *College English* 32 (1971): 879–89. Rpt. in Lillian S. Robinson. *Sex, Class, and Culture*. Bloomington: Indiana University Press, 1978. 3–21.

——, and Lise Vogel. "Modernism and History." *New Literary History* 3 (1971): 177–200. Rpt. in Lillian S. Robinson. *Sex, Class, and Culture*. Bloomington: Indiana University Press, 1978. 22–46.

Robinson, Lora H. "Institutional Variation in the Status of Academic Women." In Rossi and Calderwood, *Academic Women*, 199–238.

Roby, Pamela. "Institutional Barriers to Women Students in Higher Education." In Rossi and Calderwood, *Academic Women*, 37–56.

——. "Women and the ASA: Degendering Organizational Structures and Processes, 1964–1974." *The American Sociologist* 25 (1992): 18–48.

Roche, John P. "The New Left Vigilantes." *National Review*, 8 December 1989, 34–35.

Rohrlich-Leavitt, Ruby, Barbara Sykes, and Elizabeth Weatherford. "Aboriginal Woman: Male and Female Anthropological Perspectives." In Reiter, *Toward an Anthropology*, 110–26.

——. Introduction to Rosaldo and Lamphere, *Woman, Culture, and Society*. Stanford University Press, 1974, 1–15.

Rosaldo, Michelle Zimbalist, and Louise Lamphere, eds. *Woman, Culture, and Society*. Stanford: Stanford University Press, 1974.

——. Preface to Rosaldo and Lamphere, *Woman*, v–vi.

Rose, Steven. "The Roots and Social Functions of Biological Reductionism." In *Reductionism in Academic Disciplines*. Ed. Arthur Peacocke. Guildford, UK: Society for Research into Higher Education & NFER-NELSON, 1985. 24–42.

Rose, Suzanna. "Women Biologists and the 'Old Boy' Network." *Women's Studies International Forum* 12 (1989): 349–54.

Rosen, Ruth. *The World Split Open: How the Modern Women's Movement Changed America.* New York: Putnam, 2000.

Rosenfelt, Deborah Silverton. Introduction to *Female Studies VII*, iii–iv.

Ross, Robert J. S. "At the Center and the Edge: Notes on a Life in and out of Sociology and the New Left." *Critical Sociology* 15 (1988): 79–93.

——. "Primary Groups in Social Movements: A Memoir and Interpretation." In *Toward a History of the New Left: Essays From Within the Movement.* Ed. R. David Myers. Brooklyn: Carlson, 1989. 153–82.

Rosser, Sue V. *Biology and Feminism: A Dynamic Interaction.* New York: Twayne, 1992.

Rossi, Alice S. "Status of Women in Graduate Departments of Sociology, 1968–1969." *The American Sociologist* 5 (1970): 1–12.

——. "Summary and Prospects." In Rossi and Calderwood, *Academic Women*, 505–29.

——. "Women—Terms of Liberation." *Dissent* 17 (1970): 531–41.

——, and Ann Calderwood, eds. *Academic Women on the Move.* New York: Russell Sage Foundation, 1973.

Rothchild, Mary Aickin. "White Women Volunteers in the Freedom Summers: Their Life and Work in a Movement for Social Change." *Feminist Studies* 5 (1979): 466–94.

Rothenberg, Paula. "The New Jersey Project Enters Its Second Phase." *Women's Studies Quarterly* 18.1–2 (1990): 119–22.

Rothstein, Richard. "Evolution of the ERAP Organizers." In Long, *New Left*, 272–88.

Rubin, Gayle. "The Traffic in Women: Notes on the 'Political Economy' of Sex." In Reiter, *Toward an Anthropology*, 157–210.

——. "Woman as Nigger." In *Masculine / Feminine: Readings in Sexual Mythology and the Liberation of Women.* Ed. Betty Roszak and Theodore Roszak. New York: Harper, 1969. 230–40.

Rubin, Lillian B. "An Unanticipated Life." In Orlans and Wallace, *Gender*, 229–47.

Rupp, Leila, and Verta Taylor. *Survival in the Doldrums: The American Women's Rights Movement, 1945 to the 1960s.* New York: Oxford University Press, 1987.

Russell, Catherine. Description of conference in Smith, *Everyday World*, 71–72.

Ryan, Barbara. *Feminism and the Women's Movement: Dynamics of Change in Social Movement Ideology and Activism.* New York: Routledge, 1992.

——. "Ideological Purity and Feminism: The U.S. Women's Movement from 1966 to 1975." *Gender and Society* 3 (1989): 239–57.

R. Z. S. "Up Against the Men's Room Wall." *Time,* 3 August 1970: 70–71.

Sacramento State University Women's Studies Board, ed. *Report on the West Coast Women's Studies Conference.* Sacramento: Sacramento State University Women's Studies Board, 1974.

Salper, Roberta. "The Development of the American Women's Liberation Movement, 1967–1971." In Salper, *Female Liberation*, 169–83.

——. "Women's Studies." In *Female Studies V*, 100–105.

——. "Women's Studies." *Ramparts* 10.6 (December 1971): 56–60.

———, ed. *Female Liberation: History and Current Politics.* New York: Knopf, 1972.

———, and Barbara Kessel. "Case Study: Women's Studies—Theory and Practice." *NUC Women's Caucus Newsletter* 7 (April 1971): 40–41.

Salzman, Frieda. "Aggression and Gender: A Critique of the Nature-Nurture Question for Humans." In *Genes and Gender II*, 71–89.

Salzman-Webb, Marilyn. "Feminist Studies: Frill or Necessity?" In *Female Studies V*, 64–76.

———. "Feminist Studies Program, Goddard College." In *Female Studies III*, 157–58.

Sanday, Peggy R. "Female Status in the Public Domain." In Rosaldo and Lamphere, *Woman*, 189–206.

Sandler, Bernice. "The Hand That Rocked the Cradle Has Learned to Rock the Boat." *New Directions in Institutional Research* 3 (1974): 1–21.

———. "A Little Help from Our Government: WEAL and Contract Compliance." In Rossi and Calderwood, *Academic Women*, 439–62.

Sandoval, Chéla. "Feminist Forms of Agency and Oppositional Consciousness: U.S. Third World Feminist Criticism." In Gardiner, *Provoking Agents*, 208–26.

Sargent, Lydia, ed. *Women and Revolution: A Discussion of the Unhappy Marriage of Marxism and Feminism.* Boston: South End, 1981.

Schiebinger, Londa. *The Mind Has No Sex: Women in the Origins of Modern Science.* Cambridge: Harvard University Press, 1989.

———. "The Private Life of Plants: Sexual Politics in Carl Linnaeus and Erasmus Darwin." In *Science and Sensibility: Gender and Scientific Inquiry, 1780–1945.* Ed. Marina Benjamin. Oxford: Blackwell, 1991. 121–43.

Schlozman, Kay Lehman. "Representing Women in Washington: Sisterhood and Pressure Politics." In *Women, Politics, and Change.* Ed. Louise A. Tilly and Patrician Gurin. New York: Russell Sage Foundation, 1990. 339–82.

Schmidt, Peter. "States Discourage Welfare Recipients From Pursuing Higher Education." *Chronicle of Higher Education*, 23 January 1998, A34.

———, and Douglas Lederman. "Legal Barriers Removed to California's Ban on Racial Preferences." *Chronicle of Higher Education*, 5 September 1997, A47.

Schmitz, Betty. *Integrating Women's Studies into the Curriculum: A Guide and Bibliography.* Old Westbury, NY: Feminist Press, 1985.

Schneider, Alison. "Affirmative Action's Impact on Academe Has Been Minimal, a New Book Argues." *Chronicle of Higher Education*, 24 March 2000, A20.

Schneider, Joseph W., and Sally I. Hacker. "Sex Role Imagery and the Use of the Generic 'Man' in Introductory Texts: A Case in the Sociology of Sociology." *The American Sociologist* 8 (1973): 12–18.

Schwartz, Pepper, and Janet Lever. "Women in the Male World of Higher Education." In Rossi and Calderwood, *Academic Women*, 57–77.

Schwenger, Peter. "The Masculine Mode." *Critical Inquiry* 5 (1979): 621–34.

Scott, Joan W. "Deconstructing Equality-Versus-Difference: Or the Uses of Poststructuralist Theory for Feminism." *Feminist Studies* 14 (1988): 33–50. Rpt. in Meyers, *Feminist Social Thought*, 759–70.

——. "Gender: A Useful Category of Historical Analysis." *American Historical Review* 91 (1986): 1053–75.

Secor, Cynthia. "Preparing the Individual for Institutional Leadership: The Summer Institute." In Tinsley et al., *Women,* 25–33.

Shavlik, Donna, and Judy Toucher. "Toward a New Era of Leadership: The National Identification Program." In Tinsley et al., *Women,* 47–58.

Sherman, Julia. *On the Psychology of Women.* Springfield, IL: Charles C. Thomas, 1971.

——, and Florence L. Denmark. *The Psychology of Women: Future Directions of Research.* New York: Psychological Dimensions, 1978.

Shields, Stephanie A. "The Variability Hypothesis: The History of a Biological Model of Sex Differences in Intelligence." *Signs* 7 (1982): 769–97.

Shinn, Terry. "Scientific Disciplines and Organizational Specificity: The Social and Cognitive Configuration of Laboratory Activities." In *Scientific Establishments and Hierarchies.* Ed. Norbert Elias, Herminio Martins, and Richard Whitley. Dordrecht: Reidel, 1982. 239–54.

Showalter, Elaine. "Feminist Criticism in the Wilderness." *Critical Inquiry* 8 (1981): 179–205.

——. "Introduction: Teaching About Women, 1971." In *Female Studies IV,* i–xii.

——. Review Essay: Literary Criticism." *Signs* 1 (1975): 435–60.

——. "Women and the Literary Curriculum." *College English* 32 (1971): 855–62.

——. "Women Writers and the Double Critical Standard." In Gornick and Moran, *Woman,* 452–79.

Shumway, David R. *Creating American Civilization: A Genealogy of American Literature as an Academic Discipline.* Minneapolis: University of Minnesota Press, 1994.

——, and Ellen Messer-Davidow. "Disciplinarity: An Introduction." *Poetics Today* 12 (1991): 201–25.

Sicherman, Barbara. "The Invisible Woman: The Case for Women's Studies." In Furniss and Graham, *Women,* 155–77.

——. "Review Essay: American History." *Signs* 1 (1975): 461–85.

Sigworth, Heather. "Issues in Nepotism Rules." In Furniss and Graham, *Women,* 110–20.

Simmons, Robert O., and Delores H. Thurgood. *Doctorate Recipients from United States Universities: Summary Report 1994.* Washington, DC: National Academy of Sciences, 1995.

Simons, Margaret A. "Racism and Feminism: A Schism in the Sisterhood." *Feminist Studies* 5 (1979): 385–401.

Siporin, Rae Lee. "Women and Education: The Conference as Catalyst." In *Female Studies V,* iii–xiv.

Smith, Carol H. "Creating a State-Wide Network." In Smith and Olin, *New Jersey Project,* 1–7.

——, and Ferris Olin, eds. *The New Jersey Project: Integrating the Scholarship on Gender, 1986–1989.* New Brunswick, NJ: Institute for Research on Women, 1990.

Smith, Dorothy E. *The Conceptual Practices of Power: A Feminist Sociology of Knowledge.* Boston: Northeastern University Press, 1990.

——. *The Everyday World as Problematic: A Feminist Sociology.* Boston: Northeastern University Press, 1987.

——. "Sociological Theory: Methods of Writing Patriarchy." In Wallace, *Feminism*, 34–64.

——. "A Sociology for Women." In *The Prism of Sex: Essays in the Sociology of Knowledge*. Ed. Julia A. Sherman and Evelyn Torton Beck. Madison: University of Wisconsin Press, 1979. 135–87.

——. "Women's Perspective as a Radical Critique of Sociology." *Sociological Inquiry* 44 (1974): 7–14.

Smith, Henry Nash. "The Scribbling Women and the Cosmic Success Story." *Critical Inquiry* 1 (1974): 47–70.

Smith, Inez Reid. "Viewpoint: Science, Politics, and Race." *Signs* (1975): 397–422.

Smith-Rosenberg, Carroll. "The New Woman and the New History." *Feminist Studies* 3 (1975): 185–98.

Snitow, Ann. "A Gender Diary." In Hirsch and Keller, *Conflicts*, 9–43.

Sommers, Christina Hoff. *Who Stole Feminism? How Women Have Betrayed Women*. New York: Simon and Schuster, 1994.

Sonstroem, David. "*Wuthering Heights* and the Limits of Vision." *PMLA* 86 (1971): 51–62.

Sowell, Thomas. "'Affirmative Action': A Worldwide Disaster." *Commentary* 88.6 (December 1989): 21–41.

——. *Preferential Policies*. New York: William Morrow, 1990.

Spanier, Bonnie, Alexander Bloom, and Darlene Boroviak, eds. *Toward a Balanced Curriculum: A Sourcebook for Initiating Gender Integration Projects*. Cambridge, MA: Schenkman, 1984.

Spann, Girardeau A. "Pure Politics." In *Critical Race Theory: The Cutting Edge*. Ed. Richard Delgado. Philadelphia: Temple University Press, 1995. 21–34.

Spelman, Elizabeth V. *Inessential Woman: Problems of Exclusion in Feminist Thought*. Boston: Beacon, 1988.

Stack, Carol B., et al. "Review Essay: Anthropology." *Signs* 1 (1975): 147–59.

Stambler, Sookie, ed. *Women's Liberation: Blueprint for the Future*. New York: Ace, 1970.

Stanton, Domna. "What's in a Name? The Case for Author-Anonymous Reviewing." In Hartman and Messer-Davidow, *Women in Print II*, 65–77.

——. "What's in a Name? Re-visiting Author Anonymous Reviewing." *PMLA* 112 (1997): 191–97.

Steering Committee. "Female Studies Program, Cornell University." In *Female Studies III*, 151–52.

Stefano, Christine De. "Dilemmas of Difference: Feminism, Modernity, and Postmodernism." In Nicholson, *Feminism/Postmodernism*, 63–82.

Sterling, Dorothy. *Black Foremothers*. Old Westbury, NY: Feminist Press, 1979.

Stetson, Erlene. "Black Women in and out of Print." In Hartman and Messer-Davidow, *Women in Print I*, 87–107.

——, ed. *Black Sister: Poetry by Black American Women, 1746–1980*. Bloomington: Indiana University Press, 1981.

Stimpson, Catharine R. "The Making of *Signs*." *Radical Teacher* 6 (December 1977): 23–25.

——. "The Mind, the Body, and Gertrude Stein." *Critical Inquiry* 3 (1977): 489–506.

——. "The New Feminism and Women's Studies." In *Women on Campus*, 69–84.

——. "Women's Studies, Barnard College." In *Female Studies III,* 140–41.

——, and Nina Kressner Cobb. *Women's Studies in the United States.* New York: Ford Foundation, 1986.

Stofflet, Mary. "Women's Caucus for Art at the C.A.A." *Feminist Art Journal* 5.2 (1976): 38–40.

Stringer, Patricia. "Grooming Women for Leadership." *Change* 9.2 (February 1977): 21–26.

Strobel, Margaret. "Consciousness and Action: Historical Agency in the Chicago Women's Liberation Union." In Gardiner, *Provoking Agents,* 52–68.

Strumingher, Laura S. "The Birth and Growth of 'Friends of Women's Studies' at the University of Cincinnati." *Frontiers* 8.3 (1986): 41–55.

Summers, David. "Form and Gender." In *Visual Culture: Images and Interpretations.* Ed. Norman Bryson, Michael Ann Holly, and Keith Moxey. Hanover, NH: Wesleyan University Press and University Press of New England, 1994. 384–411.

——. " 'Form,' Nineteenth-Century Metaphysics, and the Problem of Art Historical Description." *Critical Inquiry* 15 (1989): 372–406.

Tanner, Leslie B., ed. *Voices from Women's Liberation.* New York: Mentor, 1970.

Tanner, Nancy, and Adrienne L. Zihlman. "Women in Evolution, Part I: Innovation and Selection in Human Origins." *Signs* 1 (1976): 585–608.

Teodori, Massimo, ed. *The New Left: A Documentary History.* Indianapolis: Bobbs-Merrill, 1969.

Theodore, Athena. *The Campus Troublemakers: Academic Women in Protest.* Houston: Cap and Gown, 1986.

Thernstrom, Abigail M. "On the Scarcity of Black Professors." *Commentary* 90.1 (July 1990): 22–26.

——. *Whose Votes Count? Affirmative Action and Minority Voting Rights.* Cambridge: Harvard University Press, 1987.

Thompson, Irene, and Audrey Roberts, eds. *The Road Retaken: Women Reenter the Academy.* New York: MLA, 1985.

Thompson, Mary Lou, ed. *Voices of the New Feminism.* Boston: Beacon, 1970.

Thompson, Tommy. "Land of Milk and Money." *Policy Review* 56 (1991): 31–35. Interview with Adam Meyerson.

Thurgood, Delores H., and Julie E. Clarke. *Doctorate Recipients from United States Universities: Summary Report 1993.* Washington, DC: National Academy of Sciences, 1995.

Tinsley, Adrian, Cynthia Secor, and Sheila Kaplan, eds. *Women in Higher Education Administration.* San Francisco: Jossey-Bass, 1984.

Tirelli, Vincent. "Adjuncts and More Adjuncts: Labor Segmentation and the Transformation of Higher Education." In Martin, *Chalk Lines,* 181–201.

Tobias, Sheila. Introduction to *Female Studies I,* n.p.

——. "Women's Studies: Its Origin, Organization, and Prospects." In *The Higher Education of Women: Essays in Honor of Rosemary Parks.* Ed. Helen S. Astin and Werner Z. Hirsch. New York: Praeger, 1978. 80–94.

——, and Margaret L. Rumbarger. "Rearrangements in Faculty Schedules: Full-Status Part-Time Faculty." In Furniss and Graham, *Women,* 128–37.

Traweek, Sharon. *Beamtimes and Lifetimes: The World of High Energy Physicists.* Cambridge: Harvard University Press, 1988.

Unger, Rhoda K. *Female and Male: Psychological Perspectives.* New York: Harper & Row, 1978.

University of Cincinnati Women's Studies Program. "Pioneers for Century II: A National Bicentennial Conference." Conference program, Cincinnati, OH, 1976.

U.S. Bureau of the Census. *Statistical Abstract of the United States.* 119th ed. Washington, DC: U.S. Bureau of the Census, 1999.

Van Alstyne, Carol, R. Frank Mensel, Julie S. Withers, and F. Stephen Malott. *Women and Minorities in Administration of Higher Education Institutes: Employment Patterns and Salary Comparisons.* Washington, DC: College and University Personnel Association, 1977.

Vaughter, Reesa M. "Review Essay: Psychology." *Signs* 2 (1976): 120–46.

Vetter, Betty M., and Eleanor L. Babco. *Professional Women and Minorities: A Manpower Resource Service.* Washington, DC: Scientific Manpower Committee, 1975.

Voloshin, Beverly. "A Historical Note on Women's Fiction: A Reply to Annette Kolodny." *Critical Inquiry* 2 (1976): 817–20.

Waite, Linda. "Working Wives and the Family Life Cycle." *American Journal of Sociology* 86 (1980): 272–94.

Wallace, Michele. *Black Macho and the Myth of Superwoman.* New York: Dial, 1978.

Wallace, Phyllis, ed. *Black Women in the Labor Force.* Cambridge: MIT Press, 1980.

Wallace, Ruth A. Introduction to Wallace, *Feminism,* 7–19.

———, ed. *Feminism and Sociological Theory.* Newbury Park, CA: Sage, 1989.

Washington, Mary Helen, ed. *Black-Eyed Susans: Classic Stories by and about Black Women.* New York: Doubleday, 1975.

———, ed. *Midnight Birds: Stories of Contemporary Black Women Writers.* New York: Doubleday, 1980.

Weatherford, Elizabeth. "Aboriginal Woman: Male and Female in Anthropological Perspectives." In Reiter, *Toward an Anthropology,* 110–26.

Weathers, Mary Ann. "An Argument for Black Women's Liberation as a Revolutionary Force." In Tanner, *Voices,* 303–7.

Weisstein, Naomi. "Psychology Constructs the Female." In Gornick and Moran, *Woman,* 207–24.

Wellek, René. *Concepts of Criticism.* Ed. Stephen G. Nichols, Jr. New Haven: Yale University Press, 1963.

———, and Austin Warren. *Theory of Literature.* 3d ed. New York: Harcourt, Brace & World, 1956.

Westervelt, Esther M. *Women's Higher Education: Some Unanswered Questions.* Racine, WI: Johnson Foundation, 1972. Report of the Wingspread Conference.

White, Barbara. "Up from the Podium: Feminist Revolution in the Classroom." In *Female Studies IV,* 28–34.

White, Barbara Erlich, and Leon S. White. "Survey on the Status of Women in College Art Departments." *Art Journal* 32 (1973): 420–22.

"White Professor Wins $122,000 in Bias Case." *Chronicle of Higher Education*, 27 March 1998, A14.

"Who's Come a Long Way, Baby?" *Time*, 31 August 1970, 16–21.

Williams, Juan. *Eyes on the Prize: America's Civil Rights Years, 1954–1965*. New York: Penguin, 1987.

Williams, Juanita, ed. *Psychology of Women*. New York: Norton, 1979.

Williams, Patricia J. "The Death of the Profane." In *Debating Affirmative Action: Race, Gender, Ethnicity, and the Politics of Inclusion*. Ed. Nicolaus Mills. New York: Dell, 1994. 117–25.

Williams, Walter E. "Race, Scholarship, and Affirmative Action." *National Review*, 5 May 1989, 36–38.

Willow, Samantha. "Rounding Our Corners." In *Female Studies VI*, 208–22.

Wilson, Edward O. *On Human Nature*. Cambridge: Harvard University Press, 1978.

——. *Sociobiology: The New Synthesis*. Cambridge: Harvard University Press, 1975.

Wilson, Stuart. "Richardson's *Pamela*." *PMLA* 88 (1973): 79–91.

Wimsatt, W. K., Jr. *Hateful Contraries: Studies in Literature and Criticism*. Lexington: University of Kentucky Press, 1966.

——. *The Verbal Icon: Studies in the Meaning of Poetry*. Paper ed. Lexington: University of Kentucky Press, 1967.

Wölfflin, Heinrich. *Principles of Art History: The Problem of the Development of Style in Later Art*. Trans. M. D. Hottinger. 7th ed. New York: Dover, 1932.

Women and Poverty Public Education Initiative. *In Our Own Words: Mothers' Perspectives on Welfare Reform*. Report prepared for the Stewart Mott Foundation, 1997.

Women on Campus: The Unfinished Revolution. Ed. Editors of *Change*. New Rochelle, NY: Change, 1975.

"Women Unite." Special issue, *Leviathan* 2.2 (1970).

"Women's Groups Organizing Another National Federation." *Responsive Philanthropy* (fall 1994): 1–2.

Women's Research and Education Institute. Brochure, Washington, DC, n.d.

——. "WREI Awards Ten Congressional Fellowships." Press release, Washington, DC, October 1992.

——. "WREI Congressional Fellowships, 1992–1993." Brochure, Washington, DC, n.d.

Women's Studies 2.2 (1974).

Women's Work and Women's Studies 1971. Ed. Kirsten Drake, Dorothy Marks, and Mary Wexford. Pittsburgh: KNOW Press, 1972.

Women's Work and Women's Studies 1972. Ed. Dicki Lou Ellis, Kathleen Graces, Kirsten Grimstad, Dorothy Marks, Fannette Pollack, Jan Thompson, and Mary Elizabeth Wexford. Pittsburgh: KNOW Press, 1973.

Workman, James. "Gender Norming." *The New Republic*, 1 July 1991, 16, 18.

Wyatt, Jean M. "*Mrs. Dalloway*: Literary Allusion as Structural Metaphor." *PMLA* 88 (1973): 440–51.

Yardley, Jonathan. "Women's Lib Gets Rough." *The New Republic* 1 (August 1970): 26, 30–32.

Young America's Foundation. *Campus Leader: A Newsletter for Student Leaders from Young America's Foundation.* 13 issues, 1992–96.

——. *Libertas: The Voice of Freedom on Campus.* 10 issues, 1992–96.

Young, Iris. "Beyond the Unhappy Marriage: A Critique of the Dual Systems Theory." In Sargent, *Women,* 43–69.

Zihlman, Adrienne L. "Women in Evolution, Part II: Substance and Social Organization among Early Hominids." *Signs* 4 (1978): 4–20.

Zinn, Maxine Baca, Lynn Weber Cannon, Elizabeth Higginbotham, and Bonnie Thornton Dill. "The Cost of Exclusionary Practices in Women's Studies." *Signs* 11 (1986): 290–303.

Zwerdling, Alex. "Esther Summerson Rehabilitated." *PMLA* 88 (1973): 429–39.

Lawsuits and Related Documents

BAKKE

Regents of the University of California v. Bakke, 96 Supreme Court Reporter, 2733–2815.

GUTZWILLER

Kathryn J. Gutzwiller v. Bernard C. Fenik et al. (1 November 1988). United States Court of Appeals for the Sixth Circuit Full Text Publication, nos. 86-3852 / 86-3854 / 86-3916. Pamphlet supplied by Kathryn J. Gutzwiller. 49 pp.

HOPWOOD

Cheryl J. Hopwood v. State of Texas, 78 Federal Reporter, 3d series, 932–68.

MICHIGAN STATE

Michigan State University Faculty Association v. Michigan State University (13 April 1981), 32 Federal Rules Service, 2d series, 1292–1300.

Michigan State University Faculty Association v. Michigan State University (13 October 1981), 93 Federal Rules Decisions, 54–62.

PODBERESKY

Podberesky v. Kirwan, 956 Federal Reporter, 2d Series, 52–57.

Podberesky v. Kirwan, 38 Federal Reporter, 3d Series, 147–62.

RAJENDER

Attorneys for the Plaintiff. "Memorandum in Support of Motion for Order Determining That Action Is Maintainable as a Class Action," 6 January 1978. *Rajender v. University of Minnesota,* Civil 4-73-435, United States District Court, District of Minnesota, Fourth Division. Typescript supplied by William P. Donohue, University of Minnesota Associate General Counsel. 20 pp.

Lord, Judge Miles W. "Order" (certifying the class), 13 February 1978. *Rajender v. University of Minnesota,* Civil 4-73-435, United States District Court, District of Minnesota, Fourth Division. Typescript supplied by William P. Donohue, University of Minnesota Associate General Counsel. 2 pp.

Lord, Judge Miles W. "Memorandum Accompanying Order of February 13, 1978," 24 April

1978. *Rajender v. University of Minnesota,* Civil 4–73–435, United States District Court, District of Minnesota, Fourth Division. Typescript supplied by William P. Donohue, University of Minnesota Associate General Counsel. 11 pp.

Lord, Judge Miles W. *Rajender v. University of Minnesota* (certifying the class), 24 April 1978. 24 FEP Cases, 1045–58.

"Consent Decree from *Rajender v. The University of Minnesota*" (13 August 1980). *Journal of College and University Law* 8.2 (1981–82): 219–53.

ROSENBERG

Rachelle A. Rosenberg v. University of Cincinnati (29 September 1986), 654 Federal Supplement, 774–81.

Rachelle A. Rosenberg v. University of Cincinnati (11 May 1987), 118 Federal Rules Decision, 591–97.

Rice, Judge Walter H. "Decision and Entry Setting Limited Evidentiary Hearing on Defendants' Motion to Decertify Class" (29 September 1986). Doc. no. 71, in *Rachelle A. Rosenberg v. University of Cincinnati,* Case no. C–1–77–039. Typescript supplied, on the request of Rachelle A. Rosenberg, by her attorney Charles G. Atkins. 21 pp.

Wagner, Thomas. Affidavit, in *Rachelle A. Rosenberg v. University of Cincinnati,* Civil Action no. C–1–77–39; and "Employment Practices, Decision-Making, University of Cincinnati," appended to "Affidavit." Typescript supplied, on the request of Rachelle A. Rosenberg, by her attorney Charles G. Atkins. 19 pp.

Fieldwork Sources

INTERVIEWS AND COMMUNICATIONS

Alexander, Marianne. Interview with the author. Public Leadership Education Network, Washington, DC, 12 June 1992.

———. Interview with the author. Rutgers University, 7 June 1994.

"Anne" (Midwestern State student). Interview with the author. Midwestern State University, 29 May 1991.

"Betsy" (FAS-Georgetown student). Interview with the author. Georgetown Paolo's, Washington, DC, 13 July 1993.

Boehm, Kenneth F. Interview with the author. Legal Services Corporation, Washington, DC, 14 July 1993.

Brandow, Kimberly R. NFIB Foundation, Washington, DC, 14 July 1993.

"Candace" (Midwestern State faculty member). Interview with the author. Midwestern State University, 29 April 1991.

Collins, Michael J. Interview with the author. Georgetown University, Washington, DC, 17 November 1992.

———. Interview with the author. Georgetown University, 18 June 1993.

Crawford, Sandra L. Interview with the author. Media Research Center, Alexandria, VA, 15 July 1993.

"David" (FAS-Georgetown student). Interview with the author. Georgetown Inn, Washington, DC, 15 July 1993.

"Diane" (FAS-Georgetown student). Interview with the author. Georgetown Dean and Delucca, Washington, DC, 17 July 1993.

"Diane" (Midwestern State faculty member). Interview with the author. Midwestern State University, 29 April 1991.

———. Interview with the author. Midwestern State University, 6 May 1991.

Dooley, Betty Parsons. Interview with the author. Women's Research and Education Institute, Washington, DC, 23 November 1992.

Farley, (Pamella) Tucker. Telephone interview with the author. 25 September 1996.

———. Notes written on copy of telephone interview transcript. February 1997.

Forrest, William. Interview with the author. Leadership Institute, Springfield, VA, 9 June 1992.

Goldberg, Edward D. Interview with the author. New Jersey Department of Higher Education, Trenton, NJ, 2 June 1992.

———. Notes written on copy of interview transcript. 5 August 1992.

Hartman, Heidi. Interview with the author. Institute for Women's Policy Research, Washington, DC, 23 November 1992.

Hartman, Joan E. Telephone interview with the author. 29 August 1996.

———. E-mail answers to my e-mail queries. August 1996.

Heatherly, Charles L. Interview with the author. Heritage Foundation, Washington, DC, 6 April 1992.

"Hillary" (Midwestern State faculty member). Interview with the author. Midwestern State University, 15 April 1991.

Howe, Florence. Telephone interview with the author, 14 August 1996.

Institute for Political Journalism Professors. Conversations with the author, Georgetown University, Washington, DC, week of 14 June 1993.

"John" (Midwestern State faculty member). Interview with the author. Midwestern State University, 30 April 1991.

Johnston, Judith S., and Ferris Olin. Joint interview with the author. New Brunswick, NJ, 21 May 1991.

"Kevin" (FAS-Georgetown student). Interview with the author. Georgetown Dean and Delucca, Washington, DC, 17 July 1993.

Klein, Mal. Interview with the author. National Journalism Center, Washington, DC, 3 April 1992.

Kolmar, Wendy. Interview with the author. Madison, NJ, 29 May 1992.

Lauter, Paul. Telephone interview with the author. 11 August 1995.

"Leslie" (Midwestern State student). Interview with the author. Midwestern State University, 29 May 1991.

Lester, Irma. Interview with the author. Rutgers University, 21 May 1991.

"Louise" (Midwestern State faculty member). Interview with the author. Midwestern State University, 15 April 1991.

Mandel, Ruth. Interview with the author. Rutgers University, 12 June 1994.

"Mina" (Midwestern State fundraising administrator). Interview with the author. Midwestern State University, 15 April 1991.

"Oona" (Midwestern State Women's Center director). Interview with the author. Midwestern State University, 15 April 1991.

Ream, Roger S. Interview with the author. Fund for American Studies, Washington, DC, 11 November 1992.

——. Interview with the author. Fund for American Studies, Washington, DC, 17 November 1992.

Rhoades, Katherine A. Letter to the author on Wisconsin W-2 (workfare-welfare program). 17 February 1998.

Robinson, Lillian S. Information on art history student and her husband. Telephone conversation with the author. August 1994.

"Rosa" (Midwestern State student). Interview with the author. Midwestern State University, 29 May 1991.

Rosenfelt, Deborah. Information about Sacramento State Women's Studies Conference. E-mail answer to author's e-mail query. 19 May 1999.

Rothenberg, Paula. Interview with the author. William Paterson College, Wayne, NJ, 30 March 1992.

——. Notes written on copy of interview transcript. 4 August 1992.

Salper, Roberta. Telephone interview with the author. 18 October 1996.

——. Telephone interview with the author. 17 January 1997.

Salzman-Webb, Marilyn. Telephone interview with the author. 18 October 1996.

——. Telephone interview with the author. 7 December 1996.

——. Notes written on draft on my chapter 3. February 1997.

Schwartz, Michael. Interview with the author. Free Congress Foundation, Washington, DC, 10 June 1992.

——. Interview with the author. Free Congress Foundation, Washington, DC, 24 November 1992.

Sheridan, Marina C., and Lawrence F. Guillemette Jr. Joint interview with the author. Washington, DC, 13 July 1993.

"Sheryl" (Midwestern State faculty member). Interview with the author. Midwestern State University, 6 May 1991.

Smith, Ellen. Interview with the author. Rosslyn, VA, 15 July 1993.

Stoneback, Sharon. Interview with the author. Rutgers University, New Brunswick, NJ, 10 June 1994.

"Sue" (Midwestern State student). Interview with the author. Midwestern State University, 29 May 1991.

Warden, Chris. Interview with the author. National Journalism Center, Washington, DC, 3 April 1992.

Wolfe, Leslie R. Interview with the author. Center for Women Policy Studies, Washington, DC, 10 June 1992.

OBSERVATIONS

Free Congress Foundation. "Family Forum Live." National Empowerment Television broadcast. Free Congress Foundation, Washington, DC, 17 November 1992.

Fund for American Studies/Georgetown University. Institute for Comparative Economic and Political Systems and Institute for Political Journalism. Georgetown University, Washington, DC, 14–20 June 1993 and 12–17 July 1993.

Heritage Foundation. "Ideas Have Consequences: A Conservative Battleplan for the 1990s." Fifteenth Annual Resource Bank Meeting, Chicago, 23–24 April 1992.

——. "Ideas and Strategies to Unite the Conservative Majority." Lecture by Paul Weyrich and audience discussion in the lecture series "Defining Conservatism." Washington, DC, 24 November 1992.

Intercollegiate Studies Institute. The Upper Midwest Leadership Conference. Minneapolis, MN, 10 October 1992.

Midwestern State University. "Collective Analysis and Action" class and the Department of Women's Studies. Weekly visits, April and May 1991.

New Jersey Project. 1992 Summer Institute. Rutgers University, New Brunswick, NJ, 30 May–2 June 1992.

——. The Inclusive Curriculum: Setting Our Own Agenda. Conference, Parsippany, NJ, 16–18 April 1993.

NEW Leadership Summer Institute. Center for the American Woman and Politics, Rutgers University, New Brunswick, NJ, and other locations, 6–16 June 1994.

Rutgers University, Institute for Research on Women. Ninth Annual Celebration of Our Work. Rutgers University, New Brunswick, NJ, 21 May 1991.

Index

Activism: in American Sociological Association (ASA), 101–5, 112–15; and Berkeley Free Speech Movement (FSM), 92, 95; on campuses, 5–9, 65–66, 90–91, 93, 95, 96–98, 115–19, 125–27, 261–68; civil rights movement and, 50, 92–95, 197–99, 211, 298 n.2, 309 n.8, 310 nn. 9, 10, 11; in communities, 4–6, 87–89, 115–27, 162–63, 210–11, 261–68, 287–89, 316 n.63; and conservative movement, 217–18, 225–30, 270–71; female studies and feminist studies and, 7–9, 87–89, 115–27, 123–25, 210–11, 261–67, 287–88, and Heritage Foundation Resource Bank, 225–28, 237–38; and Industrial Areas Foundation (IAF), 6–7, 235; and Intercollegiate Studies Institute (ISI), 229, 351 n.30; and Leadership Institute (LI), 228; and Midwestern State University (pseudonym), 261–67; in Modern Language Association (MLA), 105–15, 316 n.51; National Journalism Center (NCF) and, 228–29; New Jersey Project and, 235–36; NEW Leadership and, 253–60; New Left and, 64, 92–96, 131, 239, 298 n.2, 309 n.8, 310 nn. 9, 11; New University Conference (NUC) and, 93, 96–98, 105–6, 209, 311 n.13; Public Leadership Education Network (PLEN) and, 253; as site of incubation for feminism, 91–101, 309 n.8, 310 n.9, 312 n.22; teaching of, and Free

Congress Foundation (FCF), 228; Young America's Foundation and, 229

Ad Hoc Women's Institute and Resource Center (WIRC), Portland State University, 153

Affirmative action: conservative opposition to, 270–74, 359 n.2; implementation and resistance to, 63–69, 78–79, 270, 303 n.40; laws and guidelines, 63–67, 303 n.40; lawsuits, policy initiatives, and voter referenda, 67–78, 217, 270–86, 360, 361 n.21, 362 n.22

African Americans: civil rights movement and, 50, 92–95, 197–99, 211, 298 n.2, 309 n.8, 310 nn. 4, 10, 11; and feminist studies, 191–92, 195–201, 341 nn. 69, 70, 71, 342 nn. 72, 73, 74, 343 nn. 78, 80; in NEW Leadership, 259–60; in universities, 192–94, 340 n.65; and work by and about African-American women, 194–201, 341 nn. 69, 70, 71, 342 nn. 72, 73, 74. See also Affirmative action; Civil rights movement; Discrimination, race; Racism

Ahlum, Carol, 119, 154

Alcoff, Linda, 208–9

Alexander, Marianne, 253, 258

American Civil Rights Institute (ACRI), 272, 273

American Council on Education National Identification Program (ACENIP), 65

American Enterprise Institute (AEI), 222, 270–71, 354 n.63

American Sociological Association (ASA): activism in, 93, 96, 101–5, 112–15, 311 n.13, 314 nn. 38, 41; Committee on Women, 104–5, 113; feminist work in journals of, 144–46, 323 n.38; institutionalization of feminism in, 102–5, 112–15; and Sociologists for Women in Society (SWS), 105; and Women's Caucus, 102–5, 113, 144. *See also* Sociology

Anderson, James, 233, 235

Anthologies, feminist, 133–35, 170–71, 196, 198, 200, 296 n.54, 320 n.6, 321 n.7

Anthropology, 185–86, 189, 337 n.47, 338 n.48. *See also* Disciplinary constructs and conventions; Disciplines, academic

Art history and fine arts, 28–33, 45, 54–55, 148–49, 294 nn. 31, 34, 37, 38, 300 n.11

Barnard College, 127–28, 153, 326

Beale, Frances, 200, 343 n.80

Bennis, Warren, 5–6, 10–11, 13, 78, 213

Berkeley Free Speech Movement (FSM), 92, 95

Biology, 53, 159, 168–78, 182, 183, 185, 330 nn. 4, 6, 7, 331 nn. 8, 12, 15. *See also* Disciplinary constructs and conventions; Disciplines, academic

Broverman, Inge, 182–83

Butler, Judith, 176–77, 332 nn. 23, 24

Calderwood, Ann, 140–41, 142

Cambridge-Goddard School, 126–27

Caucuses, women's, 51, 93, 98, 101, 102–5, 109–111, 113, 144, 218, 299 n.3, 316 n.51

Center for Individual Rights (CIR), 271, 272, 273, 277–78

Center for the American Woman and Politics (CAWP), Rutgers University, 253

Chodorow, Nancy, 189–91, 207, 339 n.58

Choice, rhetoric of, 226–30

Civil rights movement, 50, 92–95, 197–99,

211, 218, 298 n.2, 309 n.8, 310 nn. 9, 10, 11

Cole, Jonathan, 59–62, 78

College of Women's Studies, SUNY Buffalo, 153

Conservatism: and affirmative action, 270–84, 359 n.2; coalition building and networking, 217–18, 221, 223–26, 228–30; and conservative organizations, 218, 221–24, 225–30, 237–38, 238–52, 354 n.63; funding of, 222–23, 238, 239–40, 347 n.1; women and, 211, 226–27, 228, 230, 241, 257–58, 273, 346 n.105

Cornell University, 83, 93, 153, 160–61, 208

Curriculum and pedagogy: Cambridge-Goddard School, 126–27; Fund for American Studies–Georgetown University Institutes, 241–49, 355 n.66; Goddard College, 125–26; Midwestern State University (pseudonym), 261–68; Mississippi freedom schools, 95, 313 n.26; New Jersey Project, 231–36, 238; NEW Leadership, 253–60, 356 n.87; women's studies, 83–85, 151–62, 326 n.58, 327 n.69, 328 nn. 71, 72, 73

Disciplinary constructs and conventions: in biology, sociobiology, 169–76, 330 nn. 4, 7, 331 n.12; in biological determinism (biology, psychology, sociobiology), 168–70, 172–73, 175–76, 182, 184, 335 n.37; and biology-to-culture paradigm (anthropology), 185; canon (literary studies), 178–79, 201–3, 296 n.54; of formalism and New Criticism (literary studies), 38, 40–45, 47, 203, 297 n.61; and historical narratives (art history, history, literary studies), 32–33, 45, 179–80; and interpretationism (literary studies), 38–40, 181; and male-centered conventions (literary studies), 39–40, 45–48, 179, 296 n.54; and objectivity conventions (sociology), 36–37, 45, 295 n.47; and operationalism (physics), 25–28, 45; and periodization (history),

180; and public/private spheres (history), 178–80, 332 n.27; and sex-difference research (psychology), 182–85, 335 nn. 36, 37, 337 nn. 44, 45; and sex roles (psychology), 182–83; and style (art history), 31–32

Disciplinary dynamics: evaluation, 140, 142–51, 292 n.3, 325 n.57; and feminist self-socialization, 34–35, 46–48; formatting feminist studies, 129–65, 319 n.1; and institutionalized production, 18–21, 165, 166–68, 206–13; and sex-pattern education and employment (*see also* Higher education system); sex-typing of, 58; and socializing practitioners (practices and effects), 4, 12–13, 18, 20–24, 28–30, 33–36, 38–40, 41, 43–46; specialization, 11–13, 189–91, 206–7, 212–13

Disciplines, academic: anthropology, 53, 185–86, 189, 337 n.47, 338 n.48; art history and fine arts, 28–33, 45, 54–55, 55 t.1, 148–49, 294 nn. 31, 34, 37, 38, 299 n.3, 300 n.48; biology, 53, 159, 168–78, 182, 183, 185, 330 nn. 4, 6, 7, 331 nn. 8, 12, 15; feminist studies (*see also* Feminist studies); history, 141–42, 178–82, 332 nn. 27, 29, 333 n.33; literary studies and modern languages, 4, 12, 38–48, 53 t.1, 55–56, 141, 178–82, 195, 201–3, 208, 291 n.1 (Part 1), 297 n.61, 299 n.3, 307 n.78, 334 n.35; physics, 21–28, 35–36, 45–46, 53 t.1, 53–54, 293 nn. 18, 26, 299 n.78; psychology, 53 t.1, 182–85, 189–90, 335 nn. 36, 37, 38, 336 n.39, 337 n.44; sciences, 24, 58–62, 149, 176, 302 n.32; sociobiology, 170, 172; sociology, 33–38, 45, 54, 55 t.2, 57–58, 144–46, 150–51, 188–89, 295 n.47, 296 n.53

Discrimination, race: in college admissions, 275–84, 286; lawsuits: *Hopwood v. Texas*, 272, 275–77, 360 n.6; *Regents of the University of California v. Bakke*, 275–78; legislation and constitutional amendment, 276–77; litigation, 274–75; and the precedent function, 361 n.21; strict scrutiny test,

283–84, 361 n.22. *See also* Affirmative action; Higher education system

Discrimination, sex: and disaggregating systemic sex discrimination, 60–62; grievance processes, 66–67; lawsuits: *Gutzwiler v. Fenik, et al.*, 73–75; *Michigan State University Faculty Association v. Michigan State University*, 70–75; *Rachelle A. Rosenberg v. University of Cincinnati*, 72–75; *Shymala Rajender v. University of Minnesota*, 69, 76–78; litigation, 67–70; the precedent function, 361 n.21; systemic sex discrimination in higher education system, 49–51, 78–79. *See also* Affirmative action; Higher education system; Sexism

Distributive justice, 243, 270, 280, 284–87, 363 n.25

Diversity, 246–49, 252, 256–57, 278–83

Dixon, Marlene, 96, 98–100, 102, 116

Doctorates: earned by racial minority, 193–94, 340 n.65; earned by women, 22–24, 51–56, 53 t.1, 61, 109, 300 n.18

Douglass College (Rutgers University), 230–31, 236

Equal Employment Opportunity Commission (EEOC), 63, 66, 303 n.40

Faculty: career path of, 59–60, 64–65; and department autonomy, 64–66, 68, 70–78, 154–56, 158; and feminist studies, 84–85, 112, 153–65, 169–213, 261–63, 326 n.58, 327 n.69, 328 n.73; hiring practices, 57–58, 301 n.23; race patterns in, 64, 192–94, 304 n.42, 340 n.65; reaction to women's studies, 84, 116, 118, 120–21, 125–27, 128, 140, 153–57; resistance to affirmative action, 64–66, 303 n.40; salary equity, 77, 306 n.73; sex patterns in, 18, 51–60, 53 t.1, 55 tt. 2, 3, 64, 79, 301 n.23, 302 n.27, 304 n.42, 307 n.78; women in university administration, 8, 52, 64–65, 304 nn. 42, 43, 305 nn. 44, 45

Farley, Tucker, 96, 98, 105–6, 107, 112, 114, 163–64

Female identity: consciousness raising (CR), 46–47, 125; constructed by disciplines, 20–47. *See also* Identity discourse

Female studies: envisioning, 87–91, 115; formation of, 83–86, 87–91, 309 n.1

Female Studies, 83, 88, 90, 109, 119–20, 128, 157

Feminism: civil rights movement and, 92–95, 198–99, 211–12, 309 n.8, 310 n.9; and community activism, 8, 87–89, 99–100, 115–18, 121, 126–28, 161–64, 197–98, 210–11, 213, 221–24, 255, 263–68; dissent in, 87–88, 99–100, 103–4, 115–25, 127, 167, 190–93, 197, 201–13, 346 nn. 103, 104; genealogy, 91–92, 163–65; movement organizations, 111–12, 221–24; publishing and, 130–51, 194–96; sites of incubation for, 91–100, 309 n.8, 310 nn. 9, 10, 11, 311 n.13, 312 n.22; Third World feminism, 204–5, 344 n.92. *See also* Feminist studies; Women's studies

Feminism, academic. *See* Curriculum and pedagogy; Higher education system; Publishing; Women's studies

Feminist conferences: Berkshire Conferences of Women Historians, 141–42, 180; Celebration of Our Work (Rutgers University), 230–31; on economic consequences of divorce (University of Cincinnati), 8; Genes and Gender Conference, 170–71, 330 n.6; The Inclusive Curriculum: Setting Our Own Agenda (New Jersey Project), 232; Pioneers for Century III (University of Cincinnati), 8; Wingspread Conference on the advancement of women in higher education, 57–58, 301 n.25; Women and Education: A Feminist Perspective (University of Pittsburgh), 87–88, 119–20, 124, 127, 163; Women's Studies and Feminism: Survival in the

1970s (Sacramento State College), 121–23, 318 n.81; on women's studies scholarship and publishing (MLA Commission on the Status of Women), 9

Feminist Press, 83–84, 119, 127–28

Feminist studies, epistemic shifts, 208–10, 212; feminist-studies discourse (*see* ch. 5); formatting feminist studies (*see* ch. 4); institutionalization of, 10–11, 12–13, 83–86, 87–91, 104–5, 109–10, 115–28, 129–65, 319 n.1; materiality of knowledge-production, 206–8; objects of knowledge (*see also* Gender; Multiple Identities and Oppressions; Sex); problems and solutions in, 203–6, 213; rules of discourse, 210–13; superabundance of knowledge, 166–68, 329 n.1. *See also* Sex-gender systems; Standpoint Theory

Feminist Studies, 141, 142, 196

Firestone, Shulamith, 100, 168–69

Flacks, Richard, 96, 99, 101

Foucault, Michel: on author as construct, 361 n.21; on discourse, 294 n.30, 345 n.102; on discursive context in research, 185; on genealogy, 163–64; on government, 79; on models of investigation, 169; on truth, 284, 292 n.4

Free Congress Foundation (FCF), 222, 228, 354 n.63

Friedan, Betty, 133, 134

Friends of Women's Studies: Duke University, 162, 328 n.74; University of Cincinnati, 8, 162, 328 n.74

Frye, Marilyn, 233–35

Fund for American Studies–Georgetown University Institutes, 239–52, 268, 354 nn. 62, 63, 64, 65, 355 nn. 66, 77, 78, 356 nn. 79, 80, 81

Funding: conservative organizations and, 222–23, 238, 347 n.1; feminist organizations and, 163, 222–23; Midwestern State University (pseudonym), 262–63, 264,

267; New Jersey Project, 231–32, 237–38; in the sciencs, 59, 302 n.32; of women's studies programs, 153, 155, 162, 213

Gender: in anthropology, 185–86; in art history and fine arts, 29; and feminist critiques of Chodorow's work, 189–91, 339 n.58; in history, 178–82; in literary studies, 178–82; meanings, 177–78; in psychology, 182–85, 335 n.38; and sex-gender systems, 186–91, 212, 338 n.53

Goddard College, 125–27

Goldberg, Edward D., 231–32, 236, 237

Graduate education: doctorates earned by racial minority, 193–94, 340 n.65; sex discrimination in, 51, 61–62, 302 n.27; women and, 17, 21–28, 52–57, 53 t.1, 109, 291 n.1, 300 n.18; in women's studies programs, 126–27, 161, 263–66

Harding, Sandra, 58–59, 187–88, 189

Hartman, Joan, 9, 108, 110, 217, 291 n.3

Harvard University, 21–24, 28

Heritage Foundation, 222, 228, 270–71, 350 n.24, 354 n.63

Heritage Foundation Resource Bank, 224–28, 267, 349 nn. 16, 17, 20, 21

Higher Education Resource Services (HERS), 65

Higher education system: decision-making structure in, 62–66, 78; delimitation of populations and knowledges, 192–97; disaggregating systemic sex discrimination, 60–62; institutional-disciplinary order in, 19–21, 48, 78–79, 88–90, 127, 163–65, 292 n.1; race patterns in, 64, 192–94, 304 n.42, 340 n.65; sex-patterns in, 18, 51–60, 53 t.1, 55 tt. 2, 3, 64–79, 301 n.23, 302 n.27, 304 n.42, 307 n.78; and systemic sex discrimination, 49–51, 78–79. *See also* Affirmative action; Anthologies, feminist; Discrimination, race; Discrimination, sex; Fac-

ulty; Journals, disciplinary; Journals, feminist; Publishing; Racism

History, 141–42, 178–82, 332 nn. 27, 29, 333 n.33

History and Society Program (University of Minnesota), 11–12

Holton, Gerald, 24–28, 33, 44, 293 n.18

Howe, Florence, 17–18, 83–84, 96, 106, 109–10, 112–13, 119, 122, 146–47, 152, 154, 157, 164, 201, 311 n.13, 316 nn. 51, 52, 326 n.58

Identity discourse: conservative and feminist, 224, 229–30; in feminist studies, 46–47, 118–25, 176–77, 191–92, 201–5, 207–13, 343 n.87; at Fund for American Studies–Georgetown University Institutes, 246–52, 267–68; at Heritage Foundation Resource Bank, 225–27, 236, 267–68; at Midwestern State University (pseudonym), 262–63, 265–68; at New Jersey Project, 232–36, 267–68; at NEW Leadership, 256–60, 267–68; at San Diego State College Women's Center, 89, 115–19, 123–24, 267–68

Industrial Areas Foundation (IAF), 6–7, 235

Institute for Research on Women (IRW), Rutgers University, 230–31

Intercollegiate Studies Institute (ISI), 229, 351 n.30, 354 n.63

Journals, disciplinary: *American Journal of Sociology*, 144–45; *The American Sociologist*, 144–45; *Art Bulletin*, 148–49; *College English*, 17–18, 138, 141; *Critical Inquiry*, 147–48, 325; *New Literary History* (NLH), 147; *PMLA*, 17–18, 139–40, 146–47

Journals, dynamics of: control of discourse and, 292 n.3; evaluation and citation in, 149–51, 325 n.53; formatting feminist work and, 138–49, 157–58; work by and about African-American women and, 195–96, 199–201, 341 nn. 69, 70, 71, 342 nn. 72, 73, 74. *See also* Publishing

Journals, feminist: *Feminist Studies*, 132, 140–42, 196; *Signs*, 128, 132, 142–43, 178, 196–97, 204, 322 n.26, 342 n.74; *Women's Studies*, 132, 138, 140, 141

Kampf, Louis, 96, 106–7, 108, 114, 146
Keller, Evelyn Fox, 21–28, 30, 35, 45–46, 144, 203–4, 292 n.5
Kelly, Joan, 180, 333 n.33
KNOW Press, 83, 127–28, 132, 308 n.3
Kohlberg, Lawrence, 182, 335 n.38
Kolodny, Annette, 143–44, 147, 181, 201–3, 334 n.35, 343 n.87

Ladner, Joyce, 188–89
Lauter, Paul, 83, 96, 97, 99, 106, 113, 114
Lawsuits: *Gutzwiller v. Fenik, et al.*, 73–75; *Hopwood v. Texas*, 272, 277–84; *Jennifer Gratz and Patrick Hamacher v. Bollinger, et al.*, 273; *Katuria E. Smith v. University of Washington Law School*, 273; *Michigan State University Faculty Association v. Michigan State University*, 70–75; *Podberesky v. Kirwan*, 271; *Rachelle A. Rosenberg v. University of Cincinnati*, 72–75; *Regents of the University of California v. Bakke*, 275–77; *Shymala Rajender v. University of Minnesota*, 69, 76–78
Leadership training, conservative: Free Congress Foundation (FCF), 222, 228, 354 n.63; Fund for American Studies–Georgetown University, 239–52; Heritage Foundation, 228, 270–71, 350 n.24, 354 n.63; Heritage Foundation Resource Bank, 224–28, 267, 349 nn. 16, 17, 20, 21; Intercollegiate Studies Institute (ISI), 229, 351 n.30, 354 n.63; Leadership Institute (LI), 228; National Journalism Center (NJC), 228–29, 354 n.63; Young America's Foundation (YAF), 229, 354 n.63
Lerner, Gerda, 180, 199, 332 n.27, 333 n.31
Literary studies, 4, 12, 38–48, 53 t.1, 55–56, 141, 178–82, 195, 201–3, 208, 291 n.1 (Part

1), 297 n.61, 299 n.3, 307 n.78, 334 n.35. *See also* Modern Language Association

Martin, Wendy, 138, 140
Midwestern State University (pseudonym), 261–67
Millett, Kate, 109, 135–37
Mississippi freedom schools, 92, 95, 313 n.26
Modern Language Association (MLA): activism in, 105–11, 112–15, 311 n.13, 315 n.44; and Commission on the Status of Women (CSW), 9, 17–18, 55–56, 83–84, 98, 108–9, 113, 138–40, 291 n.3, 299 n.3, 300 n.16; convention format, 138–39, 302 n.29; institutionalization of feminism in, 107, 108–11, 112–15; publications, 139–40, 146–47; and Women's Caucus for the Modern Languages (WCML), 98, 108–11, 316 n.51
Morgan, Robin, 122, 134, 196
Multiple identities and oppressions: constru(ct)ing women's groupness and oppression, 197–98; and feminist critiques of Kolodny's work, 201–3; and identity discourse, 191–92; and modeling systems of race, sexism, and classism, 199–201, 343 nn. 78, 80, 81, 82, 83, 84; and systematicity of racism, sexism, and classism, 198. *See also* Standpoint theory

National Association for the Advancement of Colored People (NAACP), 93, 95, 218
National Association of Scholars (NAS), 271, 272
National Council for Research on Women, 85, 221
National Organization for Women (NOW), 83, 92, 93, 111, 308 n.3
National Women's Studies Association, 85, 221
Networking: American Sociological Association, 101, 102, 104–5; civil rights movement, 94, 95; conservative movement, 218, 221, 223–24, 230; Heritage Founda-

tion Resource Bank, 225–26, 237–38, 349
nn. 16, 17, 20; Modern Language Associa-
tion (MLA), 110–11, 112–13; New Jersey
Project, 230–38; New Left, 64, 92–96, 131,
239, 298 n.2, 309 n.8, 310 nn. 9, 10, 11;
New University Conference (NUC), 96,
105–6, 311 n.13; Students for a Democratic
Society (SDS), 95–96, 311 n.13; women
in university administration, 65, 305
n.44
New Criticism, 38, 40–45, 297 n.61
New Jersey Project, 230–38, 352 n.45
NEW Leadership, 253–60
New Left, 64, 92–98, 111–12, 131, 211–12, 239,
298 n.2, 309 n.8, 310 nn. 9, 10, 11
New University Conference (NUC), 93, 96–
98, 105–6, 209, 311 n.13

O'Barr, Jean, 84, 142–43, 167, 203–4
Office of Federal Contract Compliance Pro-
grams (OFCCP), 63
Ohmann, Carol, 96, 110
Ohmann, Richard, 96, 106, 108, 140

Physics, 21–28, 35–36, 45–46, 53 t.1, 53–54,
293 nn. 18, 26, 299 n.3, 307 n.78
Psychology, 53 t.1, 58, 182–85, 189–90, 335 nn.
36, 37, 38, 336 n.39, 337 n.44
Public Leadership Education Network
(PLEN), 253
Publishing: evaluation and citation, 149–51,
325 n.53; *Female Studies*, 83, 87–88, 119–20,
128, 157, 201–2, 342 n.73; feminist anthologies, 134–35, 170–71, 196, 200, 296
n.54, 320 n.6, 321 n.7; Feminist Press, 83–
84, 119, 127–28; *Feminist Studies*, 141, 142,
196; of feminist scholarship, 55–56, 139,
140–50, 205–6, 320 n.4, 329 n.1; and formatting feminist work, 138–49, 157–58;
and gatekeeping, 130–32, 145; hybrid feminist genre and, 133–38, 196; and KNOW
Press, 83, 127–28, 132, 308 n.3; *Ms.* magazine, 132; racism and, 292 n.3; reorganiza-

tion of, industry, 130–38, 320 nn. 4, 6, 321
n.16; reviewers, 130, 135–37, 300 n.17;
Women's Studies, 138, 140, 141; *Women's
Studies Newsletter*, 84; *Women's Work and
Women's Studies*, 127–28; work by and
about African-American women, 195–96,
199–201, 341 nn. 69, 70, 71, 342 nn. 72, 73,
74. *See also* Journals, disciplinary; Journals, feminist
Racism: and conservative government and
organizations, 270–74, 284–85; and conservative jurisprudence, 274–84; and
modeling systems of racism, sexism, and
classism, 199–201, 203, 343 nn. 79, 80, 81,
82; and publishing, 292 n.3; and race patterns in higher education, 64, 192–94, 304
n.42, 340 n.65; systematicity of, 198–201,
278, 280, 283–84, 285. *See also* Feminist
studies; Identity discourse
Research methods: on discrimination, 60–
62; and sex-difference research, 184–85,
331 n.12, 335 nn. 37, 38, 337 n.45
Resist (antiwar organization), 106, 311 n.13
Robinson, Lillian S., 28, 30, 147, 149
Ross, Robert, 96–98, 99
Rossi, Alice, 51, 58, 96, 102–4, 113, 116, 190
Rossi, Peter, 96, 113
Rothenberg, Paula, 231, 232, 236
Rowell Council, Carol, 116–17, 118
Rubin, Gayle, 186–87, 199–200, 338 n.51, 343
n.78
Russell, Catherine, 33–35
Rutgers University, 230–31, 253

Salper, Roberta, 88–90, 96, 98–99, 116, 118–
19, 123–24, 164
Salzman-Webb, Marilyn, 88–90, 96, 98–100,
118, 125–26, 163, 313 n.28
San Diego State College Women's Center,
89, 115–19, 123–24, 317 nn. 73, 74
Sciences, 24, 58–62, 149, 176, 302 n.32. *See
also* Anthropology; Biology, Physics; Psychology; Sociobiology; Sociology

Ellen Messer-Davidow is Associate Professor
of English at the University of Minnesota.

Library of Congress Cataloging-in-Publication Data
Messer-Davidow, Ellen
Disciplining feminism : From Social Activism to
Academic Discourse / Ellen Messer-Davidow.
p. cm.　Includes bibliographical references and index.
ISBN 0-8223-2829-1 (cloth : alk. paper)
ISBN 0-8223-2843-7 (pbk. : alk. paper)
1. Feminism and education—United States.
2. Women's studies—United States. I. Title.
LC197 .M47 2002　378'.0082—dc21　2001040715